TOUCHSTONE

The THIRTIES
A TIME TO REMEMBER

Edited and with Commentary
by DON CONGDON

A TOUCHSTONE BOOK

PUBLISHED BY SIMON AND SCHUSTER

ISBN 0-671-20832-2

ISBN 0-671-20738-5 PBK.

LIBRARY OF CONGRESS CATALOG CARD NUMBER 61-12854

MANUFACTURED IN THE UNITED STATES OF AMERICA

3   4   5   6   7   8   9   10

2   3   4   5   6   7   8   9   10 PBK.

ACKNOWLEDGMENTS

"I Remember the Thirties"—Copyright 1960 by John Steinbeck; reprinted by permission of McIntosh & Otis, Inc.

"From Riches to Rags" and other selections from *The Age of the Great Depression*—Copyright 1948 by The Macmillan Company; reprinted by permission of the Publisher.

"How to Solve the Traffic Situation"—Copyright 1930 by Condé Nast Publications Inc.; reprinted by permission of Harold Ober Associates, Inc.

"New England's Tragic Towns"—Copyright 1938 by Louis Adamic; reprinted by permission of Harper & Brothers.

"Catastrophe in Coal"—Copyright 1960 by Irving Bernstein; reprinted by permission of Houghton Mifflin Company.

Selections from *Only Yesterday*—Copyright 1931 by Frederick Lewis Allen; reprinted by permission of Harper & Brothers.

"Pepper Martin—The Happiest Hooligan"—Copyright 1959 by W. C. Heinz; reprinted by permission of William Morris Agency, Inc.

"The Gashouse Gang, the Deans, and Other Heroes," from *Baseball*—Copyright 1947 by Robert Smith; reprinted by permission of Simon and Schuster.

"The Texas Babe"—Copyright 1932 by Condé Nast Publications Inc.; reprinted by permission of Harold Ober Associates, Inc.

"The *Akron* and Thɔse Who Came Back"—Copyright 1957 by John Toland; reprinted by permission of Holt, Rinehart and Winston, Inc.

"Hitchhiker"—Copyright 1946 by Eric Sevareid; reprinted by permission of Alfred A. Knopf, Inc.

"The Flight of the Bonus Army"—Copyright 1932 by The New Republic, Inc.; reprinted by permission of the Author and *The New Republic*.

"The Inaugural"—Copyright 1957 by Arthur M. Schlesinger, Jr.; reprinted by permission of Houghton Mifflin Company.

"The Great Bank Holiday"—Copyright 1960 by Curtis Publishing Company; reprinted by permission of Harold Matson Company.

"The Rise of Federal Relief" and "More on the Rise of Federal Relief"—Copyright 1958 by Arthur M. Schlesinger, Jr.; reprinted by permission of Houghton Mifflin Company.

"How to Relieve Everybody"—Copyright 1933 by Condé Nast Publications Inc.; reprinted by permission of Harold Ober Associates, Inc.

"Weary Willie"—Copyright 1939 by The University of North Carolina; reprinted by permission of University of North Carolina Press.

Material in "Scottsboro Boys" abstracted from *They Shall Be Free*—Copyright 1951 by Allan K. Chalmers; used by permission of Doubleday & Company, Inc.

"Life with Fiorello"—Copyright 1955 by Ernest Cuneo; reprinted by permission of The Macmillan Company.

"Repeal" and other selections from *Since Yesterday*—Copyright 1939, 1940 by Harper & Brothers; reprinted by permission of the Publisher.

"The Judging of Hauptmann" and "*Morro Castle* Aftermath"—Copyright 1935 by Stanley Walker; reprinted by permission of the Author.

"Dillinger"—Copyright 1956 by Fawcett Publications, Inc.; reprinted by permission of the Author.

"The Great Nickel Panic"—Copyright 1931 by Condé Nast Publications Inc.; reprinted by permission of the Author.

"The Almost-Assassination of Thomas E. Dewey"—Copyright 1951 by Burton B. Turkus and Sid Feder; reprinted by permission of Farrar, Straus and Cudahy, Inc.

"The *Morro Castle* Fire"—Copyright 1949 by Simon and Schuster; reprinted by permission of the Author.

"Rescue at Sea"—Copyright 1934 by The New Republic, Inc.; reprinted by permission of *The New Republic*.

"Boulder Dam"—Copyright 1935 by The New Republic, Inc.; reprinted by permission of *The New Republic*.

"In Search of America"—Copyright 1937 by W. W. Norton, Inc.; reprinted by permission of the Author.

Table of Contents

Table of Contents

Table of Contents

9

Table of Contents

Table of Contents

stand it. They'd hang onto the cage and ride back up on the first trip and quit right there." —*Boulder Dam spectator*

Table of Contents

14

Table of Contents

Table of Contents

Table of Contents

17

Table of Contents

FOREWORD

RECENTLY I have been urging friends to look back at the Nineteen Thirties as a time of unprecedented social reform, artistic ferment and imaginative leadership (qualities found in very small measure in the "Fabulous Fifties"). I believe that a portrait of the period would remind us of its particular vitality—and entertain readers, too.

The Thirties gave us social security and unemployment insurance, hospitalization plans, the first cyclotron, sulfa drugs and the artificial lung, insulin-shock therapy, television, the five-day week and frozen foods. But it was hardly a golden age. In the first three years of the decade the country seemed to be wallowing in a sea of turmoil, without leadership. A new political administration in 1933 suddenly galvanized the nation, supplied new hope for the future, and released dormant energies with which Americans began to deal with the tremendous problems before them. The change seemed almost miraculous.

To high-school students, such as I was then, the adventures of the Gashouse Gang in the National League seemed more important, or scraping together the fifteen dollars necessary for a trip aboard the Ford Company excursion train special to the Chicago World's Fair. But the year I was graduated from high school the banks took over the small hotel my family managed, and my father and I signed up with the WPA. Before I could be handed a shovel, I heard of a possible job in New York City, where two days later, with eight dollars in my pocket, I arrived by Greyhound bus.

My first day on the job was my last. I was sent out for Scotch Tape, needed in a hurry for an advertising layout, and came back with black electrician's tape: Scotch Tape—also an innovation of the Thirties—was unknown to this country boy.

Eventually I landed another job. It paid twelve dollars a week. Out of this, six dollars went for rent, and, while I longingly eyed the belt-backed suits in Crawford's windows, I managed to squeak by on cheap meals at places like Nedick's, where a breakfast of two doughnuts, orange drink and coffee cost ten cents. My rooming-house landlady, who claimed she had been swindled by Samuel Insull, often tried to bully me into paying an advance on next week's rent—showing that if she hadn't learned much about financial operations she had at least learned to look sharp for the angles.

I would not say I look back on the Thirties with pleasure, but rather with an appreciation of the air of excitement that pervaded the country. People spoke out freely and were quick to fight for what they believed in. I remember how, as young people, we often argued hotly over the social and political issues of the day. When I was nineteen, a skillful persuader sold me Communism for about three days, until with the help of a wise friend I learned better. The week after, I remember debating before a large group the right of assembly for Fritz Kuhn and his Nazis, who wanted to meet in Madison Square Garden. Thus I sampled the ideas of the day, testing myself against them and developing confidence in my own judgment.

Then the war years intervened. For a long time afterward no one seemed moved to recall the Thirties, and today many people—particularly the younger generation—don't bother to look beyond the label "Depression" and perceive one of America's great victories, in the face of unprecedented domestic crisis. To them, and to those Americans who are heel-draggers and nay-sayers when faced with social reform today, this book is addressed.

The Thirties is, of course, about much more than social reform and politics.

It is also about:

The lively arts of radio, movies, theater, books and popular music; sports figures Joe Louis, Dizzy Dean and Babe Didrikson; the Lindbergh kidnaping, and bankbusting John Dillinger; dust storms, the Ohio River flood of 1936, and the New England hurricane of 1938; the Morro Castle fire; Americans fighting in the Spanish Civil War; the last flight of the dirigible Akron; the construction of the great dams at Boulder, Grand Coulee and in the Tennessee River Valley; Marian Anderson and the DAR; and "invasion" by Martians.

These were all a part of the Thirties. John Steinbeck says he knows of "no other decade in history when so much happened in so many directions." His "I Remember the Thirties" serves as a fine prologue to the unfolding story of those years.

Prologue

JOHN STEINBECK

I REMEMBER THE THIRTIES*

SURE I remember the Nineteen Thirties, the terrible, troubled, triumphant, surging Thirties. I can't think of any decade in history when so much happened in so many directions. Violent changes took place. Our country was modeled, our lives remolded, our government rebuilt, forced to functions, duties and responsibilities it never had before and can never relinquish. The most rabid, hysterical Roosevelt-hater would not dare to suggest removing the reforms, the safeguards and the new concept that the government is responsible for all its citizens.

Looking back, the decade seems to have been as carefully designed as a play. It had beginning, middle and end, even a prologue—1929 gave contrast and tragic stature to the ensuing ten years.

I remember '29 very well. We had it made (I didn't, but most people did). I remember the drugged and happy faces of people who built paper fortunes on stocks they couldn't possibly have paid for. "I made ten grand in ten minutes today. Let's see—that's eighty thousand for the week."

In our little town, bank presidents and trackworkers rushed to pay phones to call brokers. Everyone was a broker, more or less. At lunch hour, store clerks and stenographers munched sandwiches while they watched the stock boards and calculated their pyramiding fortunes. Their eyes had the look you see around the roulette table.

I saw it sharply because I was on the outside, writing books no one would buy. I didn't have even the margin to start my fortune. I saw the wild spending, the champagne and caviar through windows, smelled the heady perfumes on fur-draped ladies when they came warm and shining out of the theaters.

Then the bottom dropped out, and I could see that clearly too, because I had been practicing for the Depression a long time. I wasn't involved with loss. I didn't have money to lose, but in common with millions I did

* Condensed from *Esquire,* June 1960.

dislike hunger and cold. I had two assets. My father owned a tiny three-room cottage in Pacific Grove in California, and he let me live in it without rent. That was the first safety. Pacific Grove is on the sea. That was the second. People in inland cities or in the closed and shuttered industrial cemeteries had greater problems than I. Given the sea, a man must be very stupid to starve. That great reservoir of food is always available. I took a large part of my protein food from the ocean. Firewood to keep warm floated on the beach daily, needing only handsaw and ax. A small garden of black soil came with the cottage. In northern California you can raise vegetables of some kind all year long. I never peeled a potato without planting the skins. Kale, lettuce, chard, turnips, carrots and onions rotated in the little garden. In the tide pools of the bay, mussels were available and crabs and abalones and that shiny kelp called sea lettuce. With a line and pole, blue cod, rock cod, perch, sea trout, sculpin could be caught.

I must drop the "I" for "we" now, for there was a fairly large group of us poor kids, all living alike. We pooled our troubles, our money when we had some, our inventiveness and our pleasures. I remember it as a warm and friendly time. Only illness frightened us. You have to have money to be sick—or did then. And dentistry also was out of the question, with the result that my teeth went badly to pieces. Without dough you couldn't have a tooth filled.

It seems odd now to say that we rarely had a job. There just weren't any jobs. One girl of our group had a job in the Woman's Exchange. She wasn't paid, but the cakes that had passed their salable prime she got to take home, and of course she shared so that we were rarely without dry but delicious cakes. Being without a job, I went on writing—books, essays, short stories. Regularly they went out and just as regularly came back. Even if they had been good, they would have come back because publishers were hardest hit of all. When people are broke, the first things they give up are books. I couldn't even afford postage on the manuscripts. My agents, McIntosh & Otis, paid it, although they couldn't sell my work. Needless to say, they are still my agents, and most of the work written at that time has since been published.

Given the sea and the gardens, we did pretty well with a minimum of theft. We didn't have to steal much. Farmers and orchardists in the nearby countryside couldn't sell their crops. They gave us all the fruit and truck we could carry home. We used to go on walking trips carrying our gunny sacks. If we had a dollar, we could buy a live sheep, for two dollars a pig, but we had to slaughter them and carry them home on our backs, or camp beside them and eat them there. We even did that.

Keeping clean was a problem because soap cost money. For a time we washed our laundry with a soap made of pork fat, wood ashes and salt. It worked, but it took a lot of sunning to get the smell out of the sheets.

For entertainment we had the public library, endless talk, long walks, any number of games. We played music, sang and made love. Enormous invention went into our pleasures. Anything at all was an excuse for a party: all holidays, birthdays called for celebration. When we felt the need to celebrate and the calendar was blank, we simply proclaimed a Jacks-Are-Wild Day.

It's not easy to go on writing constantly with little hope that anything will come of it. But I do remember it as a time of warmth and mutual caring. If one of us got hurt or ill or in trouble, the others rallied with what they had. Everyone shared bad fortune as well as good.

In Pacific Grove we heard that business was improving but that hadn't much emphasis for us. One of the indices of improvement was that the men who had begged the Administration to take over and tell them what to do were now howling against government control and calling Mr. Roosevelt highly colored names. This proved that they were on their feet again and was perfectly natural. You only tolerate help when you need it.

By 1936 the country must have been on the upgrade. When a writer does well, the rest of the country is doing fine. A book of mine which had been trudging wearily from publisher to publisher was finally bought and brought out by Pat Covici. It sold well enough so that it was bought for motion pictures for $3,000. I had no conception of this kind of dough. It was like thinking in terms of light years. You can't.

The subsequent history of that book is a kind of index of the change that was going on. The studio spent a quarter of a million dollars having my book rewritten before they abandoned it. Then they fired the man who had bought it in the first place. He bought it back for three thousand and later sold it for $90,000. It shows how values change. But I still think of that original $3,000 as about as much money as there is in the world. I gave a lot of it away because it seemed like too much to be in private hands. I guess I wasn't cut out for a capitalist. I even remained a Democrat.

My books were beginning to sell better than I had ever hoped or expected and while this was pleasing it also frightened me. I knew it couldn't last and I was afraid my standard of living would go up and leave me stranded when the next collapse came. We were much more accustomed to collapse than to prosperity. Also I had an archaic angry-gods feeling that made me give a great lot of my earnings away. I was a pushover for anyone or any organization asking for money. I guess it was a kind of propitiation. It didn't make sense that a book, a humble, hat-in-hand, rejected book, was now eagerly bought—even begged for. I didn't trust it. But I did begin to get around more.

I met Mr. Roosevelt and for some reason made him laugh. To the end of his life, when occasionally he felt sad and burdened, he used to ask me to come in. We would talk for half an hour and I remember how he would rock back in his chair behind his littered desk and I can still hear his roars of laughter.

A few weeks ago I called on a friend in a great office building in midtown New York. On our way out to lunch he said, "I want to show you something."

And he led me into a broker's office. One whole wall was a stock-exchange trading board. Two young men moved back and forth swiftly filling in changes, rises, falls, buying, selling. Behind an oaken rail was a tight-packed, standing audience—clerks, stenographers, small businessmen. Most of them munched sandwiches as they spent their lunch hour watching the trading. Now and then they made notations on envelopes. And their eyes had the rapt, glazed look one sees around a roulette table.

THE THIRTIES

DIXON WECTER

FROM RICHES TO RAGS*

IN mid-October 1929 the average middle-class American saw ahead of him an illimitable vista of prosperity. Herbert Hoover had announced soberly in the previous year that the conquest of poverty was no longer a mirage: "We have not yet reached the goal, but given a chance to go forward with the policies of the last eight years, we shall soon with the help of God be within sight of the day when poverty will be banished from this nation."

The aftermath of America's latest war had seen the arrival in strength of mass production, to compound the wonders of the new technology. Even now, in this third week of October 1929, with the President and other notables in attendance, Henry Ford was sponsoring the "Golden Jubilee of Light," honoring Edison and the fiftieth birthday of the incandescent lamp. Motorcars, bathtubs, electric refrigerators, radios, were the touchstones of progress. Keeping up with the Joneses, under the spur of fashion and advertisement, demanded nothing less than the latest model. Pressures of salesmanship urged even the duplication of luxuries—two cars in every garage—in a consumer's market already displaying symptoms of surfeit, not because all Americans were gorged with worldly goods, but because buying power was unevenly distributed.

Time Magazine, in January 1929, had hailed Walter P. Chrysler as Man of the Year, because during the past twelve months he had introduced the public to Plymouth and DeSoto cars, bought out Dodge Brothers for 160 million dollars and begun to build "the world's tallest skyscraper, a 68-story colossus." Now, on the cover of *Time* for October 14, 1929, appeared the face of William Wrigley, Jr., to be followed in successive weeks by Harry Guggenheim, Ivar Kreuger, Samuel Insull and T. W. Lamont— heroes all. They represented the stimuli which beat incessantly upon the mind of the average magazine reader.

Masses of Americans who bought their first bonds in the Liberty Loans of 1918 had lately turned to more speculative issues. Advertisements flaunting high prices instead of bargains—$2.50 lipsticks, and razor blades at

* From Dixon Wecter's *The Age of the Great Depression* (New York, Macmillan, 1948).

three for fifty cents—set the sumptuary scale for a generation of easy money. To keep abreast of the traffic in this climb to the highlands of permanent prosperity, the stock market was the obvious vehicle. In 1920 there had been 29,609 stockbrokers in the country; within ten years they had jumped to 70,950. It was commonly observed that a great many citizens no longer read the front page of their newspaper, but turned hurriedly to the financial columns.

If a man saves $15 a week, and invests in good common stocks, and allows the dividends and rights to accumulate, at the end of twenty years he will have at least $80,000 and an income from investments of around $400 a month. He will be rich. And because income can do that, I am firm in my belief that anyone not only can be rich, but ought to be rich.

So declared J. J. Raskob, chairman of the Democratic National Committee, in the summer of 1929. Employees were encouraged to invest in the stocks and bonds of their employers—a system regarded somewhat vaguely as the American equivalent of profit sharing, or perhaps social security.

Much of this buying of stocks was on margin, which meant that investors, including the small fry with little cash but big hopes, put up about a fourth of the price. The broker advanced the rest by borrowing from banks. This precarious credit structure of brokers' loans had trembled in February 1929, when the Federal Reserve Board ordered member banks not to lend money for such speculative purposes. But private bankers, led by Charles E. Mitchell, had promptly unlocked their millions for speculation and given a further fillip to the great bull market and the age of confidence upon which it was built. This caused another spasm of activity, unwarranted by any such tangibles as consumer demand, gains in productive efficiency or real earning of the stocks in question. While the rich were growing richer, several million citizens with small incomes were raiding their savings, reducing their immediate purchasing power and mortgaging their future in order to speculate. Ninety per cent of these market transactions in the Twenties, it has been estimated, were gambling ventures rather than permanent investments.

The overexpansion of credit was a prime cause of the disasters that followed 1929. The First World War began a process which reckless financing continued to accelerate. In the background loomed the huge structure of long-term debt in the United States—a public debt, federal, state and municipal, of 33 billion dollars, and corporate and individual debts of 100 billion—which demanded expanding markets and world prosperity for successful carrying. A relatively small reduction in buying power, or backsliding of prices, could send tremors along the whole length of the chain. The grand operations of credit, a new force of such power that one economist likened it to the prime movers of physics, were still imperfectly understood and recklessly abused.

The common man knew more about overexpansion of credit in such homely shapes as installment buying. Intensive campaigns to break down "sales resistance"—often sheer insufficient purchasing power among small citizens—led to new extensions of the time-payment plan for cars, clothes, washers, etc. In effect it was a loan from producer to consumer, because the latter lacked cash, and the former, with his urgent need for sales, preferred this method to that of increasing mass purchasing power by cutting prices and boosting wages.

Meanwhile important business enterprises were being concentrated in fewer hands. The forging of chain stores all over the nation was no less significant than recent big mergers in the automotive industry. Centralized industry made every metropolis the center of a regional web, and each of these networks fitted into a national pattern for making, selling and distributing commodities. The economy of a continent had never been so highly integrated, nor its equilibrium so sensitive. The frontier, the farm, the village and Middletown had at last been engulfed by the rise of the city.

These sweeping changes had hardly entered the consciousness of the average citizen. In his own mind he was never more loyal than in 1929 to the doctrine of individualism and unhampered private enterprise. Clashes between theory and practice, like the potential friction of capital and labor, remained almost inaudible so long as the nation's economic mechanism ran with the oil of prosperity.

Yet beyond question the major shortcomings of the American economy lay not in production but in consumption. Already in the early autumn of 1929 financial pages gloomed over "heaviness" in automobiles and radios, slackening of the building trades, disappointment along the new frontiers of aviation. Much of America's productive effort and income had lately gone into luxuries and durable goods, whose purchase could be postponed without affecting daily needs. At the first storm warnings these goods would pile up in warehouses, causing wheels to stop turning and huge areas of joblessness to appear. This was one reason why the Depression following 1929 was unparalleled for severity and duration.

Two thirds of the country's savings were made by families with incomes over $10,000 a year. Those with less than $1,500, comprising 40 per cent of the population, actually paid out more than they earned. Mass buying power was unable to absorb the nation's output, not alone because wages had advanced comparatively little but because retail prices took virtually no cut between 1922 and 1929. Savings achieved by improved technologies were not being handed on to the consumer in the form of lower prices. They were diverted into dividends, reserves, bigger salaries and bonuses. Various shapes of monopoly, like trusts in disguise, mergers, et cetera, helped keep prices up, even while new machinery, better production methods and services of "efficiency experts" increased the over-all output of American labor by more than a third in the decade after the First World War. In some trades, like automobiles, productive efficiency was reported to have tripled. But from this plenitude the average consumer gathered only the crumbs, and even the producer reaped merely a shortsighted advantage.

Upon this world of uneasy prosperity the first blow fell in late October. Like the sound of gunshot which starts an Alpine avalanche, a minor panic on the New York Stock Exchange began on the twenty-third among stocks that speculators had pushed to fantastic heights. The next day, "Black Thursday," saw hysteria rampant. Brokers wept and tore off their collars trying to keep abreast of selling orders; sight-seers jammed the Wall Street district, ogled the arrival of great bankers in the limousines before the House of Morgan, and under the rumor of mass suicide gathered to watch an ordinary workman on a scaffolding in morbid expectation of his plunge.

At first it appeared that the magicians of finance had arrested disaster, but just as the public cheered them and breathed more easily, another sickening lurch sent the market to new depths, spreading conviction that these wizards had merely propped the falling timbers long enough to get out from under. At the month's close 15 billion dollars in market value had been wiped out, and before the end of the year losses reached an estimated 40 billion.

The solvent of American humor began early to attack the crisis. Grim jokes arose about the complimentary revolver given with every share of Goldman Sachs, or the room clerk's query of every registrant, "For sleeping or jumping?" A little later, when mass unemployment began to steal the headlines from Wall Street, bravado succeeded flippancy. Billboards began to ask, "Wasn't the Depression terrible?" The departing owner of a ruined shop scrawled upon the door "Opened by mistake." Trained in the cult of the stiff upper lip, of singing in the rain, Americans hated to admit that things were not as they had always been. The International Association of Lions Clubs observed the week of October 19, 1930, as Business Confidence Week. Prosperity was just around the corner.

SUNDAY DRIVERS

IN 1930, although the Depression had begun to make itself widely felt, a few of Prosperity's problems remained. One of them was traffic congestion on our highways. More than 31 million passenger automobiles had been manufactured from 1920 through 1929, and to at least one observer it seemed that every one of them was out on the road every Sunday.

Since 1930, our federal, state and county governments have employed thousands of experts and have spent billions of dollars to alleviate the problem, but the problem remains, apparently never to be completely solved. It may be that our experts have not approached the problem as sweepingly, or as radically, as Corey Ford, who in the following piece presents his view of the situation and his ideas for remedying it; and it may be that Corey Ford was, and still is, just too far ahead of his time.

COREY FORD

HOW TO SOLVE THE
TRAFFIC SITUATION*

THE SCENE is practically any well-traveled Motor Highway in America. It is Sunday afternoon.

And what a pleasant scene it is, to be sure! The broad highway, lined with the gay autumn colors of red and yellow! The smooth concrete road, unwinding like a magic carpet, who knows whither? The hum of myriad bees, the lowing of contented cattle, the gentle Sabbath breezes! The long line of pleasure cars, extending up and down the road as far as the eye can reach, filled with fortunate American families who have left the hot stuffy city behind them and driven out here into the peaceful countryside for a breath of fresh air.

Let us draw nearer. Let us examine this pleasant scene a little more closely. Things, it appears, are not quite as they seemed. The gay autumn colors of red and yellow still line the broad highway, it is true; but they

* From *Vanity Fair*, October 1930.

are contributed by the red and yellow gasoline pumps in front of Ye Olde Hotte Dog Fyllynge Statione. The smooth concrete road unwinds like a magic carpet for five hundred feet, and then terminates abruptly in a deep morass of muddy ruts, red lanterns, steam shovels and a gloating sign: "Construction Ahead: Proceed at Your Own Risk." What we took for the hum of bees is the grinding of myriad gears; the lowing of cattle is the honk of discontented horns; and the gentle breezes are laden with our standard Sabbath mixture of two parts gasoline, one part burning brakes and the rest fresh tar.

And what of the long line of pleasure cars, extending up and down the road as far as the eye can reach? Here, too, something appears to be wrong. The cars extend up and down the road, to be sure; but they are not moving. They are, in fact, standing perfectly still. They have been standing still for the past three quarters of an hour; and they are filled with as sour a lot of American families as ever deserted their comfortable rocking chairs and paper-strewn sofas to spend their Sunday afternoon sitting out here in the broiling sun, waiting for the line to start forward again.

But stay! A ray of hope! Something is moving at last along the interminable file of halted cars. It is a motorcycle; and on the motorcycle, my pet, is seated a curious individual in a blue uniform with brass buttons, whose heart apparently was removed when he was very, very young. And what word of cheer does this lone messenger bring? His greeting is brief, but to the point; to each car in turn, as he chugs past, he tosses over his shoulder a single sunny message, squeezed out between his clenched teeth like sausage meat through a grinder: "Keep in line! Keep in line! Keep in line!"

And the driver of each car sinks a little lower behind the wheel, his eyes glazed, his cigar drooping despondently, his gaze fixed stolidly ahead. He is humming to himself. He is humming a forgotten refrain. It is the Song of the Open Road. . . .

As matters stand, he hasn't got a prayer. On every thoroughfare and country lane, on highway and byway, up and down the length and breadth of our native land, America is spending its Sabbath day on wheels. If all the automobiles purchased in 1930 were placed end to end along the Boston Post Road on a single Sunday afternoon, experts state, it would be just like any other Sunday. Bumper to bumper, fender to fender, they edge forward patiently three feet at a time, radiators pressed to spare tires like an interminable file of circus elephants with their tails in their trunks. Roadsters and sedans, touring cars and trucks, limousines and coupés extend from horizon to horizon in a solid and immovable queue, hour after hour, mile upon weary mile. Gears grind, horns honk, brakes squeak, the sun mounts higher and higher, the spirits sink lower and lower. The drivers stare ahead. As a form of Sunday relaxation, they decide, the automobile is not all it is cranked up to be.

In order to settle the whole question a Traffic Commission was recently appointed to study the traffic situation in America. Its suggestions were:

1. Enforce the speed limit. This plan was later discovered to be impracticable, owing to the fact that the cars were already standing still.

2. Establish One-Way Streets. By means of this unique system, all the cars on the odd-numbered streets would move steadily east, and all the cars on the even-numbered streets would move steadily west, the idea being that with two lines of cars advancing continuously in either direction, one would eventually fall with a splash into the Atlantic Ocean and the other would fall with a splash into the Pacific Ocean, thus disposing of hundreds of cars every Sunday.

3. Build cars with runways up the back, so that other cars could drive up on top of them and park.

4. Invent a portable road.

5. Walk.

But the Sunday driver still sits patiently in line, hour after hour, his hands clutching the steering wheel at the very top, his head lowered, bowed but not yet beaten. There is still a faint glow of hope in his weary eyes.

He is waiting, as a matter of fact, for the traffic problem in America to settle itself. Sooner or later, he knows, the roads will grow more and more congested, and the cars will move slower and slower, until that time is not so far distant when they will stop moving altogether. Then we can simply fill in the chinks between them with cement, pave the hoods, and start life all over again on top.

WHERE WOULD IT STOP?

BEGINNING in 1929 the national income dropped from 87 billion dollars to a low in 1933 of 40 billion. This collapse was so extreme as to mark 1929 as a frontier between an old and a new world. In the words of Angel Gabriel in *Green Pastures,* "Everything nailed down is comin' loose."

Even so, some industrial projects were brought to completion, and a few begun, in the early Depression years. In 1931, the new Waldorf-Astoria, world's finest luxury hotel, was opened to the public; the Empire State Building, tallest skyscraper in the world, was completed, although many of its floors, as in other Manhattan office buildings, would remain vacant; and architects' plans for Rockefeller Center were published. As Dixon Wecter says in his *The Age of the Great Depression,* "some critics of architecture prophesied that these would be the last dinosaurs of America's metropolitan era, convinced that such vainglory had overreached itself, promoting little save congested traffic, overcrowding and colossal debts. Like many other vanities of the century, perhaps the skyscraper too was bankrupt. At any rate, the nation's outlay for new construction fell 60 per cent between 1931 and 1932 as the momentum of prosperity ground to a dead stop. By 1933 architects were doing less than a seventh of the business they had enjoyed in 1928."

Behind the statistics measuring unemployment and the ever-shrinking wage levels were stories of bitter privation among the employed, as well as among the idle. "Many industries and small businesses," wrote Wecter, "denied even lip service to the Administration's plea for maintenance of wage rates. A growing backwater of unemployment led department stores to pay clerks as little as five or ten dollars weekly. Investigation of a group of working girls in Chicago showed the great majority toiling for less than twenty-five cents an hour, a fourth for less than ten cents. Makers of ready-to-wear dresses, confectionery employees and cannery workers were among the classes exploited most callously. Domestic servants were obliged to labor for room and board plus ten dollars a month. As usual, unskilled workers had been the shock troops, followed by white-collar workers and technicians. Professional classes felt the jar a little later, as teachers' and ministers' salaries were cut or fell into arrears, and the practice of other groups declined, with fees increasingly hard to collect."

In the mill towns of New England the Depression had begun somewhat earlier than in most of the rest of the nation. Due largely to the short-sightedness of the millowners, the people there in 1930 were in their fourth and fifth years of deprivation. One of the hardest-hit communities was Lowell, Massachusetts; its story has an unusual historical irony.

Back in 1820, according to a *Fortune* Magazine account, "women's first experience in large-scale industry in this country had begun with

36

the 'Lowell factory system.' It combined the advantages of a humanely run workshop and a seminary for young ladies. The mill girls were never driven and were always paid for extra work. Their hours would today seem long—from five in the morning to seven at night—and the wages, low—$2.25 to $4 a week (men got about twice that). But such working hours were considered only normal then, and such wages extremely high.

"There were nonmonetary perquisites attached to working at Lowell. For two decades, from the 1820s on, girls such as now go to colleges went to Lowell for its educational advantages. The mill girls' 'Improvement Circle' was the first factory-women's club, and the *Lowell Offering* was the first magazine ever written exclusively by women.

"But it was too good to last. Industrial competition reached Lowell, and wages were reduced. In 1836 the girls struck against a wage cut. They marched through the streets in their white muslin dresses and green stockings, carrying green parasols, and singing. The strike was lost, and the industrial status of women in America rapidly declined." *

In 1930 Louis Adamic made a tour of New England, beginning with Lowell, to survey conditions there. He was interested in people, not in bloodless statistics, and his report on the New England mill towns provides a vivid picture of men and women experiencing the full force of the Depression.

LOUIS ADAMIC

NEW ENGLAND'S TRAGIC TOWNS†

ON THE train to Lowell, but a decade ago one of the most important cotton-textile centers in the United States, I sat next to a traveling salesman. He told me that six years ago he had worked in the office of a cotton mill in Lowell; now he lived in Chelsea.

"The 1930 census figures show the population of that city [Lowell] has gone down from 113,000 to around 100,000. And most of this decrease has occurred since 1927.

"Till recently no one dared to say out loud that things were on the decline. It was merely a sort of public secret for years that everything was not as it should be. The unemployed—thousands of them—walked around like ghosts (they still do; you'll see them) or were hiding away in their shacks and hall rooms."

* From "Women in Business," *Fortune*, September 1935.
† From Louis Adamic's *My America* (New York, Harper, 1938).

Until the mid-Twenties Lowell was a comparatively prosperous town. Not a few people there had a great deal of money, lived in fine houses, wore nice clothes, drove good cars. They were mostly business and professional folk and the better-paid mill employees. The general run of mill operatives, male and female, who formed numerically the largest group in town, the underdog class, earned less than twenty-five dollars a week when they worked full time, which barely enabled them to lead decent lives. By pinching they saved a little, but very little; a small percentage of them managed to acquire homes of their own.

Then, about five years ago, the mills began to shut down in Lowell. King Cotton was sick. With Coolidge Prosperity in full swing throughout the land, the people began to wear silk, imported from Japan, and other fine materials instead of cotton. There was still some demand for cotton goods, but only for the cheaper kind. Millowners were starting new mills in the South, where raw cotton was produced and, what was still more important to them, "the pore white trash" of Tennessee, Alabama and South Carolina provided cheaper labor than the Italian, Lithuanian and French-Canadian immigrants in New England. Also, there were no laws in the South, such as there were in New England, regulating the number of working hours and female and child labor.

In 1927 and 1928 Lowell practically ceased as a cotton-textile center. I found there eight enormous mills, all idle for years, dominating the town, each six or seven stories high and covering several blocks, with tall, unsmoking chimneys. Only here and there upon the lower floors a few hundred square feet were occupied by tiny industries, such as radio-assembly shops, which the desperate community, working through the Chamber of Commerce, had recently managed to lure to Lowell in an effort to create jobs for the thousands and thousands of former textile operatives who, caught by the circumstances of their lives, had not yet moved away. But these new industries in Lowell, lost in the immensities of the former cotton mills, were, of course, only a drop in the bucket so far as the local unemployment situation was concerned.

How many jobless people there were in Lowell who needed work desperately or urgently, nobody knew exactly. Labor officials told me that perhaps two thirds of the town's working population were idle or employed only part time. Not only textile workers were "out," but nearly two thirds of the organized building-trades craftsmen had had nothing to do for nearly two and a half years. Except for the new post office, there had been no new building in Lowell for more than three years.

The mayor and the other city officials had somewhat lower estimates of the extent of idleness in Lowell. Chester M. Runels, executive secretary of the Lowell Chamber of Commerce, said to me that he knew exactly how many jobless people there were in the city—"too damned many."

Bewilderment, perhaps, was the outstanding characteristic of the Lowell psychology. Mr. Runels confessed that he was spending sleepless nights trying to think of something—anything—that would put the city back on its feet industrially, but, in common with other leading Lowellites, remained only deeply perplexed. He was starting emergency measures to relieve "immediate distress," encouraging charity, trying to induce the better-to-do people in the community to renovate their homes before Christmas and otherwise "create" jobs for needy family men during the winter months. He realized, as he told me, that what Lowell needed was industries, for it was essentially an industrial city; it had started as a mill town and could continue only as an industrial community. But, obviously a very decent person, he was loath to try to lure manufacturers—with low rentals for floor space and cheap labor—from other towns and thus create unemployment elsewhere. Instead, he strove to "create" more new industries by urging local people with money to organize companies for the production of novelties and new commodities. But so far his success in this respect was meager. Several shoe companies had established themselves in Lowell since 1928, but civic and business leaders were frank in saying that they were "afraid of the shoe industry," because, with its cruelty to workers and its utter lack of organization, self-discipline and public conscience, the shoe industry (of which more later) was seldom, if ever, an asset to a community.

Charity, as one citizen remarked to me, was "the biggest industry in Lowell," and it promised to continue big for some time to come. I was told that the priest in charge of the Catholic charity organization and his two assistants were busy from twelve to fourteen hours daily investigating cases of poverty, collecting funds from the well-to-do, who still formed a rather numerous class in Lowell, and distributing what they collected. I was assured that the donations were spontaneous and liberal. There were other charitable agencies in the city, including a municipal welfare bureau, trying to eliminate so far as possible extreme hunger and suffering for want of clothing and fuel.

Business, obviously, was poor in Lowell. Every third or fourth store in the main streets was vacant. There were few "For Rent" signs in the windows, the proprietors figuring, I suppose, that it was no use putting them up. One sign read: "For Rent at Your Own Price."

I had a desolate feeling as I walked through some of the streets. There were rows of old wooden houses, unoccupied, uncared-for, their window-panes broken. Many of the tenanted houses in the working people's districts, evidently, had not been painted for years. I saw broken window-panes pasted over with paper, the residents, apparently, being too poor to replace them.

In the main business section, the five-and-ten-cent store seemed to be the only really busy place. A butcher told me that he sold few steaks and chops; most of the customers bought tripe, soup bones and the cheaper cuts of meat. He had ordered but few turkeys for Thanksgiving. Grocery and dry-goods prices were at least one-third lower in Lowell than in New York or Boston, but even so the stores were doing little business. Two merchants confessed they were operating at a loss; they were "caught"; people owed them money for years back, and they were hoping "things would pick up soon." Said one shopkeeper, "But I don't know how much longer I can hold out on hope."

A barber told me that people obviously were cutting their hair at home; several barbershops had gone out of business. A second barber, when I asked if many of his customers took hair tonic, said, "Hell, no!"— and proceeded to elaborate upon the tragedy of the barbering trade in Lowell.

I spoke with physicians. One admitted that he, like the other doctors in town, had difficulties in collecting his fees; perhaps more than half of his patients were "charity." A dentist informed me that the number of extractions, in proportion to other dental work that he performed, was increasing rapidly. "I suppose people haven't the money," he said, "to come for treatment before it's too late and the tooth has to be removed. Also, I imagine that improper or insufficient food the poorer people have been eating the last few years hastens the decay of teeth."

A neighborhood druggist, having nothing better to do, spoke to me for several hours. "Oh, quite a few working people in Lowell still have money," he said; "at least the number of bank accounts shows that, but they're holding onto it as if it was all there was in the world. Even some of the millworkers seem to have money saved up. How they managed to save anything is more than I know. Now, with the Depression they hold on to it. They're scared. They spend only for absolute necessities. They say, God knows how long the panic will last in Lowell. They're stuck in Lowell. They probably own a little property or have old parents who can't be moved. Some of those who were foot-loose back in 1928 and had a little money cleared out soon after the mills closed down for good. Some stayed, thinking the mills would open up again soon. They waited. Then it was too late for them to clear out. Now they're stuck. Their little savings, maybe, are all gone; and if not, since Wall Street went smash the rest of the country is not much better off than Lowell, and there's no use going elsehere. . . . Of course, I'd like nothing better than to sell out, even at a loss. In the last few years I've been making less than two and a half per cent on my investment. Next year I probably shan't make that much unless things pick up. But who's fool enough to buy me out? Besides, I'm married, kids are going to school, and people in the neighborhood owe me money; so what can I do but stick? If I were single, I'd probably just take my week's receipts, close up and go."

In Lowell I saw shabby men leaning against walls and lampposts, and standing on street corners singly or in twos or threes; pathetic, silent, middle-aged men in torn, frayed overcoats or even without overcoats, broken shoes on their feet (in a town manufacturing shoes!), slumped in postures of hopeless discontent, their faces sunken and their eyes shifty and bewildered—men who winced and jerked queerly when they noticed me looking at them and shuffled off uncertainly, wringing their hands in a mingling of vague desperation and of resentment at my gaze. I spoke or tried to speak with some of them, and I went into a few of the unemployed's homes in Lowell and heard and saw things which, if I described them, would make very melancholy reading.

But even so I was scarcely prepared for the painfully awry conditions that I found in Lawrence, once the leading wool and worsted city in the United States, a half hour's trolley ride from Lowell. According to the census, since 1920, or more exactly since 1927 or thereabouts, the population of Lawrence decreased from 94,270 to 84,949, or nearly 10 per cent.

The situation was different from that in Lowell, where, as I have stated, the cotton-textile industry had almost completely deserted the community and gone South. Most of the mills at Lawrence had not yet shut down. However, since 1926 they had operated very irregularly, giving for brief periods only part-time employment, and gradually decreasing the number of even part-time workers, for during the 1920s the wool, worsted and carpet industries had also been moving out of Massachusetts, where the law provided a maximum forty-eight-hour week for workers, and were starting mills in nearby Maine, New Hampshire and Rhode Island, where employers might work their people fifty-four hours a week, and in Connecticut, where they had a fifty-five-hour law. Another motive in the tendency of the textile interests to start new mills outside of Massachusetts was that in such old centers as Lowell, Lawrence, New Bedford and Maynard labor unions had become powerful, forcing up the wage scale. The mill-owners in Massachusetts realized that they had made a mistake in getting so many mills into a few towns close together. The labor agitators' work was easy when twenty or thirty thousand operatives were concentrated in one city. And the tendency now was not to build more than one small mill in any one town in Rhode Island, Connecticut, Maine or New Hampshire. The millowners figured that this diffusion would prevent "labor troubles."

Lawrence, with its tremendous mills, was a "mistake," which the millowners had been trying to rectify by operating the mills only a little more than was necessary to pay the overhead on the old mills, and thus killing the unions; for, when jobless or working only part time, workers cannot pay their union fees. The process of rectifying this "mistake" was still going on when I came. And it was a painful process to the people—especially the working people—of the city of Lawrence.

I happened to arrive before daybreak on a Monday morning and, walking about, saw hundreds of shabby, silent, hollow-eyed men and women, native and foreign-born, going toward the immense, dark mills. I discovered later that very few of them were going to work; most were seeking work. On Mondays they usually went to the mills to learn from the employment managers if any help would be needed during the week.

By eight o'clock the great majority of them were returning from the mills. Some had been told to come to work on Wednesday or Thursday or Friday; others, perhaps a majority of them, were told there was no work for them this week. Perhaps next week.

Women hurried home. Men stood on curbs, wretchedness inherent in their every action and aspect; penniless men, most of them without any intelligent, objective idea of what was happening to them, what was going on in Lawrence or in the textile industry. One of them said to me, "I don't know nothing, only that I have no job. No job—no job," he repeated in a shrill, half-hysterical voice.

I saw men standing on the sidewalks clapping their hands in a queer way, obviously just to be doing something. I saw men talking to themselves, walking around, stopping, looking into shop windows, walking again.

For several minutes I watched an elderly man who stood on a deserted corner near the enormous and idle Everett Mills in the posture of an undotted question mark. He did not see me. Every now and then he swung his arms, not because it was cold, but no doubt because he wanted activity other than walking around, which he probably had been doing for years in a vain effort to get a job. He mumbled to himself. Then, suddenly, he stepped off the curb and picked up a long piece of string from a pile of rubbish, and his big, work-eager hands began to work with it, tying and untying feverishly. He worked with the string for several minutes. Then he looked around and, seeing me, dropped the string, his haggard, hollow face coloring a little, as though from a sense of guilt, or intense embarrassment. He was shaken and confused and stood there for several seconds, looking down at the rubbish heap, then up at me. His hands finally dropped to his sides. Then his arms swung in a sort of idle reflex motion and he turned, hesitated a while as if he did not know where to go and finally shuffled off, flapping his arms. I noticed that his overcoat was split in the back and that his heels were worn off completely.

The general aspect of Lawrence was not unlike that of Lowell: empty stores—rows of shabby, unpainted, untended old houses—broken windowpanes—no new buildings going up—people still moving out when they could—and so on and on. In Lawrence, too, charity was one of the main industries.

The Lithuanian priest, Father Juras, spoke to me for a couple of hours, evidently glad of the chance to get things off his chest. "Yes, conditions are bad," he said. "I don't know, I don't know. I can do so little. Many of my people work only one or two days a week. They earn so little. I hear that some workers in order to get and hold jobs must give a part of their small earnings to unscrupulous mill bosses who have the power to hire and fire them. . . . Mothers come to me and cry and say they have no money to buy shoes for the children, and winter is here. We make collections in the church, and I give them money for their children's shoes. Not only for shoes, but for clothing, food and gas bills. Some of my people don't work at all. For months and months—for years—no work. Some have gone out of Lawrence, to the farms near-by, where they work just for food and lodging. It is better than nothing. . . . No, very few become Communists; almost none. Lithuanians are good, patient people. They suffer, but they don't know what is going to become of them. They come to me and cry: What is going to happen to our children? One family I know has lived on lentils, nothing but lentils, all this year. They can't afford to buy bread. No work for them. The young people are restless. They want money. They want to go to picture shows and dances. . . ."

He shook his head.

"Many of my people pay very little rent," he continued. "Some pay no rent. The house owners don't throw them out. The tenants at least take care of the houses. . . . Yes, some of the men drink. They're desperate. It

43

helps them to forget. But their characters degenerate. That is bad. They feel helpless: what's the use! I try to help. But—"

Again he shook his head.

The rector of one of the two French-Canadian parishes spoke to me similarly. "Oh, yes, we, too, have to buy shoes for children," he said. "We have a Catholic school here and we watch the children. If they need clothing, we give it to them. Many parents have nothing—no money, no work, or very little work. I have six priests in this parish assisting me. All day long they go around, from house to house, where we hear there is distress, and we help as much as we can. Our well-to-do parishioners are generous. Last Sunday we received three hundred dollars for the poor." He was unwilling to fix the blame upon the mills or any other factor in Lawrence. "I have come here only recently," he said. "I don't know whose fault this condition is. All I know is that things are terrible—no work for the people."

Speaking with the jobless, I noticed acute desperation. One man said to me, "You're from New York? Say, do you think there'll be a war soon? There was lots of work and high wages during the last war. Remember? Mills were going day and night."

Few of the unemployed in Lawrence—and elsewhere, for that matter —impressed me as competent people. They were willing, eager to work, but there was something dead in them, as from exhaustion or perhaps too much idleness; they lacked personal winsomeness or any power of demand. Lost, bewildered souls, victims in the pinch of the machine, victims of the 1920s' industrial-financial processes, of "rationalization" and speeding-up in the textile industry, victims of the greed for higher and higher profits on the part of the industrialists; victims of the country's incongruity. . . . The situation was infinitely pathetic, not to say appalling.

The Census Report showed that in the 1920s the population decline of New Bedford and Fall River, both cities with populations of over 100,000, was only 6.9 and 4.3 per cent, respectively; but the conditions in these towns were perhaps no better than in Lowell or Lawrence.

Fall River, one of the oldest mill towns in New England, was also practically dead as a textile center. Were I to describe its plight from the human point of view I should be only repeating, with slight changes, what I have said about the plight of Lowell and Lawrence. The immediate reason for Fall River's decline, however, was somewhat different. A former labor leader in Fall River said to me, without any attempt at hiding his bitterness, "The trouble with this place is that the machinery in all these big mills which you see is archaic. In some of them the equipment has not been replaced since the mills were built, thirty and forty years ago. Of course, they cannot compete in production efficiency with mills equipped with modern machines, each of which produces with the aid of a single worker more than twenty machines here used to produce with ten workers. But years ago most mills were tremendous money-makers. They paid dividends of as high as two and three hundred per cent. At the same time the wages were slavery wages. They employed children in their early teens and women, pregnant and otherwise. They worked them night and day, twelve and fourteen hours at a stretch. That was before Massachusetts legislated against such things. . . . It was a high-pressure 'racket,' cruel to the workers, cruel to the city of Fall River, suicidal for the mills. . . ."

New Bedford was a victim of a combination of circumstances. There was archaic machinery in some of the mills. New Bedford, too, was a "mistake"—like Lawrence—which was being rectified; the companies whose mills dominated New Bedford had also new mills in the neighboring states and in the South where laws allowed longer working hours and there were no labor unions.

I bought lunch for a jobless worker who told me he had not eaten a decent meal for months—"or maybe it's years. I'm losing track of time." He had a family of four. A brother of his in New Jersey, he told me, had recently killed his wife and child and committed suicide. "I don't blame 'im," he said. "I'd do the same; only I ain't got the guts. I'd have to kill four of 'em. And I couldn't . . . I couldn't. Christ, ain't it awful! . . . And suppose I do get a job soon. I am in debt hundreds of dollars and it'll take me years to pay it back. There's nobody I know in town who's ever had any money that I don't owe him some. We owe to the groceryman, butcher—everybody. You don't know what it means to have a wife and kids and no work and no money, and be in debt."

In Maynard, Massachusetts, the conditions were extremely chaotic, too, though—quantitatively, at least—not as tragic as in the larger towns. There is but one considerable mill in Maynard. Once it had employed 1,500 people; when I was there, two thirds were completely "out" and the rest worked only part time, earning from $8 to $9 a week. Approximately the same was true of Housatonic, another small mill town in Massachusetts which I visited.

I spent a few days in the Rhode Island mill towns—Manville, Woonsocket, Ashton, Berkley and Lawnsdale, not far from Providence; most of which have but one good-sized mill working part time. But those who worked there, while they worked, worked long hours for lower wages than similar workers received in Massachusetts. I saw bad working conditions —men and women and even boys and girls in their teens working fifty-four hours a week. I saw "speeding-up" and "stretching-out." I saw girls in one town, for instance, running thirty wide looms from before sunup till after sundown. In most Massachusetts towns, where the unions had some power, operatives ran on the average of only twenty looms eight hours a day, and even that was considered a great strain upon a person's energy and nerves.

And the average shoe-manufacturing town was no better than the average textile town in New England. Haverhill, Massachusetts, was one of the largest shoe centers in the country, with shoe-factory employees comprising four fifths of Haverhill's laboring men and women, and from the human point of view the situation was as appalling as in the textile towns. Things were further aggravated by a dispute between shoe manufacturers and the Shoe Workers' Protective Union, which included about half of the shoe people in town. Threats to remove their plants from Haverhill had been made by eight firms as the result of union opposition to contemplated wage cuts. The whole city was beside itself. People with whom I talked, including responsible public and semipublic officials, seemed unable to discuss the situation objectively. They talked incoherently, emotionally, about emergency measures to prevent suffering during the winter.

A public official who asked me not to quote him by name said to me, "You say the textile industry is stupid and chaotic. Well, it has nothing on the shoe industry. Here in Haverhill we have over thirty shoe factories. Most of them have been started by selfish little fellows with a few thousand dollars at their command. They rented a little floor space and then had the United Shoe Machinery Company lease to them machines which turn out shoes hand over fist. The manufacturers don't own the machinery; they pay royalties to the U.S.M. on every pair of shoes made. They get a shoe model that they think will sell and then they work day and night producing that model. When they think they have enough shoes manufactured they quit, and to hell with the workers, and to hell with Haverhill. Their most pressing problem then becomes to sell the shoes. And this goes on all over the country. The U.S.M. installs machinery almost anywhere. There are hundreds and hundreds of shoe manufacturers in New England and more elsewhere. The U.S.M. machinery has been working overtime; now there is overproduction. Now there's no work. And the workers who made millions of pairs of shoes did not make enough to have decent shoes on their own feet!"

But Haverhill, perhaps, was not the worst-hit town because of this chaotic overproduction and underpayment of workers in the shoe industry. In Lynn, Massachusetts, only about two thousand of the six thousand shoe workers were employed, full and part time. In Brockton and South Boston the production of working and jobless shoe people was approximately the same. In Manchester, New Hampshire, a worker, long out of a job, told me how, a month before, he had gone to New Haven, Connecticut, in search of work; how a policeman there arrested him for vagrancy, and how a judge threatened to jail him unless he left the city within thirty minutes.

Everywhere chaos and suffering because of stupid greed—because of no vision, no sense of social responsibility on the part of industry.

I describe the social-economic-industrial situation in these New England shoe and textile towns in such detail because what was true of them in 1928–30 became largely true by 1932 or 1933 of the entire United States —and for essentially the same reasons!

In my eleven days of traveling through New England I found but one busy, happy, prosperous town—Salem, Massachusetts, which impressed me as almost a complete antithesis of such places as Lowell, Lawrence, Fall River, Haverhill and Manchester. In comparison with these, Salem was a veritable boom town. In a population of about 40,000 only 600 were unemployed, most of them shoe workers. The stores and hotels in Salem were attractive, busy places. The homes were painted and the whole community had an aspect of well-being.

The reason for this happy status of Salem was mainly that the city had a great textile mill—the Pequot—whose management was intelligent and humane, trying with no small success to run its business not solely for its own immediate, narrow profit, but also for the benefit of its two thousand operatives and, through them, of Salem. The Pequot Mill workers' average weekly wage was around $34 for forty-eight hours—an amazing stipend for the textile industry. Their employment was steady; at least no one was laid off at a moment's notice, irrespective of his or her circumstances; for the Pequot management had tried in the past and continued in its efforts, to stabilize production as much as possible and plan ahead. The sanitary and safety appliances in the mill were the most modern. I inspected the mill and spoke with the workers and their union's leaders. Nowhere within the realm of the textile industry—and in very few other industries—were employees treated half so well as at Salem.

The result was that the relations between the management and the workers, all of whom were organized, were excellent, and that Pequot had a force of contented, healthy, efficient operatives who, individually and through their union, did everything possible to help the firm decrease the production costs. The textile workers' union at Salem was recognized by the Pequot people; indeed, the mill management and the union, headed by an intelligent labor leader, maintained a joint research bureau under the direction of an efficiency engineer, with the purpose of further decreasing the production costs, stabilizing production, and increasing the profits and wages as the operating costs were lowered in the mill.

In Pequot was a strong touch of industrial democracy. The employees did not live in constant fear of losing their jobs. When I was in Salem everybody there knew that the mills had enough work to run full time until the spring, and the workers were fairly sure that there would be work after that. In consequence, the people did not hesitate to spend their money. I saw mill girls come to work in the morning clad in raccoon coats, and in the evening I saw a group of them in evening gowns dining with boy friends at the Hawthorne Hotel. Naturally, then, Salem—in sharp distinction from Lowell, Lawrence, New Bedford and Fall River—was a pleasant, thriving town.

THE MINER'S ORDEAL

THE DEPRESSION was no novelty in the coal fields of America. The Twenties had seen a slight decline in the production of coal and a substantial decline in price. Bituminous production had gone down, between 1920 and 1929, by about 6 per cent, and prices by some 55 per cent. In 1932 production dropped by about 42 per cent from the 1929 figure (45 per cent from 1920), and prices fell by about 57 per cent from 1929 (81 per cent from 1920). This table tells the sad story:

BITUMINOUS COAL PRODUCTION

	Net Tonnage	Value
1920	568,666,000	$2,129,933,000
1929	534,988,000	952,781,000
1930	467,526,000	795,483,000
1931	382,089,000	588,895,000
1932	309,709,000	406,677,000

"The structure of the bituminous industry," one writer has noted, "was totally inadequate to meet the crisis. The horizon of the typical operator was fixed at the line of his own property. The consumers of coal, mainly the large steel, railroad and utility corporations, played the operators off against each other. Since labor constituted about two thirds of mining costs (and there was an enormous oversupply of labor), the operator passed on his falling prices in lower wages. Survival depended upon wiping out union wage scales and with them the union itself." * Indeed, one way of cutting wages where miners

* Irving Bernstein, *The Lean Years.*

were paid by the ton was the falsification of weights, and the miners were at the mercy of the checkweighman.

Throughout the Eastern coal-mining areas of Illinois, Kentucky, West Virginia, Ohio and Pennsylvania, the families of miners experienced unimaginable privation. In one community a teacher asked a little girl in her classroom whether she was ill. "No," said the child, "I'm all right. I'm just hungry." When the teacher suggested that she go home and eat something, the child replied, "I can't. This is my sister's day to eat."

In many mining towns a miner could buy only at the company store, where prices were usually higher than at outside markets. The miner often made his purchases against his next pay check, and regularly found himself, at payday, with little or no cash due him. There were other ways, too, by which the company would prevent the miner from buying elsewhere; generally it was the threat of dismissal, but in Harlan County, Kentucky, the miners frequently were paid in scrip, which was negotiable only at the company store. And from the Harlan County miner's pay envelope, according to a *Fortune* Magazine report, "the company deducted an average of $11.80 monthly for rent, medical attention, powder and caps and insurance. To pay this deduction, a man had to mine forty-five tons of coal a month, which meant he had to work nine days. Most of them worked a total of six days, and the result is a load of debt with no balance for food." *

There was little opportunity for the miners to change these conditions. A "troublemaker" could easily be replaced. Attempts at organization—by the United Mine Workers of America, the Progressive Mine Workers and, in Harlan County, the National Miners Union—were met with vigorous, often bloody, countermeasures by the companies.

IRVING BERNSTEIN

CATASTROPHE IN COAL†

In 1931 a Harlan miner wrote:

We are half fed because we can'nt feed ourselves and family's with what we make. And we can'nt go to a Cut rate Store and buy food because most all the company forbids such tradeing. If you got the cash. But now we have no cash. And the companies keeps their food stuffs at high prices at all time. So you can not clear enough to go anywhere. And if you do go some where and buy food you are subjects to be canned. . . .

We have been eating wild green. . . . Such as Polk salad. Violet tops, wild onions. forget me not wild lettuce and such weeds as cows eat as a cow wont eat a poison weeds. . . . Our family are in bad shake childrens need milk women need nurishments food shoes and dresses—that we cannot get. and there at least 10,000 hungry people in Harlan County daily. I know because I am one off them. . . . I would leave Harlan County if I had only $6 to send my wife and boy to Bristol, Va. and I could walk away—But I can't clear a dollar per month that why I am here. that why hundreds are here.

There was only the dim memory of a union in the Harlan field. The United Mine Workers, which had organized the region during World War I, was destroyed locally in the early Twenties. District 19, with jurisdiction over Harlan and Bell Counties, was a "paper" organization headed by William Turnblazer. Harlan had the reputation, richly deserved, of being "the toughest spot to unionize" in the United States. A Harlan operator put it succinctly: "We can't do business if they have unions." The mining companies and the public officials they controlled had no intention of yielding this distinction to another locality.

In February 1931, the Harlan employers cut wages 10 per cent. While

* "No One Has Starved," *Fortune,* September 1932.
† From Irving Bernstein's *The Lean Years* (Boston, Houghton Mifflin, 1960).

this was merely the latest in a long series of reductions, the reaction was unique. "We starve while we work; we might as well strike while we starve." The UMW staged a meeting at Pineville, the Harlan county seat, on March 1 at which Philip Murray exhorted 2,000 miners to join up. Many did. The Black Mountain Company retaliated by firing 175 of its men and the Black Star Company discharged 35. Evictions from company houses followed. Another meeting was held at La Follette three weeks later, addressed by Turnblazer and Congressman J. Will Taylor. They denounced the discriminatory discharges and evictions and urged the men to sign. Turnblazer promised that the UMW would provide food and money for a strike. Over 11,000 miners streamed into the union, and the mines shut down. Violence, endemic in the Kentucky mountains, soon appeared. The strikers, failing to receive food from the union, looted stores and gardens. Deputized mine guards physically assaulted the striking miners.

Near the town of Evarts on May 4 several carloads of deputies, carrying rifles and machine guns, engaged in pitched battle with about a score of armed miners. The Battle of Evarts lasted thirty minutes and at its end four men (three deputies and one miner) lay dead. An obscure strike in a remote mountain region suddenly erupted into nationwide prominence. Harlan County entered the national consciousness, like the name of the state in which it was situated, as "a dark and bloody ground."

Governor Flem D. Sampson was urged to send troops into Harlan. His agents first entered into an agreement with Turnblazer: the UMW would welcome the soldiers; food would be supplied; mine guards would be disarmed and their commissions as deputies revoked. The National Guard, 400 strong, arrived on May 6. The agreement was immediately repudiated. Union leaders were arrested, scabs, many of them Negroes, were imported, and mine guards retained their arms and commissions. In fact, on May 11, Sheriff J. H. Blair announced that he knew of no agreement and had no intention of relieving deputies. On May 16, Blair conducted a raid upon the offices of the UMW local in Evarts and uncovered evidence of IWW activity. Some of the members were Wobblies and they had applied for a charter in the Industrial Workers of the World. This allowed the enemies of the union to invoke Kentucky's criminal syndicalism law by claiming a conspiracy to overthrow the government. Further, twenty-eight UMW members were charged with first-degree murder for the death of a mine guard at the Battle of Evarts.

At this point the United Mine Workers quit. Turnblazer told the men that their strike was a "wildcat" and that they should return to work. The

UMW gave no reason, then or later, for the sharp reversal of policy. This failure gave apparent substance to the charge, repeatedly leveled by its enemies, that the union had "sold out" its Kentucky members. Whatever the merits of the accusation, there was abundant evidence that the cause was hopeless: the operators were relentless, the apparatus of the state was on their side, food and funds were virtually nonexistent, and economic conditions were desperate. The strike of the mountaineer coal diggers, which slowly petered out, was not a collective bargaining dispute: it was a revolt born of desperation and doomed to defeat.

Recognizing this, the Communist Party filled the vacuum UMW left. The attractions were irresistible; here, in fact, was the class war with capitalism Marx had predicted, with the state joined against the workers. The "reformist" trade union was bankrupt. In their present mood the miners, innocent of unionism and collective bargaining, to say nothing of political polemics, were readily manipulable. The Harlan murder trial before a prejudiced judge whose wife was a member of the Coal Operators Association (the people of Harlan, Judge David Crockett Jones declared, don't need "anyone from Russia or any warped twisted individuals from New York to tell us how to run our government") might be exploited as another Mooney-Billings or Sacco-Vanzetti case. The Party, sensitive to the charge of foreign influence, would speak for an impeccably "American" constituency: the Kentucky mountain folk were indubitably Anglo-Saxon, their pioneer ancestors had followed Daniel Boone through the Cumberland Gap, they spoke Elizabethan English, did square dances and sang old English ballads. American writers and intellectuals, by 1931 moving into the Communist Party and its environs in large numbers, could be counted on to dramatize the Harlan spectacle and to evoke national and even international sympathy. The Party considered Harlan, Malcolm Ross observed, as "one of those powder boxes where a well-placed fuse can blow a hole in the Capitalist System."

Dan Brooks, organizer for the leftist National Miners Union, arrived in Harlan on June 19 and was soon followed by Jessie Wakefield of the International Labor Defense, who took over legal and relief activities. Many of the miners were eager for any outside assistance regardless of source. The local union held a secret meeting on July 2 which voted to send delegates to the NMU convention in Pittsburgh in mid-July. The organization then came into the open. A picnic attended by 2,000 miners and their families was staged on July 26 and was followed by a state convention of 500 delegates at Wallins Creek on August 2.

Behind the NMU marched the writers and intellectuals, those estimable tourists Judge Jones called "snake doctors from New York." Early in November the Dreiser Committee made a widely publicized voyage to Harlan County. Theodore Dreiser was chairman of the National Committee for the Defense of Political Prisoners. In open telegrams he invited a number of prominent citizens—senators, businessmen, publishers, college presidents—to join the trip. Almost all refused. His group consisted mainly of writers—John Dos Passos, Sherwood Anderson, Charles Rumford Walker and Bruce Crawford, among others. Their results were published in a book, *Harlan Miners Speak*. Early in 1932 a committee of New York writers, including Waldo Frank, Edmund Wilson, Malcolm Cowley and Mary Heaton Vorse, descended upon Harlan with several truckloads of food and clothing. They were followed by a delegation of pastors and several groups of students. Finally, in May 1932, a committee of prominent attorneys made the trip under the sponsorship of the American Civil Liberties Union. It seemed that a writer or intellectual who failed to reach Harlan in 1931–32 was hardly worth his salt. The attendant publicity gave the county's name a certain stench in the national nostrils and helped to launch an investigation by the Senate Manufacturers Subcommittee in the spring of 1932.

Any disposition the operators may have had to abide by the rules evaporated with the arrival of the Communist union in the summer of 1931. They were no longer merely defending low wages, union-busting, and evictions; they now guarded the American Way of Life. This required the suppression of civil liberties by terror in Harlan and Bell Counties. According to Herbert Abel, the operators conducted

. . . a systematic unrelenting campaign. The forces of the coal guards roam the countryside at night, terrorizing the inhabitants. Meetings are broken up with tear-gas bombs, raids are conducted almost every night with their consequent toll of deaths, houses are broken into and property confiscated, the mails are tampered with, the slightest resistance is met with the force of guns.

Scores of people were arrested for criminal syndicalism. Visitors were made unwelcome. The Harlan County attorney notified Arthur Garfield Hays that his "godless, self-appointed, nondescript, iconoclastic minority of grandiloquent egotists" would be treated like "mad dogs." Outsiders were beaten, ridden out of the county and subjected to seizure of property. The operators called in a notorious gunman, Bill Randolph ("He's killed three or four men," one of his defenders admitted). Relief was denied to strikers. Herndon Evans, editor of the Pineville *Sun* and chairman of the local Red Cross, admitted that he checked with the employer to determine whether applicants were on strike. "We tell the men on strike that they'd better go back to work, even if there is water in the mines and conditions aren't what we'd like to have them."

The campaign was a spectacular success. By the end of 1931, the National Miners Union was smashed and the Harlan and Bell operators had achieved control over their workers. At this point the union performed an act of irresponsibility to its few remaining loyal members: NMU called a general strike for January 1, 1932. It proved a disaster. The union disappeared from Kentucky and its members were hounded out of the mines.

By the winter of '32–33, the coal industry was in a state of complete demoralization. Its condition called to mind the old western Pennsylvania story about the final day of a worked-out mine: The last grizzled miner placed the last lump of coal on the last worn-out pit car. He threw his battered broom and his rusty pick and shovel atop the load, and guessed at its weight. With the help of his faithful but ancient dog harnessed to the car (the mine mule had died) he laboriously dragged the load to the tottering old tipple and dumped it into the last railroad car below on the rusty siding. The tipple at that moment collapsed. The pit car dropped in a heap and fell to pieces. The old dog died. Since the grizzled old miner didn't know what else to do, he went on strike.

SIGNS OF CHANGE

ALTHOUGH, in general, the hard times of the early Thirties affected the living conditions of practically all Americans, for some the necessary adjustments were minor. Some families in the higher economic strata merely had to reduce the lavishness of their entertainment; others, on a slightly lower economic level, had to forego some of the luxuries of foreign travel, club memberships, or palatial domestic establishments. But the vast majority of those with jobs and regular incomes made their adjustments by finding more of their recreation in the home or where entertainment and sport were comparatively inexpensive or free.

Hobbies, like stamp collecting and jigsaw puzzles, and table games, like checkers and chess, achieved unprecedented popularity. But it was bridge that acquired by far the greatest number of devotees. In its new, more intricate form, contract, bridge absorbed the attention of people in all sections of the country. Proficiency at it became almost a social requisite—so much so that in 1931 the American public paid ten millions dollars for lessons.

The year before, it had been an outdoor recreation that established itself in comparable measure. In 1930, according to Frederick Lewis Allen, "the Department of Commerce had found at least one thoroughly prosperous business statistic to announce: there were almost 30,000 miniature golf courses in operation, representing an investment of $125,-000,000, and many of them were earning 300 per cent a month. If the American people were buying nothing else in the summer of 1930, they were at least buying the right to putt a golf ball over a surface of crushed cotton seed and through a tin pipe." *

Together with the change in recreational interests, there was a noticeable change in the public's attitude toward heroes of the day. As Allen put it, "the noble art of ballyhoo, which had flourished so successfully in the 1920s, had lost much of its vigor. Admiral Byrd's flight to the South Pole made him a hero second only to Lindbergh in the eyes of the country at large, but in the larger centers of population there was manifest a slight tendency to yawn; his exploit had been overpublicized, and heroism, however gallant, lost some of its spontaneous charm when it was subjected to scientific management and syndicated in daily dispatches. As for Shipwreck Kelly, premier flagpole sitter of the 1920s, he was reported to have descended from the summit of the Paramount Building in 1930 because no one seemed to be watching.

"There were other signs of change; some of them had begun long before the panic; others developed some time after it; but taken together they revealed striking alterations in the national temper and the ways of American life.

"One could hardly walk a block in any American city or town without noticing the women's clothes, for

* Frederick Lewis Allen, *Only Yesterday* (New York, Harper, 1931).

55

instance. The skirt length had come down with stock prices. Dresses for daytime wear were longer, if only by a few inches; evening dresses swept the ground. Defenders of the knee-length skirt had split the air with their protests, but the new styles had won out. Bobbed hair was progressively losing favor. Frills, ruffles and flounces were coming in again, and the corset manufacturers were once more learning to smile.

"The long skirts and draperies and white gloves of 1930 and 1931 were the outward signs of a subtle change in the relations between the sexes. No longer was it the American woman's dearest ambition to simulate a flat-breasted, spindle-legged, carefree, knowing adolescent in a long-waisted child's frock. The red-hot baby had gone out of style. Fashion advertisements in 1930 and 1931 depicted a different type, more graceful, more piquant, more subtly alluring; decorum and romance began to come once more within the range of possibilities.

"What the fashions suggested was borne out by a variety of other evidence. The revolution in manners and morals had at least reached an armistice.

"Not that there was any general return to the old conventions which had been overthrown in the 1920s. The freedom so desperately won by the flappers of the now graying 'younger generation' had not been lost—the people were pretty much bored with the whole idea.

"Robert Benchley expressed a widely prevalent opinion when he wrote in his dramatic page in The New Yorker, late in 1930, 'I am now definitely ready to announce that Sex, as a theatrical property, is as tiresome as the Old Mortgage, and that I don't want to hear it mentioned ever again.' " *

Despite Mr. Benchley's weariness with the subject, the cause of women's freedom had made substantial advances in the world of business and industry; by 1930 nearly eleven million women were working, and their purchasing power became a major factor in the production and merchandising programs of entire industries. In business offices, women had won virtually inviolable jurisdiction in typing, filing, stenographic and secretarial functions. In nursing, teaching and store clerking, too, women had achieved a majority.

The deepening Depression of the early Thirties whittled away some of the economic advantages that women had gained. Their average wages dropped steadily, and job opportunities became relatively scarce. In New York offices, for instance, women's salaries, which in 1931 ranged from $30 to $60, in 1936 ranged from $25 to $35. And in many places women found that marriage made them ineligible for employment; many municipal public-school systems, for instance, would not hire married women and would automatically dismiss teachers who did marry.

And yet, even during the Depression, women penetrated still further into occupational fields from which they once had been excluded. In 1933 President Roosevelt appointed the first woman Cabinet member in United States history—Frances Perkins, as Secretary of Labor—and the first woman diplomatic representative of this country—Ruth Bryan Owen Rohde, as Minister to Norway.

* Frederick Lewis Allen, Only Yesterday.

BASEBALL IN THE EARLY THIRTIES

DESPITE hard times, baseball, the great American pastime, continued to draw as many fans as ever. The excitement of the pennant race and the World Series helped divert the people from their troubles, at least temporarily. In 1932, Babe Ruth thrilled the country by a feat since become legendary, when, with two strikes on him in the third game of the World Series between the New York Yankees and the Chicago Cubs, he pointed in the direction of the center-field bleachers and hit a home run on the next pitch to that very spot.*

The decade had opened with two great performances in golf and horse racing: in 1930 Bobby Jones got his Grand Slam, winning both amateur and open golf championships in England and America; and in the same year, Gallant Fox, with Earl Sande up, took the Triple Crown, by winning the Kentucky Derby, the Preakness and the Belmont Stakes.

But it was baseball, year in, year out, that held the lion's share of the attention of the sports audience. Superstars like Babe Ruth, Dizzy Dean, Jimmy Foxx, Carl Hubbell, Lefty Grove, Joe DiMaggio and Bob Feller helped maintain an intense public interest in the game. In the early Thirties the cry was often heard, "Break up the Yankees!" or, "Break up the Athletics!" These two teams, with their star-studded rosters, had so dominated the American League that from 1926 through 1932 no other team in the league had been able to win a pennant.

Such prowess did not guarantee world championships, however; anything could happen in a World Series. In the 1930 Series the Athletics had beaten the St. Louis Cardinals of the National League, four out of six games; in the 1931 series the two teams met again, but this time something new had been added—a man by the name of Pepper Martin.

* Years later, Charley Root, the Cubs' pitcher in that incident, said that Ruth hadn't pointed anywhere but had merely held up one finger and called out to Root, "You still need one more, kid."

W . C . H E I N Z

PEPPER MARTIN—THE
HAPPIEST HOOLIGAN*

WHEN the 1931 Series opened Pepper was just a 27-year-old rookie who'd been kicked around the minors for six years. When it closed he had 12 hits and five stolen bases, and the St. Louis Cardinals had licked Connie Mack's great Philadelphia Athletics. What the sports writers wrote then is still true today. In all the history of baseball no other ballplayer has ever come out of nowhere as suddenly and as sensationally.

Pepper had hit .300 in the regular season of '31, but when he broke loose in that Series he came as a complete surprise. The Athletics had just won their third pennant in a row and were going for their third straight win in the Series. They had Mickey Cochrane, one of the all-time great catchers, Jimmy Foxx, who ended up second only to Babe Ruth in home runs, and Al Simmons, who led the league in hitting that year with .390. Throwing for them they had George Earnshaw and Lefty Grove, who had led the league for three years and that season had a record of 31 and 4.

"How do you feel going into your first Series?" Frank Graham, who worked for the New York *Sun* then, said to Pepper just before they opened in St. Louis.

"Like a kid with a little red wagon," Pepper said. He took off his cap and scratched his head. "It seems a shame, though," he said. "Here I am, gettin' into a World Series in my first year as a regular. Think of all the great ballplayers who have been in the majors for years and never get into a World Series."

Think of all the great ballplayers who did get into a World Series, though, and never did what Pepper did. In the first game Grove beat the Cards, 6–2, but he didn't hold Pepper.

"When they raised that flag before the game and we stood at attention," Pepper said, "that silence was so strong it was noisy. I don't know how we got 'em out in that first inning, but when I came up there was two

* From *True* Magazine, October 1959.

men on and two out. I rubbed my hands and resorted to prayer. I said: 'God, be my helper.' "

"I guess He was," I said. *

"He was," Pepper said, nodding, "and that fast ball of Grove's, if you got ahold of it, it'd ring."

Pepper boomed a double off the right-field wall and drove in a run. He also got two singles and stole his first base. When the Cardinals won the second game, 2–0, Pepper got a double, a single and a walk off Earnshaw, stole second and third and scored both runs. By the time the Series moved to Philadelphia everyone in Shibe Park who hadn't seen the games in St. Louis wanted to see if Pepper was real.

"Which one," someone would say, "is he?"

"That one there," someone else would say, "with the dirty uniform."

"I must be warm-blooded," Martin says now, "because I'd always sweat a lot playin'. That's why I never wore slidin' pads. After a few minutes my uniform was wet, and then the dirt would stick to it."

Now when Pepper would get on base there'd be a hum in the stands. Then there'd be an eruption at first, the hum would rise in a roar and Pepper would be streaking for second, the dirt flying behind him. Mickey Cochrane would reach for the pitch-out, throw and there'd be a cloud of dust and Pepper, beak first, would be plowing into second on his belly. Then he'd get up with that big grin on his face, and even the Philadelphia fans would be standing and applauding.

"When I come up in that third game," Pepper says, "Grove said to me: 'You country --- -- - -----, I'm gonna throw this right through your head.' I said: 'You country --- -- - -----, you do that.' Cochrane had to laugh, and I hit the pitch out to the scoreboard in right center.

"You know, they blamed Cochrane for my stealin', but that wasn't right. It wasn't a question of me studyin' the motion of the pitchers, either. I guess it was the subconscious brain that told me to go. I only got the steal sign once in that Series, but you steal in the first ten steps, and I always knew I had the base stole about the time I got under way. Really, I felt sorry for Cochrane. Once he said to me: 'Don't you ever make an out?' "

Pepper got that double, a single and another stolen base in that game and the Cardinals won, 5–2. The next day Earnshaw beat them, 3–0, and gave up only two hits. It was Pepper who ruined the no-hitter. He got both hits and stole his fifth base.

"What's he hitting, George?" Connie Mack asked Earnshaw.

* Author Heinz talking; part of article was based on an interview with Martin in 1959.

"Everything I throw him," Earnshaw said.

"It got so," Pepper's wife says, "that when he'd come up I'd say: 'No. He's not due to get a hit again.' Then he'd get another hit, and finally I just broke down and cried."

That was in the fifth game. Pepper got a homer, two singles and a sacrifice fly and batted in four runs as the Cardinals won, 5–1. Frank Frisch was playing second base for the Cardinals then, and he still talks about that one.

"I can see it like it's yesterday," Frisch says. "In the sixth inning Pepper says to me: 'You get on, Frank, and I'll hit one nine miles.' I got a double, and damned if he didn't do it. He lined the first pitch into the left-field seats."

By now Pepper owned Philadelphia like he owned St. Louis. Crowds followed him wherever he went and waited for him in the lobby of the Ben Franklin Hotel and outside on the sidewalk for hours.

"Tell me, son," one old guy said to him, "where'd you learn to run like that?"

"Well, sir," Pepper said, scratching his head. "I guess I learned it out in Oklahoma. When you get to runnin' out there, there ain't nothin' to stop you."

When the teams left to finish the Series in St. Louis, the crowds mobbed the car Pepper was riding in and jammed traffic on Market Street. At Broad Street Station the cops had to clear a path, and Judge Kenesaw Mountain Landis, who was then Baseball Commissioner, walked up to Pepper and shook his hand.

"Young man," he said, "I'd give anything to change places with you tonight."

"Well," Pepper said, thinking, "it's agreeable to me, salaries and all."

"I don't believe you," Landis said.

Landis was making $65,000 a year and the Cardinals were paying Pepper $4,500. The A's shut Pepper out after that and won the sixth game, 8–1, but the Cards won the seventh, 4–2, with Pepper catching the last out, and he got $4,467.59 out of the winner's share. Then they paid him that $2,500 a week for the vaudeville tour, but after a month Pepper quit.

"I ain't no actor," Pepper said. "This is takin' money under false pretenses and practicin' deceit."

"It just amazed me," his wife says, "that all those people wanted just to *see* him that much."

When Pepper quit the tour he stopped in at St. Louis to see Branch

Rickey. Rickey was the general manager of the Cardinals, then, and he asked Pepper what he'd done with the $10,000.

"Why, I got it right here," Pepper said. "Can't you see all my pockets are bulgin'?"

"Judas Priest!" Rickey said. "Somebody'll rob you."

"No they won't," Pepper said.

Rickey made Pepper buy some bonds, but as soon as he got back to Oklahoma City he unloaded them and paid off the mortgage on his Dad's ranch and bought a home for himself and Ruby. Even if he'd carried the cash back in his kick, though, anyone who tried to lift it would have had to kill Pepper or he'd have been killed himself.

"Pepper Martin," Rickey once told Arthur Daley, of the New York *Times,* "is the most genuine person I've ever met in my life. There never was an ounce of pretense in the man. He was one hundred per cent in everything he did. When he fell in love he fell head over heels in love. If he wanted a new bird dog or a shotgun he bought it whether he could afford it or not. He went all out in everything, and that was why he was so great a ballplayer."

"I can't understand that about myself sometimes," Pepper says. "When I was about eighteen I run a motorcycle race with a fella in Oklahoma City. He had high handle bars and wore them glasses, and in those days I thought that was sissy. We started out by the Capitol and he got ahead of me. Then he slowed up, with a car in front of him and another comin' the other way, and I was about a hundred feet behind. I had mine opened up, and I went right between those two cars. It was so close that I had to turn my hands up on the handle grips to keep from gettin' scraped, but I beat him.

"With nothin' at stake but to win the race," Pepper says, thinking about it, "it was a crazy thing to do. I don't know why I'm like that."

When Rickey calls Pepper a great ballplayer, though, he's talking about something that doesn't show in the records. The records say that in thirteen seasons of playing the outfield and third base for the Cardinals, Pepper averaged .298. Three years he led the National League in stolen bases. In addition to hitting .500 and stealing those five bases in that '31 Series, he got eleven hits in the 1934 Series when St. Louis beat Detroit. But statistics are no way to measure Pepper Martin.

"Pepper," Ripper Collins says, "was the kind of a guy who would kill you with a slide just to get to the next base. If you survived he'd stay up all night nursing you back to health. Then, if the same situation came up again the next day, he'd do it again."

Rip played first base for the Cardinals and later for the Cubs and the Pirates. When he first showed up in a Cardinal camp, though, they tried him in left field.

"They warned me," he once told Frank Graham, "to look out for Martin. They told me never to try for a ball on the fringe of his territory and to keep out of his way if he came into mine, because I might be knocked down and trampled. They told me, too, that it wouldn't do any good to yell for a ball, because he wouldn't hear me.

"I played next to him for four days, being careful to keep from under his feet, and this day, after he'd run from center field into my territory and caught a ball, he discovered his shoe was untied. He threw the ball back to the infield, called time and then knelt and tied his shoe. I stood there, looking at him and he looked up and smiled and said: 'Hello, son. What's your name?' I said: 'Collins.' And he said: 'Collins, eh? When did you join us, today?' "

Rip Collins can tell stories about Pepper by the hour. One of them has to do with the time Bill Terry was playing first base and managing the Giants, and he and Rip met on the field.

"Terry," Rip says, "said to me: 'You don't know how lucky you are not having to play against that Martin. When he's running for first I can hear him coming like doom, and it scares me.' So a couple of years later I'm playing first for the Cubs and here comes Pepper running for first, and it scared me, too."

"I used to bring my knees up high," Pepper says. "I liked to get a good piece off the ground.

"I remember one day in St. Louis when the temperature was up over a hundred and it was too hot to take battin' practice. It was Ladies' Day and the ladies were just sittin' there without anything to amuse them and I felt sorry for them. I got some paper and went under the stands and found some wood. Then I got a blanket from the clubhouse and I built a fire in front of the dugout and sat down in front of it with the blanket around me. Then Diz and Rip Collins, they come out with blankets and sat down with me, and that amused the ladies."

Pepper's two big diversions, though, were his midget racer and his Mudcat Band. One winter, when he came into St. Louis to sign his contract, he saw some midget races at the Arena.

"When I seen 'em run," he says, "I wished I had one, and the next year I had one built. It cost me fifteen hundred dollars, and about every other week I had to send it to Milwaukee to get it fixed for fifty or a hundred dollars."

Lou Schneider, who won the Indianapolis 500 in 1931, drove for Pepper. The car was white—with "Martin Special," a ball bat and two cardinals painted in red on the side—and Schneider won a few races with it.

Once, in the clubhouse before a game, Frisch was giving the club a raking over when suddenly he ran out of words. "Why don't you -------s say something?" he said.

"Well, Frank," Pepper said, "what do you think? Should I paint my racin' car red instead of white?"

Another time, the Cards were opening a crucial series with the Pirates in St. Louis and Pepper missed batting practice. When he did come running into the clubhouse there was grease up to his elbows.

"Where you been?" Frisch said, starting on him.

"I'm sorry, Frank," Pepper said, "but I had a bet with a guy I could beat him in a two-mile race and he was late showin' up."

"That's great!" Frisch said. "We're tryin' to win a pennant and you're tryin' to win a racing bet. How much was the bet?"

"Two quarts of ice cream," Pepper said, "and I won, too."

"No," Frisch said, shaking his head. "We're not crazy. We're perfectly sane, all of us."

"The Dutchman," Dizzy Dean said to Pepper, "is goin' out of his mind."

ROBERT SMITH

THE GASHOUSE GANG,
THE DEANS, AND OTHER HEROES*

PEPPER MARTIN was a member of the Gashouse Gang, the 1934 St. Louis Cardinals, which was almost a reincarnation of the 1894 Baltimore Orioles. There was the same fiery team spirit, the same reliance on craft, teamwork and aggressive play, the same unified determination to keep umpires and opponents in their places.

Frank Frisch, the manager of the crew, was a graduate of the New York Giants, where he had been inoculated with the very virus of Mc-

* Excerpted from Robert Smith's *Baseball* (New York, Simon and Schuster, 1947).

Grawism. Leo Durocher, the shortstop, had earned the nickname Lippy from his own teammates when he was with Miller Huggins' New York Yankees; and he had got himself waived right out of the American League after two seasons. Dizzy Dean, of course, was no man to pull out of any sort of encounter, be it vocal or physical.

Jerome Herman Dean had been a raggedy little cotton picker when he should have been going to school; and when he should have been living in a secure home, running with playmates he had known since he could talk, he was traveling in a ramshackle car with his father and brothers from one backbreaking job to the next. The Army to him had been a refuge, where a kid could get regular meals, shoes, clean clothes and a proper bed to sleep on.

His ability with a baseball was the only thing Dean owned, when he was a kid (he was only nineteen when he signed first with Houston), that offered him a chance to vaunt himself on fairly equal terms with boys who had been to school, had known clean clothes and had taken meals for granted. His boasting, when he was breaking in to baseball, was almost hysterical—fantastic far beyond belief, haphazard to the point of sense-lessness. He gave himself two different names and three different birth-places in his eagerness to create a background and a personality that peo-ple would want to hear about. He contradicted himself, made promises he sincerely meant to keep and broke them immediately because he sincerely thought he was doing right to change his mind.

Steering him through this morass of adolescent antics were two people he had been lucky to meet: his wife, who was determined that her Dizzy was going to win the good things he deserved, and a newspaper writer named J. Roy Stockton, who realized how much ability the boy possessed and who owned the patience, the good nature and the human sympathy to see, through Dizzy's vainglorious babbling, the essential sweetness of the boy's nature.

For Dizzy Dean was not only the finest baseball pitcher of modern times, but an unusually intelligent boy with a great fondness for people, a sharp wit and, at the bottom of his heart, an honest desire to work his head off for the people who liked him.

In this era, between the end of the Hoover regime and the entry of the United States into the Second World War, there were several distinct types of successful professional ballplayers; and it is well to remember in judg-ing them that practically all of them were still boys, many very poor boys, and that most of them had to grow up in the public prints, with each silly boast, thoughtless threat and angry recrimination baked into hard type and left for the world to stare at.

Without his fiery speed ball and his sharp-breaking curve, Jerome Herman Dizzy Dean would have been just a goodhearted and unhappy little braggart, cheated by poverty of a chance to develop his better-than-average mind. As he grew older, he became somewhat shrewd about his own eccentricities and saw to it that his priceless publicity did not wither and die. But he learned, too, that just being Dizzy Dean out loud was not what made people love and admire him—that he had to work hard and win ball games. So he worked hard and won ball games; and people bought tooth paste carrying his name, paid money for his pictures, gave their kids clothing with his name inscribed, or fed them the breakfast food that the comic strips said Dizzy Dean consumed.

He was at his most attractive when he talked about his brother Paul (who was called "Daffy" only by the sports writers). Paul, three years younger than Jerome, had a lightning-fast ball and excellent control. His three-quarters overhand pitching motion was almost the duplicate of Dizzy's, but he did not have Dizzy's spectacular curve—or Dizzy's penchant for talking loudly, loosely and endlessly. Without his eccentric brother, he'd have been merely a very good pitcher. But to Dizzy he was "faster than me," "better than I ever was," and compared to Paul, said Dizzy, "I'm just a semipro." He saw to it that Paul got his rights, too. He even threatened a strike unless Paul's salary were increased. And Paul repaid his interest by returning the admiration sevenfold and sticking to Dizzy in whatever tempestuous stunt the older Dean felt he had to turn to.

When Dizzy went on strike against appearing in exhibition games or being shown off like a prize dog, Paul went on strike, too, and acted just as angry. When Dizzy repented and came back to work twice as hard, Paul too bore down and won a row of ball games.

Typical of Dizzy Dean's antics, which won him the dislike of a number of people who were not inclined to make allowances, was his childish bobbing of the ball up to Pittsburgh batters in a game where he thought the rest of the team wasn't trying. One of his most famous stunts—made more famous because he did it all over again in front of a photographer— was his tearing up two uniforms (Paul helped him) when Manager Frank Frisch suspended him and his brother after they had refused to take the field unless a fine were rescinded. Frisch kept both Deans out of the game after that, in spite of popular clamor, until Dizzy sought the aid of Landis. Landis, after hearing the story, told the Dean brothers quite frankly what a pair of spoiled kids they looked like. And Dizzy, swallowing his pride and his threats with dignity equal to Babe Ruth's, set to and pitched for Frisch some of the finest games of his career.

Dizzy was a good hitter. He loved baseball enough to play any position, and he knew enough about the game to have been valuable anywhere. But he was most valuable to his club in the pitching box. They got their money's worth from Dizzy, too. Not only did he pull countless customers in at the gate; with the aid of Paul, he pitched the Cardinals into a pennant they had practically abandoned hope of winning. That was the year he and Paul won forty-nine games between them. Toward the end of that season, one Dean or another was pitching almost every day.

To see Paul and Dizzy pitch a double-header was like seeing the same man do a perfect job twice. From the center-field bleachers it was not easy to tell them apart. They were built alike and were about the same size. Their motions were nearly identical, both smooth, almost effortless sweeps of the arm halfway between sidearm and overhand. To a batter, there was not much to choose between that streaking fast ball of Paul's and the crackling curve that Dizzy could pour in.

Dizzy shortened his own career by pitching when he had to favor a broken toe. The toe had been hurt when he was pitching his heart out in an all-star game. When his better nature was appealed to, Dizzy was as generous with his skill and strength as he was with his money. And with money he was another of those who "did not know the value of a dollar" —just as if a kid who had worked from dawn to dark for a grudging fifty cents did not know more about what money was and wasn't worth than any news writer alive.

Dizzy got into many a row, with his own teammates, with opponents, with newspapermen, and with the president of the league. He could take a licking with good grace, and he could dish one out. And when he locked horns with the president of the league, he did not exactly come in second. This last set-to came about because Dizzy, harried by a sudden new ruling which forced him to make a distinct pause after his pre-pitching stretch and before sending the ball to the plate, made extra-long pauses which delayed the game interminably. The umpire penalized him for this; and afterward Dizzy found occasion to declare publicly that Umpire George Barr and President Ford Frick were "a pair of crooks." Frick, he went on to say, was "our great little president—but a pain in the neck to me."

For this *lèse-majesté*, Frick suspended Dean and ordered him to New York. Dean denied making the remarks. A newspaper reporter insisted he had. Frick, who, like many other men, thought that a boy becomes a man when he gets a wad of money, insisted on a "written retraction." He wrote it and asked Dean to sign it. But there Dean balked. "I ain't signing nothing," he announced. And he did not sign it, either. Frick lifted the suspension, apparently realizing at last that you could no longer kick a man out of the game just for losing his temper at the boss.

Perhaps not the high point of his career, but certainly the episode that becomes him best, was his fulfillment of a promise to a hospital full of crippled kids to strike out Bill Terry, who was then playing manager of the Giants. The kids had assured Dizzy they would be listening to the radio account of the game, and Dizzy said he would, if possible, fan Terry with the bases full. In the ninth inning of the game next day, with two out and the Cardinals one run ahead, the first two men hit safely. The next man was Critz and after him came Terry. Critz got a base on balls. Dean walked down toward Terry and smiled. "I hate to do this, Bill," he said. "But I done promised some kids I'd fan you with the bases full. That's why I walked Critz."

Then Dizzy went back to the mound and poured this fast ball through for two quick strikes. With two strikes on a good hitter, the traditional—and safest—thing to do is to waste a ball, that is, give the batter a chance to hit a bad ball. But Dizzy fogged the next one, waist-high, across the center of the plate, and Terry just stared at it. That was strike three. Dizzy came chuckling in to the bench.

"Bill never figured I'd dare put that last one right through the middle," he explained.

Dizzy, when his arm was gone, managed to keep pitching for a time on his craft. And perhaps he could have held a baseball job for many years more, with his brains and hitting power. He chose, however, to accept an offer to broadcast baseball games over the radio.

There were other famous players who did their arguing with their fists: Tex Carleton, who once took a swing at the great Dizzy Dean himself; Showboat Ernie Orsatti; Wild Bill Hallahan; and K.O. DeLancey.

Their doings during the championship season of 1934, and particularly in Detroit in the World's Series, sharpened the public taste for vocal and physical aggressiveness on the ball diamond to such an extent that the results have never been properly measured.

The Gashouse Gang set upon umpires and upon fans with a ferocity and a unanimity that had not been seen since McGraw was still playing third. In squads of four and five they used to march out to shout into an umpire's face, unmindful of the fact that Commissioner Landis, following Ban Johnson's lead, was ever ready to back the dignity and security of league umpires with the full strength of his office. It cannot be said that their verbal assaults upon umpires were as well motivated as were those of the old-time "kickers." There were two and often three umpires in even the most ordinary game nowadays, and they were all men who had been trained for their positions by years of major-league baseball or of minor-league umpiring. They were alert, quick-witted and thoroughly honest members of an honorable profession. But Frisch knew that it helped team spirit and enraptured the customers if his gang yelled for every extra inch.

In the 1934 World's Series, the Gashouse Gang introduced to the whole nation an adjunct of professional ball which casual fans had never noticed—the art of bench jockeying, that is, digging vocal spurs into the personal sore spots of individual members of the opposing team. By their scholarly application of this talent they heated up opponents and fans until they finally boiled right over.

Detroit, that fall, when the World's Series began, was like an army camp. All normal commerce, all social activity, even the operations of the great newspapers, were either stalled or utterly unraveled. Clerks deserted their counters, mothers carried their hungering children to the ball park, workingmen stood idle in the street, trolleys neglected their schedules, salesmen forgot to make their rounds, businessmen shushed their customers, and office girls allowed correspondence to turn yellow in the sun. For the first time in twenty-five years Detroit had a World's Series in its home park, and the natives could not have been more stirred had they been called to repel an invasion from Mars. Every avenue and byway echoed with the blasts of street radios which promised great doings in the offing, reported the current play at the park, or repeated over and over again what had taken place just a few hours before.

There were three great heroes in the city then: Schoolboy Rowe, the enormous young hurler ("With a wind behind him," said Dizzy Dean, "he's pretty near as fast as Paul"); Manager Mickey Cochrane (Black Mike), a graduate of Connie Mack's Philadelphia Athletics, where he had become the greatest catcher of the day; and Hank Greenberg, the breathtakingly handsome first baseman who was threatening to push Babe Ruth right off the home-run throne.

Upon these three the brash St. Louis bench jockeys concentrated all their genius. Schoolboy Rowe, delighted to find himself able to face a radio microphone without swallowing his tongue, had concluded a broadcast with a gay little murmur to his wife, who was listening at home: "How'm I doing, Edna?" How many hundred times he must have wished he could have taken a broom and wiped those words away! For he could not make a move upon the diamond after that without a brassy chorus of "How'm I doing, Edna!" arising from the St. Louis bench amid hoarse cackles of sardonic merriment.

Some overwrought caption writer had seen fit to print a picture of Mickey Cochrane under the line OUR STRICKEN LEADER on a day when Mickey had been only mildly bruised. That particular phrase provided the St. Louis bench with a needle they must have stuck under Cochrane's skin a couple of thousand times.

Hank Greenberg reacted to his first World's Series with the tense excitement of most young and suddenly famous ballplayers. And the cries of the St. Louis players did not ease his tension. "Boy," yelled Dizzy Dean, "what makes you so white? You're trembling like a leaf! Must be you heard Old Diz is going to pin your ears back!"

On the field of play the Gashouse Gang implemented their vocal needling with plenty of rough base running; and they finally hit the jackpot when Joe Medwick, who is put together like a small brick building, slammed into Marvin Owen, the Detroit third baseman, and Owen retaliated by tagging him with force enough to leave a mark. The two men almost simultaneously began to slug at each other. And when, after the row had been quelled and the St. Louis inning completed, Medwick took his position in the outfield, the nearby fans greeted him with a shower of vegetables, worn-out fruit, sandwiches, boxes, pieces of chairs, and bottles —in fact, anything bruising they could set their hands to. Judge Landis, in the stands, finally decided that Medwick would have to be withdrawn.

It must not be thought that the Gashouse Gang was the first, the last, or the only team to instigate this wholesale participation by fans in the side issues of the game. In St. Louis there had been several instances of bottle throwing—one an almost fatal injury to Umpire Billy Evans. In the Twenties, Whitey Witt, then a New York outfielder, had been struck on the head and seriously hurt by a thrown bottle. McGraw's Giants, too, had undergone a shower of bottle in the same St. Louis park. Detroit fans in the Twenties, stirred to action by the exchange of obscenities, bean balls, and fisticuffs on the diamond, piled down into the fight to the number of many hundreds, bringing clubs made out of chairs to give the New York Yankees' Murderers' Row a little of their own medicine. And in the Yankee Stadium, not too long ago, fans heaved a gross or two of bottles at Umpire Rue because he had called a ball foul which might possibly have been fair.

But it was the Gashouse Gang and its eager publicists who began to make it clear that "color" in the form of rough talk and violence was as salable a commodity as eccentricity. In St. Louis, coupled with aggressive and winning baseball, it pulled in throngs so deep they had to sit on the grass.

Bench jockeying, of the type exemplified in that Detroit series, has always been a part of baseball, enjoyable to the players and even valuable in a way.

The accomplished bench jockey and his understudy, the loudmouthed man, take pains, however, to find the aspect of a man's personality or background which he can least bear to have discussed; and they harp on that with as much vulgarity and as little wit as they can manage.

But the public attitude toward baseball, through the Roosevelt era, was not entirely one of vaunting the loudmouth, the name-caller, and the picker of fights. Much was left of the sophisticated sentimentality of the late Twenties, when hero worship, both gay and solemn, colored the published annals of the game. As the Thirties grew older, however, and people in increasing numbers participated in the great mass movements—the NRA, the sit-down strikes, the new unions of employed and unemployed, the petitionings of Congress—they became less likely to be moved to tears by the story of the man who silently bled to death because "the show must go on" or so that fellow crooks rather than "coppers" should privately avenge his murder. Heroes now had to be of truly heroic size: not men who owed allegiance to a team, a private ethic, or the College Militant, but men who faced a whole world of enemies, with a town, a country, or even half a nation at their backs.

When Carl Hubbell, the New York Giants' lean pitcher, who was called "Long Pants" because of his habit of fastening his knee pants just above his ankles, struck out, as a representative of the National League in an all-star game, five in a row of the most murderous sluggers in the American League, you might have thought he had beat back with a rusty bayonet a squad of assassins come to do our President to death. There is no denying that Hubbell demonstrated unusual ability with a baseball. Using his famous "screwball" (the Mathewson fadeaway), he showed the most-talked-of hitters in the opposing league that there was more to the game than just slamming the horsehide sphere with all the strength in your back. But the tributes to his clear-eyed daring, his raw courage, his fierce heroism that echoed through many a parlor at broadcast time suggested he must have been bathed in blood.

In the seasons just preceding the Second World War, fans in many parts of the country used to lend themselves quite honestly to the delusion that the Browns, the Dodgers, the Pirates, or the Reds were championing them and their city against all who had conspired to keep the milk, the honey and the gold forever from there.

Other towns, while perhaps never so fervid, had their own heroes in this age. In Boston, I know, many boys felt about Wesley Ferrell—who used to throw his "nothing" ball down to his brother Rick while batter after batter waved vainly at it—the way they should have felt about their fathers. In the early part of the Depression period, the Braves' pitchers Lou Fette and Jim Turner, two "old men" (they were rookies, though in their thirties), brought solace to many a young fellow who was watching for the first gray whisker on his temple.

In Cincinnati young Johnny Vander Meer became the man most kids wanted to be when they grew up: he pitched two no-hit games in succession. Pitcher Bobo Newsom (called Bobo because he called everybody else Bobo) had a following in nearly every city in the country, for he played in almost every one, shuttling from majors to minors, from National to American Leagues, and from team to team in a manner never equaled. A few of the better folk found baseball reasonably attractive after blue-blooded young Charlie Devens, a star at Harvard, had put in a spell with the Yankees. In Washington and Chicago, Joe Kuhel was known as the ablest first baseman in the business; and Bill Jurges was another man who could have had a free drink in almost any Chicago bar when beer came back. New York kids grew to manhood and womanhood blindly admiring a quiet lad who had been a major leaguer since he was sixteen—Mel Ott, who finally became manager of the Giants.

For the fans who missed Babe Ruth—who had left baseball before the 1930s were out—the Yankees offered Joe DiMaggio, a lean, long-nosed center fielder from California. Joe, compared to Ruth, was like a ball-playing machine. He never seemed to excite himself at the bat. He swung smoothly and gracefully, with great precision and a tremendous follow-through. He was what is known as a wrist hitter, for he held his swing until the final instant, took almost no forward stride and then snapped the bat at the ball in a short swift arc. He was not a bad-ball hitter, was not given to striking out and never offered the appearance of either gaiety or anger, or tremendous effort. His smile was self-conscious, his manner withdrawn to the point of chill. He was interested in money—his own and other men's. He preferred the company of those who "counted" and had little time for small boys who wanted autographs. Like the majority of modern ballplayers, he was of a saving nature, never upset anyone with the size of his tips or the abandon of his spending, and sought out many devices for boosting his income off the field and on.

He was as accomplished on defense as he was at bat. He sped gracefully and easily across the green outfield, hardly seeming to lift his feet higher than the grasstops. Until he injured a shoulder, he sent long, low, almost geometrically perfect throws into the diamond. He was soft-spoken on and around the ball field and created no exciting stories for the press— except the wonders he worked at bat. His marriage to a showgirl and the subsequent rumors of divorce made a scattering of items for the Broadway columnists, but these were nothing to the fans. He held out frequently for higher pay, once hired a Broadway character to "manage" him, and made himself unpopular early in his career, with some fans and teammates, by missing, for one reason or another, part of the training and playing season.

DiMaggio set new records for consecutive hitting, and continued to blast the ball when he should have been laid up with a bad arm, a bad foot, or some more serious ailment.

MILDRED "BABE" DIDRIKSON ZAHARIAS

IN 1950, an Associated Press poll declared Babe Didrikson the greatest all-around woman athlete of the first half of the twentieth century.

At the age of nineteen, she was a sensation in the 1932 Olympic Games at Los Angeles, winning the 80-meter hurdles and setting a new world record with the javelin throw, and she would have had at least a first-place tie in the high jump but for a judge's ruling against her style of jumping. Paul Gallico said she could also "play basketball, tennis, pool and billiards, swim, golf in the 80s, and throw a baseball and a football." One of her tricks was to go up to an opponent before a sports event and announce, "Ah'm gonna lick yuh tomorrow." She usually did.

Shortly after her Olympic success, Miss Didrikson turned professional. In 1938 she married George Zaharias, a wrestler, and with his encouragement she became one of the country's top women golfers. She won the U.S. Women's Open golf championship three times and, after being reinstated as an amateur, was the first American to win the British Ladies golf championship.

Mrs. Zaharias was one of the most popular athletes of her day and an especial favorite of the press, for she made good copy. Her death in 1956 ended a career that spanned almost a quarter of a century, during which countless newspaper and magazine pieces were written about her. One of the very best of those is Paul Gallico's portrait of her at the 1932 Olympics.

PAUL GALLICO

THE TEXAS BABE*

DURING the recent Olympic games in Los Angeles, four of us, including Grantland Rice, played a game of golf at Brentwood with Mildred "Babe" Didrikson, the world's champion lady athlete. At the conclusion of the round, during which the Babe belted the ball consistently for 240 and 250 yards and sneaked long, easy irons up to the cup, there was a moment of slight embarrassment as we paid off our porters and settled petty bets. Nobody knew whether to invite the Babe into the men's locker room for

* From *Vanity Fair*, October 1932.

a bath and a drink, or whether to say, "Well, good-bye, kid, see you later."

Eventually, the Babe traipsed off with some of the women folk, but as we sat around in the locker room with towels around our haunches, clinking ice in tall glasses and telling lies, we missed her in a way. Up to the eighteenth green, she had been one of us—and better than most of us. The strange, nineteen-year-old girl-boy child would probably have been right at home there.

If one must be a Muscle Moll, and apparently this urge smolders in many a female chest—there were hundreds of them, the pick of the nations, at the Olympics—then I suppose the next thing is to be the best one in the world, the Muscle Moll to end all Muscle Molls, as it were. When a lady athlete can perform the feats that La Didrikson can, she begins to exercise a peculiar and mysterious fascination all her own.

Your deponent spent considerable time in the Chapman Park Hotel in Los Angeles, where the lady athletes of all nations were quartered, studying at close range the Muscle Molls, and I am still giving them to you, with the exception of three or four of the American girl swimmers and divers and the incomparable Didrikson. You can't have her. I like her. She's a champion. She is a champion of champions. She is unquestionably the greatest all-around athlete this country has ever produced. If she were a man—well, there never has been a man who could do half the things she can in sports, or do them as competently.

The Babe stands five feet seven inches in height. She weighs 126 pounds. She has greenish-blue eyes, an aquiline nose, a mop of brownish hair, close-cropped in back like a boy's, but worn floppy, and a little longer in front. Her mouth is large and thin-lipped. One of the girls on the swimming team said she had a mouth like a lizard's. The comparison is apt. There is light fuzz on her upper lip, her face, her neck. She has an enormous Adam's apple. Her legs are powerful and hirsute, with large, strong ankles. Her body is slim, compact, hard. She has the biceps of a village blacksmith. She is magnificently graceful. She looks like a boy. She is a splendid dancer. She would rather dance than do anything else. She plays, among other games, baseball, football, golf, basketball, polo, soccer, lacrosse and tennis. She was said to be entering the women's national golf tourney in Massachusetts. She is taking adagio dancing on the side. But darned if I know what makes her tick.

I went through the whole list of sports with her, trying to find something she couldn't do—fencing, bowling, skating, billiards, swimming, diving— she is an adept at all of them. Finally I said, "Great guns, Babe, isn't there anything you don't play?"

"Sure," she said—"Dolls."

There was no use asking her about boxing. We had already heard the two classic stories, and both verified. In high school she entered an amateur boxing tournament and flattened three bona fide males before they discovered what was going on. In Dallas, Texas, at some kind of athletic affair, someone suggested that she slip on a pair of 12-ounce mittens and spar with Babe Stribling, younger brother of Willie the Clutch.

She said, "I will if you can make him promise not to go easy with me." They sparred. Didrikson foot-feinted, showed Stribling her left and then banged him square on the potato with a right cross that split his mouth and brought the evening's entertainment to a charming conclusion.

She was introduced to Frank Craven in the lobby of the Chapman Park one evening, and golf was mentioned. The Babe was masticating some gum. Without breaking the beautiful rhythm of her jaws, Marvelous Mildred clouted Craven on the spine and offered to golf, wrestle, or fight him. Mr. Craven paled, coughed and retired.

Her first appearance in the Olympic games was in the javelin throw. Somebody said, "There's Babe!" I saw an individual who looked like a boy, dressed in a white track suit and shorts, with the red, white and blue diagonal band and the American shield on her chest, running across the field with fluent grace. Her short hair was flying in the breeze of her own speed. Her spear was poised. Diana! When she came to the scratch, she dropped her arm back and whipped it through the air, 143 feet, 4 inches. The old world's record for women was 132 feet, 7/8 inch. The javelin never did attain any height. It flew practically on a line. The Babe explained it, afterward. "It sliypped," she said in her husky drawl. "It sliypped outa mah hand. Ah'd a throwed it much further, if it hadn't sliypped."

It was just as well that it "sliypped." If it hadn't she would have killed six officials at the other end of the field with it.

There is nothing she cannot do in track and field athletics. She sprints, hurdles, broad jumps, high jumps, throws the javelin and discus and puts the shot. In the trials in Chicago she won eleven events. They permitted her to enter but three in the Olympics: the javelin, the 80-meter hurdles and the high jump. She set a world's record in the first two and was robbed of a third, in the jump, by an official.

But none of this explains her. Her parents are Norwegians, Ole and Hannah Didrikson. Her father was a ship's carpenter who came to Port Arthur, Texas, in 1900, where she was born, June 26, 1913. She remembers that she never cared to play with dolls but was always swiping her father's tools and driving nails into things. She has some brothers and a couple of sisters. Of her younger brother, she says that he will be a great all-around athlete. Asked whether her sisters did anything in sport, she hesitated a moment and then said, "Aw shoot, no. They caint do anythin'. They're sissies."

Girls and men who are not athletic are sissies to her. Her attitude toward her sister athletes is curiously aggressive. She went up to Helene Madison, the champion swimmer, in the lobby of the hotel one evening and said to her, "You're the swimmin' champion, ain't yuh?" Helene admitted it. "What's your time for the hundred?" Helene named it—the world's record. The Babe banged Helen on the shoulder. "I'll cut two seconds off that next year," she announced. The serious Madison nearly had a fit. The fancy divers *did* have a fit when Babe calmly announced to them that she could do a two and a half somersault, a dive that very few men do well.

The Los Angeles prints did not receive the Babe kindly. She was outspoken about her powers. For instance, she claimed an eighty-two and drives of 250 yards, after ten games of golf. Of course this was ridiculous. And so, to see for ourselves, we fixed up a golf date. It was the girl's eleventh game of golf. She turned up at the first tee with one of the finest golf swings we had ever seen. Her grip was wrong. But she whistled that clubhead through like a man. She was playing with borrowed clubs after a six months' layoff. When she came to the ninth tee she lashed a ball 260 yards. Grantland Rice said to Olin Dutra, who was standing on the tee, "Did you see that?" Olin replied, "I saw it, but I don't believe it." She played the second nine in 43.

There she was, striding down the fairway in an old pink dress (which she made herself), an Olympic "jumper," and a white hat with a red, white and blue band perched weirdly on the extreme top of her head. She would smack one down the middle of the fairway and say, "Boy, Ah sure hit that one. This is one game I sure would like to know how to play."

She is the same way in competition, eager to go and absolutely confident of her powers. In the high jump, she hardly waited for the official to get out of the way before she was running for the bar. In the 80-meter hurdles she broke once before the gun. Twice meant disqualification. So she sat in her toe holes and let the field get away, caught the leader by inches and broke the world's record.

The Babe was first discovered playing basketball in Houston, Texas, by Colonel M. J. McCombs, a former athlete himself. She came to Dallas to play on the basketball team of his insurance firm. He taught her to run, jump, throw weights and hurdle. The loyal Babe says, "Everybody's claiming how they coached me now. They's just one man coached me and that's Colonel McCombs."

Everybody in Los Angeles was talking about the Babe. Was she all boy? Or had she any feminine traits? She slaps men of short acquaintance on the back hard enough to jar them from head to foot and will roughhouse with anyone. But she saw a pair of shoes she liked in a shop window and bought six pairs because they had none like them in Dallas. She can swear like a man, ride horseback, shoot and play polo, but she came into the room of some of the American swimmers one afternoon, glowing, with a box under her arm. Clothes! New bathing suits! She spread them out on the bed. One of the bathing suits was scant and low-cut in the back. She said, "Boy, Ah guess I'll sure look pretty slick in that."

She told me she had two interests in life: (1) to crack every existing track record for women and crack them so that they would stay cracked, and (2) acquire a husband. I couldn't find out anything about the necessary qualifications for the latter, except that he mustn't be a sissy. Her travels in athletic competition have given her an age and poise far beyond her years. She never gets tired. The day she won the eleven events she admitted that she was a little tired at the end, but not very. She could have gone on.

A very paragon of Muscle Molls.

But not a very happy girl, I judge. She knows that she is not pretty, that she cannot compete with other girls in the very ancient and honored sport of man-trapping. She uses no cosmetics, creams or powders. But she competes with girls, fiercely and hungrily, at everything else.

Underneath, there dwells a child. A national celebrity at nineteen, interviewed, photographed, pursued by autograph pests, she shows flashes of wistfulness that are at times pathetic. There was a garden party at the hotel. The blond Georgia Coleman and Joan McSheehey, the lovely Eleanor Holm and one or two others of the American swimmers were clowning on the lawn with a group of the men athletes, swimmers and divers— young, good-looking kids. They were joining hands and dancing in gay, meaningless circles. The circles merged and became one large one that suddenly swept across the lawn to a shaded corner where stood the Babe in her blue track pajamas, with the shield of the United States on its breast.

Georgia Coleman broke the circle and ran over. "Come on, Babe," she coaxed. "Come on, get in here with us, we're having a Paul Jones."

Babe said, "Shoot, honey, ah caint! I'm competin' tomorrow. . . . Ah caint play tonight. . . ."

The circle formed again and went spinning around the lawn, a rim of young, laughing faces. The greatest woman athlete in the world stood on the outside, looking on.

QUEEN OF THE SKIES

THE Thirties would see undreamed-of expansion of aviation for travel and transportation. Until the decade began, most Americans who "went up" did so for the thrill, sight-seeing at the local airports and county fairs. At that time, there were many who believed the future of aviation was to be found in the development of the rigid airship, the dirigible.

During World War I, the Germans had used the dirigible effectively in air raids over England, where it proved to be a potent psychological weapon. Enthusiasts for air power not only emphasized the dirigible's weapon value, but predicted a great future for it in transportation.

The United States Navy's first dirigible, inflated with hydrogen, was constructed in England; while being tested for flight across the Atlantic, fire broke out and the ship went down. This accident put off acceptance of the ships in the United States until helium, a noninflammable gas, was put into use. In 1925, the first American-built dirigible, the *Shenandoah,* broke into three pieces, a victim of a line squall. But the Navy pushed forward; the Goodyear Company was put to work constructing the two largest airships to date—the *Akron* and the *Macon.*

The *Akron* was 785 feet long and, after being christened by Mrs. Herbert Hoover in 1931, began a series of shakedown cruises. In May 1932, the "Queen of the Skies" completed her first cross-country trip, arriving at the San Diego Naval Base. What happened at this attempted landing is told in the following article by John Toland, who goes on to give an account of the tragic end of this flying ship.

JOHN TOLAND

THE *AKRON* AND THREE
WHO CAME BACK*

AT 9:30 A.M. the "Queen of the Skies" descended through the thick fog bank, coming into the clear at 1,200 feet. Now the heat of the morning sun quickly expanded the helium, making the ship extremely buoyant. Four of the ship's propellers were inverted, like huge overhead fans, in

* From John Toland's *Ships in the Sky* (New York, Holt, 1957).

an effort to pull the *Akron* toward the ground. The power fought the buoyancy, but the dirigible stayed aloft. Since Lieutenant Commander Rosendahl, the ship's skipper, did not want to valve precious helium, the battle against buoyancy lasted many minutes.

It wasn't until eleven o'clock that the 400-foot trail ropes were dropped from the port and starboard sides of the nose, falling neatly between the two landing parties. To the surprise of those in the control car the landing crew merely stood watching the ropes instead of picking them up. Rosendahl looked at Lieutenant George Campbell. Both men knew that they were in for a rough landing. The crew was more inexperienced than they had feared.

Rosendahl made two more passes over the sandy field before the trail ropes were finally grabbed and attached to "spiders," ground lines fitted with wooden toggles. Each of the ground crew men hung onto a wooden toggle, while Peck shouted instructions frantically. The seven-eighths-inch steel mooring cable spun out of the nose of the ship and hit the ground. It was coupled to a ground cable leading to the top of the mooring mast. The winch wound slowly, dragging the reluctant ship down.

The heat of the ground now made the *Akron* even more buoyant. The nose bobbed up. Those men on the forward spiders were lifted slightly from the ground. Then the tail leaped up, almost standing the "Queen of the Skies" on her stubby nose.

Engine Number 8 sputtered. Mechanic Sid Hooper struggled to keep it going but it soon stopped: the steep angle had cut off the fuel. Emil Klaassen had the same trouble in engine room Number 4.

Rosendahl instantly gave orders to valve helium, but it was too late. The angle had automatically tripped the ballast bags and 3,000 pounds of water were dumped. All the engines had by this time rung up "stop." Rosendahl had to act quickly. "Cut the mooring cable!" he ordered. "Let everything go!"

The cable attached to the mast was released, and the two ground parties were told to let go. The *Akron* shot into the air with the long trail ropes dangling below.

From the hatch near Number 4 engine room, Mechanic Quinny Quernheim could see that the starboard trail rope was cleared. Then he noticed that there was a little cluster of men still clinging to the other rope. Fifty feet above ground a tiny figure dropped from the rope. At 100 feet, a second man slipped off the spiders even before the first one struck the ground.

Quernheim watched in horror as the second man hit and bounced.

Shakily he went into the engine room. His face was pale. "My God!" he said to his partner, Klaassen. "That kid smoked when he hit the ground!"

Others in the ship were watching the third man on the spiders. He appeared to be tangled in the web of lines several hundred feet below the ship. Rosendahl knew that if he tried to land the buoyant ship he would probably dash the man to death. He told the rudder man to head for the ocean where the air was smoother.

Two crews, under Lieutenants Roland Mayer and George Campbell, began to improvise rigs to transfer the trail line to the mooring winch so the ground crew man could be reeled to safety.

The *Akron* was now flying 2,000 feet above the Pacific. The stranded sailor, who was sitting astride a toggle, wrapped in a tangle of ropes, looked up. "Hey!" he called, "when the hell are you going to land me?"

An officer called encouragement through a megaphone, but the sailor below didn't seem to need it. He waved and then took off his white cap, stuffing it in his jumper. He didn't want to be read off for losing government property.

The men in the nose of the *Akron* were now trying to figure out a way to haul the sailor into the ship. The top twenty-five feet of the trail rope was one-inch cable—and wouldn't revolve around the drum of the mooring winch.

Boatswain's Mate Second Class Dick Deal volunteered to go down and tie a line below the steel cable section. Deal was slowly lowered out of the nose of the dirigible in a bosun's chair. As he swung dangerously, twenty-five feet below the bow platform, he grabbed at the swaying trail rope. Finally he reached it and, after fifteen minutes, tied a line to it. A few minutes later the steel cable section was cut off and the rope attached to the mooring winch. Then the sailor was hoisted up a few feet at a time.

After a tense hour and a half his head was level with the bow platform. Chief Arthur Carlson, a survivor of the *Shenandoah,* leaned down and grabbed the sailor. At last he was on the platform—safe. He was a rugged, rawboned young man of twenty-one and he was far less excited than those on the platform. He looked around curiously. He had never seen a dirigible this close before.

Captain Rosendahl came up to the young man. "Son," he said, "what do you think of your ride?"

The sailor, whose name was Bud Cowart, grinned. "Captain, that was a lily dilly!"

Young Cowart escaped without a scratch, but two others had died. The "Queen of the Skies" was now more than a jinx, she was a killer.

SKIES were overcast on the morning of April 3, 1933, at Lakehurst. Low clouds scudded across the field from the ocean. But despite the threat of bad weather, in Hangar Number 1 sailors and civilian workers were preparing the *Akron* for her fifty-ninth flight.

In the nearby Administration Building, just across Lansdowne Road, officers were anxiously looking out the windows of the commandant's office. One of the main missions of the flight was to calibrate radio direction-finding stations up in New England, the First Naval District. And work of this nature could not be accomplished unless the skies cleared.

A few minutes before eleven the phone in Commander Fred Berry's office rang. The commandant of the station talked a moment, and from the tone of his voice it was obvious that he was connected with Washington. Then he held out the phone to Commander Frank McCord, the *Akron's* new skipper. "The admiral wants to talk with you," said Berry.

McCord, a short, good-looking man, took the phone. He didn't have to be told who "the admiral" was. At Lakehurst there was only one admiral—William A. Moffett, Chief of the Bureau of Aeronautics and a staunch friend of the rigid dirigible.

While McCord was talking, his executive officer, Lieutenant Commander Herbert V. Wiley, went into the next room and called up the ship's aerologist. "What are the weather probabilities for the flight, Lieutenant?" he asked. Wiley was a big, solidly built man with a shock of shaggy gray hair and a ruddy face that was surprisingly young. With his deep, brooding eyes and broad, thoughtful forehead, he looked more like a philosopher than an airshipman—a philosopher with a barrel chest.

At the other end of the wire young Lieutenant Herbert Wescoat said the ship could be safely taken out of the hangar, but it would be definitely impossible to do any radio or compass work for at least another day.

Wiley quickly went back to the other room. In an undertone he told McCord the bad news. The *Akron's* captain repeated it to Moffett, then hung up. "The admiral," he said, "is coming up from Washington. He wants to fly with us, in spite of the weather."

Late that afternoon the office was crowded with those scheduled to make the evening flight. Admiral Moffett, accompanied by Commander Harry Cecil, had arrived from Washington, where everyone was still buzzing from the new President's stirring "nothing to fear but fear itself" speech. Besides Commander Berry, others who were going along for the ride that evening were A. F. Masury, a reserve Army colonel from the International Motor Company, and three junior officers from the station, who needed the flying time.

In spite of the threatening weather there was the usual preflight air of expectation and excitement, with a leavening of buffoonery and horseplay. For with Moffett present, the men knew the flight wouldn't be canceled unless a hurricane sprang up.

At 4:20 P.M. McCord and Wiley went to the station aerological office and examined the weather map made only twenty minutes before. The captain turned to his executive officer. "Cancel the airplane hook-on drill," he said. "But see if you can take aboard a training plane."

An hour and a half later the two men met again at the weather office. There was a light northeast wind and the temperature had fallen 20 degrees. Wiley phoned the hangar, ordered the Officer of the Deck to put 3,500 pounds of water ballast aboard.

Wiley, a meticulous airshipman who never left a thing to chance, then went to the great hangar himself. Finding the inside temperature even higher than he'd expected, he ordered additional ballast put aboard to compensate for the difference of 16 degrees between the hangar and out-side. He walked out on the field and looked up. Thick balls of fog were rapidly forming.

By six o'clock the hangar was alive. Most of the crew men making the flight had already put their gear on the *Akron*—toilet articles, sleeping-bag liners, and heavy flying clothes. Now they were standing under the ship or loafing in one of the adjoining shops.

Chief Machinist George Walsh looked in the big mechanic shop. "Hey," he called to Mechanic Sid Hooper, "you don't have to make the trip. It's only a short hop. Get Anderson."

Hooper didn't care. He had logged plenty of hours, and Vic Anderson, the third man in Number 8 engine room, needed a qualifying hop for watch-stander. Hooper found Anderson in the crowd. The youngster was nervous with excitement as Hooper handed over his heavy, fur-lined gab-ardine flight jacket, skull-cap flight helmet lined with fur, and big sheep-skin-lined flying boots. Then Hooper went to the front of the hangar to wait for his wife. She was coming to watch the ship take off—the first time he'd allowed it. Now he wouldn't even be aboard.

A few late-comers were on their way, driving over the dark, lonely roads lined with scrubby pines and dwarf oaks. Robert Copeland, chief radio operator, was being chauffeured by his wife. The misty, overcast weather made her nervous. For the tenth time she asked him how dangerous light-ning was. Copeland, who had originally studied to be a missionary, laughed at her fears. "Lightning will go right through the propellers and won't hurt us," he insisted.

Two veterans of the *Shenandoah* were on the back road trom Lakewood. Henry Boswell still looked boyish and unsophisticated. The other man was Dick Deal, who had risked his life the year before to save Cowart in San Diego. He had been scheduled to make the last flight of the *Shenandoah,* but Ralph Joffray, who had relatives in St. Louis, had asked to take his place. Joffray had been at the wheel, next to Lansdowne, when the control car tore out of the *Shenandoah.* This last-minute change suggested to Dick's shipmates that he be called "Lucky" Deal. By a curious twist of fate, five years after the *Shenandoah* crash Deal had married Joffray's widow, the former Gertrude Matthews of Lakewood. At that moment she was at their home on Thirteenth Street in Lakewood, worrying about their hound bitch who was about to have puppies.

Fog thickened as their car crawled through a hollow. Both men had made many stormy trips but neither liked the look of the weather. Boswell, usually a lighthearted fellow, became somber as they neared Lakehurst. "I hope," he said, "they've got sense enough to cancel this flight."

At 6:25 P.M. the heavy hangar doors opened slowly. Fog curled in like smoke. The ship was walked out of the hangar at six forty-one. Seven minutes later the mobile mast had carried its burden to the center of the mooring circle. The temperature was 41 degrees.

Every man was at his landing station. Captain McCord stood at the port side of the control car, giving commands to Lieutenant George Calnan, in charge of ballast. Wiley was at the captain's right, conning the rudder man. Boswell was at the elevator wheel just behind Captain McCord. Admiral Moffet stood back out of the way next to Navigator Harold Mac-Lellan. The admiral watched the weighing-off operations with his usual absorption.

Copeland was in his radio shack, a tiny cabin above the control car. He looked out the window, trying to see his wife, who was standing in front of Hangar Number 1. But it was so dark and foggy that the great shed was only a formless mass. At the bow stood Dick Deal, and at the other end of the ship, almost a sixth of a mile away, Metalsmith Second Class Moody Irwin was at the emergency control station, in the forward section of the huge lower fin. It was a tiny room, just large enough for one man at the elevators and one at the rudder wheel. Irwin leaned out the port window. It was his job to release the X frames that supported the fin during handling operations. These X frames had been devised as insurance against a freak gust of wind.

In all there were seventy-six aboard the *Akron* that evening, including the Navy's Air Chief; the commandant of Lakehurst; Lieutenant Calnan, a

former world's champion fencer; Lieutenant Wilfred Bushnell, the copilot
of the American balloon that had won the Gordon Bennett Race over
Switzerland the year before; five survivors of the *Shenandoah* crash, Boswell, Carlson, Quernheim, Shevlowitz and Russell; twenty-two-year-old
John Weeks, who had just married without telling his mother; and a young
sailor, Paul Hoover, who couldn't swim and had a morbid fear of water.

At seven twenty-eight the ship slowly left the ground, pushed up by four
inverted propellers. In front of the hangar, Mechanic Sid Hooper, his
wife, Mrs. Copeland and others—wives, friends, civilian workers—waved
and shouted farewells that could not be heard. They watched the great
ship disappear into the dense fog at 300 feet. Now only the dull roar of
its motors could be heard.

A moment later the roar was heard by Norman Walker, who was driving
his wife to Toms River. The veteran airshipman, the only American to
live through the ZR-2 (R-38) crash, tried to peer up through the thick
fog. "I hope," he said jokingly, "that thing holds up."

Not a man aboard the *Akron* had the slightest feeling of apprehension.
A few enlisted men did think it was damned foolishness to be setting out
on a calibrating mission in a pea-soup fog. But they knew that Admiral
Moffett would rather ride in a big rigid than eat; and it was easy to
sympathize with him, feeling almost the same way themselves.

By now the ship was circling above the fog bank; the Naval Air Station
was a dim glow 1,200 feet below. McCord realized that it would be too
dangerous to bring any planes aboard, and at 7:39 P.M. he ordered Copeland to wire the station that planes weren't required. Since the fog extended
over the ocean, McCord headed the ship west with only six motors running. He had decided to cruise inland where visibility was reported better.
Then, when the coastal regions cleared, the ship would turn north to arrive, at seven the next morning, over Newport, Rhode Island.

"*Akron* flying Lakehurst to Philadelphia to Delaware Capes, thence
along coast," wired Copeland at seven forty. It was the last clear message
Lakehurst received from the ship.

Although the watch didn't change until eight o'clock, Metalsmith Moody
Irwin decided to relieve his partner early. Irwin, a slender, thin-faced
man of twenty-eight with a tiny mustache, walked up the port keel to
frame 170 and took up his post in front of the telephone. Unlike the
Shenandoah, the *Akron* had three keels, all V-shaped. One keel was near
the top of the ship, running from bow to stern like a backbone. By means
of this keel gas valves could now be inspected without going topside. The
other two keels were near the bottom of the ship—one curving along the

port side and the other along the starboard. Nine cross-walks connected the two lower keels, making the inside of the ship a complicated maze of tunnels.

The frames, like those of the *Shenandoah*, were numbered starting with the rudder. Engines Number 1 and 2 were at frame 57.5, 57.5 meters from the rudders; the airplane hangar ran from 123 to 147.5; the control car ladder was at 170; and the tip of the nose was 213.5. The frames aft of the rudder were given a minus designation: for example, the machine-gun nest at the extreme tail was —25.75. The cells were also numbered from the stern, running forward from cell 0 in the tail to cell 11 at the nose.

At eight o'clock Dick Deal took over the telephone watch on the starboard side of the ship. He hadn't been on duty more than ten minutes when a familiar, stocky figure came down the keel, heading for the officers' wardroom. It was Admiral Moffett. "Well, we're on our way!" said the admiral. He stopped and the two chatted for a few minutes. He and Deal had shared many flights and were old friends. Rank meant little to the Chief of the Bureau of Aeronautics. "These are my happiest hours," confided the admiral. "Nothing like being on board a dirigible!"

The admiral passed forward, and Deal looked out a window. Visibility had cleared; Philadelphia could be plainly seen. He looked at his watch. In forty-five minutes he was due to relieve Ralph Stine at the elevators.

In the blacked-out control car, Wiley decided to take a smoke. He walked back to the room, which also served as the officers' smoking room, in the after end of the car. Soon he noticed that the ship was moving faster. His curiosity aroused, he walked forward. He found that now eight engines were running at standard speed, and the ship had turned east.

In explanation McCord pointed to the south where lightning was flashing. At that moment Aerologist Wescoat reported that there had been thunderstorms over Washington at 7:00 P.M. Deal climbed into the car and took over the elevator wheel from Stine. McCord and Wiley stood by anxiously watching the lightning.

Wiley walked back to MacLellan's cubicle. "Where are we?" he asked.

"We'll cross the coast at Atlantic City, I think," said the navigator.

They were again shrouded in fog. McCord told Deal to bring the ship down to 1,500 feet. Deal slowly lowered the *Akron*. At last the dull lights of a town could be seen through the mist. Lightning flashed again. It seemed to be only about twenty-five miles away. Rain began to strike the windows.

The captain ordered the course changed northeast.

"I think we'd better go west, sir," said Wiley tensely. Old airshipmen had a theory that, with such a storm approaching, the dirigible should be headed toward shore. But McCord shook his head. "No," he said pointing to the west. "I saw two flashes of lightning there."

At least a dozen men aboard the *Akron* that night knew that the ship should have turned west. But the captain, although he'd passed the airship pilot's course, had spent almost all his Navy time at sea, learning to be a master mariner.

Deal began to have trouble with the elevators. The air was smooth, but the buoyancy of the ship kept changing capriciously as the *Akron* bobbed in and out of the fog. Stine was called back to the control car to stand by in case Deal needed help.

At ten o'clock Deal was exhausted and glad to be relieved by Rufus "Red" Johnson.

"The ship's one and one-half degrees light, sir," Deal told Lieutenant Clendening, the Officer of the Deck. "Can I go up into the ship now, sir?"

"Stand by Johnson," replied Clendening. He had just seen two thunder-heads and was afraid the ship was in for some heavy weather.

MacLellan stuck his head out the navigator's cabin. "I think we're over Asbury Park, sir," he called to McCord.

The skipper nodded. Then he turned to Wiley, who was staring ahead at the turbulent skies. "I'm going up and take a look at the weather map," he said.

The lightning was now only a few miles off. Great, jagged bolts would strike horizontally and then be answered, a moment later, by vivid vertical flashes. But in spite of the lively electrical display the air was still calm and Johnson was having little trouble with the elevators.

Deal walked back to the navigator's room. Colonel Masury was seated at the port window, looking nervously out into the storm.

Suddenly thunder rumbled almost overhead. Long vertical bolts of lightning flashed on both sides of the ship, and the rain increased in force. The storm had caught up with them at last.

"It's pretty bad, isn't it?" the colonel said.

Deal tried to reassure Masury. "There's nothing to worry about, Colonel," he said. "We've been in worse electrical storms than this one." Lightning flashed, illuminating the colonel's drawn face. Deal wondered why older people, who had a lot less to live for, were always more frightened than the young. Deal peered forward. McCord, who had returned from the weather room, was anxiously looking out the starboard windows. Wiley looked out the port. Then the two officers silently changed positions.

"You should have been with us in the *Shenandoah*," said Deal to Masury. "The time we were coming from Buffalo back in nineteen twenty-four, the lightning was so bad over Wilkes-Barre that the control car seemed to be a ball of fire."

Masury found little reassurance in the story. "I'd just as soon not fly in a thunderstorm," he shouted above a resounding clap.

On the starboard side of the room MacLellan was dropping flares over the side to check his position. But the sea of fog below was too thick.

"Look!" cried Masury. He pointed down. "I can see lights on the ground!"

Deal looked out the port window. He saw the lights and called Mac-Lellan. The navigator joined them. After a moment he began to laugh.

"That's just the reflection of the light from the officers' quarters on the fog."

In the radio room above them, Copeland, fearing that the antenna might be hit by the lightning, had hauled it in. Anyway the radio had been useless the past hour because of the static.

Copeland nodded in greeting as Admiral Moffett clambered past his room and down the ladder into the control car. The radio man figured that the admiral had been wakened by the lightning.

When Moffett reached the bottom of the ladder he looked forward. There Wiley and McCord were changing positions rapidly, like dancers in a peculiar ballet.

Thunder crashed, as if announcing the admiral's entrance. "It's almost as bad as one we struck in Alabama," he said to no one in particular. His feet apart, he rode the easy roll of the ship. There was no nervousness on his face. The admiral was enjoying himself.

McCord told Wiley to go up and have a look at the weather map. The executive officer went aloft and found out from Wescoat that only about two thirds of a map had been received before the radio went off. Wiley examined the map fragment, shook his head dolefully and returned to the control car.

"What do you think, Commander?" McCord asked him.

"We certainly have a storm center down there, sir," answered Wiley. "It's something to play with."

"We'd better take her to sea," said McCord.

Again Wiley suggested heading west. But McCord had made up his mind. They would run east and then south to get ahead of the storm center.

The *Akron* headed out into the black skies over the Atlantic.

At 11:30 P.M. conditions were still normal in the ship. Deal was having coffee and a sandwich in the crew's mess hall above the airplane hangar, on the starboard side. He chatted with Chief Machinist Walsh for a few minutes. They agreed it was a sad night for flying. Then Walsh started on another inspection of his eight engines, and Deal strolled back to the starboard telephone at frame 170. Glancing out the window, he noticed lightning near the radio antenna. Copeland had just been given permission to lower one antenna fifteen feet, to the level of the bottom of the control car, so that he could try to get some weather information.

Lieutenant Calnan looked over Deal's shoulders. "Stand by the fire unit," he ordered, "in case anything catches fire."

Moody Irwin brushed by Calnan and started down the ladder to the control car. "I'm ready to relieve you, Red," he told elevator man Johnson a moment later.

"The ship's a little heavy," said Johnson, handing over the wheel. Because a "heavy" ship was inclined to climb, Irwin carried 5 degrees down elevator, which held the *Akron* at her given altitude, 1,600 feet. Ralph Stine, an expert elevator man, stood behind Irwin in case of an emergency.

The lightning was now flashing all around the ship, blinding Irwin for several seconds at a time. He found he was having more and more difficulty holding the tail up.

"She's tail-heavy," he called to Lieutenant Calnan.

Calnan immediately sent for Henry Boswell, the most experienced elevator man on the ship. In a minute Boswell was at the controls.

"Check on the slack adjusters and counterbalance springs," said Calnan. Boswell nodded. He made the adjustments, then turned the wheel back to Irwin.

The storm seemed to get worse, and McCord finally ordered the dirigible headed back for the coast. But Navigator MacLellan had no idea where they were. Not only had the tricky, veering winds muddled their bearing, but also one of McCord's orders had been misunderstood; when the captain had called for a 15-degree change in course, the helmsmen thought he'd said 50 degrees.

Copeland was still doing his best to reach the home radio station. At 11:45 P.M. Radioman Third Class Robert Hill, the Lakehurst operator on duty, heard the *Akron's* call, but the static was too heavy to read the message. Five minutes later an amateur radioman, Arthur Hullfish of 224 East Montgomery Avenue, Wildwood, New Jersey, thought he could hear someone trying to establish communications on short wave. He distinctly heard the call letters "NAL," but then the message was broken up by static.

At a few minutes before twelve, Hill heard another call from the *Akron*. Again the Lakehurst operator couldn't make sense out of the message. It was just about this time that the men in the *Akron's* control car sighted the Jersey coastline. Neither MacLellan nor McCord had figured that they were so close to land.

"One hundred twenty degrees compass!" ordered McCord quickly. For all he knew they might be heading straight for the Empire State Building.

The *Akron* turned slowly and headed back over the Atlantic. In a few minutes she was submerged in fog.

At twelve the watch changed. Tony Swidersky and Joe Zimkus relieved Irwin and Stine at the elevators. Irwin started wearily toward the galley for sandwiches and coffee before turning in.

Dick Deal headed for the enlisted men's smoking room, which was above the plane hangar on the port side. Stine was there. So was Elmer Fink, an engineer and the ship's comedian. The thunder was now rumbling louder than ever.

"That's beer kegs being rolled around!" said Elmer.

It was a legitimate topical joke—3.2 beer was to be legalized the next day—and Stine and Deal laughed. And they smoked contentedly as little Elmer, in rare form despite the storm, continued to entertain them. After a pleasant ten minutes the two elevator men left the smoking room.

"Bad night for airships," remarked Deal. "Good night." The men separated, each heading for his bunk. Deal went into a tiny, canvas-walled room. He sat on his bunk and took off his shoes. He'd already removed his heavy flying trousers in the smoking room, and he flopped on the bunk with his head toward the keel walkway. On either side of him were two empty bunks. They belonged to men who'd just come off duty and were in the galley having a midnight lunch.

The keel lights shone dully over his head as he lay back and listened to the roar of Number 8 engine. It was a pleasant, comforting sound. He wasn't very tired. He never was tired on the first night of a flight. He flopped over on his stomach, leaning on his elbows with his face resting in his hands. There was no use corking off until his shipmates got back from the mess hall.

Irwin was lying on his bunk a few yards forward. He was too tired to take off anything except his shoes. It'd been a rough watch.

In Wildwood, the storm rose to such intensity that Arthur Hullfish decided to disconnect the radio belonging to the people who lived on the other side of his house. He ran out into the storm. Over the crackle of lightning and the crash of thunder, he could hear the heavy boom of the surf 1,000 feet away. He looked out toward the Atlantic. It was blanketed with fog. Hullfish quickly unhooked the aerial and ran back into the house. He wanted to see if he could pick up those strange short-wave calls again.

At twenty minutes past midnight Admiral Moffett again came down from his cabin above the control car. Even an old seadog couldn't sleep through a storm so wild. He stood in the darkened control car watching every maneuver intently.

Young Joe Zimkus was spelling Swidersky at the elevators. But Tony, by far the more experienced man, stood watchfully behind Joe. McCord and Wiley were still peering out the front windows, trying to find a break in the storm. The control car began to jerk spasmodically. Deafening peals of thunder were now following almost instantly after the rips of lightning. It seemed to Wiley that the sky above was cracking in two. The screaming wind told him that they must be near the center of the storm itself.

Suddenly young Zimkus cried, "We're falling!"

The elevator wheel tore out of Joe's hands and began spinning. Zimkus stood transfixed and watched the wheel whirl madly. Swidersky pushed Zimkus aside, threw himself on the wheel. It tried to tear itself from his hands. Wiley grabbed two of the wheel's spokes. Together the two powerful men yanked the nose of the ship up.

"I got it, sir," said Swidersky a moment later. He was in a sweat.

Wiley looked at the altimeter. It read 1,100 feet and was sinking fast even though the ship was almost at an even keel.

"Should I drop ballast, Captain?" asked Wiley quietly.

"Yes," replied McCord, who had already rung up for more knots from the engines.

Wiley yanked at the toggles, emptying the service bags. The executive officer turned and looked at the altimeter again. They were down to 950 feet. But he knew that instrument was unreliable and could be off as much as several hundred feet. He reached up and pulled at the emergency toggles. Sixteen hundred pounds of water dumped out of frame 187. The needle on the altimeter wavered, stopped at 800 feet, and then began to shoot up almost as fast as it had fallen.

Wiley stood behind Swidersky, conning him cagily to reduce gradually the rate of rise. At 1,300 feet the executive officer tensed. "All right," he said. A moment later he saw that Swidersky had good control of the ship. "Now bring her up to 1,600 gradually, and then level off." Wiley stepped back a pace and began to breathe more normally. The crisis was over.

Inside the ship, Irwin had noticed the fall and rise. Several bunks aft, Deal had heard the telegraph ring in Number 8 engine room. Then he felt the ship surge forward with increased speed. After a few minutes he heard another ring in the engine room. The roar of Number 8 motor slacked off, and he knew they were back on standard speed.

Below them, the control car was swaying harder and faster than ever. Blinding flashes of lightning lit up the dark car, elongating the black figures of the men and distorting their faces weirdly. The ship was tossed up and down violently. Wiley knew they had finally hit the storm center.

"All hands to landing stations!" he called.

Although the rocking motion was less noticeable in the crew's sleeping quarters, which were near the ship's center of gravity, Deal wondered sleepily what the devil was going on. Leaning on one elbow he glanced up at Number 7 cell. It was surging and gasping like a creature in pain. It reminded him of one of those respiratory bladders attached to a patient during an operation. His drowsiness instantly disappeared. Something was happening. He rolled out of bed.

As Deal stood erect, the ship lurched sideways heavily, as if she had been hit by a big club. There was an alarming crackle overhead. He looked up. Girders 7 and 8 had snapped in two.

Irwin was half dozing when he heard a sound like the crack of a paper bag bursting. He looked up and saw that girder 7, the big longitudinal, had parted.

Up forward Chief Bosun's Mate Carl Dean was shouting, "All hands forward!"

The lurch almost knocked Wiley off his feet. The gust that had caused it was the most vicious he'd ever felt. As soon as he recovered his balance he saw that the lower rudder control rope had been carried away. He told the captain. Then he began unclutching the broken rudder control.

"She's falling," reported elevator man Swidersky with no emotion in his voice.

Captain McCord looked at the altimeter. The ship was falling fast— faster than the first time.

"Full speed!" he ordered. The engineering officer instantly rang up the eight engine rooms.

Just as Wiley finished unclutching the lower control, the upper control snapped. He could hear a high, shrill whine inside the ship. It sounded to him like sheaves carrying away. He knew the ship's structure had been damaged somewhere.

By this time Swidersky had the bow of the ship up almost 20 degrees in an effort to stop the fall. "Eight hundred feet!" he called.

There was no confusion in the control car as the ship plunged into blackness below. Lieutenant Calnan, who had appeared a moment after the landing station signal, was standing patiently by the ballast board. With both controls broken and useless, Wiley hung to the girder alongside the port window. He stared down fixedly, waiting for the water to loom into sight.

Arthur Hullfish was back at his short-wave set. Once again he picked up faint staccato signals. Then he began to hear plain language instead of meaningless code. Hullfish knew he'd cut in on a distress signal of some kind. Frantically he began to copy words. "Two bays [or guys] control broken—ship bad condition—heavy storm strong wind—going up now— [something] broken." Then only isolated words and short phrases could be heard. "Out—700 feet—nose—nose up—breaking center—run into something—crashing [or cracking]."

There were a few more signals, then dead air. Hullfish looked at his watch. It was 12:26 A.M. He studied the gibberish he'd written. It made no sense whatever. He decided to forget the whole thing.

When Deal had seen the girders snap, he decided to call the control car. But when the ship began falling rapidly by the tail he knew he should drop fuel tanks first. Looking up the keel, he saw a tank, suspended above the walkway, start to break loose. He hurried forward so he wouldn't be crushed. The gangway was now so sharply angled that he had to pull himself up girder by girder.

Irwin was ten yards behind Deal. He, too, saw the gas tank tilting crazily, and he scrambled up the steep catwalk. Passing the tank, he heard a shriek of metal as the after-suspension gave way. The 120-gallon tank crashed to the keel. It missed Irwin by inches, but in his rush to get forward he never saw it. He climbed to the telephone at frame 170.

Deal, who hadn't time to put on his shoes, was at frame 175 with half a dozen men. Chief Paul Jandick squeezed past him going aft. The others stood silently about, hanging onto girders for support. Girders were breaking and wires singing from strain. Though the lights were still glowing above the catwalk, everyone knew the ship was breaking up. Bill Russell, survivor of the *Shenandoah*, looked at Deal. Neither spoke. Chief Dean waited motionless.

Deal wondered whether they were over land or sea, and which would be worse for a crash. The men at 175 stared at each other and hoped for a little good luck.

Several miles away the German oil tanker *Phoebus,* out of New York and bound for Tampico, was fighting the heavy seas. Thirty-four-year-old Captain Karl Dalldorf had taken the mate's watch because he wanted to be on the bridge all through the storm. Then a flashing of lights appeared in the air off his bow. He had no idea what the lights were, but he was sure they weren't the Barnegat Inlet Light: he had just passed it a few miles back.

Now the lights seemed to be on or near the water. Dalldorf, figuring it was a plane crashing into the sea, instantly changed his course. The 9,226-ton, twin-screw motorship plowed through the twelve-foot waves full speed ahead.

Wiley, looking out the port window, could see nothing but fog below. Suddenly the choppy, wind-lashed sea appeared through a hole in the fog. "What's the altitude?" asked Wiley.

"Two hundred feet," answered Swidersky.

"Stand by to crash!" called Wiley. Since broken wires had ruined their regular telegraph system, he ordered the engineering officer to ring up the crash signal on the emergency bell-pull system. Just as the engine cars began repeating back the order, there was a heavy jolt. The tail, dragging far below the control car, had struck the ocean.

Lights went out all along both lower keels. Irwin jumped through the ship's outer covering. He plummeted through the criss-cross tangle of wires and out of the dirigible.

Ten yards forward, Deal felt icy water bursting through the keel at his feet. He had a horrible, panicky feeling. He and the others with him were caught inside a trap of metal and wires. There was still no sound from the men at frame 175. The *Akron* didn't carry life preservers. They all knew that it would soon be over.

Water flooded in over Deal's head. He felt his right leg being clutched and held by wires. He kicked frantically. He yanked at the wires. Somehow he got loose and shot to the surface of the water. The starboard side of the ship was drifting away from him.

Irwin struggled as the great hull of the *Akron* slowly rolled on top of him, pushing him below the waves. He jackknifed his legs until his feet were on the ship's structure. Then, his lungs bursting, he pushed off and dived as deep as he could. Moments later his head popped out of the water. He had barely cleared the sinking wreckage. He kicked off his low-cut crepe-soled shoes. It was easy because he had made a habit of leaving them untied when off duty. He took a deep breath and then, as he sank, started removing his bulky flying coat. Finally he got the coat off and shot to the surface again. Then he swam as hard as he could, away from the foundering ship and the undertow.

A few seconds after the crew's quarters were flooded, water rushed through the open port window of the control car, which was listing to starboard. The torrent picked up Wiley and carried him out the starboard window. He felt a mass of rubberized fabric on top of him and knew that he was being dragged down with the ship. He swam under water until his lungs seemed about to burst. Then he surfaced. Lightning flashed and, in the brief glow, he saw the dirigible, her bow pointed in the air, drifting away. He saw two lights on the stern section. Beyond were the lights of a vessel. Even farther off was a glare he thought came from Barnegat Lighthouse. Wiley swam toward the *Akron*.

Irwin was swimming away from the dirigible. He wasn't particularly afraid of drowning: he knew that they were near the Jersey coast, and he figured that if necessary he could swim to land. But he *was* afraid of sharks. He'd been afraid of them since he was a little boy. He kicked his feet frantically to scare them away. Looking around for something to help keep him afloat, he saw phosphorous flares blazing near the submerged control car. They had probably burst out of the locker in the navigator's room and ignited upon hitting the water. Finally he saw a fuel tank— perhaps the same one that had almost hit him a moment before the crash. It was bobbing like a giant cork twenty yards away. He struggled through the heavy seas toward it.

When at last he reached the 120-gallon tank, two men were already clinging to it. During the next flash of lightning he recognized Copeland, the radio operator, and Mechanic Lucius Rutan. Irwin grabbed onto the slippery tank with one hand and slowly took off everything but his underclothes. It wasn't until then that he realized how cold he was. Several hundred yards away he saw the "Queen of the Skies," her bow sticking out of the water like an inverted ice cream cone. A moment later, in another flash of lightning, he saw about a dozen men struggling in the water about fifty yards away. The sea was momentarily quiet, and the cries of the swimming men were faint and frightened. Irwin would never forget the sound of their cries.

Deal heard the cries for help all around him. But he couldn't help; he was hard put and lucky just to keep himself afloat. He figured that he'd been swimming about twenty minutes, and if he didn't find a piece of wood or floating debris he'd soon go under. A bolt of lightning lit up the great white-flecked swells. In the flash he saw several men floating by on a tank. Desperately he struck out for the tank, and he was tiring with each stroke. A few yards from it he reached the end of his endurance and started to go under. Then he felt himself being pulled. His hands hit metal. He hung onto the tank and took a deep breath.

"Who's here?" he asked.

"Irwin," said the man who had pulled him onto the tank.

Rutan didn't answer so Irwin added, "And Rutan."

The last man said, "This is Copeland."

Deal was hopeful for the first time since the crash. It was a good feeling to have company.

Wiley had heard the fading cries for help. He had found a board about three feet square, and when he saw a man struggling not far away he swam toward him. A wave tore the board from his frozen hands, and dragged him under. After he had fought his way to the surface again, he couldn't find the man who had cried out.

Wiley was now about 400 yards from the wallowing dirigible. The wind changed, and as the waves began hitting him squarely in the face, he realized that he didn't have a chance of swimming toward the ship. He wondered, without panic, how long a man could live in that icy, heaving sea. He knew he was in good condition; and if he budgeted his strength he had as good a chance for survival as anyone. So he swam easily, trying only to keep afloat.

The four men were having trouble hanging onto the bouncing fuel tank. Each big wave would sweep somebody off. Whenever Rutan was knocked off, he tried to climb on top of the tank; and each time the tank threatened to roll over. If it did, thought Deal, they'd all go under.

Then a wave tore Deal off the tank. As he swam back he noticed that the feed-pipe, which had connected with the main gas line, had snapped off.

"We've got to keep this feed-line above water!" he told the others. Should water flow into the broken pipe, the tank would fill up and sink. He clamped his hand over the jagged pipe to keep out the water.

"It's just a matter of time," said Deal encouragingly. "Somebody'll find us."

The men said nothing.

Irwin was no longer cold. In fact, he was beginning to feel pleasantly warm. His eyes started to close, and he realized with a start that he was freezing. Quickly he ducked his head under water to rouse himself. If he stopped fighting he'd be finished.

Deal was now at the other end of the tank. He reached across it with both hands. Irwin saw what he meant and clasped hands with him. The two men locked each other onto the bucking tank.

They'd been in the water over an hour.

Suddenly Deal shouted, "There's a ship!"

Irwin turned and looked. As the tank reached the crest of a wave, lightning ripped across the sky; and far away he saw the unreal outline of a ship.

Deal prayed that the ship would find them in the deep troughs and foaming water. He kept straining to follow the ship. One moment it would be riding high, the next it would plunge down and out of sight behind a great swell.

"It's just a matter of time," Deal kept repeating over and over.

A big wave smashed against the tank. Rutan slipped off. Slowly he sank. For a moment his hands writhed at the surface, then he was gone. No one could help him.

Now Deal could see a green light on the ship. He shouted. In a semi-delirium Irwin saw two green lights, though vaguely he knew there should be only one. Perhaps the second was the reflection in the water. Then he began to shout, too. Copeland remained silent, his teeth clenched, a look of helpless strain and fatigue on his face.

The ship's deck lights flashed on. Deal felt a surge of hope. Then the ship's whistle began blowing. That must mean, he thought, that they'd spotted the tank.

A wave broke Irwin and Deal apart, and both floundered in the water. Irwin grabbed wearily at the tank. "I can't hold out any longer!" he gasped.

"Hold on!" Deal cried. "We'll be all right in five minutes."

Wiley saw the lights, too, and he heard the continuous, plaintive cries of the men on the fuel tank. He still had nothing to cling to, but he had been swimming with as little effort as possible, riding each giant wave cautiously. The rescue ship was floating toward him, almost broadsides. Wiley swam toward it with strong strokes. In a minute a circular life buoy was tossed near his head. Wiley reached out and caught the buoy. He was hauled aboard the *Phoebus*.

As if in a dream Irwin saw a life buoy scaling toward him from the darkness. It flopped in the water ten yards away. He left the tank and swam lazily to the buoy. His arms and legs were heavy, lifeless. He wished he could go to sleep. As he was dozing off he hooked his right arm through the buoy. He grabbed his chest with his right hand, locking himself to the preserver. Then he lost consciousness. When sailors pulled him onto the *Phoebus* at 2:00 A.M. his fingernails were dug into his bleeding chest, and his eyes were closed. He was in a deep sleep.

Deal, still holding onto the tank, saw a group of sailors hauling Irwin aboard and another group lowering a lifeboat from the ship. Dim figures were struggling with tackle lines, and Deal figured something must have fouled. It seemed an hour before the boat was finally over the side. At last it hit the water and speared toward the tank.

At that moment a big life raft floated serenely by. It was the fourteen-man raft kept in the airplane hangar—the only raft on the *Akron*. It was empty. A moment later he imagined he saw somebody grab Copeland. Then he felt himself being lifted. Then everything blacked out.

After the four men were picked up, the two lifeboats of the *Phoebus* continued searching in the forty-five-mile-an-hour gale. Several men sank just before they could be reached. Mattresses and bits of wreckage covered the sea. No more survivors were found.

When Deal came to, he was in a bunk in a pitching stateroom. Packed around his naked body were whisky bottles filled with hot water. German seamen were vigorously rubbing his legs.

Deal was shivering so violently that he couldn't talk. A fifth of whisky stood on a chair next to his bed. He sat up, his teeth chattering. He grabbed the bottle with numbed, fumbling hands. He took big gulps of the whisky. The German sailors laughed, encouraging him with broad gestures to drink more. He finished the entire fifth. But it had no effect on him— except to make him feel warm inside at last.

"What ship are we on?" he asked.

A young sailor who had lived in New York four years told him that it was the *Phoebus*. They'd left New York late that afternoon and luckily had been blown a little off their course. Then the door opened and Commander Wiley walked in.

"How do you feel?" he asked Deal. There were deep hollows under Wiley's dark, sad eyes, but he was in good condition.

"O.K.," said Deal. "How many survivors are there, sir?"

Wiley hesitated. Then he said, "Not many, Deal."

In the adjoining stateroom Irwin came awake and immediately felt warmth on his stomach. He didn't know it came from a bottle filled with hot water. As soon as he opened his eyes, the chief engineer of the *Phoebus* boosted him to a sitting position. The German started pouring a tumbler of whisky down his throat. Irwin thought he was still in the ocean, imagined he was swallowing salt water. He moaned and struck the glass out of the German's hand. He clutched at the chief engineer's hat, tearing it apart with violent jerks. Then he lost consciousness.

When he opened his eyes again there was no one in the room. He didn't know where he was or what had happened to him. He figured he'd been knocked out in an accident. He lay back on the bunk for a few minutes trying to make sense out of vague memories. A few minutes later he sat up. Seeing a bottle of 5-Star Hennessy on a table across the room, he slowly slung his legs out of the bunk. (Actually, it was 3-Star—there has never been a 5-Star Hennessy.) He wanted a good, long drink. He put his feet on the floor and took a step. But his numb legs crumpled under him. He lay on the floor unable to move.

The fourth man—Copeland, who had almost become a missionary—never regained consciousness. Before the Germans could lay him in a bunk his life faded away. Only three of the *Akron's* complement of seventy-six were now alive.

The papers that evening were full of the tragedy. The nation was stunned. President Roosevelt said, "The loss of the *Akron* with its crew of gallant officers and men is a national disaster." Billy Mitchell sprang to the defense of the rigid dirigible. "They were helping to develop a defensive arm that still will be invaluable in the future," he declared. "We should not let an accident of this kind hold up our airship development. We must go forward."

Red-bearded Anton Heinen was also heard from. "There should be no whitewash of the *Akron* disaster," he said, "as there was of the *Shenandoah* tragedy."

By the end of the day few believed anyone else had survived the deadliest crash in the history of aviation. But at Lakehurst the women still kept vigil. They still scanned the dark, empty skies as if expecting the big ship to return any moment. Although all the workmen had left Hangar Number 1 long before, half a dozen automobiles still stood inside the vast, tomblike building. They belonged to members of the *Akron's* crew. Outside the hangar half a dozen dogs sat waiting.

The day after the crash the three weary survivors were flown to Washington to see the Secretary of the Navy. The next morning they were driven to the White House. Franklin D. Roosevelt insisted on taking time to talk with them.

"I'm thankful you're here," said the President. "Sit down and tell me all about it."

Wiley, in clipped tones, told of their crash and rescue. Deal, who wore tight-fitting civilian clothes, put in only a few words. Irwin said even less.

The President congratulated them on their narrow escape. Then, to relieve their tension, he told an amusing story of the inept Congressional investigation of the *Titanic* sinking. The President told them that many of the Congressmen involved thought that starboard meant the left side of a ship.

The three men laughed a little.

When Wiley praised the seamanship of the *Phoebus* crew, Roosevelt turned to his Assistant Secretary of the Navy, Henry Latrobe Roosevelt. "I shall personally write a letter to the captain and crew of that ship," he said, "and thank them for their gallant work."

A few days later Deal returned to Lakehurst and his greatest ordeal. He didn't know what to say to the widows. It would be especially hard with the wives of his old mates of the *Shenandoah*.

Irwin also had a hard chore. He felt he had to go to Seaside Park, New Jersey, to see the wife of his dead friend, Red Johnson. She was on the beach when he arrived. After they talked a minute about Red she started like a sleepwalker across the sand, tears pouring down her cheeks. To Irwin's horror she walked into the ocean. Before he could kick off his shoes and take off his pea jacket she had sunk out of sight.

Irwin dove in after her. He had a struggle bringing her back to the beach—she was bigger than he and she fought to stay in the sea.

That same day, not many miles away, the body of William Moffett, the airshipmen's favorite admiral, was washed ashore. The few who, like young Mrs. Anderson, still prayed for a miracle, knew at last it was the end of all hope.

SOME PRETTY EXPENSIVE SYSTEMS

As unemployment rose from four million in 1930, to eight million in 1931, to more than twelve million in 1932, "a gap had opened between the official mood in Washington and the human reality in city streets and in the countryside . . . between the presidential vision of accelerating private construction, mounting confidence, and the actuality of privation and fear." *

President Hoover had defined the function of government in 1931 as that of bringing about "a condition of affairs favorable to the beneficial development of private enterprise," and he insisted that the only *moral* way out of the Depression was by self-help. The people should find inspiration, furthermore, in the devotion of "great manufacturers, our railways, utilities, business houses and public officials."

The trouble was that the business leaders, who in the Twenties "had never had it so good," were unable to suggest a sound way out of the dilemma of unemployment; few of them appeared to believe they had any responsibility to the general welfare, and certainly they did not want the government to take any action. Henry Ford said, for instance, "government should stick to the strict function of governing . . . let them let business alone"; and "unemployment insurance would only insure that we would have unemployment."

The irony here was that while businessmen regarded federal aid in the form of relief to the unemployed "as spelling the end of the Republic," they did not object to federal aid to business.

What avenues of self-help were there? *Fortune* Magazine said, "The theory was that private charitable organizations and semipublic welfare groups, established to care for the old and the sick and the indigent, were capable of caring for the casualties of a world-wide economic disaster. In application, social agencies manned for the service of a few hundred families and city shelters set up to house and feed a handful of homeless men, were compelled by the brutal necessities of hunger to care for hundreds of thousands of families and whole armies of the displaced and jobless. And to depend for their resources upon the contributions of communities no longer able to contribute, and upon the irresolution and vacillation of state legislatures and municipal assemblies long since in the red on their annual budgets.

"The psychological consequence was even worse. Since the problem was never honestly attacked as a national problem and since the facts were never frankly faced, people came to believe that American unemployment was relatively unimportant. They saw little idleness and therefore believed there was little. It was possible to drive for blocks in

* From Arthur M. Schlesinger, Jr.'s *The Crisis of the Old Order* (Boston, Houghton Mifflin, 1957).

the usual shopping and residential districts of New York and Chicago without seeing a breadline. And for that reason, and because their newspapers played down the subject as an additional depressant in depressing times, and because they were bored with relief measures anyway, the great American public simply ignored the whole thing."

By 1932, only about 25 per cent of the unemployed were getting relief, and it was restricted primarily to food benefits. *Fortune* went on to say:

"Such is the problem created by three years of increasing unemployment and two years of hand-to-mouth relief: city after city attempting to feed a half or a third or a quarter of its citizens upon gifts made from the reduced earnings, or from taxes levied on the overappraised homes of the other half or two thirds or the other three quarters; city after city maintaining the lives but not the health of its unemployed on a survival ration; city after city where the whole mechanism of relief has failed or is about to fail or has survived only by abandoning a major part of its task; and beyond the cities the mill towns and the coal mines and the 'cropper farms where relief is merely a name.

"The Depression, along with its misery, produced its social curiosities, not the least of which was the wandering population it spilled upon the roads. Means of locomotion vary but the objective is always the same —somewhere else. There were the hitchhikers whose thumbs jerked on-

ward along the American pike, and the number of spavined Fords dragging destitute families from town to town in search of a solvent relative or a generous friend.

"Dull mornings last winter, the sheriff of Miami, Florida, used to fill a truck with homeless men and run them up to the county line. Where the sheriff of Fort Lauderdale used to meet them and load them into a second truck and run them up to *his* county line. Where the sheriff of Saint Lucie's would meet them and load them into a third truck and run them up to *his* county line. Where the sheriff of Brevard County would *not* meet them. And whence they would trickle back down the roads to Miami. To repeat.

"It was a system. And it worked. The only trouble was that it worked too well. It kept the transients transient and it even increased the transient population in the process. But it got to be pretty expensive, one way or another, if you sat down and figured it all out—trucks and gas and time and a little coffee. . . ." *

About two million people were roaming the country—several hundred thousand of them were young people—looking for a job, hope, or anything that would suggest that life had not passed them by. The young traveled alone, or with one companion, and most of them wanted work. The following narrative by Eric Sevareid is not one of despair, as so many of their stories must have been. From it one can take a certain pride in the generation formed by these years.

---

* "No One Has Starved," *Fortune,* September 1932.

ERIC SEVAREID

HITCHHIKER*

AT TWENTY, the eye is sharp, perceptions are keen, and the heart is never again so warm. Every man one meets, the lowliest tramp, is alive and vibrant with personality, with meaning, with Self. The colors of the sky are brilliant, there is extraordinary beauty in a cowshed at sunrise, and in the warm night the clicking cadence of the freight car's wheels sends one easily to confident sleep with no more than an arm for pillow. I traveled alone; it is the right and only way. You do not have to talk if you would rather be silent; you can stop where you will, doze when you wish, and think your own thoughts. All that the eye sees, the mind registers, and the heart envelops is filtered by the screen of Yourself, untreated, unmodified by the conditioning presence of another being. There is no other way to find out the world and to touch the boundaries of your own limitations for finding out. I discovered all this—and America.

The grain was full and high in North Dakota, this place which I had never desired to see again. I had forgotten that the grain rose and settled with the undulating swell of the ocean, that the distant barn became a rising and falling ship on the rim of this sea, its cupola a mounted stack. I had forgotten that the clouds of summer were fat and laundered white and that small shadows moved over the surface of this inland ocean. I had forgotten the precision design of a furrowed field on a canvas so spacious that lines were long and clean and never crowded. I had forgotten how the rails were fixed to the earth, how they bent and fastened the world down at the far edge, where the curvature of the planet was apparent to the human eye. It was incredible, at first, to find that Velva was still there, every house intact. It had grown not older, but younger. The river had not yet reached the width I knew, and the great trees in our yard had begun all over again as saplings. All should have been in decay and ruin, dying and dead among weeds. Instead, all was green, pruned, and trimmed. There was concrete sidewalk over the coulee where there had been only a treacherous board; radio antennae had replaced the lightning

* From Eric Sevareid's *Not So Wild a Dream* (New York, Knopf, 1946).

rods upon the roofs; there were yellow parking signs where the hitching posts had stood, and gleaming Buicks had replaced the dusty buggies.

It was not by their faces that one knew them all, instantly and without mistake. Things fade from the retina of the eye's recollection, but there are sixth and seventh senses which retain it all. The faces were strange, but not what was *in* the faces. The special, strong, untransferable *feeling* of each was the same. It is by this that a child knows those around him, and through this mysterious medium it all comes back when he is grown.

A young man with whom I used to make a daily trade—his pony for my Ranger bicycle—drove me to Minot (the "Magic City") in his six-ton truck. He had a farm of his own now and he considered me with the faint condescension and suspicion with which men of property regard the unpropertied. I wandered into a park in the darkness and slept in a clump of brush, to be wakened in fright by fearful noises from what sounded like very large animals. They were. I was sleeping next to the bears' cage in the zoo. A telephone lineman drove me forty miles in his Ford half-truck, remained silent the whole distance, and uttered his first words when he invited me in to dinner with himself and his wife at his roadside shack. A young traveling salesman picked me up and drove me seven hundred miles into the heart of the vast Montana country, in a long limousine, the back of which was stacked with cases containing samples of his wares, which were ladies' underclothing. His extra suits, carefully pressed, hung on hangers in the car's interior. He wore dark sun-glasses and small, stiff collars which he changed twice a day. He worried about the manicured nails of his soft, white hands and talked constantly and confidently. He told me, repeatedly, that he had the world by the tail, and I believed him. "What you want to be a newspaper reporter for? Naw, naw, that's no good. I know some of them guys around the *Tribune* in Chicago. I can buy and sell any two of them guys. Naw, I got the racket. I can clean up two-three hundred a week, commissions alone, not counting the bonus. You gotta know how to go at these local yokels, gotta impress them —big car, swell clothes—gotta breeze in on them, talk fast, give 'em the idea you're in a rush and doing them a favor. Of course, my goods are straight, best that money can buy. Don't want to get mixed up in any cheap racket, then you can't go back a second time. I make it, but I spread it around. I ain't tight with it. Take the girls to the best spot in town, tip a lot. Never turned down a bum for a handout yet, pick up guys all the time on the road. Here. Here's five bucks. Go on, take it. Take it. I know you're broke. Take it. What's the diff? Lots of guys are broke." Unable to resist his sales technique, I took it, humbly.

He was an inland sailor, with a girl in every department store. For hours he discussed them—intimately—and I was fascinated and impressed by this insight into a life of irresponsible, sexual freedom which I had scarcely suspected. The one in Fargo he called "Silky," in homage to the texture of her skin, more particularly the skin of the small of her back. There was Margie in Minot, and somebody else in Great Falls whose private qualities and capacities are better left undetailed. He always wired ahead to these ladies to give them time to prepare for his coming. It never occurred to him that he might be disappointed, and, so far as I knew, he never was.

I watched him haggle with a granite-faced garage man for a tire. His complete, overriding confidence was remarkable, and I listened in mute, uneasy wonder. He got the tire at much below the asking price—something I knew I could never do. I felt sympathy for the garage man, but my friend and protector took the keenest pleasure in his victory. He hadn't cared about the price at all; it was the fun of the contest, the testing of his powers. I understood that here was a man who would never go hungry, who would always be able to take care of himself and his round little stomach at no matter what cost to those around him. It was my first acquaintance with the Wise Guy incarnate. I was to see them later, in many countries, where honest people starved, where honest men stole that their families might eat. But these, the Wise Guys of the world, the Slick Operators, never starved, never had to steal. War and the collapse of their countries, their society, scarcely touched them. They are an international breed, owing allegiance to no one, not even to one another. They manipulate currencies, they operate black markets; they live for money, and money seems to exist for them. It is the only reality in life to them, and they are contemptuous of anyone who does not share their knowledge, incredulous of those who do not share their belief. They are the outlaws of society, but they are not the hunted. They are, indeed, the hunters, the merciless hunters.

Helena was a sudden discovery, isolated, alone in a lost valley, connected with the world by the frail liaison of a highway, a thin white tape that disappeared in the distant hills, and a rail line, a silver wire that flashed its presence to the sun before vanishing in turn among the crags. Here I entered the Ford roadster of a pink, chubby man named Smith whose business it was to advertise the benefits of milk to the American people. He was on a leisurely survey of the American West, with an incidental aim. There was a girl living in Missoula. He had not seen her since their college days, eight years before. They had rarely corresponded. But he had decided, in those eight years of experience, that she was the only girl he wanted to marry. He wasn't sure, now, whether she was married or not. At Missoula I slept among the smells of unwashed bodies and disinfectant in the Salvation Army, while Smith went off to pay his visit of surprise. He picked me up in the morning and said, after a few miles: "She wasn't married—but she's going to be." He could not prevent happy smiles from breaking out on his cherubic face. "Like a goddam novel, isn't it?" he said. He drove me many hundreds of miles and we were briefly chagrined at parting, before the door of my uncle's house near Seattle. (My parents came from extremely large families, far scattered since, and I had the benefit of intimate staging points.)

For five dollars, one could ride a double-decker bus all the way from Seattle to northern California. I rode for twenty-four hours or more, stifled by day, shivering by night, sustained on the thick sandwiches prepared by a worried aunt. At Portland, a slim girl with unnatural blond hair and greasy lipstick climbed into the seat beside me. She carried only a handbag and wore only a set of green pajamas. At least to me they were pajamas; they may have been what we now call slacks. She was bound for San Francisco, or maybe Los Angeles, or maybe San Diego. She wasn't quite sure; it didn't matter. She chewed her gum, fiddled with her handbag, examined her eyebrows in the little mirror a half-dozen times, then peered over my shoulder. "Watcha reading?" I was trying, between headaches, to understand an erudite article in *The Atlantic Monthly* on science and religion. "Jesus," she said, "you're pretty young to be a dope." She fidgeted awhile and offered: "What's the difference between a mountain goat and a soda jerk?" I did not know. "The soda jerk mucks around the fountain." She was something new; I did not know how to talk with her, and very soon she abandoned me for gayer company in the lower deck, a party of sailors from the *Pennsylvania,* whom she assisted with guitar, song, and flask throughout the night despite the timid protests of other, less enduring travelers. Undoubtedly the sailors solved the problem of her destination. She was a plain, honest whore, operating on her own. The Ritz hotels of the world are full of them, not so plain nor so honest; they do not wear green pajamas in public, and their jokes are slightly more subtle, but they travel by the same means, with the same happy indifference to the next destination.

I bathed in the brown, thick waters of the Sacramento River, slept under its willows, followed on foot the macadam road that wound through the vineyards, and crossed over the dreary wastes of lava rock, making for the purple mountains in the distance. At seven in the morning sweat blinded my eyes, the soles of my feet were burning, my tongue was swollen and parched. The nearest hummock shimmered and dissolved in a subaqueous world of refracted light. I became half-faint, stumbled frequently, lost sight of the mountains, and made my goal the next telephone pole, and the next, in whose six-inch shaft of shade I could lay my face. I was lying thus, when the first driver came along and took me on to Oroville. The rural postman's truck traversed the Feather River, where the gold had once been shoveled up like sand, mounted the Sierra heights, skirted a great hole in the side of the roadbed where a mountain lion had chosen to bury his kill, and deposited me a mile high, at the cabin of a certain Fitzgerald, fair-weather prospector, who surveyed my skinny frame with disappointed doubts in his narrowed eyes. But he kept me, all summer, and I earned my keep.

In those Depression years of the early Thirties, many men had drifted back into the high reaches of these mountains, and a minor resurgence of placer mining began. We were more like scavengers; some filtered and fingered through the piles of sand and stone, the "tailings" from earlier boom days when pressure hoses had washed away whole sides of mountains, leaving them bleached and scarified. Others, such as Fitzgerald and I, hopefully enlarged the abandoned beds of precipitous streams, heaved out endless blobs of the slabby clay in long-handled shovels, ran tons of the stuff over the washboard riffles of our wooden sluices. But, like our neighbors, we worked only four or five hours a day. The hope of finding gold, which almost none of us ever did, was more of an excuse to live in the hills where life was cheap, than anything else. There was a kind of mutual understanding among the men that they were there waiting until the unnatural economic troubles in San Francisco or Sacramento blew themselves out. They brewed beer and turned their sluice boxes into iceboxes where the bottles stood all day in the running water. If Big Foots at the Buster Brown Mine shot a deer one day, we would all gravitate over for a venison feast and would aid, without asking questions, in burying the bones, hide, and antlers so the game warden would find no evidence. Beer parties developed with spontaneity at this cabin, then at another—loud parties, attended frequently by large, blowsy middle-aged women who often arrived on the fenders of decrepit Ford cars which somehow bumped over the rutted trails. They had powerful voices, and an enormous capacity for beer, and spoke the four-letter words simply because they were ignorant of the politer synonyms. If one were not careful, he would experience a heavy, flabby, red arm on his neck, dragging him with astonishing power down upon a cot amid screams of delight from the assembly.

I was just "Slim," the newcomer, the tenderfoot, and fair game for all pranks. When the news somehow got out that I had been to college and had even written things for newspapers, the relationship became unnatural and they left me alone. In a way, it was relief; in a way, I regretted it. Few of the couples were married, which surprised me, since I believed "living in sin" was an exclusive indulgence of the rich.

It was mostly a world of men, of artisans. It did not seem to matter what they had been before—shipyard workers, printers, saloonkeepers— they all had an easy, instinctive comprehension of wood and iron, dynamite and cement, air currents, water pressures, the properties of ore, of soil and seed. They could make trees fall precisely where they wished, transform a motorcycle engine into a power saw, build a fireplace with no question of its failing to draw, produce a complicated plumbing system from a creek and a few lengths of pipe, worm a dog one hour, bake a chocolate cake the next, install a carburetor the next, and repair a gold watch in spare time. So easily, all this was done! None of them ever read a book of directions, studied a blueprint, or consulted with a colleague. They just did it, with leisurely, natural system, and it stayed done, it worked. None of them could have quoted a single law of physics or chemistry, and the words would have sounded like embarrassing nonsense to them anyway. Yet they understood, they *knew*, their *hands* knew. The world of the knowing hands, a world I could never enter—yet half my countrymen dwell in it always. A world of its own, inside America, from which we were to draw a host of sergeants and corporals to make an army work in a manner that was the envy and despair of the others—the British, the French, the Germans, the Russians, all the others.

I had to take these men on their own terms, try to communicate in their language, because they could not in mine. "Fitz" would bait me:

"Jesus H. Christ, don't hold that bit like it was a lily flower! Now turn it, turn it every time you hit it. Keep turning it. Now douse the rock, let the pieces run out. How far in does the dynamite have to go? How far in! Well, that beats me—and you one of them college boys. Jesus H. Christ, when I was your age I was bossing a gang of fourteen men. What in the name of Almighty God do they teach you in them colleges!"

But there were private moments that came frequently during the fresh morning hours of work, moments that never return to one in later years, of pleasure keen to the point of anguish. Fog would vanish, the mountain was unveiled and cleansed, and sweet, dank odors flowed out like perfumed oils upon bright waters. The day sounds would begin: the shrill chippering of a squirrel overhead, the dull smacking of a woodpecker, and down in the valley the tinkle of a cowbell. Near the ditch, in a patch of saw grasses, little globules of dew gathered and dropped, gathered and dropped, like the ticking of sweat drops in the secret hair. The taste of salt was sharp in the corner of the mouth, and the wooden shovel had a good, grainy feel in the hand. In these moments the power of life exploded slowly through the veins, and one worked in a savage orgasm until exhaustion came.

By the end of summer Fitz noticed that I could swing up the leaden-heavy shovel with easier grace than he and could stand longer spells at the bucksaw than he. He said nothing, but the baiting ceased, and that was understood between us as the highest form of compliment. In September he drove me down to Quincy, still unable to make out a young man who offered to perform the most back-breaking labor for no return, even paying his share of the board. I left with a deeper chest, heavier shoulders, and a souvenir phial containing about eighty cents' worth of gold flecks in black dirt—all that our mine had produced.

I awoke before dawn from a bed among the damp weeds by the Union Pacific tracks at Sparks, the division point near Reno, and found an "empty" in the long freight train making up for the thirty-six-hour run across the Great American Desert to Salt Lake. I entered a new social dimension, the great underground world, peopled by tens of thousands of American men, women, and children, white, black, brown, and yellow, who inhabit the "jungle," eat from blackened tin cans, find warmth at night in the box cars, take the sun by day on the flat cars, steal one day, beg with cap in hand the next, fight with fists and often razors, hold sexual intercourse under a blanket in a dark corner of the crowded car, coagulate into pairs and gangs, then disintegrate again, wander from town to town, anxious for the next place, tired of it in a day, fretting to be gone again, happy only when the wheels are clicking under them, the telephone poles slipping by. Some were in honest search of work, but many were not. They had worked—once—but jobs did not last, pay was low, they had had to move on and on for new jobs, until finally it became easier just to move, to move for the moving. Perhaps this world has gone now; one never hears of it. Perhaps wartime prosperity has wiped it out; I do not know. In the Thirties it was a vast, submerged, secondary United States with its own categories of cities, advertised by its own kind of chambers of commerce, its own recognized leaders, its strong men and its recognized bad men, its ragged dowagers and grimy debutantes, and its own laws—such as they were—which dealt primarily with self-preservation. The true world of private enterprise and individual initiative. It will come back, unless America is very wise, but next time it may have lost its "picturesque" quality; they may not beg cap in hand; they may fight with something else but razors because they will know other weapons, and they may not confine their fighting to themselves.

There were strange men among them, remarkable men, unknown to the rest of America. No one has written the biography of Tex, King of Tramps, for example. I never saw him, but I knew there was an obsession in him not unlike Hitler's, a terrible straining of the ego to find expression— either that or he was a wandering imbecile having a glorious time. At least fifty times in the course of a couple of thousand miles I came across his insigne, his coat of arms: Tex—KT. You would find it carved on the wooden seat of a privy on the edge of a Nevada town, penciled on the wall of a shower room in a Salvation Army flophouse in Idaho, chalked on the iron side of a locomotive tender in South Dakota, painted in six-foot letters of red on a white cliffside high up in a Montana canyon. Men told me you found it from Maine to California, everywhere, printed, written, carved thousands of times in the course of what must have been fifteen or twenty years of wandering.

In the jungle, cities were judged and rated on the basis of their citizens' generosity with handouts and the temperament of the railway "deeks" who guard the freight yards. You did not, for example, attempt to travel through Cheyenne, Wyoming, if you had any alternative. You were apt to be chased from the yards there not only with clubs, which was fairly common, but with revolver shots, and it was a long walk to the next station. You traveled through a certain Idaho town only at careful intervals to avoid the monthly raid by the sheriff, who filled his jail with indigents, fed them on nineteen cents a day, and collected a dollar a day from the local government for each occupant. There was no rancor against the sheriff—he had to have his dodge, his racket, like everybody else—but you just avoided him, unless, of course, the weather was rugged and handouts were not forthcoming and you desired a month indoors with steady meals.

One of the most renowned and fearsome characters to dwellers in the jungle was Humpy Davis, railway dick at Harvey, North Dakota. He, it appeared, was a bearlike hunchback, who took a fiendish pride in his ability to clean out a crowded box car, singlehanded, in one minute flat. Normally he used a club, and the score of broken arms and heads was running extremely high, when a conclave of hoboes out in Vancouver decided that Humpy must be eliminated for the good of all concerned. They elected a tall Negro, famous for his marksmanship, to do the job.

News travels fast by the jungle grapevine. Humpy knew, and waited. One day he observed a Negro, alone, walking steadily toward him between the tracks. This was it. Humpy stood still, letting him come on. Suddenly the Negro stopped, swung up his hand, and fired. The legend relates that Humpy did not move, did not raise his arm. Instead, he shouted: "Shoot at my head, you black bastard, shoot at my head!" The assassin fired again. Humpy, unmoving, repeated his instruction. The Negro fired his six shots, yelled in astonishment and terror and, as he began to run, was brought down by a single shot. Humpy walked across the yards to a beer parlor, unbuttoned his shirt, and exhibited his bulletproof vest with six indentations over the heart so closely grouped that a coffee mug could cover them all. It is a favorite story in the jungle. If one doubts it, he is wise not to express his doubt.

My empty box car at Sparks rapidly filled, the train operators having deliberately left it open and vacant in order to avoid having the inevitable load of hoboes clambering around on top of the cars or clinging to the tender. All were bums by choice save one weather-beaten couple of advanced age who came from New Mexico. They had just lost their small farm and were looking for new opportunities. The man carried a great pack with a washboard strapped on it, while his wizened little wife held their scabby hound dog by a length of frayed clothesline. They represented Respectability among us, were accorded a whole corner to themselves and not included in the unending argument, jeering, boasting and scuffling.

I sat in the open doorway, swinging my legs in the sun, and listened to a youngster of sixteen. He was well built, with a remarkably attractive, open face, which had a way of slipping quickly into a sneer, becoming then almost sinister. He was boasting of his racket, and I was failing to understand. Finally he took out a crumpled sheet of paper. I read: "For services rendered, I have delivered the following articles to—— [the boy]." Then came a list including watch, fountain pen, set of evening clothes, silver-backed hairbrushes, and so on. "That was in Frisco last month," the boy explained. "I work fast. I find the café where the queers go, mix in with the bunch that looks richest, go home with one of them, and before I get through with him he's given me everything he owns and the written statement. I'm a minor. It's a criminal offense. But he can't do a thing about it, not a thing." He discussed it openly, casually, as if he were boasting of his prowess at baseball. I had only the vaguest notion of what homosexuality was all about, had never been acquainted with anyone I knew to be abnormal in this way, and rather imagined it was something confined to certain boys' schools in England and the Bohemian quarters of Paris. Suddenly it was all around me. I noticed men with glazed, slightly bulging eyes and uncertain voices who traveled in company with boys in their teens. The men were referred to as "wolves" (long before that word became slang for Casanovas of normal physiology). A Negro boy named Freddie, no more than fourteen, joined our group one day. He was complaining loudly about the perfidy of a white man who had picked him up while he had been hitchhiking the evening before. "Offered me a quarter if he could ——, then he wouldn't give me the quarter, the skunk. Kicked me out of his car. But I slammed a rock through his back window, the bastard," Freddie finished boastfully, and was rewarded by general acknowledgment that it had served the so-and-so right. All this told so naturally, as if it were an open, common matter understood and accepted by everyone. Except for me, apparently it was.

Freddie was very nearly the cause of my death one night. We had reassembled in the box car after a brief foray through a bleak Nevada hamlet, and now, as the train rumbled through the night, we squatted around a small fire in the middle of the car floor, exchanging tidbits. Freddie was missing; somebody thought he had caught the train at the other end, and when we heard a banging on the roof we knew he had, and that he had run over the tops, leaping in the darkness from car to car. Somebody slid the big door wide open, and we heard Freddie yell: "Grab my legs, I'm coming down." We looked at one another. There was silence for a moment. A man said: "How about you, Slim? You got long arms." I had no choice of action. I stood by the door, while a chain of three or four men fastened themselves to one of my legs. The wind blew in my face. The train was racketing along a narrow bridge over a dark canyon. Suddenly there were Freddie's dangling feet, then his legs, swinging in close, then away again as the box car tilted, then close again. I grabbed them, felt myself being torn out of the car, then was toppled over backwards, on top of the human chain, Freddie on top of me. Except for a moment, ten years later, when I found myself at the door of a plunging airplane, trying to jump, I have never known a greater terror. Freddie had stolen a bottle of cherry brandy. He was the hero of the evening, and we ate, drank, and sang to the accompaniment of a harmonica until long after midnight.

I was traveling with two boys of seventeen, bound like myself for Minneapolis where they had recently been suspended from high school for unauthorized absences. We had made a secret pact: they did the begging for food (at which they were expert) and, whenever there was no time to beg or the fruits were meager, I would buy food for the three of us from my store of six or eight dollars which was tied in a handkerchief and secured out of sight inside my belt. (Murder for much less than that was a commonplace in the jungle.) One night we sat by the rails of the "Oregon Short Line," next to the water tank on the outskirts of Ogden, Utah, where we knew our train would pause. We were after the manifest, the "hot shot" —a sealed, nonstop freight train, representing to this social dimension what the Century does to another. We became aware that an enormous Negro was standing a few feet away. He said: "Good evening," sat down beside us, and chewed on a straw. Eventually he said: "Catching the hot shot?" I said we were. Finally: "Rode it once myself. Long, cold ride. Get mighty hungry." More silence and then he said casually: "Tell you what. One you boys want to walk over to my house, have my wife fix up a few sandwiches for you." I got up and said that was kind of him and that I would go along. My companions said nothing.

We walked along a narrow road, bordered by weeds and ditches. He seemed to be in no hurry and said nothing. I was worried about missing the train and asked him where his house was. "See that light?" he answered. The light appeared to be at least a half-mile away. We walked on, and it began to seem very strange to me. Why should a Negro, obviously poor, go so much out of his way to aid three young white tramps? I was becoming very uneasy, trying to think of some way to withdraw, when the man turned abruptly, walked across a plank over the ditch, and halted by a clump of willows. "Come here a minute, Slim," he said.

My throat had become suddenly dry and I could not answer. He called in a soft tone two or three times: "Come here—got something to show you." All manner of ideas flashed through my head. Did he know about my money and intend to murder me for it? Had he some grisly object there he wanted me to carry away on the train?

He walked deliberately back and stood towering over me so close I could smell his breath. "Want to make a quarter, Slim?" he said softly, coaxingly.

My voice returned enough for me to say in what I hoped were even tones that I couldn't do anything for him. I turned and began to walk back down the dark roadway, the hair on the back of my neck tickling, expecting something to strike me at any moment. Then two figures stepped from the ditch and stood there, waiting, in my path. My heart beat faster, but my head got very cool. I had walked into a trap and was about to be "rolled." I kept on, approached them, lifted my hands over my head, and said in an abnormally confident voice: "All right. You can have anything I have on me."

One of them said: "For Christ sakes, Slim, what do you think you're doing?"

My two loyal, very wise companions had followed us. They got out their knives and wanted to attack the Negro, but let themselves be dissuaded. They scolded me at length for being so dumb that I hadn't recognized a queer, and I had nothing to say. My hands shook for an hour afterwards.

There were glorious days of sunshine, days when we stretched out nude on a flat car cooled by chunks of ice someone tossed down from the "reefer" adjoining, days when we swung our legs idly and yelled to the girls working in the passing fields, days when we abandoned the trains and swam naked in deep mountain pools of cold, clear water. In the night there was hazard and danger, always. There was a midnight halt while the train reorganized at a sleeping Montana division point on the Milwaukee line. The hoboes gather in a hamburger shop, the only concern still open for business. It was a cold night. With their pennies and nickels the tramps provided themselves with thick mugs of coffee. I ordered sandwiches for myself and my companions. Then to my horror I discovered I had only a five-dollar bill. I passed it over the fake marble counter to the waiter as surreptitiously as I could, and no one noticed. But Montana is a silver state, and the waiter returned with four heavy, gleaming silver dollars in his hand. He did not put them in my anxiously outthrust palm but proceeded to drop them, ringing, clattering on the counter, one at a time. I was conscious that the sounds of eating and drinking around me had ceased and that every eye had turned in my direction. I stuffed them in my pocket and we rose, leaving our food unfinished, sauntered out the door and then ran with all our strength to the train. We hurried along from car to car, scrambling, panting, until we found one with the door unlocked. It was half-filled with lumber. We climbed in, shifted the boards until we had made a hole, then pulled them over us. As the train began its slow, jerking start we heard boots scuffing the boards above our heads. Later we could catch a few words. The voices we recognized as belonging to two of the more evil-looking tramps of the earlier evening. They were talking about the kids with the silver dollars. The voices ceased after a time, and we drifted to uneasy, uncomfortable sleep. In the morning the men were gone.

I arrived at my father's house with my face black from the coal dust of a locomotive tender—my berth during the final roaring, kaleidoscopic night of clinging to a passenger express.

DOWN AND OUT AT ANACOSTIA

Was there anyone who believed it was necessary to take action?

The critics of American business seemed as unprepared as the businessmen themselves. Labor leaders were befuddled—with two exceptions: John L. Lewis of the United Mine Workers and Sidney Hillman of the Amalgamated Clothing Workers, both of whom felt the government must assume leadership to cure the sick economy.

While the Administration stood foursquare against taking initiative, the Congress seemed to be in a state of paralysis, unable to create, let alone pass, any helpful legislation. One Senator had shown a persistent concern with the business cycle, the labor movement and other facets of the industrial society—Robert F. Wagner of New York. There were a few others—La Follette of Wisconsin, Norris of Nebraska and Hugo Black of Alabama, for instance— who believed in relief and who offered programs; but it was Wagner who proved the rallying voice in 1932, as he would in later years.

In February 1932 the Reconstruction Finance Corporation had been organized to make loans to banks, railroads and insurance companies. But later that year it was disclosed that more than half of the 126 million dollars distributed had gone to three large banks.

"We shall help the railroad; we shall help the financial institutions; and I agree that we should," said Senator Wagner. "But is there any reason why we should not likewise extend a helping hand to that forlorn American, in every village and every city of the United States, who has been without wages since 1929?"

Finally, in July 1932, the Emergency Relief and Construction Act established an RFC fund of 300 million dollars for loans to the states, but President Hoover cautioned the states not to call on the money "except in absolute need."

Still there were no signs of serious revolt in the people. They were sad and defeated, not rebellious.

A qualifying footnote to such a generalization was the increase in shipments of gold beyond our shores by some of the wealthy in the country who wished to avoid paying taxes. Colonel Robert R. McCormick, publisher of the Chicago *Tribune,* carried on a campaign to get people to pay their full taxes, while at the same time, in his own tax report, he listed his personal property as being little more than $25,-000, on which he paid a tax of about $1,500. Samuel Insull, one of the country's biggest speculators in the world of finance, was indicted for embezzling funds, but not before he fled the country.

There had been isolated strikes and a few hunger marches on local and state seats of government; not until summer of 1932 was there an incident big enough to focus the country's attention on growing resentments. A group of World War I veterans called on the government for immediate payment of their bonus for services in the war, a payment not scheduled to be made until 1945. At the time, the Patman bill, which provided for immediate payment, was before the Congress.

The proposal caught fire. Fifteen thousand veterans, some with wives and children, arrived in Washington in late spring of 1932 and camped on the Anacostia mud flats, to lobby for the passage of the bill. On June 16, the Patman bill was defeated. Five thousand veterans left Washington, but the remainder simply waited on the flats. Congress voted money to pay their fares home, and then adjourned. Still, the veterans did not stir, their leaders exhorting them to hold fast.

MACARTHUR, EISENHOWER
AND PATTON VERSUS THE VETS

THE Hoover Administration had chosen to ignore the "invaders" and some people suggested the whole thing was a Communist plot, even though the veterans behaved in an orderly fashion. Not until an accident set off a scuffle between the police and the veterans, did the government take a step. Then Hoover ordered General Douglas Mac-Arthur, Chief of the Army, to evacuate the veterans and their families.

MacArthur is said to have excused the unnecessary brusqueness of the evacuation by suggesting that a mob was about to seize control of the government.

The veterans were undoubtedly a source of embarrassment to the President but they had been unarmed, and this cavalier handling of down-and-out Americans seemed to many to be further proof of the government's callous unconcern for the plight of the people.

In *The Lean Years,* Irving Bernstein has provided a description of this unusual military operation:

"The armed forces that gathered in the vicinity of the White House consisted of four troops of cavalry, four companies of infantry, a mounted machine-gun squadron, and six whippet tanks. MacArthur himself was in command. At his side was his aide, Major Dwight D. Eisenhower, and one of his officers was the dashing George S. Patton, Jr.

The operation was delayed an hour while an orderly rushed across the Potomac to Fort Myer for Mac-Arthur's tunic, service stripes, sharpshooter medal, and English whipcord breeches.

"He then led the troops in dramatic display down Pennsylvania Avenue before a huge crowd, arriving at the troubled area at 4:45 P.M. 'We are going to break the back of the B.E.F.' [Bonus Expeditionary Force], MacArthur told Glassford [Superintendent of Washington Police]. The soldiers, using tear gas, quickly cleared the old buildings and set them on fire. By 7:15, all the encampments within the city had been evacuated and burned.

"MacArthur then sent his forces across the Anacostia bridge. Thousands of veterans, their wives, and children fled before the advancing soldiers. The troops attacked with tear gas and set fire to a number of huts. There was virtually no resistance. The veterans then spread the conflagration. By morning Anacostia was a smoldering ruin.

"The military operation was carried out swiftly and efficiently. Total casualties, including those in the earlier fracas, were two veterans shot to death, an eleven-week baby in grave condition (he later died), an eight-year-old boy partially blinded by gas, two policemen with fractured skulls, a bystander shot through the

117

shoulder, a veteran's ear severed by cavalry saber, a veteran stabbed in the hip by a bayonet, more than a dozen persons injured by bricks and clubs, and over 1,000 gassed. Property damage of value was slight, perhaps the most important loss being twenty old sycamores and elms seared by flames near the Pennsylvania Avenue encampment."

Thus was the "invasion" of Washington repulsed. How the Bonus Army was then dispersed is told in the following selection.

MALCOLM COWLEY

THE FLIGHT OF
THE BONUS ARMY*

WHEN the veterans of the Bonus Army first tried to escape, they found that the bridges into Virginia were barred by soldiers and the Maryland roads blocked against them by state troopers. They wandered from street to street or sat in ragged groups, the men exhausted, the women with wet handkerchiefs laid over their smarting eyes, the children waking from sleep to cough and whimper from the tear gas in their lungs. The flames behind them were climbing into the night sky. About four in the morning, as rain began to fall, they were allowed to cross the border into Maryland, on condition that they move as rapidly as possible into another state.

The veterans were expected to disperse to their homes—but most of them had no homes, and they felt that their only safety lay in sticking together. Somehow the rumor passed from group to group that the mayor of Johnstown had invited them to his city. And they cried, as they rode toward Pennsylvania or marched in the dawn twilight along the highways, "On to Johnstown."

Their shanties and tents had been burned, their personal property destroyed, except for the few belongings they could carry on their backs; many of their families were separated, wives from husbands, children from parents. Knowing all this, they still did not appreciate the extent of their losses. Two days before, they had regarded themselves, and thought the country regarded them, as heroes trying to collect a debt

* From *The New Republic,* Aug. 17, 1932.

long overdue. They had boasted about their months or years of service, their medals, their wounds, their patriotism in driving the Reds out of their camp; they had nailed an American flag to every hut. When threatened with forcible eviction, they answered that no American soldier would touch them: hadn't a detachment of Marines (consisting, some said, of twenty-five or thirty men, though others claimed there were two whole companies) thrown down its arms and refused to march against them? But the infantry, last night, had driven them out like so many vermin. Mr. Hoover had announced that "after months of patient indulgence, the government met overt lawlessness as it always must be met if the cherished processes of self-government are to be preserved." Mr. Hoover and his subordinates, in their eagerness to justify his action, were about to claim that the veterans were Red radicals, that they were the dregs of the population, that most of them had criminal records and, as a final insult, that half of them weren't veterans at all.

They would soon discover the effect of these official libels. At Somerset, on the Lincoln Highway, some of them asked for food. "We can't give you any," said a spokesman for the businessmen. "The President says that you're rebels—don't you understand? You're all outlaws now." A veteran's wife and children were refused admission to a hotel, even though they offered to pay for a room in advance. At Johnstown, the wealthier citizens were dismayed to hear of their arrival. Possibly half the workmen in the city were unemployed; a fifth or a sixth of the population was in need of charity. Ten thousand hungry people were a threat in themselves, but the editor of the Johnstown *Tribune* was about to conjure up new terrors. He wrote:

Johnstown faces a crisis. It must prepare to protect itself from the Bonus Army concentrating here at the invitation of Mayor Eddie McCloskey. . . .

In any group of the size of the Bonus Army, made up of men gathered from all parts of the country, without discipline, without effective leadership in a crisis, without any attempt on the part of those leaders to check up the previous records of the individuals who compose it, there is certain to be a mixture of undesirables—thieves, plug-uglies, degenerates. . . . The community must protect itself from the criminal fringe of the invaders.

Booster clubs, community organizations of every sort, volunteer organizations if no sectional group is available, should get together in extraordinary sessions and organize to protect property, women and possibly life.

It is no time for halfway measures. . . .

The heroes of 1918, now metamorphosed into "thieves, plug-uglies, degenerates," were preparing to gather in the outskirts of the city, in the camp site offered them at Ideal Park. And the leading citizens, aided by the state police, were planning to use any means short of violence to keep them from reaching it. Mr. Hoover's proclamation had done its work.

At Jennerstown is a barracks of the Pennsylvania State Police, looking for all the world like a fashionable roadhouse. In front of the barracks is a traffic light. The road ahead leads westward over Laurel Hill and Chestnut Ridge; the right-hand road leads nineteen miles northward into Johnstown. It was the task of state troopers to keep the Bonus Army moving west over the mountains, toward Ligonier and the Ohio border.

In half an hour on Saturday morning, I saw more than a thousand veterans pass through Jennerstown—that is, more than fifty trucks bearing an average of twenty men apiece. Later I was told that the procession continued at irregular intervals until Sunday evening. The troopers would wait at the intersection, twenty men on their motorcycles like a school of swift gray sharks, till they heard that a convoy was approaching; then they would dart off to meet it in a cloud of dust and blue gasoline smoke, with their hats cutting the air like so many fins. One of the troopers stayed behind to manipulate the traffic light. As the trucks came nearer, he would throw a switch that changed it into a mere yellow blinker, so that all of them could shoot past the intersection without slackening speed. They were full of ragged men, kneeling, standing unsteadily, clinging to the sideboards; there was no room to sit down. Behind each truck rode a trooper, and there were half a dozen others mingled with the crowd that watched from in front of a filling station.

The contrast between these homeless veterans, hatless, coatless, unshaven, half-starved—most of them hadn't eaten or slept for thirty-six hours, a few hadn't had so much as a drink of water—and the sleekly uniformed, smug, well-nourished troopers who were herding them past their destination, produced a sharp effect on the crowd of backwoods farmers, who otherwise cared little about the Bonus March.

"Hey, buddies," they shouted, "turn right, turn right. Johnstown"— pointing northward—"Johnstown." The hungry men smiled and waved at them uncomprehendingly.

But a few had seen that something was wrong, that they were being carried beyond their meeting place. They tried to pass the word from truck to truck, above the roar of the motors. As they went bowling through the level village street, there was no way of escape; but just beyond Jennerstown, the road climbs steeply up Laurel Hill; the drivers shifted into second gear—and promptly lost half their passengers. The others, those who received no warning or let themselves be cowed by the troopers, were carried westward. The following week I met a New York veteran who hadn't escaped from the convoy till it passed the Ohio line. A Negro from Washington, a resident of the city for thirty years—he wasn't a bonus marcher at all, but made the mistake of walking through Anacostia in his shirt sleeves—was arrested, piled into a truck, and carried all the way to Indianapolis before he managed to tell his story to a reporter.

As for the veterans who escaped at Jennerstown, they lay by the road-side utterly exhausted. Their leaders had been arrested, dispersed, or else had betrayed them; their strength had been gnawed away by hunger or lack of sleep; they hoped to reunite and recuperate in a new camp, but how to reach it they did not know. For perhaps twenty minutes, they dozed there hopelessly. Then—and I was a witness of this phenomenon—a new leader would stand forth from the ranks. He would stop a motorist, learn the road to Johnstown, call the men together, give them their instructions—and the whole group would suddenly obey a self-imposed discipline. As they turned northward at the Jennerstown traffic light, one of them would shout, "We're going back!" and perhaps half a dozen would mumble in lower voices, "We're gonna get guns and go back to Washington."

Mile after mile we passed the ragged line as we too drove northward to the camp at Ideal Park. We were carrying two of the veterans, chosen from a group of three hundred by a quick informal vote of their comrades. One was a man gassed in the Argonne and tear-gassed at Anacostia; he breathed with an effort, as if each breath would be his last. The other was a man with family troubles; he had lost his wife and six children during the retreat from Camp Marks and hoped to find them in Johnstown. He talked about his service in France, his three medals, which he refused to wear, his wounds, his five years in a government hospital. "If they gave me a job," he said, "I wouldn't care about the bonus."

The sick man, as we passed one group of veterans after another, pointed northward and said in an almost inaudible voice, "This way, comrades, this way. Comrades, this way," till his head fell back and he lapsed into a feverish sleep.

It seemed the ragged line would never end. Here the marchers were stumbling under the weight of their suitcases and blanket rolls, here they were clustered round a farmhouse pump, here a white man was sharing the burden of a crippled Negro, here white and Negro together were snoring in a patch of shade. The road curled downward into the valley where Johnstown swelters between steep hills. On either side of us were fields of golden grain, cut and stacked for the threshers; a moment later we were winding through a forest. It was a landscape not unlike the high hills north of the River Aisne. In that other country, fifteen years before, I had seen gaunt men coming out of the trenches half-dead with fatigue, bending under the weight of their equipment. The men on the Johnstown road that day were older, shabbier, but somehow more impressive: they were volunteers, fighting a war of their own. "And don't forget it, buddy," one of them shouted as the car slowed down, "we've enlisted for the duration."

At Ideal Park, where the new camp was being pitched, there was the same determination, combined with a hysteria caused by sudden relief from tension. A tall man with a tear-streaked face was marching up and down. "I used to be a hundred-percenter," he said, "but now I'm a Red radical. I had an American flag, but the damned tin soldiers burned it. Now I don't ever want to see a flag again. Give me a gun and I'll go back to Washington."—"That's right, buddy," said a woman looking up from her two babies, who lay on a dirty quilt in the sun. A cloud of flies hovered above them. Another man was reading the editorial page of a Johnstown paper. He shouted, "Let them come here and mow us down with machine guns. We won't move this time."—"That's right, buddy," said the woman again. A haggard face—eyes bloodshot, skin pasty white under a three days' beard—suddenly appeared at the window of our car. "Hoover must die," said the face ominously. "You know what this means?" a man shouted from the other side. "This means revolution."—"Yes, you're damned right it means revolution."

But a thousand homeless veterans, or fifty thousand, don't make a revolution. This threat would pass and be forgotten, like the other threat that was only half concealed in the Johnstown editorial. Next day the bonus leaders would come, the slick guys in leather puttees; they would make a few speeches and everything would be smoothed over. They would talk of founding a new Fascist order of Khaki Shirts, but this threat, too, can be disregarded: a Fascist movement, to succeed in this country, must come from the middle classes and be respectable. No, if any revolution results from the flight of the Bonus Army, it will come from a different source, from the government itself. The army in time of peace, at the national capital, has been used against unarmed citizens—and this, with all it threatens for the future, is a revolution in itself.

ELECTION YEAR—1932

PERHAPS the people themselves were not ready for radical leadership, but the plain fact was that even if they had been, none of the radical or the old reform parties had anything attractive to offer. But the people would be given a chance to express their feelings in the forthcoming election. Cracks were beginning to appear in the composure of some of the nation's leaders. Said Senator David A. Reed in 1932, "I do not often envy other countries their governments, but I say that if this country ever needed a Mussolini it needs one now."

President Hoover was nominated by the Republicans to run again; the Democrats nominated the Governor of New York, Franklin D. Roosevelt. Some of the liberal commentators of the day thought Roosevelt was too weak and vacillating. His record in Albany had been good on welfare and conservation, but his co-operation with the Seabury investigation of corruption in New York City had left something to be desired. Consequently, no one could forecast just what Roosevelt had in mind when, in his acceptance speech at the convention in Chicago, he spoke of establishing a "new deal" for the people.

In the months that followed Roosevelt's nomination, he consulted frequently with a group of advisers, which was called his "brain trust"— men like Moley, Tugwell, Rosenman and Berle. They were as much concerned with the economic and social dilemmas of the time as were the politicians; and, well versed in political theory and economic philosophy, unhampered by traditional ideas of the market place, they were not afraid to advise experiment.

One of the main questions to be settled was how big a role the federal government should assume in planning and, in particular, just how much control it should exercise in making decisions "to promote the general welfare" of the people. Roosevelt made his position clear: businessmen "had to assume the responsibility which went with power; when they failed, the government must be swift to protect the public interest."

The Republicans abhorred government "interference" and insisted that the country would right itself eventually if it was just let alone. Roosevelt and his advisers observed that this policy had had no noticeable effect in arresting the downward trend of the economy and that active measures were necessary—tougher regulatory policies for business, more social planning, sounder practices for banking, plus keeping the budget balanced (no one had the courage to declare against this—in public, at least); all these came under debate within the "brain trust."

THE CAMPAIGN

In campaigning for the election, Roosevelt made a good impression upon the public, but the people made just as strong an impression on him. "For Roosevelt," Arthur Schlesinger says, "the faces before him were an unforgettable experience—the great mass of Missourians under the lights before the Capitol at Jefferson City, the Kansans listening patiently in the hot sun at Topeka, the Nebraska farmers in the red glow of sunset at McCook, the stricken but dauntless miners of Butte.

" 'I have looked into the faces of thousands of Americans,' Roosevelt told a friend. "They have the frightened look of lost children.' Roosevelt himself, endlessly watching out of train windows, from the back seat of automobiles, from the platform of the crowded auditoriums, smiling, waving his battered Italian felt hat, seemed to gather new strength from the people." *

Hoover's campaign was received with a mixture of approval and hostility. The people held him respon-

sible for the bad times. The President could not believe the government deserved such ill feeling, and he campaigned hard, charging that Roosevelt's New Deal ideas would bankrupt the country and vitiate the very foundations of the American government.

On Election Day the American people went Democratic: Roosevelt polled 22,809,638 votes to Hoover's 15,758,901.

Roosevelt announced his Cabinet members soon afterward; among them were Cordell Hull, as Secretary of State, and Frances Perkins, as Secretary of Labor, the first woman Cabinet member.

Before the inauguration, efforts were made to bring Hoover and Roosevelt together to discuss mutual action to arrest the ever-deepening crisis, but their personalities and their philosophies were too far apart for them to find common ground.

ARTHUR M. SCHLESINGER, JR.

THE INAUGURAL†

THE WHITE HOUSE, midnight, Friday, March 3, 1933. Across the country the banks of the nation had gradually shuttered their windows and locked their doors. The very machinery of the American economy seemed to be coming to a stop. The rich and fertile nation, overflowing with natural wealth in its fields and forests and mines, equipped with unsurpassed technology, endowed with boundless resources in its men and women, lay stricken. "We are at the end of our rope," the weary President at last said,

* Arthur M. Schlesinger, Jr., *The Crisis of the Old Order.*
† From Arthur M. Schlesinger, Jr.'s *The Crisis of the Old Order* (Boston, Houghton Mifflin, 1957).

as the striking clock announced the day of his retirement. "There is nothing more we can do."

Saturday, March 4, dawned gray and bleak. Heavy winter clouds hung over the city. A chill northwest wind brought brief gusts of rain. The darkness of the day intensified the mood of helplessness. "A sense of depression had settled over the capital," reported the New York *Times*, "so that it could be felt." In the late morning, people began to gather for the noon ceremonies, drawn, it would seem, by curiosity as much as by hope. Nearly one hundred thousand assembled in the grounds before the Capitol, standing in quiet groups, sitting on benches, watching from rooftops. Some climbed the bare, sleet-hung trees. As they waited, they murmured among themselves. "What are those things that look like little cages?" one asked. "Machine guns," replied a woman with a nervous giggle. "The atmosphere which surrounded the change of government in the United States," wrote Arthur Krock, "was comparable to that which might be found in a beleaguered capital in wartime." The colorless light of the cast-iron skies, the numb faces of the crowd, created almost an air of fantasy. Only the Capitol seemed real, etched like a steel engraving against the dark clouds.

On the drive from the White House to the Capitol, the retiring President, his eyes lowered, his expression downcast, did not try to hide his feelings. The nation which had helped him rise from a poor Iowa farm to wealth and power, which he had repaid with high-minded and unstinted service, had rejected him. "Democracy is not a polite employer," Herbert Hoover later wrote. "The only way out of elective office is to get sick or die or get kicked out."

It was customary for the retiring President to ask his successor for dinner on the night of the third of March; but Hoover had declined to issue the usual invitation. At length, the White House usher insisted that the President-elect must be given the opportunity to pay his respects. Instead of the traditional dinner, a tea was arranged for the afternoon of the third. It had been a strained occasion in the Red Room, complicated by fruitless last-minute discussions about the banking crisis. Finally the President-elect, recognizing that Hoover was not in the mood to complete the round of protocol, politely suggested that the President need not return the visit. Hoover looked his successor in the eye. "Mr. Roosevelt," he said coldly, "when you are in Washington as long as I have been, you will learn that the President of the United States calls on nobody." Franklin Delano Roosevelt, hurrying his family from the room, returned to the Mayflower Hotel visibly annoyed. "It was . . ." a close friend later reported, "one of the few times I have ever seen him really angry."

Now Hoover sat motionless and unheeding as the car moved through crowded streets toward the Capitol. Doubtless he assumed the occasional cheers from the packed sidewalks were for Roosevelt and so not his to acknowledge. But for Roosevelt, sitting beside him in the open car, these last moments belonged to the retiring President; it was not for the President-elect to respond to the faint applause. On they drove in uncomfortable silence. Passing the new Commerce Building on Constitution Avenue, Roosevelt hoped that at least this sight might tempt the former Secretary of Commerce into an exchange of amiabilities. When a friendly remark produced only an unintelligible murmur in reply, the President-elect suddenly felt that the two men could not ride on forever like graven images. Turning, he began to smile to the men and women along the street and to wave his top hat. Hoover rode on, his face heavy and expressionless.

The fog of despair hung over the land. The images of a nation as it approached zero hour: the well-groomed men, baffled and impotent in their double-breasted suits before the Senate committee; the confusion and dismay in the business office and the university; the fear in the country club; the angry men marching in the silent street; the scramble for the rotting garbage in the dump; the sweet milk trickling down the dusty road; the noose dangling over the barn door; the raw northwest wind blasting its way across Capitol plaza.

In the Capitol, the President-elect waited in the Military Affairs Committee Room. Sober and white-faced, he sat in silence, glancing at the manuscript of his inaugural address. Huey Long, the senator from Louisiana, glimpsed him and started to sweep into the room; then paused at the threshold and tiptoed away. Ten minutes before noon Roosevelt started down the corridor toward the Senate, only to be stopped. "All right," he said, "we'll go back and wait some more." When the moment arrived, he was to ride in his wheelchair to the east door; then walk thirty-five yards to the speaker's stand.

A few moments before, in the Senate Chamber, the new Vice-President, John Nance Garner of Texas, had taken his oath of office. There followed a rush from the Senate to the inaugural stand outside. The mass of people, swarming into the narrow exit from the east doors of the Capitol, blocked the runway. In a moment the congestion was hopeless. Garner and the retiring Vice-President, Charles Curtis of Kansas, had meanwhile reached the stand. The Texan, with no overcoat, shivered in the harsh wind; he borrowed a muffler and wrapped it around his neck. Near him Curtis disappeared into the depth of his fur coat, looking steadily at the floor, apparently lost in memory. Gradually, invited guests began to force their way through the jam: members of the new Cabinet, half a dozen senators, the new President's wife, his mother, his tall sons. Eventually Charles Evans Hughes, the Chief Justice of the United States, made his appearance, erect and stately, a black silk skullcap on his head, his white beard stirred by the wind and his black robe fluttering about his legs. In a leather-upholstered chair to the left of the lectern sat Herbert Hoover.

The tension in the crowd mounted steadily with the delay. Presently a Supreme Court attendant arrived bearing the family Bible of the Roosevelts. Then, at last, the bugle sounded; and Franklin Delano Roosevelt, intensely pale, leaning on the arm of his eldest son James, walked slowly up the maroon-carpeted ramp. The Marine Band, in its scarlet jackets and blue trousers, finished the last bars of "Hail to the Chief." There was a convulsive stir in the crowd, spread over forty acres of park and pavement; then cheers and applause. Mrs. Woodrow Wilson waved a handkerchief. Bernard Baruch leaped upon a bench and swung his black silk hat. Josephus Daniels, the new President's old chief, his eyes wet with tears, pounded vigorously with his cane. A few rays of sunshine broke for a moment through the slate clouds upon the inaugural stand.

The Chief Justice read the oath with dignity and power. Instead of returning the customary "I do," Roosevelt repeated the full oath. ("I am glad," Hughes had written when the President-elect suggested this. ". . . I think the repetition is the more dignified and appropriate course.") The family Bible lay open to the thirteenth chapter of the First Corinthians. "For now we see through a glass, darkly; but then face to face: now I know in part; but then shall I know even as also I am known. And now abideth faith, hope, charity, these three; but the greatest of these *is* charity."

Six days before, Roosevelt in his Hyde Park study, writing with pencil on a lined, legal-sized yellow pad, had made a draft of his inaugural address. Waiting in the Senate committee room on inauguration day, he added a new opening sentence to his reading copy: "This is a day of consecration." But, as the great crowd quieted down, the solemnity of the occasion surged over him; he said, in ringing tones, "This is a day of national consecration."

Across the country millions clustered around radio sets. The new President stood bareheaded and unsmiling, his hands gripping the lectern. The moment had come, he said, to speak the truth, the whole truth, frankly and boldly. "Let me assert my firm belief that the only thing we have to fear is fear itself—nameless, unreasoning, unjustified terror which paralyzes needed efforts to convert retreat into advance." The speaker flung back his head. "In every dark hour of our national life a leadership of frankness and vigor has met with that understanding and support of the people themselves which is essential to victory."

The bounty of nature, he continued, was undiminished. "Plenty is at our doorstep, but a generous use of it languishes in the very sight of the supply." Why? Because the rulers of the exchange of mankind's goods "have failed through their own stubbornness and their own incompetence, have admitted their failure, and have abdicated. . . . They have no vision, and when there is no vision the people perish. The money changers have fled from their high seats in the temple of our civilization." The crowd delivered itself of its first great applause. "There must be an end," Roosevelt went on, "to a conduct in banking and in business which too often has given to a sacred trust the likeness of callous and selfish wrongdoing." Again the crowd shouted.

"This Nation asks for action, and action now. . . . We must act and act quickly. . . . We must move as a trained and loyal army willing to sacrifice for the good of a common discipline, because without such discipline no progress is made, no leadership becomes effective." "It may be," he said, "that an unprecedented demand and need for undelayed action may call for temporary departure from that normal balance of public procedure." If Congress should fail to enact the necessary measures, if the emergency were still critical, then, added Roosevelt solemnly, "I shall ask the Congress for the one remaining instrument to meet the crisis—broad Executive power to wage a war against the emergency, as great as the power that would be given to me if we were in fact invaded by a foreign foe." The crowd thundered approval in a long, continuing demonstration—the loudest applause of the day.

Roosevelt—"his face still so grim," reported Arthur Krock, "as to seem unfamiliar to those who have long known him"—did not acknowledge the applause. Nor, indeed, did all share the enthusiasm. Some who watched the handsome head and heard the cultivated voice mistrusted what lay behind the charm and the rhetoric. "I was thoroughly scared," the retiring Secretary of State, Henry L. Stimson, wrote in his diary. ". . . Like most of his past speeches, it was full of weasel words and would let him do about what he wanted to." Edmund Wilson, covering the inaugural for the *New Republic,* saw "the old unctuousness, the old pulpit vagueness," the echoes of Woodrow Wilson's eloquence without Wilson's glow of life behind them. "The thing that emerges most clearly," wrote Wilson, "is the warning of a dictatorship."

But the unsmiling President showed no evidence of doubt. "We do not distrust the future of essential democracy," he said in summation. "The people of the United States have not failed. In their need they have registered a mandate that they want direct, vigorous action. They have asked for discipline and direction under leadership. They have made me the present instrument of their wishes. In the spirit of the gift I take it." Herbert Hoover stared at the ground.

The high clear note of the cavalry bugles announced the inaugural parade. Franklin Roosevelt, in the presidential car, waved greetings to the crowd along the way—men and women now curiously awakened from apathy and daze. The horsemen wheeled into line, and the parade began.

In Washington the weather remained cold and gray. Across the land the fog began to lift.

WILLIAM MANCHESTER

THE GREAT BANK HOLIDAY*

IT IS SLIGHTLY more than a quarter century since panic closed America's banks—since that improbable month when Norman Vincent Peale denounced capitalists, John D. Rockefeller ran out of dimes, Macy's announced that demanding cash from its customers would be unpatriotic, and what were then known as step-ins were solemnly accepted as legal tender in Madison Square Garden.

Even then it had an air of fantasy, and was quickly forgotten, just as it had been unforeseen during the lame-duck winter of 1932–33 which led to it. And yet there had been omens of the panic. There was, for example, the jigsaw-puzzle craze, which reached its crest at the very moment America was plunging into the terminal trough of the Depression. During that winter some 6,000,000 puzzles were sold, and in retrospect the significance of the vogue seems painfully clear. It was a time of searching for elusive answers in politics and economics. The jigsaw turned out puzzles a man at least could solve.

In Detroit the weekend of February 11–12 newsstands enjoyed a heavy sale of 500-piece (*Lincoln*) puzzles. They were tough to do. Thousands of automotive workers were still frowning over card tables Monday night as their children, huddled by radios, hoarded the currency of the young— Ralston box tops, Ovaltine seals, Rice Krispies labels, Tastyeast wrappers. None of the puzzle workers, of course, suspected that very soon American parents would be reduced to even stranger exchange. But the time was at hand, and for Detroit it was the very next day, St. Valentine's Day, 1933.

President Hoover was singing his swan song over the networks at ten o'clock that evening before the Republican National Committee. Among those not listening was the Democratic Governor of Michigan, William A. Comstock. It was nothing personal. At three o'clock that afternoon he had received an urgent telephone request to join a conference of bankers in downtown Detroit, and he had been there ever since. Detroit's Union Guardian Trust Company was in straits. If it failed it probably would take every other bank in the city with it, and the bankers were asking Com-

* From *Holiday*, February 1960.

stock to declare a banking moratorium throughout Michigan. At midnight he agreed, drove to the state capital at Lansing and issued a proclamation closing the state's 550 banks. He called it a holiday.

The idea was not new. For more than a year the nation's harassed business community had been begging for breathers, and in two states, Nevada and Louisiana, it actually had been given them. Nevada, however, had a population of only 91,000, and Louisiana's moratorium covered just one weekend. Michigan, on the other hand, was the heart of the automotive industry. Its citizens, moreover, were depleted of cash after the long weekend and unprepared for Comstock's valentine. The proclamation was too late for the regular editions of the morning papers; extras greeted workers arriving downtown with the news that they were cut off with whatever cash they had in their their pockets. In some cases this was almost nothing, but there was no hysteria, no gathering in front of the closed banks. The general mood was casual, even gay. After all, it *was* a holiday.

To be sure, it was awkward. Many of the newsboys peddling the extras were obliged to sell on credit. Those who did collect coins found themselves hailed by cruising merchants waving bills and pleading for change. A few storekeepers, unable to locate silver, had to close their stores; those who sought relief in Windsor, Ontario, were coldly told their checks would be accepted "subject to collection," and under the phony holiday air there was a feeling of uneasiness about the value of what currency there was. The Dow Chemical Company of Midland began coining magnesium into "Dowmetal Money," with an arbitrary value of twenty cents—the first of a series of substitutes which were to plague the economy for a month.

Still, there were reassuring signs. Merchants talked of organizing a change bureau. Milk companies promised to continue deliveries. Before noon a shipment of gold estimated at $20,000,000 was flown from Federal Reserve coffers in Chicago, and that night another $5,000,000 arrived from Washington to meet money orders and Postal Savings withdrawals. Surely, everyone said, the bronze doors would yawn wide the next day. Wags told other wags the story of the man who had to call his wife, couldn't cash a bill, and borrowed a nickel from an apple seller on Woodward Avenue. "Brother," the optimists sang blithely, "can you spare a dime?" And in Dearborn, Henry Ford heard the piping voices of two hundred children chant, "When the bough breaks, the cradle will fall."

But the doors didn't yawn. Later in the week they were held slightly ajar—depositors could withdraw five per cent of their accounts. It wasn't enough even to meet local payrolls. Detroit's Colonial Department Store, frankly resorting to barter, offered dresses for salted Saginaw herring, suits for livestock, assorted merchandise for eggs and honey. By the following week jokes were discarded. The holiday had been extended.

Michigan's plight had been aggravated by plunging real-estate values, but the Depression was nationwide. Since the crash of 1929 more than 5,500 American banks had failed, and the public, understandably, was edgy. It responded by hoarding. Gold was vanishing from vaults at the rate of $20,000,000 a day, and depositors who couldn't get metal were taking paper, so that the government was called upon to expand its currency at the very time the gold on which it was based was disappearing.

Bank panics are always suicidal. In 1933, however, the situation had been complicated by three years of deflation. Even the soundest institutions held mortgages and securities which had fallen to a fraction of their former value. The nation's 18,569 banks had about $6,000,000,000 in cash to meet $41,000,000,000 in deposits, and bankers who were forced to sell mortgages or securities to raise cash would suffer heavy losses. President Hoover was trying everything he could think of to turn the tide—R.F.C. loans to banks, debtor relief, higher duties on Jap sneakers and Czech rubbers—but nothing seemed to work.

Now Michigan had fallen. Abruptly the daily outflow of gold from the rest of the country's banks jumped to $37,000,000; currency withdrawals to $122,000,000. Banks everywhere were swarming with wild-eyed depositors taking out cash—in the Bronx a young mother rented her baby, at twenty-five cents a trip, to women who used it to claim preference at the head of bank lines; and the week of February 20 in Maryland the Baltimore Trust Company paid out $13,000,000, nearly half of it on Friday. Late Friday night Governor Albert C. Ritchie declared a three-day holiday for the state's two hundred banks. The second state had collapsed.

Responsible men were making a painfully self-conscious effort to keep their heads. The Detroit *News* commented, "It is an experience we shall have to look back upon, and no doubt grin over," and the Baltimore *Sun* said cheerily, "Life . . . will be filled with pleasant and unpleasant things as it was before. And it will have the additional advantage that everybody will have something to talk about."

The president of the Baltimore Association of Commerce saw no reason why business should not continue as usual; the Bureau of Internal Revenue issued a stern reminder that income taxes were due in two weeks.

Nothing from Hyde Park dispelled the illusion of unreality. Indeed, the pixie mood of the press seemed superbly matched by President-elect Roosevelt's selection of a man to be Secretary of the Treasury, a puckish little railway-equipment manufacturer who wore a gray toupee, loved puns, collected five-dollar gold pieces, and spent his leisure time composing on a guitar. A week later, when the new administration took office, the country was to know another William H. Woodin—hard-driving, ingenious—but on the eve of office his most striking achievement known to the public was the composition of a song for children:

> *Let us be like bluebirds,*
> *Happy all day long*
> *Forgetting all our troubles in*
> *A sunny song.*

In Indianapolis and Akron that Sunday, February 26, banks announced that withdrawals would be limited to five per cent of balances. During the night institutions in a dozen other Ohio cities fell into line, and on Monday—as flames gutted the Berlin Reichstag and Japanese troops marched into a Manchurian blizzard—the number grew to one hundred. Across the river from Cincinnati, five Covington, Kentucky, banks adopted similar restrictions. Monday evening Governor Gifford Pinchot of Pennsylvania signed a bill permitting individual institutions to close at will, and Thomas W. Lamont informed Hyde Park that in the view of J. P. Morgan, "the emergency could not be greater."

It could be, and soon was. By Wednesday, frantic governors had declared bank holidays in seventeen states. Pinchot acted so hurriedly he had to watch the inauguration five days later with only ninety-five cents in his pocket. Governor Allen of Louisiana, on the other hand, openly withdrew his expense money for Washington and then entrained, leaving behind his dictated proclamation closing all banks.

It was on Wednesday, March 1, that the President-elect—who, Arthur Krock reported, was being asked by responsible men to assume power *now*—drove to his Manhattan home at 49 East Sixty-fifth Street and went into conference with Woodin. They did not emerge until Thursday afternoon, when, preceded by the screaming sirens of twenty motorcycles, they raced down Fifth Avenue and turned west toward the river. During the morning a light snow had sifted over the city. New Yorkers stood silently in it, staring at the cavalcade. Outside Radio City Music Hall, King Kong, enjoying his first Manhattan run, leered toothily. In the Hudson the French Line steamer *Paris* lay quietly at berth, her cargo space reserved—though no one in the party knew it yet—for $9,000,000 in fleeing gold. On the other side of the river a special B. & O. train was waiting, and all that afternoon, talking now with Woodin of banks, now with Farley of religion,

Franklin Roosevelt thundered through a cold fog, toward Washington. It was sleeting when they reached Union Station. In the Presidential Suite of the Mayflower Hotel a sheaf of telegrams awaited Roosevelt: banks were closed, or closing, in twenty-one states and the District of Columbia, and Federal Reserve figures showed the week's gold loss to be $226,000,-000. He was scarcely unpacked when Woodin drew him aside. Secretary of the Treasury Ogden Mills and Eugene Meyer, of the Federal Reserve Board, had telephoned to suggest a proclamation closing all banks. President Hoover felt less drastic action, under the Trading-with-the-Enemy Act of 1917, would do. Roosevelt's approval was solicited, but he, still declining to act until he had the authority, refused to advise anyone. Fair skies had been forecast for Saturday's inauguration, but now the barometer was falling.

The last page of the New York *Times* of Friday, March 3, carried an ad depicting "John Doe" and "Jane Doe" acclaiming the "Good Work" of the Bowery Savings Bank. Presumably its purpose was to hearten depositors. It failed. By noon long lines of New Yorkers had formed opposite Grand Central Station and were filing into the world's largest private savings bank, demanding cash. By 3 P.M. the Bowery closed its doors, with a huge crowd still unpaid. At the same hour Governor Henry Horner of Illinois sat in the Federal Reserve Bank of Chicago, plucking nervously at his mustache, reading figures which showed that Chicago banks had paid out $350,000,000 in two weeks. After seventeen days in the hinterland, the storm was hammering at the nation's two financial strongholds.

That morning Miss Catherine Shea, a messenger for the Treasury Department, had brought Herbert Hoover his last $500 pay check. He had received it with a semblance of cheer; reports reaching him before noon suggested that the panic was lessening. After lunch, however, it became clear that this was only an illusion. Minnesota and Kansas were gone. North Carolina and Virginia were going.

In Washington the National Symphony Orchestra had scheduled as its first number that evening a composition by the incoming Secretary of the Treasury. Woodin had reserved a box, but wasn't in it. He was in the Presidential Suite with Roosevelt, Raymond Moley, Cordell Hull and Jesse Jones, debating the wisdom of a nationwide bank moratorium, while in the White House the same question engaged Hoover, Mills and Meyer. Hoover called Roosevelt twice, to compare notes. Thomas Lamont, who was at the New York Reserve Bank with sixteen other bankers, telephoned the Mayflower. Daniel Ellis Woodhull, president of the American Bank-note Company, was with them and was prepared to print scrip, but the bankers didn't feel this was necessary; they were sure they could stay open.

At 1 A.M. Roosevelt suggested to Hoover that they turn in and get some sleep. They did. And as they slept, their advisers decided everything for them.

Moley, stepping from the elevator into the Mayflower lobby, found Woodin waiting for him. "This thing is very bad," Woodin said wearily. "Will you come over to the Treasury with me? We'll see if we can give those fellows a hand."

At the Treasury were Mills and Meyer, back from the White House, A. A. Ballantine, Mills's Undersecretary, and F. G. Awalt, his Acting Comptroller. Before them lay the latest bleak Federal Reserve figures. During the last two days, $500,000,000 had been drained from the nation's banks. They were convinced that the New York bankers did not understand the immensity of the disaster, and must be protected. Governor Herbert Lehman, who had canceled his trip to the inauguration at 11 P.M., awaited the decision of the Lamont group. Mills and Woodin agreed that regardless of what the bankers decided Lehman must be persuaded to close New York's banks, and that Horner must also declare a moratorium for Illinois.

At 1:45 A.M. Horner's hotel telephone jangled—his groggy bankers were ready to capitulate. He taxied to meet them, and together they held a telephone conference with Lehman and the Treasury. At 2 A.M. he proclaimed his holiday. The sixteen New York bankers, meanwhile, piled into five limousines and drove to Lehman's home, where arguments continued. Moley, spent, fell asleep in Mills's office. Finally, at 4:20 A.M. the Governor of New York had reached his decision.

Woodin shook Moley. "It's all right, Ray. Let's go now. Lehman's agreed."

Hoover was told at 6 A.M. "We are at the end of our rope," he said. "There is nothing more we can do."

On Saturday, March 4—the day Franklin Roosevelt took office and Howard Scott, technocrat, was formally declared bankrupt—inauguration visitors in Washington found this notice posted over hotel counters:

Members find it necessary that, due to unsettled banking conditions throughout the country, checks on out-of-town banks cannot be accepted.

THE WASHINGTON HOTEL ASSOCIATION

The financial heart of the country had ceased to beat. Banking in every state was wholly or partly suspended. Flags flew in Wall Street, honoring the inauguration, but the Stock Exchange was closed, and so, for the first time in eighty-five years, was the Chicago Board of Trade. By 10 A.M. Woodhull's presses were roaring, turning out $250,000,000 in scrip for the New York Clearing House.

In Washington, the sky was the color of slate. Money worries had kept half the anticipated crowd at home; Vice-President Garner wore a borrowed muffler; Woodin, unable to reach his seat, perched on a railing with a cameraman; and during his address Roosevelt, uncovered and coatless, braced himself in the chill wind.

"President Hoover, Mr. Chief Justice, my friends . . ."

He was flaying the money-changers, gone from the temple. Later it occurred to some that his speech had political implications, but actually it was mild abuse. That weekend—Norman Vincent Peale, no revolutionary, demanded from his Fifth Avenue pulpit the following morning that the bankers and corporation heads get down on their knees before God and confess their sins. Yet the fact is that the Treasury, at least, had never been freer of politics. Awalt, the Republican Acting Comptroller, was working on under the Democrats, his uncut hair hanging over his ears. Ballantine, the G.O.P. Undersecretary of the Treasury, was drafting Roosevelt's first fireside chat on the banks. And Mills's invocation of the Trading-with-the-Enemy Act, originally written for Hoover, was issued by Roosevelt Sunday night.

His cigarette holder atilt, the new President declared the next four days a holiday for all banks and empowered Woodin to make exceptions. An embargo was declared on the export of gold—the *Paris* sailed without her precious cargo. Congress was being called into special session on Thursday, when emergency legislation would be ready. Meanwhile the people of the United States would have to manage without money-changers.

How was it done? A great deal depended on who you were—and where you were. As a rule, the farther a man was from home, the greater his plight. If you were in Havana, you found that Cuba had declared its own holiday. In Cairo you were offered seventeen piasters to the dollar—the previous day's rate had been twenty-eight—and in Montreal your dollar dropped thirty-five cents in value overnight. Traveling salesmen had to hitchhike—one, in New York, hawked his shoe samples in a hotel lobby to earn his fare home. Ten New Yorkers stranded in Chicago were sent home in a bus by their hotel.

In Reno that week, fewer than a half-dozen court cases were filed each day; women had court costs and fees, but lacked funds for train tickets. Miami was in an uproar—the American Express Company declared a fifty-dollar limit on the cashing of its checks there Monday as five thousand tanned visitors lined up. Pasadena's exclusive Huntington Hotel printed scrip for stranded millionaires; among these seen in the lobby queue were Edward Bausch, of Bausch and Lomb; Sir Montagu Allan; and Prince Erik of Denmark. In Washington, Cordell Hull's first official chore was to deal with enraged diplomats, who argued that their money was entitled to diplomatic immunity from sequestration. He held them off—their plight was no worse than that of many an American alone in a strange city where his credit meant nothing. In New York a drunken Hawaiian entertainer killed his partner for accepting a check. As Prince Mike Romanoff, the noted impostor, noted piously, "A great many people's checks are now as good as a great many others."

At home Americans struggled along with varying success, depending upon the length of local holidays. Detroit, in its fourth week of moratorium, was suffering. Two thirds of the city's 1,400 laborers had been unable to raise anything on their pay checks, and several fainted on the job from hunger before emergency food cards were issued. Merchants estimated their business at 60 to 70 per cent below normal, restaurant cash registers were crammed with signed lunch checks, and doctors, unable to get gasoline, had to restrict their calls. In Springfield, Massachusetts, on the other hand, a newspaper survey showed that the average citizen had $18.23 cash—in trousers, purses, teapots and baby banks—when the city's banks closed on Inauguration Day.

In such communities the problem was not cash, but change. Many a man was walking the streets with a full wallet, unable to buy cigarettes, ride a bus, or use a pay telephone, because no one would break his bills. As early as Saturday, March 4, New York suburbanites began redeeming their commutation tickets to obtain silver. That night a crowd flourishing $100, $500 and even $1,000 bills formed in Pennsylvania Station—buying tickets to Newark.

Automats were invaded by women in mink who got twenty nickels change for dollar bills and left without eating anything, subways by men in Homburgs who had never ridden a subway and didn't intend to start now. Clerks, watching their stocks of coins shrink, became wary. On Lexington Avenue a man with a fifty-dollar bill tried to buy $3.52 in shaving supplies; he was advised to grow a beard. The Commodore Hotel turned away a changeless man with a $30,000 certified check. Hotel managers sent bellhops to churches to exchange bills for silver. Churches, however, were having their own difficulties; even the devout were close-fisted that March 5. One Methodist minister in New York advised his congregation to keep its silver; another solicited an offering of IOU's.

As the week wore on the shortage of change became crippling. On Monday storekeepers in Elgin, Illinois, learned that a sixteen-year-old boy had saved 11,357 pennies toward his college education, and within an hour they had his home surrounded. There weren't many such caches, however; by Wednesday even the eleemosynary Mr. Rockefeller had run out of dimes and had to give his caddie a whole buck. About the only people with fluid currency were the Alaskans, who were using gold dust, and bootleggers.

Credit indeed, was the only solution to the holiday, as smart retailers had realized at the beginning. "If I try to get all my cash I shall certainly make matters worse," declared Jesse Isidor Straus, president of R. H. Macy & Company, which normally dealt only in hard money. "Use your charge account at Lord & Taylor!" "Use your credit!" cried newspaper ads. "Do not declare a moratorium on your appetite," advertised the Hollywood Cabaret Restaurant. And in Texas, pharmacists accepted IOU's for prescriptions. Gimbel's extended credit to patrons of its restaurant, and taxi dancers in Manhattan's Roseland Dance Hall accepted IOU's—from men who could produce bankbooks.

Harry Staton, manager of the Herald Tribune Syndicate, was in California when the banks closed there. They kept on closing ahead of him, but he returned to New York on ten dollars, signing his name all the way. When he visited a gambling casino, the manager agreed to give him chips on credit, but warned that he would be paid in chips if he won. In Florida, two race tracks folded. More significant to the economy were the steel industry, whose orders hit a new low; the real-estate business, which was paralyzed; and the automotive industry, some of whose plants were forced to close. Barbershops and railroads reported sharp declines. Hollywood was near ruin—box-office receipts dropped 45 per cent, and every studio shut down. King Kong went into his second week at Radio City, but he was snarling at empty houses.

Where credit failed, people fell back on barter or improvised scrip. During the first week of the new administration, stamps, phone slugs, Canadian dollars, Mexican pesos and street-car tickets were used for currency. Mormons in Salt Lake City designed a paper money that could be used locally; the Greenwich Village Mutual Exchange issued $1,000 in tokens to member businesses; in Princeton the *Princetonian* printed twenty-five-cent scrip notes for students, to be redeemed when the banks reopened. A Wisconsin wrestler signed a contract to perform for a can of tomatoes and a peck of potatoes; an Ashtabula newspaper offered free ads in exchange for produce; and a New York state senator arrived in Albany with twelve dozen eggs and a side of pork to see him through the week.

The most spectacular experiment in barter was conducted by the New York *Daily News,* which was sponsoring the semifinals of the Golden Gloves tournament in Madison Square Garden. The price of seats was fifty cents, but any article worth that amount was accepted as admission, provided the five-cent amusement tax was paid. An appraiser was engaged, who inspected, during the evening, frankfurters, mattresses, hats, shoes, overcoats, fish, noodles, nightgowns, steaks, spark plugs, cameras, sweaters, canned goods, sacks of potatoes, golf knickers, mechanics' tools and foot balm. A boy presented his New Testament, a girl her step-ins. The items most frequently offered were jigsaw puzzles.

Nearly everyone assumed the holiday would end with the formal adoption of scrip—local currencies, managed by states, cities and individual firms. Atlanta, Richmond, Mattituck, Long Island, and Knoxville, of all places, were already on the stuff; before the week of March 6 was out Nashville would have $1,000,000 in circulation; Philadelphia, $8,000,000. The Louisville *Courier-Journal* was paying its employees in private scrip. More than a hundred communities were having notes printed, including Chicago, Boston, Providence, New Haven, Detroit and New York. Governor Lehman had appointed Al Smith chairman of an Emergency Certificate Corporation, and tellers' cages were being constructed in the New York Clearing House to distribute rainbow-colored bills ranging in value from one dollar to fifty dollars. In Nutley, New Jersey, a safety-paper company which had been working three days a week for months went on three shifts, turning out six tons of scrip for Wisconsin and Tennessee.

To Secretary of the Treasury Woodin, however, the thought of state and municipal currencies and company certificates floating around the country was appalling and at breakfast on Tuesday, March 7, he told Moley that he had been up half the night, brooding over alternatives. Scrip wasn't needed, he had decided. "We can issue currency against the sound assets of the banks," he said. "It won't frighten people. It won't look like stage money. It'll be money that looks like money." There was nothing to lose. After all, he said publicly, "We're on the bottom. We're not going any lower."

Working endlessly in his Carlton Hotel suite with Carter Glass, Woodin met Thursday's legislative deadline. As congressmen filed into the special session the finished bill was handed to the clerk—"My name's Bill, and I'm finished, too," Woodin muttered—and was read aloud. Few representatives heard it above the hubbub. They had no copies of their own—there had been no time to print them; even the copy given the clerk bore last-minute changes scribbled in pencil. In thirty-eight minutes they whooped it through while Eleanor Roosevelt sat knitting in the gallery like a benign Madame Defarge, counting votes. Then they crowded into the Senate chamber to hear Glass explain just what it was they had done.

The little Virginian backed it, though he acknowledged there were parts which shocked him. It was, in fact, a shocking measure, ratifying all acts "heretofore *or hereinafter* taken" by the President and the Secretary of the Treasury. It provided prison terms for hoarders, "conservators" rather than receivers for weak banks—a euphemistic triumph almost as great as "holiday"—and authorized the issuance of $2,000,000,000 in new currency based on bank assets. At 8:36 P.M. a rumpled Roosevelt signed it in the White House library, surrounded by unpacked books and pictures from Hyde Park. That evening the Bureau of Engraving and Printing recruited 375 new workers. The official printing presses of the United States finally were going into action.

All that night and the next the lights of the Bureau twinkled across the tidal basin. There was no time to engrave new dies—plates bearing the imprint "Series of 1929" were pressed into service. There wasn't even an opportunity to acquire facsimile signatures of two officials from each of the twelve Federal Reserve banks; signatures were taken from files in the district and sent by messenger to the American Type Foundry in Jersey City, where logotypes were cut. Early Saturday morning planes began taking off from Washington bearing bales of cash. The first were delivered to New York's Federal Reserve bank shortly before noon. Transfer to member banks began immediately.

The real trick was prying open the rigid fists of hoarders, who in one week had taken 15 per cent of the nation's currency out of circulation. Even a bewitched Congress couldn't make the penal clauses apply to hoarding that already had taken place, and so the government turned to the spur of publicity. On Wednesday, March 8, the Federal Reserve Board announced that its banks would prepare lists of persons who had withdrawn gold since February 1 and who failed to bring it back by March 13, the following Monday. Newspapers had scarcely appeared with this announcement before bank switchboards were jammed. Anonymous callers wanted to know what would be done with the names, what it was all about. The replies were ominously vague. Callers were told only that if they had gold and wanted to return it, the banks would open for them, and newspapermen would be kept out of lobbies.

In the next few hours thousands of mattresses were torn open, cans dug up, hidden boxes brought forth. Banks everywhere reported long queues, reminiscent of the preceding week's panic but comprised this time of men and women carrying Gladstones and briefcases. In Cleveland $300,000 was deposited that day; in Minneapolis, $182,000. Thursday, the day Woodin's bill was cheered through Congress, Cleveland took in $500,000, Philadelphia $700,000, Richmond $163,000. The real flood of double eagles, however, was in New York, which, despite a fifty-six-mile gale—which tore loose the stitching in a woman's petticoat and sent a sheaf of gold certificates scudding across Sixth Avenue—banked $30,-000,000 that day. One man brought in $700,000; one firm, whose identity remains a secret, delivered $6,000,000 in bullion to the Federal Reserve Bank.

Encouraged, the bank extended its order on Friday, asking for reports covering withdrawals of the past two years. The widened hunt brought bigger game; the nation's gold supply rose dramatically. By 9:30 A.M., when the Federal Reserve Bank of New York opened, there was a line of 1,000 people, their pockets and luggage sagging with gold. An hour later, the crowd had grown to 1,500. Filing through the grilled gates, the depositors filled out deposit slips, presented the same bags and rolled paper stacks they had withdrawn, and waited while the money was counted. When the bank closed at 5 P.M., two hours late, 4,000 people had passed in and out.

The flow continued, uninterrupted, on Saturday, enhanced in Wilmington by a twenty-year collection of gold pieces turned in by Irenée du Pont. By that night, Federal Reserve banks had recovered $300,000,000 in gold and gold certificates—enough to support $750,000,000 additional circulation. Even before the planes took off with new bank notes, Woodin had permitted individual savings banks to dole out ten dollars to each depositor. Business began to stir, and not all the money was spent for necessities. In Boston Saturday afternoon a *Herald* reporter found several hundred women crowded around five counters in a bargain basement buying jigsaw puzzles.

Roosevelt extended the national moratorium while the Treasury separated strong banks from the weak. After the passage of Thursday's bill Woodin invited applications for permission to reopen; actual openings would start Monday. It was the next week that killed Woodin—he was under a doctor's care before it was over, and in his grave the following year. Yet despite his heroic effort, the staggering task of examining 18,000 institutions would have been impossible without the technical knowledge of the Republicans, who stayed at their desks. Awalt, in the first few days, returned home only to shower and change his clothes; James Douglas, who had been assistant secretary under Mills, served as the contact man with the twelve Federal Reserve Banks, forty state banking departments, and clearinghouses everywhere. In the whirlwind tempers were short, but did not follow party lines. "We were," Moley later recalled, "just a bunch of men trying to save the banking system."

In New York on Monday, all but nine national banks were allowed to reopen; in Philadelphia, all but six. At the end of the week 13,500—75 per cent—of the country's banks were back in business, and the sweet notes of gongs again were heard in stock exchanges. Price rises on the Chicago Board of Trade strained at the legal limit, and in New York stocks jumped 15 per cent. We have John T. Flynn's word for it that the New York ticker clicked off the message, "Happy Days Are Here Again."

Of course they weren't really. One dollar in every ten was tied up in frozen deposits on March 14—when the Bureau of Internal Revenue finally agreed to give income-tax payers sixteen days grace—and as late as October the government still was trying to reorganize 376 banks. But the panic had been ended without currency chaos or nationalization of the banks. Undoubtedly the medicine had been strong; the inflationary movement, once started, was irresistible; in April America left the gold standard. The months that followed saw an entirely new concept of the economy developed in the NRA, AAA, CCC, the Federal Securities Act, the Stock Exchange Act, and, in 1935, the Public Utility Holding Company Act. The power of the bankers had been irrevocably broken.

It was in Roanoke, Virginia, that J. P. Morgan was discovered during the holiday on his annual automobile trip south. He was shy as ever, and declined comment on the Depression. He did, however, remark that he was glad the morning's fog was lifting.

"I like to read the signs along the road," he said.

THE HUNDRED DAYS

THE Roosevelt Administration wasted no time in tackling the many problems that lay before the country. Once the bank holiday had been declared by the new President, Congress was convened and a flood of legislation was swiftly enacted. The first bill, the Emergency Banking Act, was whipped through both houses and signed by Roosevelt at the White House in a matter of just eight hours. This bill declared the bank holiday at an end, and set forth regulations for new transactions.

During the Hundred Days, the period of the special Congressional session which terminated on June 15, 1933, the following legislation was enacted:

March 9—the Emergency Banking Act

March 20—the Economy Act

March 31—creation of the Civilian Conservation Corps

April 19—abandonment of the gold standard

May 12—the Federal Emergency Relief Act

May 12—the Agricultural Adjustment Act

May 12—the Emergency Farm Mortgage Act, for the refinancing of farm mortgages

May 18—the Tennessee Valley Authority Act, setting up a system of dams on the Tennessee River to produce electrical power and sell it to consumers

May 27—the Truth-in-Securities Act, necessitating full disclosure of facts in all stock issues

June 5—cancellation of the gold clause in public and private contracts

June 13—the Home Owners' Loan Act, to refinance home mortgages

June 16—the National Industrial Recovery Act, instituting a system of industrial self-government under federal supervision, and $3.3 billion public works program

June 16—the Glass-Steagall Banking Act, separation of commercial and investment banking, and guaranteeing all bank deposits

June 16—the Farm Credit Act, reorganization of agricultural credit

June 16—the Railroad Co-ordination Act*

In addition to helping formulate the new legislation, President Roosevelt delivered speeches, initiated informal press conferences, held his Cabinet meetings, and set up the new machinery for his Administration, which seemed to be galloping off in all directions at once. He was making such an impact upon the country, the press and even the business world, that Secretary Ickes said, "It's more than a New Deal, it's a New World; people feel free again, they can breathe naturally. It's like quitting a morgue for the open woods."

One of the first critical problems to be dealt with by the New Deal was relief of the unemployed.

* As listed in Arthur M. Schlesinger, Jr.'s *The Coming of the New Deal.*

ARTHUR M. SCHLESINGER, JR.

THE RISE OF FEDERAL RELIEF*

THE NEW DEAL thus launched in 1933 a series of experiments in agricultural, industrial, commercial, and monetary policy. These programs were addressed both to the immediate task of recovery and to the larger task of reconstruction. Yet they could not, in the best of circumstances, be expected to take effect overnight. There remained in the meantime the problem of the millions of men and women who had no work and could find none. No one knows how many there were on Inauguration Day— at least 12 to 15 million, over a quarter of the labor force—subsisting wanly and desperately on relief. How to keep these people going until jobs were available again?

Most people close to the subject had long since concluded that the only hope was a federal program. During the short session before Inauguration, a parade of experts—social workers, municipal officials, representatives of charities—came to Washington to testify for Senator Costigan's federal relief bill. None spoke more authoritatively than Harry L. Hopkins, head of Franklin Roosevelt's Temporary Emergency Relief Administration in New York. Hopkins dismissed the idea of loans to penniless states as unrealistic and called for a federal welfare agency—not a banking agency, like RFC—to make direct grants to states for relief purposes.

Hopkins had already made the same points in a letter to the President-elect in December 1932. But in the early weeks of 1933 the banking and agricultural crises shouldered the relief problem out of Roosevelt's attention. Unable to get through to the President, Hopkins turned to his former Albany colleague, Frances Perkins. Accompanied by William Hodson, a veteran social worker and director of the Welfare Council of New York City, he met Miss Perkins at the crowded Women's University Club on a March evening. The only place they could find to talk was a cramped space under the stairs. There Hopkins and Hodson tersely laid out a federal relief program. Miss Perkins, impressed by the precision of their knowledge, got them an appointment with the President.

* From Arthur M. Schlesinger, Jr.'s *The Coming of the New Deal* (Boston, Houghton Mifflin, 1959).

Other members of the Administration were arguing for action. Even John Garner spoke up one day: "When we were campaigning," he said, "we sort of made promises that we would do something for the poorer kind of people, and I think we have to do something for them." Roosevelt agreed, and on March 21, 1933, sent a message to Congress requesting the establishment of the office of Federal Relief Administrator. At the same time, he called in Costigan, La Follette, and Wagner and asked them to draw up a bill.

The bill proposed a Federal Emergency Relief Administration with $500 million for grants-in-aid to states. It produced some violent reactions. "I can hardly find parliamentary language," said Simeon D. Fess of Ohio, "to describe the statement that the States and cities cannot take care of conditions in which they find themselves but must come to the Federal Government for aid." "Is there anything left of our Federal system?" asked John B. Hollister of Ohio. "It is socialism," said Robert Luce of Massachusetts, adding with his scholarly meticulousness, "Whether it is communism or not I do not know." "God save the people of the United States," said C. L. Beedy of Maine. These were minority views. The bill passed the Senate on March 30 by a vote of 55 to 17 and the House three weeks later by 326 to 42.

Roosevelt quickly decided on Hopkins as head of the new agency. He had a little trouble with Governor Lehman of New York, who was disinclined to let Hopkins go. Finally on May 19, Hopkins telegraphed Lehman: PRESIDENT STATES HE WAS WIRING YOU AND WANTS ME TO REPORT TO HIM MONDAY MORNING. Lehman wired Roosevelt in anguish: YOU HAVE THE ENTIRE COUNTRY FROM WHICH TO MAKE CHOICE. But Roosevelt knew what he wanted. On May 22, 1933, Harry Hopkins went to Washington.

Hopkins was a lean, loose-limbed, disheveled man, with sharp features and dark, sardonic eyes. He talked quickly and cockily, out of the side of his mouth; his manner was brusque and almost studiously irreverent; his language, concise, pungent, and often profane. "He gives off," noted one observer, "a suggestion of quick cigarettes, thinning hair, dandruff, brief sarcasm, fraying suits of clothes, and a wholly understandable preoccupation." He was at his best under pressure. Wearing what friends described as his hell's-bells or you-can't-put-that-over-on-me expression, he would screw up his face and fire a volley of short, sharp questions until he had slashed through to the heart of a problem. Understanding what had to be done, he wasted no time in formalities, but assumed responsibility, gave orders, and acted. He expended nervous energy carelessly and restored it by chain-smoking and by drinking cup after cup of black coffee. Beneath his air of insouciance and cynicism, he had a buoyant—almost gay—conviction that all walls would fall before the man of resource and decision. And underneath the hard-boiled pose, there lay a surprising quick sensitivity to human moods and relationships.

Action was instantaneous. Before evening on the second day, Hopkins had thrown together a staff, begun the collection of information, alerted forty-eight state governors to set up state organizations, and sent emergency aid to seven states. He warned his staff that he would soon be the most unpopular man in America: he planned to keep reminding the nation of unemployment and poverty, "and they won't want to hear it." Still, for all his forebodings, he set to work with aplomb.

The Federal Emergency Relief Administration did not deal directly with relief applicants. It made grants to local public agencies. Half of its $500 million was to be assigned on a matching basis—one dollar of federal funds for every three dollars of state money spent for relief during the three months preceding. The other half was to go where need was urgent and the matching requirement could not be met. Exhorting, cajoling, scolding, threatening, Hopkins and a small field staff used their power to pump new life into the faltering state agencies. Where a local organization seemed hopelessly incompetent, Hopkins asked the governor to make the necessary changes. Most of the time, his evident disinterestedness won co-operation. In a few cases, FERA had to go into the state and appoint its own administration. Hopkins remained profoundly convinced of the values of decentralization. He kept his Washington staff small and gave great responsibility to state administrators, while at the same time holding them as well as he could to the national mark.

The critical problem of relief, as he saw it, was preserving the morale of people forced to live by government handouts. Men and women who lacked jobs for reasons far beyond their own control should not, Hopkins believed, be made to feel like paupers; it was necessary not just to feed them but to maintain their self-respect. "I don't think anybody can go year after year, month after month, accepting relief without affecting his character in some way unfavorably," he wrote in June 1933. "It is probably going to undermine the independence of hundreds of thousands of families. . . . I look upon this as a great disaster and wish to handle it as such."

A measure of degradation in relief seemed inescapable. Since limited funds had to go as far as possible, it was essential that no one obtain relief who could get along without it. Thus FERA could not escape the means test. Investigation was left to local case workers, who could presumably conduct it with least humiliation to the applicant. Once need was established, the problem became the form in which relief was to be granted. Some states had set up special commissaries where reliefers could go for food. This was a cheap enough form of relief; but Hopkins, feeling that it portended a ghetto for the unemployed, liquidated the commissary system as fast as he could. The grocery order removed those on relief less from normal society. Still, it placed the family under a paternalism, compelling them to buy what the nutritionists decided they needed. Hopkins much preferred giving straight cash, even if the reliefer used it for tobacco or liquor; on the whole, he felt, more damage was done to the human spirit by loss of choice than by loss of vitamins.

Basically, however, Hopkins objected to direct relief in any form. Keeping able-bodied men in idleness, he believed, could not help but corrode morale. In 1932 the mayor of Toledo, Ohio, said: "I have seen thousands of these defeated, discouraged, hopeless men and women, cringing and fawning as they come to ask for public aid. It is a spectacle of national degeneration." It was this which Hopkins wanted to avoid in demanding a more creative response to the catastrophe. Instead of putting the unemployed on the dole, why not offer the weekly government check in exchange for labor performed for the public welfare? Work relief, Hopkins said, "preserves a man's morale. It saves his skill. It gives him a chance to do something socially useful." Of course, it would cost more than the dole. But the advocates of economy in relief, Hopkins said, never counted in the cost of depriving citizens of "their sense of independence and strength and their sense of individual destiny."

Although FERA, thrown so suddenly into the breach, could not escape direct relief as its main instrument, a wide variety of work relief projects were devised under Hopkins' relentless prodding. Thus teachers on relief rolls were assigned to country schools which would otherwise have had to close their doors; by December 1933, about 13,000 teachers, paid from relief funds, were holding classes in rural areas. FERA too had a special program to take care of transients—the thousands of jobless men roaming the country in search of work and hope. There were provisions for drought relief, and for grants to local self-help and barter associations. Hopkins invited experiment, calling on state administrators to show "imagination." Some local organizations remained resistant. This was partly because of the added expense of work relief, partly because of the added administrative difficulties. And often, when they tried it, the projects were ill-conceived and unconvincing.

As the fourth winter of the depression approached, new unrest stirred among the jobless. According to a *Fortune* report, men and women on relief "do not like the dole. They are almost unanimous in demanding *work*." Radicals and Communists were tireless in exploiting disappointments and grievances. In August 1933 several thousand members of the Ohio Unemployed League marched on the State House at Columbus. "We must take control of the government," shouted Louis Budenz, one of the agitators, "and establish a workers and farmers republic." Was it safe to try and negotiate the winter of 1933–34 on the direct relief basis? It seemed more and more evident that a new and better federal effort would be necessary to meet the winter's challenge.

Hopkins, in Chicago on a field trip late in October, pondered the next step. His staff wanted him to make an all-out fight for a federal works program. Hopkins agreed in principle. But he was not sure he could sell the idea at the White House, and he was disturbed by the threat of labor opposition. In his Pullman drawing room between Chicago and Kansas City (where he was to confer with the Federal Re-employment Director of Missouri, Judge Harry S. Truman), Hopkins brooded over the problem. In Kansas City he received word from Aubrey Williams, a top FERA aide, that Samuel Gompers himself had once favored a works program, a fact which might turn aside labor objections. Encouraged, Hopkins called Washington and asked for a White House appointment.

Hopkins outlined his scheme at lunch with the President on the day of his return. Roosevelt asked how many jobs he thought he could provide. Hopkins answered four million, if he could get enough money. Roosevelt, thinking aloud, remarked that Ickes' Public Works Administration was slow in getting under way; perhaps Hopkins could get funds out of the PWA appropriations. Indeed, the whole effort might be conceived as a means of tiding the unemployed over one more winter, by which time PWA could begin to take up the slack.

This was the beginning of the Civil Works Administration. By November 15, Hopkins announced his objective: "the employment of four million by December 15, 1933." He set himself a prodigious job. Though CWA, unlike FERA, was empowered to operate works projects directly, Hopkins had no planning staff, no shelf of light public works, no formulated program. CWA jobs, moreover, had to be easy to learn and short in duration; winter weather limited the type of project available; necessary tools were in short supply. Yet Hopkins, always at his best when confronted by impossibilities, allowed nothing to get in the way of rapid expansion. He immediately converted much of his FERA staff to CWA and adopted the existing state relief organizations as CWA's local arms. Project ideas, generated in the atmosphere of pressure, came both down from Washington and up from the field. Hopkins missed his first target date—by December 14, there were only 2,610,451 on CWA rolls—but by the middle of January he was well over the 4,000,000 mark.

CWA tackled a tremendous variety of jobs. At its peak, it had about 400,000 projects in operation. About a third of CWA personnel worked on roads and highways. In the three and a half months of CWA's existence, they built or improved about 500,000 miles of secondary roads. Next in importance came schools—40,000 built or improved, with 50,000 teachers employed in country schools or in city adult education, and large numbers of playgrounds developed. CWA gave the nation nearly 500 airports and improved 500 more. It developed parks, cleared waterways, fought insect pests, dug swimming pools and sewers. Three thousand writers and artists found CWA employment utilizing their own skills. ("Hell!" said Hopkins. "They've got to eat just like other people.") Above all, it supplied work to four million Americans who would otherwise have festered in humiliation and idleness.

Of course, Hopkins paid a price for speed. In money, the cost was considerable—in the end, nearly a billion dollars. And there were administrative lapses too which Hopkins characteristically exposed before his critics could discover them. In January 1934, he lashed out at evidence of political interference and graft in CWA operations. "I never anticipated anything of the kind," he told newspapermen. "I suppose I'm naïve and unsophisticated, but that's the truth. I didn't, and I feel very badly about it." He ordered investigations, shook up incompetent or tainted state organizations and began to bring in Army officers to strengthen the program against corruption.

Lieutenant Colonel John C. H. Lee, a stern West Point engineer assigned to study CWA for the War Department, watched Hopkins' unorthodox methods with astonished admiration. "Mr. Hopkins' loose fluidity of organization," he concluded, "was justified by the results achieved. It enabled him to engage for employment in two months nearly as many persons as were enlisted and called to the colors during our year and a half of World War mobilization, and to disburse to them, weekly, a higher average rate of wage than Army or Navy pay." CWA, Lee said, reached every county and town in the United States in a period of two months during one of the most severe winters on record.

The accomplishments of the CWA were possible through the arduous efforts of the young Administrator and the group of able young assistants which he has assembled and inspired. They have worked daily long into the night with a morale easily comparable to that of a war emergency. These assistants address Mr. Hopkins fondly as "Harry." There is no rigidity or formality in their staff conferences with him, yet he holds their respect, confidence and seemingly whole-souled co-operation.

As for the reliefers themselves, FERA field investigators like Lorena Hickok and Martha Gellhorn provided graphic reports of their condition. Poignant images spilled out of these documents—the cry in September 1933 in Pennsylvania, "Our children must have shoes, or they can't go to school"; the Catholic priest in Scottville, Pennsylvania, begging for medical supplies to keep his people alive; the little boy in Houston, Texas, who refused to go to school wearing trousers of black-and-white-striped ticking because everyone would know his family was on relief; the man in Camden, New Jersey, explaining that he went to bed around seven at night "because that way you get the day over with quicker"; the South Dakota farm wife who had a recipe for soup made from Russian thistles—"It don't taste so bad, only it ain't very filling"; the sixteen-year-old girl keeping house for her family in a dark tobacco barn in Wilson County, North Carolina, the place scrubbed spotlessly clean, the girl saying sadly, "Seems like we just keep goin' lower and lower"; pinned on her bosom, as one wears a brooch, was a 1932 campaign button, a profile of Franklin Roosevelt.

In 1933 Lorena Hickok noticed evidences of Communist activity. "They are very, very busy," she wrote from Aberdeen, South Dakota, in November, "getting right down among the farmers and working like beavers." In Pennsylvania the unemployed, she felt, were "right on the edge"; "it wouldn't take much to make Communists out of them." Martha Gellhorn, moving around the country a year later, found less organized protest. The idolatry of Roosevelt, she thought, was taking the spirit out of opposition. "The problem," she wrote Hopkins, "is not one of fighting off a 'red menace' . . . but of fighting off hopelessness; despair; a dangerous feeling of helplessness and dependence." Everywhere there seemed a spreading listlessness, a whipped feeling like the hitchhiker who said to Theodore Dreiser, "I'm going downhill. I'm going to hell, really. I don't care as much as I used to." Miss Gellhorn was disturbed most of all by this smell of defeat: "I find them all in the same shape—fear, fear driving them into a state of semicollapse; cracking nerves; and an overpowering terror of the future . . . each family in its own miserable home going to pieces."

The relief rolls were changing in character. First, there had been the unemployables; then had come the working-class unemployed; but now, increasingly, white-collar workers, their savings exhausted by four years of depression, their scruples conquered by want, their self-respect eroded by fear, were going on relief. They hated it, but in the end they saw no alternative. "I simply had to murder my pride," an engineer told Lorena Hickok. "We'd lived on bread and water three weeks before I could make myself do it." "It took me a month," said a lumberman. "I used to go down there every day or so and walk past the place again and again. I just couldn't make myself go in." And with white-collar relief there came new tensions. Above all, the compulsion to cling to some semblance at least of past ways of life complicated relationships with the relief administration. "We can provide overalls, but not tailored business suits," said Miss Hickok. "We can't keep those white collars laundered."

FERA and CWA had at least kept conditions from becoming worse. On the whole, there was less revolt, less starvation, and less Communism than might have been expected. As Hugh Charles Boyle, the Roman Catholic Bishop of Pittsburgh, told Lorena Hickok, "Inadequate though it may be, the emergency unemployment relief has been and is the most stabilizing force we have. . . . The Federal Government will have to put up the money, or—well, God help us all!" And CWA, because it provided work, was received by the unemployed—or at least by those who could get on its rolls—with special gratitude. Miss Hickok was in Iowa on the first CWA pay day. "And did they want to work?" she wrote Hopkins. "In Sioux City they actually had fist fights over shovels!" "It was pathetic to watch some of the reactions," reported a CWA administrator. "I saw a few cases leave the office actually weeping for sheer happiness."

Still, Hopkins's view was that federal relief was doing only a minimal job. "We have never given adequate relief," he said in 1936. Many social workers and public officials agreed. Thus Lawrence F. Quigley, mayor of Chelsea, Massachusetts, wrote Hopkins in January 1934 that only 155 people in his town could get CWA jobs; another 2000 were congregating sullenly in City Hall; "a spark might change them into a mob." "I believe," said Mayor Quigley, "that the Federal Government, once having acknowledged its responsibility by giving jobs merely for the sake of a job, must now put every unemployed man to work doing the most useful task that can be found for him. . . . If some such remedial measure is not immediately adopted I make bold to predict fundamental and sweeping changes in the structure of our government before the end of the present year."

This was one view. Other Americans believed that any national relief program at all was too much. As the economic situation began to improve in 1934, some of this opinion began to be vocal. When someone asked him about the homeless boys riding the rails in search of employment, Henry Ford said equably, "Why, it's the best education in the world for those boys, that traveling around. They get more experience in a few months than they would in years at school." Even a liberal businessman like Robert E. Wood of Sears, Roebuck could identify relief as the New Deal's "one serious mistake." "While it is probably true that we cannot allow everyone to starve (although I personally disagree with this philosophy and the philosophy of the city social worker)," Wood wrote, "we should tighten up relief all along the line, and if relief is to be given it must be on a bare subsistence allowance." Winthrop Aldrich of the Chase National Bank called for the elimination of work relief. Lincoln Colcord, reporting to Hopkins in 1934 on talks with businessmen, summed up business opinion as one of opposition to work relief, not only because of its cost but because all work projects—even ditch digging—were deemed competitive with private industry.

There was considerable resentment too in farm areas, especially in the South. Planters complained that relief made it impossible to get cheap Negro farm labor. "I wouldn't plow nobody's mule from sunrise to sunset for 50 cents per day," as one aggrieved farmer wrote to Governor Eugene Talmadge of Georgia, "when I could get $1.30 for pretending to work on a DITCH." (Talmadge forwarded this letter to Roosevelt, who dictated a biting reply. "I take it, from your sending the letter of the gentleman from Smithville to me," the President said, "that you approve of paying farm labor 40 to 50 cents per day." Figuring in the seasonal character of the employment, Roosevelt reckoned this to be $60 to $75 a year. "Somehow I cannot get it into my head that wages on such a scale make possible a reasonable American standard of living." On reflection, Roosevelt decided to send the letter under Hopkins's signature.)

Most pervasive of all was the feeling that the whole theory of federal relief was incompatible with American individualism. Much of this concern was doubtless the rationalization of objections to high taxes, to high wages, and to any increase in federal power; but much too reflected authentic anxieties over what dependence on government handouts might do to the American people. "Our present efforts in the direction of relief," wrote the banker Frank A. Vanderlip in a statement repeated ten thousand times by business leaders in these years, "have broken down self-reliance and industry. I profoundly believe that society does not owe every man a living."

It was easy to ridicule such arguments. When Hoover attacked federal aid to the unemployed for weakening the "moral fiber" of the people, Harold Ickes retorted that Hoover as President had not hesitated "to weaken the moral fiber of banks and insurance companies and manufacturing and industrial enterprises" by handing them millions of dollars. Hoover's policies no doubt justified Ickes's retort. Yet the issue raised by conservatives was a real one. Hopkins himself worried about moral effects: that, of course, was why he preferred to offer the unemployed jobs rather than the dole. Lorena Hickok was alarmed when she heard little boys in Salt Lake City boasting about whose father had been on relief longer. Some people on relief, she commented sorrowfully, became "gimmies"; "the more you do for people, the more they demand." Social workers said, "They are beginning to regard CWA as their due—[they feel] that the Government actually owes it to them. And they want more." Some projects were themselves too obviously sham to help the morale of either the workers or the public. The term "boondoggling" arose to describe the most futile of the leaf-raking or ditch-digging efforts.

TOO MUCH, TOO SOON

THE opponents of the New Deal didn't waste any time; relief measures had been barely started when newspaper editorial writers, political cartoonists and satirists swung into action, writing off the whole idea as a "sinful" waste of the taxpayer's dollar. Frank Sullivan's "cliché expert," Mr. Arbuthnot, exemplifies the old-line conservative's reaction to relief, and the whole New Deal, in the following excerpt from a fictional dialogue.

Q: Do you mean "orgy of spending?"

A: That's just the phrase I was searching for. You know how it's all going to end up?

Q: How?

A: Inflation. We're going to have the worst inflation in this country you ever saw. These taxes. Twenty-five cents out of every dollar goes for taxes. . . . Now, you take relief. I certainly think it's all right to help people who deserve help, but I don't believe in all this coddling. . . . The trouble with half the people on relief is they don't *want* to work. You can't tell me that most of these people can't find work. If a man wants a job bad enough he'll find one all right. . . .

Q: What about the WPA, Mr. Arbuthnot?

A: Oh, the shovel brigade. I'm against the WPA and the PWA and all this alphabet-soup stuff. Say, speaking of the WPA, did you hear the one about the WPA worker and King Solomon? Why is a WPA worker like King Solomon?

Q: I heard it. Now then—

A: Because he takes his pick and goes to bed.*

The Hundred Days legislation had hardly got on the books when *Vanity Fair* published the following spoof of relief measures.

JOHN RIDDELL

HOW TO RELIEVE EVERYBODY†

EVER since I can remember (which is about the day before yesterday), the newspapers have been filled with columns and columns of figures, statements and statistics explaining the latest Government plans for Farm

* Frank Sullivan, *A Pearl in Every Oyster* (Boston, Little, Brown, 1938).
† Condensed from *Vanity Fair*, August 1933.

Relief. We have read about the Debenture Plan, the Equalization Fee Plan, the Voluntary Allotment Plan, and the Plan Against Surplus Production. After studying all these Plans to relieve the Farmer, therefore, I have finally put forth my own Plan, whish is known as the Plan to Relieve People Who Have to Read All These Plans. Personally, I feel a little relieved already.

Before I go into this particular Plan of mine and explore its possibilities, armed only with a flashlight and a ball of twine, I think I should attempt first to explain the whole Farm Problem in such a way as to confuse everybody even further about it, if possible; and in order to mix up the reader completely I should like to offer the following simple illustration of just what is meant by Farm Relief.

For example, let us say that Mr. A., a farmer, has just raised a parsnip. Nobody wants a parsnip, least of all Mr. A.; and so the Government steps in and offers Mr. A. five dollars if he will take his parsnip somewhere and get rid of it. Mr. A. gets rid of the parsnip and spends the five dollars for parsnip seeds, with which he raises one hundred more parsnips. He gets rid of these parsnips to the Government for five hundred dollars; and with this five hundred dollars he goes into the parsnip business on a large scale, raising millions of parsnips and getting rid of them to the Government at five dollars a parsnip. Thus Mr. A. is relieved because he raises parsnips, everybody else is relieved because he gets rid of them again, and the Government is relieved in time of all the money in the Treasury. This is known, roughly, as Farm Relief.

I have devised my own Farm Relief Plan, which contains several handy methods designed especially to cut down this surplus production as far as possible. For example:

CUTWORMS

One suggestion for limiting production would be to include a few high-grade cutworms henceforth in every package of seed sent out by Our Congressmen in Washington. (In certain sections of the country, boll weevils, corn-borers or Japanese beetles could be substituted.) By sowing these busy little worms in his garden, the Farmer would soon find his entire production was being cut in half, usually right at the roots.

SUBSTITUTING SOMETHING ELSE FOR "SEED"

One reason the Farmer produces too much wheat or cotton is because he sows wheat-seeds and cotton-seeds, which grow up to be wheat or cotton. A second suggestion for limiting production, therefore, would be to sow things in the garden which would *not* grow up to be wheat or cotton, such as china cup-handles, rusty nails, suspender buttons, or old galoshes.

SUBSTITUTING SOMETHING ELSE FOR "SOIL"

For that matter, production may also be curtailed considerably by removing the "soil" or "dirt" in which these seeds flourish, and substituting something else in which they will *not* grow, such as a solid cement walk or an old mattress. A good substitute for soil consists of two parts gravel, equal parts of crushed brick, large pebbles and sand, one part ground glass, and just a dash of soapy water from the kitchen window.

WEEDS

In weeding the Farmer could cut down his surplus production considerably if he would pull up the plants, and leave the weeds.

FORECLOSURES

If all these other methods of limiting production fail to work, however, we can always fall back on the sure plan of having the banks foreclose all the farm-mortgages which they hold. Once we get the bankers to take over the farms in this country and run them the way they ran their banks, we won't need to worry about surplus production. They'll have every farm closed in a week.

In the meantime, besides cutting down surplus production, my Farm Bill goes ahead at the same time and increases public demand for what the Farmer *does* produce. In other words, according to my plan, the Farmer not only produces nothing at all, but in addition he gets a much better price for it. This is accomplished by the simple principle known as Rotation of Crops.

Rotation of Crops consists of planting all the different crops which a Farmer might raise—i.e., oats, peas, lima beans and corn (succotash), squash, pumpkins, apples, cider, or hooked rugs—on the different levels of a large machine built like a Ferris Wheel, and then rotating the crops slowly in front of the consumer. The moment the consumer shows the least bit of interest in one of the crops, such as radishes, the Farmer presses a button and the wheel turns, elevating the level with the radishes up into the air, just out of the consumer's reach. This teases the consumer, and he wants the radishes more than ever. By rotating his radish crop two or three times before the consumer's nose, the Farmer will soon have the harassed radish-lover completely in his power, and not only can he get any price he wants for his radishes, but in addition can probably palm off a few old beets or turnips as well.

Unfortunately, there is one angle of the Farm Adjustment Act which has never been made very clear, and that is the leasing proposal. According to this suggestion, the Government will go out with a lot of money (all those billions and billions of dollars which have been lying around for years just gathering dust) and rent out of bearing all the poor lands and surplus farms. These leased farms would then be posted by the Government as officially "out of production," and thereafter any ear of corn or spear of wheat poking above the surface in the spring would be arrested on sight.

One method of putting this land to use would be to cut it up into small portable sections, and ship it to the larger cities to use for parking spaces.

Another use for this surplus land would be to turn it over to the public for peasant-dancing. There is almost no peasant-dancing going on in this country today, and this would be a very good chance to get it started. In every news-reel that I have seen for the last year, there has always been a scene showing Bavarian peasants or Tyrolean peasants wearing short pants and little hats with feathers in them, stamping up and down and snapping their fingers and occasionally shouting "Hey!"

Last but not least, our Farm Bill must solve the problem of how to persuade the farmers to *accept* all this money which the Government wants to pay them. Judging from the attitude of our agricultural experts, the American farmer is a highly sensitive creature, whose pride would be cut to the quick if the Government simply went out and handed him this money as a gift. In fact, the whole purpose of the Farm Bill seems to be to attempt to disguise this gift to the farmer under vague and elaborate terms such as the Debenture Plan or the Voluntary Allotment Plan or the Equalization Fee Plan. Working on this theory, therefore, my own Farm Bill has devised several further methods of tricking the Farmer into accepting money from the Government without embarrassing him, let alone the Government:

1. Put the money in a colored Easter Egg and leave it on his doorstep some night.

2. Bury the money at various points about his farm—under the gatepost, behind the barn, or in his mattress—and then write the Farmer an anonymous letter telling him where it is hidden. The Farmer will enter into the spirit of the treasure-hunt, and he will not know where the money is coming from. (Inasmuch as the Government won't know either, this will make it unanimous.)

3. If these methods fail, the agricultural expert can put on a false

mustache and tell the Farmer that he is a long-lost uncle named Abner and that he has just decided to leave the Farmer his entire fortune in his will.

4. Give the money to the Farmer as a prize for making the largest number of words out of the sentence: "Everybody loves the Farmer."

5. Put the money in a bank, and then make the Farmer president of the bank. In this way, the Farmer will find himself taking the money out of force of habit.

In this way the Farmer will be persuaded sooner or later to accept this money which we are all trying so hard to give him. In the course of time the Government doubtless will manage to turn over all the money in the Treasury to the Farmer. Thus the Farmer will have all the money in the country. Then it will be up to him to pass a *Non*-Farm Relief Bill, to relieve everybody else.

ARTHUR M. SCHLESINGER, JR.

MORE ON THE RISE
OF FEDERAL RELIEF*

YET WHAT was the answer? Hopkins and the Administration considered
relief of some sort inevitable; the alternative was revolution. If this were
the case, work relief seemed the form most compatible with self-respect and
individualism. And the argument for work relief was more compelling in
1933–34 than it might be later. At a time when morale was low and before
other spending programs were showing results, an emergency works program could have marked stimulative effect, both economically and psycho-
logically.

For their part, the businessmen had no clear alternative to present.
Some doubtless wished to abolish relief altogether. But few were prepared
to avow this as their objective. This left most in the unsatisfying position
of deploring the moral consequences of relief while advocating the form
of relief which by their own theory was morally most deleterious—the
cash handout, the detested dole. This contradiction did not, however,
notably restrain many from doing all they could to forestall a works
program.

Work relief really presupposed a national effort, since forty-eight separate works programs were inconceivable. Consequently returning relief to
the states would effectively doom the works idea. And it would save money
over-all; since state governments could not create the market for their own
securities, the resources available to them for relief were limited. Best of
all, such a policy would diminish the power of the national government.
So the restoration of relief to the local communities became the key conservative issue. In December 1934, for example, a group of business leaders
meeting at White Sulphur Springs under Chamber of Commerce and
N.A.M. auspices, demanded that the states take over relief. But when
Today Magazine wired state governors asking them what they thought
about this proposal, only one of the thirty-seven replying—Gene Talmadge
—agreed. Thirty-three said that their states had already reached the limit
of their contributions.

* From Arthur M. Schlesinger, Jr.'s *The Coming of the New Deal* (Boston, Houghton
Mifflin, 1959).

The fiscal point was only one of the arguments for federal relief. Many observers in addition considered a national program better proof against waste and graft. "Turning federal funds over to the states for administration," as Senator James F. Byrnes of South Carolina put it, "would mean more politics instead of less politics in administration." "If the relief system were not centralized where centralization is necessary," said the political writers Joseph Alsop and Turner Catledge in *The Saturday Evening Post,* "the inevitable result would be the greatest pork-barrel riot Congress has ever seen."

Still, some wanted a pork-barrel riot. Others wanted to kill work relief. Others wistfully hoped that defederalization might bring on a new access of local responsibility. And so a debate began which continued through the rest of the decade.

The first phase of the debate boiled up over the extension of CWA in January and February 1934. Criticism of CWA had been muted at first—a fact plausibly explained by Al Smith in December 1933 on the ground that "no sane local official who has hung up an empty stocking over the municipal fireplace is going to shoot Santa Claus just before a hard Christmas." (The embattled Hopkins replied with feeling, "The hell they won't. Santa Claus really needs a bullet-proof vest.") But the charges of waste and corruption—despite the fact that Hopkins was the first to reveal them—strengthened the hands of those who had disliked the works program all along. More important, Roosevelt, under pressure from southern Democrats and from his Director of the Budget, Lewis Douglas, was beginning to feel that the expensive CWA operation must end for the sake of the budget.

Hopkins, and most social workers and liberal Democrats, disagreed with this decision. So too did many Republicans; Governor Alfred M. Landon of Kansas, for example, wrote Roosevelt, "This civil-works program is one of the soundest, most constructive policies of your administration, and I cannot urge too strongly its continuance." To the left of the New Deal, Norman Thomas organized a march on Washington to protest against termination. In a single week nearly 60,000 letters and wires deluged the CWA office and the White House. CWA workers engaged in strikes and demonstrations. Yet, once the President had made his decision, Hopkins accepted it and, with his usual brusque efficiency, destroyed the organization he had so brilliantly built up. Roosevelt, in the atmosphere of neurotic administrators weeping on all available shoulders—the Johnsons, Richbergs, Peeks, Hulls—was grateful for Hopkins's uncomplaining loyalty.

What remained of CWA was transferred to the Emergency Work Relief Program of FERA, though work relief continued here only in diminished form. Where CWA had offered jobs at regular wages both to reliefers and to jobless persons who, for whatever reason—probably pride—had refused to go on relief rolls, FERA had to confine itself to those on relief and pay them only substandard wages; and, where CWA had planned and operated its own projects, FERA could finance only state activities. FERA nonetheless carried on substantial parts of the CWA program, including the white-collar projects.

In addition, FERA developed new programs of its own during 1934. An experiment of special interest was the Federal Surplus Relief Corporation, first conceived in the fall of 1933 as a means of circumventing the irony whereby crops piled up in the countryside while the cities went hungry. "Will you and Peek and Harry Hopkins," Roosevelt wrote Henry Wallace in September, "have a talk and possibly prepare a plan for purchase of surplus commodities such as butter, cheese, condensed milk, hog products and flour, to meet relief needs during the course of the winter?" Jerome Frank proposed doing it through an independent corporation; and, starting in December, the Federal Surplus Relief Corporation began to acquire surplus commodities with the double purpose of helping the farmer by removing price-depressing stocks from the market and of helping the unemployed by giving him food. The Corporation began with pork from the martyred pigs and soon moved from food to surplus cotton, blankets, and even coal.

As FSRC operations expanded in 1934, some businessmen began to charge it with the sin of competing with private enterprise. When FSRC purchased cotton and sent it to FERA workrooms to be made into mattresses for the unemployed, the mattress manufacturers erupted in indignation; nor were they satisfied by FERA's demonstration that the mattresses went only to people who, because they had no money, could not possibly subtract from the mattress market. The drought of 1934 intensified both FSRC activities and business criticism. Taking over cattle which otherwise would have perished uselessly in the drought areas, FSRC proposed that they be converted into canned beef and shoes for men and women on relief. These plans provoked a storm of denunciation. Shoe manufacturers virtuously refused to rent the government the necessary machinery. Such adverse reaction restricted the scope of FSRC activities. In the two years before it was transferred to AAA in 1935, the total value of surplus commodities which FSRC was permitted to distribute amounted to only about 265 million dollars.

FERA's support of self-help production roused equally strong business resentment. The self-help movement had sprung up spontaneously in the early Depression. People who had no money could still work, and it seemed logical to some to try to trade what they could make for what they needed. In time, it began to seem similarly logical for state governments to provide facilities to enable the unemployed to manufacture things necessary for their own subsistence. FERA was consequently authorized by Congress to make capital grants to states to promote the "barter of goods and services."

In June 1934 the State Relief Commission of Ohio set up the Ohio Relief Production Units, Incorporated; and in a few months the state leased a dozen factories, in which unemployed men and women made dresses, overalls, furniture, and stoves for their own use or for exchange with relief agencies in other states. Half a dozen more states were similarly preparing to bring together idle labor and idle factories (often mattress factories or canning plants) to produce for the unemployed. It was estimated in the summer of 1934 that probably 50,000 families through the nation were members of self-help groups, some organized privately, some under state sponsorship. In the fall, these production projects accounted for 15 per cent of the employment under the Emergency Work Relief Program.

As these programs developed, however, the phrase "production-for-use" began to acquire sinister connotations. The impression grew in business circles that the self-help program was the entering wedge of socialism. The "Ohio Plan" was suspicious enough; and when Upton Sinclair, running for governor in California, envisaged production-for-use by the unemployed as the nucleus for a radical reconstruction of the economy, reaction was vigorous and unequivocal. FERA, because of business hostility, could grant in two years only a little more than three million dollars to self-help co-operatives (this figure does not, however, include the rather more significant support production-for-use received in the works programs). By 1935 the production-for-use and the self-help programs were both on their way out. (Only the President himself remained interested as when, confronted with new supplies of electric power from the new federal dams, he asked Ickes and Hopkins in the spring of 1935 to consider the government's going into the business of producing aluminum, nickel, or magnesium with unemployed labor.)

FERA's Rural Rehabilitation Division was charged with the responsibility of relief on the countryside. Its most useful efforts went to what was known as "rehabilitation in place"—that is, loans to farm families for seed, fertilizer, livestock, or farm tools. It also engaged less profitably in attempts to set up rural communities, based on Roosevelt's old dream of decentralized industry and subsistence homesteads. Eventually these activities were absorbed by the Resettlement Administration in 1935. The Transient Division of FERA continued through 1934 to deal with the still large numbers of men on the road; this program disappeared in 1935.

Some of FERA's most striking successes were in particular localities. Thus imaginative FERA leadership saved Key West, Florida, from decay and probable extinction. In 1934 two-thirds of the inhabitants of Key West were on relief. The town government was bankrupt, and local services had wholly broken down, leaving the streets cluttered with garbage and rubbish. J. F. Stone, Jr., the regional FERA administrator, persuaded the governor of Florida to declare a state of "civil emergency," under which municipal powers in Key West were to be delegated to the Florida Emergency Relief Administration. It was an act of dubious legality, but it was enough. The Key West Volunteer Work Corps was then organized to clean up the streets and beaches; houses were painted and renovated, hotels reopened, an air service subsidized (by FERA funds), a federal art project set up, the FERA Marimba Band formed—and Key West entered a new, profitable and perhaps ultimately even more ruinous phase as a resort town.

Following the demobilization of CWA, FERA in 1934 resumed its efforts to hold the relief line, at the same time continuing under Hopkins's driving leadership to diversify and improve the quality of its projects. If much of FERA activity at this point had the air of marking time, it was because the relief picture could not be clear until the Public Works Administration swung into full operation.

THE NEW DEAL—JUNIOR DIVISION

OF ALL the legislation of the early days of the New Deal, the law which created the Civilian Conservation Corps probably was most directly and completely the brain child of President Roosevelt. For more than twenty years the conservation of natural resources had been for him a subject of special interest; and in the particular problem of reforestation as a method of land conservation he was an expert, with a background of personal experience as well as governmental program. In 1932, as Governor of New York State, he had put 10,000 unemployed to work on reforestation projects. Years before that, he had given over many acres on his Hyde Park estate to trees in order to renew the land, so that, as he once explained it, his great-grandchildren would be able to farm the land as productively as it had been farmed in the nineteenth century.

In his acceptance speech at the 1932 National Convention, Roosevelt had spoken of putting a million unemployed to work in the forests of the nation; and it was to this idea that he turned, after his inauguration, immediately after the more urgent banking crisis was brought under control. He had the assistance of several experts and advisers in formulating the organizational details, but it was substantially his idea that was offered to Congress in a message less than three weeks after he became President. Public opinion was not overwhelmingly favorable when the measure came up for hearings in Congress. Some influential people, including members of the President's Cabinet, thought that the organizing of large groups of unemployed and probably embittered young men might lead to armed rebellion. The labor movement feared the regimentation of labor and a depressing effect on wages. Observers on the Right saw the specter of communism, and those on the Left saw the threat of fascism. Nevertheless, under the sponsorship mainly of Senator Robert F. Wagner, of New York, the bill authorizing the establishment of the CCC became law on March 31, 1933.

The CCC was placed under the jurisdiction of the Labor Department, which quickly set up its apparatus for administering and recruiting. The War Department mobilized regular and reserve officers to operate the camps.

Enlistment in the CCC was limited to single men between the ages of eighteen and twenty-five, from families that were on relief; and it was, of course, voluntary. Everywhere, the recruiting personnel found eligible young men eager to join the organization, especially after the earliest joiners began to write home about their experience.

"By the middle of June," Arthur Schlesinger says, "1,300 camps were established; by the end of July over 300,000 boys were in the woods. They discharged a thousand conservation tasks which had gone too long unperformed. They planted trees, made reservoirs and fish ponds, built check dams, dug diversion ditches, raised bridges and fire towers, fought blister rust and pine-twig blight and the Dutch elm disease, restored historic battlefields, cleared beaches and camping grounds, and in a multitude of ways protected and improved parks, forests, watersheds and recreational areas.

"They did more, of course, than reclaim and develop natural resources. They reclaimed and developed themselves. They came from large cities and from small towns, from slum street corners and from hobo jungles, from the roads and the rails and from nowhere. One out of every ten or eleven was a Negro. Some had never seen mountains before, had never waded in running brooks or slept in the open air. Boys from the East Side of New York found themselves in Glacier Park, boys from New Jersey at Mount Hood in Oregon, boys from Texas in Wyoming. Their muscles hardened, their bodies filled out, their self-respect returned. They learned trades; more important, they learned about America, and they learned about other Americans." *

A monthly wage of thirty dollars was given each enrollee, part of which was a family allotment, and a green uniform was worn in winter, olive-drab in the summer. From 1933 through 1941, some 2,750,000 recruits served in the CCC. Because

* From *The Coming of the New Deal.*

the per-capita cost was about $1,075 per year, the CCC could be said to be one of the more expensive forms of relief, but this cost was more than offset by the gains in conservation, as well as the preservation of the health of America's young men.

A second major youth program was the National Youth Administration, begun in June 1935. At the height of its effectiveness, the NYA had enrolled more than 600,000 boys and girls between the ages of sixteen and twenty-five. At least seven eighths of the enrolled were given student aid to enable them to finish high school or college. The remainder were given aid in part-time employment out of school—lettering signs, sewing, soil-erosion control, et cetera. Many critics charged that the NYA was inefficiently managed and leaned too far to the left politically; its success depended largely on local administration, and with only the small appropriations granted under the NYA there was undoubtedly a tendency to boondoggle.

But if you were young and a member of a depression family in the early Thirties, the CCC and the NYA restored hope and a faith in the future. An instance of this is provided in the following first-person narrative of a young Negro CCC enrollee as transcribed by two writers on a WPA (Works Progress Administration) project.

NELLIE G. TOLER AND JAMES R. ASWELL

WEARY WILLIE*

MILLARD KETCHUM had just come in from his day's work in the field. He was still in his blue CCC work uniform. "This is better clothes than I ever had at home," he said, "before I got to the CCC. You see, at home they was so many of us, we couldn't have much clothes to wear and in summer time we jist didn't wear no shoes, and no shirts much, nor nothing else much.

"Let me git you some where to set if you want to talk a while. Hey, Sarge! kin I git a few minutes off to talk here to this lady here? Okay, Sarge."

When asked about his family, he said, "Well, my mama she come from Bundy County. She was a Dunlap. My papa, he come from Chester County, over here nigh Henderson. They live at Zama now and been there about two year. I ain't got so big a family to keep up, not so big as lots of the boys has. I jist got five brothers and one sister. I'm the oldest and I ain't but nineteen year old.

"My brothers, they's named Winston Gormer, Jim Ables, Luther Crocker, Ray Slowey, and Jonathan Junior. My sister she's named Pearlie Jo and she's thirteen.

"We's farmers and renters. Ain't ever owned no home as yet. We lives at Zama now with a Mr. Lew Truitt. We've got two big houses on each side of us and they's shore pretty, too. We ain't got so big a house to live in—jist a small house, but my mother she's a good housekeeper and keeps everything spick and span. Ain't much trouble, you know, with a little house to keep it clean. We ain't got so much in it neither. Jist enough to make it comfortable for us. We got plenty of beds, though, arn bedstids, and all. You know jist like most any pore farmer's got, but enough to do us all.

"I ain't never been much to school. Jist went to the second grade, that's all, excepting what I learned here in the CCC. I could have gone, I guess, but for some reason didn't keer nothing about it. Jist didn't want to go.

* From *These Are Our Lives* (Chapel Hill, North Carolina University Press, 1939).

166

I would have went if I wanted to. They didn't make me not go. We jist didn't none of us go. I got one brother that went to the second grade, too, and my sister she went to the first. Then she quit. We jist wasn't a family that like school.

"I quit that old second grade when I was fourteen. I left home and went to work. Been on my own ever since. I went down here to Woolard and went to work on a farm. The man he was sick and not able to work and had to have somebody to help him. That's why I got to work so long, and even got the job at all. Got twenty dollars a month."

I asked. "Would you go on to school and finish now if you had the chance?"

"Don't know whether I could or not. I would really like to learn." He flushed and scowled. "The boys they make fun of us when we can't read the funnies nor nothing. I look at pictures in books, and things like that in the recreation hall, so they won't laugh at me. I wish I had gone on to school now and would go as far as I could if I git the chance. Guess I couldn't git much learning now though, could I? I'm too old most to learn now."

I asked if he wanted to stay with the CCC.

"Yes'm, as long as I kin, because I git plenty to eat here. I didn't always at home, not the same kind of stuff, anyhow. Guess we had plenty, such as it was, at home, but it jist wasn't good like this, nor enough of it for the kind it was. I git to go more, git to see more. I'm learning too. I watch the others, and then, I have more clothes and can keep cleaner too.

"You see where we is at home they don't go to school. None of them has gone any since they moved to Rivers County. They's three at home now to go to school, but they ain't went none and guess they won't ever. I got higher'n any of 'em. My littlest brother, he three year old now. I git thirty dollars a month and send twenty-two of it home to them. They need it! My papa he don't make enough to do for all, jist renting and farming like he does.

"You see, my pap drinks some. Not all the time, but he gits drunk at times, and that makes it hard on mama. I got drunk a few times. First time I jist all at once didn't know what was wrong. I jist couldn't walk, so I set down and went to sleep. I don't drink now. I quit since I got in the C's which I've been in nineteen months now.

"I ain't never voted yet. Ain't old enough and don't think I will till I git old enough, neither. My papa, he's a 'Publican, but I'm going to be a Democrat myself. He don't vote in every election neither. But I'm going to when I git old enough. I'll take them all in as they come.

"Do I go to church?

"Well, no'm. Not now. But while in the C's I do. The chaplain preaches to us two times a month, and I like to hear him. He makes tears come in my eyes, too. I quit drinking all on account of him. I'm a good boy now. I don't go to church at town much because I'm afraid they'll laugh at me. My mother she's a Baptist, but I jist go to any of them. I always give some money when I have it to give.

"Down home it's different. I've rambled all over that place and they ain't got no churches down there. I been there two years and ain't ever seen no church yet. Some of my little brothers ain't never seen no church yet.

"No'm. Ain't ever been sick to speak of. Ain't never had nothing but measles and 'pendicitis and had them both in Camp and got my bills paid. If I'd been at home, I wouldn't had no operation, couldn't have paid for it. I skipped all other sorts of being sick. I ain't never had pneumonia sickness yet. I jist about got all the doctor bills at home paid up now because I sent my whole check home and done without going to shows or smoking and everything to git them all paid up. The family's sick lots."

"Are you ever homesick?"

"Yes, heck! I have enough to eat, but by gosh, when the rest gits to raising cane to go home, sometimes it makes me homesick, too. I don't git there much because I can't pay my way. I like to see my mother though. You see, at home we have peas with bugs and weevils in them. We have sweet potatoes and I don't like peas, and sometimes we have pudding and meat when Mama has time to make pudding for us.

"You ought to go to my house some time. We got a pump, and the water ain't much good. But Mom she's clean. They jist don't make them no cleaner than my ma. And I got a girl at home. She jist lives half a mile of me. We go walking every time I go home, because we ain't got no car. We go boat riding sometimes, but I don't like swimming. I can't swim and, anyway, I don't want to see my girl in swimming and nearly naked like most of them goes. I ain't going in for anybody looking like that. I kissed her last time I was home, but didn't do that till after dark. I ain't never asked no girls here at Belgrade to go with me nowhere. I'm afraid they won't. Anyhow, I'm going to marry some day when I git a good job to keep her up. It would be too many children to keep up on what I make now. Mama needs what I make for the ones at home."

"What does your father do?"

"Blame if I know. Nothing. Jist sets around the house after he gits off work at night. You see, he farms. After the crop is laid by, he don't do nothing much. Jist sets around. He might go out to the stores some. They's three or four little stores around there, about half a mile apart. He won't let me go off in a car. I went riding in an auto one time with my girl and a whole lot of us. It runned off in a ditch and I ain't got in none of them no more. I jist ain't going no more. I'm afraid.

"I git up about five in the morning, eat breakfast, go to morning classes, then go to the field. I don't work nearly so hard in this as I do in the field at home. I git to be with lots of boys that I wouldn't at home. They help me lots, show me how to do things I wouldn't have never knowed about. I like all my bosses and I like all the fellers. They tease me sometimes, but they like me, too.

"They call me Weary Willie. I guess it's because I look so sleepy-headed. I go to the shows some and I guess I make much as I need. I spend every blame penny I git my fingers on. I get eight dollars a month to spend. I sure do run through with it. Bet I could spend twenty dollars without half trying."

ON A TRAIN TO MEMPHIS

IF THE CCC had been in existence as early as 1931, could there ever have been a Scottsboro Case? It's an interesting speculation.

The nine Scottsboro boys were marked by the Depression, members of that army of 200,000 roving the country; with perhaps another fifty to sixty young people, they were hoboing on a freight train bound for Memphis.

It was March 25, 1931—their last day of freedom for several years; almost twenty years would go by before the last one, Andrew Wright, gained his release.

SCOTTSBORO BOYS*

1931

March 24—Two white girls, Victoria Price and Ruby Bates, from Huntsville, Alabama, hobo their way to Chattanooga and stay there overnight.

March 25—They return on a freight train leaving Chattanooga for Alabama. On the train are a number of Negro and white boys who engage in a fight, the white boys being thrown off the train. Alleged rape of the two girls by the Negro boys follows. When the train pulls into Paint Rock, Alabama, at 1:30 P.M. nine Negro boys, aged thirteen to twenty, are arrested and locked up at Scottsboro, the county seat. Victoria Price and Ruby Bates are examined by doctors that afternoon.

The attitude of the community becomes so threatening that the governor calls out the militia late that night.

March 26—The Negro boys are taken to Gadsden, Alabama, under military protection.

March 31—The grand jury, called into session at Scottsboro the previous day, indicts the nine boys for rape.

April 6-9—The boys are tried at Scottsboro and all are convicted except

---

* Abstracted, by the editor, from Dr. Allan K. Chalmers' *They Shall Be Free* (Garden City, N. Y., Doubleday, 1951).

Roy Wright, in whose case the jury disagreed. All are sentenced to death. The boys were represented by a white attorney from Chattanooga, one Stephen Reddy, retained by a local ministers' association, and local lawyers appointed by the court.

April–May—Atttorneys for the International Labor Defense and the National Association for the Advancement of Colored People enter the case. George W. Chamlee of Chattanooga, former county solicitor general, is retained by some of the defendants.

June 22—Motion for a new trial is argued by J. R. Brodsky of the ILD and is denied.

July 10—Executions for this day are postponed pending appeals to higher courts.

July 1931–March 1932—Protests from all over the world are registered by radicals, labor unions, important personages, ministers, et cetera.

1932

March 24—The Alabama State Supreme Court affirms the conviction of seven defendants but reverses the conviction of Eugene Williams on the ground that he was a minor and as such could not be tried in the Circuit Court until after a hearing in the Juvenile Court. The court denies a rehearing on April 9.

April 27—Ada Wright, mother of Andrew and Roy Wright, sails for Europe with J. L. Engdahl, general secretary of the ILD, to address meetings in many countries.

July 3—150,000 German workers fill the Lustgarten in Berlin to hear Mrs. Wright plead for the lives of her sons and the other defendants.

According to Dr. Chalmers, Mother Wright's trip to twenty-eight foreign countries was so successful that the Communist ILD arranged for at least eight other "Mother Wrights" to appear simultaneously in widely scattered parts of the world. Nobody knows accurately how much money the Communists raised for the Scottsboro Case. Some have estimated as high as a million dollars. According to Dr. Chalmers, a reasonable estimate of ILD expenditures during the years they were actively engaged in the case was in the neighborhood of 50–60,000 dollars. The ILD gets credit for organizing the defense of the boys in the early years and maintaining the early fight, but because of the clumsiness of some of their work, suspicions were aroused that the Communists had hold of such a good thing they weren't in a hurry to let it go.

October 10—The appeal to the United States Supreme Court is argued by Walter H. Pollak, retained by the ILD.

November 7—The United States Supreme Court reverses the conviction of the seven defendants on the ground that appointment of counsel appearing for them in the original trial at Scottsboro was inadequate and ineffective and violative of their constitutional rights. A new trial is ordered.

1933

January 5—Ruby Bates, at Huntsville, Alabama, writes a letter to a boy friend denying that the Negro youths attacked her. Local police secure the note.

January 23—The ILD secures a court order to photostat the Ruby Bates letter for use as defense evidence.

At Birmingham, Judge M. P. McCoy hears a writ of habeas corpus asking for the release of Roy Wright, still held in jail though unsentenced.

January 30—Writ is dismissed. Roy Wright is still held.

March 13—Samuel S. Leibowitz, New York criminal lawyer, is retained by the ILD.

March 27—The case of Haywood Patterson, the oldest defendant, is separated from the others by the State of Alabama, and he is placed on trial at Decatur.

April 9—Patterson is convicted and the jury imposes the death penalty. (He was defended by Leibowitz, J. R. Brodsky and G. W. Chamlee, all retained by the ILD. Ruby Bates appeared at the trial and reversed her previous testimony, denying that the boys committed rape on her or Victoria Price. Her story is challenged by Victoria Price who maintains her original testimony.)

April 16—J. R. Brodsky files with Judge Horton a motion for a new trial for Haywood Patterson on the ground that the conviction was against the weight of evidence.

April 28—The Scottsboro boys protest ill treatment in Jefferson County jail, in Birmingham, with a hunger strike.

June 1—Judge Horton orders two of the boys under sixteen years of age to be transferred to the Juvenile Court.

June 22—Judge Horton grants the motion for a new trial of Haywood Patterson and sets aside the conviction with a lengthy opinion reviewing the case and concluding that the conviction was not justified by the evidence.

November–December—Haywood Patterson, on trial for the third time, from November 20 to December 1, before Judge W. W. Callahan at Decatur, is convicted and again the jury imposes the death penalty. Clarence Norris, another defendant, is put on trial immediately after and is similarly convicted after a week. Both boys are represented by Leibowitz, Brodsky and Chamlee.

1934

February 24—Motions for a new trial are denied by Judge Callahan.

May 1934–January 1935—The Alabama Supreme Court again affirms the convictions; in November petitions are filed in the United States Supreme Court for review of both convictions.

1935

January–February—The United States Supreme Court on January 7 grants petitions for review, and the appeals are argued on February 15–18 before the Court by Leibowitz and Walter H. Pollak.

April 1—The Supreme Court reverses the convictions of both boys on the ground that Negroes were excluded from the panels of grand and petit jurors which indicted and tried the boys.

May 1—New warrants are sworn out by Victoria Price, the only complaining witness since the withdrawal of Ruby Bates from the prosecution.

November 13—The grand jury at Scottsboro returns new indictments for rape against all the boys *including the two transferred to the Juvenile Court.*

December—The Scottsboro Defense Committee is formed, composed of all agencies co-operating in the defense: the ILD, the NAACP, the American Civil Liberties Union, the Methodist Federation for Social Service, the League for Industrial Democracy, and the Church League for Industrial Democracy (Episcopal).

The head of the new Defense Committee was Dr. Allan K. Chalmers of the New York Broadway Tabernacle Church and from this point on the tide begins to turn ever so slightly in favor of the boys. As soon as the Committee was functioning, it had a neuropsychiatric case study made of each of the boys. The following is an excerpt of a "stream of talk" report on one of the boys. (Remember they had now been in prison for five to six years.)

"While out in the street I suffered with asthma. Some nights I can't catch my breath. This steel and concrete just kills me. No outlet, no exercise, no window in front of my cell; some nights I just can't get my breath. I have a hurting in my right side and my left side of my head. When I lay down I just can't catch my breath—all stove up. Would like to know the cause of that.

"How is my mind, Doc? I know I done lost my health. My health ain't so good. Then to some things I can remember just as good and then some I am forgetful. Like I know what year I was born in but I just couldn't think of it just now. Doc! I tell you the truth I am just lucky to be living. I know you hate to hear the truth, but I just as soon be dead at times as be living. It seems that they like to pick at me. I ain't done nothing and I can't understand what I am in solitary for.

"Been in solitary a year the twenty-fourth of this month and every doctor in the U.S. knows that as long as I been in here I ain't in good condition. Every now and then a pain hits me back of my head. I can't understand. I feel like I am not going to get up or get out of here anyway. I'm in here on a frame-up, Doc, I just got to say I think I am doing well to keep the mind I got now. Can't get no exercise, no outlet, go up to take a bath and right back. Don't never get out.

"I'm going to hold up as long as I can."

The Committee hired a local lawyer from Huntsville, the accusing girls' home town, to assist Leibowitz and to reduce some of the hostility that prevented Leibowitz from obtaining his usual success with such cases. Leibowitz had attempted to handle the Scottsboro boys' defense without reference to or consideration of Southern prejudices, and Southern hostility was fierce. By January 23, Patterson was convicted for the fourth time, but instead of the death sentence, he was sentenced to seventy-five years' imprisonment.

Dr. Chalmers now formed a local committee in Alabama to help with the fight. Eventually forty-nine Alabama citizens, white and colored, subscribed to the work and helped form a common ground for sympathy and help from other Southerners.

The "leniency" of Patterson's seventy-five-year sentence distressed the prosecution, and the state began to look for ways to get a compromise. Dr. Chalmers was told, "Plead the boys guilty and they'll get only seven years," which would have let them out of jail very soon.

Dr. Chalmers personally rejected such an arrangement, but for the boys' sake he suggested the prosecution put the proposition up to them directly.

It was then revealed the proposal had already been made to the boys, but none believed it was on the level. Finally, Dr. Chalmers agreed to confirm the proposal to the boys as being an honest one, but he was prepared to advise them against acceptance.

He described his visit to Andy Wright; all the boys had been in solitary for four months, which meant each spent his time in a room little more than the size of a nine-by-six rug. A shelf bed folded against the wall. Once a week they were taken out, given a shower and allowed to walk for thirty minutes along an empty corridor.

He greeted Wright, told him of the progress that had been made in the formation of the committee, and then he said, "The authorities have promised that if you plead guilty you can go free. But you are not guilty. You are under no obligation. . . . I'll stick with you as long as we live, but I must be honest with you—I don't know when we'll get you out."

Wright clutched the bars, his face up against them. He said, "Doc, I'll rot here till I die before I'll say I did something I didn't do just to get out."

That summed up the boys' opinion, and Dr. Chalmers did not even bother to communicate their decision to the prosecution. But other attempts by the prosecution to make deals continued.

1937

June 14—Alabama State Supreme Court confirms Patterson's fourth sentence.

July 15—Clarence Norris, convicted for the third time, receives the death sentence.

July 22—Andrew Wright convicted, receives sentence of ninety-nine years.

July 24—Charles Weems tried, convicted, receives seventy-five-year sentence.

July 24—Ozie Powell pleads guilty to a charge of assault with intent to murder and is sentenced to twenty years in jail. (After the January 1936 trial, Powell had slashed a man while in a Sheriff's car being taken back to prison; Powell was shot and permanently injured.) The rape charge against Powell and four others is dropped. Roy Wright, Olen Montgomery, Eugene Williams and Willie Roberson are freed. The other defendants are returned to prison.

December—An interview is held with Governor Graves of Alabama by Dr. Edmonds of Birmingham, chairman of the Alabama Scottsboro Defense Committee, Grover Hall, editor of the Montgomery *Advertiser,* and Dr. Chalmers. At the end of that conference the Governor freely states his intention of releasing the boys as soon as the cases are out of the hands of the judiciary. In the following months Governor Graves continues to make plans to assist in the boys' release via parole before the end of his term, December 31, 1938.

In late October, however, former Senator Heflin, of Alabama, began to pressure the Governor against the release, and the Governor then began to employ delaying tactics. The Committee sought the help of President Roosevelt, who invited Governor Graves to visit him at Warm Springs, Georgia. The Governor, who had great admiration for the President, ducked the meeting. According to Mrs. Roosevelt, the President then sent him a strong letter urging him to live up to his promises to release the boys. To no avail. Graves was told by Heflin and other Alabama political figures that "if he were to go through with his original plans, he was through politically, and he found himself unable to stand up to that."

In December, Dr. Chalmers released, with the backing of the Committee, a pamphlet, "A Record of a Broken Promise." He was fully aware that such a denunciation was a "luxury" but it did bring about a change in the attitude of the press of Alabama, which now swung in behind the Committee's efforts. The new governor wanted no part of the case, but now the Parole Board seemed to offer some hope; when, in March 1940, the case was taken up before that body, the board was "favorably inclined," but they decided nothing could be done "for the present."

Dr. Chalmers and the Committee were discouraged, but through Grover Hall they approached the Parole Board with the suggestion that one of the boys be paroled in his care so that rehabilitation could be begun as an example to those in the nation who were still aroused at the endless frustrations in the freeing of the remaining boys. The Parole Board (the Alabama State Board of Pardons and Paroles) reported to Mr. Hall, the go-between, that they had made their decision and that was that.

When an interview was finally granted to Dr. Chalmers, he was forced to wait in the outer office for nearly three hours. He said, "I never knew during this time what reception I would receive. The polite hostility with which I was finally met was not encouraging. The crux of the conference may be summed up in the words of one of the Board members. He was angry as he leaned forward and said vigorously: 'Dr. Chalmers, we have made our decision and you must abide by it.' He pounded the table when he said 'must.'

" 'Judge,' I answered quietly, 'you are a teacher in a Bible School, aren't you?'

" 'Why, yes,' he answered, startled at this sudden mention of things sacred.

" 'I am a minister of that same gospel,' I continued. 'In the Bible from which you teach, and from which I preach, there is a text referring to the fact that man may be judged by the words, "whatsoever you would that others do unto you, do you even so unto them." If I were the chairman of your defense committee if ever you were in trouble, would you want me to accept the decision of the authorities no matter how vigorously they made it?'

"He looked at me soberly and then said, 'No, I wouldn't.'

" 'That is the reason,' I answered, 'why I cannot accept your decision as final.'

" 'Our decision will stand for now,' he said, smiling for the first time. 'But we'll be glad to see you whenever you want to come back.' "

Finally, in November 1943, Charlie Weems was released, and in 1944, Andrew Wright and Clarence Norris, and in 1946, Ozie Powell. Wright was back in prison soon after his first parole, because of a fist fight and his leaving the state of Alabama. But he went back to prison voluntarily, knowing at the time that his being wanted jeopardized the others' chances of getting out.

1948

July 17—Haywood Patterson escapes from prison for the second time. His stay at Kilby has been full of misery and cruelty. He reaches Dr. Chalmers and asks for help. He is given it, but told to make a new life where he is not known. The FBI checks Dr. Chalmers regularly but Patterson remains at large for two years. Then his book, *Scottsboro Boy,* is published, and the FBI catches him outside the Detroit office of the Civil Rights Congress. But Governor G. Mennen Williams refuses to allow the State of Alabama to extradite Patterson and the matter drops right there. Patterson, after eighteen years in prison, is free.

There remains only Andrew Wright.

1950

June 9—The Associated Press reports that Andy Wright left prison on parole today "with no hard feelings toward anyone." Thirty-eight years old, he says, "I'm not mad because the girl lied about me. If she's still living, I feel sorry for her because I don't guess she sleeps much at night."

His release has been in jeopardy right up until the last minute because Patterson's book was a savage denunciation of the people and the system which is the Alabama prison administration.

Andrew Wright's first letter to Dr. Chalmers, after his release, is short but eloquent:

"Doc, when are you coming to see me. I feel like a rabbit in a strange wood."

"NEW YORK, NEW YORK, WHAT A HELL OF A TOWN!"

IN New York City, one of the country's greatest public servants, Fiorello H. La Guardia, a Republican, was elected mayor in 1933. The city had suffered the agonies of the Depression, and the corrupt political machine of Tammany Hall must have seemed even more distasteful to New Yorkers when the Seabury investigation disclosed that Tammany politicians had milked appropriations for building and construction, had accepted bribes from organized crime, had corrupted the courts, all during the height of the Depression. If ever a city needed an honest administrator to "throw the rascals out," New York City did.

The following selection is from the affectionate memoir by Ernest Cuneo, La Guardia's onetime law clerk.

ERNEST CUNEO

LIFE WITH FIORELLO*

FIORELLO's campaign [for Congress, in 1932] had for me an epic quality of almost Homeric proportions. He made it seem that way. He dramatized every instant of it. He was the dauntless captain of a gallant, horribly beleaguered ship, and though we yawed on the very brink of eternity, because of his supreme skill and courage we did not go under.

My services in the campaign were assumed. Bundles of ordered campaign literature arrived, and I signed for some. Fiorello told me not to do that because money was very limited; everything had to be checked in a central place. Otherwise, diversity of control would result in our buying things we couldn't pay for. He also told me that if I signed for anything I'd be liable, which was something to think about, too. It made me feel very uneasy, however, to see him concern himself about a $68 order when he was fighting for his political life.

* From Ernest Cuneo's *Life with Fiorello* (New York, Macmillan, 1955).

Then Fiorello told me that in the campaign I was to be a speaker. Speaking on street corners is certainly nothing new in political campaigns. In fact, street-corner stumping sounded a little unattractive intrinsically, and I wondered if I might not be getting some kind of brush-off.

I asked him what he wanted me to talk about and he seemed a little surprised, and said, why, anything I pleased. The implication was that I was thoroughly conversant with the situation and could play the whole thing by ear. I was pleased.

The Twentieth District ran from about 100th Street to somewhere up around 120th, and from Lexington Avenue over to the East River. Its heart was 116th Street. It encompassed at that time a large Italian and a considerable Puerto Rican population. It included many huge tenements, where yellow lights shone dimly from the backs of long dark corridors deep within. The black store windows of small ventures which had gone under stared out onto the shabby streets like empty eyeball sockets.

But though the backdrop was depressing, the people weren't. Their economic situation generally was bad, of course, but the average person seemed not nearly so wretched as those who had gone downtown to seek out Fiorello for personal help. In fact, the people in that area gave the impression of throbbing life. They were active, determined not simply to survive but to go on loving life itself. Kids ran in droves. Tolerant, amiable, good-natured mothers looked on with the air of having completed self-evident, all-fulfilling missions in life. Pushcart transactions were at once traditional ceremonies and enjoyable battles of wits.

The next evening I climbed into the back of a big delivery truck equipped with a movable loudspeaker and ordinary wooden benches along the sides. There were a couple of other people already there. Bunting festooned the outsides, and pictures of Fiorello with Republican eagles, and his own symbol, the Liberty Bell, at the four corners completed the *décor*. A small group cheered as we drove off. The truck jounced downtown a few blocks, where a very large crowd was awaiting us. Our truck went slowly through the crowd, turned into a sidestreet, and stopped. The tailgate was let down, and the microphone was moved to the very end of the truck. All was ready. The crowd eddied up to the very edge of the tailgate; the street was packed with people on all sides of us.

I sat on the bench, reviewing my notes, as things got under way. I remember the purplish arc lights, and the shadow of a wire in front of it swinging back and forth like a pendulum. I wasn't nearly as nervous as I thought I'd be. I heard myself described as a distinguished young visitor who was thoroughly familiar with all of the grave national problems of the day and who enjoyed the confidence of our great leader, Fiorello H. La Guardia, short cheer, your mike. I grabbed it and started to talk.

It was generally agreed in newspaper circles that La Guardia and Bob La Follette had the most informed, socially conscious electorates in the country. It was an education to me, during that campaign, to see the concentrated attention which was bestowed on every speaker. There was no nonsense about the content of speeches. They could not be general: the sense of the meeting was that either you had something to say or you hadn't. The red carpet that might have been laid out for you could be snapped out from under your feet at any moment if you failed to live up to your billing.

I opened up on the City Trust, as I had planned. I had intended merely to outline it in general, but I found such rapport that I was able to go into it in detail. From the record, I named the names and charged the crimes. The Democratic leaders were heavily involved, and I cited chapter and verse. The obvious conclusion I hammered home: Who could be found to oppose the election of La Guardia, save those content to send a thief to office? "Thief" is as strong a word in Harlem as anywhere else. I was greatly satisfied with the reception I received.

Later that evening, back at headquarters, some men came over and asked me if I didn't think the only way out of the transit problem was receivership for the city subways and eventual municipal ownership. I said I wasn't sure, that I hadn't looked that far into it. Another group asked me if I didn't think the Federal Reserve should make risky equity loans direct, as a pump primer; I said I did. There were a half-dozen questions which indicated that many of those present were at least as familiar with government finance as most Congressmen, and certainly more knowledgeable than I.

When I saw Fiorello the next day, I could tell he was not pleased. "Ernest," he asked, almost plaintively, "what the hell did you do up there last night?" He pushed his glasses up on his forehead.

"Nothing," I said. "I just attacked the City Trust banditry, that's all."

Fiorello sighed. "Now They will be pouring money in there to beat me." He looked both gloomy and nettled.

"Who?" I asked in amazement. "Who'll pour in money against you because of *my* speech?"

"Why, Wall Street, the Big Banks." He made a sweeping gesture. "They were fighting me generally, but now it's personal. The Big Banks have done the same damn' things as the City Trust, and now you've gone and frightened them at just the wrong time. Money will *pour* in against me. Well, it can't be helped now."

I just couldn't picture the Boards of Directors of the big banks downtown scurrying into executive session because of an obscure speech by a law clerk on a street corner in Harlem. I said as much. Fiorello shook his head. "No," he said, "the Democratic leaders are probably downtown right now, collecting thousands." I had mad visions of fleets of armored cars rushing gold bullion uptown posthaste, with Morgan and Aldrich wringing their hands and praying it was enough. It was, I thought, too silly for words. Yet the idea was enormously flattering. I felt like a young Disraeli, regretful that his first speech had upset the balance of power in Europe but determined to be resolute about it all. "Well," I soothed, "let's wait and see."

Presumably the Money Barons refused to be stampeded into parting with their cash, because nothing was ever heard of it again. I decided, however, to concentrate thereafter on Fiorello's voting record and his Congressional leadership. There was material enough there, Heaven knew, because Fiorello had taken a position on practically every bill before Congress during his tenure of office.

The speakers were eventually assigned to specific trucks, and the trucks made specific stops. Most of the speaking took place between 8:00 and 10:30 P.M. Fiorello himself would often speak at the final gathering of the evening, and he drew immense crowds. He was eloquent, factual, and sincere; he always ended on a fighting note, and he had them with him all the way. Our "enemies" deliberately scheduled a meeting one night for the same time and place as a meeting we had announced, at which Fiorello was slated to speak. Fiorello got there early and climbed up on the truck with us. A large crowd of La Guardia supporters was on hand. Sure enough, as the appointed hour drew near, a huge mob of people accompanied by a band could be heard coming up the avenue. Our opponents stopped about a block from the edge of our crowd. Between the two groups stood one lone policeman. Suddenly both crowds became absolutely silent. They faced each other like two shaggy, unfriendly animals.

"Ernest," said Fiorello, very quietly, "go and tell that cop we were here first and we're staying. Tell him," he said, "that if the Law can't protect us, we can protect ourselves." I rose to go, but he caught me by the sleeve and added: "Get tough with him. And if you have to hit him, don't hesitate."

182

My stomach muscles froze. "You mean *hit* the *cop*?" I bleated unbelievingly.

"Yes," said Fiorello. "Punch him in the eye if he tries to finagle us."

There is an old superstition among newsmen that it is very bad luck indeed to sock a New York cop, and I had seen strong evidence, as an ex-reporter myself, in support of it. But down I clambered from the truck and made my way through the crowd; or rather, a way opened for me. I passed the outer fringe of our followers with all the enthusiasm of a space cadet leaving the earth's gravitational field in a faulty rocket. I advanced on the cop, thinking we two were like Sohrab and Rustum meeting between the opposing lines. Just before I reached him, I looked back at Fiorello under the arc light, and he nodded his head vigorously by way of reassurance. I straightened my shoulders, walked the rest of the way, and aggressively stuck out my jaw.

"Listen," I snarled. "La Guardia says we were here first and we're gonna stay here. If you can't enforce the law, we'll do it for you."

He was a bulky young Irishman, about my age. He poked his face right into mine.

"*You* listen," he said. "I got eyes. Tell him to keep his shirt on. And I don't need no help from nobody." He turned on his heel, faced the other crowd, and moving his arms as if he were shooing chickens, he started walking toward them. "Beat it," he said to them. "Go on, beat it." They hesitated for a moment, then broke. A couple of blocks away, their band struck up and they all marched off. I was dizzy with relief. There was no question about it: Fiorello would have resorted to violence then and there had it been necessary.

An elderly lady came into the office one afternoon, apparently a shopkeeper of small means. She was on a mysterious errand; she said she wanted to give the money, *this time,* to Mr. La Guardia himself. "*This* time?" frowned Fiorello. "Show her in."

She explained to him that one of our ward leaders had asked her for twenty-five dollars for a secret La Guardia campaign fund, and she had given him fifteen dollars. The balance, she had made up her mind, she would hand to Fiorello himself, to be sure he got it. Fiorello called in one of the girls, and the woman told her story while it was taken down. La Guardia explained to her that he wanted to keep our records straight. It was immediately typed up, and La Guardia read it to her. He told her if what she had said was true, he would like her to sign it. She signed. Then

Fiorello phoned the Police Commissioner and asked him to investigate. The Commissioner apparently asked why, because Fiorello barked, "Because there's a chance one of *my* leaders may be a crook!" That, I thought, took real political guts.

Toward the end of the campaign I was having an early dinner down at the Little Venice with some friends one night when the headwaiter came over with a message: Mr. La Guardia wanted me uptown right away. I said to tell him I'd be along as soon as I finished eating. The captain came back and said it was urgent, that I was to leave immediately. With the air of a Foreign Secretary being called away from his house guests by a fussy Prime Minister, I excused myself. The deferential captain hurried me into my coat. I felt like Sheridan hurrying up to Winchester. The spirit of the Alamo and the Relief of Lucknow pervaded me. To the Rescue! I arrived at headquarters, and half a dozen people said in hushed voices, "The Major wants you." It was like walking through a verbal arch of crossed swords: "The Major wants you."

The Major greeted me with a hearty "Ah!" as if my arrival meant he could stop worrying. He quickly motioned me into a huddle. I knew I was the envy of all.

"Ernest," he whispered, "they're going to pull the fire alarm when I speak tonight." He drew back as if aghast at the terrible secret he had just imparted to me, and his expression suggested that I too must be confounded by such a diabolical plot. I couldn't imagine what this had to do with me and my mad dash uptown. I had expected that Fiorello was at least going to seek a temporary injunction against the United States Navy, or some such outlandish dramatic move that would rock the nation back on its heels.

"Why," I said absently, "they'll never get away with it."

This was greeted with vociferous enthusiasm by Fiorello. He clapped me heartily on the back. "Attaboy!" he said. "Get right over there."

"Get over where?" I asked, completely bewildered.

"Over to the fire alarm box," he said, "and punch anybody in the eye who comes near it!"

My Foreign Secretarial robes slid from my shoulders to the floor in an untidy heap. Visions of the Alamo and Lucknow dimmed. I wasn't even a bodyguard, I reflected; I was a bouncer. "Wait a minute," I said. "Suppose there *is* a fire? *Then* what do I do?"

"There won't be any," he assured me impatiently. "There hasn't been one in that vicinity for fifty years. Hurry up, now. Get going!"

I made my way outside, running a gauntlet of eager questions, but I just held up one hand and shook my head: Atlas staggering under the secret burden of the world. But to myself I thought bitterly, Big Deal for a Big Shot. I perspired with humiliation: if anybody were to find out the real reason why I had been called, I'd never live it down.

I took up my lonely vigil by the fire alarm box, feeling definitely sub-human. To make matters worse, one of those cold autumn rains began to fall with a quiet, discouraging persistence.

About nine-thirty a cab drew up in the drizzle. The door flew open and a cheerful voice called out: "Hey, Mr. President! Come on, get in. He's not speaking tonight after all." With cheerful malice, it added, "Never mind; 'they also serve who only stand and wait.' "

Fiorello was a dynamo throughout the campaign—absolutely tireless. People waited to see him in long lines, and he saw every one of them. He kept tabs on the smallest detail, but could switch from a trivial registry question to a fiery speech concerning basic issues on no notice at all. He was everywhere at once, encouraging, strengthening, and inspiring us all.

In the last days before the election he told me that I was to function as a Deputy Attorney General of New York. Each side was allowed a few to patrol the election. I went downtown and was sworn in. The night be-fore election I will never forget. Fiorello sent for me and we went off by ourselves behind a big screen. His powerful jaw was set. He said, "Ernest, what are you going to do if they try to steal the election tomorrow?" His eyes glittered with a thousand lights, like the hard, cold glitter in the eyes of a poised black panther. I was almost hypnotized; I know I had difficulty swallowing before I could speak.

"Listen, Major," I said. "I took an oath and I'll live up to it. I know a crime when I see one. Nobody has to tell me what to do!"

"What will you do?" he persisted.

"I'll arrest them," I said angrily, "or get killed trying to."

He put his hand on my arm. "No," he said, "we don't want arrests; we want votes. If they rush the machine, knock them away from it. Then cast as many votes for me as they stole. You hear? Vote until they knock you out! Tomorrow," he continued, "I've given you a post of honor. Ernest, it's dangerous." I was about to deprecate this when he said slowly: "They might shoot you. You could be killed."

Well, that's just dandy, I thought; from baby carriages on the bean to bullets in the chest. "For God's sake, then, give me a gun!"

"No," Fiorello said deliberately, "you can't have a gun. I'd sooner see you dead than tried for murder."

185

"Well, *I* wouldn't," I assured him. "I want a gun."

"No," he said firmly and soothingly, as to a child, "you can't have a gun. And," he added sharply, "I don't want you to get one anywhere else. You hear? If you don't want to go, you don't have to, but you can't take a gun. Understand?" He must have been reading my mind; I had been thinking, Why ask him? Somewhere I'd get a pistol that night. Now that was out. I promised I wouldn't get a gun, and we parted.

But I got sorer and sorer the more I thought about it. I tried to catch his eye, but he evaded me. I went over later in the evening and tapped him on the shoulder. "No gun," he said levelly, without even looking at me, and went right on talking to the person he was with.

Fiorello's climactic speech that night was unforgettable. The finale of every La Guardia campaign was a great ceremony. It always took place at his Lucky Corner, 116th and Lexington. Thousands of people were on hand, a moving demonstration of faith by people who regarded Fiorello not only as their own champion, but as the champion of humanity as a whole. There was almost a religious fervor about it. Fiorello spoke, and his soul was in every word. Never had his integrity, all his gifts, found better expression. He was a charging lion. As he concluded, a searchlight played down on him from somewhere above. And at the end the tumult of the crowd was such as must have toppled the walls of Jericho.

I slept very little that night. I just lay in bed and stared at the ceiling of my darkened room. It was unthinkable that Fiorello would send me into a gun fight without a gun. I tried to believe it was just like the night before a big game, but that wasn't true. Noel Coward once described his sensations before an opening—as though his stomach were a paper bag with a sparrow fluttering inside. But my stomach seemed to have shriveled to a hard, wrinkled walnut. Dawn came at last and I got ready to go uptown. The polls opened at 6:00 A.M. I ate no breakfast because I had read somewhere that if you were shot the difference between life and death could be the presence of food in your stomach. The theory was that the food poisoned the wound. I didn't believe it, but I was taking no chances.

I arrived at my assigned location at 5:45. There was already a short line of voters outside. I noticed a little boy playing with a hoop by the door, and I thought it was a hell of an hour for a kid to be up. The polling place was a long store with windows on both side of the entrance. The registration books were to the right as you entered, and the voting booths were further back and on the left, over against the wall. Near the window to the right of the door stood three young seminary students, representing the Honest Ballot League, as I recall. The inspectors were already seated. Two policemen in bull harness were at their stations near the curtained voting booths.

So was our opponent's man, a little older than I, and about my size. I took off my topcoat and hung it up.

The voting started. The first voter came in, checked with the inspectors, and entered the booth. The opposition man brazenly moved the curtain aside with his hand and peered in. I challenged the vote at once and told the cops to make an arrest. They suggested that I just take it easy. The Tammany man walked out with the voter. I followed. I told the three young clerics to stand by, there was going to be trouble. I went outside and discovered my adversary passing down the line, openly handing out money from a large roll of bills.

By this time the second voter had completed inspector's check and was going into the booth. Back came the Tammany man and again he poked his head inside the curtain. And again I challenged the vote, with the same negative results.

A third man came in, checked, stepped into the booth. As the Tammany man raised the curtain to watch the vote, I belted him on the jaw with everything I had. He went flying into the machine and collapsed to the floor. All hell broke loose. The two cops jumped me, and I locked with one of them. We scuffled and cuffed, and the cop yelled that I was under arrest. I said *he* was. Neither cop, I noticed, went for his gun; in fact, the other cop was now engaged in picking up the fallen man. With the heightened perception one tends to have in moments of crisis, I saw that the young clerics were praying and that the little boy outside was jumping excitedly up and down and waving his hat.

The cop and I had just broken apart, still arresting each other, when a huge limousine hurtled to a screaming stop at the curb. Men tumbled out of it and came running into the store. This is it, I thought. I just stood there, waiting for the bullets. I felt naked, and my arms were going up and down in short jerks like a pawing bear. "Now and at the hour of our death, Amen," came fleetingly to mind from out of my childhood. It was all over in seconds. In all, seven men rushed in, their right hands in their pockets. *But* they wore great big La Guardia buttons in their lapels! They formed a semicircle around me, facing the cops, and just stood there, crouched. Not a word. I regained my voice, and from behind my barrier I told the cop again that those first three votes were challenged. He said he'd heard me the first time. The fellow I had hit was on his feet now, and the second cop was helping him wash his face at a sink at the back of the store.

Now another black car roared up and out jumped Fiorello. He apparently knew all about what had happened because he burst in shouting, "Attaboy, Ernest, give 'em hell!" He tongue-lashed the cops and said they'd go to prison if there was any more nonsense. He said they'd date time for the rest of their lives from the second anything funny happened there again. I saw that the La Guardia men were leaving, and I asked one of them in a low voice where they were from.

He whispered: "Friends of Fiorello. Amalgamated Clothing Workers of America."

Fiorello looked around defiantly and then motioned for me to leave with him. We got into the car. "There won't be any more trouble there," he said. Then, "Are you all right?" I started to say that of course I was all right, but instead I broke into a torrent of tears. I was as surprised as Fiorello. He said what was I crying for, I had done fine. For a moment or two I couldn't stop. I had seen football players cry in the dressing room after a tough game, and it isn't exactly crying so much as a release of tension, but I had never been affected that way before. Fiorello gazed out of the window while I pulled myself together, and for the rest of the ride he was gruffly kind.

He was right; there was no more trouble that day. The fellow I had hit was gone when I went back in the afternoon, but he soon reappeared. It was awkward at first, but it seemed to me that he was actually trying to be friendly. He smiled, and I went over and said I was sorry that I had had to belt him. He said to forget it, it was all part of the game. He stuck out his hand and I shook it.

Fiorello carried that particular precinct by less than fifty votes. But it was obvious that over-all it was a Democratic landslide from Buffalo to the Battery. By eleven, we knew the bad news. Fiorello had lost a very close race.

I felt terrible. We walked up the dark street together. At the corner he stopped. "Well, Ernest," he said, "we did our damnedest. And you can't do better than that. Now go home and get some rest." I told him I didn't want to, but he ordered me to go. I didn't know what to do. I wanted desperately to help him. I went on down the block alone and crossed the street. Then I looked back. He was talking to some people who had come along. They parted and he walked on by himself. I followed him, keeping well back on the opposite side of the street, hoping something would occur to me to do, but nothing did. He climbed the steps to his house and walked in, closing the door gently behind him. I never felt so miserable in my life as I did standing there on that street. I don't know how long it was before I turned and started the long walk home.

Within a month after his defeat, Fiorello was busy regaining lost ground. Postcard invitations were sent to a special list of people known to be actively interested in better government for New York City, and a meeting was held in Town Hall. An audience of over five hundred showed up and warmly applauded Fiorello's calm, cool speech. In the main they were old faithfuls—the hard nucleus of Fiorello's support. As had happened in the past, Fiorello was down to base strength, laying careful foundations for a new edifice to be built on the ruins of an old defeat.

However careful or logical his plans may have been, his immediate future was to be shaped by a seemingly unrelated series of events which he could not possibly have anticipated. This chancy chain of events began four years before with a gambling game and a pistol shot. It is not too extravagant to borrow a page from history by saying that this was a shot heard eventually round the world, for it had a direct bearing on the subsequent election of two men to the highest elective office in the land. The figurative ricochet of this bullet radically changed the complexion of party politics in New York City and in Albany; and at least the echo of the explosion rang through the corridors of the White House.

The gentleman on the receiving end of the literal bullet was, of course, Arnold Rothstein, banker to the underworld, one of the most verminous characters that ever infested New York City. One October evening in 1928, two notorious big-shot gamblers, "Titanic" Thompson and "Nigger Nate" Raymond, anxious for some action, invited Arnold Rothstein to participate in a game of High Spade. The evening's diversion was expensive for Rothstein; he lost $340,000. He resolved this dilemma in characteristic fashion: he welshed. But this proved even more expensive. On a Saturday night early in November, he received, while dining at Lindy's, another cordial invitation, this time from gambler George Mc-Manus, to attend a floating crap game at the Park Central Hotel, a few blocks north. Rothstein bustled out, his sporting blood aroused. At 11:10 P.M. Mr. Rothstein was found at the service entrance of said hospice, his right side punctured by a .38 bullet, a wound of which he subsequently died at Polyclinic Hospital on the following Tuesday. On his deathbed Rothstein had only enough strength to caution his friends and well-wishers everywhere, including his lawyer, to keep their mouths shut; and, having completed his last furtive act, he died, thereby performing the one act of public service ever connected with his name.

In the meantime thirty-five New York City detectives were halfheartedly going through the motions of finding out who did the shooting. The murderer was never caught.

Up to the day of his timely demise, Rothstein had always made it a point to know the price of every corrupt official in the city, and always had the money to pay it. He knew to a penny the market on lost souls, from rigged security operators and horse race fixers down to what a Bowery bum would do for the glass of rotgut whisky that was killing him. And Rothstein traded on it all. If Rothstein alive had been an unsavory article, Rothstein dead was a calamity. His activities had not been limited to the dregs of society; on the contrary, certain of his dealings had involved some very eminent citizens indeed. The publication of his records might make for embarrassment, it was felt. Not to put too fine a point on it, City Hall was in an uproar. Mayor Walker was unhappy and upset.

After the killing the police went to Rothstein's fortress home and seized his voluminous files. A judge ordered that they be put in the custody of a Tammany district leader—for "safekeeping." Although it took two trucks to move them, the trustee shortly reported to the court that they had been stolen, and the court solemnly accepted this explanation.

But at least one record actually was missing, for in 1929, when he went down to crushing defeat in the mayoralty race against Jimmy Walker, Fiorello produced it. It was the record of a loan of $19,940 from Rothstein to a pitiful excuse of a magistrate named Albert Vitale, of the Bronx. That was the touch-off match to the powder train which was to blow the old Tammany Hall to smithereens forever.

There were two Democrats in New York State who bore no more love for Tammany than Fiorello did. One was the distinguished Judge Samuel Seabury, who had been done out of the Governorship by the Wigwam in 1916; the other was Franklin D. Roosevelt, whose first act in public life fifteen years before had been to stamp on Tammany's toes for opposing his election as State Senator. The paths of Fiorello, Seabury, and Roosevelt were to converge with effects important to the nation's history. The man who brought them together was Adolf A. Berle, Jr., Professor of Corporate Finance at Columbia University. In 1928, however, no one of the men involved had any more notion that this would occur than Arnold Rothstein himself, laid out in Brooklyn in his pine box, for once in a game he couldn't fix.

The Appellate Division named Judge Seabury to investigate the Magistrates' courts. It was open knowledge at the time that magistrates' appointments were sold to loyal and zealous ward heelers. Some of the magistrates really represented a family enterprise. All relatives who had two dimes to rub together went into the pool, the family had the honor of including a judge in their number, and everyone sat back for dividends. The caliber of this bench can be imagined, but not described.

Seabury went after his quarry cautiously, even though he had the backing of the press. It is a phenomenon of all investigations that the "breaks" come in the form of volunteer witnesses once the investigations are announced. The Magistrates' courts investigation went true to form. One night there walked into the New York *Daily News* office a desperately ill little pimp by the name of Chile Acuna. Acuna said he was tired of framing innocent women for the Vice Squad and helping to railroad them before crooked magistrates. A pimp is not the world's most reliable witness, and the *News* checked carefully. What they found disgusted a city which was used to stenches: one woman magistrate had actually doctored the court records in her zeal to protect the police-vice ring. Innocent women had been framed, all right, and by the dozen.

This set off a second investigation: the Hofstadter Committee to investigate corruption in New York City, with, again, the implacable Sam Seabury as its counsel.

Mayor Walker tried to wisecrack it out of existence. He paraded across the line of fire with leers and knowing winks to vociferous if cynical applause; but when he was in complete command of his faculties—which was seldom in those later days—the strain made his skin look like old parchment. From Washington, Fiorello threw what assistance he could to Seabury; but there was a game of far larger stakes developing, and no one knew it more than the agile incumbent at Albany, Governor Franklin D. Roosevelt.

Roosevelt certainly loved Tammany no better than did La Guardia or Seabury, but, unlike them, he needed the Hall badly. He was an all-out candidate for the Presidency and, if he got it, a hands-down choice to win. Now Roosevelt was in a dilemma. Every bit of the shocking evidence Seabury was unearthing made headlines across the nation. Tammany, an absolute necessity to Roosevelt until his nomination, would be a millstone around his neck west of the Hudson once he had it. With his usual perfect timing, however, F.D.R. pulled the neatest political trick of the year, and it landed him squarely in the center ring of the Big Top for two performances and a double encore.

Meanwhile, Seabury had assembled a highly competent staff of accountants and lawyers and told them to see what they could find. To no one's surprise, they found plenty. The various machine leaders had large amounts of money, the explanation of which convulsed the nation with hoots of angry laughter. Wonderful Damon Runyonesque characters were uncovered: Tin Box Farley (no relation to James, of course) whose only explanation for his funds was that he had simply found them in his little tin box; the fifty-four starving McQuades who were the ridiculous excuse offered by that rascal for his bulging deposit box; and mighty Jimmy Hines, caught far up the creek, not only without a paddle, but in the same boat with the master gangster Dutch Schultz. The Board of Standards and Appeals, which had jurisdiction of zoning and building permits, was exposed as a million-dollar-a-year racket, but only after Tammany had challenged Seabury's subpoena up to the Court of Appeals and lost.

The contest had all the drama and violence of a heavyweight championship fight. Crafty old Judge Seabury kept boring in with heavy body punches, and the Democratic Party winced as far north as Albany when his crashing right landed on its soft underbelly, Tammany. There was no doubt as to what Seabury's knockout blow was to be. He had, in the parlance of the fight game, telegraphed his punch: it was going to be a crushing overhand right, tagged for the political glass jaw of one James J. Walker.

The Seabury technique was coldly methodical. It took time, but under the paralyzing body blows of exposure after exposure Tammany was at last brought to bay, breathing heavily and badly hurt. The trail of blood left by the dying Rothstein led straight to the paths of corruption within the city machine, and those paths were narrowing rapidly in the direction of the back door of the Wigwam. All at once it was too late for Jimmy's fancy footwork; he was going down for the full count unless saved by the referee—i.e., Governor Roosevelt.

In desperation, Tammany went into a clinch. It hung on with the claim of constitutional privilege and the rule applying to burden of proof in a criminal case. Seabury had proved big, unexplained, and inexplicable bank accounts, but he still had to prove, and beyond a reasonable doubt, that these sums actually represented graft in order to make a case.

As 1932 rolled in, Governor Roosevelt viewed the untidy New York scene with absolutely unmixed emotions: everyone knew he was out for himself. He preferred to remain 150 miles north, in Albany, away from the furious scuffle in progress, and thus avoid the consequences of any wild swings. For Seabury's sake he deplored, and for Tammany's he demurred, an elegant exhibition on the high wire if there ever was one.

But ringwise Sam Seabury knew that F.D.R. was in a tough spot, and he decided to capitalize on it. He suddenly declared that he was not conducting a criminal trial, but a legislative inquiry, thereby taking off his back the heavy burden of proof. He stated that the proof he had was not intended for a Grand Jury action: it was meant for Governor Roosevelt, and he laid it at Roosevelt's feet, thereby making himself the most unwelcome visitor in the Upper Hudson Valley since Gentleman Johnny Burgoyne.

The nation held its breath; it looked as if the New York Governor was cornered. A rapid look at the spring calendar—instead of the issues—quickly decided the man on the high wire. F.D.R. simply had to have Tammany support for the convention, still three months away. To the amazement of all, and the admiration of many, he resoundingly denounced graft and corruption in general, but ruled that Seabury had failed to make a case in particular. Tammany breathed a sigh of relief heard across the nation. With this heartening demonstration of party regularity in the face of tremendous pressure, the big city machines of Jersey City, Chicago, Kansas City, and New Orleans took a more kindly view of the Squire of Hyde Park. Which only goes to prove how little politicians know about politics. Jim Farley took planes, trains, and busses to the far hinterlands and ultimately piloted F.D.R. through to the nomination for the Presidency at Chicago. With that accomplished F.D.R. lost no time in letting it be known that the Tammany millstone around his neck would shortly find itself at the bottom of the sea. Everybody understood this but the Wigwam, which, in its innocence, was apparently unable to comprehend such a fast double play.

Immediately after the convention, Seabury examined Walker, and then renewed his attack at Albany. In brief, Seabury stated that there were large, unexplained amounts of money in the hands of public officials, and that he wanted another ruling from the Governor: though not enough to convict, were they not enough to remove? Fiorello also pressed the point. He sent me chasing for statements by Presidents Grover Cleveland and Theodore Roosevelt and, backed by them, he submitted that a public office was a public trust, and what did Governor Roosevelt intend to do about it all? F.D.R., the marvel of the high wire, was waiting for just this cue. With a great flip, he described a complete arc and a full about-face, declared that public office was *indeed* the highest of trusts, and descended gracefully to his waiting Admiral's cape as Commander-in-Chief, which he never thereafter doffed. His feat left Tammany holding the bag, in fact a lot of little black ones, which contained one-way tickets to Sing Sing. Only Roosevelt could have managed the stunt, and it was a question as to which he had more of—skill or brass.

Fiorello and I were at the intersection of Seventh Avenue and 47th Street when the news trucks came tearing into Times Square and the newsboys started shouting "Extra!" I ran over and got a paper with the headline "Roosevelt Sustains Seabury," and the subhead "Rules Public Officials Must Explain Private Funds." Fiorello scanned it and said very solemnly, "Ernest, this is a great day for our country."

Before the ink was dry on the extra, Jimmy Walker's sponge came sailing into the ring in the form of a one-sentence letter to the City Clerk: "I hereby resign as Mayor of New York City, James J. Walker." The Walker-La Guardia political duel was ended.

When the Lame Duck Congress opened, F.D.R., through Adolf Berle, Jr., made Fiorello his spokesman for certain legislation. Oddly enough, Fiorello became the savior of the railroads he so ardently disliked by jamming through the Railroad Bankruptcy and Reorganization bill. Far closer to his heart was the Farm and Home Mortgage Relief bill. And together Fiorello and Berle patterned the legislation that resulted in the famed "77B" of the Federal Bankruptcy Act, providing for an extension of private credit obligations under supervision of the court. Altogether, it was perhaps the most active Lame Duck session in the nation's history. As the time came for Fiorello to step down and for F.D.R. to step up, the two men knew they had much in common, including one trustworthy friend in Berle.

During this period Judge Seabury kept slugging away. His revelations were such that the new Democratic Governor of New York, Herbert Lehman, a man of absolute personal honor, decided to appoint a Special District Attorney for New York County. The Seabury exposures had made corruption not a party issue, but a public cause. Governor Lehman, as a mark of his integrity, picked a man of the opposite party to root out and prosecute all civic irregularity. He was as honest as he was cold. Thomas E. Dewey was to go on to Albany three times as Governor and he stopped twice at the very threshold of the White House. These things aside, he would still be remembered as the man who broke the hold of the Lepke, Luciano and Dutch Schultz gangs.

Fiorello was out and F.D.R. was in as the jockeying for the New York mayoralty race began in the spring of 1933. Early in May, Fiorello urged an anti-Tammany ticket to be headed by Al Smith, with Socialist Norman Thomas for Aldermanic President and Bob Moses for Comptroller. These nominations were duly made, with the fullest knowledge on Fiorello's part that none of the men named could possibly accept them. Fiorello, however, indicated that he stood ready to save the situation; if Al Smith wouldn't head the ticket, he, Fiorello, would.

A number of independent groups started a "Stop La Guardia" movement, working toward a joint ticket with the Republicans. It didn't look too good for Fiorello as the climax approached in late July. But Berle had arranged a series of private conferences between Seabury and Fiorello, as a result of which Seabury agreed to cast for Fiorello. When the showdown occurred early in August at the City Club, Berle and Seabury carried all before them. Fiorello came out of it with the Republican and Fusion nominations. It looked to be another rough, tough battle.

Fiorello adopted as his campaign song "Who's Afraid of the Big Bad Wolf," and the interminable tootling in the streets had people ready to start screaming. Overnight, however, it became "The Battle Hymn of the Republic," and the most fervid crusade in New York City's history was under way. The final lines seemed drawn.

But they weren't. The new man in the White House had a few ideas of his own. Without a word of warning, F.D.R. had Boss Ed Flynn of the Bronx split the Democratic ticket by nominating Joe McKee on a Recovery platform against the bumbling Tammany candidate, John O'Brien. At the same time, F.D.R. sent Berle to Cooper Union with a public White House repudiation of McKee! Roosevelt nominated McKee through Flynn and then denied him support through Berle—thus splitting the Democratic ticket. To nominate and then repudiate while allowing the nomination to stand is one for the books. It was. The books at final audit read: La Guardia—858,000; McKee—604,000; O'Brien—586,000.

Fiorello entered City Hall straight down the middle of F.D.R.'s split ticket. It was one of the nattiest double plays on file. Up in the Bronx and down on Fourteenth Street they still call it a double cross. Though the debate raged as to whether the President had pitched a ball or a strike, all were agreed that Fiorello was very nimble on the bases. Well, you have to be to steal home.

In Judge Samuel Seabury's home at exactly midnight on January 1, 1934, Fiorello H. La Guardia took the oath of office, administered by Supreme Court Justice Philip J. McCook, as Mayor of New York City. At exactly one minute after midnight, he ordered the arrest of the most notorious gangster in town—Lucky Luciano. His take-off next morning was jet-propelled, and the momentum never let up until he stepped out of office twelve years later. He would dictate to secretaries in relays for at least twelve hours every day. No longer a legislator who had to persuade and negotiate, he now had what amounted to virtual dictatorship within his domain, and he pushed his prerogatives to the limit. When his labors ended, he had greatly altered the face of the city, from its charter to its highways, from its hospitals to its high schools. The outpouring of his prodigious energies was strictly in line with the convictions he had always held. He set about realizing his theories at boiler-works tempo.

At the end of his first six months, he rendered a report to the people. Among other things, 400 new playgrounds had been opened in that period and the city had begun to distribute milk, at cost, to the poorer sections. The hospital system was completely revised; so was the setup of the Health Department. All sorts of food-market racketeers were on the run. Almost every department had felt his none too gentle hand, and had heard during surprise visits harsh demands for greater economy and efficiency. Remarkably, though, considering all these new departures, he had wiped out the budget deficits; and the city bonds, which were at 78 when he took office, were now over par. The bankers had enough confidence in him to give him an interest rate of ¾ of 1 per cent, whereas historically Tammany had had to pay 4 per cent. Adolf Berle deserves much of the credit for this. One of Fiorello's first official acts was to appoint Berle City Chamberlain, with instructions to put the city's financial house in order.

Fiorello's fiscal policies were a pride and a joy to him. Public utilities found themselves the recipient of a brand-new tax, and had their old ones lifted. Since, under the law, they are entitled to a fair return, however, it was also something of a consumer's sales tax for all the fanfare. But it paid off, and along with the cutting of nonperforming officeholders, the city treasury soon began to show color in its cheeks—or, if you prefer, its checks. New Deal money flowed into the city. Berle continued on as a White House financial adviser, and the two Chief Almoners, Ickes and Hopkins, were old friends of Fiorello's. It was a source of immeasurable relief in the Capital to be able to make large grants, knowing that under Fiorello's gimlet eye every dime would go for its designated purpose. Federal aid, of course, did a lot to lift the strain on the local treasury, but there was no doubt, in any event, that the city's credit was sound.

When the time came for Fiorello to refund some long time obligations, he thought it would be a novel idea to get the money from the R.F.C. The R.F.C. politely declined. The banks thereupon upped their interest rate to 4½ per cent. Fiorello at once threatened to go around the country selling his own bonds in key cities. It never came to that, however, because a compromise was finally reached. During the hassle one of Fiorello's young socialite secretaries sought to act as mediator. He remarked that he thought he could smooth the whole thing out: by a strange coincidence he was spending the weekend with the opposition's leading investment banker. "Don't apologize," snapped Fiorello. "A lot of young men aren't particular where they sleep around on weekends!"

From the first, Fiorello dropped in on municipal lodginghouses unannounced, taking his place in the lines, to see how the luckless were being treated. With the plight of the city's unemployed uppermost in his mind, he spent much time and thought in preparing a request for a record-breaking relief budget. Typically, he left as little to chance as possible.

He completed his careful preparations for the presentation of his relief budget and then rolled up his sleeves. Anticipating the constitutional issue, he declared that all lawyers were semicolon boys—that they had retarded civilization more than cancer and smallpox combined. He had determined to press for an over-all of about three billion dollars. He called to the first public hearing the chairman of the board of the largest bank in the city, intending to bait him into some sort of "Let-'em-eat-cake" remark. Aggressively, he asked the banker how much money he thought it would take to keep his fellow citizens from starvation. The banker, tipped off as to Fiorello's three billion estimate, calmly stated that it might run to six billions, and Fiorello's sails flapped feebly and hung slack. The expected opposition developed from the political quarter. As Fiorello started to read his findings, he was interrupted by an alderman who declared that relief money was already being misdirected. The alderman had documentary evidence, sworn affidavits, no less, proving that prostitutes were receiving relief money. He demanded that the practice be stopped, and that the budget be curtailed to the extent that these women were included. Fiorello bent upon the alderman his best busy-browed glare. "I thought that question was settled two thousand years ago, but I see I was wrong. Mr. Sergeant-at-Arms," he thundered, "clear the room! Clear the room—so this big bum can throw the first stone!"

As had been widely predicted, Fiorello's activities as Mayor were consistent with all his previous views. He continued to go down the line for Labor with a capital L; in any given dispute he did exactly what might have been expected of him, though theoretically his was now an impartial position. All of his craft, and he was a very crafty man indeed, was employed for the benefit of working people. With the power of City Hall behind it, his opinion very frequently was decisive. It all came under the head of ministerial prerogative, but the ruthlessness with which it was applied left no doubt as to his personal bias or the inevitable result of any given issue. At one point all the waiters in the city went out on strike. Their strike may or may not have been doing too well. At any rate, the city's hotels and larger restaurants managed to carry on—that is, until Fiorello entered the scene. What he did was classically simple: under the Health Law the city could inspect anyone handling food at any time. Fiorello, without warning, chose the height of the evening dinner hour to order a health inspection of all the scab waiters on duty, thus paralyzing service. The managements didn't like the findings either: several waiters were found to be suffering from contagious diseases. The inspections ceased as soon as an agreement with the regular waiters was reached, which was very shortly. The Building and Fire departments were preparing to make elaborate inspections when the managements came to terms.

At another time girl laundry workers went on strike. They were badly underpaid, and their working conditions were very poor. Hearkening back to the sweatshop era, and Fiorello's part in the fight against them, it was no surprise that as Mayor he would be their vigorous champion. Under the guise of keeping order, he practically blockaded the laundries with squads of police. The laundry owners went to City Hall to protest. Fiorello received them with elaborate courtesy and listened most patiently to their complaint. That alone should have put them on their guard, but it didn't. They told him that he was interfering in a labor dispute, and that the city was supposed to be neutral. Fiorello heartily agreed. The labor-union leader tried to say something, but Fiorello told him to shut up. Fiorello then turned to the spokesman of the laundry owners and asked him if he had an application to make. The spokesman swept himself firmly into the saddle of Fiorello's Trojan horse by repeating that his sole desire was to have the city remain neutral. Fiorello asked that this request be made in writing. The laundry owners hastily complied with a written request that the city withdraw all support from either side. As soon as it was handed to him, Fiorello announced that the application was granted, and that the city henceforth would be absolutely neutral. Thereupon he picked up the telephone, called the Water Department, and blandly ordered the Water Commissioner to turn off the water in all laundries, since the city was neutral in the fight. The laundry owners collapsed on the spot.

Fiorello ran true to form in his ideal of public service, too. He expected to be besieged by officeseekers, and, to a degree, he was. But he disposed of this problem at once. Immediately after his election, he addressed his entire campaign headquarters force. He said, in a very few sentences, that a Cause, not a man, had succeeded; and now he had been elected the Chief Magistrate of the city. "My first qualification for this great office," he declared, "is my monumental personal ingratitude!" There was disgruntlement, of course, and even a few heartbreaks, but Fiorello never swerved from his position: he got the best people he could for the jobs at hand, especially the top ones. Some of his highest appointments went to men outside the city, a new precedent which caused much wailing and gnashing of teeth. But Fiorello maintained that he hired a man on his abilities and not on the basis of where he slept at night. He felt the strain, however. He told Adolf Berle one evening that he'd like to be able to say "yes" to everything which was asked of him, but that he had taken an oath of office which he intended to honor. "The devil," said Fiorello, "is easy to identify. He appears as your best friend when you're terribly tired and makes a very reasonable request which you know you shouldn't grant."

After he got settled in, Fiorello was practically his own Police Commissioner. As an ex-Commanding Officer, he knew that nothing goes down to the ranks faster than the disposition of the command tent. He used to say that any variation at the center made for terrific wobbles around the circumference. He also believed that the most sensitive department in the city was the Police, so there was little astonishment in his insistence of City Hall support for honest cops. Very early in his administration, a physician who was a casual personal acquaintance got a ticket for illegal parking. The doctor forcefully told the young patrolman that the ticket was inacceptable, whereupon the boy arrested him and brought him to the station house. The physician afterward went down to City Hall in person to report this grievous wrong. Fiorello called the station house and asked to speak to the young patrolman. The captain of the precinct, who by this time had heard all the details, came on instead and was all apologies. He explained to the Mayor that the arresting officer was a rookie cop who just hadn't known any better. Fiorello, of course, hit the ceiling. "He's a better cop than you are," he raged, "and I called him up to tell him I was sending him a box of cigars. He's the kind of cop I want—and you're not!" The rookie got his cigars, delivered significantly by the Mayor's car, and Fiorello very nearly broke his superior. This story ran through the department like wildfire.

General O'Ryan, the Police Commissioner, was a stickler for form, and he and the Mayor did not get on any too well. One bitter February day, when the city was in the grip of one of the worst cold waves on record, O'Ryan issued an order stating that policemen must wear their coats in summer. The Mayor at once issued countermanding orders. The freezing city roared with laughter at this battle over what uniform would be worn in sweltering July. Trivial though the incident was, it resulted in O'Ryan's eventual resignation, which had long been brewing. Fiorello was not displeased; and it was fitting that the situation had come to a head over a quarrel relating to the comfort and well-being of the rank and file, whom Fiorello was always to defend at the expense, if necessary, of his own top brass.

A story once went the rounds to the effect that Police Commissioner Valentine, O'Ryan's successor, had put a bodyguard on Fiorello without his knowledge. A couple of detectives were established in an apartment near his with orders to keep a protective eye on him. Fiorello found out about it somehow and hit the roof. He summoned the detectives to his office. "Very well," he said, "at the expense of the *taxpayers* you're protecting me. Where was I last night at eight-thirty?" They didn't know. "I was hiding out," Fiorello told them acidly, "in a front box at the opera. Five thousand other people knew where I was, but not you two. I guess you must be the same detectives that looked for Dutch Schultz."

Savage is the word for Fiorello's feeling about gangsters. His instructions to the Police Department were, in effect, Be sure you've got the right man, then give him the works. This ruthless point of view exercised several civil liberties groups, and protests were lodged regarding irregular police procedure. Fiorello once called Valentine over to City Hall to face one such group. "Louie," he said, "these people claim you violate the Constitution." "So do the gangsters," said Valentine. Fiorello nodded, much pleased, and dismissed the petitioners forthwith.

There is no doubt that Fiorello did in fact go far beyond constitutional limitations in his unremitting war on gangsterism. Inside or outside the legal framework, however, he never deviated an inch. When it became common knowledge that a notorious criminal by the name of Terranova was in effect barred from New York by an order for his detainment at the city limits, a delegation of liberals protested. Their argument was that if every mayor did the same it could become an arbitrary injustice that would put a stop to freedom of movement in the United States. "You're absolutely correct," Fiorello told the body; and, turning to his Police Commissioner, he added: "Terranova has a perfect right to come into New York City. Let him come in, by all means! *Wait until he gets to 125th Street—and then go to work on him.*"

His standards for police action were almost the same as for an armed reconnaissance patrol in time of war. One time a thug had got the drop on a Jersey City cop, and at pistol point the patrolman had yielded up his own weapon. Mayor Hague of Jersey City condoned it; he said the cop had had no alternative to surrendering his pistol. Fiorello at once issued an order to New York's Finest that this philosophy was not in their tradition —that they should yield their lives before yielding their guns. He said he expected them to shoot it out under any and all circumstances. It was what Fiorello would have done himself if he were a cop. The order made me think of his scathing attack on Dutch Schultz in 1931. The gangster numbered among his friends powerful Bronx officials and even sported a deputy sheriff's badge. The papers blazoned Fiorello's disparaging remarks, and there was muttering to the effect that the outspoken Congressman was a candidate for a bullet. I felt a little alarm, and one night, after a particularly blistering attack on New York judges who had gangster pals, I insisted on walking home with him. He wanted to know why. I didn't want to tell him, but he pressed me and I finally said I was afraid he might get shot at. He looked very tired. Then he brightened up and said, "Oh, well, a bullet in the head is a good way to die."

By and large, though, Fiorello thoroughly enjoyed himself as Mayor. His office gave him plenty of opportunity to indulge his fondness for the spotlight. Leading a contingent of New York policemen in a Washington, D.C., parade was a routine gratification, but conducting the combined Police and Sanitation departments' bands to a capacity Carnegie Hall audience was meat and drink. The city was virtually tied up for days as its two key departments braced themselves for the ordeal. Everybody was afraid that Fiorello the Conductor might let loose on them as Fiorello the Mayor. The stage manager of this stupendous spectacle took no chances and went down to City Hall for final instructions. He asked Fiorello how he wanted the spotlights used. "Shall I play them on you as you come down the aisle, and follow you right up to the podium, Mr. Mayor?"

"Hell, no!" said Fiorello. "Just treat me like Toscanini!"

THE NOBLE EXPERIMENT

THE story of Prohibition belongs mostly to the Twenties; but the excesses, the contradictions, the failure of that "experiment noble in motive" came to their natural conclusion in the Thirties.

The excesses—in the evolution of a multibillion-dollar industry outside the law and against the law—reached their greatest heights in the early Thirties; and everywhere the public saw the criminal manifestations.

The contradictions—in the almost universal use of the liquor that the Eighteenth Amendment had supposedly banished—were everywhere apparent; everywhere the "best people" enjoyed liquor, seemingly without fear of censure. The speakeasy, operating outside the law through undercover payments to local law-enforcement officers, had taken on a peculiar glamour for its customers; and the man who had "his own bootlegger" achieved a special status in the eyes of his fellow citizens.

The failure—in that the law had become the supporting props of a criminal industry; that it had been largely annulled in most aspects; and that it had become an enormously expensive "nonlaw" to enforce—had become inescapable to the vast majority of Americans.

The over-all question of Prohibition was explored and re-explored in countless forums. Proponents invoked the authority and wisdom of the Scriptures and presented sociological statistics. Opponents cited criminological statistics and invoked the Articles of the Constitution. But nowhere was there an acknowledged consensus.

By 1932, an election year, forces were set in motion to roll back the Eighteenth Amendment. The Democrats—the "wet" party—agreed at their national convention to include within their platform a plank that called for repeal. Roosevelt made reference to it in the course of his campaign, and it was one of the issues on which the electorate voted.

However, in February 1933, before Roosevelt's inaugural, the lame-duck Congress approved the submission of the Twenty-first Amendment to the states for ratification.

In the selection which follows, Frederick Lewis Allen tells us what happened when the thirty-sixth state ratified the Amendment that abolished Prohibition—and ended an era.

FREDERICK LEWIS ALLEN

REPEAL*

AT THIRTY-TWO and a half minutes past three (Mountain Time) in the afternoon of the fifth of December, 1933, the roll call in the ratification convention in Utah was completed, and Utah became the thirty-sixth state to ratify the Twenty-first Amendment to the Constitution, repealing the Prohibition Amendment. A telegram went off to Washington, and presently the Acting Secretary of State and the President declared that Prohibition was at an end, after a reign of nearly fourteen years.

Crowds of men and women thronged the hotels and restaurants waiting for the word to come through that the lid was off, and when at last it did, drank happily to the new era of legal liquor. They thronged, too, to those urban speakeasies which had succeeded in getting licenses, and remarked how readily the front door swung open wide at the touch of the doorbell. But the celebration of the coming of repeal was no riot, if only because in most places the supply of liquor was speedily exhausted: it took time for the processes of distribution to get into motion. And as for the processes of legal manufacture—which for distilled liquors are supposed to include a long period of aging—these were so unready that an anomalous situation developed. The available liquor was mostly in the hands of bootleggers; even the legal liquor was mostly immature. Among the people who, during the first days and months of repeal, rejoiced in at last being able to take a respectable drink of "good liquor" instead of depending upon "this bootleg stuff," thousands were consuming whisky which consisted simply of alcohol acceptably tinted and flavored. To a public whose taste had been conditioned for years by bootleg liquor, good bush needed no wine.

Drinking, to be sure, did not become legal everywhere. Eight states remained dry—all of them Southern except North Dakota, Kansas, and Oklahoma. (These states received—at least in the years immediately following repeal—very little assistance from the federal government in protecting their aridity.) Fifteen states made the selling of liquor a state monopoly—though seven of these permitted private sale under varying regulations,

* From Frederick Lewis Allen's *Since Yesterday* (New York, Harper, 1940).

most of which, in a determined effort to prevent "the return of the saloon," forbade perpendicular drinking and insisted—at least for a time—that drinkers be seated at restaurant tables.

Despite these qualifications, the change in the American mores which began in 1933 was tremendous.

Hotels and restaurants blossomed with cocktail lounges and taprooms and bars, replete with chromium fittings, mirrors, bright-colored modern furniture, Venetian blinds, bartenders taken over from the speakeasies, and bartenders who for years had been serving at the oyster bar or waiting on table, and, now, restored to their youthful occupation, persuaded the management to put on the wine list such half-forgotten triumphs of their ancient skill as Bronx and Jack Rose cocktails. So little building had been going on during the Depression that the architects and decorators had had almost no chance for years to try out the new principles of functional design and bright color and simplified furniture; now at last they had it, in the designing of cocktail lounges—with the odd result that throughout the nineteen-thirties most Americans instinctively associated modernist decoration with eating and drinking.

Hotels in cities which in days gone by would have frowned upon the very notion of a night club now somewhat hesitantly opened night clubs with floor shows—and found they were a howling success. Neat new liquor stores opened—in some States operated by government authority, in others under private ownership. It took some time for customers to realize that it was no longer necessary for a man carrying home a package of rum to act the part of a man carrying home a shoe box; and in some towns where the dry sentiment was still strong, there were men who continued to patronize bootleggers rather than subject themselves to the embarrassment of walking into the state liquor shop.

Whether there was more drinking after repeal than before cannot be determined statistically, owing to the obvious fact that the illicit sale of liquor was not measured. The consensus would seem to be that drinking pretty surely increased during the first year or two and probably increased in quantity thereafter, but that on the whole it decreased in stridency.

One change was manifest; there was more mixed drinking than ever, just as there was more smoking by both sexes. (In the six years from 1930 to 1936 the production of cigarettes went up from 123 billion to 158 billion, while the production of cigars decreased a little.) On the whole, men and women were spending more of their time in one another's company and less of their time segregated from one another. Perhaps it was not an altogether unrelated fact that most men's clubs were still somewhat anxiously seeking members throughout the nineteen-thirties and that many of the lodges were in dire straits. Was it not possible to infer that the male sex, for one, was enjoying mixed company too well to want very urgently to get away from it? Possibly the cause of feminism was triumphing in a way which the earnest suffragists of a generation before would never have expected—and at which they might have been dismayed.

And what became of the bootleggers? Some of them went into the legitimate liquor business or other legitimate occupations, some of them went into business rackets and gambling rackets, some joined the ranks of the unemployed—and a large number of them went right on bootlegging. For one of the most curious facts about the postrepeal situation was that the manufacture and smuggling and wholesaling of illicit liquor continued in great volume. The federal government and the states, in their zeal to acquire revenue from the sale of liquor, had clapped upon it such high taxes that the inducement to dodge them was great. Year after year the Internal Revenue agents continued to seize and destroy stills at the rate of something like 15,000 a year, and straightway new ones sprang up. In his report for the fiscal year ending June 30, 1938, the Commissioner of Internal Revenue, reporting that only 11,407 stills had been seized, noted, "This is the first year since the enactment of the Twenty-first Amendment that there has been a decline in illicit distillery seizures." Likewise rum-running—or, to be more accurate, the smuggling of alcohol—continued to provide a headache for the customs officers and the Coast Guard; in February 1935, more than a year after repeal, the Coast Guard found twenty-two foreign vessels lying at sea *at one time* beyond our customs waters, waiting for a chance to sneak in.

THE WORST CRIME OF ALL

KIDNAPINGS increased at an alarming rate in the early Thirties. In Chicago alone, police recorded two hundred kidnapings in 1930 and 1931, with ransom payments amounting to two million dollars.

In 1932 the Lindbergh kidnaping shocked the nation and an aroused Congress enacted a law prescribing graded penalties, including execution, for abductions across state lines. Thereafter if a kidnaping was classed as a federal offense the F.B.I. was automatically brought into the case.

The FBI compiled a formidable record; from 1932 to 1937 they solved all but one of the kidnaping cases in which they had performed investigative work. The Lindbergh case was solved, and the death sentence was meted out as punishment. Such achievements discouraged would-be kidnapers, and by the end of the decade this crime was almost a rarity.

In the two selections that follow, Frederick Lewis Allen and Stanley Walker review, from different angles, the most celebrated—and consequential—kidnaping in our criminal annals.

FREDERICK LEWIS ALLEN

THE LINDBERGH CASE*

ON THE EVENING of the first of March 1932, an event took place which instantly thrust everything else, even the grim processes of Depression, into the background of American thought. The baby son of Colonel and Mrs. Charles A. Lindbergh was kidnaped—taken out of his bed in a second-story room of the new house at Hopewell, New Jersey, never to be seen again alive.

Since Lindbergh's flight to Paris nearly five years before, he had occupied a unique and unprecedented position in American life. Admired almost to the point of worship by millions of people, he was an uncrowned prince; and although he fiercely shunned publicity, everything he did was so inevitably news that the harder he tried to dodge the limelight, the more

* From Frederick Lewis Allen's *Since Yesterday* (New York, Harper, 1940).

surely it pursued him. His new house at Hopewell, remote and surrounded by woods, had been built largely as a retreat in which the Lindberghs could be at peace from an intrusive world.

And now, suddenly, this peace was shattered. Within a few hours of the discovery that the Lindbergh baby's bed was empty—the blankets still held in place by their safety pins—a swarm of police and newspaper men had reached the house and were trampling about the muddy grounds, obliterating clues. And when the news broke in the next morning's newspapers, the American people went into a long paroxysm of excitement.

More police and reporters arrived; the nearest railroad station was transformed into a newspaper headquarters; news from Hopewell crowded everything else to the back pages of the papers; President Hoover issued a statement, the governor of New Jersey held police conferences, anti-kidnaping bills were prepared by legislators in several states, the New York *Times* reported the receipt on a single day of 3,331 telephone calls asking for the latest news. Bishop Manning of New York sent his clergy a special prayer for immediate use, declaring, "In a case like this we cannot wait till Sunday." William Green asked members of the American Federation of Labor to aid in the hunt for the criminal. Commander Evangeline Booth urged all commanding officers of the Salvation Army to help, and referred to "the miraculous accomplishments with which God has honored our movement along these very lines through our lost and found bureau." Clergymen of three denominations prayed over the radio for the baby's deliverance. Wild rumors went about. Babies resembling the Lindbergh child were reported seen in automobiles all over the country. The proprietor of a cigar store in Jersey City brought the police on the run by reporting that he had heard a man in a telephone booth say something that sounded like a kidnaper's message. And the Lindberghs received endless letters of advice and suggestion—the total running, in a few weeks, to one hundred thousand.

From day to day the drama of the search went on—the Lindberghs offering immunity to the kidnaper in a signed statement, giving out the pathetic details of the baby's accustomed diet, asking two racketeering bootleggers named Spitale and Bitz to serve as intermediaries with the underworld; and soon the chief actors in the Hopewell drama became as familiar to the American newspaper-reading public as if the whole country had been engaged in reading the same detective story. Mr. and Mrs. Oliver Whateley, the butler and his wife; Betty Gow, the nurse; Arthur Johnson, her sailor friend; Colonel Schwarzkopf of the New Jersey State Police; Violet Sharpe, the maid at the Morrows' house, who committed suicide;

and Dr. John F. Condon ("Jafsie"), the old gentleman in the Bronx who made the first personal contact with the kidnaper—these men and women became the subjects of endless conjectures and theorizings. When a stranger asked one, "Have they found the baby?" there was never an instant's doubt as to what baby was meant, whether the question was asked in New Jersey or in Oregon. One would hear a hotel elevator man saying out of the blue, to an ascending guest, "Well, I believe it was an inside job"— to which the guest would reply heatedly, "Nonsense, it was that gang in Detroit." If the American people had needed to have their minds taken off the Depression, the kidnaping had briefly done it.

On March 8, a week after the crime, old Dr. Condon—college lecturer and welfare worker in "the most beautiful borough in the world," as he called the Bronx—conceived the odd idea of putting an advertisement in the Bronx *Home News,* to the effect that he would be glad to serve as an intermediary for the return of the Lindbergh child. The next day he received a letter, misspelled in an odd Germanic way, containing an enclosure addressed to Colonel Lindbergh. He called up the house at Hopewell, was asked to open the enclosure, described some curious markings on it, and at once was asked to come and see Colonel Lindbergh—for those markings were identical with the code symbols on a ransom note which had been left on the window sill of the baby's room! On March 12, Dr. Condon received a note which told him to go to a hot-dog stand at the end of the Jerome Avenue elevated railroad. He found there a note directing him to the entrance of Woodlawn Cemetery. He presently saw a man in the shrubbery of the cemetery, and he went with this man to a bench near by, where they sat and talked. The kidnaper had a German or Scandinavian accent, called himself "John," and said he was only one of a gang.

Further negotiations—which left no doubt that "John" was indeed the kidnaper, or one of the kidnapers—led to the payment of $50,000 in bills to "John" by Dr. Condon (accompanied by Colonel Lindbergh) in St. Raymond's Cemetery in the Bronx on April 2—whereupon "John" handed Dr. Condon a note which said that the baby would be found safe on a "boad" (meaning *boat*) near Gay Head on Martha's Vineyard. The Colonel made two flights there by plane and found no "boad"; clearly the information given was false.

Then on the evening of May 12, 1932, about six weeks after the kidnaping, the newsboys chanted extras in the streets once more: the child's body had been found by chance in a thicket near a road five and a half miles from the Lindbergh place. Whether he had been killed deliberately or accidentally would never be known; in any event, the kidpaper had chosen that spot to half-bury the little body.

"BABY DEAD" announced the tabloid headlines: those two words sufficed.

A great many Americans whose memories of other events of the decade are vague can recall just where and under what circumstances they first heard that piece of news.

The story seemed to have reached its end; but still the reverberations of horror continued. Soon it was clear, not only that the kidnaper had added the cruelty of Lindbergh's hopeless search by plane to the barbarity of the original crime; not only that Gaston B. Means had wangled $100,000 out of Mrs. McLean of Washington on the criminally false pretense that he could get the child back; but also that John Hughes Curtis of Norfolk, Virginia, who had induced Colonel Lindbergh to go out on a boat in Chesapeake Bay to make contact with the kidnapers, had concocted—for whatever reason—one of the most contemptible hoaxes ever conceived. These revelations, coming on top of the shock of seeing the Lindberghs forced to deal with representatives of the underworld (as if the underworld were quite beyond the law), brought thunders of dismay from preachers, orators, editorial-writers, columnists: there was something very rotten indeed in the State of Denmark. And the tragic sense that things were awry was deepened.

There the Lindbergh case rested in 1932. But we must go ahead of our history to recount the sequel. It came over twenty-eight months later, on September 19, 1934, when the kidnaper was arrested. Ironically, one of the things which facilitated his capture was that in the meantime the New Deal had come in, the United States had gone off the gold standard, and the gold certificates which had been handed over to the kidnaper had become noticeable rarities.

The kidnaper proved to be not a member of the organized underworld but a lone criminal—a fugitive felon from Germany, illegally in the United States—one Bruno Richard Hauptmann. He was arrested in the Bronx, was tried at the beginning of 1935 at the Hunterdon County Court House at Flemington, New Jersey, was convicted, and—after an unsuccessful appeal and a delay brought about by the inexplicable unwillingness of Goveror Harold Hoffman of New Jersey to believe in his guilt—was electrocuted on April 3, 1936.

The evidence against Hauptmann was overwhelming. Leaving aside the possibly debatable identifications of him and other dubious bits of evidence, consider these items alone: 1. Hauptmann lived in the Bronx, where

Dr. Condon's advertisement had appeared, where Dr. Condon had met "John" and where "John" had received the ransom money. 2. The numbers of the ransom bills had been recorded: many of these bills had been passed in parts of New York City accessible to a resident of the Bronx; it was the passing of one by Hauptmann in a Bronx garage which led to his arrest. 3. When arrested, Hauptmann had a $20 ransom bill on his person. 4. No less than $14,600 in ransom bills was found secreted in his garage. 5. He was a German, his tricks of speech corresponded roughly to those in the ransom letters, he had once used in an account book the spelling "boad," and he used other misspellings and foreign locutions like those in the ransom notes. 6. His handwriting was similar to those in the notes. 7. He had had no regular means of support after March 1, 1932, but had nevertheless spent money freely and had had a brokerage account of some dimensions (with which he was quite unsuccessful). 8. His story of how he got his money, through an alleged partnership in a fur business with one Frisch, and how he kept it in a shoe box on a shelf, was vague and unconvincing. 9. Furthermore, the kidnaper had left behind, at Hopewell, a ladder of odd construction. An expert from the Department of Agriculture, Arthur Koehler, not only found, from the sort of wood used in the making of this ladder and from peculiarities in its cutting, that it had been a part of a shipment to a Bronx firm, but also that irregularities in the planing of it corresponded to irregularities in a plane in Hauptmann's possession. 10. Finally, one piece of the wood used in the ladder fitted precisely a piece missing from a floor board in Hauptmann's attic, even the old nail holes in it matching to a fraction of an inch!

STANLEY WALKER

THE JUDGING OF HAUPTMANN*

THE trial of Bruno Richard Hauptmann, for the murder of the Lindbergh baby, which began in Flemington, New Jersey, in the first part of January 1935, was so spectacular, so bizarre, that in restrospect it seems almost incredible that things could have happened as they did. Everything conspired to make the trial dramatic. In its bare, simple outlines the case had

* From Stanley Walker's *Mrs. Astor's Horse* (New York, Stokes, 1935).

all the ingredients of a starkly realistic mystery story. But that was not enough. It remained for the press, the radio, the officials and the spectators to make of it a fantastic extravaganza.

The 300 or more reporters covering the trial filed more than 10,000,000 words. Foreign correspondents sent hundreds of thousands of words by radio, cable and mail. Many radio stations were busy broadcasting transcripts of the testimony. In addition, news commentators and extralegal authorities discussed all aspects of the case. Hearst's New York *Journal,* which was instrumental in employing defense counsel, and which paid the wife of Hauptmann $25 a week, had thirty reporters and a posse of photographers on the scene. The New York *Times* devoted more space to the trial than the other papers, simply because it had more room. It was, surely, the trial of the century.

One of the unforgettable characters of the trial was Edward J. Reilly, a criminal lawyer from Brooklyn, who had been retained as chief of defense counsel. Known as the "Bull of Brooklyn," Reilly had a long, successful record of defending criminals. His strength in his home county usually lay in political pull, oratory or convenient witnesses. As soon as he took over the defense of Hauptmann he began issuing statements. There were, he said, new witnesses. He knew who did the kidnaping. He knew many dark secrets. The forces of the prosecution, headed by David Wilentz, Attorney General of New Jersey, began answering Reilly, and this interchange continued up to the start of the trial.

The sideshow motif became evident early. Sheriff John H. Curtiss, of Hunterdon County, a fat man who came from New England, perceived almost immediately that he could make a good thing out of the trial. His first move was to keep the minions of Mayor Frank Hague of Jersey City out of the scheme. Mr. Hague is a man of considerable dignity, but some of his "boys" have a habit of "muscling in" on important trials, no matter in what part of New Jersey they are held. A committee of reporters, with one of the Hague men at the head, set out for Flemington to discuss seating arrangements. When they arrived, Sheriff Curtiss eyed the Hague fixer with contempt. After some blustering the Hague man departed, leaving the Sheriff in complete power.

The Sheriff informed each reporter, when he came to get tickets for his paper, that there would be a $10 tax on main floor seats and a $5 fee for balcony seats. Most of the reporters paid it, knowing that they could put the item on their expense accounts. But one young fellow from the New York *World-Telegram* telephoned his office before paying; the editor, in crusading mood that morning, ordered a story on the Sheriff's fee-fixing.

Then the fun began. The Board of Freeholders, all Democrats, announced an investigation of the Sheriff, who was a Republican. The Sheriff explained that he was only trying to save the county a little money, and that the "contributions" were merely to meet the cost of installing benches and a temporary press table. He offered free seats to the *World-Telegram*. The reporters, realizing that they would have to keep on good terms with the Sheriff for many weeks, let the matter drop.

Afterward the Sheriff was more cautious. A third person, connected with a telegraph company, could get anyone a ticket for a price. Even Mrs. Ogden L. Mills, wife of the former Secretary of the Treasury, had to pay to get in. Tickets could be obtained for $10, $5, a pint of good bonded rye, or a box of cigars. The Sheriff smoked cigars. Tickets were good for one session only; the reporters were lucky to have received season passes for $10 each. A ticket, of course, did not guarantee a seat. Many paying customers saw the show from the aisles, radiators and window sills. Panes of several windows were broken by eager spectators, adding a pleasant tinkle of falling glass to the regular trial noises.

On one occasion a woman drove up in front of the courthouse in a Rolls-Royce. Her uniformed chauffeur leaped out and open the door. The woman, wrapped in mink, stepped out and drew from her pocketbook a $100 bill, which she waved, announcing in a loud, clear voice that she would give all of it for a ticket. She got the ticket.

The first to realize the possibilities in the housing situation was Bert Pedrick, owner of Flemington's only hotel, a ramshackle three-story wooden building. He bought up options on most of the rooms available in the town. He paid the owners $1 a night and charged newspaper men $5 a day for room and board. After the trial Bert paid off the mortgage on the hotel and bought a new sedan.

Everybody in town was out to make money. The Women's Exchange, where homemade pastries, breads and rolls were brought by matrons during normal times for sale to their sisters, emerged as a tearoom. The Methodist Episcopal Church became a luncheon spot, with women from the auxiliary serving meals. This enterprise was subsidized by the state, which fed all its witnesses and officers there. After the trial the church bought a new organ. An evangelist from the Middle West saw an opportunity to save some souls while the trial was in progress. The Reverend J. Fred Bindenberger of Flemington liked the idea and promised the sky pilot his church. Other pastors objected. A compromise was reached under which the visitor agreed not to mention the Hauptmann trial in his exhortations. The revival was a failure.

The souvenir salesmen overran the place. One enterprising fellow made up a batch of miniature ladders. They were simple affairs, about eight inches long and two inches wide, the pine in them being of cigar box thickness. These miniatures were handed out to salesmen, who went about shouting that it was possible to purchase "exact duplicates" of the famous ladder used in the kidnaping for twenty-five cents. The ladders differed greatly from the principal exhibit in the case, but the buyers didn't mind. The ladders sold. One young man, highly excited, bought a ladder and tied it to his lapel with a red ribbon. He said to his companions:

"I'm going to leave it on too, by God! I'll march in on Gertie with it. Then won't she kick herself when she sees what she missed. The double-crossing bitch!"

A man with a metal press did a fair sort of business. He set up for business on the porch of the hotel. He had constructed a die depicting the Hunterdon County courthouse, surrounded by the legend, "Hauptmann Trial, Flemington, N. J." On the stand beside the press lay several hundred bright new pennies and several fine strips of copper. By running the copper strips through the press, together with the pennies, he turned out Lincoln heads backed by the courthouse and the legend. The pieces sold for five cents each, three for a dime.

The Flemington pottery turned out a set of book ends on which the courthouse appeared. These bits of clay were bought by the more wealthy visitors and today serve as parlor exhibits in many a home. A quick-sketch artist turned out portraits of Hauptmann and other principals of the trial by the dozen; post cards with scenes of Flemington were sold at five cents each; pictures of the jury ranged from a dime to twenty-five cents. The higher-priced jury pictures were "suitable for framing."

Boys from the high school made pocket money running copy for reporters. They had managed to get days off from school. These sharp lads hit upon a scheme of financing their yearbook. The town was overrun with autograph seekers. One day several of the boys appeared in the bar of the hotel with a large drawing board. They went from reporter to reporter and asked for autographs for the yearbook. It seemed that the book was to be dedicated to the reporters who covered the trial. As each man jotted down his name, he was asked for a contribution of twenty-five cents. The reporters didn't feel they could refuse. The boys also got signatures of most of the principals except Colonel Lindbergh and Hauptmann. A week later there was offered for sale at twenty-five cents each, copies of the sheet with the autographs, headed by the inscription, "The Trial of the Century." The youth of Flemington made a lot of money.

The crowds of curious were bad enough on weekdays, but on Sundays they were worse. After the first Sunday, when visitors stole everything in the courthouse they could get their hands on, the Sheriff wanted to close the place on Sundays, but the American Legion and the Kiwanis and Rotary Clubs volunteered to supply guards who would not only stop souvenir hunters but would answer the questions of the sightseers. When the visitors began arriving the second Sunday they found huge placards scattered about the courtroom. Over the chair of the defendant was the sign, "Hauptmann." Likewise there were signs indicating where the judge and jury sat, the witness chair, Colonel Lindbergh's chair, and the spot where Walter Winchell usually kept himself. The crowds were especially eager to see Mrs. Hauptmann and her little son. Every time the two appeared on the street, the crowd would rush for them. Somehow the sightseers seemed to find it astonishing that the child should appear as a pleasant-faced, chubby baby rather than as some sort of monster. Reilly wanted to have the baby brought into the courtroom, but Justice Trenchard, presiding, refused to allow it. Nevertheless, the jury got several glimpses of the child.

A man who got relatively little attention during the trial was Warden Harry O. McCrae, who guarded Hauptmann. Of course he got a few cigars now and then for divulging how Hauptmann had slept, or what he ate, but that was about all he got during the trial. Later, however, it developed that McCrae also had entered into the spirit of the thing. Because the officials feared that Hauptmann might attempt suicide if allowed to eat with ordinary knives and forks, he was forced to use paper utensils. The warden supplied this equipment, but when Hauptmann had finished eating, the warden hid the utensils in a little basket under his desk. After the trial he handed out paper spoons, forks and plates to any friends who happened to call—each and every one of them guaranteed to have been used by none other than Bruno Richard Hauptmann.

The macabre spectacle finally came to an end. The most dismal scene of all was the courtroom from the time the jury went out until it returned with the verdict of guilty. Justice Trenchard left the bench and went to his chambers to read. Attorney General Wilentz sat in the jury box. Reilly was in the witness chair. The floor was strewn with papers, cigarette stubs and remnants of sandwiches. Some, with paper bags in their hands, ate sandwiches and cakes and drank coffee, milk or applejack. The more sportive element played games of checkers and tick-tack-toe. Some of the journalists started a dice game in Justice Trenchard's library without his knowledge. Soon reporters, radio men, stenographers, lawyers and Broadway hangers-on were trying their luck. One man won $200 on two passes. A member of the defense counsel collected $75 and said, "That's more than I earned during the whole trial." At this point Justice Trenchard left his chambers and started for the library to get a book. The players, however, were warned. They quickly hid the dice and money and when the old justice entered the library he saw an unusually studious group of young men, all poring over law books. As soon as the justice left, the game was resumed.

Meanwhile, Wilentz, sitting in the jury box, amused his listeners with such jests as, "This is where I should have been in the first place." Reilly, in the witness chair, burlesqued the testimony of state's witnesses. He shot questions at himself, then pretended to be too deaf to hear them. He would cup his hand to his ear and say, "What was that? What? Repeat the question." Reilly is known far and wide as a card, and his barroom stories and repartee were among the most engaging aspects of the Flemington period. Before the jury came in Reilly and a woman reporter stood up in front of the judge's bench and sang "When Irish Eyes Are Smiling."

As soon as the jury had found Hauptmann guilty its members were besought by agents to go on the stage. The foreman was offered $800 a week and the other members $500 a week each. Some of them considered it seriously. So far had the carnival spirit run that many persons could see no impropriety in the jury going on the stage. This attitude was expressed by County Judge Adam O. Robbins, who had relinquished his post in order that Justice Trenchard might sit at the trial. Asked what he thought of the jury accepting the offer, he said:

"Couldn't blame them if they did. You don't make that much farming in a lifetime. Nope, I think it might be a good idea."

The vaudeville scheme collapsed, but the members of the jury did write (or rather, had ghostwritten) articles in which they discussed the trial. They also wrote a book, each contributing a chapter. These twelve men and women had become so impressed with their importance that they found it difficult after the trial to return to their ordinary tasks.

American newspapers were criticized because of the sensational fashion in which the trial was handled. There were many astounding excesses, violations of ethical canons, double-crossings by reporters and officeholders, and an unbelievable amount of trickery. Indeed, sound films of the trial were taken surreptitiously during the first few days, shown at a few theaters, and then suppressed. Undoubtedly the press and the radio people overstepped all limits of dignity, but they were not alone. The lawyers in some respects were worse. And there was printed during the trial a long, learned discussion of the evidence in the New York *Law Journal,* the official law periodical of the First Judicial Department of New York. This article discussed the evidence editorially as it had developed thus far, and pointed out that some of the testimony given was hardly credible. Many old-fashioned lawyers were perturbed at this.

It is difficult to see what could have been done to make the trial a model of decorum. It was too big, and the interest was too great. Justice Trenchard was not to blame; indeed, he did the best he could in a trying situation.

Two exhibits in the life of Flemington deserve mention. One was the menu devised by the owner of a hash house several doors from the hotel. The proprietor was not getting as much business as he had hoped for. His itinerant chef suggested a novel way of getting customers. One morning a sandwich board appeared in front of the place. It was headed "Trial Lunch." Some of the items were: "Writers' cramp soup, 10¢"; "Lindbergh steak, 50¢"; "Hauptmann beans, 35¢"; "Trenchard roast with Bruno gravy, 40¢"; "Jafsie chops, 50¢"; "Jury pie, 10¢"; "Reilly pudding, 20¢"; "Press custard, 10¢; and "Photog's ice cream, 10¢."

Another exhibit is a song sung around the bars, the hotel and the rooming houses of Flemington. It is a parody of the old German "Schnitzelbank" song, long a favorite in the beer halls. It is entitled "Du Schoene Hauptmann Trial," and goes as follows:

DU SCHOENE HAUPTMANN TRIAL

Ist das nicht ein dowel pin?
Ja, das ist ein dowel pin,
Fitted das nicht nicely in?
Ja, es fitted nicely in.
Dowel pin, etc.

THEY CALLED IT BANKBUSTING

IN THE early Thirties, individual desperadoes achieved national notoriety as never before; their exploits were front-page stories in the press and their relative "popularity" was determined by the order in which their names appeared in the FBI's list of Public Enemies. They were not members of the organized city gangs that ran the rackets and levied "protection" taxes on small businessmen, as did the Capone gang, for instance. With hard times upon them, these modern Jesse Jameses simply decided to take money from banks, killing in cold blood when anyone got in their way. This was outlawry in its oldest form.

At times the press and a willing public seemed to create a spirit of Roman holiday around these manhunts; the very names of some of the criminals suggest the publicity man—"Pretty-Boy" Floyd, bank robber and killer; "Baby-Face" Nelson, bank robber, kidnaper and killer; "Machine-Gun" Kelly and his whole family, kidnapers; Clyde Barrow and his gun-moll, Bonnie Parker, killers and hold up specialists; and the most publicized of them all, John Dillinger, bank robber and killer. The Dillinger manhunt was followed so avidly that when he was slain the whole country appeared to have experienced a kind of emotional catharsis.

Until 1933 a state line was the bankbuster's best friend. If he managed to get away from the scene of the crime and into a neighboring state, he was relatively safe from apprehension. There was little effective co-operation among the separate state police departments, and no central clearinghouse for the coordination of activities. The Seventy-third Congress, however, passed some twenty anticrime laws, including one that reorganized the Federal Bureau of Investigation, to provide for the apprehension and prosecution of interstate criminals. With such organization on the side of the law, the "percentage" in favor of the roving desperado was reduced. And with the centralization of responsibility for the pursuit of fugitives, the opportunities for flamboyant enterprise in the newspaper coverage of such man hunts disappeared. The heyday of the bankbuster was over, but it had been an exciting time while it lasted.

ALAN HYND

DILLINGER*

JULY 1933

THE time bomb that was to terrorize the Middle West began ticking a few minutes after eleven o'clock one morning early in July 1933. John Dillinger, Jr., twenty-nine years old, fresh from a nine-year stretch in the Indiana state penitentiary at Michigan City, had returned to his father's scraggly ten-acre produce farm outside Mooresville. His father, a small, stoop-shouldered man in his middle sixties, was standing near the water pump, thumbs hitched in his patched overalls.

A truculent fellow, John Dillinger was five feet eleven, weighed 170, and had reddish-brown hair, yellowish-brown eyes and a tight, mean mouth. In the months that lay ahead Dillinger's features, scowling from newspaper front pages, were to become familiar the length and breadth of the land.

"Hello, Pa," Dillinger said.

Old John didn't answer, just nodded.

"What's wrong, Pa?"

"It's your mother."

Up on the second floor, a worn woman lay panting on a four-poster. She was John Dillinger's stepmother—the only person for whom he had ever developed a genuine affection. She barely managed a smile. Before the sun went down that afternoon, she died.

That night, after the undertaker had called for the body, Dillinger sat with his father in the kitchen. "What was wrong with Ma?" he asked. "You never told me about her while I was away."

"It was her heart," said old John. "Her heart went bad after the banks."

Old John had lost his savings in a bank. The mortgage people now were threatening to foreclose on his farm. Savings banks all over America had failed during John Dillinger's last months in prison.

Next day, Dillinger went into Indianapolis, sixteen miles away, and walked into an employment agency.

"I'd like to get a job as a machinist," said Dillinger.

* Condensed from *True* Magazine, September 1956.

218

"How much experience have you had?" the interviewer asked him.

"A couple of years."

"Where?"

Dillinger cleared his throat and looked at his feet.

"I said, where have you had your experience?" the other insisted earnestly.

"Well, it's like this. I've been in prison. But—"

The man shook his head. "Not a chance," he said. "Employers aren't hiring ex-convicts. Jobs are too scarce. Sorry."

Dillinger got the same brush-off at other employment agencies. He checked the newspapers, but there were no ads for machinists.

Dillinger thought about the shirt factory in the penitentiary at Michigan City, where he had spent five of his sentence years. He thought of the four men—Pierpont, Hamilton, Makley and Clark—who'd been his closest friends while he was in prison. . . .

A few days later, John Dillinger walked into a rooming house on the South Side of Chicago and called on Homer Van Meter. Little Homer stood just five feet, one inch high. Twenty-six years old, he looked eighteen, with a round boyish face, guileless blue eyes and soft brown hair. As ex-cons, unable to get work, Dillinger and Van Meter were starting with a lot in common.

Dillinger was full of plans. "We could make an awful lot of money holding up banks. Me and you and a couple of other fellows could get together and make a nice living. You only got the cops to think about when you rob a bank, and cops ain't very smart. The people who work in the banks have got a lot of relations who lost money in banks. I'll bet some of the people who work in banks would be glad to see us. And anyway, it ain't their money."

AUGUST 1933

One afternoon early in August, Dillinger and Van Meter went to Wrigley Field to see the Chicago Cubs. This was the year that Bill Terry's New York Giants were to cop the pennant and beat Joe Cronin's Washington Senators in the World Series. Dillinger and Van Meter settled themselves in the grandstand along the third-base line and drank Cokes and munched hot dogs. What he was plotting, as he sat there with Van Meter, one eye on the ball game, was to spring his four old friends—Hamilton, Pierpont, Clark and Makley—from Michigan City.

"What we could do," Dillinger decided, "is put some guns in a crate of that thread they ship to the prison shirt factory. I've got a contact in that thread factory outside Indianapolis. Harry always opens the crates. I think I'll drop him a note."

A few days later in the prison shirt factory, Harry Pierpont (doing twenty years for armed robbery) opened a crate of thread and got the note. Dillinger was shipping in a load of guns and ammunition; Harry should stand by for a crate with a few splashes of black paint under the address lettering.

Pierpont passed the news along to an armed-robbery specialist named Harry Makley. Makley, in turn, told John Hamilton—a square-faced thirty-eight-year-old murderer known as Three-Finger Jack because he had lost the middle finger on his trigger hand in a Chicago gun fight. Dillinger's fourth friend who got the message that day was Russell Clark.

Dillinger went to a hot-car dealer in Chicago and bought a black Ford sedan, paying for it with cash.

Late one dark, sticky night, the third week in August, Dillinger was up on the loading platform of the thread factory doctoring up a crate of thread. He put in some guns, some ammunition and an envelope containing $1,000 in cash. Then he nailed it up and splashed some black paint under the address lettering.

SEPTEMBER 1933

A few minutes before noon on September 4, Dillinger and Van Meter drove into Indianapolis, got out of the black Ford and strolled casually into the State Bank in the heart of Indianapolis. There were six tellers' windows and the desks of three officers behind a mahogany railing out on the floor.

Dillinger and Van Meter stood at a counter facing the tellers' cages. Dillinger made a rough sketch of the premises on a deposit slip.

"I don't like the great big windows in this place," he told Homer. "People on the street can look right in and see everything. I'm going outside. You go over to one of the tellers and get a bill changed and while you're doing it act tired and yawn and stretch your hands over your head."

When Van Meter returned, Dillinger said, "I could see your hands. We got to make sure nobody puts their hands in the air when we hold up this place."

Dillinger spent the rest of the day cruising around downtown Indianapolis. He made notes of the distances between blocks—down to a tenth of a mile—how long it took traffic lights to change, how heavy the traffic was on certain streets and various crossings.

The nearest police station was five blocks from the State Bank. Dillinger, driving at normal speed over the distance, estimated that it would take the cops at least a minute and a half to reach the bank. So he put a time limit on the job—ninety seconds from the time he walked in until he ran out. He figured it would take the cops ten seconds at least to get into action.

A ten-second jump was all Dillinger asked for. By virtue of his study of the traffic conditions and his souped-up car, he could move in and out of downtown Indianapolis at least as fast as any pursuer. And if worse came to worst, he could always shoot his way out.

At four minutes after one the afternoon of September 5, Matt Leach * got a flash from the Indianapolis police. Two armed men had walked into the State Bank at one o'clock sharp. The taller of the two had announced a holdup but warned everybody not to put their hands in the air. While his companion covered everybody, the tall one forced one of the bank officers to take him behind the cages. There, he scooped up fistfuls of bills. Every few seconds he glanced at his watch and called to his companion: "Thirty seconds . . . twenty seconds . . . two seconds!" Then: "Let's go!"

Matt Leach quickly identified Dillinger and Van Meter. Through his experience as a municipal cop in Gary, Leach had established several solid contacts in the underworld. He couldn't get a line on little Homer but from a stool pigeon he learned that Dillinger was hiding out in Dayton, Ohio, in the apartment of a sister of one of his four pals in Michigan City.

Acting on Leach's tip, the Dayton cops hung around the apartment house and pounced on the unsuspecting Dillinger, taking him without a struggle. Dillinger, viewing his capture philosophically, grinned at his captors. "All right," he said. "You've won this hand. But you can bet I'll win the next one."

News of Dillinger's capture was soon buzzing over the grapevine at Michigan State [Penitentiary]. On the morning of the twenty-sixth Dillinger's four friends—Pierpont, Hamilton, Makley and Clark—equipped with the stuff he had smuggled in to them, overpowered two guards and a visiting sheriff and used them as hostages on a break.

At a few minutes after eleven o'clock that night the four escapees barged into a little gospel mission just off Fountain Square in Indianapolis. The intruders stripped four derelicts and changed from their prison clothes. In a few minutes Dillinger's four friends were barreling through the moonless countryside, planning to spring Dillinger from jail. One bad turn deserved another.

* Captain Leach was operating head of the Indiana State Police.

OCTOBER 1933

Sixteen nights after the Michigan City break, Pierpont, Makley, Clark and Hamilton drew up in front of the jail in Lima. Dressed in new suits and wearing snap-brim hats, the four walked into the warden's office.

"Who's in charge here?" asked Pierpont, the cruel one.

"I am," said Sheriff Jesse Barber.

"We're deputies from Michigan City," said Pierpont. "We've come to take Dillinger back to the penitentiary."

"I'll have to see your credentials," said the sheriff.

Pierpont reached toward his inside jacket pocket, drew a gun and emptied it at the sheriff—the first murder of the Dillinger mob.

When the sheriff's wife and a deputy came running in, the four outlaws grabbed them, herded them into a cell and slammed the door shut. With the sheriff's key Pierpont then freed Dillinger.

Shortly after midnight they pulled up to a darkened farmhouse that was not wired for a telephone.

Through an unlocked back door, Dillinger went inside. A dog sprang at him. He fired once and killed the animal.

A light went on in the house. The five intruders heard footsteps approaching. Presently a figure came into the kitchen. Dillinger snapped on the light and leveled his gun at the man in the doorway—a middle-aged farmer in bare feet and nightshirt.

"How many people in this house?" asked Dillinger.

"Just my wife," said the terrorized farmer, "and my two sons."

"How old are your sons?" asked Dillinger.

"Seventeen and eighteen."

"Get them down here. And your wife, too. I'm hungry."

Next morning, Dillinger sat in the parlor, listening to radio news flashes about the murder of the sheriff and the hunt for the killers. His four pals had split up to cover the family; the farmer and the sons were out in the fields as usual, not daring to tell.

Posses were scouring the countryside for Dillinger and the men who had sprung him, with orders to shoot on sight. Every so often one of the four others would come in and ask Dillinger what the news was.

"Everything's all right," Dillinger reported. "We'll just stay here until we can move."

Late in the afternoon, he decided they could safely get to Pierpont's mother's farm near Leipsic, about ten miles away. "We can dig a cave under the barn and stay there in case the cops do come around."

Mother Pierpont, a wrinkled old crone who spent most of her time sitting in a rocker in the parlor, smoking a corncob pipe, was not surprised to see them.

"Hello, son," she said to Harry. "What did you have to go and kill that sheriff for? Now, everybody'll be after you, so be careful."

The boys worked through the night, fashioning a cave under the barn floor. They scattered the dirt in the fields so it wouldn't attract attention. By morning, with Ma covering up the boards on top with straw, the five fugitives were safely hidden in the cave.

That very afternoon, Matt Leach, acting on a hunch, visited Ma Pierpont's place. First thing he did was to check the barn. Noticing the pile of hay over the cave, he gave it a few jabs with a pitchfork. But Matt jabbed horizontally, not vertically, and hit the straw, not the camouflaging floor boards.

Mother Pierpont kept the boys in food and reading matter, and one day Dillinger spotted a newspaper item.

"Listen to this! The cops in Peru, Indiana, just laid in a new stock of machine guns and ammunition to make things hot for us." He grinned. "We could sure use some machine guns and ammunition. . . . "

Next day, Homer Van Meter, who had been lying low in Chicago, appeared at the Pierpont farm.

"How'd you know where we were?" Dillinger asked.

"Instinct," said Homer.

"You're just in time," said Dillinger. "I got a job for you in Peru."

Dillinger, Van Meter and Pierpont arrived in Peru late at night. Van Meter, coached by Dillinger, went into the police station and palmed himself off to the lone man on duty as a writer for a detective magazine.

"I want to write up a story about how you are protecting your community," little Homer said.

The cop showed Homer the new arsenal.

"You on duty here alone?" asked Homer.

"Yeah," answered the unsuspecting cop. "I get relieved at eleven o'clock."

At half past ten Pierpont walked into the station and asked the cop directions to Indianapolis. As the cop got up from his desk, Pierpont grabbed him. Dillinger appeared and helped Pierpont lock the cop in a cell. Then they cleaned out the police station and drove off with all the guns and ammunition.

Dillinger now went off alone on a reconnoitering tour. He spotted just what he was after in the town of Greencastle, some forty miles southwest of Indianapolis—the National Savings and Trust Company, a compact red-brick building right across the street from the courthouse. Putting on a pair of dark glasses, Dillinger went in and drew a sketch of the interior layout.

Two days later, Dillinger returned to Greencastle with Van Meter and Pierpont. He assigned little Homer to remain in the car, which was parked down the street from the bank, and make note of how many people went in and out. He and Pierpont strolled around town, looking over traffic conditions. Dillinger, on this second visit, noticed that there was more activity around the bank than he ordinarily cared for; too many people lounging around the courthouse. Nonetheless, the plum looked too ripe not to be plucked.

Back in the cave, at Mother Pierpont's farm, Dillinger and the others tossed the problem around. How could they pull a job with so many people looking on?

Dillinger finally got an idea. "We'll make believe we're movie people making a movie. We can rob that bank and everybody who sees it will just think we're making a movie."

The rehearsal, entered into by the boys with all the enthusiasm of amateurs getting set to stage a high-school play, had Makley standing in front of an imaginary jug with a make-believe camera and tripod and wearing his cap turned backward. Hamilton, who was to be attired in white shirt, open at the neck, and puttees, was carrying a director's megaphone. Little Homer, the assistant director, was standing by while Clark, the assistant cameraman, was carefully measuring the distance between the camera and the entrance of the repository of concentrated wealth.

A couple of imaginary people were to wander over from the courthouse and ask the boys what was going on. "We're from Paramount Pictures," little Homer was to explain. "We're shooting a scene of a couple of bank bandits escaping."

Dillinger and Pierpont, wearing yellowish make-up, and carrying machine guns, were then to appear and, on directions from Hamilton, go inside the bank.

The holdup accomplished, everybody was to be off in a car, in a cloud of dust, before anybody on the outside realized that the caper had been real instead of make-believe.

Something changed John's mind, though. Then, on the morning of the twenty-third, the boys pulled just another routine robbery—for them. They took to the hills with $74,382.14.

NOVEMBER 1933

Early in November, four months after he had begun operations, John Dillinger was wanted by two states and by the government of the United States. Ohio wanted him to take up where he had left off in Lima. Matt Leach wanted him for bank hold-ups in Daleville, Rockville, Indianapolis and Greencastle. The FBI wanted him for the Indianapolis and Greencastle heists, because the banks in those cities were national institutions.

The four bank jobs so far had yielded a total of slightly more than $127,000, of which Dillinger, after splitting with his co-workers, had kept roughly one fourth, or more than thirty grand. At the going rate for machinists, he had made as much in four months as he would have made as a machinist in twenty years.

Dillinger decided to make Chicago his headquarters. In addition to being big, Chicago had other advantages. Its police department was honeycombed by crooked cops who, should they be lucky enough to spot him, could be bought off.

Unable to trust anybody but himself, Dillinger wondered where to keep his wealth. He had no faith in banks, and he could not carry the money around with him.

Finally, under a variety of aliases, John rented about a dozen mail boxes in post-office substations around Chicago. He stuck about $20,000 in envelopes, and mailed the money to himself. Then he mailed all the box keys, except one, to one of the boxes. He went to a shoemaker and had him insert the key to the master box between layers of leather in one of his shoes. He retained more than $10,000 in cash, which he carried around with him for emergencies.

Assuming the name of Jack Lawrence, John moved into a semirespectable rooming house on the North Side. The other members of the gang—Pierpont, Hamilton, Makley, Clark and Van Meter, whose faces were totally unfamiliar to the average cop—were scattered in other rooming houses in the immediate neighborhood.

DECEMBER 1933

In the first week of December, Dillinger and Makley happened to notice a bank that was, surprisingly, both open and closed. The Unity Trust and Savings on West North Avenue had recently gone out of business, but a sign in the front window proclaimed that a room in the rear, used exclusively for safe-deposit boxes, was still open for business.

John went in. The safe-deposit room was in the rear, and Dillinger saw that there was just one attendant on duty, an elderly man.

Dillinger came out and told Makley to go in to the safe-deposit room and pose as a salesman of burglar alarms. Charlie was to find out if the place was wired for sound. In a few minutes Mackley reported back. The room wasn't wired. There was no electrical alarm system to thwart an assault on the place.

Dillinger got the boys together.

It was during that conference that Dillinger conceived something new in lookouts—a fake Santa Claus. Since Christmas was coming on, Makley, the fat one, was to dress himself up as Santa Claus, complete with pot and bell, and station himself outside the bank building. The fraudulent Kris Kringle was to keep an eye on things while the robbery was in progress. If anybody tried to enter the bank, Makley was to divert them by volunteering the information: "They closed early in there this afternoon. They'll be open at nine in the morning."

At one o'clock on the slate-gray afternoon of December 13, the caper got under way. Dillinger, carrying a suitcase, arrived and dropped a coin in Santa's pot. "Everything clear?" he asked Makley.

Charlie nodded. "Nobody's inside but the attendant."

John went inside, removed the sign from the window, and waited for his co-workers. Three-Finger Hamilton, Pierpont, Van Meter and Clark appeared within two minutes. All but little Homer went back to the safe-deposit room. Van Meter remained in the bank proper to act as a liaison between the boys in back and the Santa Claus out front.

The back room was a bare, stuffy, windowless affair, with only the one door. All four walls were lined with steel safe-deposit boxes. The attendant —a man named Johnston—sat at an oak desk in the far corner of the room, facing the door. He was quickly bound and gagged and Dillinger took his place at the desk.

Dillinger took a portable radio out of the suitcase, and tuned in on the police frequency. Pierpont and Hamilton got out an acetylene torch and began to work on the safe-deposit boxes. Grimly efficient, they had a whole row of the boxes open in less than fifteen minutes. Dillinger examined the contents. He had developed a good eye for what was negotiable and what wasn't. The valuable stuff he put in the suitcase.

At a few minutes after two, an elderly gentleman who had got by the outside boys ambled into the back room. "What's going on here?" he snapped.

"What's your box number, dad?" asked Dillinger, friendly but business-like.

"Five hundred and three. Why?"

Dillinger asked Hamilton if he had come to Box 503.

"We're just opening that row now," said Hamilton, not even turning around to look at the depositor.

"Just stand over here in the corner, dad," said Dillinger, tying up the old man.

At a quarter to three, Pierpont and Hamilton had torched their way into about three hundred boxes. Dillinger had collected more than $70,000 in cash and about $150,000 in negotiable bonds.

At five minutes before three o'clock—the hour a signal would go off if the bound-up attendant didn't punch in—the boys packed up and left. They departed the premises one by one, split up and walked casually out of sight, Dillinger carrying the suitcase.

The caper in the safe-deposit room caused quite a furor in Chicago. Matt Leach quickly identified the culprits and kept pestering the Chicago cops to flush them. Late one afternoon, when the dusk was thickening, a detective recognized Three-Finger Jack on the street. But Three-Finger Jack saw the cop first and murdered him on the spot.

The murder made things too hot even for Dillinger. He decided to go to Florida with a woman he'd picked up—Evelyn Frechette—Makley, Pierpont, Clark and three ladies of casual morals whom the latter three had acquired. Three-Finger Jack was to lie low until things quieted down. Little Homer was to make a business trip through the Middle West, looking for new banks to bust.

Criminals on the lam, Dillinger had learned, usually traveled in high-powered cars by night. "We'll go in secondhand Fords," Dillinger said, "and we'll travel in the daytime."

The eight travelers, riding in two Ford sedans, arrived in Daytona Beach a few days before Christmas. Makley, cast by Dillinger in the role of a Wall Street broker, went to a real-estate office and rented a seventeen-room house on the waterfront. It was quiet on the waterfront in late December and the boys had nothing to do except lie around.

There they were, then, with no money worries, with no work crying to be done, and with their physical wants taken care of. And were they happy? You bet they were.

But finally Pierpont and Makley, the frisky ones, began to crave action.

Their share of the loot was burning holes in their pockets. They went into Daytona Beach and bought Cadillac roadsters, paying cash.

On New Year's Eve, Evelyn Frechette appeared wearing a slinky black evening gown. She asked Dillinger, "What are we goin' to do tonight? It's New Year's Eve, you know, Johnnie."

"Nothin'," said Dillinger. "We're stayin' right here."

Pierpont and Makley felt like getting drunk. Dillinger, who never drank, decided it might be fun to try some liquor.

Along toward midnight, the four boys and the four girls were out on the veranda, feeling no pain. Pierpont, hunched over the balustrade, was looking out at the water. The tide was coming in and the whitecaps, visible in the moonlight, were big and loud. He thought it would be fine sport to shoot at the whitecaps. Dillinger, feeling his liquor, agreed. So Harry went inside and brought out three machine guns. The boys waited for midnight. Then, when they heard the whistles blowing, they emptied the machine guns at the whitecaps. A neighbor, hearing the racket, called the cops.

When Pierpont saw a prowl car pulling up in front of the house, he said to Dillinger, "It's the cops. Let's kill the bastards!"

Dillinger, suddenly regaining sobriety, vetoed the suggestion. "I'll take the guns inside," he told Pierpont and Fat Charlie. "Just tell the cops you're sorry you made so much noise. And be real nice about it, too."

JANUARY 1934

Everybody slept until noon New Year's Day. The girls made scrambled eggs and coffee. Dillinger, settling himself in a big chair, began to leaf through a local newspaper that Makley had brought home the previous day. Suddenly, he stiffened. "Hey, Pierpont," he yelled. Pierpont came in from another room. "Look at this in the paper here!" said Dillinger. He pointed to a photograph of a man sitting at the wheel of a white Cadillac roadster.

Dillinger was furious. "You stupid fool! I ought to blow your brains out." Pierpont had actually posed in his new Cadillac for the publicity-conscious dealer who had sold it to him.

"Matt Leach reads every paper printed and he'll see that picture," Dillinger said. He turned to the hallway leading upstairs. "Hey, Evelyn!" he yelled. "Pack up right away. We got to get out of here quick!"

Dillinger decided not to stay with Makley, Pierpont, Clark and their molls. He and Evelyn drove west to Nebraska, then turned around and headed back east. On the way back Dillinger dropped several taunting postal cards to Matt Leach. Every card said the same thing:

Having wonderful time. Wish
you were here.

JOHN DILLINGER

Leach knew the cards were genuine because the handwriting matched
with authentic Dillinger penmanship. The postmarks on the cards indicated
that John was traveling from west to east. Leach deduced that Dillinger
was using the cards as a red herring and after mailing the last card he
would turn around and head west.

But John did no such thing. He kept going straight to Chicago, landing
there the second week in January. Pierpont, Makley and Clark had meantime gone to Tucson, Arizona, because Evelyn had told John that Tucson
was a nice place and thought they should eventually go there. One attractive feature of Tucson was its proximity to the Mexican border. If
things got too hot, Dillinger planned to go there with his girl.

Settled in Chicago, Dillinger contacted Three-Finger Jack, who had
been lying low after murdering the detective, and little Homer, who had
been off on a scouting trip. Little Homer told John that there was a bank
in East Chicago, Indiana, that was just begging to be taken.

Dillinger rubbed his hands together. "In Indiana, eh. Won't Matt Leach
be surprised if I hit his territory again!"

Arriving in East Chicago with Three-Finger Jack and little Homer,
John made a tour of the downtown district. The First National Bank and
Trust Company was a handsome, two-story marble building that accom-
modated, on each side of the entrance, a drugstore and a dime store. The
traffic in front of the bank was quite heavy. There was a cop on the beat
—a fellow named O'Malley—whose movements, Dillinger noted, seemed
to be erratic.

Until now, it had never occurred to Dillinger to wear a bulletproof vest.
But, with the instinct that some criminals have, he decided to equip himself
with one for the East Chicago job. He sent little Homer, the innocent-
looking errand boy, to Chicago to buy one.

Dillinger and Hamilton were to go into the bank at 11 A.M. sharp and
spend exactly four minutes inside. Little Homer was to remain outside to
keep an eye on things.

The day of the robbery, Dillinger's souped-up Ford pulled to a stop in
front of the bank. Dillinger and Hamilton, carrying machine guns in two
suitcases, walked inside. They laid the suitcases on a counter reserved for
customers, and casually extracted the machine guns.

"Keep your hands at your sides!" Dillinger told the dozen customers and
the bank help. Hamilton kept an eye on everybody, while Dillinger went

behind the cages and scooped up stacks of bills. He lined his pockets with more than $40,000 in fives and tens.

Dillinger's four minutes were just about up when Van Meter popped in, jerking his thumb in the direction of the door. Dillinger came out from behind the cages to cope with the emergency.

Patrolman O'Malley walked in. As O'Malley drew his service revolver, Dillinger raised his machine gun. The machine gun jammed. Three-Finger Jack couldn't help out because he was standing directly behind Dillinger, and little Homer was unarmed.

Everybody dropped to the floor except the three outlaws and the cop. O'Malley emptied his service revolver at Dillinger. John's hunch about that bulletproof vest paid off.

The last of O'Malley's bullets had just bounced off Dillinger's vest when John got his gun going. Grinning, he practically cut Patrolman O'Malley in half. Fifteen seconds after the murder he and Hamilton and Van Meter were driving off.

A few hours later, Matt Leach exhibited a stack of rogues-gallery pictures around the East Chicago bank and got positive identifications on Dillinger, Hamilton and little Homer.

Van Meter and Three-Finger Jack blew to the wilds of Wisconsin. Dillinger, with Evelyn, ran for Tucson. There, at the Congress Hotel, he joined Pierpont, Makley and Clark.

On the night of January 23, they all gathered in Dillinger's room on the second floor of the Congress Hotel in Tucson for a little game of poker. Considering how well fixed they were, they played for comparatively small stakes. The game had hardly got underway when Dillinger, dealing, began to sniff the air. "I thought I smelled smoke," he said.

A minute or so later, Clark, who seldom said anything, spoke up. "Damn, it's awful hot in here."

Pierpont went and opened the door. A tongue of flame licked at him. "Christ!" yelled Pierpont, "this place's on fire!"

The boys and Evelyn got out, though, and holed up in rooming places around town. Somebody, however, had gotten a good look at Dillinger at the time of the fire and when the delayed take set in, the hunt was on. Evelyn went back to the Midwest, safely, but Pierpont, Makley and Clark were picked up, one by one, without a struggle. And then one night Dillinger, with his guard down, got out of his car after a little drive somewhere and, going into his hide-out, walked into a nest of gun muzzles and gave up without a word.

Thirty-six hours after the capture, Matt Leach walked into the jail at Tucson and faced John Dillinger for the second time.

"Hello, copper," said Dillinger, grinning. "Did you get all the cards I sent you?"

"Yes, Johnnie," answered Leach.

"What's on your mind, copper?"

"To get you back to Indiana to stand trial for the murder of that policeman in East Chicago. And your three friends are going back to Ohio for murder."

Dillinger was still grinning on the train rolling eastward. "There ain't a jail in this whole country strong enough to hold me," he told Matt Leach.

"We'll hold you in Crown Point, Johnnie," Leach replied.

When Dillinger, now coming into his own as a celebrity, got off the train with Leach at Chicago, the press was there in force, aiming questions and cameras at the outlaw as if he were a movie star. A fat woman with stringy reddish hair shouted: "Oh, Johnnie, I want to marry you!" Dillinger just grinned.

At Crown Point, Leach and two other cops drove up to the county jail with Dillinger and turned him over to the sheriff. The sheriff was a woman—Lillian Holley—who had succeeded her husband when a crazed murderer had shot him to death.

The cameramen wanted more pictures. They had no sooner begun to scream for their shots than the prosecutor of Lake County—a local politician named Bob Estill—got into the act.

Acme News Pictures got Sheriff Holley, Prosecutor Estill and Dillinger together and had a little chat with them. "The three of you line up," he said. "You stand on the left there, Mrs. Holley, and you stand next to her, Mr. Estill. You stand next to the prosecutor, Johnnie."

The photographer grew thoughtful. "Suppose," he said to the prosecutor, "you put your arm around Johnnie's shoulder. You, Johnnie, you rest your arm on the prosecutor's shoulder—just to show there's no hard feelings." The prosecutor and the outlaw followed instructions and the picture was snapped.

That picture was to have political repercussions for months afterward—the prosecutor posed as being palsy-walsy with the country's Number One criminal while the woman sheriff smiled on benignly.

FEBRUARY 1934

Dillinger was in the county jail in Crown Point, Indiana, awaiting trial for the murder of the cop during the bank holdup in East Chicago.

Mrs. Holley, the lady sheriff, had put on twenty extra outside guards—ten by day and ten by night. They patrolled outside the jail, carrying machine guns. But in her elaborate precautions, Sheriff Holley overlooked one thing—Dillinger's cunning.

When the lights were out one night, Dillinger wrote a letter of instructions to Homer Van Meter. Next day he slipped it to a prisoner who was being released. When Van Meter received the letter, which had been addressed to a hot letter drop in Chicago, he got busy following Dillinger's instructions.

Van Meter sat down and wrote a batch of letters, signing himself "Taxpayer," and mailed them from Crown Point. The letters, addressed to the local newspaper and to the city fathers, all struck one note: Taxpayers' money was being squandered on all those unnecessary guards around a stout jail.

One of the letters to the newspaper editor was published in the paper. The paper, impressed by the letters, ran an editorial suggesting that the outside guards around the jail were now unnecessary. The city fathers, impressed by the paper's stand, and fearing to run afoul of public sentiment, quickly disposed of the extra guards.

Now Dillinger addressed himself to the second half of the problem—the fact that the warden and his deputies came into the exercise area armed. One morning, while Warden Lou Baker was unlocking Dillinger's cell, Dillinger asked, "Warden, ain't you afraid that somebody might take your gun off you when you come in here?"

The idea struck the warden like a ton of bricks; he had never considered the possibility. He promptly dumped the problem in the lap of the lady sheriff. She then issued an order that neither the warden nor any of his deputies were to go into the exercise area carrying arms so long as John Dillinger was in residence. Thus, before the month of February was over, John Dillinger had removed the guards from the outside of the jail and disarmed those on the inside.

Sometime that February—probably during the last week—John Dillinger came into possession of a gun. . . .

MARCH 1934

At a few minutes after nine o'clock on the morning of Saturday, March 3, Warden Baker entered the exercise area and let Dillinger out of his cell. Baker was just inserting a key in another cell when Dillinger stepped up behind him and jabbed the gun in his back.

"Don't turn around, Warden," said Dillinger. "Just do as I say and you'll stay alive."

"All right, Johnnie. All right. What do you want me to do?"

"Call Blunk in here."

Ernest Blunk, the jail's fingerprint expert, came in, to be surprised by the gun in Dillinger's hand.

"Throw me your keys, Warden," Dillinger told Baker. He locked the warden and the fingerprint expert into his cell, where they stood meekly.

Dillinger, having learned the layout of the jail building and the location and the movements and the names of all the jailers, told Warden Baker to summon the others, one by one. There were five other special guards in the building. After leaving their arms outside the exercise area, they came in, singly. As each man entered, Dillinger locked him in the cell. In ten minutes he had the seven men locked up.

Half an hour later, Dillinger was far out in the open country.

The ticking of the time bomb was growing louder. . . .

Three nights after his break from Crown Point, Dillinger drove alone into Lima, Ohio, in a stolen car. He parked the car two blocks from the jail there. He pulled his hat down over his eyes, put on a pair of horn-rim glasses, and ambled through the darkness toward the jail. He walked to the edge of a flood of light illuminating the building. There was a crowd around the jail and the area was electric with excitement.

Dillinger eased himself into the edge of the crowd. "What's all the excitement about?" he asked.

"They're afraid that man Dillinger is goin' to come here and get his friends out," a woman told him.

"Is that so," said Dillinger.

"But he'll never do it," said the woman. "Why, they got a hundred guards around the place. National Guards, too."

Dillinger was considering trying the same stunt in St. Paul that had worked so successfully in Crown Point—drawing all those guards off. But Leach found out about those spurious "Taxpayer" letters. Getting hold of one, he'd had the handwriting analyzed. It was Homer Van Meter's writing. Leach not only tipped Lima off to watch out for such letters but broke the story in the papers.

Dillinger went to Chicago and contacted Evelyn Frechette. Then, he summoned Homer Van Meter and Three-Finger Jack Hamilton and the three of them roared through Indiana and Ohio, knocking over six banks in eight days for a total score of $103,000. He took his loot—one third —and mailed it to one of his post-office boxes in Chicago.

Matt Leach, at the State House in Indianapolis, was growing desperate. Governor McNutt was putting the pressure on him and the newspapers were putting the pressure on McNutt.

The Hoosier outlaw now had a hold on the imagination of the entire country. Practically every detective in the Middle West was carrying a rogues-gallery shot of John. Dillinger's likeness, pasted up inside the cages of banks, scowled down at the tellers. Bank tellers in Indiana and Illinois got jittery every time a strange man sauntered up to the windows. Some tellers, spotting somebody who aroused their suspicions, instinctively pressed alarm buttons. One day, the Chicago police rushed to eight different banks on false alarms.

The latest news about John—usually a baseless rumor of some kind— came out of radio loudspeakers. As the month of March drew to a close, the Hoosier outlaw's notoriety had spread across the Atlantic. The London *Times* and the Manchester *Guardian* were asking their correspondents in this country for all the news on Dillinger.

Newspaper offices around the country were being bombarded with tips, some sincere, others by practical jokers, that Dillinger was here, there, everywhere. With the exception of the Lindbergh baby kidnaping two years previously, no police case in the annals of American crime has ever stimulated the volume of tips that poured in while John Dillinger was at large. The Chicago *Tribune*, tongue in cheek, mirrored conditions this way:

Mr. Dillinger was seen yesterday looking over the new spring gloves in a State Street store in Chicago; negotiating for a 12-cylinder car in Springfield, Ill.; buying a half dozen sassy cravats in Omaha, Neb.; bargaining for a suburban bungalow at his home town of Mooresville, Ind., and shaking hands with old friends; drinking a glass of soda water in a drug store in Charleston, S.C.; and strolling down Broadway swinging a Malacca cane in New York. He also bought a fishing rod in a sporting goods store in Montreal and gave a dinner at a hotel in Yucatan, Mex. But, anyhow, Mr. Dillinger seems to have kept very carefully out of London, Berlin, Rome, Moscow and Vienna. Or at least if he did go to those places yesterday he was traveling incog.

The Detroit *Free Press,* taking the stand that things had gone far enough, addressed an editorial to J. Edgar Hoover, angrily ordering him to bring in the outlaw. The London *Daily Telegraph* inquired on its front page: "What Is Happening in America?" The Governor of Indiana, who since boyhood had nursed an ambition to be President, wondered how he could ever go to the voters and ask to run the country, when his own State Police couldn't run an outlaw to the ground.

MAY 1934

J. Edgar Hoover, tight-lipped and unsmiling, saw to it that the heat did not lessen in intensity when the not-so-merry month of May rolled around. Hoover continued to beseech the public to keep shooting in tips.

Evelyn Frechette was picked off a Chicago street and given a jail term for harboring a fugitive. Makley and Pierpont, found guilty of murdering the sheriff in Lima, were sentenced to the electric chair. Clark got off with life.

Dillinger began to feel very sorry for himself. His world was rapidly shrinking. He decided to hide out in Skid Row in Chicago. Not even the G men or Matt Leach would think to look for him and Hamilton and little Homer there.

Skid Row, only a few minutes by taxi from Chicago's Gold Coast, was a derelicts' purgatory. Here, from all corners of the land, came men with broken lives to find surcease in the "smoke" that retailed for as little as a nickel a shot. Detectives seldom thought to hunt down anybody in Skid Row. The reason was simple. The men who populated Skid Row were so far gone physically, mentally and morally that they didn't have what it took to commit nickel stick-ups, let alone a high-class job.

Dillinger and his pals were lying in a quarter flophouse one rainy afternoon when Dillinger fell to contemplating Hamilton's missing finger. "Be sure and keep that hand in your pocket when you're outside," Dillinger suggested.

Hamilton in turn suggested that Dillinger keep his face well hidden. "Every flatfoot in the country could probably draw a picture of you from memory," he said. "Them FBI passed around millions."

Dillinger didn't answer. But he grew very thoughtful. In a little while he said, "You fellows stay here—right in this flophouse here. I'm goin' away."

"For how long?" asked Van Meter.

"A few weeks."

JUNE 1934

Early one afternoon, the first week in June, John Dillinger returned to the flophouse. Three-Finger and little Homer were sitting at a smoke-stained table playing cards. Dillinger walked up to the table and stood behind Hamilton, facing Van Meter. Although both players had noticed Dillinger, neither paid any attention to him, marking him down as a kibitzer.

Van Meter looked up at Dillinger again. His eyes lighted up. "Look who's standin' behind you!" he told Three-Finger.

Hamilton studied Dillinger a few hot moments. "Well, I'll be a son-of-a-bitch! I wouldn't of known you."

Dillinger's hair was not auburn but jet black. He had grown a small bushy mustache. His eyebrows had been thinned. And he was wearing silver-rimmed eyeglasses.

"You look a lot younger, Johnnie," said Van Meter. "At least ten years younger."

Dillinger had been in a private hospital where a gangster physician had given him a face lift.

JULY 1934

When the month of July dawned, John Dillinger had a premonition of death. He was all alone now. Homer Van Meter, taking a walk one night, had been picked up by the cops. Three-Finger Jack Hamilton, sauntering out of the Skid Row joint for a breath of air, had been shot down in the street.

Dillinger left Skid Row, drew all his money out of his post-office boxes and carried it around with him. He got into a black Ford sedan and began to drive through the Indiana countryside, traveling by night, sleeping by day.

Early in July, Dillinger pulled into a gas station in southern Indiana to get the tank filled up. Just as he was leaving, he caught the attendant looking at him. He knew the attendant had recognized him. He was about to reach for his gun when two other cars pulled into the station. John drove off, certain he would be followed. The roadblocks would be up in a matter of minutes.

He turned in at a farm and knocked on the door. An old lady answered. "Who lives here with you?" asked Dillinger.

"Nobody, son," said the old lady, not recognizing John. "I'm a widow woman. I live alone."

"Mother," said Dillinger, pressing ten ten-dollar bills in the old lady's hand, "I need help. I want you to hide me. And if anybody comes looking for me you ain't seen me. Understand?"

"Yes, I understand." The old lady counted the money. "Why," she said, "you're John Dillinger!"

"That's right, Mother. I'm John Dillinger."

"Why," said the old lady, "you're not really bad at all, giving a poor woman like me money like this."

Next night, after Dillinger left, the old lady told her neighbors all about him. The papers got the story. A Robin Hood legend, phony as it was, began to attach itself to Dillinger.

On the tenth day of July, John Dillinger drew up to his father's farm outside Mooresville. It was noon and the sun was baking the dry brown fields. Old John Dillinger, working a tomato patch near the weather-beaten house, looked up at the car and squinted in disbelief. "Johnnie," he said, "it ain't safe for you to come here."

"I can take care of myself," said Dillinger. "I just wanted to see you."

The old man nodded toward the homestead. "We'll go inside."

"No. Let's walk in the fields. I want to walk in the fields."

"But somebody might drive by and see you, Johnnie."

Dillinger half laughed. "Nobody'd think of lookin' for me here, Pop."

The elder Dillinger peered into his son's face. "You look different. I can't say just why, but you ain't the same."

"It's this mustache, Pop."

"No, Johnnie. It's somethin' about the eyes."

Dillinger didn't answer. He took his father by the arm and walked into the fields. "I won't be seein' you again, Pop," Dillinger said. "Somethin' tells me that."

"Don't say that, Johnnie, I don't like it."

Seven nights later, on July 8, John Dillinger walked into a lunch wagon on the South Side of Chicago. "Coffee," he said to the waitress. "With cream and sugar." As he drank the coffee, Dillinger kept looking at the waitress, who was busy serving customers. She was blond and had a hard, pretty face. "Gimme another cup," said Dillinger.

Three quarters of an hour later, when Dillinger was ordering his fifth cup of coffee, the girl said to him, "You sure drink an awful lot of that stuff."

Dillinger glanced at a big wall clock; it was ten-forty. "What time do you get through?"

The girl smiled. "I get relieved in twenty minutes. Why?"

"I thought I'd take you home."

The blonde looked him over. "Okay, Buster."

Her name was Pauline Hamilton. She led Dillinger to a frame house a block and a half from the lunch wagon. They went up two flights of stairs to a small flat that smelled of good cooking. "Anybody home?" she called out.

"I'm in here readin'," came a voice from a bedroom.

"Come on out, Ann," said the blonde. "I want you to meet somebody." Turning to Dillinger, the blonde asked, "What did you say your name was?"

"Lawrence," replied Dillinger. "Jack Lawrence."

"What do you do for a livin', Jack?"

"Salesman."

A compact, square-faced woman of middle age, swathed in a fancy blue satin dressing gown, appeared in the doorway. "This is Ann," Pauline told Dillinger. "Ann Sage. She used to run a place in East Chicago. I worked for her, only we got closed up."

Ann Sage crossed in front of Dillinger and sat on a red plush sofa. "What's your name?" she asked Dillinger. "I don't think I got your name."

"Lawrence. Jack Lawrence."

"You new in Chicago?"

"Yeah. Just visitin'."

"We want to use the bedroom, Ann," said Pauline.

"Go right ahead," said Ann, picking up a magazine.

Next morning, over coffee in the kitchen, Ann Sage said to Pauline Hamilton, "That fellow you had here last night, I can't get him out of my mind."

"Why?"

"If he didn't have that mustache, and if he had big bushy eyebrows instead of them thin ones, I'd swear it was John Dillinger."

Next night, when Pauline walked into the flat with Dillinger, Ann Sage went out of her way to be nice to him.

The next day, Ann Sage walked into police headquarters in East Chicago and sought out Detective Martin Zarkovitch, a hard-faced man who was a good friend of hers. The friendship between Zarkovitch and Ann Sage had remained undisturbed despite the fact that the Sage woman had been closed up three times by the East Chicago police as the madam of a house of ill fame. Ann Sage was, as a matter of fact, in very hot official water that day when she went to East Chicago to talk to her detective friend. Miss Sage was a citizen of Romania and, under the law, was subject to deportation as a thrice-guilty lawbreaker.

"I think I know where John Dillinger is," Ann Sage said to Detective Zarkovitch.

"You don't say!" said Zarkovitch. "Where!"

"He's come to my flat twice now to see Polly Hamilton. He was there last night and night before last. And he'll probably be there again tonight."

The detective leaned across his desk. "You sure about this, Ann?"

Ann Sage was absolutely sure. Dillinger had grown a mustache and had

had his eyebrows thinned. But there were other things about Lawrence that checked with the known facts about Dillinger. Lawrence didn't smoke, drink or swear. His speech was definitely that of a Hoosier. And he was flashing a big roll of bills. No, there was no doubt that Jack Lawrence was John Dillinger.

At the very hour Ann Sage was sitting in the office of Detective Zarkovitch, Matt Leach entered the Chicago field offices of the FBI. He was ushered into the office of Melvin Purvis, the special agent in charge of the Chicago field office.

"I was wondering," Leach began, "if you had any line on Dillinger."

"No," said Purvis, "I wish we had. But we haven't the slightest idea where he is."

"No leads at all, huh?"

"Yes, we get leads. But every time we run them down we find they're false."

The next morning Melvin Purvis had two visitors—Ann Sage and Detective Zarkovitch. Ann Sage told Purvis she thought she could lead him to Dillinger, but she wanted to make a deal: if the FBI would pull strings in Washington with the Immigration Department to wash out that deportation rap, she'd put the finger on Dillinger. Purvis said he couldn't make a deal even if he wanted to; the FBI and the Immigration Department weren't that close to each other.

"All right," said the madam, "I won't put the finger on Dillinger."

Purvis said coldly, "If you don't, I'll arrest you for harboring a fugitive."

Purvis wanted to know where Dillinger lived. Ann Sage didn't know. Dillinger had never volunteered the information, and she had been too cagey to ask. Well, then, when was Dillinger expected at her flat again? Dillinger was coming the following night, Sunday, July 21. What time? About seven o'clock. Fine, said Purvis. He and several of his men would plant themselves in Ann Sage's apartment and surprise Dillinger when he came in.

Ann Sage shook her head. "Like hell you will," she said. She didn't want to have any part in the actual capture. She didn't want any publicity. What with trying to beat a deportation rap, it wouldn't look very good to have the papers come out and say that Dillinger had been visiting a girl friend in her apartment. No, Purvis would have to think of something else.

"Well then," said the G man, "when Dillinger comes to your place tomorrow night we'll take him in the street before he goes in."

Ann Sage, who was more or less in a position to call the shots, was against that, too. "I'll tell you what," she said to Purvis. "I think maybe I can talk Dillinger into going to the movies. *Manhattan Melodrama* is playing at the Biograph. Clark Gable's in it, and Dillinger's nuts about Clark Gable." The Biograph Theater, a neighborhood movie house, was less than two blocks from Ann Sage's apartment.

That was the plot, then: Ann Sage and Pauline Hamilton were to go to the Biograph Theater with Dillinger. He was not to be taken until after he came out of the theater and the G men could move in on him.

At a few minutes after nine o'clock on the night of July 22, 1934, John Dillinger sat in the fifteenth row of the Biograph Theater, between Ann Sage and Pauline Hamilton. Up on the screen, the picture was ending. Clark Gable, in the role of Blackie Gallagher, a gangster in *Manhattan Melodrama*, had been convicted of murder and was leaving his cell in death row to walk the last mile to the electric chair. "Die the way you've lived," Gable was saying to his cellmates as he started on the last mile. "That's the way to take it."

Dillinger, his gaze glued to the screen, didn't move a muscle.

The picture ended and the house lights went up. Dillinger walked up the aisle first, Polly Hamilton behind him and the Sage woman, dressed in a bright-orange-colored dress, behind Polly. G men, planted in the audience, spotted the madam's bright dress and fell in behind her. Several moviegoers brushed right up against John Dillinger as he made his way up the aisle, but they were too preoccupied by what had happened to the fictional killer on the screen to give a real killer a second look.

Outside, Melvin Purvis and twenty-two G men, sitting in parked automobiles, were straining their eyes for some sign of Dillinger or a signal from an agent emerging from the theater. It was Purvis who spotted Dillinger. "There he is . . . right behind Ann Sage!"

"Some picture," Dillinger was saying to Pauline Hamilton. "That Clark Gable sure is some actor." On one side of the Biograph Theater was an alley that had led to the theater's stage entrance when the place had played live attractions. Dillinger and his two companions had to pass the alley on their way back to the apartment. As Dillinger approached the alley, three G men were close behind him. The idea was to sneak up behind him and grab him before he could reach for his gun.

Dillinger was talking about the picture as he reached the mouth of the alley. Apparently he had addressed a remark to either Ann Sage or the Hamilton girl and was expecting an answer. None was forthcoming. He looked to the right. The Hamilton girl was not there. He turned quickly to the left. Ann Sage was not there.

With the instinct of an animal, John Dillinger knew he had been ambushed. He never stopped to look behind him. He just knew. He ducked into the alley and began to run.

He hadn't gone ten feet when the G men began to blaze away. That was all there was to it. John Dillinger was hit so fast and so often that he probably never even felt any pain.

THOSE WERE THE DAYS

REMEMBER how important a nickel was in the Thirties? A five-cent piece, the twentieth part of a dollar, purchased many things and many services. If you were a child and wanted to buy the biggest and best candy bar, a nickel would do the job. To get from the Bronx to the Battery by subway in New York, it took just a nickel. A local telephone call could be made by depositing only a nickel. Could Horn & Hardart have thrived without the stream of nickels passing through the glass windows in the Automat? And what about the cup of coffee, and the weekly magazines such as *The Saturday Evening Post, Collier's, Liberty* —just five cents. The juke box began to hum when the nickel dropped in, and the one-armed bandit (slot machine) earned fortunes, in nickels, for organized crime.

Let us assume, then, that it was a solid underpinning of daily business. In deep Depression, when any and all kinds of nostrums were proposed to cure the economy, someone might have decided that the ubiquitous five-cent piece was behind our troubles, and then decided on a program of action. The Great Nickel Panic didn't happen, but, believe it or not, there were even *crazier* schemes proposed for ending our troubles.

CREIGHTON PEET

THE GREAT NICKEL PANIC*

ONE AFTERNOON late in the spring, John B. Rutherford, billionaire and philanthropist, decided that the civilization extant in New York in the year 1931 was so excessively unsatisfactory as to require changing. The city was too large, traffic was very trying and life was not the simple, leisurely thing it should be. For one thing people were always taking subways and "L's," thereby getting themselves into the most outrageous and unpleasant crowds. For another thing telephones were forever ringing and taking the minds of the citizenry off the thinking of great thoughts. Again, such institutions as soda fountains and automats were rushing all the leisure and

* From *Vanity Fair*, September 1931.

fine flavor out of eating. In fact, this machine age thing had gone far enough.

For fully fifteen minutes the famous Rutherford mind revolved about the project of altering the current state of affairs, and at the end of that time Rutherford pressed a few mother-of-pearl buttons on his desk, calling in a selected assortment of private secretaries. In the following five minutes commands and instructions calculated to completely paralyze the more objectionable aspects of city life were given, and the secretaries set about their duties.

All modern life, reasoned the great philanthropist, depended upon the use of the nickel, or five-cent piece. Remove the nickel and life would eventually be forced to assume a more leisurely pace. It would take time, of course, to absorb all the nickels in circulation, but old Rutherford's patience was as unlimited as his vast fortune.

Two hundred actors out of work—men and women of all ages and types, and all sworn to the strictest secrecy—were engaged to go about the city collecting nickels. They were specifically instructed never to go to banks and ask for nickels in quantities. They were to take only such nickels as they received when asking for them. One day a worker would get nickels in automats, drugstores and cigar stores ("to 'phone") on the west side of Broadway, and the following day he would make a visit to the uptown local stations of the east side subway. A couple of weeks later he or she would attend to the drug and cigar stores on the east side of Broadway. Nothing was hit-or-miss. The campaign was executed with military precision, and every ten days each worker evolved a new disguise.

Four delivery trucks were fitted up and chastely inscribed AMERICAN SERVICE CORP., and set to patrol such well-traveled thoroughfares as Broadway, Seventh Avenue and Thirty-fourth Street. Whenever a worker spied one of these trucks parked for a few moments at the curb, he would climb up beside the driver and, after giving the password, he would be allowed to crawl through a small door into the interior of the truck. Here sat an accountant who exchanged twelve dollars for every ten dollars' worth of nickels produced. Some collectors were able to gather as many as a thousand coins a day, but the average haul was about five hundred. After dark, the trucks slipped, one by one, into the private driveway of the old Rutherford mansion on Fifth Avenue, the big gates were closed, and more sacks of nickels were noiselessly dumped into an unused cellar. Within a week the pile was as high as a man's head, and Rutherford ordered another storeroom cleared of old trunks and boxes.

It was fully three weeks before any public notice was taken of the shortage of nickels. By this time 2,100,000 subway fares had been salted away in the cavernous Rutherford cellars. By the end of the fourth week, when 2,800,000 nickels had been withdrawn from circulation, the public at large became suddenly and acutely aware that something was wrong with the economic world. Lines at subway change booths trebled in length, and each patron was allowed but one nickel at a time. Elevateds, surface cars, and some bus and ferry lines were slowed up considerably, and officials were losing much sleep trying to think of some way out of their difficulties. The telephone company was simply miserable, for it turned out that a lot of nickels, burning holes in people's pockets, were the cause of a tremendous number of phone calls. When nickels became difficult to find, or a call could only be made with a dime or a quarter, a lot of girls were left sitting all alone by the telephone, with nothing at all to keep them from reading good books.

The attitude of the press to the nickel shortage was at first frivolous. Columnists and cartoonists had quite a bit of fun with people who stayed home from work because they couldn't find a nickel to get down town with, and for some weeks city desks refused to take anything as trivial as a nickel shortage seriously. Who would hoard nickels, and why? Besides, there were so many millions of nickels about that no matter how many were lost or confiscated, there would always be enough to carry on business. . . .

But this optimistic attitude was suddenly altered on Friday of the fifth week of the Rutherford secret crusade. By this time some 3,360,000 nickels were lying in the vaults of the old Fifth Avenue mansion. On the evening of this day, rush hour crowds, furious at the long queues waiting at the subway change booths at Grand Central, pushed aside the guards, jumped over turnstiles, and forced open the emergency exists. The following day similar riots occurred in several other subway stations. The telephone company was facing a crisis in its affairs, and the Automat people were forced to close down all but the cafeteria sections of their high-speed restaurants. The same day advertisers were thrown into a panic by the news that *The Saturday Evening Post, Liberty*, and *Collier's* were dropping circulation heavily, and that the sales of five-cent candy bars were shrinking. You could, of course, buy two things costing five cents each by using a dime, or give a quarter in payment and receive two dimes in exchange, but an amazing number of people wanted to buy just one single five-cent article, and unable to do so, discovered that they hadn't really needed it at all.

Needless to say, the Rutherford agents had begun to have as much trouble finding nickels as anyone else, and even by patronizing the nickel scalpers outside the subway stations who sold two or three nickels for a quarter, they were often unable to find more than a thousand or so coins a day. By the end of old Rutherford's eighth week of crusading, 4,475,000 nickels had been withdrawn from use, and both city and Federal detectives were working on what the newspapers, now alarmed, referred to as the NICKEL PANIC and the FIVE-CENT MYSTERY. The directors of subways and other public utilities, unable to wait till the mints could issue extra coins, tried manufacturing slugs or counters, until it was discovered that fully as many bogus coins as they were making were being stamped out and sold in sacks, a dollar for a hundred. After a week this plan was abandoned, no more slugs were issued, and many of the makers of the fake counters were caught and prosecuted.

The end of the ninth week found 4,975,000 nickels out of circulation. At this time the Rutherford agents decided to exercise more caution in the collections. The agents made up sacks of nickels in distant apartments and hotel rooms and smuggled them into the Rutherford mansion in boxes of groceries, cases of liquor and other commonplace containers.

But it was not until twelve weeks after the work had started that old Rutherford's scheme showed any signs of success. A man named Smith, living on West 178th Street, announced that he was tired of the city's toil and strife and that existence must certainly be more pleasant out in the country where there were no subways, very few telephones, and where nickels were but an unpleasant memory. The newspapers got wind of Mr. Smith's ideas and printed big stories of his plan to take his family to the country and live the simple life. The following day eighty-seven more families announced that they were going back to their home towns, and the Real Estate board was pulling out its hair in large fistfuls. By the end of the week three thousand apartments were deserted, leases were but an idle jest, and some twelve thousand men, women and children had left the city. By the end of the seventeenth week thousands of "permanent" New Yorkers had gone to live in the country.

Old Rutherford was feeling pretty happy about things and pretty proud of himself as a public benefactor, when the papers joyfully announced that the U. S. mints, working overtime, were producing five million new nickels, one million of which were to be placed in circulation immediately. For a while things looked bleak for old Rutherford. People stopped moving out of town, the subways began to clog up again, and the whole plan began to look like a failure. But this setback was only temporary. On the eighteenth week the Rutherford collections jumped from a trifling 3,000 coins to 190,000, and a few days later it was obvious to everybody that the same mysterious agency which had swallowed all the previous nickels was fast making way with the new coins.

This news alarmed the civic authorities, and a mass meeting of the great men of the city was called to decide on a course of action. Foremost among the speakers was old Rutherford himself. He even mustered up a few tears for the occasion, and spoke touchingly of the wheels of progress, mass production, the majestic Hudson, and his early New York ancestors.

By the twenty-second week of the great crusade 6,682,000 nickels were safely hidden away and nearly a million people had left the city. About forty collectors were still on the job, but they were resorting to the most elaborate devices to escape suspicion.

Old John B. Rutherford had taken the curse of hurry from the greatest city in the world. He was a benefactor, an unsung hero. The following spring trees were replanted in Park Avenue, the elevated line discontinued running trains and planted flowers and vines in boxes along the tracks, and a thousand extra benches were ordered by the park commission. Business had more or less disintegrated, it was true, but life had at last become endurable for all those who were forced to remain in the city. People grew little gardens on the setbacks of their apartment houses, and a few years later such things as canned vegetables were unknown. The telephone rang so seldom that its sound became as welcome as the spring sunshine. Couples who had never even dreamt of such things had babies, and business slackened so much that even on a weekday you could see the sun just as plain as plain. The millennium, in fact, had arrived.

THE SYNDICATE

WITH THE onset of the Depression, there were fewer customers who could afford bootleg liquor. The repeal of the Eighteenth Amendment reduced the take of organized crime even further. The take from gambling, prostitution and narcotics may not have decreased, but the loss of illegal liquor sales prompted the gang overlords to move into the labor unions. They invaded the unions through transportation, a key operation in industry. By 1932, it was said that in Chicago Al Capone controlled two thirds of the unions or at least collected tribute from them; such trades as cleaning, barbering, baking and paving were under the thumb of gangsters.

In Detroit, the Purple Gang muscled into cleaning and dyeing, coal and the building trades, according to Irving Bernstein. In Cleveland, the undertaking business was taken over by the rackets, and New York was probably as racket-ridden as any other city. But it was not until the close of the decade that the extent of organized crime was made known to the public, in all its sordid details and subhuman riffraff, revealing a country-wide network, with a board of directors—the Syndicate. "To insure their organization, one and all concentrated on developing connections, on municipal, state and national levels. The cartel is so finely organized that it can swing elections in many places—and regardless of which political party holds the reins." *

One of its most ruthless arms, uncovered in investigations in the Thirties, was a group of murderers located in Brooklyn, known as Murder, Incorporated. Its members were employed to kill anyone standing in the way of "business."

BURTON B. TURKUS AND SID FEDER

THE ALMOST-ASSASSINATION
OF THOMAS E. DEWEY†

No ONE expected Dutch Schultz was ever coming back when he took off running at the start of 1933, about a step and a half in front of the Internal Revenue men.

* Turkus and Feder, *Murder, Inc.*
† From Turkus and Feder's *Murder, Inc.* (New York, Farrar, Straus & Cudahy, Inc., 1951).

The Dutchman had tried everything before he took flight. No amount of pressure from his political connections, however, had been able to soften Uncle Sam. After all, Schultz's income then was something more than just loose change. His return from beer alone, from 1929 through 1931, was a matter of $481,000, with all overhead paid. Then there were such other remunerative grabs as the protection racket and the numbers.

Even Dutch's sincerest supporters could see only certain conviction and a long stretch as guest of the government, if he so much as poked his face out of his hole. Gangland didn't especially care. When the boss mobsters voted the national Syndicate into existence in 1934, the absent Dutch was not wanted. He was isolationist—antagonistic to the new aim toward amalgamation. The bosses knew that, at heart, he was a mad dog whose maniacal outbursts and twitching trigger finger would get everyone associated with him into serious trouble sooner or later.

For most of his thirty-three years, he had been that way—this hoodlum scion of a Bronx saloonkeeper and a pious, patient woman whose great grief it was that the son she adored turned out as he did. Born Arthur Flegenheimer, he had a brief exposure to education in P. S. 12, where the principal was Dr. J. F. Condon, who was to achieve international notoriety as the "Jafsie" ransom man of the Lindbergh baby kidnaping.

At seventeen, Arthur was already serving fifteen months for burglary. When he emerged, his playmates nicknamed him Dutch Schultz, after an infamous member of the old Frog Hollow Gang of the Bronx. He began to put together a gang of his own. Notable among his early hired hands was Joey Rao, whose police record went back to 1920. It included sixteen arrests, and convictions for burglary and felonious assault. Once, while spending some time in New York City's House of Correction on Welfare Island, Rao was the "prisoner boss," in connection with such items as kangaroo justice and distribution of drugs.

In recent years, Rao suddenly acquired entrée to many and unexpected places. In November of 1950, a probe of politico-crime tie-ups was launched in New York, after Samuel Kantor, a district leader, charged that "underworld characters are exerting influence on City Hall." Almost the first names to pop up were Joey Rao and his brother-in-law, Joe Stracci, who is more notorious as Joe Stretch.

The probe uncovered a drive by Tammany Hall to oust former General Sessions Court Judge Francis X. Mancuso from his post as Democratic leader of the 16th Assembly District. For this purpose, a meeting of election captains, district leaders and officials of prominence in Tammany Hall and in the city government was held next door to Rao's home in

East Harlem. The District Attorney [Frank S. Hogan] described the meeting as a "gangster-controlled" political session. He said that Rao and Stretch showed up at the meeting and "laid down the law in strong-arm language."

"The presence of Rao and Stracci," declared Hogan, "had the same effect as if they had leveled a gun at the heads of the persons at the meeting."

Rao's explanation was novel, anyway. "I went over and looked into the house because I thought it was a crap game," he reported innocently. "It was a political meeting. So, I ain't interested . . . I go home."

For Dutch Schultz, back in the late Twenties and early Thirties, Rao advanced to the post of manager of Harlem for slot machines. Dutch had aligned himself with leading moguls of the one-armed bandits—Dandy Phil Kastel, the bucket-shop impresario, and Phil's boss, Frank Costello.

As Repeal neared, Schultz moved into the restaurant racket, snatched control of a window cleaners' union and grabbed the $20,000,000 numbers racket in Harlem. The profit in a single numbers bank ran as high as $4,000 in one week. He had a stable of prize fighters, raced his own horses and owned pieces of various night clubs. His gang of gunmen was the envy of mobdom.

When it came to principle, Dutch hit new lows, even for a mobster. He was a cheating guy always. His beer was the worst. His liquor was cut horribly. Even the 1,000-to-1 odds against the player in the numbers game didn't satisfy him. He hired Abbadabba Berman, a mathematical wizard, to make it absolutely foolproof—for Schultz. The daily winning number was based on the total of mutuel odds at certain race tracks such as Coney Island, in Cincinnati, and Tropical Park, in Florida, both racket-controlled then, and the New Orleans track, in which Mayor Robert Maestri, who was Huey Long's political heir, had more than a passing interest. Abbadabba was a human comptometer, and was able to rig the final odds so that it would bring out the most lightly played policy number for that day. It mulcted the players of millions.

Now, there has always been a suspicion that something more than just the insane Schultz violence was behind his omission from the national Syndicate. Dutch's comparatively new restaurant racket, which had mushroomed into a $2,000,000 annual extortion, caught the eye of Louis Buchalter, known as Lepke—an eye easily caught by profitable "gimmicks" in industrial extortion. With the explosive hoodlum left out of the cartel, Lepke could embrace this racket without violating Syndicate law against muscling. He simply moved in and took over while Schultz was in flight. Nor was Lepke the only one who made hay while the Dutchman had his back turned. Charley Lucky's Unione did the same with a major portion of the lush Harlem numbers banks Dutch had developed.

"He won't be back, anyway," was the gangland excuse.

The bosses also summoned Bo Weinberg, whom Dutch had named acting commander in chief of his crack cadre of killers.

"You deliver the mob to us, and we'll take care of you," they suggested persuasively. "The Dutchman ain't coming back, ever."

Bo was not only a good gunman; he was an adroit businessman. There would be little percentage in holding out for something as nebulous as the return of Schultz. Nor did it smack of sharp business to buck the Syndicate. The moguls just reached out and took what they wanted, anyway. Bo made a wholesale delivery of the troop. The torpedoes were adopted en masse, and spread among the Syndicate's various subsidiary branches. The annexation of the Schultz empire was then complete.

And then—Dutch beat the rap!

From the moment he had started his flight, his former associates had buried the Dutchman. The interment turned out now to have been grossly exaggerated.

For a while it had looked very bad. However, with Dutch safely out of sight, his lawyers had continued plugging away. Their chief goal was to defeat the government's demand to try him (as, if and when he exposed himself) in metropolitan New York, where his reputation and record would be a serious handicap with any jury. In spite of the government's determined efforts, the attorneys finally succeeded in winning a change of venue. When he came out of hiding, the trial would be taken upstate, to Syracuse, where Dutch Schultz was a name known only through the newspapers.

With that guarantee, the Dutchman emerged after eighteen months under cover. Out on bail pending trial, the conniving mobster moved into Syracuse early, and craftily set out to achieve a notoriety completely new and different from that to which he was accustomed. He did a great deal of socializing with the townsfolk. He took up charity—making sure that word of his noble gestures reached the newspapers, so the citizens who might serve on the jury would be apprised of what a lovely fellow he really was. The result was that, when the trial was held, Schultz escaped, temporarily anyway, on a hung jury—a disagreement.

Much to his satisfaction, the retrial was moved, thanks to his lawyers' efforts, even farther upstate—to the tiny border town of Malone. Once more, Schultz arrived early, and slyly plotted his defense. He spent money all around the place. He sent gifts to hospitalized children. He entertained expansively and expensively. He was, as a result, thought of most sympathetically among the citizenry of Malone. And the jury acquitted him. It drew a blistering denunciation from Judge Frederick Bryant.

"The verdict was dictated by other considerations than the evidence," the jurist charged.

Dutch dropped out of the clouds on the mob. No one, however, was particularly perturbed. The Syndicate was a going concern by then. New York still had a number of embarrassing matters to take up with him. So, the Dutchman had to settle in Newark, New Jersey. He called in Bo Weinberg immediately, and demanded an accounting of his staff.

Bo was forthright and no longer in awe at talking up to the boss. He advised his deposed employer it would not be healthy to try a comeback in the New York rackets. Perhaps he was too blunt. At any rate, that turned out to be Bo's last recorded appearance. The better gangland society has always maintained, over its teacups, that he got a gift of a cement overcoat shortly thereafter, and that he is still wearing it—on the bottom of the East River.

It was soon clear to the Dutchman that, during his vacation, a new era in gangdom had risen, based on an organized, concretely knit front. No single mob could crack it. Schultz could no more blast this efficient system out of his way than he could recoup the empire it had purloined from him. As touchy a torpedo as he was, Dutch still was not sufficiently bereft of his reason to try it. There was enough room left, anyway, for him to maneuver. He was able to save some of his numbers, and he managed to dig up assorted action in New Jersey without drawing rude stares from Longy Zwillman.

He had no particular financial worries, anyway. Dutch's personal bankroll was estimated in the millions—sometimes as high as seven million dollars.

Early in 1935, a Manhattan grand jury was investigating the numbers racket in New York, when some shenanigans began to take place.

An assistant District Attorney had been presenting the evidence—and doing an excellent job that was rapidly nearing indictments against "important" people. Suddenly, the assistant D. A. was called off the case. In his place, the District Attorney, personally, appeared. At once the investigation began to sag badly. The District Attorney then was William C. Dodge. Later, it was to be revealed that Dodge's election campaign had enjoyed contributions of some $30,000 from Dutch Schultz's organization.

The grand jury took the bit in its teeth. It demanded removal of the District Attorney from the investigation on the ground that he was not supplying the evidence it wanted. It became, in fact, one of the few "runaway" grand juries in New York history. (Grand jurors rarely realize they have the power to order before them any witnesses they wish to hear and to pursue any inquiry they deem necessary. Both the District Attorney and the court are subservient to the grand jury. Actually, a "runaway" jury is nothing more than a jury aware of its authority—especially when a prosecutor is unaware of his obligations.)

The grand jury that ran away in 1935 demanded that Dodge be superseded by a special prosecutor who would really dig into the rackets. The suggestion was made that the appointment go to a young lawyer named Thomas E. Dewey, who had compiled a hard-hitting record in the Federal Attorney's office. Immediately there were indications that Dewey would not be welcomed in certain quarters. The newspapers, however, picked up the jury's demands, and Governor Herbert Lehman designated Dewey, in a wide-sweeping mandate, to delve into the rackets in New York City.

Excitable even when normal, Dutch blew up completely at this. He got his current lawyer on the telephone.

"Hey, mouthpiece," he bellowed, "what does the word nemesis mean?"

"Why, Arthur," replied the attorney, who insisted on complete formality with his client at all times, "it means a hoodoo, a jinx."

"Just what I thought," Schultz nodded dolefully as he hung up.

It affected him most morbidly. Night after night, he wept in his cups about it.

"That Dewey," he would moan. "He is my nemesis."

Dutch had something there, at that. As an assistant Federal Attorney, Dewey had obtained the indictment for income-tax evasion which had started all of Schultz's woes. Now the same Dewey was looking into the numbers, which was one of the very few lines of business Dutch had left. For many days, The Dutchman brooded. The mad dog began to froth; the nemesis became an obsession. One night, it got him.

"Dewey's gotta go," Schultz slammed the table and screamed. "He has gotta be hit in the head."

In the old days, such a pronunciamento would have had an official ring to it. Now, though, it was no longer the ultimatum of the Boss with one hundred of the top triggermen of the era to back his play. Now he was just one gangster—and at the fringe of the cartel, at that. However, Dutch was not the only mobster who wanted Dewey removed. Others—accredited members of the Syndicate—felt his elimination was called for; but for business, rather than personal reasons. That made it a subject for the board of governors, like any murder matter involving intermob affairs. A meeting was called in New York to consider the case. Schultz was so beside himself that he slipped over from his home base in Newark, despite the standing order for his arrest on sight if he ever set foot in Manhattan. Although not part of the cartel, he was permitted to sit in as an interested party in a similar line of business.

Following protocol and procedure very carefully, the new democratic order limited discussion to the question of whether Dewey should be stopped and if so, the extent of the stopping. This was not a meeting held in desperation or dread. The bosses sat down as coolly and methodically as any board of directors considering important business policy. These gang lords had seen investigations come and go. No one was panicky. In fact, no one—except Schultz—was even very excited. Everyone had his say.

There was no unanimity of judgment at the conclave. The division of opinion ranged from outright assassination of the prosecutor as the sound means of ending the investigation, all the way to, "forget about him." The discussion dragged on. Finally, some of the wiser heads felt more time should be taken to weigh so important a problem. After all, murdering a prosecutor was not just any mob job. Eventually, in order to allow for profound thought, it was decided to adjourn for one week, and meet again.

"But suppose next week we vote to take him?" interposed the single-track-minded Dutchman. "We should be ready to do the job quick."

That was logical. It would be wise to blueprint in advance the mechanical details of so delicate a matter, in the event the ultimate decision favored assassination. The directorate agreed to have Dewey cased between sessions. His movements, his comings and his goings (and his stops) were to be thoroughly checked and clocked. All necessary details for the execution were to be prepared. It was Murder, Inc.'s customary painstaking and studied preparation, by which risks of failure due to carelessness were eliminated.

Obviously, this assignment would require utmost subtlety and finesse. The job was, in fact, so top priority that no less an individual than Albert Anastasia, czar of the Brooklyn waterfront and boss of the Syndicate's newly added death squad, was proposed as the ideal man to do the casing and take charge of preparatory details, such as the getaway car and murder weapons. No one opposed the nomination. It was an important piece of work and required an important man. Albert A. was important enough to be officially described as "the overlord of organized crime" in Brooklyn.

In those days, Dewey never moved without his two bodyguards. The caser would have to be especially adroit to avoid attaching suspicion to himself. Someone got the idea for the perfect subterfuge. A child was borrowed from a friend to accompany the caser. What could be less sinister than a devoted father romping with his offspring?

For four straight mornings, this "proud parent," with his decoy child pedaling a velocipede, took up an innocent stand in front of Dewey's apartment building. Each morning, they were already there when the prosecutor and his guards emerged. It must have been a fine show of parental devotion to Dewey and his companions—this man willing to rise early enough to spend a bit of time with his heir before heading off for the daily toil.

For the inoffensive "father," the setup was ideal. Given four mornings of uninterrupted observation, he noted that Dewey's daily routine followed a pattern. The prosecutor and his guards left the apartment at practically the same minute each day. They headed for the same drugstore a couple of blocks away. There, the guards took up a stand outside the door, while Dewey went inside. He remained for several minutes, then reappeared, and the trio would be off.

The pharmacist could hardly be suspicious of the proud parent and his child who dropped in on two different mornings just after Mr. Dewey left. The man was very disarming; seemed interested, mostly, in seeing that the tot did not ride his tricycle into a floor display of beauty soap. It was no trouble for the man to learn that the prosecutor's regular stop in the drugstore was to make the first phone call to his office each day. Later, when someone mentioned it, Dewey recalled that morning call.

"I did not want to disturb Mrs. Dewey by using the phone in our room at the apartment so early," he explained. Besides, it was very likely that his home phone was tapped, once his probe began.

By the fourth morning, the caser felt he had established that Dewey's actions were regular habit. The prosecutor could be counted on to do the same thing every day. Meantime, the other necessary details were being handled with the same efficiency. From a public garage, the Brownsville troop stole a black four-door sedan, especially selected for inconspicuous color and high-speed power. This would be the getaway car for the killer, if the decision was to proceed with the assassination. The car was stored carefully away in a prepared "drop," to remain under cover until needed. License plates were stolen from another car, and transferred to the "hot," or stolen, vehicle, completing the almost impenetrable disguise. Guns for the job were secured by rifling one of a number of crates of weapons, waiting on a pier for shipment to some European government. Even if their absence were eventually noted—which was unlikely—it would be months, and thousands of miles, away.

Not even that insurance satisfied the combination's sticklers, however. The guns were also specially treated. The usual precaution against tracing a pistol is to file off the numbers. Crime-fighting science has discovered, though, that the metal beneath the number on a weapon is compressed when the numerals are stamped in. Thus, when the number is simply filed away, an application of acid—nitric or hydrochloric—will bring out the ghostlike imprint of the figures. The Brooklyn hoods, well aware of this, had a gunsmith who could circumvent it. He merely gouged out the metal completely—and an acid bath produced nothing but blank steel. Finally, the business end of each weapon was threaded so that silencers could be attached. With that flourish, everything was ready to carry out the mandate, if the decision of the adjourned meeting of the board of governors dictated the assassination of Dewey.

The report of the caser showed exactly how it would be done. On the day selected, the gunman would get to the drugstore a few minutes before the regular time for Dewey's arrival. He would be inside and waiting and the bodyguards, who always remained outside, would not know there was a stranger even in the neighborhood. Keeping his back to Dewey, the trigger-man would be "buying" a tube of toothpaste or a box of cornplasters, or something, until the prosecutor went into the phone booth, as usual.

"Dewey'll be a sitting duck in there," it was pointed out.

Out would come the gun—equipped with silencer. That was a must. The flat crack of the silencer would never carry enough to be audible to the guards through the closed door of the store, above the street noises. The assassin would turn and blast Dewey, cornered there in the booth. The druggist would be drilled where he stood, behind the counter. There would be no outcry, no sound of gunfire, no alarm—and no identification later.

Having completed the contract, the killer would ease out. The guards, having heard nothing, would barely look his way as he ambled past. Casually, he would turn the corner to the waiting getaway car, which he would abandon with the untraceable guns wherever convenient. Before the bodyguards grew perturbed enough to investigate, there would be ample time for a smooth, easy disappearance.

All of this was before the board of governors as the adjourned meeting opened. Dutch Schultz was on hand again, as anxious as ever for the elimination of his nemesis. The debate was resumed. However, this time the Syndicate's cooler heads dominated. The new-order mob moguls balanced the necessity for any killing against the consequences it might stir up. Besides, Lepke and Lucky Luciano were firmly convinced they knew the technique with which to meet the danger that threatened.

"All investigations collapse when no witnesses are around," argued the czar of industrial extortion. Lepke always maintained the same philosophy. He had learned it through probe after probe that had died slow deaths in the past.

"We are bombproof when all the right people are out of the way," he pointed out. "We get them out of the way now—then this investigation collapses, too."

Lepke's logic was deadly. Under our system of jurisprudence, witnesses before a grand jury must make out a prima facie case of crime before law enforcement can secure an indictment. Without the essential witnesses, a prosecutor cannot muster such a case.

The other directors of crime respected Lepke's judgment. His record was excellent. On the basis of his "success" alone, he must have the right answers.

"Besides," both he and Lucky propounded another powerful point, "the best Dewey can do is try to go after the New York rackets; he can't touch anything outside of New York."

No one in the Syndicate could ignore as particularly pertinent a consideration as that. Dewey was bound to Manhattan by jurisdictional limits. The take from the New York rackets was important, but it was a drop compared to the businesses the cartel was operating across the nation. And assassinating a prosecutor would stir up such righteous indignation throughout the country that it could very well dam up the financial flood from the lucrative rackets in all other places.

"If we knock him off," cautioned another of the gang lords in support of this view, "even the Federals will jump on the rackets. We'll be chased out of the country."

The proposed assassination, then, was potentially disastrous enough to blow up the entire national empire of crime. Sacrificing the whole chain-store system to halt an as yet embryonic threat solely against New York was not sound business. That was the main concern of the directors: good business. They saw the light. Lepke's sage and forceful persuasion, backed by Lucky, won out. They took a vote, and the directors decided to permit Dewey to live.

The decision was not unanimous. Dutch Schultz did not approve. Nor did Gurrah, Lepke's snarling partner. This might have been expected. Of the entire group, these were the two strong arms famed for doing most of their thinking with their muscles. All the rest, however, turned thumbs down on the idea of murdering the special prosecutor. They were not inspired by any humanitarian motives. The executives of national crime spared Dewey's life solely for the sake of—national crime.

Dutch Schultz was of that era and ilk of power-mad paranoiacs so pampered and fawned upon by favor-seeking punks that they came to believe their orders were royal decrees and their wishes ordained commandments.

Dutch was neither satisfied nor happy with the edict sparing Dewey's life. He made no secret about it.

"I still say he ought to be hit," the mad dog barked defiantly. "And if nobody else is gonna do it, I'm gonna hit him myself."

Anyway, he contemplated, it would be a shame to waste all that valuable data gathered by the "proud parent."

"That drugstore phone booth is a natural," thought the outlaw hoodlum. So, in defiance of the board of governors, Schultz set out to murder Dewey on his own—using the very scheme the board had discarded. It looked foolproof.

Dutch Schultz was a blowhard. Like all blowhards, he talked too much. He couldn't keep this one to himself. To an associate, he whispered that he was not only going to do it—but he even said when. He boasted that he was going to get the big rackets-buster in forty-eight hours!

No such startling undertaking could be kept off the grapevine for long. Anyone who heard such a whisper must realize it was guilty knowledge, much too hot to keep. In short order, the Syndicate buzzed with the report that the Dutchman was going to "take" Dewey on his own. The gang lords were shocked—not so much at the assassination plot as at the defy.

"That Dutchman is just daffy enough to do it, too," Lepke warned the others. "This is no good."

Obviously, Schultz's insane plot would bring on the cartel the entire heat of the Law that the leaders had always avoided. It would wreck the rackets and launch the biggest war on crime in history. Or, as one informer told us:

"They got scared that rubbing out Dewey would hit them where it hurt the most—in their pocketbooks."

Having ordained that Dewey should live, the chiefs of crime now had to insure his life. And since Dutch was rushing the demise of his nemesis, the insuring would have to be done in a hurry. The fact that Schultz was plotting to defy Syndicate decree for personal reasons made this a matter of prime importance. It was especially significant in that this was the first real challenge to and test of Syndicate law.

The directors discussed it—and ruled that the Dutchman himself must die to guarantee Dewey's life. The mob actually ordained that it would rub out a mobster—to save a prosecutor!

Schultz was a veteran of gang gun fights, tough to corner. Over in Newark, his guard was always up. For public appearances, his favorite spot was the Palace Chophouse in downtown Newark, and things were so arranged there that he could transact business and social obligations in a sort of back-room niche, easily guarded at its one entrance.

This was a special job; it would take special men. Without a word of palaver on personnel, each of the bosses immediately picked, mentally, the exact men called for. Lepke had two operatives on his staff made to order for it. Lepke knew it, too. He designated both for this all-important mission —"Charlie the Bug" Workman, one of gangland's most deadly executioners, and Mendy Weiss, a hulking, snarling murderer with a touch of directional ability.

Mendy was a strangler and a strong-arm veteran of the labor wars. He was an operational boss on Lepke's staff—although perhaps not quite as important as he liked to have others believe. He fancied getups like one flashy all-green outfit that practically blinded an entire courtroom one day. It was Mendy who reveled as acting boss when Lepke was in hiding in 1939, and ordered murder done as far away as California.

Bug Workman, one of the most valuable gunmen in the entire underworld, was a curly-haired completely casual killer, custom-tailored from head to foot. Because of his ability at assassination, his place in gangdom was high, for a gunman. Although not a member of the directorate, he sat in council chamber with the executives and did only important work for the boss. Detectives called him the Powerhouse. When it came to doing a job of slaying, gang style, the Bug was practically a mob all by himself.

"A guy has to be a bug to do what Charlie does," his admiring gunmates used to say, shaking their heads in awe over the score of contracts he had handled.

For the Dutch Schultz expedition, a third party would be needed, someone who knew his way around Newark to pilot the getaway car for the two New Yorkers. The story is that this third man was supplied by the Jersey mob, and was especially familiar with the best routes. He is identified to this day only as Piggy; there are, however, suspicions as to who he is.

On the night of October 23, 1935, one of the hundreds of cars rolling through the Holland Tunnel, outbound from New York, was an inconspicuous black sedan, carrying three inconspicuous-appearing men. Their talk was equally inconspicuous, idle chatter of fights and baseball and maybe a bit of politics, like any three men thrown together in an automobile.

Their mission, however, was not so innocuous. They were on their way to beat a deadline—on assassination. Dutch Schultz was just thirty-six hours away from murdering Thomas E. Dewey, special rackets prosecutor, and the trio had strict orders from the overloads of the underworld to stop the Dutchman—for keeps!

The car slid swiftly through the aromas from the slaughterhouses and glue works which make automobiling across the Jersey meadows more comfortable with the windows rolled up, even on hot days. In Newark, Piggy, the driver, found the Palace Chophouse easily enough. They pulled up in front of the place not long after ten o'clock.

Mendy was designated as "cover" for the getaway. He stayed at the door. Piggy, as wheelman, remained in the car, ready to pull away. Charlie the Bug barged right into the place.

There was a bar in the long front room, and beyond it this sort of backroom niche, which the Dutchman used as a combination office and cozy nook. The "finger" had reported that Dutch would be there that night.

The Bug strolled the length of the bar, breezily and completely carefree, like a man on his way to the free-lunch counter in the better days. Just off the end of the bar was the men's room. Workman flipped open the door to it. Even the bold Bug would not overlook an uncovered quarter, from which a flanking attack might be launched. Inside, a fellow, his back to the door, was washing his hands. Something about him looked familiar.

"One of the bodyguards, I guess," thought Workman. And he pulled out his pistol and fired. The handwasher toppled without even turning off the faucet.

The Bug, gun ready, now advanced on the boys in the back room. The bar had emptied in a hurry. The bartender, with admirable presence of mind, disappeared behind the mahogany. A World War I veteran, he knew the advantages of defilade under fire.

In the rear room sat three Schultz aides. A business meeting had been in progress. Before them, papers were piled on the table—apparently the monthly accounting of Dutch's enterprises. One strip of adding-machine tape carried a long list of figures, among them entries of $313,711.99 and $236,295.95. Obviously, the Dutchman had reorganized well. The three lieutenants, however, were no longer interested in financial statements. As Workman appeared, they opened fire. The Bug fired back. He kept banging away, and pretty soon, Lulu Rosenkrantz, who was Dutch's chauffeur and bodyguard, and Ab (Misfit) Landau, one of his torpedoes, and Abba-dabba Berman, the human comptometer who fixed the daily number, were all dead.

Workman was troubled, though, as he retired once more to the empty bar. The word had been that Dutch was to be there. The Bug had not seen Schultz. And there was no one else in sight.

"Funny," thought the Bug. "The Dutchman ought to be around. I got to take him."

Then, it dawned on him:

"Why, sure . . . that guy in the toilet. No wonder he looked familiar."

He was right. The man in the men's room had been Dutch Schultz. The first to go had been the mob magnate whose extermination the Syndicate had ordered to save the life of a law-enforcement officer. Almost simultaneously with the realization, a recollection hit Charlie the Bug of an incident in the Dutchman's life which is legend among New York's police. One June night in 1931, Dutch and his torpedo, Danny Iamascia, had just slipped out of Schultz's hideout on upper Fifth Avenue when they noted two vague figures detach themselves from the shadow of a building across the street.

"The Mick," snapped Schultz in warning, presuming they were representatives of his sworn enemy, Vincent Coll, the maddest mobster New York ever saw. Dutch and Danny went for their guns. The two figures made no threatening move, though, until the hoodlum and his stooge started shooting. For, the two figures were not the Mad Mick's men. They were Detectives Julius Salke and Steve DiRosa. The battle did not last long. Detective Salke put a bullet through Iamascia. Dutch, seeing his triggerman fall, threw his own gun away and started running. Detective DiRosa could have shot him right then. Instead, he took off after the speeding Schultz, caught him in a matter of yards and dropped him with a superb bit of tackling.

The police legend is that Dutch reached into his pocket after his arrest, brought out all the cash he had on him and offered it as a bribe for his release. And all the cash he had on him was a mere $18,600! The officer was so incensed at the bribe attempt, the legend runs, that he roared, "You miserable bum, I'll shove that dough down your throat." And, the legend concludes, the officer had the Dutchman down and had one end of this king-size roll of bills in the Dutchman's mouth, and was doing just that, when a fellow officer persuaded him it was not a nice way to treat money.

All of this ran through Charlie the Bug's mind as he stood in the middle of that Newark saloon that night in 1935, with Dutch on the toilet floor, mortally wounded. Now it may have dawned on him that all the pistol-popping was going to bring a lot of curious policemen rapidly. But the threat was not nearly strong enough to outweigh the possibility—and the hope—that maybe lightning could strike twice in the same place. Back into the gents' room barged the Bug, and he gave Dutch's pockets a thorough and total frisk. He never mentioned to anyone afterward whether it proved worth while.

Mendy was supposed to be at the door of the chophouse covering the getaway when Charlie the Bug started out, leaving Dutch Schultz and his trio of hired hands fatally wounded. But Mendy was not there.

The Bug did not think that was right. Suppose he had needed cover for his escape. Outside, there was no Piggy at the wheel of the getaway car, either. In fact, there was no getaway car. And right then was neither the time nor the place to be on foot in Newark, in the vicinity of the Palace Chophouse.

The hue and cry was going up all over the neighborhood by now—and no wonder, with all that gunfire. The Bug could see any number of curious citizens bearing down rapidly, from all directions. He slid into an alley, and from there he had to dash across back yards, slip through vacant lots and leap over fences, before he finally made his getaway back to New York. Those guys, he pondered in annoyance, must have run out on him. What irked the Bug was that they had taken the car with them. Not only did he have to run practically all the way home, but it had made him late for a date, besides. Charlie the Bug was fit to be tied.

The incident raised hob in the underworld. Mendy and Piggy had a lot of explaining to do—especially Mendy, because he was a staff gunman. Under the Syndicate's law, abandoning a post and a mobmate, while on organization business, is fatal. Not even the fact that he was a trusted lieutenant of the mighty Lepke could ease Mendy out of this one. Unless he had a perfect explanation, the bull-shouldered strangler would have to stand trial before the kangaroo court.

The supreme court of crime was made ready for Mendy. The mere fact that he was not there when the Bug came out of the chophouse made it an open-and-shut case. The situation looked bad. Mendy foresaw his danger, and immediately reported his side to his boss, in a desperate move to avoid a trial. Surprisingly, he maintained that he had definitely remained at his post until the contract was all finished. The bulky badman admitted he wasn't at the chophouse door when Workman finally came through it. That, however, was no contradiction, he held.

"I claim," Mendy concluded, "that hitting the Dutchman was mob business, and I stayed there till it was over. But then the Bug went back in the toilet to give the Dutchman a 'heist.' I claim that was not mob business any more—that was personal business."

That being the case, Mendy maintained, he had a perfect right to depart forthwith, before the Law arrived, and to take Piggy and the getaway car with him. On a point of law, the Bug's act was simply *ultra vires*—it was not in furtherance of the purposes for which the corporate mission was organized.

There was no argument against such logic. Not even the Bug would dispute the point. Mendy was discharged without even standing trial.

Dutch Schultz did not bow out immediately the night Bug Workman blew a big hole in him with his .45.

The dying Dutchman lingered, in fact, for close to twenty-four hours, with Police Stenographer John Long glued to his bedside in a Newark hospital, shorthanding his every gasp, and Police Sergeant Luke Conlon asking him questions in his few conscious moments. Mostly, though, it was delirious babbling, interspersed with an occasional lucid word or phrase or paragraph, as Schultz struggled for life. For only about two hours, on the afternoon following the shooting, did any of his garbled ramblings have any coherency at all.

Apparently the violent gangster never knew what hit him, there in the men's room of the saloon. At least, that was the impression he left in the brief chances Sergeant Conlon had to put any questions to him through his coma.

Q—What did they shoot you for?

.A—I don't know, sir . . . honest . . . I don't even know who was with me, honestly . . . I went to the toilet . . . I was in the toilet. When I reached the can, the boy came at me.

Q—The big fellow gave it to you?

A—Yes . . . he gave it to me.

Q—Do you know who this big fellow was?

A—No.

Once, in reply to another query about who shot him, the writhing hoodlum groaned:

"The boss himself."

Both FBI agents and police investigators grabbed at the babbled phrase as pointing directly to Lucky Luciano. Wasn't Lucky head of Unione Siciliano, they reasoned? Wasn't the head of Unione always known as the Boss?

Later, The Dutchman brought in another name, and sent the investigators off on another tangent:

Q—What did the big fellow shoot you for?
A—Him . . . John? . . . Over a million—five million dollars.

"John," FBI and police figured, could be Johnny Torrio, the sharp little gangster who had turned Chicago over to Al Capone. No one knew then, of course, that he had given gangland the recipe for national organization. In fact, no one even dreamed a national organization existed. But they did know that in underworld stature, John was a "big fellow." As for the "five million dollars," that probably was Dutch's estimate of his loss through the mob's snatch of his rackets.

Mostly, Schultz just lay there gasping and raving. From his wandering snatches came few, if any, pieces to fit the puzzle.

"If we wanted to break the ring . . . no, please . . . I get a month," he stammered once, through teeth clenched with pain. And again, "My gilt-edge stuff . . . and those dirty rats have tuned in."

And still again, "No . . . no . . . there are only ten of us and there are ten million of you fighting somewhere. . . . So get your onions up and we will throw up the truce flag."

The thread through all this was that the muscling of his rich rackets by Lepke and Lucky preyed on Schultz's distorted brain. The "I get a month" may have referred to a time limit given him by the Syndicate to clear up his business. He may have tried to get paid off—"get your onions up"—for agreeing to pull out of the rackets entirely.

Later, there was:

"Please crack down on the Chinaman's friends."

One of Dutch's bitter enemies was Charles Sherman, a Waxey Gordon strong-arm and narcotics executive known to the underworld as the China-man, or Chink. Schultz's "crack-down" request was followed to the letter within a couple of months, incidentally. Sherman's body was found buried in quicklime on the Sullivan County farm of Jack Drucker, a Brooklyn boy who was Murder, Inc.'s Sullivan County manager for a time. It was Drucker who carried an ice pick, the night one Walter Sage was stabbed to death and dropped into a lake with a slot machine tied around his neck.

Off and on during that twenty-four hours on his deathbed, Schultz stammered parts of other names that only added to the mystery.

"Now listen, Phil . . . Fun is fun . . . What happened to the other sixteen?" was one bit of incoherency. Phil, in this case, could have meant Dandy Phil Kastel, Frank Costello's general field manager (then and now), with whom Schultz had been in deals over slot machines.

He failed to mention his wife directly at any time, but at one point, a request to "get the doll a roofing" was taken as a plea to his mobmates, in his delirium, to see that she was cared for. His wife, however, never saw any of his millions. Dutch's pals and underlings, who were generally understood to be holding his money for him (since he never did trust banks), demonstrated exactly how much honor there is among thieves by making off with his fortune as soon as his trigger was no longer there to defend it.

On the other hand, there were half a dozen occasions when he cried out for "mama." Once, toward the very end, tossing with pain, he sobbed: "Mother is the best bet . . . And don't let Satan draw you too fast."

Perhaps the quiet, churchgoing woman who tried so hard to make her son respectable could take some solace, at last, from that.

The most puzzling development of the Dutchman's last hours, however —even more puzzling than trying to make sense out of his deathbed delirium—were the antics and verbal ambulations of his twenty-one-year-old, hatcheck-girl wife, Frances.

Frances has frequently been pictured, and especially in one recently published book, as a shy, shrinking violet, brought up on that block of West Forty-seventh Street which Damon Runyon dubbed Dream Street. The romance of Frances and the cheating, conniving criminal flowered in a couple of hours one night in a restaurant on Dream Street where she was a combination hatcheck-cigarette girl. Dutch came into the place and promptly went "on the make" for her. Sweet Frances would have nothing to do with this miserable plug-ugly—for at least an hour after she first set eyes on him. Then he told her he was *the* Dutch Schultz. From that moment, it was a beautiful romance.

The day after Dutch was shot, Deputy Police Chief John Haller of Newark, plunging into the investigation, thought he ought to ask her a few questions. That was only natural. Frances told him, explained the deputy chief with a mystified air, that the wedlock joining her and her mobster mate operated under a "legal contract." The usual satisfactory results were achieved evidently. The legal contract had produced two children.

Deputy Chief Haller said that, at first, Frances told him she had not been near the Palace Chophouse the night the love of her life was murdered. Then police had an employe confront her, and the employe said, sure, she was there only two hours before the fireworks.

Frances, the deputy chief stated, now did a neat verbal flip-flop. She explained that she had left Dutch two days before, had gone to New York and had stayed there until the evening of the shooting. On the murder night, she stopped in to see Dutch at the saloon about eight-thirty, on her return from her New York visit. She refused to tell the police official, he said, with whom she had stayed in New York for those two days and two nights, or whom she had seen there. She left the chophouse on the murder night, after visiting with Dutch for about half an hour, and she went to a nearby movie.

"I got out about eleven o'clock, and there was a crowd in front of the tavern [chophouse]," the deputy chief quoted her. "I thought it was a saloon raid, so I walked right by."

She walked to the tube station, and took a train back to New York, evidently preferring the bright lights of Manhattan, at that moment, to the company of the mobster with whom she shared such a great and abiding love that it was written about in books, like Romeo and Juliet. Reaching New York about midnight, she bought a newspaper. It was then she learned that the "saloon raid" actually had been the slaughter of her husband and his chums.

Did Frances now hurry back to Newark to be at the bedside of her mate, who was near death? Did she run—her pure little heart thumping in panic —to the nearest phone to try to learn the very latest word of his condition? Deputy Chief Haller said she told him she went in the opposite direction, to the apartment she maintained in Jackson Heights—a short subway trip to Long Island—and she went to sleep. Some time the following afternoon, Frances finally got back to Newark.

This was all very interesting, the deputy chief agreed. It left him still wondering, however, who had fingered Dutch; who had let the mob know that he would be in the chophouse that night when the killers arrived?

Not long after Dutch Schultz ended up in the gents' room, Kid Twist Reles gave a party at his home. It was a strictly social evening—no business. (No one to be shot, slugged or strangled, that is.)

A lot of the boys were there, relaxing from the everyday toil. It was noted, though, that Charlie the Bug Workman was not getting into the swing of things as merrily as the rest, and this was surprising. As the evening wore on, the curly-haired hoodlum loosened up some. Finally, he leaned forward in his easy chair and brought his pet peeve onto the floor. He hadn't believed Mendy's excuse.

"Nice thing, huh," he was hurt and bitter. "Here I go on a job with two guys and they're supposed to be good. I do all the work. That's okay. But these two bums run out on me. You know what those bums did? . . . That Mendy and Piggy—they 'pigged' it!"

And out popped the story. It showed how worked up the Bug really was, when he got as eloquent as that. It was the costliest conversation of his life. Two of his listeners were his host, Kid Twist, and Allie Tannenbaum—who was called Tick-Tock by the mob because he talked with the easy regularity of a clock at work. Of course, the Kid, being an individual who got around in the gang, already knew many of the details from other sources.

And when the Kid began to sing for us that Good Friday night five years later, he included the story of the Dutch Schultz slaughter, and the Bug's bitter and voluble monologue at the party. Only then did the startling motive for the quadruple blood bath come out for the first time anywhere, except in the innermost sanctums of crime.

As might have been expected, the assassination of the Dutchman had stirred up all manner of furore. For five years, the possible motives advanced had almost outnumbered the suspects.

When Reles talked and the "inside" cracked, the actual reason finally leaked through gangland's forbidding silence. The mad-dog Dutchman was hit, not by a New York mob, but by a national syndicate. He was hit, not because he stood in the way of the rackets—the mob already had taken over his major operations—but simply because he insisted on murdering Dewey in defiance of this syndicate, and the gang lords believed that would hurt their business. Only then did it come to light: Thomas E. Dewey had been within thirty-six hours of never living to be almost President of the United States and a three-time Governor of New York State!

A long time later, I related the story to Dewey. I was tremendously impressed by his obvious personal courage. Through all the details, step by step, he said not a word, gave never a sign of the slightest shock at learning he was mere hours away from certain death. But when I mentioned the baby on the velocipede—the decoy for the man casing him—Dewey's eyes widened a fraction. It was a barely perceptible flicker; hardly any motion at all. It gave me the idea, though, that he had recalled the tot—and its "proud parent."

And what ironical justice developed! Organized crime had saved Dewey's life in 1935. Four years later, Dewey dealt organized crime the most severe blow it ever had been hit up to that time. He convicted Lucky for his rackets and Lepke for industrial extortion. And Lepke and Lucky had led the campaign to save him, when Dutch wanted him murdered.

It took four more years for the touch that rounded it all out. Then, Lepke, doomed for murder in our Brooklyn probe, made one last desperate plea for executive clemency. That is a right enjoyed by every man, even a Lepke, under American justice.

Nine years before, Lepke had the life-or-death say over Thomas E. Dewey—and Lepke had said life. Now Lepke was begging for his own life for the crimes he had committed. And the man who now had the life-or-death say over Lepke was—the very same Thomas E. Dewey!

WILLIAM MCFEE

THE *MORRO CASTLE* FIRE*

SATURDAY, September 8, 1934, was a blustery autumn day along the Atlantic coast. There was some rain, the leaves were falling, and so was the barometer. It was the kind of day on shore which indicates dirty weather at sea. September is the hurricane month.

Three days earlier, September 5, the *Morro Castle*, of the Ward Line, sailed from Havana on her homeward run to New York. September 8, in a storm of wind and rain, she was three miles east of Barnegat, heading for the Ambrose Channel, where she would pick up her pilot. It was nearly three o'clock in the morning. Her 318 passengers and most of her crew of 231 men and women were asleep.

The usual Friday night conviviality, the "farewell dinner," the paper hats and toy balloons, the drinking, dancing, and love-making, the traditional culmination of a pleasure cruise in the West Indies, had been clouded by an unusual event. Captain R. Willmott was taken ill at dinner and died within a few hours.

It was a grave psychological strain for the chief officer, Mr. William F. Warms, who had come off watch at eight o'clock. He was about to turn in, for he had a strenuous day ahead of him in New York, when he made the discovery. To find his captain dead in his bunk, to face the sudden responsibility of taking over the command of the ship, would impose a burden on the strongest of men.

Mr. Warms, moreover, had another anxiety.

The gap between chief officer and master of any ship is wide enough, but in this particular case much of the executive authority usually assumed by a chief officer by custom and tradition had been retained by the dead captain. We have to keep this in mind when we come to the actions of Captain Warms, suddenly confronted with the most terrifying emergency to be faced by the master of a vessel crowded with helpless, sleeping passengers.

At five minutes to three Mr. Hackney, acting second officer, saw smoke issuing from the stokehole fiddley. He called down from the bridge to the

---

* From "The Peculiar Fate of the *Morro Castle*," in *The Aspirin Age* (New York, Simon and Schuster, 1949).

engine room to know "if there was a fire in the engine room." Cadet Engineer William F. Tripp, an eighteen-year-old Massachusetts Institute of Technology student, who was on duty near the telegraph and telephone, for they were about to pick up the pilot, replied in the negative. He knew of no fire. This is a highly important detail which, for some reason, was not emphasized by the experts. One minute later, at 2:56, Mr. Hackney pulled the fire alarm, which would be relayed all over the ship.

By this time, of course, Captain Warms was on the bridge. Accepting the above official record, confirmed by Mr. Tripp's log sheet, we face the extraordinary facts that (1) some eighteen minutes elapsed before the captain ordered a radio call for assistance; (2) the radio operator, Mr. Rogers, whose cabin, fifty feet aft of the navigating bridge, was on fire, sent three times to ask for instructions; (3) other ships near by saw the fire and sent calls before the *Morro Castle* call went out; (4) the ship was kept at nineteen knots, into a twenty-mile wind, in darkness, pouring rain, and pounding seas, before being stopped.

By that time, around half past three, the fire had made such headway that the ship's upper structure, from the forward funnel to the mizzenmast, which rose abaft the deck ballroom and the veranda, was a furnace. The passengers were crowding to the tourist section of the ship, right on the stern rails, on B and C decks. They were pouring through the passageways. Some, who were later seen at portholes, screaming for help, had been trapped in their cabins and were to die horribly there. Six young ladies, who had been carried by stewardesses from the bar to their cabins at the end of the evening's festivities, were not seen again. Some, of course, probably less fuddled, more athletic, and more enterprising, squirmed their way through their portholes and dropped into the sea, and were lucky enough to be picked up by the boats.

Most of the passengers, however, suddenly awakened by the raucous loud-speakers, frightened by the roaring of the flames and the running of men who had lost their wits and had no one to command them, surged aft through the smoke-filled passages. In such a case the word "panic" is inadequate. It conveys nothing of the actuality. These people, running through corridors of a burning ship, half-clothed and many of them half-demented, were in a bad way. When they came out on the after rail it was raining in torrents. There was no light save the lurid flames leaping at them from the superstructure. Below them was the dark turbulence of the sea, dotted with crying people in life belts, calling to the boats dimly seen, standing off fearfully from the heat of the burning ship. Desperation came to these people, and a measure of courage too. Down they went, jumping, or sliding down ropes, and, being inexpert at such business, scorching their soft hands, so that some of them were forever incapacitated for their professional work. There were many women there too, and they threw off their flimsy shoes by the rail, discarding their lipsticks and compacts, their lighters and cigarettes and girdles, as though, when faced with the final, grim, eternal verities of the sea, they instinctively abandoned the nonessentials.

WARREN R. MOULTON

RESCUE AT SEA*

(*A Coast Guardsman's Story of the* Morro Castle)

I WAS called at midnight September 8 to go on patrol two and a half miles north. I left the station at 12:10 A.M., noting the barometer was falling as I went out. Wind was northeast, sky overcast, weather thickening fast. Marked increase in wind with high surf rolling in, which indicated heavy weather off shore. Some lightning and thunder for about ten minutes at 1:50 A.M., followed by heavy rain squalls, and fog banks. All boats close in running for harbor.

When I got off watch at 4 A.M. I heard the lookout man telling the skipper that he had seen either a boat on fire or distress signals. The man off patrol and I both looked out to sea, but it was so thick we could see nothing. As I went down I heard the skipper sending a call to all stations, and reporting to the commander of this district that he was going to try to get out to sea, but did not think that any of our boats would make it on account of the bar. I did not think so either.

Five of us, all told, started in the surf boat. As we left the dock, the skipper hollered to another member of the crew to bring out the station Pickett boat just as soon as it was light enough to get her out. He did not think she could make it at that time. She is about forty-eight feet long and a mighty fine sea boat, with a very poor engine in her, plenty of power when the damn thing runs, which is not any too often.

We managed to get across the bar and for the next seven or eight miles

* From *The New Republic,* Oct. 31, 1934.

we had an awful fight, until we were within half a mile of the burning ship. Then we ran into something I never want to see or hear of again. The ocean was fairly lit up by the light of the burning ship, and the water was simply alive with screaming men and women. We stopped, and it very nearly spelled the end of us and a great many others, for so many grabbed the boat at once that we were nearly capsized and sunk. I do not know how many minutes we stopped, but certainly not more than five, and I heard the skipper bellowing at me to go ahead on her. I got her under way and for the next half-mile there was a fight on that I will never forget. Every sea broke over us, washing us from stem to stern. The crew did all they could to keep others off, and prevent our running over someone in the water; the skipper was at the tiller, I at the engine controls. The water was so deep that my hands on the gas throttle were covered. All around, ahead, on each side and astern, were men and women, all excited, a few with their hands stretched out toward us, calling for help; and we, already overloaded, unable to help at all. The rain beat down, the spray flew, and the way those upturned faces looked as they rose on the crest of a wave with the firelight flickering on them was awful. This lasted for about half a mile, then we were abreast of the burning ship and no one in the water to be run down.

There was nothing to do now but keep the boat headed into the sea, every wave breaking over us, for the next two and a half or three miles to the *Andrea F. Luckenbach,* the only steamer there at the time. We managed to crowd a little more speed on. Just as day was breaking we drew up to the *Luckenbach*'s Jacob's-ladders. I looked at our cargo for the first time; women back of me in the stern piled three deep, men and women over the engine box, cordwood fashion, all alive. Just how many there were I do not know, for we had our hands full to get them aboard the ship and keep our boat from being smashed alongside.

As soon as the last passenger was off and aboard ship, our skipper went aboard to get the master to move in closer to the *Morro Castle* so as to be more help to us. Later he did. We started back for another load. Before we got back to the burning ship two more steamers had arrived and put out lifeboats; I do not know how many, but quite a few. Most of them were heavily loaded then, but a few were not, and these were either hauling people out of the water or doing all in their power to draw up to the stern of the *Morro Castle*, where there must have been two hundred people crowded, either along the deck rail, in the water, or hanging by ropes over the stern. We stopped and loaded with women, all women, except three men who were just about gone, right alongside of us.

We went to the nearest ship, the *Empress of Bermuda*, British register, just as quickly as we could. We could not get our load of passengers aboard as no one would throw us a line to hold on to, and they kept the ship's head too much in the wind to give us a good lee so as to enable the women to make the Jacob's-ladder hanging over the side. Finally we had to leave the ship and run over to the *City of Savannah* and put them off. Those fellows and the captain really gave us wonderful help. The minute we were alongside they threw us a line both forward and aft to make fast to before the boat even lost headway. They opened one of their cargo ports and lowered ropes to tie around the women and men who could not climb the ladder.

When we got rid of the next load the ship's lifeboats had gotten the last of the passengers and crew who were aft on the *Morro Castle* and in the water around her. There were about a dozen men on the forward deck, which was not on fire at that time. We tried to get them, but the captain and the rest of the crew refused to leave.

Up to this time there had been no other Coast Guard boats on the scene, just us, in a little twenty-six-foot boat. We made a circle around the *Morro Castle* to see if we had missed anyone, and found the chief wireless operator hanging on the forward boat tackle block. This was on the weather side, and every time a sea came he would go completely out of sight. We had a time getting him aboard without getting busted ourselves.

Along about now the Pickett boat from our station drew up alongside the *Luckenbach* with one of her lifeboats in tow. They had picked it up drifting toward shore, overloaded, with the crew unable to handle her on account of the high seas that were running. The crew was completely played out when they took them in tow. I have since heard there were fifty people on that boat.

By now our gas was getting low. We started to the leeward to take a look at the inlet to see if we could possibly get in. When we were about two and a half miles from the *Morro Castle,* we saw two ship's lifeboats bob up away off on our starboard, but could not make out what they were doing, as it was raining so hard. They seemed to be drifting helplessly toward the breakers, about half a mile inshore. When we were within about a hundred yards of the first boat we saw a girl throw up her hands just a little way from us. We went to her and just as we got her on board, the rain slacked; as we rose on top of a sea, as far as we could see the ocean was dotted with both living and dead.

We were but a few minutes in getting a load of the living, took the lifeboat in tow, and started for the *City of Savannah,* two and a half miles to the windward. The boat we had in tow was one of hers.

On the way we saw our Pickett boat and signaled them to go to the assistance of the other lifeboat. After years, it seemed to me, we reached the *Savannah* and were unloaded in a hurry by her crew, as we were all just about done in by now. As soon as we unloaded, we went back to where the Pickett boat and lifeboat were last seen. The lifeboat was gone, and the Pickett was there rolling helplessly, about to be capsized by each sea. We ran down by them and hollered to know what the trouble was. They said their engine had stopped and they had gotten a fishing boat to take the lifeboat with them. Even if we had had the power to take the Pickett in tow, we could not have done it, as our gas was getting low. We decided the only thing to do was for me to board the Pickett and see if I could get her engines to running. The regular engineer was not on board, he having gone on liberty before the fire started. I got aboard her some way, and straightened up to take a look around. I saw a dead woman lying across the stern, dead lying on top of the cabin; the port side of the deck and cabin were red, dripping blood. In the after cabin were the most forlorn men and women I have ever seen, and all with hardly a rag on. Bilge matter was on the after-cabin floor and in the engine room forward, and everywhere one of the worst smells I have ever smelt where they had vomited. A fish factory is cologne compared to the smell on that boat.

One of the boys was on the stern in his underwear, trying to get the rest of his clothes on. I did not know the reason at the time, but have since heard from the crew that he deserves a lot of credit, which he is not getting. When the engine stopped on them, they were trying to come up to three women with life preservers on; he went overboard and managed to pull them close enough for the rest to get them on board. His name is Monroe Wilson of Marshalburg, North Carolina.

I managed to get the engine running after a while. How long I was, I do not know, nor how close we were to the breakers when we got started, as we could not see very far on account of the heavy rain. Judging from the way the sea was running, it could not have been far. We ran around after that for a while, but could find nothing but dead with life preservers on. We picked up a few of them, but it was such a job to get them on board and they would soon be on the beach anyway. The fellow in charge thought it best to get those in the cabin to a doctor, and leave those already dead alone. Shank River Inlet Bar was out of the question by now, as it was a great deal rougher than when we came out that morning. We thought of Sandy Hook, but it was twenty-five miles up the beach, and from the pounding the old boat was getting we were all doubtful whether she would stand it long enough to make it, even if the engine did not fail, and I was pretty certain it would, as the lubricating-oil pressure had dropped from forty-five pounds to fifteen, on account of gasoline's getting in when they were trying to start it before I got there. I said to go in Manasquan Inlet, which was about five miles from us, but he said he had never been there and did not know the way. I told him I had been there once and thought I could go again, so he gave her up to me and we made it some time that evening.

How many we pulled out of the water, I don't know. I kept count up to fifty-six, the skipper says one hundred and sixteen in all.

STANLEY WALKER

MORRO CASTLE AFTERMATH*

ONE HUNDRED THIRTY-SEVEN persons lost their lives. From four o'clock in the morning until long after nightfall, New Jersey residents of communities along the shore dropped their normal occupations to aid in rescue work.

The burning hulk, known to contain many charred bodies, broke loose from the cutter that was towing her at six-thirty in the evening and wallowed to a shallow berth less than forty yards from the Convention Hall at Asbury Park.

The next day, Sunday, crowds estimated at from 125,000 to 250,000 flocked to Asbury Park to see the burning ship. The majority came by automobile, jamming traffic in almost endless snarls. In New York 2,038 persons took advantage of the special half-price, one-day excursion run offered by the Pennsylvania Railroad. From various parts of New Jersey the Central Railroad hauled an additional 1,058 sightseers to Asbury Park at bargain rates. Philadelphia also sent excursion trains.

It was the largest crowd in any one day in the history of the resort. Local businessmen, from hot dog venders to hotel proprietors, saw their

* From Stanley Walker's *Mrs. Astor's Horse* (New York, Stokes, 1935).

chances for money. The beach where the smoldering liner lay was, of course, the center of interest.

Many spectators seemed to share the opinion of a fat woman who, after sitting for hours on the damp sand, explained to the girl beside her, "Yeah, I'm tired all right, but I ain't going to see nothing like this for a long time." On the boardwalk the man with the telescope, who usually made a bare living charging ten cents to look at the moon or passing vessels, did a thriving business in views of the *Morro Castle* at twenty-five cents a look.

Soon the officials of Asbury Park realized that they had stumbled on pay dirt. Very early a project was on foot to rope off the beach and boardwalk for one hundred yards to the north and south of the Convention Hall and to charge twenty-five cents for the privilege of a good look.

By Monday, September 10, there were stories around that there had been looting on the *Morro Castle*, and the governor sent two hundred soldiers from Fort Hancock. They were immediately put to work by Asbury Park officials directing traffic. Among the loot from the ship were supposed to have been purses, wallets, jewelry, luggage and passengers' clothing.

On Monday afternoon the City Council of Asbury Park by a vote of three to one decided to take over the *Morro Castle* as a permanent tourist attraction.

But there was an unforeseen joker in the "happy improvement plan." When the city fathers claimed the *Morro Castle* they did not know that she carried a cargo of green hides. When the wind blew in from the sea, the stench of scorched and rotting hides nauseated the citizens. Even the boardwalk concessionaires, known as men of exceptionally strong stomachs, turned a bit queasy and went around with pained, baffled expressions. Soon the whole town was tired of the *Morro Castle*. One official, however, still had faith. He sent squads of men aboard the ship to remove the cause of the odor, but not all of his policemen and firemen and all their chloride of lime could stop that all-pervading odor.

The city officials and the Chamber of Commerce, panicky now, begged the salvagers to take the nasty thing away. But the perverse ship remained stuck in the sands for many months. It was not until one chilly morning in March 1935 that the salvage tugs gently nosed the old hulk into deep water and started her on her last voyage to New York and the scrap heap.

THE MAGNIFICENT PUBLIC WORKS

THE Public Works Administration, organized in June 1933, was a part of the grand plan of attack on unemployment, and with its help large-scale undertakings such as TVA and the Grand Coulee Dam were begun, as well as smaller projects such as schools, highways, sewage systems, bridges and the like. The Agency was slow to get off the ground but the Chairman of the Public Works Board, Harold Ickes, was to become acclaimed for incorruptibility, not speed. With the tremendous funds at his disposal, he wanted to avoid scandal at any cost.

The PWA could loan or make outright grants of money to states and public organizations to begin their own construction work; the agency could use its money for its own projects; and it could loan money to private corporations. In addition, the PWA went to work for the Navy, constructing aircraft carriers—the *Yorktown* and *Enterprise* —cruisers, destroyers and submarines.

Such public works, while attacked by conservatives all over the country, were, under Secretary Ickes, honestly operated for the public good. Ickes was not going to "hire men to chase tumbleweeds on windy days."

Conversely, conservatives among the businessmen were apt to find it easy to accept government money to complete private business operations—the Pennsylvania Railroad, for instance, accepted 80 million dollars as a loan to electrify its road between New York and Washington. The Triborough Bridge in New York City was finished with PWA funds after private investors and banks refused to buy bonds for its completion; and PWA money was put up to hasten the completion of Boulder Dam, later christened Hoover Dam—there had been an appropriation under Hoover to begin work on this dam near Las Vegas, Nevada, on the Colorado River. Hoover Dam was the first of the magnificent achievements completed in the Thirties to meet the need for better conservation of the country's resources.

BRUCE BLIVEN

BOULDER DAM*

WHEN I crossed southern Colorado from east to west, my train, dropping several thousand feet from the top of the transcontinental divide in the course of a few miles, wound downward through a canyon beside the bed of an insignificant, an inconsequential river, trickling along in an amiable and unimportant way. Days later and hundreds of miles distant I met the same river again, now become the lordly Colorado, whose course, carved at one point through a vertical mile of colored rock, provides the Grand Canyon, the most awesome single spectacle in the whole world—the Colorado, which in flood has in the past wreaked incalculable damage but will never do so again, will on the contrary be of tremendous usefulness to that part of the human anthill which lies within a vast circle whose central point is a few hundred miles from the river's mouth in the Lower California Gulf.

What Hath Man Wrought.—You reach Boulder Dam by automobile from Las Vegas, Nevada (of which more in a moment). For two thirds of its length the road runs straight across the semidesert upland through sparse and stunted vegetation; then you twist upward and to the left amid barren small hills. You pass a barrier where a uniformed representative of Uncle Sam looks you over (and politely turns you back if you happen to be unemployed and looking for work), and in a twinkling here you are in Boulder City. A few years ago this was bare desert, without a tree or a teaspoonful of water; now it is a pleasant community of curving boulevards along the hillsides, bastard-Mediterranean architecture, green lawns, palms and bright flower beds. The men who are making the dam live here in big air-cooled dormitories, traveling to and from the dam itself, a few miles away, in huge buses. As many as 5,000 persons have been employed simultaneously, though with the end of the job perhaps only eighteen months away the number is now reduced. The men work in three shifts—day, swing and graveyard; they eat in a huge restaurant whose staff

* From *The New Republic*, Dec. 11, 1935.

tosses off lightly the task of preparing up to 10,000 "sit down" meals and 5,000 box lunches every day.

The work is exceedingly hard, often dangerous, and not particularly well paid; the average payroll works out at about $35 per week per person, which, in view of the many highly skilled men who get more than this, means that large numbers get less. Nevertheless, in several ways the workers here have had unusually good conditions—including the air-cooled sleeping rooms in a climate where the summer temperature often goes above 120 degrees (I have seen it myself at 127). The men's living quarters reminded me strongly of conditions in an average dormitory for men in a Western college; and when I mentioned this I was told that in fact a large proportion of the workers had been college men who, because of the vagaries of our economic system, had been unable to get jobs more appropriate to their training.

Thumbing the Nose at Mother Nature.—Up still higher into the hills, a few miles on winding mountain roads; a long and sharp descent with a hairpin turn, and here you are, a quarter of a mile downstream from the dam. At this spot a few years ago the river roared and hissed at the bottom of a deep notch cut between ugly, tumbled, black hills, with hardly a blade of vegetation on their sharp-edged shoulders of volcanic material. Men came and clambered over the rocks, squinted far down at the green and white water against the black, deeply shadowed walls, and this is what they have done: they have built vast tunnels through the canyon walls, paralleling the course of the mighty stream; they have turned the water out of its bed; in that dry bed they have constructed by far the largest dam on earth, six hundred feet through at the base and towering almost two thirds as high as the Empire State Building. Upstream from that dam is now accumulating a lake which will take ten years to fill. It will then be 115 miles long, 8 miles wide at its widest point, and it will contain enough water to cover all of New York State to a depth of one foot. If by some miracle of nature the river itself were to disappear from the face of the earth, its mighty current would continue to sweep onward at the normal volume for *two years* before this lake would be exhausted.

What you see as you come around that hairpin turn is a vast wall of new gray-white concrete, curved in a beautiful bow with its arch upstream for strength. Just beyond it are four concrete towers which look "modern" because they are functional—two on either side of the dam, close inshore —the intake towers through which will pass the water for the hydroelectric plant. That plant will lie nestled against the downstream side of the dam, a U-shaped structure which in fact will be twenty stories high but will, I should say, look like a pygmy beside the flank of that incredible man-made mountain. At present, the floor of the canyon below the dam is the usual appalling litter that goes with big construction—temporary roads, wooden scaffolding, a tangle of power cables. Even from our height, a little below the top of the dam itself, the workers moving about amid their rubbish heaps seem incredibly small and weak; the mind refuses to grasp the fact that these tiny dolls and others like them have actually turned aside the river, built that vast cliff of concrete, chiseled and blasted out all these roads, many of them cut into the very face of the cliff, bored the mighty tunnels through which the entire river is now racing silently, far below our feet in the bowels of the hill.

Abstractedly, as we see huge cages move out on cables strung across the canyon, and then descend 700 feet with their massive cargoes, we hear the Voice of Explanation in our ears: The purposes of Boulder Dam are flood control, irrigation, silt control, water supply and electricity. The new aqueduct, many miles downstream, will carry one billion gallons of water per day to Los Angeles, a distance of 239 miles, over desert and through mountains, lifting it a quarter of a mile, by means of pumping stations, in the process. Still farther downstream, a new irrigation canal will carry water to 1,000,000 acres and ultimately to 500,000 more. In addition, flood danger will be eliminated from another vast area. The dam, when completed, will have a maximum electric capacity four times that of Niagara, three times that of Muscle Shoals, two and one-half times that of the great Russian dam which was once called Dnieprostroy. The sale of electricity and water should pay the expense of construction within about fifty years (the aqueduct will cost some $60,000,000 more than the dam itself, and is next only to the Panama Canal among the great projects of the modern world).

The dam is by far the largest single piece of masonry ever attempted. It weighs 6,000,000 tons, and if this were poured in a cube, it would cover a square block and rise higher than the Empire State Building. Because of the heat engendered in pouring, the dam would take a hundred years to cool, if left to itself. To hasten the process, more than 500 miles of tubing have been built into the structure, through which ice water circulates from a plant capable of turning out 1,000 tons of ice every twenty-four hours (compare that with your electric refrigerator). This dam, which is being built by a combination of private companies, was first tailor-made in the Denver offices of the Reclamation Service, where the plans were all drawn. The actual construction, of course, was mostly done on the spot. Before construction could begin, a branch railroad had to be built thirty-three miles in length; many miles of first-class highway were constructed and, oddly enough, a power-line 222 miles long was strung to bring electricity, for the building job, to the place which will ultimately produce the world's largest supply of it.

The top of the dam is broad enough for a roadway, and is already used for that purpose. Eventually, the main highway between Chicago and Los Angeles will go through here and tin-can tourists rattling along at fifty miles an hour toward the Coast will glance down casually at the lake on the right, the river resuming its flow on the left. Probably few of them will ponder very much about 6,000,000 hours of heartbreaking, risky work performed here by steel-helmeted men in overalls, who, the task completed, will have gone their anonymous way toward the next job.

Worm's-Eye View.—My friend Buddy the chauffeur, tearing down a winding mountain road, deposes and says:

The brakes on this car are all shot. Hope you don't mind? I can most always hold her by going into second gear.

Sure, I worked on the dam. Say, everybody around here has taken a crack at it one time or another, or anyhow tried to. Men came here from pretty near everywheres, 'specially a couple years ago when it was just getting started. Lots of them were hired, and then got in the cage for their first trip down. You seen it: the cage goes out over the canyon, 700 feet high and then in the middle it goes on down. Lots of men couldn't stand it. They'd hang onto the cage and ride back up on the first trip and quit right there.

Good many men been killed here. What do you expect? It's dangerous work. Don't know exactly how many, but it must be close to 200. Quite a lot of them fell. A fellow was running the hoist that pulls the cage up and down on the cables. One time he was bringing up a cage with three men in it, and when it got to the top he forgot to pull the lever. The hoist wheels went on turning, the cable raveled out, and the cage dropped. Sure, all killed. Did they fire the hoistman? Say, they never caught him to fire him. Anybody that gets in an accident like that, he lights out for all hell and you never see him again.

Used to be a cable bridge across the river—also 700 feet up. Floor was two planks, each twelve inches wide, no handrail, or nothing. Many a man come here, took one look at that bridge and quit. Sometimes somebody would start across, standing up, of course, and leaning against the wind. Then he'd look down, or get thinking about it, and lose his nerve. He'd drop to all fours, hugging them planks, and crawl off an inch at a time. When two of you met, walking from opposite sides, you'd take hold of hands, swing out and past each other, straighten up and let go of hands again. One fellow got scared in the middle of the swing, and the other man fell. After that they strung another cable for a sort of handrail. Wasn't much good, though; kept hitting you in the leg as you walked and you'd come off of there all black and blue.

A fellow was sitting in a painter's chair, hung down over the side of the dam, 'bout twenty-five feet from the top. He looked up and seen a man slip and come down, over the edge. Son of a gun if he didn't kick the face of the dam, swing out and catch the guy right in the air. Saved his life. Tore his coat though. And then the man he caught turned out to be a supervisor. Son of a gun!

It's funny about them hoistmen. Even when they are just running a cage out and down, up and in, they differ a lot. You'd get so you'd know who was at the levers, just from his style. You seen them big buckets to carry wet concrete; did you notice how the whole bottom opens out to let the stuff through? Course, when she empties, the bucket jumps up a little with the weight off. This fellow Smitty, now, he could jerk the lever so when she bounced, she come up twenty-five feet. Nobody else could do it. He could unload ten buckets to anybody else's nine, right along. The other men said it was the helpers he had, but Smitty said No, they could give him any helpers they wanted, and he'd still beat them. Did, too.

Well, I missed that truck. Guess you thought I was going to hit, didn't you? I'll have to have somebody look at these brakes and see if they can't be fixed.

Wide-open Town.—So far as anyone can discern from casual observation, the only occupations of Las Vegas, Nevada, are drinking, gambling and prostitution. They must do something else there, but if so it is not discernible to the innocent tourist's eye. Probably the dam, with up to 5,000 men, mostly single, has helped, though old inhabitants tell me that Las Vegas has always been one of the most wide-open towns in a wide-open state. It is a bit startling, at first, to walk down the main street at 11 A.M. and see in almost every block one or more gambling houses, doors open to every passerby, crowded with men and women, old and young, playing Keno, roulette, poker, shooting craps, or betting on horse races, described by a raucous-voiced gentleman who gets his facts by direct wire from the track. Las Vegas' Painted Ladies go in for raspberry-colored sailor pants, coral-tinted blouses and high-heeled slippers; their faces, beneath the metallic-looking orange rouge which is universal in the Southwest, are haggard and burned like the faces of all desert people. Every second or third man you meet has had about three drinks too many, and is glad of it.

The ladies, as always, drink less or hold it better, and obligingly help keep their gen'l'men friends from rolling into the gutters.

Perhaps I had better break down and confess that going in for sin in a Big Way, as Las Vegas does, seems to me a pretty awful spectacle. It is carrying over the habits of the old West into an era of long-distance buses, radio sets and ubiquitous Ford V-8s. The cowhand or miner who once got to town on an occasional Saturday night now can, and apparently does, come in and raise hell any odd Tuesday morning that he feels like it, and whatever glamour there once was to the business of buying excitement has departed. (A Western friend to whom I said this, replied: "You're just kidding yourself. There never was any glamour, except in Wild West novels.")

Probably I am being both unfair and sentimental, but I found myself making comparisons between Boulder City and Las Vegas, to the disadvantage of the latter. Boulder City was built and is still largely controlled by the federal government, and it has none of the things of which its rival has so many too many. Even if you assume that Las Vegas is Boulder City's necessary slum, you still can't help feeling that in this place private industry shows itself in one of its less savory forms.

(Las Vegas Chamber of Commerce: Please don't write.)

THE PEOPLE, YES

ONCE the government had pushed through programs to help the poor and distressed, it was still not always easy to see that they actually got their benefits. For example, the sharecroppers or tenant farmers in the South gained very little from the Agricultural Adjustment Administration. They existed in a semifeudal state, dependent upon their landlords for food, shelter and clothing, and while their plight had been a national disgrace for years, the landlords were not about to give up their economic advantages that came from exploiting such cheap labor. Also, these poor souls were the first to suffer when the government's crop and acreage reduction measures went into effect.

In 1936, the Secretary of Agriculture, Henry Wallace, having returned from a trip through the cotton states from Arkansas to the East Coast, declared he had never seen, even among the peasants of Europe, such poverty as existed throughout the sharecropper belt. Through the AAA and the Resettlement Administration, efforts were made to deal with the problem but progress was slow.

In some cases, the 'cropper families piled into their old rattletrap cars, if they owned such, and set off for the Far West, in hope of getting work as fruit and vegetable pickers. These migrant workers, their ranks swollen by displaced farmers from the dust-bowl areas, inevitably created new social problems wherever they went. And as migrant workers, they were outside the reach of the AAA.

Just getting work was not enough; after years of hard times, a feeling of security about the future was important too. Thousands of workers flocked to the huge construction jobs, but how were they to live when their part of the work was completed?

These, and many other questions as to the way people were existing in the changing times, needed to be answered. Writers like Erskine Caldwell, James Agee, Benjamin Appel, Nathan Asch, and others, moved out into the heartland to talk with the people and write about them. In the case of Nathan Asch, he simply got aboard a Greyhound bus one day in 1936 and started across country.

NATHAN ASCH

IN SEARCH OF AMERICA*

I WALKED along the street in Texarkana, Texas, where Louisiana, Arkansas and Texas almost make a corner, and I wondered how I could get to live a week with a sharecropper family. I had crossed Arkansas and come here because I wanted to see the most isolated, the deepest cotton country, untouched by the world and not knowing the outside world. Probably I should have gone back to Alabama, but I had heard that of late years cotton had been grown each year further westward, until now Texas was the great cotton state.

But where was I to go? How does one look for a sharecropper's shack? Where does one find the impudence to step off the road, and enter a home and demand shelter there? There are highways that leave Texarkana and go off in every direction; which highway to take? And where does one stop?

I stood and I watched a young man with blond hair and red face look at his car—it had Minnesota plates—and sadly shake his head. I asked what was wrong.

He said, "The axle's broken."

I offered to help him push it to a garage. He said, "What's the use? I can't buy another axle."

I said, "You're a long way from home."

He said, "I've just got enough money to buy gasoline home. I better get a bus ticket instead."

I said, "Let's go and have a glass of beer."

His name was Peder, and he and his brother had a small farm in northern Minnesota. They couldn't get back what they put into wheat, and it didn't pay for them to raise hogs. They had a few cows and a lot of hens; and there was just enough work for one, so they took turns, one staying at home and the other traveling all about the country.

Peder said, "I've been just about everywhere, and I guess I've stopped now."

I asked him how much would a new axle cost, and he told me. I said, "Have you seen how the sharecroppers live?"

* From Nathan Asch's *The Road* (New York, Norton, 1937).

He said, "They live terrible."

"Let's really find out how they live," I suggested. "What they eat and how they sleep, and what they talk about."

He said, "All right. We're bad enough up in Minnesota, but I'll be ashamed to look these people in the face."

We put in a new axle and we got a map, but all we could see were names of towns and of roads. We asked a man at a filling station.

He looked at us strangely but he said, "It's all cotton around here. You go down by the Red River and you'll see nothing but farms."

We drove east out of town on a United States highway, and then it became just a country road. It was too early for plowing, and in the fields there was nothing but stubble. Alongside the road there were tumbled-down shacks.

Peder asked if I wanted to stop. I said No. Let's go on for a while. Down below us was Red River, but first we came to Garland, Arkansas. It was the meanest town that I have ever seen. No city slum, no suburb, no condemned row of tenements ever had a more wretched appearance. With one exception there wasn't a house that was painted, a house that was whole, that had a whole roof, that was not on the verge of collapse. With but that one exception there was not a house that could be called a house. There was no glass in the windows, no doors that had hinges, no wall without a yawning crack. The exception was the church, which was new, and the minister's house. There must have been a thousand people who lived in Garland, Arkansas, but these white and black creatures wore clothes that could not be said to have ever had color or no patches, or been sold new in a store. This was not in the bleak, hopeless Ozarks, it was in rich cotton country; and about a half mile beyond, down by the toll bridge, there was a newly built filling station, and the attendant and a man in breeches and boots were admiring a brand-new automobile. I asked Peder to stop.

We got out of our car and we strolled toward the two men and we stood admiring the beautiful car. I asked the man in boots if the car was his. He smiled Yes.

I asked, "You farm around here?"

He said Yes, he had about four hundred acres.

I asked, "How many tenants have you got?"

He said he didn't know yet. Last year he'd had thirty families, but he said he was considering not having any tenants this year. He was playing around with the idea of having nothing but day labor.

I asked, "Where are the families from last year?"

He said, "Oh, I let them stay on through the winter."

I asked how did he think they had lived on through winter; it didn't seem to me that the heat would stay in with all the holes in the walls.

He said, "Those sons of bitches can live through anything. They've got hides like hogs."

I asked if he didn't think it would increase the value of the land if the improvements on it were weathertight, were in habitable condition?

"No," he said. "Anybody who'd do that would be crazy. He'd be laughed at. Two years ago I had one of those brain storms. I built a new outhouse for each tenant shack. Do you know what those bastards did? The first cold spell, and they knocked down the outhouses and they burnt them for fuel."

"Where can they get fuel?"

"They can buy it. I sell it."

We got back in the car and Peder asked, Where now? I suggested we get on a side road. We drove almost down to Red River, and then turned off on a dirt road.

I said, "What do you think of this for an idea: 'The worse you exploit somebody, the worse you hate him.' You have to. Your conscience wouldn't let you alone."

Peder said, "If I was his tenant I'd shoot him."

We saw a sign, "Lost Prairie—1 mile." We saw a man walking down the road and we gave him a ride. He wore overalls and half of his face was covered by a birth mark. We asked him if he lived in the neighborhood. He said he was a renter. Where did he rent? Well, he didn't rent nowhere right now. The doctor in Texarkana who owned the land he lived on had hired day labor. Sometimes he got day work in the fields.

"How much do you get?"

"Anywheres from fifty to sixty cents a day."

"How many hours do you work?"

"From dark to dark."

We drove along, then the man said he was home. We asked if we could meet his wife, and he took us inside. The shack had four walls, with newspapers stuck in the cracks, and two beds and a stove and a packing box at which the wife was standing and ironing. Two children were in school, and the eldest boy was out rabbit hunting. "Maybe he'll bring us a rabbit." Peder and I sat on a bed and we smoked cigarettes. The wife kept on ironing, then she stopped and straightened her back.

The man said, "Her back gives her misery."

I asked why she didn't go to the doctor that owned the land they lived on.

The man said, "He charges two dollars." Then he lost his temper and shouted at his wife, "Why don't you stop ironing?"

She turned to us. "The children have to look clean or they won't let them in school."

The man muttered, "School!"

The woman said, "If they get an education, it's something nobody can take away from them. I'll keep them in school if I have to die for it."

Peder said, "Why don't you do something about it? Why don't you and your friends get guns and go on the towns?"

The man shook his head. "Well, by God. Something will have to happen pretty soon."

We left. We drove on; that whole country must have been called Lost Prairie, because there was no town on the road.

We came to a shack that was leaning on piles, elevated from the ground, and seeming as if it had to collapse the next moment. There were two Negro children lying on the side of the road; a Negro woman and man sat on the threshold. The man held a twig in his hand. We got out of the car and came toward the house; and the man smiled pleasantly at us.

We said we were from the North; we had been driving around and were talking to people and asking them questions. Could we ask him some questions?

Again he smiled nicely and said, "Sure enough. You want to know the truth and we'll give you the truth."

For the last six years he had been renting eleven acres from the lawyer in Texarkana. It was the time of the year to discuss the renting, but the lawyer had not come; each year he was late; he wanted to scare them into buying a mule. Each year they refused, and the lawyer threatened to stop renting to them. He wanted a hundred and sixty dollars for it, but "it can't be a good mule if he's so anxious to sell it."

The woman said, "If we had money, we'd buy a cow with it."

We asked if we could go inside their home. They nodded "Of course."

There were two rooms; the room they slept in and the room where they cooked. An opening in the wall was the entrance, there was no frame to it, no place for a door. Inside the room there was a mattress on the floor, and that was all. In the inner room there was a stove and an oil lamp and a packing box. That was all in that house. There were no beds, no second mattress for the children, no table, no dresser, no chairs, no mirror; there was no closet; there were no clothes in that house. In the room where they cooked there hung from a nail a side of bacon, they said from a hog they had killed last fall. And the place was a sieve; light could be seen through the four walls and the ceiling.

Peder and I did not look at each other, and we came down from the house, and I said, "I don't see how you people can live."

The Negro said, "We don't live here. We're just here."

I said, "How can he demand a hundred and sixty dollars? Where would you get a hundred and sixty dollars?"

"He'd take it off our share in the fall."

"What is your share in the fall?"

The man didn't know. The reason there was no meal in the house was that until the shares were agreed the storekeeper would not give them credit. Whatever they bought through the summer he put into the book; and in the fall the lawyer settled out of their share. Last fall there was enough left to buy the children a pretty for Christmas.

We left that house and we drove on to another house; and this one had a real door, and I knocked on it; and the door opened, and inside the room was papered with old newspapers. The people living there had a sense of decoration, and the newspapers had been cut into patterns of print and pasted on the walls with frills and with curls. There was a place on the floor where a fire was burning and three Negro women sat around the fire.

They were suspicious of me and remained silent. I tried to explain. In faraway New York City there was a newspaper interested in how they lived. I would write stories about them.

They said they couldn't afford it. I said it would cost them nothing. I would just talk to them and then write about them. They didn't believe me. They didn't believe anybody wrote pieces for nothing. I went back to the car and there was the Negro man talking to Peder. He too was suspicious.

I said, "We're your friends. We can't stand to see how you live. We're going to write about it; we're going to make people so mad they'll have to do something about it."

I took his hand and I pressed it. He pulled it away.

He said, "I was trained by Southern white folks, and I know my place. Maybe if I had been trained up North, I'd have been different. But I'm here. And I know my place and I keep it."

He went back to the house with the paper inside, and we drove on. We stopped at other houses and we saw the same picture and heard the same story. It was the time for renting; and the planters were trying to get advantageous shares; and they were considering abandoning the share system altogether; and hiring day labor to work from dark to dark at fifty to sixty cents for the day. We asked the people what they would do, and we were told: "We don't know what we'll do."

It was in Oklahoma that I went inside the dust storm that for three weeks obscured the sun and made everything, food, water, even the air taken into the lungs, taste gritty. It blew into the eyes, underneath the collar; undressing, there were specks of dust inside the buttonholes; in the morning it had gathered like fine snow along the window ledge; it penetrated even more; it seeped along the wiring of the house; and along the edges of the door button there was a brown dusty stain. Sometimes it did not blow; it stood between the buildings, dulling them, and dulling the mind, making thoughts oppressive, giving the city a mood of foggy melancholy. As in a disaster one only thought of dust, one saw it, felt it, tasted it and lost his sense of smell. In the country, the road, the ditches, the fields, the grass, the plants, even the sky above, everything was covered by the dust; cattle stood head down, immovable, not tasting the gritty leaves; automobiles went slowly; and when even the road was obscured from the driver's vision and all the world, everything that one could possibly see was just a brownness, one had to stop and wait.

Until I had gone over the crest of mountains in Wyoming, the dust was always there. Everything I thought was complicated by the thought of dust; in everything I ate I tasted dust. It was the last thing before I fell asleep, and the first thing with consciousness at waking. I missed Oklahoma City, because arriving in the morning after a sleepless night on the bus, and looking at the choking morning town, I couldn't bear to enter it. I went on in the bus. The thought of air became precious; the memory of pleasant mornings in New England, of plants that were green, of dew on leaves, of the sun brightly rising in a sky that was clear, was so sweet that I half lay on the bounding seat in the grimy bus and daydreamed of it. It became something that had perhaps never happened; something in a life so far in the past it was a previous life. Everyone in the bus seemed dejected, and even the usually squirming children did not squirm now. They sprawled on their seats and whimpered.

Now the dust was lighter; we could see outlines of objects through it, even a quarter of a mile away. The bus had left the flatness of western Oklahoma and had ridden into the Panhandle of Texas, also flat and ever stretching. We were passing wheat land from which the storm had stripped away the top soil, cattle land deposited with dust and ruined as range, and oil three thousand feet below, safe from the elements and with gas pressure waiting to push it to the surface.

We came near Borger; everywhere in the haze we saw camps of sheds with black enormous columns rising from them, and then as the wind again rose, the columns wavered, diffused, sprawled; we approached them, entered them, and were blind as in a night that had no moon to light it. The driver must have guessed the straightness of the road, because we couldn't see our hands laid on our laps; and as we left the blackness into comparative clearness of the dusty air, we saw the cement road was as black as pitch, where previously the wind had played the black stuff on it. Carbon black plants, someone in the bus explained; from millions of badly lighted wicks burning natural gas, soot was deposited, nine tenths of it wasted to dirty the Panhandle air, and what had been retained on slowly revolving cylinders was scraped off; the carbon black, the smallest-particled substance that man knew, invisible even in the microscope, was used in the making of high-speed printing ink.

It was a waste of precious natural gas; in the Panhandle they said that enough natural gas was wasted, in one field alone, to light all of Chicago, with the rest of Illinois. And it wasn't only partially wasted, as in the smudge of making carbon black; at night driving through the range the world was a fantastic night scene of gas-burning flambeaux, illuminating the waste land even through the dust. Almost everywhere there was a derrick, and near it a pipe stuck out of the ground, a tremendous lighted torch, throwing off and consuming gas from the sands below. It was a waste of gas; and it was indirectly ruinous, because the pressure needed to bring oil to the surface was slowly weakening, fading. But what could you do, they said shrugging, when below all that country was the sea of oil and the atmosphere of gas, and it belonged to anyone that could drill to it, that could get to it first? Why should anyone save gas, never to be replaced, when by wasting untold millions of cubic feet of it, he could get a few barrels of oil that he could sell? Even the great oil companies that to keep on existing had to conserve what was down below, even they wasted oil and gas, because they had to compete with other oil companies and had to get the stuff quickly to the ground.

I had a letter for Jim Bailey, a drilling contractor in Pampa. He lived in the hotel where the oil men stayed, and there I found him, ready to go to bed after a hard day's work, with a bottle of bourbon. He was kind; everyone was kind; everyone welcomed a stranger just off the bus, did not ask him questions, made him feel at home; within half an hour there were five men in leather jackets in the room, looking at their glasses and telling stories of the old boom days before the great oil companies had grabbed off all the possible oil-bearing lands. The telephone rang, and Jim Bailey answered it and listened to it and then pulled off his pajamas and pulled on his pants. His crew had broken off a drilling bit three thousand feet below, and the drilling was held up; the hole that had cost thousands, that had taken weeks of endless pounding by the cable tools in the effort to reach the sands below, was lost for good, and he was maybe ruined, unless the bit was fished out and brought back to the surface.

I drove with him through darkness, spotted by the flambeaux burning gas away, past ghostly operating derricks silently pumping oil, past rotary drilling outfits, the whole illuminated derrick shaking as the pile whirled crazily into the hole; off the main highway and through more darkness to the silent, lighted derrick with the crew standing helpless waiting for the boss. Soon the bull wheel spun, and the drilling line descended with the fishing tool, and for hours they fished, as blindly as one does fish, only deeper, over three thousand feet. The drilling line rose time and time again, pushing to the surface nostril-tickling gas, spilling oil over the derrick floor and over us. The donkey engine again rotated its elbows, again the line quickly descended with another tool. I set myself into a derrick strut and I fell asleep; and woke hours later, in the grayness of a Panhandle dawn, with nothing getting lighter as the dust still permeated the entire world. I was tired from the endless traveling, shaking in the bus, no relief from dust in my lungs. And still they were fishing for the broken bit; and someone took me to the hotel in Pampa; and, rested now, twenty-four hours later, I came back to the derrick, and they were still fishing. Jim Bailey, foul now with all the oil on him and a two days' growth of beard, was drinking coffee from a thermos bottle, and beneath his leather jacket the edge of his silk pajama top was still sticking out.

I was walking in the hazy evening along Larimer Street in Denver, hearing music playing and voices through the suddenly opened doors of the Mexican cafés and trying to decide to go into one; then with the noise torn off by the doors again closing, hesitantly going on—when through one of the doors two girls came out and almost fell on me. They were Mexicans; one of them was drunk and asked me if I would buy them wine. We went inside the crowded smoky room; three men sat on chairs and played nostalgic Mexican music; two fat cops, giants among the Mexican boys and girls, walked up and down the room and stood over tables and stared; the dancers and the drinkers, Spanish eyes set in Indian faces, with strong hook noses, high cheekbones, and always even on overalls and cheapest dresses a touch of color, tried to dance and drink, and make believe the police were not in the room, watching them, determined to find trouble.

The two girls led me to a booth and sat themselves and ordered red wine; they drank one glass of wine and then ordered another; and then drank that, and the drunker one of the two said she wanted to dance. I said I didn't want to dance. She said I had to.

I asked the other one, "What's the matter with her?"

She said, "She's in love."

And then I looked up and there was a young fellow with black polished hair looking as if he wished he had a knife.

I rose from my seat and went up to him, and I took his hand and I said, "Look, there's an extra place in our booth and I wish you'd take it."

He said, "Who are you?"

I said, "I'm nobody at all. Just a man from the East."

Suspiciously, he went with me. I ordered more wine, and I acted as if I were terribly interested in the other girl.

I asked her, "What's wrong with them? Why don't they get married?"

She said, "They haven't got no kids."

I said, "What?"

"They can't get a contract," she said, "if they don't have no kids."

I asked for explanations. All these Mexicans worked in the sugar-beet fields in northern Colorado. During the winter they lived in colonies on relief; and in the spring when the time came to make an agreement with the growers for work in the fields, the contract unit was a family, a father, mother and their children. I said I thought that child labor was forbidden; I thought there had been an agreement made.

She said, "Well, maybe there is. All I know is that when beet-picking time comes around they close all the schools, and if you're young and ain't had no time to get kids of your own, you don't get no contract."

I said, "Why don't you people do something about it?"

The boy who was in love shrugged his shoulders. "They say all the time if you don't make a contract, if you don't get off relief, they'll ship you back to Mexico."

I asked, "How old were you when you came?"

"I was born here. They can't deport me."

But the girl who was in love had been five years old when her family had been brought over to work in the beet fields. The next year she had picked beets and had continued ever since. Now she was drunk. And she wanted to dance.

I said, "You two dance. But I want to talk to some of your friends."

He brought some friends over, and the cops came, too.

One of the cops wanted to know, "What's going on around here?"

I rose, and I took my credentials from my pocket.

The cop said, "You mind coming out with us?"

I went out with them. We walked to the corner of the block we were on, and the cop said, "Buddy, you don't want no trouble. And we don't want no trouble. Why don't you go home?"

I asked, "Are you going to run me in?"

He said No, he wasn't. But I was not going back into the Mexican café. He added, "Why don't you be a good fellow and go home?"

Chiver, Aragon and I got into the old dilapidated sedan and started off for northern Colorado. The sedan had been on the go for weeks in other parts of Colorado, and Chiver had tried to sleep in it, had lived in it, had stood on its uncertain top and made speeches to the assembled beet workers. His eyes were red with tiredness, his hands were not steady, and he almost fell asleep in the Denver traffic. Aragon must have been tired too; he had hitchhiked from the North the night before, had reported to his office and had been told to find Chiver coming from the South and to start out again. It must have been the Indian blood in him that made his eyes seem inscrutable, that prevented me in the following two days from guessing Aragon's feelings.

To me, everything about Aragon was amazing; this man whose face was of red copper, whose head was like an eagle's, whose shoulders were so wide that when he spread his arms to prove a spoken point he looked like an eagle with the wings outstretched, who had broad hands and enormous body, had the most musical voice I have ever heard and spoke correct and unaccented English. Look at him and he was a big red Indian, but speak to him and you heard old Spain. He was well read, and though Chiver had been a year to college, Aragon could outargue him on every necessary subject and decide the point and act on it; and though Chiver was the leader of this expedition it was Aragon that led, and Aragon that kept Chiver to the chosen line and called him down when Chiver enthusiastically and devil-take-the-consequences got off the line.

Aragon was a peon and the son of a peon, while Chiver's father had been a beet grower and Chiver himself had grown sixty acres of beets until

293

two years before, and had kept Mexican families on his own farm and had paid them what other growers paid. But the combination of the sugar company and the current times had proved too much; he had been sold out; his wife was on relief; and Chiver was organizing the sugar-beet workers; Aragon was organizing too. They were going into northern Colorado, to visit the colonies of Mexicans and to try by some means to organize them into a common front against the growers.

Yet the growers were as much victims of the situation as the Mexican workers were. The growers did not buy new automobiles as did the planters in the cotton country. When in the fall the price was paid for the delivered beets and divided among the grower and the Mexican, the Mexican got almost nothing, but the grower after he had paid the interest on the mortgage on his house and land, after he had paid for seed and the interest on the loan for seed, did not get anything either. He owned the house he lived in and the land he planted, but the bank in which the mortgage on these chattels lay was controlled by the sugar company, and the company set the price for beets, arbitrarily, without the semblance of an open market, of competition. He could accept the price that was offered by this one company, or his beets could rot.

And all the stories that for years had appeared in the newspapers of the nation describing the awful living standards of sugar workers of other nations and begging for a protective tariff, all these stories were misleading, were lying stories, because when lawyers for the sugar company elected to the United States Senate had finally succeeded in getting the protection, and incidentally ruined the economy of Cuba, the living standards in the sugar country did not rise, the difference between the world price and the American price for sugar was transformed not into increased education, better homes and more nourishing food, but into dividends for the sugar company; and in the blackest year of the Depression, when world trade was paralyzed and profits did not exist, the sugar company, protected by the tariff and profiting from the living standards it had imposed on both growers and workers, made profits of nine millions of dollars.

In the beet industry a lot of work was needed in the fields, and all this work had to be done in the summer months. The grower himself in the spring drilled the land with seed, but when the fourth leaf appeared, and beets had to be blocked, then thinned, hoed, topped, and later in the summer pulled to be trucked to the factories nearby, no natives in America wanted to do this sunburnt, aching work. Years ago Mexican families had been recruited from Mexico, shipped up north in trucks; during the season they lived right in the fields, in shacks, sometimes in wagons to be pulled right to the edge of work so as not to waste time; and when the summer was over they had to leave the shacks and wagons and live in colonies in towns and wait till the following spring. Relief was only an innovation. Up till two years ago six in a family together earned less than three hundred dollars a year, and when they returned to winter quarters with what was left after the storekeepers had been paid, they were forced to pay rent by the same sugar company which also owned the colony they lived in. When relief was introduced the Mexicans were well used to living on almost nothing. And when this year, squeezed by the company, the growers tried in turn to squeeze the Mexicans, by offering them contracts that would pay less even than in previous years, many Mexicans refused. Spontaneous strikes broke out in sugar counties.

And now the announcement had come that those who refused to accept the contracts would be taken off relief and would be deported.

Chiver and Aragon were to visit the colonies in Weld County, richest in all of Colorado, and were to get the Mexicans together at mass meetings and find out if the sporadic strikes and the refusal to accept new contracts would make it possible to organize all the beet workers into one large sugar union that could make itself, they hoped, as strong as the sugar company. The problem was to find the colonies in each town they came to, to get inside of them without the officials of the sugar company knowing, to hold meetings, to organize local unions, to have representatives appointed from each district who could later meet and work out the proposed union's program. The problem further was to convince the terrified Mexicans that beets always would be grown, and that even if the sugar company were to disappear, they, the Mexicans, could not be made to disappear; their work was needed, and whatever happened they would not be deported.

The little car arrived in Brighton, Colorado, and there were natives and Mexicans walking along the street, and we drove to where there were still more Mexican faces, in front of a poolroom, and Aragon got off and talked in Spanish to some boys. He came back.

"They've got a hall somewhere in the colony," he said. "But they don't know if we can get it for a meeting. Let's go down there."

We turned off the main street and the cement highway, got onto a dirt road, passed a polling place (there seemed to be a local election being held that day and a crowd of citizens was there). We drove past progressively poorer houses, a railroad spur and a factory, past the breathless sour smell of old beet pulp, to a place that looked like an empty yard in spite of shacks crazily leaning over it. We talked to a little boy and to a Mexican lady and then Aragon disappeared.

When he came back he said, "They want a dollar for the meeting hall, and they want to know what we want it for. And they look as if they were going to telephone to somebody. We'll hold the meeting in the vacant lot."

We drove back to town and to the pool hall, went inside and Aragon asked for quiet and told everybody in Spanish to come to the vacant lot. In the street he told little boys to summon their fathers. We drove again to the vacant lot and waited.

There was the wall of a house facing where we were and as the Mexicans arrived they went up to the wall and sat on the ground against it and did not look at us nor at each other but rolled cigarettes and waited. When about thirty had arrived Aragon stood before them and spoke to them in Spanish. I did not understand what he said, and they did not seem to listen, but looked at the ground and smoked cigarettes. At first they were in a line before him; then the pattern changed, he was like a star in the half-crescent of a moon; his voice did not change, they did not seem to listen, but soon he was in the center of a circle; though they looked away, they were all around him. I never saw brighter eyes nor more immovable faces; I never knew less of what went on in the minds of people I was watching than when I watched these Mexicans' faces as they listened to Aragon. Then he stopped and Chiver spoke, in English. Chiver told them about the other meetings he had been to, in the South; he said they had been enthusiastic meetings; he said the beet workers in southern Wyoming, in Nebraska, in western Kansas all were organizing, all were going to stand together strong against the growers.

He said, "Once the beet plants are peering out of the ground they can't do a thing without us. But we can do a lot. We can force them to do whatever we want to. And if they don't listen, do you know what we can do? We can go at night, with hoes; five hundred hoes in the dead of night can do an awful lot of damage to a beet field."

The Mexicans weren't listening. Those that were sitting rose; quietly, with no change of expression they drifted, one by one, away. We got back into the car.

Aragon said to Chiver, "You'll never be anything but a bankrupt beet grower, trying to revenge yourself on other beet growers. If I ever again hear you say anything about hoes, I'll smash you in the face."

I didn't hear Chiver speak again, and I never understood what Aragon said, but I felt between him and the other Mexicans a sort of silent understanding. I seemed to feel what he said more in the pauses between his words, in the silence which he, a man not really fitted for speech but more for doing, needed to arrange his thoughts.

We drove on, and we spent that night in Johnston, Colorado. The colony there looked more like an imaginary colony. There was a whitewashed wall and inside there were little whitewashed houses, looking like hives in a bee colony, and really not much larger than bee hives, having only one room. Aragon knew a man who lived in one of the houses, and while word was being sent to the workers to come together, the lady of the house dished food out of a pot that stood on a brazier, while little Mexican girls stood shyly in the doorway and watched us, eyes shining.

It is hard to describe how little this house was, because there were two beds in it, and there was a dresser, and there was the brazier where they cooked, and there was room to stand between the beds, but the whole room was not ten feet square, and in this room lived a family of nine. It was clean, walls whitewashed, curling curtains in the windows, and holy pictures on the walls. And the beds were covered with embroidered spreads, and on one of the beds there lay a little naked baby with a teething ring in the mouth, and on the other were two older children, that looked like twins, asleep. And into this room, now crowded, perhaps fifteen men came in to hear Aragon speak; and after he had spoken they organized a local of the beet workers' union and elected a secretary. It was all done so quietly that the twins never woke.

I spent that night with a motherless family, the children sighing in their sleep, and the father in the morning clumsily feeding canned milk to the youngest child; Chiver and Aragon slept elsewhere, and in the morning we drove to Fort Collins.

It is a larger city. The meeting was held in a lodge hall, two American flags crossed over the speaker's table. When we arrived, we drove through the Mexican streets, and, modern Paul Reveres, we called out whenever we saw a Mexican going by:

"Come on at once to the meeting hall."

There were about three hundred people there when Aragon started to speak. The night before in the two preceding towns the workers all seemed more Spanish in appearance, with little shaven mustaches and long sideburns. Here they were Indians, the faces incredibly red, with bold high cheekbones. They were the faces that one sees on the Indian pennies, in portraits of old Indian warriors. The eyes were not the piercing Spanish eyes, but covered with some inner-looking film, and dull. They sat, tremendous men, like sculptured statues, and heard. And when the time came, they rose and they told their names, and when these had been written down, they clumsily made their crosses.

The reception girl asked, "Is there anything I can do?"

I said, "I'd like to see the manager of the lumber company. I just came from New York. . . ."

"Oh, you're from New York. Just a minute." She pressed a switch, and she said something into the receiver. "You go right in," she told me.

I went into a room where there were many maps, and there a man sat at a desk and nodded to me.

I said, "I'm from New York. I've been traveling all over the country trying to find out what makes things run."

"What makes them run?" he asked.

I said, "I don't know. And the further I'm traveling the less I'm finding out."

"Well, sit down," he said. "What can I do for you?"

I said, "For instance, the lumber industry. I want to get a picture of it. Nobody in the East knows anything about it."

He said, "It's a pretty big industry. We're just one company, but we hire ten thousand men."

"I want to live for a while with the loggers in a lumber camp. I could stay around Tacoma and talk to the men out of work. But I don't want to do that. I want to watch them working," I said.

"And you want to write about it?" he asked.

I said, "Yes."

He thought a moment, then he said, "All right. We're not ashamed of our company."

The following day, the purchasing agent who was returning to headquarters and I drove about sixty miles away from Tacoma and arrived at dusk at the company town, a large office building and company store, little houses for the married men, larger homes for the purchasing agent and the superintendent, and a long row of bunkhouses for the single men. The purchasing agent was hungry, and he drove me toward the office, went inside and brought me a check for tomorrow's breakfast, yelled once or twice, "Bull cook!" got no answer, told me, "You'll find the bull cook somewhere around, and tell him to give you a bed for the night"; and then the purchasing agent went home to supper. It was getting dark, I walked up and down the porch and smoked cigarettes. I had no idea what a bull cook was, but I yelled the words "Bull cook!" just like the purchasing agent.

A little fat man appeared. He wore a skullcap on his head, and he asked me what the hell I wanted. I wanted to know if he was the bull cook, and he said, "God damn it, yes!"

I showed him the check and demanded a bed. He took me toward the bunkhouses and opened one door, and said, "You sleep in that bed. Nobody's using it tonight."

The bull cook disappeared. It was night now and he hadn't even shown me where the washroom was. There were some old newspapers lying in the corner. I took off my clothes and got into bed, and read the old newspapers to forget my hunger. Then I tried to sleep.

It was dark yet when the whistle blew, but I was ready for breakfast, and ate as much as anyone else did. Then I was told to wait for Number 4. I went out to the track and saw logging trains go by, and then an engine came with a sign Number 4. I got into the caboose with three other men, and we started for the camps in the mountains. We rode over narrow trestle bridges, past logged-off, burned-off land, and we turned past a spot where I was told a year before an engine had fallen and killed its crew and still lay, red now with rust, past logs that had rolled off the cars and rotted black in the ditches, up to siding 8. I was to live at camp 2, and I had to wait for Number 110 to get me. Number 4 rolled away, and I waited, near a telephone booth, all alone in the world, and then I saw an engine coming nearer with the sign Number 110. It didn't stop, it just slowed down a little, and I jumped on the steps, holding on with one hand, my bag in the other. That was how I got to camp 2.

The city shoes were the worst part of the stay, because I could scarcely walk in the woods with them on. I stumbled on the stones, and then I tried to walk on the ties; and everywhere I heard axes hitting into wood, and was certain I had now arrived, and I would see men working around a curve. Finally I saw the smoking top of the giant skidder. I saw a section gang working on the grade. I had arrived.

There were about a hundred men flipping the claws of the skyline tight over the logs, watching the great logs suddenly lifted into air, dangling; and then, a lever pushed forward at the track below, the logs rushed down the skyline, down the hill, not like great hulks weighing many tons but like fragile twigs, hitting a huge tree in the way of the skidline and smashing it out of the way, down, down, where they were lowered at the track, where the loaders' claws seized them, lifted them, dexterously placed them on the railroad cars.

I climbed up the tremendous skidder, the world's largest piece of movable machinery, set on four flatcars, and sat with the operator and watched his hand move forward and, gesture multiplied a million times by power, a mile up the hill, at the other end of the steel-cabled skidline, a log was lifted and began rushing down. The other day the cable had snapped and like a mile-long snake had twisted below, cutting off whole trees and killing a man. I watched the loaders riding on the logs, and as these were set down on the cars the loaders jumped up to avoid the shock.

It was three days before I understood the various divisions of work, all the operations from the moment the boss faller marked a tree to fall, to the time when the loaded train chug-chugged up the grade. But by the time I left I could have probably done the simpler work, like loading, or perhaps helped with oiling of the skidder. The skilled work—falling, bucking, marking—I could not have done for years, especially falling, because you almost have to be born a faller to become one; and you usually have to have a brother about your size to be your partner.

I left the roadbed and carefully stepped on a fallen hemlock, walked down it in my city shoes, afraid of stepping on a piece of loose bark that, more slippery than a banana peel, would send me flying into the brush. There was over a hundred feet of this log and then I jumped on a Douglas fir and walked down it, to where I joined the two Bottleson brothers, Big Quart and Little Quart. Little Quart set the head of his axe against an enormous cedar, pointing the way it would fall, hung the oil bottle on, and began knocking off the bark. Big Quart joined him. His axe swung inside of his wrist and hit the naked wood, chipping off a piece. The brothers made the cut—Big Quart and Little Quart, then one and two— even and so smooth it was almost polished out. On opposite sides they made a hole in the bark and set their shaking stands, stepped on them, set the saw opposite the cut, and swung easily this way and that way and in and out in elbowed rhythm. They let me try to saw. They told me to exert no effort, to swing the saw as you would swing a baby, as softly, and themselves they did it, I felt, as tenderly, and to one to the other, oiling it constantly. They took the saw out, and set a wedge in the cut; they hit the wedge with a hammer—one—two—three; they lifted the tremendous tree a small bit of an inch; waited. The tiniest crack was heard. They shouted, jumped. The cedar stood still. Then it leaned—like a swan diver spread itself very slowly down—and fell—crashed—smashed—breaking itself in two. A tree had been in the way; it had snapped off that tree. It had shaken the side of the entire hill.

At four-thirty they heard Number 110 coming down the grade and knocked off work; Big Quart picked up the lunch boxes and the heavy wedges; Little Quart threw the saw upon his shoulders making it dance.

The bucker had finished sawing a log across, and joined the brothers, and together they stepped uphill on the fallen hemlock, walking easily in their calk-bottomed boots.

On the track, the loggers were climbing into the ancient coach, behind Number 110, falling into the plush, torn, oil-filthy seats, staring at the fresh stickers that asked them to join the lumber workers' federation, that had been mysteriously pasted on each glass pane somewhere through the day. They half lay, and steam rose out of their clothes. They were too lazy to light cigarettes.

"Oh, for Mae West," somebody called out.

Everybody smiled.

"Oh, for a Turkish bath and a glass of beer."

Slowly they passed the lunch boxes to be piled up forward.

"Look at this damned thing," said one they called San Quentin Joe. "Why can't I get a thermos that doesn't leak? I want some coffee, too."

Somebody suggested, "Thow it out of the window."

"I'd like to," said San Quentin Joe, "throw it the fifteen miles straight down to headquarters, so it will smash against the purchasing agent's head."

"Pipe down, Joe," whispered the other. "I'll bet there's a stool pigeon around."

San Quentin Joe slowly stood in the aisle, turned around and announced in a loud voice, "Listen, stool. I've served time, and I'll serve time again. You tell that purchasing agent if he ever comes to camp 2, I'll cut him into pieces and make him over again."

After supper we went to the bunkhouses, and it seemed to me everything was too quiet. Men lay on their bunks and read magazines. I asked if that was all they did. I was told these were the married men, who had to save their money. Some others were in Bunkhouse 9.

I went to 9. I slid back the door; and there were about twenty men sitting on the bunks, watching, and in the center of the room, on the table covered with a blanket, there was a poker game going on. I joined the game. They were the wildest crew I'd ever played with. It was table stakes, and they thought nothing of putting twenty dollars on an ace in the hole, twenty dollars it had taken them weeks to save, and which they were going to spend on a wild weekend on the Seattle skid road. Sometimes they won and their imaginations soared, and again they lost and went to sit on the bunks and to watch, forced now to remain in the camp for many weeks to come.

I was returning to my bunkhouse that night, and one of the loggers suggested I go with him. He took me to another car; there half of the men in camp were listening to a union organizer. And he had not ridden up on trains as I had. There was no transportation for an organizer. He had walked up the hill along railroad ties, hiding each time a logging train went by. If the timekeeper had found him, he'd have been beaten up. They listened to him urging them to support the federation; and when at eight forty-five the lights flickered, warning us that in fifteen minutes all lights would be out, the organizer had the signed slips in his pocket and had disappeared in the mountain night, to somehow find his way back to the road fifteen miles below.

But I saw them also when they didn't work. They had a five-day week, and Friday night the camp would be empty; they would be with their families, or dead drunk in a hotel with a two-dollar whore; or they would be laid off, on the skid road in Tacoma, in Seattle, in Spokane.

I saw these towns at the height of the season, when millions of feet of rough lumber were shipped every day to Japan, to Australia, to South America, to Europe; when other millions of feet were cut into planks and made into chairs and sent to every town in the Union; when lumber companies operated at capacities; and still the skid road in Seattle was black with unemployed loggers on relief, on the soup line, in shelters. I saw the pitiful dime shows, where not only ancient pictures were shown, but the piano played, and a line of unbeautiful girls, dressed in dirty rompers, kicked their ungraceful legs not very high. And the men didn't watch them. Their eyes were not alive. They slept, or if they didn't sleep their minds were fogged with hunger, no home, nothing to live for, no tomorrow to expect. Somehow they had gotten a dime, and they were better off than were those with empty pockets outside in the rain.

The night I stayed in a flophouse I couldn't bear to breathe through my nose, and I couldn't bear to look at the other men on the mattresses about me. I was there to see them and see how they lived, but I didn't care if I missed this sight, because if I stayed there another hour I didn't want to live. The lights were out, except in the hall, and I lay on my arms behind me, and I closed my eyes and I closed my mind. And then I began to hear that these men sleeping were beginning to breathe in and out together, as if they somehow had become one homeless unemployed, as if all this breathing in and out together had become one gigantic sigh. I rose, and put on my shoes, and I walked out into the rain, and in doorways lay these men's future, lay what they would become: junk, with still beating arteries, huddled in doorways.

It wasn't the purchasing agent the men hated so much. It was the fact that the pay was small, and the week had been shortened to five working days, and the season was short, only a few months, and there were too many loggers for the work to be done, and there was no other work to be done; and they hated the fact that for the moment they were working, were eating, were sleeping in beds; but soon, as inexorably as death, a notice would come from the Tacoma office through the purchasing agent, through the timekeeper, that the season was ended, that they were to be laid off, that they had better prepare for the Seattle skidline.

Six months before there had been no Coulee City, Washington, nor Grand Coulee, Washington, nor Mason City, Washington. There had been, since the earth first formed, a flatness made by lava, through which from off the mountains flowed the Columbia River. A glacier inched down from the north, and with it crept rocks and gravel, and for a million years the river dug another bed in lava. The glacier disappeared, the river swung back to its earlier course, and left the weird Grand Coulee, a valley in the lava, a fifty-mile-long trench, miles wide, with walls a thousand feet high. The walls were dark, streaked with green and red, and in some crevasses there grew a little bit of grass. But the world at this place was volcanic dead world, until word came that the Grand Coulee was to be dammed off, turned into a great irrigating ditch, and the dam itself would create more electric power than could be made by any other dam in North America, or maybe in the world.

It was eighty years since first this thought had come of damming the Columbia River waters and transforming the million acres of volcanic-ash-topped desert into farming land, and it might have taken another eighty years before the thought was realized in digging; only in the Pacific Northwest there were too many people out of work, and to take up the slack the federal government was creating work and had set aside millions for this digging project. Almost all the men chosen to work on the dam would be the unemployed and taken off relief.

Experts came, surveyed and drafted and blueprinted; builders came and put up the company town for three thousand men—so many dormitories, two men to a room, so many houses for the married men, a store of such a size with furniture to sell and clothes and groceries, a movie house, a jail, a beauty parlor for the women folks, a bank if you wanted to save your money; and on the other side of the proposed dam wall there also grew up the town of Grand Coulee, Washington, for those who didn't want to save their money, with beer parlor, saloons, gambling joints and whore-houses. When I got to the Grand Coulee Dam, operations had not started very long before, but there were almost ten thousand people in that former waste; and in Coulee City, which was neither company town nor night town, I met a man who had five thousand dollars and was going to build a restaurant and grill, and he told me:

"In business you can't be afraid. You've got to spend money to make it."

The proposed irrigation of the Columbia River basin was a relief proj-ect, but you'd think the place was a boom town. Speculators had gotten hold of land along the highway leading to Grand Coulee, and as the bus drove along walls eaten away by millions of years of water, suddenly there was a proposed townsite. Somebody had put up the sign, Grand Coulee, in tall letters; underneath, in smaller letters, Good Water, Business and Resi-dential Sites, Acreage; had measured off imaginary plots of land and stuck in small stakes marked Bank, Hardware Store, Garage; a little further off on more empty land there were the words Residential Section; and there was absolutely nothing there but these signs and basalt rock and high coulee walls. And in Coulee City men stood before offices marked Real Estate, and sauntered over toward any car that stopped and asked people to think of the home of their dreams and said this place was it.

The combined companies that had contracted to put up the power plant and the first unit of the dam really surpassed magnificence when they built the company town. The little rooms were neat, the showers clean and of the latest type, the glorified store had as many counters as a department store, the recreation hall was lined by a long copper-covered bar; there were pin games standing around the hall, there were card tables, and pool tables and a candy counter. The dining hall shone like an elegant restaurant in New York; and the kitchen looked like a laboratory, with most modern equipment; there was a special machine for taking tendons out of chicken thighs, and there was a special room for making ice cream.

The combined companies had not been afraid to spend money. But then there was no reason to be afraid when they had a contract with the federal government, when they were assured that their dormitories and their elegant dining hall would be filled for years; when every pin game, and every ticket the man sold in their movie house was bringing back money they had paid out as wages. They could give nourishing food and have clean linen on the workers' beds; they were taking back in the form of pay for room and board more than half of the twenty dollars weekly wage they paid. And the men who worked with a shovel eight hours day outside in the coulee, married men whose families had been for years on relief, who had lost homes and had had to give up their insurance policies, whose children needed to have their teeth repaired, and needed shoes for school in the Northwest winter, these men ate well; but now that they had jobs and had been taken off the odious relief, they could send their families less each week in cash than they had received on relief.

And there again I saw how people hate the people they rob. I was in the office of the combined companies, and I said I would like to visit the night town of Grand Coulee. Everyone was horrified; everyone warned me against going. I was told, "They hate people that wear white collars and shirts. They take their meanness out in drink there; and when they're drunk they're dangerous; they'll think nothing of smashing you in the jaw, or of stabbing you."

I went there at night, and I was scared. There were no lights on the one street of Grand Coulee; but light came out of the saloon windows and fell on the wooden planks and threw shadows on the overalled men that stood on the street. They stared at me, and I walked nervously, trying not to meet their eyes. I heard voices shouting in a place called Black Mack's, and I forced myself to enter. There were perhaps fifty men there all drinking beer and all gathered around a blond woman who was playing the piano. I stood and I listened to drunks trying to sing. I began to notice one was staring at me, and I felt cold and did not look at him. I tried to keep on listening to the singing, and I tried to edge out of the place. But the man came toward me as I was trying to get out. He put his hand out and stopped me and said:

"Let's have a beer."

I said, "O.K. Let's have it on me."

He said, "If you don't have it on me, I'll cut your heart out."

We had a beer on him. Then on me. Some others joined in and everybody drank and everybody paid. We became friendly. They asked me since I had a home what did I want to come to this hellhole for. I told them.

The man who had wanted to cut out my heart said, "Come on outside."

Outside, beyond the few lights around us and the string of flares in the Coulee, lighting up the construction, everything was dark. No one lived a mile, nor fifty miles away. There was no light in the sky, there was no wind where we stood. There was nothing except the badly used piano inside, and drunks singing.

The man said, "I didn't want to tell you in there, but I'm a poet."

I said, "Yes?"

"Yes," he said, "I'm alone a lot. And I get to thinking about things. It comes out in words, sort of."

"Could I read it?"

"It's for nobody to read." He hesitated. "I do it for myself."

"I'd like to see it," I said.

He was shy. "No. It would be too much like showing my insides. I guess not. Let's go in and have another beer."

SECURITY AT ANY COST

MANY PEOPLE became disheartened when, after two or three years of the New Deal, Utopia was not at hand. This mood made them peculiarly more susceptible to political demagogues and political "prophets" than they had been even in the earlier hopeless days of the Depression. H. G. Wells said, "The New Deal has not gone far enough fast enough for them, and that is what the shouting is about."

Thousands upon thousands of Americans turned to the nostrums of the Catholic "radio priest," Father Coughlin, to the panaceas of Dr. Francis Townsend, with his Old Age Pension Plan, and to the Share-the-Wealth plan of Senator Huey Long.

Dixon Wecter said, "Whatever evil they did, these salesmen of panaceas, even the most cold-blooded and cynical of them, helped in their fashion to hasten the adoption of social security."

Nobody knows just how far Huey Long might have traveled along the road to fascism. His activities won him many loyal followers, but also earned him the bitter resentment of many others, even in his home state of Louisiana. Hodding Carter, an anti-Long newspaperman in Hammond, knew what it was to fight the Kingfish head on. He now publishes a newspaper in Greenville, Mississippi, but he didn't leave Louisiana until after Long's death.

HODDING CARTER

HUEY LONG:
AMERICAN DICTATOR *

FOR newspapermen, those were Gargantuan, memorable days. You stood beside his hotel dining table, as he slopped up great tablespoonfuls of cereal with a sidewinding sweep or tore broiled chicken to pieces with his fingers, and you jotted down the incessant harangues against the lying newspapers, the city machine, and the battered enemy politicians, while the bodyguards glowered protectively near by. You didn't like him, if only because the slugging of newspapermen didn't seem justifiable even for vote

* Condensed from *The Aspirin Age,* ed. Isabel Leighton (New York, Simon and Schuster, 1949).

getting, and especially when the strong-arming became personal. You were chased by militiamen across the parade grounds of Jackson Barracks in New Orleans and held a prisoner after you had sneaked in to discover whether the Governor was calling out the troops on the eve of the Senatorial election—in which the Governor was a candidate.

In a corridor of the garish Roosevelt Hotel, managed by an oily former shoe clerk who was now his paymaster and treasurer, you watched a fellow reporter being hustled out of the Governor's suite. Inside the suite the reporter had struck the Governor in retaliation for being cursed, and the Governor had struck back, but only after his bodyguards had pinioned his attacker.

You interviewed him after he had precipitated a silly international incident by receiving a German admiral in disheveled green pajamas, and you laughed in spite of yourself at his shrewdly appealing account of his gaucherie. You heard a pale-faced man, thrust before a microphone, identify himself as Sam Irby, who had been kidnaped by state police on the eve of an election because he had threatened to tell what he knew about his daughter and the Governor, who employed her as his secretary. And after Irby had told who he was, in front of the microphone in the hotel headquarters, you marveled at his exoneration of the Governor, and speculated upon the reasons therefor.

Afterward, in the corridor, a fellow reporter was to have a gun thrust into his stomach as he sought to enter the elevator on which the mysterious Mr. Irby was being whisked away.

And then you testified in United States District Court that a telegram, also absolving the Governor and purportedly coming from the mother of another kidnaping victim—the secretary's ex-husband—was signed with the name she had borne before her second marriage. Counterfeit, neither pure nor simple, was this telegram which you had seen and read on a speaker's stand in New Orleans on one of the last heated nights before election. And so, endlessly, through brawling campaigns, brawling legislative sessions, brawls . . .

By the spring of 1935, Huey Long owned Louisiana. And in that spring another and lesser man, except for his honesty, gave a fey, lonely warning.

The Louisiana legislature had granted Senator Long, through his administrative and judicial proxies, incontestable control of all elections, including the appointment of commissions, the power to disqualify unfriendly voters, and the privilege of padding the voting lists wherever and whenever necessary. Already he possessed the courts, the municipal police forces, the schoolteachers, the taxing authorities, the Governor, the state government, even the banks. Now, the vote itself.

And Mason Spencer, an unimportant, honest man, rose in the legislature and said this:

> When this ugly thing is boiled down in its own juices, it disenfranchises the white people of Louisiana. I am not gifted with second sight. Nor did I see a spot of blood on the moon last night. But I can see blood on the polished floor of this Capitol. For if you ride this thing through, you will travel with the white horse of death. White men have ever made poor slaves.

Representative Spencer was a better prophet than historian. In September of that year, the Capitol's marble floors were soiled with blood. Huey Long's blood, and the blood of the quiet, studious young doctor who shot him.

But the prophet of tragedy had overlooked the history of his state. Most Louisianians had been docile political slaves for years. Few knew enough about their state to recognize this almost uninterrupted and hitherto gently managed servitude. Nor was it something which those who did know want to be bruited about.

Louisiana politics from the Purchase until the Civil War was a story of genteel corruption, of steady political degeneration, of venality, of a studied neglect of civic advancement. Reconstruction further debilitated self-government; and where Reconstruction ended, rule under the gold-directed manipulation of the Louisiana Lottery began. At the beginning of the twentieth century, Louisianians could count on the fingers of one hand those major public servants who in all Louisiana history had been honest and progressive, active in behalf of the small people, and given to implementing campaign promises with administrative performance. This is not to say that all were politically immoral or amoral, though most of them were. They resembled atavistic mastodons, towering above and unknowingly becoming trapped in a surging human slough. In this they were not unlike their fellow politicians elsewhere. The difference was that Louisiana had been so very safe for the mastodons.

Such was the political Louisiana in which Huey Pierce Long was born in 1893, in impoverished Winn Parish in north Louisiana, a breeding ground of economic and political dissenters. His background was tailor-made for a politician. A log cabin, albeit a substantial one, was his birthplace. His father was a farmer of small means but with considerable ambition, who managed to send six of his nine children—but not Huey—to college.

Young Huey hated both farm work and conformity. In high school he discovered his talent for spell-binding oratory, and the power of a vocabulary enriched by Biblical allusion and directness, acquired naturally in a devout Baptist home. This gift was useful in school politics, and soon thereafter in the art of the traveling salesman, an occupation which he chose upon graduation because his father was not able to send him, the eighth child, to college.

The years between his graduation and his becoming a member of the Louisiana bar at twenty-one tested to the limit his extraordinary physical energy and driving mental discipline—the only discipline which he ever perfected himself. He married before he reached the voting age, and supported himself and his wife by peddling Cottolene, a cooking compound, throughout north Louisiana, meeting thereby and making friends of many farm folk who were to become the core of his political organization. He attended Oklahoma University Law School for one tempestuous term. Then, incredibly, he completed the three-year law course at Tulane University in eight months and, securing a special examination from the Louisiana Supreme Court, became a lawyer at twenty-one. No other student at Tulane has ever matched this record.

As Huey Long put it in his autobiography, he "came out of that courtroom running for office."

He hung out his shingle in Winnfield, county seat of Winn Parish. And here he received his first lessons in an economic-social philosophy that would later burgeon into a gaudy national movement. His first benefactor in Winnfield was a state senator named Harper, a prosperous man for the locality, but a "radical" who proposed a redistribution of national income as the only cure-all for the country's ills. During the First World War, Harper published a pamphlet calling for conscription of the nation's wealth as well as its manpower. A federal grand jury indicted him. He was defended by his young disciple, Huey, who was deferred in the draft because he had a wife and child. (Huey also tried to gain exemption as a public official. He was a notary public.) Huey, through questionable strategy, won Harper's acquittal.

Most of his other early cases were minor ones, the only kind available to a beginner in a crowded profession. But at twenty-four Huey sought the one state office open to one of his age, a state railroad commissionership. The Railroad Commission was Louisiana's three-man utilities regulating body. He won. In the campaign he gained another ally, an older Winnfield man named O. K. Allen, who lent him five hundred dollars to help finance his campaign. Later, when Long was elected United States Senator, he rewarded O. K. by making him his Governor, stooge, and errand boy.

As Railroad Commissioner, Huey was something uncomfortably new and strange. Some regarded him as a radical menace; others saw only a coarse publicity-seeking clown, a thickening, comical-looking youngster with a face that was a puffy caricature of a cherub, with its dimpled chin, snub nose, and unruly, curling reddish hair. But among the masses there were multiplying thousands who saw a champion, a new Great Commoner. He damned and insulted Bigness in all its Louisiana manifestations: Standard Oil, the state's dominant and frequently domineering industry; the large corporations; the corporation lawyers. He clamored for a common-carrier pipeline law—Standard had denied the use of its own to the independents, among them a company in which Huey owned stock—and for a higher severance tax on oil. He won a telephone rate reduction.

In 1920 he supported, for Governor, John M. Parker, a onetime Bull Moose, because he believed the comparatively liberal Parker would deal strongly with Standard Oil. But Parker, to Huey's thinking, was too lenient after he became Governor. Huey broke with him, was indicted and convicted of libeling the Governor, and was fined a dollar and given a thirty-day suspended sentence. He refused to pay the fine, so the judge and opposing counsel made up the dollar themselves.

But he was winning friends and influencing voters. In 1924, at the height of the bitter Klan fight in Louisiana, Huey Long, now thirty, announced for Governor. He tried to go down the middle on the Klan issue. He almost succeeded. Before Election Day he predicted that he would win if rain didn't keep the mud-farmers away from the polls. It rained. Yet, in a three-cornered race, he polled seventy-three thousand votes against eighty-four thousand and eighty-one thousand for the other two candidates. His day had not yet dawned. But already the uneasy feeling had arisen among his opponents that he would be unbeatable the next time.

From 1925 to 1928 Huey mended political fences, kept himself in the headlines, and built up a large and lucrative practice as attorney for some of the vested interests against which he ranted. He explained it in his autobiography this way: "When the millionaires and corporations fell out with each other, I was able to accept highly remunerative employment from one of the powerful to fight several others who were even more powerful. I made some big fees with which I built a modern house in the best residential section of Shreveport at a cost of forty thousand dollars." There were other and less charitable explanations of his affluence.

The 1928 campaign was more like a cyclonic disturbance than another three-way race for the governorship. Huey was probably the most indefatigable campaigner and best catch-as-catch-can stumper the demagogically fertile South has yet produced. He belabored and promised and defamed, speaking in the harsh, bitter language of the poor man, eighteen and twenty hours a day. His promises were bright ones, long overdue: good roads for the farmer, lower utility rates, free bridges, free schoolbooks. He mixed filthy imputations with rhapsodic pleading. Beneath the erroneously named Evangeline oak, he drove his program home to open-mouthed, whooping Cajuns:

And it is here that Evangeline waited for her lover Gabriel who never came. This oak is an immortal spot, made so by Longfellow's poem. But Evangeline is not the only one who has waited here in disappointment. Where are the schools that you have waited for your children to have that have never come? Where are the roads and the highways that you spent your money to build, that are no nearer now than ever before? Where are the institutions to care for the sick and disabled? Evangeline wept bitter tears in her disappointment. But they lasted through only one lifetime. Your tears in this country, around this oak, have lasted for generations. Give me the chance to dry the tears of those who still weep here.

No rain fell on Election Day this time. The evil city, New Orleans, again rejected him, but Catholic and Protestant farmers united to give him a lead, though not a clear majority. His two opponents wouldn't join forces; and at thirty-five Huey Long sat in the Governor's chair that he was to transform into a throne. Louisiana's poor whites had come into their own. "Every man a king, but no man wears a crown," Huey's campaign banners had proclaimed. No man, that is, but Huey himself. And already he was boasting, "I'm going to be President someday."

The campaign had been only a movie trailer, teasingly heralding what was to come. Long summarily discharged every state jobholder under executive control who had not actively supported him. Loyal lads from the bayous and burnt stump lands began to replace the town and city slickers. Lacking a majority at the first session of the legislature, he swapped patronage for concessions, and in both House and Senate placed his own men in the chair. The legislature approved his proposal for a thirty-million-dollar bond issue to provide farm roads, increased hospital and other institutional support, and free schoolbooks, levying a severance tax and higher gasoline taxes to pay for the program. Behind Huey were the people, and the people wanted these things.

And with the people behind him, Huey expanded ominously. Defying rule and convention, he personally directed strategy from the floors of the House and Senate. Once he bragged that he was the state constitution now, and again that he had bought a legislator like a sack of potatoes. He coerced banks which hesitated to make the state a tide-over loan. When the legality of his free textbook law was challenged because it included parochial schools among the recipients, he argued his own case before the United States Supreme Court and won brilliantly. Without constitutional authority, he ordered the state militia into the unfriendly, wide-open parishes adjoining New Orleans, and closed the casinos until the gamblers co-operated.

All this was shocking enough to those Louisianians who favorably recalled less troublesome days and ways. But when Huey summoned the legislature into special session to enact a five-cent occupational tax on oil to aid "the sick, the halt, the blind, and the children," all hell broke loose. A barrel-house free-for-all took place on the floor of the House when Long's Speaker, smelling impeachment in the air, declared the House adjourned *sine die*. Bloody-faced legislators groped blindly for assailants who had struck them from behind. Men were felled by inkwells, canes, bare fists. A protesting representative hopped from desk to desk like a mountain goat, vainly trying to reach the Speaker and wreak personal vengeance on him. Men were cursing, screaming, some sobbing in anger.

The next day the Speaker decided that the House had not adjourned, and the House proceeded to impeach Huey Long. The charges ranged from the grave to the ridiculous. Huey had sought to bribe legislators. He had plotted the murder of an opposition Senator. He had misused, misapplied, and misappropriated state funds. He had squandered monies allocated to a national governors' conference in New Orleans on a riotous, bosomy party, testimony concerning which left some governors red-faced. He had acted unbecomingly in public places, even to the extent of getting cockeyed drunk. Without authority he had ordered the classical old Governor's Mansion torn down to make way for a new one. He habitually used unquotable profanity, required signed, undated resignations from his political appointees, made illegal loans. The House impeached.

Huey fought back with promises, intimidation, and circulars, distributed by the hundreds of thousands by state employees to the faithful. Again he barnstormed Louisiana. His primary targets, not altogether without justification, were Standard Oil, the newspapers—particularly the New Orleans newspapers—and the old political guard.

To most of the state it looked as if Huey was finished. Then, dramatically, he produced a round robin, signed by fifteen senators, who declared that no matter what evidence was submitted to the Senate they would not vote to convict the Governor because they believed the charges against him were invalid. The number was one more than enough to prevent the two-thirds majority necessary for conviction. The deserving fifteen reaped earthly rewards, and never again was Huey in dire political danger.

From this fiasco emerged the dictator, vindictive and intent upon a domination that could not again be challenged. No holds had been barred by either side in the impeachment fight. From now on there were to be no holds except those in which Huey was master. The impeachment fight technique would be improved upon later, but never radically altered. Frighten the wavering legislator by appealing over his head to the voters. Woo him with certain gratuities to be arranged on the side. What was the legislature, anyway? Just a hodgepodge of ward heelers from New Orleans, a scattering of lawyers, a couple of wagonfuls of simple-minded and simpleton farmers, most of them alike in that they had a price. Own them. Fashion them into a ready blade with which to carve empire.

Louisiana's frightened, vengeful Governor surrounded himself with a half-dozen gun-ready, slugging bodyguards. He established a weekly newspaper, the *Louisiana Progress*, staffed it principally with skillful, conscienceless young newspapermen, and sicked it on his enemies. State employees found it good insurance to subscribe to the *Progress,* the number of subscriptions depending upon the size of their salaries, but with a minimum of ten to be sold, eaten, or used as wallpaper. No opponent big enough to be worthy of notice escaped its libeling. The voters of the nation's most illiterate state could understand its cartoon obscenities even when they couldn't spell out the text.

The public-works program went into high gear. The Depression was rocking Louisiana. Public works meant needed jobs. And the administration could count on at least five votes for each employee; the votes of the aunts and uncles and cousins and wives and children of jobholders who made it clear to their relatives that their fifteen to thirty dollars a week was secure only so long as they could prove their loyalty with political performance.

The first program was followed by a second and more ambitious one: a sixty-eight-million-dollar highway construction project, a five-million-dollar skyscraper capitol, and another twenty million dollars in assorted projects, all to be financed by an additional three-cent hike in the gasoline tax. With a year and a half yet to serve as Governor, and with the opposition organizing against the program, Huey decided to run for the United States Senate with the state program as his platform.

The use of the sound truck and the financial strangulation of the enemy city of New Orleans were the principal innovations of the campaign. Conservative, goateed, seventy-year-old Joseph Ransdall, the incumbent whom Huey dubbed "Feather Duster," burbled unavailingly. Huey won hands down; and when his inimical Lieutenant Governor claimed the Governorship because of Long's election to the Senate, Huey called out the state police and the National Guard, read the Lieutenant Governor out of office, and put in the president *pro tempore* of the Senate as acting Governor. He designated his old benefactor, O. K. Allen of Winnfield, as the apostolic choice for the next full term.

Meanwhile he concocted what might have been a good if desperate expedient for the cotton South. With Biblical precedent to back him up, he proposed that in protest against ruinous five-cent cotton the South should let its cotton fields lie fallow for a year. But Huey managed to insult Texas, the South's principal cotton producer, and the Texas legislature, thumbing its nose at "the arrogant jackass who brays from Louisiana . . . ignoramus, buffoon, meddler, and liar," would have none of the plan. So it died.

The wider horizon beckoned. In January 1932, the Kingfish from Louisiana breezed into Washington. For the next three and one-half years he performed simultaneously in two rings of a dazzling political circus, the capital of Louisiana and the capital of the nation. He soon broke with President Roosevelt, each sensing in the other a challenge, and from the Senate floor ridiculed "Prince Franklin, Knight of the Nourmahal," and his New Deal, unconcernedly violating the Senate's rules of personal decorum by lampooning such Administration stalwarts as Carter Glass, Henry Wallace (Lord Corn Wallace), Ickes (the Chicago Chinch Bug), Hugh Johnson (Sitting Bull), Joe Robinson, and Pat Harrison. No Senator could match him in debate or in monopolizing the front page. Day after day Huey made news. Sometimes amusing news, as in the controversy over whether corn bread should be dunked or crumbled in turnip-greens pot-likker. Sometimes bad news for Huey, as when an unidentified guest at a Sands Point, Long Island, club resented with hammering fists the Kingfish's impatient and misdirected attempt to make use of a urinal before the other had moved aside. On another occasion his national and state prestige sagged momentarily when the Old Regular machine in New Orleans rebelled, returned its mayor, T. Semmes Walmsley, to office, and Walmsley followed up his victory by journeying to Washington and waiting around unavailingly to thrash the well-guarded "yellow coward."

In 1934 Long formalized the program which he hoped would eventually win him the Presidency. The hazy concept of a national redistribution of wealth, presented fifteen years before by the obscure state Senator from Winn Parish, took definable shape in a national "Share Our Wealth" organization. No dues were necessary. Huey produced the expense money as easily as the nation disgorged the followers, both by the hundreds of thousands. No matter that the Share Our Wealth program was demonstrably impracticable as presented. It *was* believable: a limitation of fortunes to $5,000,000; an annual income minimum of $2,000 to $2,500 and a maximum of $1,800,000; a homestead grant of $6,000 for every family; free education from kindergarten through college; bonuses for veterans; old-age pensions, radios, automobiles, an abundance of cheap food through governmental purchase and storage of surpluses. The Share Our Wealth members had their own catchy song, "Every Man a King," their own newspaper, the mudslinging *Louisiana Progress*, expanded now to the *American Progress*.

The movement was nothing less than a new political party, heir to the yearnings and frustrations of the Populists, the Whiskey Rebels, the Know-Nothings, the Free Silverites, of all the have-nots of capitalism. Almost singlehanded, Long won the election of Hattie Caraway of Arkansas to her deceased husband's Senate seat. The Share Our Wealth clubs began cutting across old lines in Mississippi, Alabama, Georgia. The New Deal became worried and began to use its Louisiana patronage accordingly.

By legislative action Long made sure that no federal relief money could be obtained by any Louisiana municipality or county except with the approval and supervision of an agency of his own. The administration retaliated by withholding PWA project funds. Revenue agents roved through Louisiana from 1932 until long after Long's death, and with eventually decisive results. A Senatorial committee timorously held hearings in New Orleans relative to the corruption which accompanied the election to the Senate of a Long ally, John Overton; and, after being defied, browbeaten, and ridiculed by Huey and his jibing lieutenants, exonerated Overton with a weak-kneed finding that he "had not personally participated in or instigated any fraud."

As the Share Our Wealth chorus swelled, Huey, like a wise military tactician, took care to protect his rear. In a spectacular, degenerative series of special sessions in 1934 and 1935, his legislature reduced Louisianians almost literally to the status of Indian wards. Together with this final elimination of the actualities of democratic self-government—to the unconcern of a majority of the unconsulted electorate—came new benefits: homestead tax exemption, theoretically up to two thousand dollars; abolition of the one-dollar poll tax; a debt moratorium act; and new taxes—an income tax, a public utilities receipts tax, an attempted "two cents a lie" tax on the advertising receipts of the larger newspapers, which the United States Supreme Court pronounced unconstitutional.

Perhaps it seems inconceivable that any legislature, no matter how great the material rewards for its complaisant majority, could have so completely surrendered a people's political powers and economic and personal safety to one man. But Louisiana's legislature did. Administration-designated election supervisors were given the sole right of selecting voting commissioners, sole custody over the ballot boxes themselves, and the privilege of designating as many "special deputies" as might be necessary to guard the polls. Huey's figurehead Governor, O. K. Allen, was given the power to call out the militia whenever he—or Huey—wished. The Governor could —and did—expand the state police force into a swarm of private agents, some uniformed and some not, their number and the identity of the ununiformed alike a secret. The State Attorney General was empowered to supersede any district attorney in any trial. The State Tax Commission was given the right to change any city or county tax assessment, so that a misbehaving corporation or individual might know just who held the economic stranglehold. An ironically designated civil service board was created, with appointive control over all fire and police chiefs, and a school budget committee with the right to review the appointments of every schoolteacher and school employee. The Governor was even enabled to replace the entire city administration of Alexandria, a recalcitrant municipality in which Huey had once been rotten-egged. There were other repressive measures, many others. But these are sufficient to indicate what had happened to self-government in Louisiana.

It is perhaps a corollary that in the last year of his life Long became obsessed with a fear of assassination. He increased his armed bodyguard, and took other unusual precautions to insure his personal safety. In July 1935, he charged on the floor of the Senate that enemies had planned his death with "one man, one gun, and one bullet" as the medium, and with the promise of a Presidential pardon as the slayer's reward. This plot he said, was hatched in a New Orleans hotel at a gathering of his enemies

A dictograph, concealed in the meeting room, had recorded the murderous conversation. I was at that meeting. It was a caucus of die-hard oppositionists, dolefully trying to decide what to do for the next state campaign. And the "plotting" was limited to such hopefully expressed comments as "Good God, I wish somebody would kill the son of a bitch."

And somebody did. That July, the white horse of death, foreseen by Mason Spencer earlier in the year, was but two months distant. On the night of September 8, a slender, bespectacled man in a white suit stepped from behind a marble pillar in the capitol as Long, accompanied by his closest aides and bodyguard, hurried to the Governor's office. Dr. Carl Austin Weiss, the man in the white suit, drew a small pistol and fired once. Seconds later, the assassin lay dead, his body and head riddled by sixty-one shots. Huey Long staggered away with one bullet wound, perhaps a second, in his stomach. Thirty hours later he died.

The ghost is not yet laid, although Huey Long is dead these many long years. Nor will it be for many years to come. For this hideous thing that we remember as the roughshod reign of the Kingfish was not hideous in its beginnings. Whether or not Huey Long himself was ever sincere in his protestations for the poor and downtrodden is, basically, beside the point. For he led a social-economic revolution in Louisiana; and after his death the entire South was debated ground.

It was not his political genius and ruthlessness alone that made him possible. There were two other factors equally important.

The first factor was that, after two hundred years, the people of Louisiana were ready and waiting for a messiah who would translate their needs into accomplishments. Theirs was the ground swell of the little people, a people undisturbed by his tactics as long as they got the roads, the free bridges, the hospitals, the free schoolbooks, the public works; as long as the men whom he pilloried and broke and banished were identified with the leaders of the past, bumbling representatives of an indifferent, negative ruling class. The little people shrugged at graft because of their certainty that there always had been graft of a kind. This time, whatever the politicians skimmed off the top, they were getting theirs too. And they were getting something else. Revenge. A fantastic vengeance upon the Sodom and Gomorrah that was called New Orleans. A squaring of accounts with the big shots, the Standard Oil and the bankers, the big planters, the entrenched interests everywhere. Huey Long was in the image of these little people. He talked their language. He had lived their

318

lives. He had taken them up to the mountaintop and shown them the world w..ich the meek would inherit.

The second factor was the make-up of the forces actively opposed to Long. His disunited enemies had difficulty from beginning to end to maintain an alliance that had its base in military necessity alone. We were strange bedfellows: cynical spoils politicians of the Old Regular ring in New Orleans; ardent, idealistic New Dealers; inept leaders of the country parishes, turned out in short grass; nonpolitical gentility awakened from their slumbers by rude knocking; the hitherto secure representatives of Big Business; honestly disturbed, solid bourgeoisie. Our combined cries for good government made a dissonant chorus. Huey bowled us over like tenpins, with rare misses, from the time of the failure of the impeachment proceedings to his assassination.

Looking back, I know now that part of our failure arose from an unwillingness to approve any Long-sponsored proposal for change, regardless of its merits. We offered none of our own except a plea for democratic rule, and that sounded hollow in contrast. Yet, at the end, it became the one thing of importance to Louisiana.

And Long triumphed over men far wiser politically than we. President Roosevelt and his pulse-feeler, Jim Farley, became uneasy about Long's threat soon after the Share Our Wealth movement overran the borders of Louisiana. On the Senate floor he made the most adroit, belligerent, and fluent opponent look and sound like a political freshman.

Even had Huey Long relied only upon his mesmeric appeal to Louisiana's masses and his ability to make promised delivery of the material things those masses wanted, it is probable that he could have dominated his state as completely and for at least as long as he did. But he was not content to rely upon these weapons alone. His compelling lust for power as such—a primary, animating force in his political life—and the intense vindictiveness which from the start characterized his public career lured him to a morally indefensible position.

When impeachment seemed a certainty in those early months as Governor, he simply bought and paid for enough legislators "like sacks of potatoes" to prevent the majority vote necessary for conviction. From then on, Long bought those whom he needed and could buy, and crushed those who had no purchase price or whose price was too high.

Nor was the control of a governor, a majority of legislators, a court majority enough. It should be repeated that no public officeholder, no teacher, no fire chief or fireman, no police chief or policeman, no day laborer on state projects held his job except in fee simple to the machine. Except among the political jobholders, he used this economic power sparingly. Yet even private citizens made their living by his sufferance. Long could have taxed to extinction any business, large or small, and business knew it. Men could be—and were—arrested by unidentified men, the members of his secret police, held incommunicado, tried, and found guilty on trumped-up charges. A majority of the State Supreme Court became unabashedly his. Through his State Printing Board he cracked an economic whip over the rural and small-town press, lashing all but a few into sullen silence. A thug, making a premeditated skull-crushing attack upon a Long opponent, could draw from his pocket in court a pre-signed pardon from the figurehead Governor. Entire city administrations could be removed, not by the electorate but by legislative action.

In the end, these things indirectly destroyed Huey Long himself. There are many conflicting tales as to why and how he was killed. This much is a certainty: His assassination was not plotted. It is not probable that Dr. Weiss went to the capitol the night of September 8, 1935, deliberately to kill Long. But he must have intended to protest a grave injury, the double-barreled kind of injury Long delighted in inflicting. Dr. Weiss's father-in-law, an implacable enemy of Long, had been gerrymandered out of his judgeship. Two of the judge's daughters had been dismissed from their teaching positions in further retaliation. And worse, Long had circulated noisome rumors about the family's ancestry.

Political punishment compounded with savage slander—an old, tested formula for reducing enemies to impotence. But this time the formula distilled a deadly reaction. Those who knew young Dr. Weiss best say that he could have sought Long only to protest verbally or with his fists this grave slander. They say that he could have drawn his gun only because the bodyguards threatened him. Few people in Louisiana believe that the full, true story has been told, for Long's henchmen were the only spectators. Perhaps the single bullet, fired from Weiss's small pistol, fatally wounded Long. Perhaps there was a second wound, as many Louisianians believe, caused by a ricocheting bullet from a bodyguard's gun. One bullet, two bullets. It is unimportant now; it was unimportant even then. Out of the terror he created, out of the driving passion to destroy other men, out of the futility that warped the minds of the Louisianians who opposed him, Huey Long himself forged the weapon which felled him.

AMATEURS—THERE AIN'T NONE

IN THE golden era of sports, the Twenties, when money was easy-come, easy-go, the ballyhoo whipped up for a Dempsey-Tunney world championship fight was almost a show in itself; the sports writers of the day contributed to the atmosphere by depicting the stars in hero-worshiping prose. Came the Thirties, and a lot of the hoopla faded away; in its wake, some of the golden figures in the sports world had a tarnished look about them. For one thing, it became increasingly clear that "amateur" was a meaningless term. Paul Gallico said, "We ask only one thing of an amateur, and that is that he doesn't let us catch him taking the dough."

For Gallico was incensed by the hypocrisy of the colleges, which paraded under the banner of amateurism, while they raked in larger and larger sums of money from the stadium crowds watching football, and surreptitiously arranged subsidies for their players. In 1938 he published *Farewell to Sport*, which announced his retirement as a sports writer and expressed his contempt for much of the sporting world. One of his most corrosive chapters dealt with Primo Carnera, onetime world's heavyweight champion.

PAUL GALLICO

PITY THE POOR GIANT*

THERE IS probably no more scandalous, pitiful, incredible story in all the record of these last mad sports years than the tale of the living giant, a creature out of the legends of antiquity, who was made into a prizefighter. He was taught and trained by a wise, scheming little French boxing manager who had an Oxford University degree, and he was later acquired and developed into the heavyweight champion of the world by a group of American gangsters and mob men; then finally, when his usefulness as a meal ticket was outlived, he was discarded, in the most shameful chapter in all boxing.

This unfortunate pituitary case, who might have been Angoulaffre, or

* From Paul Gallico's *Farewell to Sport* (New York, Knopf, 1938).

321

Balan, or Fierabras, Gogmagog, or Gargantua himself, was a poor simple-minded peasant by the name of Primo Carnera, the first son of a stone-cutter of Sequals, Italy. He stood six feet seven inches in height, and weighed two hundred and sixty-eight pounds. He became the heavyweight champion, yet never in all his life was he ever anything more than a freak and a fourth-rater at prizefighting. He must have grossed more than two millions of dollars during the years [1930–1935] that he was being exhibited, and he hasn't a cent to show for it today.

There is no room here for more than a brief and hasty glance back over the implications of the tragedy of Primo Carnera. And yet I could not seem to take my leave from sports without it. The scene and the story still fascinate me, the sheer impudence of the men who handled the giant, their conscienceless cruelty, their complete depravity toward another human being, the sure, cool manner in which they hoaxed hundreds of thousands of people. Poor Primo! A giant in stature and strength, a terrible figure of a man, with the might of ten men, he was a helpless lamb among wolves who used him until there was nothing more left to use, until the last possible penny had been squeezed from his big carcass, and then abandoned him. His last days in the United States were spent alone in a hospital. One leg was paralyzed, the result of beatings taken around the head. None of the carrion birds who had picked him clean ever came back to see him or to help him.

No one who was present in Madison Square Garden the night that Primo Carnera was first introduced to American audiences will ever forget him as he came bounding down the aisle from the dressing room and climbed into the ring. It was a masterpiece of stage management.

He wore black fighting trunks on the side of which was embroidered the head of a wild boar in red silk. He disdained the usual fighter's bathrobe and instead wore a sleeveless vest of a particularly hideous shade of green, and on his head a cap of the same shade, several sizes too large for him and with an enormous visor that made him look even larger than he was. Leon See, the Frenchman, then his manager, was a small man. The bucket-carriers and sponge-wielders were chosen for size too—diminutive men; everything was done to increase the impression of Primo's size.

Carnera was the only giant I have ever seen who was well proportioned throughout his body for his height. His legs were massive and he was truly thewed like an oak. His waist was comparatively small and clean, but from it rose a torso like a Spanish hogshead from which sprouted two tremendous arms, the biceps of which stood out like grapefruit. His hands were like Virginia hams, and his fingers were ten thick red sausages.

His head was large, even for the size of his body, and looking at him you were immediately struck with his dreadful gummy mouth and sharp, irregular, snaggle teeth. His lips were inclined to be loose and flabby. He had a good nose and fine, kind brown eyes. But his legs looked even more enormous and treelike than they were, owing to the great blue bulging varicose veins that wandered down them on both sides and stuck out far enough so that you could have knocked them off with a baseball bat. His skin was brown and glistening and he invariably smelled of garlic.

This was the horror that came into the Madison Square Garden ring and sent a sincere shudder through the packed house. That is to say, he was horrible until he commenced to fight, when he became merely pitiful and an object demanding sympathy. Behind what passed for the wild battle blaze in his eyes and the dreadful gummy leer, emphasized by the size of the red rubber mouthpiece (tooth-protector) with which they provided him, there was nothing but bewilderment and complete helplessness. The truth was that, handicapped by rules and regulations, a sport he did not understand and was not temperamentally fitted for, and those silly brown leather bags laced to his fingers, never at any time could he fight a lick. His entire record, with a few exceptions, must be thrown out as one gigantic falsehood, staged and engineered, planned and executed by the men who had him in tow and who were building him up for the public as a man-killer and an invincible fighter.

But I think the most dreadful part of the story is that the poor floundering giant was duped along with the spectators. He was permitted, in fact encouraged, to believe that his silly pawings and pushings, when they connected, sent men staggering into unconsciousness and defeat. It was not until late in his career, when in spite of himself he learned something through sheer experience and number of fights, that he ever knocked anyone out on the level. But he never could fight, and never will. In spite of his great size and strength and his well-proportioned body, he remained nothing but a glandular freak who should have remained with the small French traveling circus from which Leon See took him.

This big, good-natured, docile man was exhibiting himself in a small wandering cirque in the south of France as a strong man and Greco-Roman wrestler, engaging all comers and local talent in the nightly show, having found that it paid him more and offered a better life than that of his chosen profession of mosaic worker. Here he was discovered by a former French boxing champion who signed him up and apprenticed him to one Monsieur Leon See to be taught the rudiments of *la boxe*. It is highly probable that the time spent as a wrestler set his muscles and prevented him from ever becoming a knockout puncher. But Monsieur Leon See was taking no chances. He taught and trained Carnera strictly as a defensive boxer.

Now, it must be understood that Leon See was one of the most intelligent, smart and wily men that ever turned a fighter loose from his corner. He was not much more scrupulous than the bevy of public enemies who eventually took Carnera away from him simply by muscling him, but he was much more farseeing and he had certain well-thought-out notions and theories about the ridiculous game of boxing. Among them was the excellent and sensible thought that the human head was never intended by nature to be punched, and that secondly, from the manner of its construction out of hundreds of tiny, delicately articulated bones, the closed fist was never meant to be one of man's most effective weapons. In this last idea, Monsieur See was not alone. The coterie of tough guys and mobsters who eventually relieved him of his interest in Carnera rarely used the fist, reckoning it, as did See, an inefficient weapon. The boys always favored the pistol or Roscoe, also known as the Difference, the Equalizer, the Rod, and the Heat.

See was a keen student of the human body—for a prizefight manager—and he knew something about men. He was aware that abnormalities of size were usually compensated for by weaknesses elsewhere. He found out —exactly how is not known—that Primo Carnera would never be able to absorb a hard punch to the chin. He may have had some secret rehearsal in a gymnasium somewhere in Paris and, having ordered some workaday heavyweight to clout Primo one just to see what would happen, saw that the giant came all undone, wobbled and collapsed. Be that as it may, Monsieur See knew. And never at any time while he was connected with Carnera would he permit anyone to punch Primo in the head—neither his sparring partners nor his opponents. Since both received their pay from practically the same source, this was not so difficult to arrange as might be imagined. But See also had something else. He was a Frenchman and so he had a heart. He loved big Carnera.

Years later See proved to be right. When Carnera through exigent circumstances was forced to fight without benefit of prearrangement, and the heavyweights began to sight along that big, protruding jaw of his and nail him for direct hits, he was slaughtered. He was brave and game and apparently could take punches to the body all the night long. But one hard, true tap on the chin and he fell down goggle-eyed. For a long time during the early years, however, nobody was permitted to hit him there, and Carnera himself began to think he was invincible.

Primo's first trip to the United States was arranged through an American contact man and importer of foreign fighting talent, a character from Tin-Ear Alley named Walter Friedman or, as Damon Runyon nicknamed him, Walter (Good-Time Charley) Friedman. See was smart enough to know that without an American "in," without cutting in an American manager, he would not get very far in America. What he was not quite smart enough to know was how deep his "in" took him, that the ramifications of Friedman's business and other connections were to lead through some very tough and rapacious parties.

Carnera's first fight in New York involved him with a lanky Swede named Big Boy Peterson. In this fight poor Carnera was hardly able to get out of his own way and caused his opponent the most frightful embarrassment through not being able to strike a blow that looked sufficiently hard to enable him to keep his end of the bargain, if there was one. Eventually Peterson succumbed to a push as Carnera lumbered and floundered past him, and to make assurance doubly sure, the Swede hit himself a punch on the jaw as he went down. Someone had to hit him.

Now, this was a shameless swindle from start to finish, one way or another. If Peterson was making an honest effort to fight he never should have been permitted to enter the ring. The press unanimously announced beforehand that it would probably be a sell and a fake, and when it was over, suggested strongly that it had been. But it said so in a gay and light-hearted manner as though the whole thing were pretty funny (as indeed it was), and there was no one on the New York State Athletic Commission either sufficiently intelligent or courageous enough to throw Primo and his handlers and fixers right out of the ring and thence out of the country. The Peterson fight in Madison Square Garden, the stronghold of professional boxing, was a sort of a test case by the Carnera crowd to see how much they could get away with. On that score it was a clean-cut success. They found out that they could get away with anything. And so they proceeded to do just that. Primo's first American tour was organized, a tour that grossed something like $700,000, of which handsome piece of money Carnera received practically nothing. He was barnstormed across the country in the most cold-blooded, graceless, shameful series of fixed, bought, coerced, or plain out-and-out tank acts ever. If one of them was contested on its merits it was only because the opponent by no possible stretch of the imagination, or his own efforts could harm Carnera or even hit him.

Where the fight could not be bought—that is to say, where the fighter was unwilling to succumb to a tap on the elbow for a price—guns were produced by sinister strangers to threaten him, and where neither threats nor money were sufficient to bag the fight, he was crossed or tricked, as in the case of Bombo Chevalier, a big California Negro who was fascinated by the size of Carnera's chin, and nothing would do but he was going to hit it, just to see what would happen. Between rounds one of Chevalier's own attendants rubbed red pepper or some other inflammatory substance into his eyes so that he lost all interest in tapping anybody's chin.

In Newark, New Jersey, a Negro was visited in his dressing room before the bout by an unknown party not necessarily connected with Carnera's management, and was asked to inspect shooting irons, and in Philadelphia another Negro, Ace Clark, was amusing himself readying up Carnera for a knockout—he had already completely closed one of Primo's eyes—when somebody suggested he look down and see what the stranger beneath his corner was holding under his coat, and what caliber it was.

Every known build-up fighter was lined up for this tour, including faithful old hands like K. O. Christner, Chuck Wiggens, and poor Farmer Lodge. Political and gangster friends in the cities visited volunteered with their private heavyweights for quick splashes that might look well on the record books. It was all for the cause. The more money Carnera made, the more the boys would have to cut up amongst themselves. It was all just one big happy family. It seemed almost as though every scamp in the boxing game contributed his bit somehow to that Carnera build-up.

Friedman, as has been indicated, was the go-between, and although Leon See was quite capable of all the planning necessary to keep Carnera in the victory columns, nevertheless it would have been considered bad form, and downright dangerous, if See had not cut the local boys in. And, at that, I suspect the said local boys showed the amiable and gifted Frog a few things about building up a potential heavyweight champion that made the two Stribling fights arranged by Monsieur See, one in Paris and the other in London and both ending in fouls, look like Holy Gospel.

As adviser and codirector of this tour, Broadway Bill Duffy was cut in. Bill was then in the night-club and fight-managing business, but in his youth he had been convicted of a little alfresco burgling and had been sent away for a spell. He was still to achieve the highest pinnacle of fame that can come to an American—to be named a Public Enemy. It is a curious commentary upon the conduct of boxing around New York that Duffy was allowed to operate as a manager and a second when there was a rule on the books of the State Athletic Commission, if indeed it was not written directly into the boxing law, that no one ever convicted of a felony was to be eligible for any kind of license.

Duffy usually split even on things with his dearest friend, Owen Madden, better known as Owney, who had also been away for a time in connection with the demise of a policeman. Owney was out on parole at the time—he was sent back later—making beer (and very good beer it was, too) and acting as silent partner in the operation of a number of prizefighters. Also in this crowd was a charming but tough individual known as Big Frenchy De Mange who made news one evening by getting himself snatched and held for ransom by Mad Dog Vincent Coll. The Mad Dog was subsequently rubbed out in a West Side drugstore telephone booth. But the subject, after all, is Primo Carnera and not gangsters and racket men, though pretty soon it was all one subject and all one sweet and fragrant mess. The boys had their connections in every town. The Philadelphia underworld collaborated through the medium of the always friendly and helpful Maximilian Boo-Boo Hoff, and the same courtesies were extended all the way through to the Pacific Coast, where occurred the Bombo Chevalier incident, which was too nauseous even for the local commission there to stomach. There was an investigation resulting in the suspension of a few unimportant people. But Carnera and his swindle went merrily onwards.

And it continued until he won the heavyweight championship of the world by ostensibly knocking out Jack Sharkey, then world's champion, in the sixth round, with a right uppercut. I say ostensibly because nothing will ever convince me that that was an honest prizefight, contested on its merits.

Sharkey's reputation and the reputation of Fat John Buckley, his manager, were bad. Both had been involved in some curious ring encounters. The reputation of the Carnera entourage by the time the Sharkey fight came along, in 1933, was notorious, and the training camps of both gladiators were simply festering with mobsters and tough guys. Duffy, Madden, et Cie., were spread out all over Carnera's training quarters at Dr. Bier's Health Farm at Pompton Lakes, New Jersey. A traveling chapter of Detroit's famous Purple Gang hung out at Gus Wilson's for a while during Sharkey's rehearsals. Part of their business there was to muscle in on the concession of the fight pictures.

If that fight was on the level, it wasn't like either of the companies operating the two pugs. If it was honest, the only explanation was that the boys were going sissy. As far as Primo knew, the right uppercut with which he tagged Sharkey in the sixth round was enough to kill a steer. He had knocked out many men with the same punch. Now he was the heavyweight champion of the world, and even if he didn't have any money to show for it, Italy and Mussolini were going to be very pleased. I have often wondered how long he remained innocent, how long it was before he began to catch on.

For instance, it must have been a terrible surprise and considerable of an eye opener to Carnera the night he fought Tommy Loughran in Miami as heavyweight champion of the world. It was a no-decision match and a bad one for the gang to make, but they had to do something because they were desperate for money at the time. If the Sharkey fight was crooked, it is probable that the entire end of Primo's purse had to be paid over for the fix.

The Loughran fight had to go on the level because no one had ever managed to tamper with Loughran, and neither he nor his manager was afraid of guns. And Tommy had another curious and valuable protection. He was a good Catholic, and many priests were his friends. The gunmen were a little shy of those padres, who might usually be found in twos and threes at Tommy's home or his training camps. But the mob figured that with a hundred-pound advantage in weight Carnera could take care of Loughran, who was little more than a light heavyweight and never was a hard hitter. During the fight Carnera hit Loughran more than a dozen of the same uppercuts that had stretched Sharkey twitching on the canvas, and never even reddened Tommy's face. Loughran was a cream-puff puncher and yet he staggered Carnera several times with right hands and was himself never in any kind of danger from a punch. He merely got tired from having Carnera leaning on him for half an hour. If nothing else, that fight beneath the Miami moon exposed how incompetent Carnera was as a bruiser, and how utterly false were the stories about his invincibility, besides casting fresh suspicion upon his knockout of Sharkey. We had all seen Loughran put on the floor by a 175-pounder. If a man weighing around 280 pounds, as Primo did for that fight, hit him flush on the jaw and couldn't drop him, and yet had knocked out one of the cleverest heavyweights in the business, it wasn't hard to arrive at a conclusion. It was obvious that he was a phony and the first stiff-punching heavyweight who was leveling would knock him out.

Max Baer did it the very next summer. The following summer Joe Louis did it again, and then an almost unknown Negro heavyweight by the name of Leroy Haynes accomplished the feat for the third time. And that was the beginning of the end of Primo.

His lucrative campaigns and the winning of the heavyweight championship had enriched everyone connected with him except poor Primo, who saw very little of the money he earned. There were too many silent partners and "boys" who had little pieces of him. Monsieur See had long since been dispensed with and shipped back to France for his health; he had served his purpose. But it was an evil day for Carnera when they chased Leon back to Paris, for Leon never would have permitted anyone to belt Carnera on his vulnerable chin. As suggested, the little Frenchman had a love for the big fellow whom he had taught and trained and watched over so carefully. The Duffy crowd had no love for anything. Fighters' chins were made to be smacked and they might just as well get used to taking the punches there.

It seemed as though their power was beginning to lose some of its effectiveness, exhausted perhaps by its own virus and viciousness, shortly after they had made Carnera champion. Primo escaped to Italy with his title and nothing else and later returned here for the disastrous fight with Loughran under the guidance of a little Italian banker by the name of Luigi Soresi, who appeared to be genuinely trying to get and keep for poor Carnera some of the money he was making.

The by-products of the Miami affair were typical and pathetic. Duffy and company were living over a Miami night club in style and spending money like water—Primo's money. Carnera was relegated to a cheap cottage back of the town with a trainer. No one really looked after him. No one cared particularly whether he trained or not. He came into the ring against Loughran twenty pounds overweight. Shortly after that Duffy was clapped into the jug for a spell for some boyish pranks with his income tax, and from the cooler he wrote pleading letters at the time that Carnera was preparing to defend his title against Baer, maintaining that he was needed to guide, advise, and teach Primo, to prime him for the first serious defense of his title, and that he should be given furlough from quod to attend to this matter. Carnera vigorously denied that he needed him. He was only too delighted to have Duffy held in durance vile. Of course what was really killing Uncle Will was that he was where for the first time he couldn't get his fingers on a nice big slice of the sugar that big, stupid Wop would make for boxing Baer.

It is difficult to bag or fix a heavyweight championship prizefight, though it has been done. But in the postwar sports renaissance there was so much money at stake in a heavyweight championship fight that it took more cash than most could produce to purchase either champion or challenger. It stood to reason that if the champion figured to make a million dollars or more out of his title he wasn't going to sell out for any less. Too, the power of the gangs was weakening. Repeal dealt them a terrible blow and took away their chief source of revenue. Three or four years before, Carnera's title would have been safe because his handlers would not have accepted any challenger for the title unless he agreed to preserve the state of the champion's health throughout the encounter. And there were always ways and means of keeping a challenger from double-crossing.

But Duffy was in the sneezer, as the boys sometimes quaintly called the jailhouse, Carnera was broke and needed money. He could only get it by fighting Baer. And the Baer fight could not be fixed. Baer's reputation was good; at least, he had not been caught out in any shady fights. He was a powerful hitter and it was apparent that now at last the rest of us were going to be made privy to what it was that happened when Carnera was struck forcefully on the chin. We didn't have to wait long. He was knocked down three times in the first round, and lost his championship in the eleventh round on a technical knockout when he was helpless, having been knocked down a total of thirteen times during the ten and a half rounds.

Not, however, until he fought and was knocked out by Joe Louis was it apparent what a dreadful thing had been done to this great hulk of a man. Strange to feel pity and sympathy excited for one so gross and enormous and strong. But the outsizes of the world are not the happy men, and their bulk is often of little use or help to them. If anything, it is a handicap when up against the speed and timing and balance of a normal man. Carnera's great strength was practically useless to him in the ring. The hardest blow he could strike was little more than a push. True, if he caught you in a corner he could club you insensible, but no smart fighter is caught in corners, and the big man was never fast enough anyway to catch anyone but out-and-out tramps.

When he fought Joe Louis he was defensively but little better than he was the first time I saw him, which, as it happened, was not in Madison Square Garden, but in the smoky, stuffy, subterranean Salle Wagram, a little fight club in Paris where I happened to be one evening when Jeff Dickson was promoting a fight between Primo Carnera, who had then been fighting a little less than a year, and one Moise Bouquillon, a light heavy-weight who weighed 174 pounds. Monsieur See was experimenting a little with his giant. It was obvious that Bouquillon was going to be unable to hurt him very much, but what I noted that evening and never forgot was that the giant was likewise unable to hurt the little Frenchman. Curiously, that fight was almost an exact duplicate of the one that Carnera as champion later fought with Loughran. Walter (Good-Time Charley) Friedman was there too. Many years later he told me quite frankly: "Boy, was that a lousy break for us that you come walking into that Salle Wagram that night and see that the big guy can't punch! Just that night you hadda be there. Leon wanted to see if he could go ten rounds without falling down. And you hadda be there. We coulda got away with a lot more if you don't walk in there and write stories about how he can't punch."

Joe Louis slugged Carnera into bleating submission, cruelly and brutally. Handsome Uncle Will Duffy was back in his corner again, jawing angrily at him when he was led trembling and quivering back to his chair after the referee had saved him again, one side of his mouth smashed in, dazed and dripping blood. The very first right-hand punch Louis hit him broke Carnera's mouth and hurt him dreadfully.

Here, then, was the complete sell. He had nothing. His title was gone, his money squandered by the gang. And the one thing he thought he had, an unbeatable skill in defense and an irresistible crushing power in attack that no man living could withstand, never existed. It was a fable as legendary as the great giants of mythology that he resembled. The carrion birds that had fed upon this poor, big, dumb man had picked him clean. They had left him nothing, not even his pride and his self-respect, and that probably was the cruelest thing of all.

In his last fight, the one with Haynes, he was again severely beaten about the head. One of his legs refused to function. The fight was stopped. While he lay in the hospital in New York for treatment, as I have said, he lay alone.

I often wonder what that hulk of a man thinks today as he looks back over the manner in which he was swindled, tricked and cheated at every turn, as he recalls the great sums of money that he earned, all of it gone beyond recall. The world has no place for him, not even as a freak in a circus, from whence he emerged and where he might happily have spent his life and become prosperous. Because as a giant, a terror and a horror, he stands exposed as a poor, unwilling fraud who was no man-killer at all, but a rather helpless, sad creature who, when slugged by a 185-pound mortal, either toppled stricken to the floor or staggered about or bled or had to be saved from annihilation by a third man who obligingly stepped between him and his tormentors.

He was born far, far too late. He belonged to the twelfth or thirteenth century, when he would have been a man-at-arms and a famous fellow with mace and halberd, pike or bill. At least he would have fought nobly and to the limit of his great strength, properly armed, because Carnera was a courageous fellow to the limit of his endurance, game and a willing fighter when aroused. In those days he would have won honor afield and would have got himself decently killed, or, surviving, would have been retired by his feudal lord to round out his days and talk over the old brave fights.

Today there is nothing left for this man but reflection upon his humiliations. He was just a big sucker whom the wise guys took and trimmed. What an epitaph for one who came from the ancient and noble race of giants.

All this took place in our country, Anno Domini 1930–1935.

THE BROWN BOMBER

CAPTURING the crown in the heavyweight division was not so easy then as it is today; Joe Louis, for example, did not become champion until he had fought a number of contenders, several of whom had been champions. His fight with ex-champion Max Baer on October 9, 1935, would produce the first million-dollar gate of the Thirties. The previous June, Baer had lost his crown to James J. Braddock, a longshoreman who had been on the relief rolls a year before.

Braddock's underdog victory was immensely popular—a Depression victim had caught the brass ring to fame and glory; if he could do it, anybody might. Braddock would lose the crown to Louis in 1937, and the next year Louis would take his revenge on Max Schmeling (who in 1936 had administered the only defeat in Louis' record prior to his ill-advised emergence from retirement in 1950) by knocking the German out in the first round.

Boxing fans saw good matches in other fight divisions—middleweight, welterweight, lightweight, and light heavyweight—where such memorable fighters as Barney Ross, Tony Canzoneri, Henry Armstrong, Jimmy McLarnin and Maxie Rosenbloom earned followings.

But it was Louis, a lethal puncher with great skills in every department, who marks these years and compares favorably with the great fighters of the past.

JONATHAN MITCHELL

JOE LOUIS NEVER SMILES*

THESE people are here, 95,000 of them, because they have money. Down there on the field, men have paid $150 and more for a pair of tickets. Twenty thousand seats were stamped "ringside," and the customers out beyond third base were bilked. They should have known that Mike Jacobs, who is running this fight, is a smart man. No one can do anything to him because he has the support of Hearst.

It feels good to have money again. Everyone in this crowd has money. The people who were swindled by Jacobs can afford it. Happy days are here again. Of course, things aren't so good, with twenty million on relief.

* From *The New Republic*, Oct. 9, 1935.

333

A man can be fired, and next morning there are ten men in line waiting for his job. But the unemployed have been around for a long time. No one can expect us to sit home and be sympathetic indefinitely.

It is a cold, clear night. The Stadium rises steeply around one half of the field. The floodlights on its upper edge are directed on the field and the bleachers, and the Stadium itself is black except for a steady row of red exit signs. Almost the whole of the immense field is covered with chairs. Jacobs has pushed the customers so closely together that all that can be seen of them, under the floodlights, is their microscopic, bright faces. They form neat rows, divided into plots by the aisles, like commercial Dutch tulip beds. There are acres of them, shining pinkly. Men in white, with high cardboard signs in their caps, move gravely about selling pop, like gardeners. The ring is at second base, and the movie operators' metal cage, high on a pole, that you used to see at fights, is missing. The only movement comes from white tobacco smoke, rising in heavy waves. Through it you can see the American flags along the top of the Stadium, after the fashion of the opening verse of "The Star-Spangled Banner."

Near at hand the crowd is a respectable, bridge-playing one. About a fifth are Negroes, more carefully dressed and more mannerly than the whites. The little drunk with the long woolen muffler is certainly a Bronx dentist. He thinks correctly that the preliminary match now going on is poor, and keeps screaming, "Lousy." He brandishes a handful of crumpled bills, and will give odds to anyone. There seems to be something painful in his past that he would like to explain, but the woolen muffler keeps blowing in his face, and communication between him and us is eternally frustrated.

There is a stirring in the aisles near the ring. The people who amount to something, and who are bowed through the police lines outside the Stadium, are entering. There are five state governors, the Republican National Committee, important business figures and a large number of people whose press agents made them come so that their names would be in tomorrow's papers. Max Baer and his attendants are now at home plate. A dozen little pushing figures open up the crowd for him, and another dozen follow behind. Baer wears a white bathrobe and has his hands on the shoulders of the state trooper in front of him. He nods to his many friends. Joe Louis, with another state trooper and other attendants, pushes in from third base. We learn afterward that his bride, Marva Trotter, is in the first row in a bright-green dress and orchids. Louis seems to see no one.

The floodlights are extinguished. Nothing exists except the brightly glowing ring. That is old Joe Humphries being lifted through the ropes, the man who announced fights before the Depression. Since then he has been sick, and had a bad time. We have all been having a bad time, for that matter. Jack Dempsey squats in Baer's corner, but no one notices him. Humphries' assistant is bawling into the microphones: "Although Joe Louis is colored, he is a great fighter, in the class of Jack Johnson and the giants of the past." His voice fades away, and returns: "American sportsmanship, without regard to race, creed or color, is the talk of the world. Behave like gentlemen, whoever wins." Nearly two thousand police at the entrances of the Stadium are there to break up a possible race riot.

Baer has stripped. He has made a lot of money, Baer has. From all reports, he has spent a lot. He has played Broadway, Miami and the other hot spots. Why shouldn't he have done so? Joe Louis takes off his flashing silk bathrobe, blue with a vermilion lining. It is the only extravagant gesture he makes. For all his youth, he is thick under the jaws, thick around the waist. His face is earnest, thoughtful, unsmiling.

Max Baer hasn't been, I suppose, what you would call a good boy. Joe Louis has, though. This is his greatest advantage. He once was taken to a night club, and it is reported that within ten minutes he wanted to go home. He said he was sleepy. He is supposed to have saved his money. Louis' father died when he was only two years old, down in Alabama. Until she married again, his mother had a hard struggle to support the children, and they were very dear to her. Louis is fond of his mother. She is a Lily of the Valley at her church in Detroit, where the family now lives. The Lilies are having a supper, or some such event, in a few days. She wants him there, and he is going with his new wife.

We are too far away to hear the gong. They are out in the middle of the ring, with a stubby little man in a white sweater moving softly around them. Baer holds both hands, open, clumsily in front of him. Look at Joe Louis. He is leading with a straight left arm, his right hand before his face ready to block, and his right elbow tucked in to his ribs. That is scientific. That is what they teach in correspondence courses, or the night gymnasium classes of the Y.M.C.A. In the first thirty seconds, you can tell that he reeks of study, practice, study. Any romantic white person who believes that the Negro possesses a distinctive quality ought to see Louis. He suggests a gorilla or a jungle lion about as much as would an assistant professor at the Massachusetts Institute of Technology.

Baer stands flat-footed, with his great death-dealing right fist doubled by his side. He swings, and you can almost count three while the fist sails through the air. Louis moves sidewise and back, because he has been taught that if you move with a blow it can never hurt you. Baer's glove slides up the side of Louis' head harmlessly. He swings again and again, and, carefully and unhurriedly, Louis slips away. Look! Louis at last is going in. A left, a right and another left in close. Louis has pulled in his head, and, with both arms up before him, he looks like a brown crayfish. All you can see is the twitching of his shoulders. So incredibly fast he is that the blows themselves are almost invisible. His hands cannot possibly move more than a few inches. Look! Baer is backing into a neutral corner. Louis is raining down blows. Baer's nose spurts blood, his lower lip bleeds, his face is red pulp.

Baer must have meant something to many people. He made wisecracks and went to parties and was a harbinger of the return of the old days. He was Broadway, he was California and Florida, he represented the possession of money once more and spending it. This saddle-colored, dour-faced, tongue-tied, studious youth, who is punishing Baer, punishing him more cruelly than human flesh and bones can endure, what does he represent? Baer stands with his hands hanging at his sides. He is helpless. He cannot hit the dissolving form before him, and he has never learned to protect himself. He holds his fine head, with its sweep of tightly curled hair and its great, brooding nose, high above his torturer. Pride alone keeps his head up, pride that has no tangible justification whatever. It was the same pride that kept Colonel Baratieri at Adowa, twenty years before Joe Louis was born.

It is the first round, and the fight is as good as over. Maybe it was foolish to spend money going to a fight. There must be many people, even down there in the ringside seats, who couldn't afford to spend what they did on tickets. No one can be sure of his job with twenty million on relief. This is a crazy country, with people handing out a million dollars to Mike Jacobs and Hearst, while families right here in New York City are without enough to eat.

Round one is ended. Jack Dempsey vaults into the ring in a single, startling leap. Perhaps it is a trick. He must have vaulted from the ground to the edge of the ring platform, and from there into the ring itself. But from a distance, it seems one motion, and it is beautiful. Beside the man that Dempsey was, Baer and Louis and Schmeling are phonies. Nowadays everything, including men, is somehow different.

The next three rounds are slaughter. In the second, Baer makes a wild, swinging, purposeless attack. For probably fifteen seconds, he appears formidable, but his attack has no substance inside it. With the third round, he is beaten, but Louis does not rush in, as Dempsey would have, to kill. Deliberately he circles Baer, with his earnest, thoughtful face, seeking an opening through which to strike without possible risk of injury. He takes no chance of a last, desperate fling of Baer's prodigious right hand. He is a planner. He is a person who studies the basic aspects of a problem and formulates a program. Apparently his studies are satisfactory, for he carefully steps up and knocks Baer down twice. Baer is on the canvas when time is called. Dempsey slides across the ring, picks Baer up like a mother, fusses over him until the fourth, and final, round. Baer once more is down. When the stubby referee, swinging his arm, reaches seven, he tries to rouse himself. This turns out later to have been a fortunate gesture. The customers who suspected the honesty of the fight, and were unconvinced that a man could be half killed by fifty blows full on the jaw, were reassured as they watched Baer struggling to his feet. Had he been trying to throw the fight, they reasoned, he would have lain still. At the count of ten, Baer is on one knee, his swollen face wearing a comical expression of surprise.

The floodlights return us to time and space. Near at hand, there is remarkably little cheering, even from Negroes. They act as if, despite the police, they think it more prudent to restrain their feelings. There in the ring, placing his hand on Baer's shoulder in a stiff gesture, is the best fighter living, and the first Negro whose backers and trainer are men of his race. No white man shares in Louis' winnings. If the whites of the Boxing Commission will permit the match, he will be champion of the world.

All across the Stadium, the neat tulip beds are being broken up as tiny figures push into the aisles and toward the exits. A man with a small blond mustache is sobbing: "Maxie, why didn't you hit him?" Downtown in the Forties and Fifties, redecorated speakeasies will quickly be crammed to the doors and customers turned away. In Lenox Avenue in Harlem, Negroes will be tap-dancing from curb to curb, and singing: "The Baer goes over the mountain," and "Who won the fight?" Tomorrow the financial sections of the newspapers will report that business leaders regard the fight as final proof that the country's economic worries are past, and a comfortable and prosperous future is assured.

THE NEW LEISURE

MORE TIME TO PLAY

IN THE first years of the Depression, some businesses had cut working hours in order to spread employment and reduce pay checks; later, when the NRA (National Recovery Administration) codes, which had provided for a maximum forty-hour work week, failed to withstand court challenge, the five-day week was already well established in factory and business office. There was more free time.

War clouds over Europe discouraged overseas travel, and Americans turned to their homeland. Air travel expanded, the car trailer was developed, and trailer camps and roadside cabins (the motels of today) were built; public beaches and national and state parks were built in large numbers by the government's public-works projects. By the middle of the decade there were some thirty million people traveling around the country, visiting, vacationing by car.

People, as always, loved the new, the odd, the curious in their entertainment. The Thirties saw thousands of men and women crouched over bingo boards, teen-agers perched in trees vying for records for the longest roost, college boys swallowing goldfish and burying each other alive for kicks, and the chain-letter craze threatening to swamp the mails.

Baseball was still the great summer pastime, but American football, in the Thirties, became the biggest money-maker of all the sports. Professional football drew larger and larger gates after 1933 with end-of-season championship playoffs between East and West divisions of the National Football League. And college football saw a sudden mushrooming of postseason Bowl contests to compete with the famous annual Rose Bowl game.

In tennis, the United States finally won back the Davis Cup in 1937, only to lose it to Australia in 1939; the great players of the day were Ellsworth Vines and Don Budge, who in 1938 was the first player ever to hold the American, British, French and Australian singles titles.

And the same Associated Press poll that named Babe Didrikson an outstanding performer, also chose Jesse Owens as the top track performer in the first half of this century. Owens, a Negro, was the sensation of the 1936 Olympic Games at Berlin, winning the broad jump, the 100-meter and 200-meter runs, and sharing winning honors in the 400-meter relays. Hitler, furious at such a public setback to his Master Race propaganda, walked out of the stadium just before Owens was awarded his gold medals.

There were, indeed, many great sports heroes in the Thirties; at the same time, however, there was a tremendous increase of participation by many Americans in such "new" sports as bowling, skiing, softball, bicycling and golf—the opening of more and more public golf courses brought thousands of new golfers into the game. It was a time when more people seemed to want to get out to play, themselves, not just watch others.

CAFÉ SOCIETY

The leisure of the upper classes, too, was affected by the changing times. According to *Fortune* Magazine, "in the day of hunger marches and breadlines, the elaborate dinner dance seemed to the owners of most great houses vulgar if not dangerous ostentation." Society members began giving smaller dinners in public hotels or cafés; Prohibition had forced the upper classes to go out to find a drink, and "rising real-estate values drove them out of their old brownstone houses into apartments, reconciling them to standardized mass entertainment parallel with the new standardized mass housing. Then came the Depression, shrinking the inherited incomes, dealing a blow to the debutante ball that had been the old order's focal point, and making Dutch-treat dates conventional." *

Often, in the Thirties, the salaries of screen stars surpassed the Depression-shriveled incomes of the older invested fortunes. It was inevitable that screen personalities were sought after—they were already rubbing elbows in the cafés, and, of course, they also brought variety and excitement to the upper crust. "The old 400 was no longer an end in itself. This brought about a distinct change, in that the urbane man about town was supplanted by playboys and professional extra men, and, together with this, the café society was taken over lock, stock and barrel by the women." *

Certainly society lost no glamour and gained heavily in publicity for itself. After all, stars' reputations were built on publicity and now with "so many faces and fortunes coming from the world of entertainment, society became more receptive to publicity—indeed, with a few exceptions, it was avid for favorable mention in the proper newspaper columns and magazines." *

Out of this new seeking for publicity were bred the special columnists whose business it was to become familiar with the chichi world, resulting in the society gossip column. Inevitably the columnist himself became sought after, to the extent that his appearance at social functions "threw the hostess into delirious joy." In this period Elsa Maxwell thrived; she was heard to say that "no party was ever more successful than the published accounts of it in the papers." †

NEWSPAPERS AND COMIC STRIPS

Perhaps newspapers had gained a certain new glamour in their attention to the antics of café society, but they were losing readers, who were turning to radio and the movies, both of which competed directly with news and entertainment features of the press. Only in the registering of independent opinion did some of the newspapers continue to maintain superiority over the other two media, which were harried respectively by advertising pressures and mass box-office standards.

The newspapers that survived the Depression did not lose much in individual circulations, but many others became victims of mergers with larger papers, or were casualties of the bad times. By the end of

* "The Yankee Doodle Salon," *Fortune,* December 1937.
† "The Yankee Doodle Salon."

the decade fewer than 125 cities had more than one newspaper ownership, and 2,000 weekly papers had dropped by the wayside.

News and picture magazines also ate into the available readership. As a consequence news space gave way to increased use of the news photograph and the comic strip. The comic strip was not new, but now there was a stronger emphasis on the adventure serial strip, a new phase of "entertainment"—just about the time the old cliff-hanger motion-picture serial was dying out.

Of the five most noted comic strips originating in the Thirties, one was strictly an adventure strip —Milton Caniff's "Terry and the Pirates"—and it spawned more variations and imitations than any other strip in history.

The other four also set styles: "Blondie," followed over the next twenty years by a half-dozen light-hearted family strips; "Dick Tracy," the first of many cops-and-robbers strips; "L'il Abner," from which came a few regional satires by Al Capp's imitators; and "Joe Palooka," father of the straight sports strip.

The Palooka strip suggested "the old wistful portrait of power that did not corrupt. Here were all the human virtues embodied in a man who, if he were not so pure, could become a menace to society, but who, being so pure, was the kind of idol an American invariably bowed to. Even the name Palooka was perfect." *

In "Blondie," the American husband and father was presented often as "downright incompetent, but his instincts are good." This strip had a fantastic success, running in over a thousand papers all over the world, and becoming the subject of a number of motion pictures and a television series. "Dagwood, the father, sustains a six-to-one ratio in defeats over victory, but those defeats spring from his good nature, and not from real deficiencies; he lacks a capacity for cruelty; once a man has padded a cave with evergreen boughs, brought home skins and meat, perpetuated his kind, he becomes a useless supernumerary, tolerated for his weaknesses and barely permitted to delude himself with the ludicrous notion that he is of value to society." *

In "L'il Abner," Capp supplied satirical exuberance. He loved to prick frauds, lance nerves, and perhaps more than any other humorist of his day, he is "bitterly resentful of the fact that Americans have become afraid to laugh at each other." *

Chester Gould, the creator of "Dick Tracy," was led to produce the strip because of the success of gangsterism in national crime, and "his anger was directed specifically at the laxity of the local police and the seeming impunity by which hoodlums operated." * The Dick Tracy strip had a real impact upon various institutions, not excluding the police departments.

Caniff's "Terry and the Pirates" first appeared in October 1934. And while other adventure strips were popular—"Tarzan," "Flash Gordon," "Prince Valiant," for example —it was Caniff who caught the "restless, adventuresome spirit of the times better than anyone." * When, eventually, ownership of "Terry" came into dispute, Caniff easily created a new strip of his own— "Steve Canyon."

* Stephen Becker, *Comic Art in America* (New York, Simon and Schuster, 1959).

JOKES, GAGS AND A BIT OF SATIRE

Advertisers began to sell their products through comic strips in the late Thirties—the comic strip was no longer just a collection of jokes, gags, or satirical whimsey; "the public wanted a reflection of the contemporary world." *

Some of the obvious targets of national humor either were missing or didn't catch on. The New Deal and events in Europe proved poor subjects for satire. *Vanity Fair* tried hard to needle the New Deal, but went out of business before the decade was over. The black-out gags of vaudeville and burlesque were not so popular, but the great underground of jokes and gags that pass from citizen to citizen rolled on. The nationally prominent were worked over—the President and Mrs. Roosevelt were the subject of thousands of stories, many of which were offensive; but it always seems to be open season on Presidents.

For a while a new magazine called *Ballyhoo* tried to leaven some of the "hard sell" of magazine and radio advertising by poking fun at the ad man's follies; *Ballyhoo* suggested their motto in the following rhyming nonsense:

"Little drops of hooey
Little grains of bunk
Make the silly public
Buy a lot of junk." †

And the *Ballyhoo* editors wrote a mock Ten Commandments, as from the advertiser to the consumer, the first commandment being:

"Thou shalt not have for thyself any unpleasant breath, any congested cough, any film on thy teeth,

any athlete's foot, or the likeness of any disease that is in heaven above, or on the earth beneath, or in the waters under the earth."

The second commandment:

"Thou shalt not take the name of pink toothbrush in vain."

And so on until, by the tenth, the velvet glove was off:

"Thou *shalt* covet thy neighbor's car, and his radio, and his silverware, and his refrigerator, and everything that is his." †

The demagogues, the social prophets, the poor man in the street and the arrogant businessman, all got their lumps, but there was hardly any noticeable body of gags built up around them; chances are that no single individual or national incident appeared big enough to sustain the creative satisfactions of the jokesters.

Vaudeville had died, radio and the motion-picture comics seemed smothered in moth balls, unless they were working out sketches that fitted their public characters; the times perhaps demanded too much in dedication, and just possibly the people were still too much in a state of shock to appreciate real wit, even if there had been much in evidence. Great comedians such as the Marx Brothers, W. C. Fields, Bobby Clark, and even Chaplin, were at work, but their best work had been developed and polished in the great days of vaudeville.

Instead, a kind of foul-ball humor was popular, often indirect and whimsical—the shaggy-dog story, for instance.

"By the mid-'30s the shaggy-dog story ran a close second to the off-color story in oral acceptance.

---

* Stephen Becker, *Comic Art in America.*
† *Ballyhoo* Magazine.

Winchell, Lyons and other columnists began to reproduce more and more specimens, and *Esquire* and other magazines featured articles which were little more than collections of such jokes. They were still chiefly devoted to the nonsense of intoxicating rumhounds, rather than shaggy-dog stories really, but by the end of the decade only one in five of the animal characters was a dog. The others were horses, cats, pigeons, etc. Even among the dog stories the shaggy species was rare. The shaggy-dog story is really a counterpart of the fable, in that a fable has animals talking and acting like human beings for satirical purposes. Perhaps the most famous of all such is the tale of the horse that can pitch and field baseball superbly but, when asked by the manager if he can bat, replies, 'Who ever heard of a horse that can bat!'

"Or the horse that walked up to a bar and asked for a martini with a dash of horse-radish. The bartender mixes it and hands it over. The horse polishes it off, smacking his lips, saying, 'I suppose you think it's strange that I should ask for a martini with horse-radish.' 'Hell, no,' says the bartender, 'I like them that way myself.' " *

Then there was the "Knock-knock" story, still around today. A person would announce, "Knock-knock," and the listener was to respond, "Who's there?" "Freda." "Freda who?" "Freda you, but five dollars to anyone else." † Unquestionably, it was punning in its lowest form, and people winced as often as they laughed.

In the early Thirties, Americans were heard saying "check and double-check" from the Amos 'n' Andy show. Later, Joe Penner, a radio comedian, who had come out of burlesque, had us saying "Wanna buy a duck," and "Oh, you na-a-asty man"; and for some strange reason a lot of us were convulsed—for a while. And from the newsreels Lew Lehr provided "Monkeys is the cwaziest people."

A girl called her date "smooth," and an article of dress might be "neat." The teen-agers called each other "creeps" but a "killer-diller" might be anything "terrific." Admiring a dancing couple or a band's hot rhythm, one said they were "in the groove."

* Evan Esar's *The Humor of Humor* (New York, Horizon Press, 1952).
† Joke contributed by Walt Grove.

THE JOINT IS JUMPING

A JAZZ critic once wrote that no matter what distinctions are made between jazz and popular music, certain basic elements were common to all American music—a strong, swinging beat, supporting a rhythmically free, improvised melody, such melody stemming from a popular song. Furthermore, he was of the opinion that these qualities jelled best in the swing era, a time that provided just the right mold for all the previous variations of American music—blues, ragtime, brass band, et cetera. Whether one agrees with this or not, it is certain there has never been a response to popular music to equal America's enthusiasm for swing in the late Thirties.

Frederick Lewis Allen has written about a demonstration of that enthusiasm:

"One morning in the winter of 1937–38 a crowd began to gather outside the Paramount Theater in Times Square, New York, as soon as it was light. By 6 A.M. three thousand people were assembled in the otherwise empty streets—mostly high-school boys and girls in windbreakers and leather jackets. By 7:30 the crowd had so swelled that ten mounted policemen were sent from the West Forty-seventh Street Station to keep it under control. At eight o'clock the doors of the theater were carefully opened to admit 3,634 boys and girls; then the Fire Department ordered the doors closed, leaving two or three thousand youngsters out in the cold.

"Benny Goodman and his orchestra were opening an engagement at the Paramount.

"In the same year a Carnival of Swing was held at Randall's Island in New York with twenty-five bands present; over 23,000 jitterbugs listened for five hours and forty-five minutes with such uncontrollable enthusiasm that, as a reporter put it in the next morning's *Times*, the police and park officers had all they could do to protect the players from 'destruction by admiration.' " *

Many dancers were turning into listeners and it was easy to understand why. The music was generally recognized as something more than just dance music; it was "swing" and it was "hot jazz," and people were beginning to understand that the country had a great, though not so old, tradition in jazz music; people were writing about it, and more and more people were buying records and discussing the work of the performers. They had been going to the movie houses to see the bands perform in person, and they had also stayed home at night to listen to certain bands over the radio; and young people gathered wherever they could to appreciate the rhythm and the beat. I recall leaving a dance once, while in high school, to join a group around a car radio, where we stood around clapping hands to the beat of the Casa Loma band on the old "Camel Caravan" program, and exclaiming over the Clarence Hutchenrider riffs.

* Frederick Lewis Allen's *Since Yesterday.*

MARSHALL STEARNS

THE SWING ERA*

DURING THE "Swing Era," the greatest mass conversion in the history of jazz took place. For swing music was sold—as a new kind of music—from coast to coast, with all the high-pressure tactics of modern publicity. It was brought to the attention of the public in the press and at the movies, on the stage and in the ballroom, on the juke-box and over the radio. And it made converts for whom new words such as "jitterbugs" and "bobby-soxers" were coined. And again, because most of them were young and liked to dance, swing music lasted quite a while. In many ways it is still with us, although the fans are older.

Generally speaking, swing music was the answer to the American—and very human—love of bigness, for the formula of the big Harlem bands which had solved the difficult problem of how to assemble a large orchestra and still play hot jazz was adopted. At the same time, there was a real demand. With the repeal of Prohibition in 1933, jazz was brought out of the speakeasy. There was room to expand. The Depression was fading out as far as middle-class America was concerned, and a vociferous market sprang up among the college kids.

The "sweet" dance bands succeeded in building themselves up to nine men and a violinist without much trouble. They used stock arrangements that offered no creative problems. With little improvising and less rhythm, these orchestras (referred to as "mickey-mouse" bands by jazzmen) cheerfully churned out dance music that was melodious and did not interfere with the conversations of the patrons.

The big, sweet dance band was a profitable business. Where was the big, swinging dance band? As early as 1923, Fletcher Henderson had a band of ten musicians and ran head-on into the problem of making them play together as a team. With the aid of arrangers such as Don Redman, he gradually solved the problem. By 1926, Henderson led a truly swinging band of eleven jazzmen—a fact that can be documented by listening

* From Marshall Stearns's *The Story of Jazz* (New York, Oxford University Press, Inc., 1956).

344

to "The Stampede" (Col. 654). The band played regularly at the Roseland Ballroom on Broadway, where it became something of a legend among a few white musicians. White jazzmen in the Twenties marveled at the fire and guts of the Henderson band and copied what they could, but they considered much of the music clumsy and crude. The band, they said quite sincerely, played out of tune and the individual musicians were always hitting "clinkers" or wrong notes.

By European standards the white jazzmen were right. But the ears of most musicians are better educated today. What sounded rough and out-of-tune then sounds relaxed and swinging now. The jazzman's notion of the liberties that may be taken with the perfect pitch of European music has been steadily broadening toward a predictable goal—the freedom of the street cry and the field holler. Jazz that once sounded tortured has a habit of soon sounding tidy. Yet, in 1939, Benny Goodman still spoke of "digging" the music out of a Henderson arrangement. This attitude was both typical and honest. A few years before, Isham Jones had enthusiastically purchased Don Redman's arrangement of "Chant of the Weed," only to discover that his band couldn't play it.

Fletcher Henderson and his big band were not alone. Before the Twenties were over, Negro bands led by Chick Webb, Earl Hines, Cecil Scott, William McKinney, Charlie Johnson, Luis Russell and, of course, Duke Ellington were all playing a style in which the whole band swung together. And before 1935, when Goodman arrived, these bands were joined by Cab Calloway, Jimmie Lunceford, Teddy Hill, Les Hite, Andy Kirk, Don Redman and especially, Bennie Moten. This music was swinging, relaxed, powerful, but for the most part unheard.

The distinction between these colored bands and the Goodman band which started the swing craze is indicated by Goodman's own comment:

> . . . that's why I am such a bug on accuracy in performance, about playing in tune, and with just the proper note values . . . in the written parts, I wanted it to sound as exact as the band possibly could make it.

Goodman stressed precision and the accurate pitch essential to European harmony, and worked unceasingly toward that goal.

There were at least two pioneering white bands preceding Goodman: The Dorsey Brothers and the Casa Loma band.

Jimmy and Tommy Dorsey had been making records under their own names with a variety of musicians as early as 1928. By 1934, they had a fairly stable band of their own with twelve musicians—two trumpets, three trombones, three saxes, and four rhythm. This is one saxophone short of the standard swing instrumentation. "We were trying to hit somewhere between Hal Kemp and the Casa Loma band," Tommy Dorsey once told me. Unfortunately, the arrangements now sound heavy and cluttered and the rhythm was almost of the "shuffle" variety.

The Casa Loma band from Detroit was a different story. With the same instrumentation as the Dorsey Brothers, but without the star soloists, the Casa Loma band adopted the arranged "riff" almost too wholeheartedly. With the skill and foresight of such arrangers as Southern-born-and-bred Gene Gifford, the band learned to read harmonized solos and play riffs, the brass and reed sections calling and responding to each other in a variety of ways. What is more, they learned to roll along together, generating considerable swing as a whole. (In the early Thirties, they recorded, first "White Jazz," then "Black Jazz," and Decca issued albums with the same titles, but not even the jazzmen saw anything unusual about it.) The Goldkette band and the Casa Loma band came from Detroit and played the same arrangements. "The Casa Loma band could swing more," Redman once told me, "perhaps because they were a great team without so many highly paid and temperamental stars."

How did the whole Casa Loma band learn to swing, using the call-and-response pattern between the sections? They must have had a collective ear that was relatively undisturbed by the so-called "crudities" in the music of the Fletcher Henderson band and others. Above all, their arranger, Gene Gifford, was no stranger to the blues and gospel singing of the Southwest, which he toured in his teens with the Bob Foster and Lloyd Williams bands. In this territory, the call-and-response pattern was standard for practically all music, and the swing formula for big bands was no novelty. In 1932, moreover, they could have heard the first outstanding recordings of a big, swinging band with the "five brass, four saxes, and four rhythm" that Benny Goodman later helped to standardize. These records were issued on Victor's popular series and stocked by record stores where white people traded: Bennie Moten's Kansas City band with Count Basie at the piano. And in the same year, this band played the Savoy Ballroom in New York and upset the jazz applecart. "The only time we were bothered," says Count Basie, "was when we played opposite a little guy named Chick Webb."

The Moten band raised the riff to a fine—and even improvised—art, while retaining the blazing solo work of top jazzmen, and frequently combined the best of both. The leaders of the brass and reed sections would invent a series of ascending riffs on the spur of the moment (i.e., a "head" arrangement) which the entire section would forthwith play.

The popularity of the Casa Loma band among the Eastern colleges was outstanding as early as 1931. And the Casa Loma band was Benny Goodman's model. Speaking of his booking agent and friend, Willard Alexander, who had just graduated from an Eastern college, Goodman writes:

> Since the Casa Loma was so popular with the college kids, it was tough trying to sell a sweet band against them, and he had the idea of building up some young band that would go into the same field, playing the kind of music that the youngsters liked.

In 1936, the Goodman band took the place of the Casa Loma band on the well-paid "Camel Caravan" radio show.

In 1930 the average small-town white boy (especially on the East Coast) who loved jazz heard only the Casa Loma band. Virtually alone, they played swinging jazz—mixed with a large amount of engaging sweet music such as "Smoke Rings" and "In the Still of the Night"—on phonograph records, in ballrooms, and on the air. As the first big white band to swing, they had an enormous influence in the East, where it counted heavily at that time.

While the Casa Loma band was building up its college following, Goodman made a living playing club dates (one-night local engagements) and radio programs in the studios with big commercial orchestras led by B. A. Rolfe, Rubinoff, Al Goodman, or Johnny Green. Goodman had learned how to read music, swiftly and well, which meant more jobs. This did not endear him to his colleagues from Chicago who were inclined to sneer— and with some reason, considering the attitude of symphony men—at people who could read music. ("I can read them notes," cried Wingy Manone indignantly, "I just can't separate 'em—five flats look like a bunch of grapes to me.")

In 1933, Goodman met the resourceful critic, John Hammond. On a trip to England, Hammond had sold the idea of special hot-jazz recordings to a vice-president of the English Gramophone Company. Hammond promised to supervise the recordings himself and to feature the playing of Benny Goodman. At the time Hammond hadn't met Goodman, but he soon did and convinced him, too. What musicians should they hire? Hammond held out for Gene Krupa and Jack Teagarden, while insisting that a drummer who had played with Meyer Davis be dropped. Goodman insisted upon a heavy Arthur Schutt arrangement. They had to use a "society" tenor saxophonist because he was the local contractor who got the musicians together according to union regulations.

In those days, if a musician wanted to record a popular tune, the music publishers insisted that he use a "stock" arrangement, which would make the melody recognizable—and uninspired—wherever it was heard. He might be permitted to record a tune of his own, played hot if he signed away the rights to the recording supervisor. Pressure was sometimes exerted to make him play in a "corny," or old-fashioned, style which would be sure to sell. Goodman recorded "Shirt Tail Stomp" (Brun. 3975), for example, in a hillbilly style at the urging of record-company executives. When it was issued in 1928, Ted Lewis, whom Goodman burlesques on the record, liked it enough to offer him a job. The job helped pull Goodman though the Depression.

Hammond had insisted on special arrangements, however, and Goodman's first record for the English Gramophone Company—"I Got a Right to Sing the Blues" and "Ain'tcha Glad"—was a notable success in England. When the American record executives woke up and decided to issue it in the United States, only Hammond's violent objections kept them from coupling each side with a commercial number by Clyde McCoy or Harry Reser "to insure the recording's success." Goodman went on to make a series of recordings for Columbia at a new low of $100 a side, employing such musicians as Teddy Wilson and Coleman Hawkins and such singers as Billie Holiday, Jack Teagarden and Mildred Bailey.

As the series progressed, Goodman began to appreciate and employ first-rate Negro musicians. On this point, he is quite frank about the importance of Hammond's influence:

It was during these months, around the end of 1933 and the beginning of 1934, that I first began to make records with colored musicians. For this the responsibility must be given almost entirely to John Hammond, who really put me back in touch with the kind of music they could play . . . It just happened that in working along as I had during those seven or eight years, I had gotten out of touch with them. . . .

Later on, Benny Goodman broke the precedent against bands of mixed color—not without some difficulty—by employing Teddy Wilson at the Hotel Congress in Chicago.

By 1934, Goodman had his own orchestra and a job which paid less than scale at Billy Rose's Music Hall. An air-shot over WMCA, however, made new friends. Three months later "the mob found a cheaper band." Then came the big break. The National Biscuit Company was ready to launch its new Ritz cracker, and an advertising firm sold them the idea of a "Let's Dance" radio program with three bands: Xavier Cugat playing rhumbas, Kel Murray playing sweet dance music, and Benny Goodman playing a little more rhythmic jazz. The three bands alternated from 11 to 2 A.M. every Saturday night, and the program was carried by fifty-three stations from coast to coast.

The rumor of "kick-backs" still survives, but the biscuit company financed eight new arrangements of Goodman's choosing during the first thirteen weeks. His choice is revealing. With the constant prodding of Hammond, Goodman hired better hot-jazz men and went to Fletcher Henderson for his new arrangements. At this stage in the development of swing music, we can pinpoint certain musical relationships. Henderson sold Goodman arrangements that Henderson had been using for three to five years. It was Goodman's precise style of playing the arrangements that hit the great American public as something new and exciting.

The "Let's Dance" radio show, together with a series of recordings, began to build up a small but devoted following. "I had to do what I thought I was best at," says Goodman, "and just then it was having a hot band." From week to week, the band sounded better over the radio (at that, only every third number was played "hot"). But the general public was as yet untouched. MCA, the Music Corporation of America, persuaded by a young collegian in their employ, Willard Alexander, decided to book the Goodman band, much to the annoyance of most of the people at the agency. At the time MCA booked only sweet bands. They put Goodman into the Hotel Roosevelt in New York City, the home of Guy Lombardo. "Every time I looked around, on the night we opened," says Goodman, "one of the waiters or the captain would be motioning to us not to play so loud." The band was not a success.

In desperation, Alexander booked Goodman for a series of one-nighters, with a month stopover in Denver, to the West Coast where there seemed to be a little interest. The band worked its way out, playing in Pittsburgh, Columbus, Toledo, Lakeside (Michigan), Milwaukee, and then Denver— where Kay Kyser was pulling them in. The spot was called Elitch's Gardens and the owner phoned MCA at once, announcing that "the music was lousy and the leader was a pain in the neck," to quote Goodman himself. And business was terrible. By switching to stock arrangements, the band held the job but morale hit a new low.

The band's morale was still low after playing Salt Lake City and San Francisco. They recalled trumpeter Wingy Manone's observation: "Man, good jazz just can't make it over them tall Rockies." When they arrived at the Palomar Ballroom in Los Angeles, their new location for a month or so, the band became downright frightened. The ballroom had an enormous dance floor, plus a huge section with tables where food and liquor were noisily served. And they charged admission. For the first hour, the band played the sweeter tunes with the softer arrangements. Goodman was desperate:

If we had to flop, at least I'd do it in my own way, playing the kind of music I wanted to. For all I knew this might be our last night together, and we might as well have a good time of it while we had the chance.

I called out some of our big Fletcher arrangements for the next set, and the boys seemed to get the idea. From the moment I kicked them off, they dug in with some of the best playing I'd heard since we left New York. . . .

The first big roar from the crowd was one of the sweetest sounds I ever heard in my life. . . .

The Swing Era was born on the night of August 21, 1935.

The immediate reason for the sudden success of the Goodman band, according to Benny himself, is that "it was a dancing audience—that's why they went for it." Again, Goodman's phonograph records preceded the band's success, and disc jockeys had been playing some of the best of them. Further, the "Let's Dance" program hit Los Angeles between the hours of 7 and 11 P.M.—the time of maximum listening and the time when the teen-agers could hear it. They were still dancing the Lindy, and Goodman's music was just right for it. In a matter of months, the jitterbugs and bobby-soxers were dancing the Big Apple and the Shag—up and down the aisles of theaters, too—while the Goodman band played on. Above all, they were the first band to give the current hits of Tin-Pan Alley, such as "Goody Goody," for example, a jazz treatment which sold enormously.

If Benny Goodman became the "King of Swing" in 1935, reaping all the publicity and profits, the man behind the throne was Count Basie. For it was the Basie band that gave depth and momentum to the whole Swing Era while planting the seeds that later gave birth to bop and the "cool" school of jazz. In 1935, after the death of Bennie Moten, Bill Basie gradually built up his own band. He and his band were playing the Reno Club in Kansas City in 1936, when John Hammond heard them over experimental station W9XBY and alerted Benny Goodman and Willard Alexander of MCA.

The Basie band was scuffling. "It was a cracker town but a happy time," Basie recalls. At the Reno Club, imported Scotch was fifteen cents a shot, domestic ten cents, and a hot-dog stand was located next to the bar. "We played from nine o'clock in the evening to five or six the next morning, including the floor shows," says Basie, "and the boys in the band got eighteen dollars a week and I got twenty-one." When Buck Clayton joined on trumpet, the boys sacrificed twenty-five cents apiece and Clayton got two dollars a night. Down the street at the Sunset Club, boogie-woogie pianist Pete Johnson and blues-shouter Joe Turner (who made a great hit with rock and roll in 1954), were working for less. Actually, things weren't as bad as they seemed, because prices were low and tips from gangsters high.

MCA booked Basie for a trial run at the Grand Terrace Ballroom in Chicago. Nothing much happened. Then the band was brought to the Famous Door on New York's Fifty-second Street. The word got around fast. On the way to New York, Basie augmented his band from nine to fifteen men:

—I wanted my fifteen-piece band to work together just like those nine pieces did. I wanted fifteen men to think and play the same way. I wanted those four trumpets and three trombones to bite with real guts. BUT I wanted that bite to be just as tasty and subtle as if it were the three brass . . . I said that the minute the brass got out of hand and blared and screeched . . . there'd be some changes made.

The Famous Door was about the size of a large closet and, once inside, patrons found themselves sitting under the guns. When the band started to play, some listeners felt as if they were inside a loudspeaker-enclosure with the volume up. You either loved it or hated it—there was no middle ground—but to New York musicians the power and swing of the Basie band was a revelation.

Aided by the ground-breaking success of Benny Goodman and the astute managing of Willard Alexander, the Basie band with its more relaxed and powerful beat became an immediate and lasting success. "When we first came to New York we tried to experiment," drummer Jo Jones recalls, "so after a week of experimenting we found out that there was nothing old hat about what we had been doing." In a short time, Basie was influencing Goodman deeply. Goodman adopted Basie's numbers, such as "One O'Clock Jump" (which was the first Goodman recording to sell over a million), and then began to use Basie and some of his musicians on recordings. Fortunately, Basie had recorded his own version of "One O'Clock Jump" (in part, a riff taken from Redman's arrangement of "Six or Seven Times") about seven months earlier and, although it did not sell nearly as well, the original had wide distribution and musicians could hear and appreciate it.

The very birthplaces of the musicians associated with Basie made a roll call of the Southwest: Herschel Evans, Denton, Texas; Jimmy Rushing, Oklahoma City, Oklahoma; Buck Clayton, Parsons, Kansas; Jack Washington, Kansas City, Kansas; Oran "Hot Lips" Page, Dallas, Texas; Don

Byas, Muskogee, Oklahoma; Joe Keyes, Houston, Texas; Joe Turner, Kansas City, Missouri; Walter Page, Gallatin, Missouri; Eddie Durham, San Marcos, Texas; and Lester Young, Woodville, Mississippi.

The Basie band accomplished a revolution in jazz that we are still trying to estimate. Specfically, the Basie piano style, with its frequent openings for the bass fiddle, led to the de-emphasis of the left hand in modern jazz piano. The style of drummer Jo Jones, who rode the high-hat cymbal, left its mark on bop drummers. And the relaxed style of tenor saxophonist Lester Young helped to produce the "cool" school of jazz. A younger saxophonist, Dexter Gordon, says that he stopped playing after he heard Lester Young. "It was too much . . . I threw my horn away and didn't touch it for two years." Benny Goodman reacted differently: "This is the first time," he told John Hammond, "that I've ever heard a tenor sax played the way it should be and not overblown." (He swapped his clarinet for Young's tenor saxophone and, they say, sounded like Young for a whole evening.) Above all, the Basie band developed the use of the "head riff" (the improvised unison phrase, tossed back and forth by brass and reed sections) to the level of fine art. On a less evident but more important level than the Goodman band, the band of Count Basie underwrote the Swing Era. Goodman's "King Porter Stomp" was recorded in 1935, Bob Crosby's "Dixieland Shuffle" in 1936, Tommy Dorsey's "Marie" in 1937, Artie Shaw's "Begin the Beguine" in 1938, and Glenn Miller's "In the Mood" in 1939. (The importance of the disc jockey becomes evident.) The musical sources for many of these swing bands were documented, in part, by another band under the leadership of Charlie Barnet. He made a recording with "The Duke's Idea" on one side and "The Count's Idea" on the other (Bluebird 10453), paying homage to Duke Ellington and Count Basie. For the next ten years, swing music made big money and bandleaders became as popular—and as unpredictable—as movie stars.

LISTENING TO B.G.

IN THE fall of 1936, Otis Ferguson, an editor of *The New Republic,* had visited the Café Rouge, as it was then known, at the old Hotel Pennsylvania in New York City to listen to the Benny Goodman band. His description of the intense feelings one brought to listening to the good jazz of the day is inspired and lyrical but true.

OTIS FERGUSON

THE SPIRIT OF JAZZ*

SWING IN, swing out, the band is up again and drawing the people out like the sun in the fable. With Krupa, Reuss (guitar) and the inspired quiet Stacey (piano) laying down a thick rhythmic base, it plays on through whatever songs are the demand of the day, making most of them sound like something. This is an organization in the line of the great jazz bands—Jean Goldkette, Fletcher Henderson, McKinney, Cotton Pickers, Ellington, Kirk, *et al.*—a little lighter than some of these but more beautifully rehearsed and economical, and with cleaner edges. The reed section, scored as such, is more prominent than in older hot bands, giving a fuller lyric quality; but the section (five men counting Goodman) has a hard skeleton of attack and swing that supports any relative lightness of brass. The band as a whole gets its lift from the rhythm men and the soloists as they take off; it is built from the ground rather than tailored.

The quartet, composed of Goodman, Gene Krupa, Teddy Wilson and Lionel Hampton, plays every night—clarinet, piano, vibraphone, drums— and they make music you would not believe. No arrangements, not a false note, one finishing his solo and dropping into background support, then the other, all adding inspiration until with some number like "Stomping at the Savoy" they get going too strong to quit—four choruses, someone starts up another, six, eight, and still someone starts—no two notes the same and no one note off the chord, the more they relax in the excitement

* From *The New Republic,* Dec. 30, 1936.

of it the more a natural genius in preselection becomes evident and the more indeed the melodic line becomes rigorously pure. This is really composition on the spot, with the spirit of jazz strongly over all of them but the iron laws of harmony and rhythm never lost sight of; and it is a collective thing, the most beautiful example of men working together to be seen in public today.

It isn't merely hell-for-leather either. Gene Krupa, a handsome mad-man over his drums, makes the rhythmic force and impetus of it visual, for his face and whole body are sensitive to each strong beat of the ensemble; and Hampton does somewhat the same for the line of melody, hanging solicitous over the vibraphone plates and exhorting them (Hmmm, Oh, Oh yah, Oh dear *hmmm*). But the depth of tone and feeling is mainly invisible, for they might play their number "Exactly Like You" enough to make people cry and there would be nothing of it seen except perhaps in the lines of feeling on Benny Goodman's face, the affable smile dropped as he follows the Wilson solo flight, eyes half-closed behind his glasses. There was a special feeling among them the first morning they recorded this piece, the ghost of the blues perhaps; and when the clarinet takes up you will hear the phrases fall as clear as rain, with a sustained glow of personal essence that starts where command of the instrument (the ten-sion of mouth, delicate fingering, etc.) leaves off. Then Hampton sings a chorus, his vibrant hoarse voice and relaxed emphasis so appropriate to the general color; and when they take up again the instruments blend so perfectly as to be indistinguishable, singing in unison with a sweet breadth of tone that goes beyond the present place and time to some obscure source of feeling and native belief. The term swing—no more definable in words than the term poetry—is defined at its best in this piece, where the actual beats are lost sight of in the main effect, so that the inexorable and brute lift of the time signature as carried in Krupa's great drum seems fused in the harmony and melodic line of the song. And you may say of the excitement this thing starts in the blood only that these four men are quite simple and wonderful together, that they are truly swinging.

The quartet is a beautiful thing all through, really a labor of creative love, but it cannot last forever and as the band starts again you realize that even in jazz there are several kinds of musical appreciation. For if they'll agree to put on the "Bugle Call Rag" before the end of the evening I'll be willing to say there's nothing finer. There is some hidden lift to this old band standby, with its twenty quaint notes from the "Assembly" call dropping the barrier to a straight-out progression of simple chords—and they are off, riding it with collective assurance and fine spirit, the men in their sections, the sections balancing, the soloists dropping back with care for the total effect. The guests are presently banked in a half-moon around the stand, unable to be still through it or move away either; and as it builds to the final solid chords, Krupa becoming a man of subtle thunder and Benny lacing in phrases, the air is full of brass and of rhythms you can almost lean on. The music seems more than audible, rising and coming forward from the stand in banks of colors and shifting masses—not only the clangor in the ears but a visual picture of the intricate fitted spans, the breathless height and spring of a steel-bridge structure. And if you leave at the end, before the "Good-Bye" signature, you will seem to hear this great rattling march of the hobos through the taxis, lights and people, ringing under the low sky over Manhattan as if it were a strange high thing after all (which it is) and as if it came from the American ground under these buildings, roads and motorcars (which it did). And if you leave the band and quartet and piano of the Goodman show and still are no more than slightly amused, you may be sure that in the smug absence of your attention a native true spirit of music has been and gone, leaving a message for your grandchildren to study through their patient glasses.

LET'S DANCE

THERE WERE many other big bands, and they were eager to play hotel engagements—if the hotel had a direct wire for broadcasting over a radio station. Remember listening late at night to the bands at the Coconut Grove in Hollywood, the Glen Island Casino in Westchester, the College Inn at the Hotel Sherman in Chicago, or the dance music at the huge ballrooms in Chicago, the Trianon and Aragon?

A band's reputation could be made almost overnight by the jukebox, where a successful record sometimes was worth six solid months of radio exposure. Jukebox hit records helped to make the reputations of such bands as Artie Shaw's, Larry Clinton's, Tommy Dorsey's, and even Ozzie Nelson's.

In the early Thirties people had very little to celebrate; they felt vulnerable and, as much as anything, wanted to be soothed. One could take a date to the movies, or just stay home of an evening and dance to radio music, but there came a time when you wanted to get out and be with others. The big cities provided sporting events and the theater (if the prices weren't too steep for the pocketbook), but not the smaller communities. The big social events were apt to be the dances, especially if you were of high-school or college age. Until the jukebox took over later in the decade, a few live musicians were necessary to provide the music. All over the country, in the small towns, you might hear "Are you going to the dance?" and "Who're you taking?" in anticipation of the coming weekends and holidays.

And in the summer there were dances at the amusement parks, dance halls and roadhouses, on lakes, near beaches, with big dance floors that could hold hundreds of couples. It was not that these places did not exist in the Twenties (there are comparatively few today) but then there were more things to do and see, and there was more money for traveling.

A stag line was permissible, and often there was a dance program card on which to note the exchanges of partners. High-school gyms, town halls and such often doubled as dance floors, and frequently a dance would be scheduled as an afterpiece to a basketball game; the people were already there, and gas for the car didn't come cheap.

It seemed, too, that almost everybody attended the dances. More men danced, unconcerned with poor technique, and in the early years of the decade there were few obstreperous new dances to shame "the old folks" off the dance floor. When "jitterbugging" arrived with the Big Apple, Shag and Lindy Hop, later in the decade, it was every man for himself. By then, I suppose, we were beginning to believe the Depression was on its way out for most of us; we felt a sense of release, and welcomed the big bands and the new dances with an excitement and exuberance unmatched in the Twenties and the later decades. Wherever there was a patch of dance floor and a jukebox, in taverns, restaurants, roadhouses and even soda joints, young people took time to listen and dance to the latest records by Goodman, Glen Gray, Artie Shaw and others. If you couldn't get a date with your favorite girl, you settled for the fourth favorite so long as she liked to dance.

And if you wanted to learn the latest step in those days, you didn't go to Arthur Murray's; if you were lucky enough to be in New York City, you visited the temple of swing, the Savoy, up in Harlem.

OTIS FERGUSON

BREAKFAST DANCE, IN HARLEM*

THE PLACE is uptown, up the one and only Lenox Avenue, and you can dance from nine o'clock Saturday evening right through to eight o'clock Sunday morning. The breakfast dance, and swing it, men. On most nights, even most Saturday nights, there are two bands and the show is over at two or three. But tonight, one night out of every few weeks, breakfast is the limit, there are four bands in all and in short they will be able to serve it up as long as you can take it. If not longer.

It is a respectable place too. No barrelhouse, no basement creep-joint. A ballroom, in fact. Inside, up the wide flight of stairs after you have put up your seventy-five cents, the manager is nice enough and the people are nice enough, and there is no trouble. The long crowded bar at one end of the table space sells only beer (ten cents) and California wine (twenty cents a glass, out of gallon jugs). Some bring their own bottles of hard, but these can weave into the Gents, all in good time, and take care of whatever gets too much for them. There are two Gents, side by side. No trouble.

It is twelve o'clock and you can still get on the floor. The rain. The manager is very sad that people can still get on his floor. There should be more of a jam than on Ladies' Nights; but it drizzles badly and there is not more of a jam.

The hall must be seventy-five yards long by twenty-five wide, the ceiling and lights are low. In the few seconds between numbers, or in the minute when one band takes over from another, the place a rich babble, with "You saids" and "How come womans" and "Ain't that it thoughs." And

* From *The New Republic,* Feb. 12, 1936.

when the band gets pretty well into it, the whole enclosure, with all its people, beats like a drum and rises in steady time, like a ground swell.

Impossible to see everything at once. The bands; the people drinking, or half-asleep at tables over their beer, or promoting their private bit of business slapstick, romance; the musicians off duty, making horseplay or eating part of their supper with a sort of genial and quiet boisterousness.

"Doggone," says the one they call Choo, sitting like a four-poster, one of the first artists in this country on the tenor saxophone, "doggone, ain't no meat here *at* all. What that man mean, dishing me out this for charmaine?" Choo says, shoveling it in. And the dance floor is a hopeless intricate mass of flying ankles, swirls, stomps—really beautiful dancing. As dancing, superb. Everybody immensely noisy, sweating, full of spirits. Here today and here tomorrow too.

It is a strange sort of atmosphere. You cannot see everything at once but you can feel everything at once, a sort of unifying outflow of energy, you can almost see it burn. Its focal point is around the stand of rough and well-splintered wood, where the lights are and the music stands, and the bass drum spiked to the floor and the stringbass fixed in a socket and the big pianos with the keyboards worn like flights of old wooden stairs.

The single stand, for the two bands, is about sixty feet long, and narrow, down one side of the hall. It is the center of most of the light, but still dim enough. The wall behind it is painted into an extravagant blue background, and by means of trick spotlights thin clouds seem to be drawn across it perpetually, giving the effect of motion and smoke, and the bands play under that, dominating the hall and bearing down on it, inexorable, all steam and iron, like freight trains.

On the floor and at the tables and along the bar there are all the people, hundreds of them (fifteen-sixteen hundred on a capacity night maybe); and off toward one corner there is a row of hostesses, two bits for three dances; and there are rose-colored lights let into the ceiling and things going on everywhere. But the real life of the hall is over here on the stand, where the boys are lined up in two rows, stomping away and sweating their brass horns till the floor shakes, where the great moon of the sousaphone bell shines down on the dancers and the beat of guitar-piano-stringbass-drum nails all this lavish and terrific energy down to the simple restraints of a time signature. And when Teddy Hill's men begin swinging the last choruses of the specialty number "Christopher Colombo," with those driving brass figures and the reed section going down to give it body, the dancers forget dancing and flock around the stand ten deep, to register the time merely with their bones and muscles, standing there in one place with their heads back and letting it flow over them like water—invitation (and the waltz be damned) to blow the man down. The floor shakes and the place is a dynamo room, with the smoky air pushing up in steady waves, and swing it, men, get off, beat it out and in a word play that thing. It's a music deaf men could hear.

The spirit belongs as much to the place as to any particular music makers. Because this hall has something to it. Shadows maybe. The rafters have echoes of Fletcher Henderson's great swing band, and of Louis (the Reverend Satchelmouth) Armstrong, roaring through his fantastic horn, and of Mr. Ellington, the Duke, the Great Dusky, and of Cab Calloway, leading crazy man, who got his start here, of McKinney's Cotton Pickers and the Chocolate Dandies—and who not. Name a band, the manager says, you just go ahead name a band which I can tell you personally that band played here, including Paul Whiteman. There is something in the air here, a demand to be given something on the part of the people, that shapes matters, so that when a group needs to get really together and tightened up, this is where it books in.

But the spirit of all this is not just an urge to flash-bang-blare and shiver the windows. There are shrewdness and loving care going into this, and many subtleties. Not the usual fuss and gargle about art and the artist's line on war'n'fascism. Just so many of the boys apparently playing a job, playing a date, making a record for Victor, a tune for the networks or the dancers—talking about it among themselves with a peculiar reserve and modest dignity. Some of them, the best of them, burn themselves up to keep it strong and unspoiled, finely marked with the obscure beauty of their invention. The best of them would not be Lombardos, Duchins, Vallees, Reismans, even if they had the showmanship, brute luck and gall to do it. Here somehow a good tenor man can make a tone pattern that will have a dancing strength and freshness, the only one of its kind because it is made directly from his own command of an instrument, his own exuberance and sadness. Anything outside of this stern, continually inventive tradition (also to be found, shall we say, in Bach) and above all anything without this drive peculiar to the form, may be effective, tricky, may pay well. But it will be fake. It will lack the element of creation, and be fake. "Some of these tenor men," Choo says, off the stand again, "I see they go copying off Hawkins and them. Shuck. A man never get playing it really good till he putten something into it, you think? A man don't watch out, all he putten in is spit. I don't know, shuck. I work really hard trying to blow it out clean, like I can be proud of it, but a man playing around every night—shuck, I don't know . . ."

Having expressed it without saying it, or anything really, Choo breaks off in embarrassment. "Doggone this man," he says, "about this here no-good charmaine. If I eaten any meat here tonight I'll—"

But this part of it does not bother you at the time. It is three, four, five o'clock and nobody seems to know it. More people are asleep at the tables, fewer people are on the floor; but otherwise there is this same hot stuffy genial air, this same squandering of energy under the dim lights. Teddy Hill's boys have hung around a while, their spot having been taken over for the night, and dispersed in pairs and groups gradually, after observing the other man's music. And the dominant spirit of rhythm in the place is now Chick Webb, the old-timer, the little hunchback who sits bolstered up before his set of very elegant white traps, beating at them with a fierce tremendous love of the thing that sends a whole band, and gives the beat to the floor, which still shakes.

But this is Harlem. Down the stairs and outside, where the music is only a throb in the air, it is morning and already light enough to see that this is Harlem, a community. There are only a few people about—several coming out of the hall, carousing off to breakfast from the breakfast dance, several who have not been in the hall.

"Say Mac, how about a cigarette now," one of these latter says to me, stepping up as though he'd buy up the block in another minute, if the mood took him. "Guess I'd light up now, if you got a spare." He hasn't any matches either. "Well how is it up there?" he says. "Pretty crowded up there? Can't get on the damn floor I bet."

"It's pretty good—plenty of room though," I say.

"Pretty crowded though, ain't it? I figured you couldn't get on the floor, you know."

"Well, there's some there but there's plenty of room."

"Is that so? I figured it would be too crowded. . . ."

"Well say now," he says. He has made the touch for a smoke with no trouble. "You wouldn't be having a dime now, extra, I suppose? Just so's I can—well say Mac, thank *you*—so's I can get me some coffee. Funny about that. I figured it'd be too crowded up there, a guy couldn't get on the floor, you know?"

His line by now is obvious. The loud front, the wistfulness and poor pride behind it, the place not to his classy liking. He finishes the touch for the dime and waves me on my way regally. I'm to come look him up some time. Knows everybody up there. Sure. Come up some night, just mention his name. Fix me up with some nice girls too, sure.

The cuffs of his frayed cheap trousers walk jauntily off up the Avenue past rubbish and newspapers, dusty and rustling in the early morning, and off down a sidestreet of gray poor doorways, empty stores, pinched tenements. And it is not possible now to overlook where a breakfast dance ends and where it came from—the rags and mean tatters of Harlem, an American community bled dry. The thump of Chick Webb's drum is fainter in the open air, but to listen to the fine terrific beat of jazz from here is to recognize all at once another element, always present in the music but usually below its surface, most vivid in the blues (I woke up this mornin', I had to pawn my shoes). There is a gay abandon and all that, up the one and only Lenox Avenue; there are lights and people carrying on and what not. To be sure. And that is about the half of it. It is out of the lives of the people here that the music comes, and so if you will stand here you may suddenly feel it, the whole of it with undertones and overtones, its abandon and bitter sorrow.

THAT LUSH LIFE IN CELLULOID

Lots of us enjoyed our leisure at the movies. The experience of going was like an insidious candy we could never get quite enough of; the visit to the dark theater was an escape from the drab realities of Depression living, and we were entranced by the never-ending variety of stories. Hollywood, like Scheherazade in *The Thousand and One Nights*, supplied more the next night, and the next night after that.

Soon the distributors took away the comedies and short subjects, which many of us relished not only for the laughs but also for the anticipation they enabled us to feel before the big show. In their place we were given the double feature, which some of us enjoyed because it kept us in the theater twice as long. After a while we perceived that the double feature was also a device for dumping second-rate films on the public. But we still went—"hooked" by the habit—and the distributor, for his sins, was soon forced to accept the block-booking technique; to get the A picture, he had to accept a quota of B, C and Z products.

Three out of five people disliked the double feature; but a minority, it seems, was strong enough to force the program on the rest of us. While there may have been those who refused to have their hours raped by Hollywood fantasies, it was years before the rest of us got over the craving.

By the end of the decade there were between 52 million and 55 million attending the movies every week

of the year. To the girl in the glass-enclosed cage (she started the gentle separation from reality) we handed over our hard-earned money—averaging, annually, five dollars a person or twenty-five dollars a family for the total population of the country (big money in those days, remember). There were more than 15,000 theaters to choose from, more movie houses than banks, twice as many as hotels and three times as many as department stores. If you didn't like the product, you must have been un-American—because the picture industry had a capital investment in the United States of two billion dollars.

Business looked good, right? as Mort Sahl would say today. Back in 1933, the theater owners thought it should be better. So they invented Bank Night and Dish Night, and Bingo, Keeno, Screeno and such games to go along with "our daily double." (Patrons of today, please note, when you complain about the popcorn and candy wrappers under foot.)

Not everyone swallowed Hollywood whole; some took offense. Ruth Suckow, writing in *Harper's* Magazine, objected to the Galatea machine which turned out the gods and goddesses:

"It would seem at times that this nation, losing the strong Puritan orthodoxy it brought to the new continent, yet still crude and young in the mass, has turned to the worship of those picture gods, real and yet unreal, common as life and yet larger than life, known in minuter detail than next-door neighbors and yet shiningly remote, because they have come to represent certain national ideals reduced to the lowest common denominator. For that is what the screen does—it reduces while it magnifies, grinds down what it exalts into the typical.

"Motion pictures constitute the only art in which the players are actually able to see themselves. Nearly everybody prefers a flattering photograph." * After analyses of the stars of the day—Garbo, Gable, et cetera—she decided that "in spite of the skill that goes into the making of American motion pictures, they form an unconscious social document rather than an art." *

It is doubtful that, even though Miss Suckow was right about most of the product, anyone in Hollywood was one whit concerned; and anyway everyone was too busy making pictures for the double bills. Or making news—on the forty-second day of the bombardment of London, the London *Mirror* cabled its Hollywood correspondent for 280 words concerning Ann Sheridan's contract dispute with Warner's.

"No other community in America," Leo Rosten has said, "is reported upon each day so intensely, so insistently, and with such a deplorable premium on triviality.

. . . The sheer magnitude of this adoration invites awe. Each day, millions of men, women and children sit in the windowless temples of the screen to commune with their vicarious friends and lovers. Each night they read the newspaper pages (or the screen magazines) devoted to the stars and all their petty histories. Is it any wonder that one of the great appeals to the individual club member is 'Say, I could do that!'—no other industry presents so simple an invitation to the ego.

"It's one of the very few fields of enterprise left in America in which youth is promised high rewards, in which youth is, indeed, an advantage rather than a burden . . . and in which inexperience is of little account." The would-be movie star "needs no capital, no training, no skill." †

The industry flourished; in 1939 alone, Hollywood produced almost four hundred pictures. But did it produce anything that resembled art? Undoubtedly—Miss Suckow to the contrary—and if for no other reason than that a certain percentage derived from the nation's published fiction, was directed by brilliant men from the theater—and the motion picture world too—and that frequently excellent performances were given, even by some of those "gods and goddesses."

* "Hollywood Gods and Goddesses," *Harper's* Magazine, July 1936.
† Leo Rosten, *Hollywood* (New York, Harcourt, Brace, 1941).

ARTHUR KNIGHT

THE MOVIES*

THE SILENT FILM had created a world of persuasive reality despite the absence of voices and the verifying clangor of natural sound. Indeed, much of the art of the silent film lay in the invention of means to circumvent these artificial limitations. Then, suddenly, they were all removed, and the sounds of the real world became as much a part of the film as its sights. The public positively reveled in the new sensation, the opportunity to hear its favorite stars talking and singing, to hear the crack of a pistol, the roar of a motor or even the ring of a telephone. It was exactly like the first years of the movies all over again. Then, anything that moved was fascinating.

Many of the studio heads were quite willing to agree that talkies were simply a thing of the moment—but at the moment, they pointed out, it was the thing that the public wanted. Indeed, those producers who hesitated to bow to this obviously popular demand, preferring to hold off until the whole thing blew over, were soon out of business entirely. The public's enthusiasm for sound was so strong that attendance leaped from 60,00,000 paid admissions per week in 1927 to 110,000,000 in 1929. When the stock market crashed in the fall of 1929, the impetus provided by the introduction of sound proved strong enough to carry the industry safely through the first years of the Depression. By 1930 the silent film was a thing of the past, Charlie Chaplin's *City Lights* (1931) and the Flaherty-Murnau *Tabu* (1931) coming as last, lovely reminders of an art that was no more. By the start of the Thirties, in every film-producing nation the studios had converted to sound. It was to take them many a year, however, before they could regain the artistry and power of the best of the silent era.

In 1929, after little more than a year of talkies, *Variety* wryly reported, "Sound didn't do any more to the industry than turn it upside down, shake the entire bag of tricks from its pocket and advance Warner Brothers from the last place (among the film companies) to first in the league."

* Condensed from Arthur Knight's *The Liveliest Art* (New York, Macmillan, 1957).

The films had learned to talk, and talk was uppermost in everyone's mind. Script-writers who had trained themselves to think in terms of pictures gave way to playwrights who thought in terms of stage dialogue. Established directors were either replaced by directors from the New York stage or supplemented by special dialogue directors. Many a popular star—especially the European importees—suddenly found himself unemployed; while the Broadway stage was again swept clean to replace those actors whose foreign accents, faulty diction or bad voices the temperamental microphone rejected.

And then a new and imposing figure appeared in the studios, the sound expert. It was the sound expert who concealed the microphone in the vase of flowers on the boudoir table, who dictated where actors must stand in order to record properly, who decided where the camera must be placed in order to keep the microphone outside its field. He was the final arbiter on what could and what could not be done, and his word was law. The camera itself, now imprisoned within a soundproof booth, was robbed of all mobility. And the experts, concerned with nothing beyond the sound quality of the pictures they worked on, continually simplified their problems by insisting that scenes be played in corners, minimizing long shots for the more readily controllable close-up. In no time at all the techniques, the artistry that directors had acquired through years of silent films were cast aside and forgotten in the shadow of the microphone.

Sound gave the banks and the investment houses their first real hold upon the motion-picture industry. Every studio needed sound, and most of them also needed vast sums of new working capital to make the equipment purchases and studio alterations required to convert to sound. Both the equipment and the financing led ultimately to the same sources, to Western Electric, RCA and their affiliated banking houses. Soon their representatives were sitting on the boards of the motion-picture companies, making policy with—and sometimes in place of—the veteran showmen who had brought their studios from obscurity to world-wide prominence. They appointed the sound experts who dominated the studios through 1929 and 1930. These men knew only about acoustics and microphone characteristics. But because they had the backing of the people who were paying for it all, they often usurped the functions of both producer and director. As a result, a transition that would have been difficult in any case was made more difficult still. Producers whose main stock in trade was their knowledge of entertainment values suddenly found their hands tied. Directors who understood the necessity to keep the picture moving and alive found themselves arbitrarily overruled in favor of the microphone.

It is to the eternal credit of genuinely creative and courageous men like Ernst Lubitsch, Rouben Mamoulian, Lewis Milestone and King Vidor that they had the ingenuity and vitality to circumvent the experts and lift the new medium out of the rut of dully photographed plays and vaudeville routines into which it had fallen. They had no rules to go on, no precedents to quote. They had the opposition of the sound men to contend with, and the indisputable fact that at the box offices across the nation almost any film was making money as long as it talked. But these men sensed that talk alone was not enough, and that the public would soon tire of the novelty of sound for sound's sake and demand again to see a *movie*. It was their pioneer work that brought forth the techniques to make the movies move again.

Ernst Lubitsch, by 1929 the top director at Paramount, made the important discovery that a talking picture did not have to be *all* talking, nor did the sound track have to reproduce faithfully each sound on the set. In his first talkies, *The Love Parade* (1929) and *Monte Carlo* (1930), he included many passages that were shot without dialogue or any other synchronized sound. For these, he was able to bring the camera out of its soundproofed box and proceed in the old silent techniques, moving his camera freely, changing its position frequently. Music or effects were put in later. One of the high points of *The Love Parade* was a running gag with Maurice Chevalier telling a risqué joke to members of the court. Each time he approaches the tag line, his voice sinks to a confidential whisper, a door closes, or the camera leaps outside to view the effect of his story through a window. Audiences of 1929 were delighted to find a new element in the talkies—silence!

Lubitsch also knew how to use the sound camera to serious purpose. In *Broken Lullaby* (1932), his one dramatic film of this period, he emphasized its antiwar theme in many brilliantly conceived shots. The sights and sounds of an Armistice Day parade are glimpsed between the crutches of a one-legged soldier. Early in the film, while a minister is praying for peace, the camera in ironic counterpoint moves slowly down the center aisle of the cathedral, past row on row of kneeling officers, their spurs gleaming, their swords stiff by their sides. By shooting such sequences silent and adding the sound later, Lubitsch obtained not only greater freedom for his camera but the kind of control of the elements in his scene essential to artistic creation. The "Lubitsch touch," that sparkling combination of wit and irony already famous in the silent film, reached its fullest expression in his early talkies.

Meanwhile, King Vidor in his first talking picture, *Hallelujah!* (1929), explored the possibilities of the sound track to evoke mood and atmosphere. It was an all-Negro picture made, for the most part, in Memphis, Tennessee, and the swamps of Arkansas. The fact that the film was done largely on location, away from rigid studio supervision, gave Vidor an enviable amount of freedom for that time. Much of it he shot silent, later creating an impressionistic sound track for all but the direct dialogue passages. He showed that the source of a sound is less important than its quality, that sound can create an emotional aura about a scene quite independent of the words and faces of the actors. Lewis Milestone worked in much the same way in making his *All Quiet on the Western Front* (1930), photographing his scenes of troops on the march and in the trenches with a silent camera and adding in later the whine and crash of bombs, the clatter of small-arms fire and the shrieks and moans of the wounded and dying.

Postsynchronization became the first point of departure in the development of the new art.

The other was an improvement in the camera itself. During the first years of sound, the camera had been forced into a small soundproofed booth to keep the whirr of its mechanism from reaching the sensitive, cranky microphone. During 1930, however, the cameras began to emerge from these boxes, enclosed now in soundproofed "blimps" which, while still cumbersome, permitted a far greater freedom of movement. It then became the director's problem to force the reluctant sound experts to give that new mobility full rein, to demand from them more flexible microphone setups. Before long, the stationary microphones were being replaced by mikes suspended on long booms that could be swung to follow the players anywhere.

Perhaps the first director to appreciate fully the implications of sound was the Frenchman René Clair. Originally opposed to the whole idea, he insisted on the predominant importance of the visual element, declaring that the sound film need not and should not be, to use his own term, "canned theater." He demonstrated to everyone's satisfaction that much of silent technique was still valid, that it was the image and not the word that kept the screen alive. Because René Clair had instinctively grasped this principle in his first three films, and turned them out with a flair and finish unmatched anywhere at the time, his pictures had a profound effect upon other directors. He had achieved what they were groping toward. He had brought back into films spontaneity, movement, rhythm.

Perhaps the leading director of dramatic films in this country to revolt against "canned theater" movies during the early years of sound was

Rouben Mamoulian—ironically, one of the many Broadway directors brought to the studios in 1929 specifically to make "canned theater." Despite his theater background, Mamoulian felt that the camera could and should move, appreciated the importance of the close-up for dramatic emphasis, fought against the prevalent notion that the source for every sound must be seen. For him, the camera was far more than a passive observer looking on while actors recited their lines—and the function of the director was more than merely helping the actors to say their lines better. He had to help the audience find what was dramatically significant in a scene, picking out what was important with his camera, making it seem fresh and illuminating through the imagination and inventiveness of his visuals.

By the time he made *Dr. Jekyll and Mr. Hyde* (1932), Mamoulian had full control of his new medium. From start to finish, it was a virtuoso work; almost every scene revealed the director's desire to break away from a literal use of the camera and a conventional use of sound. The entire first reel was shot in the first-person technique, the camera assuming the identity of Dr. Jekyll. From that position we see his hands as he plays the organ, the shadow of his head upon the music rack. When Jekyll is ready to go out, the butler hands hat, cloak and cane directly to the camera. After a carriage ride through the streets of London, it enters the doors of a medical school and passes on into the operating theater. Here a complete 360-degree turn around the hall brings the camera to rest for the first time upon the face of Dr. Jekyll (Fredric March). Quite apart from its indisputable pictorial effectiveness, this use of the subjective camera built a growing suspense, a curiosity about the appearance of the man we know will turn into the monstrous Hyde. The transformations themselves were ingeniously achieved upon the screen (Mamoulian has steadfastly refused to divulge the secret of his technique), accompanied by a vivid, synthetically created sound track built from exaggerated heart beats mingled with the reverberations of gongs played backwards, bells heard through echo chambers and completely artificial sounds created by photographing light frequencies directly onto the sound track. The recordists referred to it as "Mamoulian's stew," but it was probably the screen's first experiment with purely synthetic sound.

Outstanding for its understatement both of sound and visual was Mamoulian's handling of the scene in which Hyde murders Champagne Ivy (Miriam Hopkins). Hyde forces the thoroughly frightened girl to sing her pathetic music hall song. Suddenly he bends over her, passing completely out of the frame. For a long moment the shot reveals only the bedpost, a highly ornamental carving of the Goddess of Love. Then the singing stops abruptly, and Hyde's triumphant face rises once more into view. We need be shown no more.

Mamoulian's own films after *Love Me Tonight* are again indicative. *Song of Songs* (1933) with Marlene Dietrich, *Queen Christina* (1933) with Greta Garbo, *We Live Again* (1934) with Anna Sten had a visual beauty, a sensuous quality that often surmounted the banality of their scripts. Certain scenes—Garbo with the grapes in *Queen Christina* or the long tracking shot to the completely immobile close-up of Garbo that closes the film—linger in the mind as directorial touches that added cinematic life to stories that made their main points through dialogue. Certainly, Mamoulian's concern for the dramatic effect of his imagery made him the logical choice as the director of the first feature-length film shot in the improved, full-color Technicolor, *Becky Sharp* (1935). His handling of the great ball before the Battle of Waterloo with its artfully designed shifting patterns of color, its gay pastels mounting to a climax of blood-red cloaks disappearing into the darkness, reveals again his ability to work imaginatively with the raw materials of his art. And when in 1936 he turned once more to musical comedy in the satiric *Gay Desperado,* he showed that he was now able to move as lightly and freely in a realistic world of thieves and radios and high-powered motorcars as in the fantasy world of *Love Me Tonight.* Always the creative director, Mamoulian best exemplifies those talented men of the early Thirties who were consciously seeking to transform the talking picture into a genuinely cinematic art.

It was perhaps inevitable that, during the first hectic years of sound, the film cycles reappeared with renewed vigor. They seemed to chase each other across the screen, one right after the other—transcriptions of Broadway musicals, prison pictures, gangster pictures, newspaper pictures, backstage musicals. With the entire industry unsure of itself, any outstanding success was soon followed by the simultaneous release of literally dozens of other films on the same subject from every studio in Hollywood. Curiously enough, this had a salutary effect on the films themselves. The studios did not try merely to imitate what had gone before; they tried to make their films better than their competition. They tried to polish techniques and stories until their own efforts were more attractive, more effective, more "box office." The number of films in each cycle may have driven the moviegoer of the early Thirties almost out of his mind by making it seem that every new picture he went to was the one that he had seen the week before. But through these cycles the film forms were themselves able to develop characteristic styles and techniques, an increased mobility and cinematic power.

One of the first and most obvious fields for exploitation by the new sound camera was, of course, the Broadway musical. During 1929 and 1930, a great many of these made the transition to film—*The Vagabond King, The Desert Song, Rio Rita, Sunny, Golden Dawn, Gold Diggers of Broadway, Song of the Flame* . . . The list is endless. Actually, however, very little original thinking went into them. It was enough that they had popular titles, famous stars and familiar tunes. In 1930 Samuel Goldwyn brought to Hollywood a dance director from the New York stage, Busby Berkeley, to handle the musical numbers for *Whoopee,* starring Eddie Cantor. And things began to happen. Berkeley, one of the most original and daring of the directors in this field, saw no reason why the dances should be a mere reproduction of the stage originals. Not with a camera capable of taking scenes from any angle and any position. In *Whoopee* he carried his camera high up into the flies and shot straight down on the dance floor. In subsequent films, he photographed from below, from the sides, from above. For one astonishing moment in "The Shadow Waltz" from *Gold Diggers of 1933,* he tilted the camera at a 90-degree angle to the floor and photographed the girls mirrored in a lake, pirouetting down either side of the screen. Since such dance sequences were generally inserted into well-worn backstage stories, purists frequently pointed out that Berkeley's work was ridiculous, that his dances could never conceivably take place on any stage in the world. They were, of course, absolutely right. What they ignored was the fact that the story was merely an excuse for the production numbers, and that Berkeley was producing the purest combination of visual and sound that had yet come from the American studios. Berkeley's vogue was to be gradually superseded by the growing popularity of the more intimate style of dance films introduced by Fred Astaire and Ginger Rogers during the mid-Thirties.

The popular gangster films of the early Thirties—*Little Caesar* (1930), *The Public Enemy* (1931), *Scarface* (1932)—and the almost concurrent cycle of newspaper melodramas also did much to return to the screen some of its former mobility and vitality. Generally written directly for the screen, they eliminated the long, fragrant speeches of the legitimate theater in favor of such pungent phrases as "We're gonna take you for a ride"; "He got bumped off"; and "You can dish it out but you can't take it." In keeping with the tone of this dialogue, the editing was similarly taut and to the point. In a typical scene from *Little Caesar,* the gang is discussing the fate of one of its members:

"Eddie's turned yellow. He's goin' to rat on us."

"He can't get away with that."

"I just seen Eddie goin' into the church."

"Get Eddie," says Little Caesar. And the scene cuts abruptly to a church exterior, with Eddie coming down the steps. A long black car swings ominously into view; there is a burst of machine-gun fire and Eddie lies sprawling on the steps. Followed by a flat cut to the next scene, Eddie's funeral.

There was a speed, a vigor, a sense of the contemporaneous scene, a realism of character and incident about these films that was in sharp contrast to the talky problem plays that surrounded them. They had action, racy dialogue, the sharply naturalistic performances of people like James Cagney, Edward G. Robinson, Joan Blondell, Lee Tracy, Paul Muni and George Bancroft. They boasted that their incidents were based on fact, that their stories came from the headlines. And they excited audiences in ways that the drawing-room comedies, boudoir romances and static musical comedies did not. They were like a breath of fresh air sweeping through the heavily padded studios of the early sound era, blowing away some of the conventions, some of the stiffness that had crept into the medium with the advent of the microphone.

And directors—even directors who were not working on gangster films—responded to their tonic. In *The Front Page* (1931), one of the first and fastest of the newspaper cycle, Lewis Milestone solved the problem of translating the Hecht-MacArthur play into a film by keeping the camera almost constantly in motion, by cutting frequently and by staging the dialogue at breakneck speed. King Vidor, faced with much the same problem in bringing to the screen Elmer Rice's *Street Scene* (1931), used few moving camera shots but worked out a shooting script in which every single shot was taken from a fresh angle.

Nowhere were the dislocations caused by the addition of the sound track more apparent than in the field of film comedy; and yet here too a balance was soon reached that proved of value to film makers in all fields. Prior to the introduction of sound, of course, comedy had been almost entirely a visual medium, with emphasis on character and physical humor. Subtitles—especially those subtitles that introduced the various characters—might carry an occasional wisecrack. ("He had water on the brain. In the winter it froze and everything slipped his mind.") In the sophisticated or folksy comedies of the Twenties, there might even be a snappy retort. Will Rogers, for example, punctuated his silent comedies with typical Rogersisms—but, significantly, Rogers was never as popular on the silent screen as he was after sound came in. In sound, the humor shifted abruptly from visual to verbal, and a whole new crowd of comics—largely imported from the New York stage and from vaudeville—came clamoring through the studios. The Marx Brothers, Ed Wynn, Lou Holtz, Eddie Cantor, W. C. Fields, Jimmy Durante, Frank Morgan, Bobby Clark, Charlie Ruggles and, soon after, Bob Hope were all brought west because they could handle a humorous line or witty repartee. Keaton and Lloyd, Harry Langdon and Raymond Griffith drifted into either the obscurity of studio office jobs or complete retirement. At the same time, such relatively minor comics from the silent days as Laurel and Hardy, Edward Everett Horton and Joe E. Brown were suddenly boosted to stardom. They were stage trained. They could talk.

Typical was the case of Buster Keaton. At the close of the Twenties, he was M-G-M's highest-paid comedian. Early in the Thirties he was cast in a series of comedies with Jimmy Durante. Nominally, Keaton was the star; but whatever success the pictures scored was so clearly due to Durante that Keaton's contract was simply allowed to expire. He had established himself as a silent, frozen-faced comedian. Durante's natural style was volatile, explosive. It was Durante, not Keaton, that the talkies wanted.

Nor were all the stars of the stage completely at home on the talking screen. Ed Wynn's simple-minded funny man, Beatrice Lillie's cool sophistication, Fanny Brice's broad dialect humor and even broader bathos found scant acceptance outside New York. Even Eddie Cantor—successful in theater, radio and now television—was never as warmly received in the movies. Radio stars like Amos 'n' Andy, Jack Benny, Fred Allen and Kate Smith were notably unsuccessful when they tried the screen. The characters that had sparked the imagination of millions when heard in the living room never quite seemed to satisfy those same millions when they came to see them in the movie houses.

On the other hand, the Marx Brothers, W. C. Fields, Will Rogers, Bob Hope, Jimmy Durante and Marie Dressler—each had some special quality of voice and personality that found an immediate response in audiences around the world. Their humor was verbal, but it also had a strong visual quality. It is difficult to think of Will Rogers and Marie Dressler without recalling their shrugs and gesticulations, their special forms of mugging. Jimmy Durante is a veritable fury of activity, magnifying every emotion until it becomes a parody of itself. Bob Hope, with the smooth patina of years of vaudeville trouping, has a cock of the eye, a twist of the lip or a flip of the hand to accompany every line.

It is in the films of the Marx Brothers, however, and of W. C. Fields— and in such rare, offbeat items as *Million Dollar Legs* (1932), *Six of a Kind* (1934) and the Hope-Crosby *Road* series—that one finds the real flowering of comedy in the sound films. Indeed, the Marx Brothers presented a perfect filmic combination—the fast-talking Groucho, the silent, nimble-witted pantomime of Harpo, and Chico, the saturnine fall guy (with statesque Margaret Dumont generally around to play straight). Even though their very earliest films, *The Coconuts* (1929) and *Animal Crackers* (1930), were nothing more than crudely photographed versions of previous stage hits, the swiftness of the dialogue and Harpo's eloquent byplay all but concealed their technical deficiencies. Such a fantastic colloquy as the one from *Animal Crackers* in which Groucho and Chico discuss the mysterious disappearance of a valuable painting needs nothing beyond a sound track and a well-focused camera:

"We'll search every room in the house," says Groucho.

"What if it ain't in this house?" says Chico.

"Then we'll search the house next door."

"What if there ain't no house next door?"

"Then we'll build one," says Groucho—and the two immediately set about drawing up plans for building the house next door.

All their better pictures had similar sequences. In *Duck Soup* (1932) Groucho as the Prime Minister of Fredonia holds up a document and says to his assembled council, "Why, it's so simple a child of ten could understand it"; then, *sotto voce* to Chico, "Run out and find me a child of ten. I can't make heads or tails of it."

Just as in the gangster films, this dialogue had a racy fascination of its own. It was talk, true; but it was also more than talk. It had, in the most literal sense, a picturesque quality—a quality that was best conveyed by a wholly passive camera. But alternating with and counterbalancing all this dialogue were sequences of frantic activity and pure pantomime—the trick with the mirror in *Duck Soup*, with all three Marxes dressed as Groucho and circling suspiciously about one another; the travesty on opera in *A Night at the Opera* when Harpo inserts "Take Me Out to the Ball Game" into the orchestra's score for *Il Trovatore* and then runs amuck in the scenery; the inspired mayhem of the operating scene from *A Day at the Races*, with Groucho calling for X rays and Harpo and Chico rushing in with the evening papers.

As a team, the Marx Brothers achieved an almost perfect balance of sight and sound, marred only by the occasional *scènes obligatoires* of Harpo playing the harp and Chico the piano. (In one of their pictures Groucho, as if aware of the letdown in tempo, says directly to the audience, "Look, I have to stay here, but why don't you go out to the lobby for a smoke until this whole thing blows over?") Although directors invariably sought to enliven such sequences with trick shots of Chico at the keyboard, with close-ups of Harpo's unique fingering of his instrument, with zoom shots and striking angles, they were never able to force cinematic life into what remained essentially stagy performances. Apart from such moments, however, the skillful interplay of the Marx Brothers created a kind of humor that was ideally suited to the requirements of the sound camera.

If the Marxes provided perfect foils for one another, W. C. Fields was the perfect sound comedian in himself. The irascible, bumbling braggadocio that was his screen character was also, it would seem, his off-screen character as well. He was an unpredictable eccentric whose confirmed pessimism had been nourished by years of adversity. A lifetime of rigorous training as a juggler in circus and vaudeville had made his every gesture and movement a masterpiece of precise timing. The result was an incomparable blend of half-articulate howls of rage, mumbled bits of private philosophy ("No man who hates small dogs and children can be *all* bad"), and eloquent pantomime. Many of the best sight gags in his earlier pictures were developed from his old stage routines, such as the golfing scene with the bent clubs in *You're Telling Me* (1934), his attempts to sleep on a noisy back porch in *It's a Gift* (1934) and the hilariously crooked poker game in *Mississippi* (1935).

There was always an air of improvisation about a Fields picture, as if his comedy patter and throw-away lines had been caught almost by accident by the camera. One had the feeling that the next time the picture was run, they might not even be there! It gave his films the peculiar fascination of a newsreel, a one-time happening to a truly unique character. The pictures themselves were invariably abominably constructed, a hodgepodge of plot and gags that shot off in all directions. Indeed, his final film, *Never Give a Sucker an Even Break* (1941), almost defies description, its narrative has so many breaks and changes. But, like all the Fields films, it is full of the most inspired inanities—Fields diving out of an airplane after his whisky bottle and comparing an ordinary cigarette to the new king size as he plummets to earth, his running warfare with the formidable waitress at the local hash house. ("I did *not* say this meat was tough. I just said I didn't see the horse that usually stands outside.") And, as in all the Fields films, there were the familiar props—the agile cane, the straw hat that constantly popped out of his hands or flew off his head, the stump of a cigar that half concealed his more scurrilous oaths.

Fields wrote most of his own pictures, using such improbable noms de plume as Otis J. Cribblecoblis or Mahatma Kane Jeeves; probably no one else could have realized quite so well the picaresque qualities inherent in the character, or dreamed up the mass of petty harassments through which Fields fought his way with beady eye and wide-swinging cane. Like the Marx Brothers, like Will Rogers and Bob Hope, Fields' humor was verbal; but what gave it character and substance was the bulbous nose, the look of outraged dignity and larcenous innocence that accompanied everything he said or did.

The fact is that in the work of the best comedians of the Thirties the sound film was coming closer to striking a proper balance between its visual and aural elements. Much of this was instinctive, much was the result of happy accident; but also, out of the accumulating skill and experience of directors and technicians alike, a sure craftsmanship was emerging. And as accident gave way to method, so too did the flamboyant trickery of the early years of sound give way to style. In the series of Fred Astaire and Ginger Rogers musicals that brightened the mid-Thirties, for example, a camera technique was evolved that broke sharply with the exuberant, exhibitionistic patterns of the Busby Berkeley dances and permitted the closer integration of musical and story elements. The Astaire films were intimate, the dances coming not as interruptions but as extensions of the story. Astaire and Rogers danced because words alone could not convey their feelings.

At first, the problem of getting into the dance was often solved mechanically, with the awkward expedient of the song cue—a bit of dialogue incorporating the title of the number or explaining its presence in the picture ("Listen, dear, they're playing our song!"). Soon, however, the Astaire films were simply letting the music steal in under the dialogue without any attempt at explanation or excuse. The dancers respond to it, and the number is under way. And they utilized the camera's innate ability to cover great areas, to fall back as the dancers move forward, to cut nimbly from place to place.

After his first few pictures, Astaire began to direct as well as to choreograph his dance sequences, with notable success. He brought his camera increasingly into the play of the dance, judiciously placing it to provide a tight frame for his own solo work, pulling it back to create new dimensions for the ensembles, moving it freely to sustain at all times the line of the dance. It was an unobtrusive, discreet and beautifully functional use of the camera—and one that, for the first time, achieved the balance between camera, image and the sound track that is the true art of the sound film.

What the Astaire films reveal, with their grace and lightness and sureness of touch, is the approaching technical maturity of the American film makers. From an overemphasis of sound, many had moved to the opposite extreme, to an overemphasis of the visual element. By the middle of the Thirties, a happier balance was being achieved. Directors no longer feared sound, nor did they try to conceal long dialogue passages behind a myriad of artificially created scenes. The better writers had long since discovered the difference between stage dialogue and talk on the screen while, at the top level, people like Dudley Nichols, Robert Riskin and Joseph Mankiewicz were writing with a strong awareness of the visual requirements of the medium as well. A whole corps of superbly trained cameramen— many of them, like James Wong Howe, Karl Freund and Arthur Edeson, with experience extending far back into the silent era—were fully prepared to transform their work into striking images. The sound engineers and technicians had, in a brief half-dozen years, supplied the studios with equipment that, for all its complexity, was incredibly flexible and allowed a maximum of control at every point; they stood ready to supply the director with virtually any effect he might request. As is always the case, masterpieces were few and far between. But the period of experimentation was over and the period of integration and consolidation could begin.

One of the first directors to achieve this integration in dramatic films was England's Alfred Hitchcock, whose mystery thrillers began to appear on American screens in 1935. Perhaps because the mystery form has always laid emphasis on visual shocks and surprises, the full extent of his contribution has been somewhat underestimated. Hitchcock did far more than simply bathe his stories in somber lighting and deep shadow to create in his audiences a dread of the unexpected. And also, it should be added, he did more than invent a series of brilliant, equally disquieting surprise effects on the sound track (although some, such as the woman's scream in *The 39 Steps* that merges with the shriek of a locomotive's whistle, have become classics in the field).

One has only to read through the first few pages of John Buchan's *The 39 Steps*, however, and compare the novel with Hitchcock's screen treatment of it to recognize his full stature. From Buchan's description of his hero wandering about London, looking in windows, stopping in bars, taking in a show, Hitchcock selected the one incident—scarcely more than a passing phrase—that lent itself best to dramatic screen treatment. He opens the film at a variety theater—something for the eye, something for the ear—and leads the narrative back there for the dramatic finale. Throughout the film the incidents are suggested by the novel rather than reproducing it scene for scene. Hitchcock, who has always worked on his own screenplays, prefers to invent around an idea, letting it develop in filmic terms rather than in terms of the novel or short story used as source material. His favorite device was the "magguffin," his own term to describe a visual or sound gimmick—a snatch of music, a man with a twitching eye, a ticking time bomb—that runs throughout the picture as a sinister leitmotif. In *The 39 Steps* this "magguffin" is a man with a missing finger. The key figure in the mysterious spy ring, he is wholly Hitchcock's invention: there is no counterpart for him in the original novel.

What contributed to the fascination of such vintage Hitchcocks as *The 39 Steps* (1935), *Secret Agent* (1935), *The Woman Alone* (1936), *The Girl Was Young* (1937), and *The Lady Vanishes* (1938) was his deliberate underplaying of climactic scenes. A woman staggers toward the camera and then, as she collapses, we see the hilt of the dagger in her back. A boy unwittingly carries a time bomb across London; we see him mount a bus and then, in long shot, the bus blows up. We are not shown the kidnaping of the old woman in *The Lady Vanishes*; we only know that suddenly in her place in the railway carriage has appeared a dreadful grim-faced substitute wearing her clothes and claiming to be Miss Froy. In *The Woman Alone*, while Sylvia Sidney is preparing to murder her husband in the shadowy movie house, on the sound track is heard the macabre refrain from Disney's cartoon *Who Killed Cock Robin*? There was a casual urbanity about Hitchcock's most carefully prepared moments, whether visual or aural, that quickly established his supremacy not only as a director of thrillers but as a master of the sound-film medium. His pictures, eagerly awaited during the late Thirties, led inevitably to a Hollywood contract. Although Hitchcock frankly admits that he is now doing what he calls "the commercial thing," few directors today can rival him in the grace and polish, the slick surface finish of his star-studded comedy melodramas.

Unquestionably the greatest single difficulty that faced the directors of the mid-Thirties was the problem of handling dialogue gracefully.

Before any approach could be successful, however, there had to be a drastic revision in the dialogue itself. The script writers, whether recruited from the theater, from radio, or from the silent movie, had to discover a truly filmic language, a language with a lively fascination of its own. Primarily, it was a dialogue that had to approximate more closely the patterns of ordinary speech than is either necessary—or desirable—on the stage or in literature. The theater demands a richness of verbal imagery to help cloak the immobile and restrictive nature of its settings. Stage dialogue is full of descriptions of off-stage events that must be reported because they cannot be shown. It is laced through with psychological insights into character and motivation that sound highly artificial in the movies.

Nor is the language of literature, particularly as discovered in the novel, any more suitable for direct filming (although there is growing evidence that many of today's writers have been strongly influenced in their conception of dialogue by repeated exposure to the motion picture). Ideally, no screen character can be permitted the paragraphs of introspective speeches that the protagonist of a novel so often indulges in. And certainly the long, discursive passages in which the author explores the ramifications of his theme—always one of the primary attractions of the novel form—defy translation into film in terms of dialogue.

Screen writers had to invent dialogue that was at once rich and colorful, pungent and amusing, but also stripped of inessentials. They had to learn not only what to say, but also how much could be left unsaid—how much could be left to the camera and the actor and the director to put on the screen through action and gesture or by implication. The script for a film is like an orchestral score. It is the conductor's interpretation of the music that finally brings it to life for the concert audience. It is the director's visualization of the script that creates the movie, blending dialogue with action to produce the most affecting combination of both.

The Informer demonstrated the advantages of a strong writer-director team, a collaboration that in John Ford and Dudley Nichols produced such memorable films as *The Lost Patrol* (1934), *The Plough and the Stars* (1936), *Stagecoach* (1939) and *The Long Voyage Home* (1940). Another outstanding writer-director team of the Thirties was Robert Riskin and Frank Capra. In such enormously popular comedies as *Lady for a Day* (1933), *It Happened One Night* (1934), *Mr. Deeds Goes to Town* (1936), *You Can't Take It With You* (1938) and *Mr. Smith Goes to Washington* (1939), Capra demonstrated his confidence in the ability of his colleague to write dialogue that held its own upon the screen by filming long passages without any change in camera position whatsoever. His special skill lay in re-creating the speed and humor of silent comedy in the sound medium, feeling out the subtle relationship between dialogue and camera, sensing when cutting or camera movement was required and when words alone could carry the momentum of his scene. If the talk was good, he reasoned, why try to hide it? A favorite technique of his was to start an extended dialogue passage with the camera some distance away from his principals, then slowly, almost imperceptibly, track in to a large two-shot, as if irresistibly drawn by his interest in what the people were saying.

In *It Happened One Night*, with entire sequences played within the confines of a bus or a small tourist cabin, Capra ingeniously contrived to keep his screen alive by scanning the faces of the passengers on the bus, or discovering his stars almost haphazardly among the people and the packages and seats that surrounded them. Only when the dialogue was important, when it bore significantly on the development of the story, did he move in for protracted close-ups. But these close-ups were completely functional: they emphasized the words. Capra sensed when he could count on Riskin's lines to carry a scene without additional visual pyrotechnics, when they could be shot with a static camera or when the full effectiveness of the scene required the extra mobility of the moving camera and staccato editing of silent days.

A particularly delightful sequence illustrates his ability to blend the two: Clark Gable and Claudette Colbert are sitting on a fence by the side of the road holding an animated conversation on the best way to thumb a ride from the passing cars; Capra filmed this entire scene in a single shot without moving his camera. But when Gable walks out to the road to demonstrate his hitchhiking methods (capped by Colbert's conclusive evidence that the knee is mightier than the thumb), Capra builds the scene from short snatches of pantomimed action brilliantly edited together—climaxed with an adroit montage in which a glimpse of Miss Colbert's leg brings a car to a screeching halt.

Capra was also among the first to perceive that the use of dialogue on the screen involved not only the preparation of a taut, vivid, idiomatic prose, but also a more specialized handling of the actors delivering that dialogue. And here was perhaps the final adjustment that directors had to make to sound. In silent days the director could (and often did) build a star's performance out of bits and pieces—a close-up of the actor, a reaction shot, an insert of an object or an image that underscored the emotional content of the scene. With sound, much of this "synthetic" kind of acting was automatically eliminated. Not only did the actors now have to speak their lines, but—as Al Jolson in *The Jazz Singer* so clearly revealed—the sound track itself produced a far greater awareness of their essential personality than the silent camera ever had. Voice, face, mannerisms and temperament were fused together by the sound camera to create that elusive, indefinable quality known as "box-office appeal." These were the elements that the actor brought to his part—along with whatever measure of talent he possessed.

More important than acting ability, however, was the photogenic magnetism of the star, around which the director could create a characterization. It was a quality which, when properly used, added its own dynamism to the film. And directors like Capra, Ford, George Cukor and William Wyler who gained the reputation of being "good with actors" were good because they knew how to fit their stars to their roles, and how to utilize their personalities to sustain the momentum of a scene.

Though American pictures are often casually dismissed as "escapist entertainment," the forms of that escape vary from era to era and have their own significance. The public did not suddenly demand "realistic" pictures, but it could no longer be amused by high society exchanging bons mots at the cocktail hour nor stirred by the matinee idols or pretty sopranos and impoverished young tenors. Sound had made possible a new degree of realism in motion pictures and when, late in 1930, Warner Brothers' *Little Caesar* brought throngs to the box office once more, the course was clear. What the public obviously wanted was a hard-hitting, naturalistic form of drama that took its themes from the headlines of the day.

The studios quickly brought to the screen not only a staggering succession of gangster pictures (fifty in 1931 alone!), but equally sensational exposés of rackets, political corruption, prison brutality, bank failures and newspaper scandal sheets. If there was any element of escapism in these films, it lay in their tendency to blame isolated individuals for what were in fact national problems. Audiences seemed to find some reassurance in the thought that everything could be solved by the jailing—or shooting—of a brutal warden, a hoodlum gangster or a power-hungry politician. In *The Big House* (1930), *Little Caesar* (1930), *The Front Page* (1931), *The Public Enemy* (1931), *The Secret Six* (1931) and many more, the public was given strong, unadulterated dramatizations of the stories behind the daily headlines. Often such films were cynical and cheap, but occasionally they proved to be sincere and perceptive investigations of evils and abuses aggravated by the Depression. Indeed, the facts revealed by *I Am a Fugitive from a Chain Gang* (1932), based on an actual case, were so shocking that an aroused public forced a reformation of the chaingang system.

Not only did the many topical films of this era reflect their times, but even the Depression romances had a metallic twist. Their heroines—Constance Bennett, Tallulah Bankhead, Joan Crawford, Marlene Dietrich, Greta Garbo, Barbara Stanwyck—were frequently ladies who took to the streets or became rich men's mistresses in order to provide food for their babies, an education for their sisters or medicine for their husbands. Despite these sentimentalities, however, such films as *Susan Lenox* (1931), *Blonde Venus* (1932) and *Letty Lynton* (1932) were quite explicit in establishing the milieu of poverty that drove their heroines into a life of shame. Nor was it sheer coincidence that these virtuous prostitutes invariably encountered public enemies or crooked politicians in their rise from gutter to penthouse. In their own way, they were merely confirming the gangster theme that the only escape from Depression-bred despair was to live outside the law.

And the general public, if box-office returns are any index, not only condoned but applauded these fallen creatures, just as they were fascinated by the exploits of the gangsters and racketeers. The heroines may have sobbed a bit over their lost virginity, the Little Caesars may have ended up perforated by bullets, but while they lived there was a glamour and fascination to their lives that was in glaring contrast to the drab realities of 1931 and 1932.

Obviously, in making heroes of gangsters and heroines of prostitutes, the movie companies departed far from both the letter and the spirit of the Production Code they had so virtuously agreed to in the halcyon year of 1927. The Depression had produced a new world, a new morality—and the studios, in giving the public what it wanted, reflected the seamiest side of the picture with unprecedented accuracy. Far too accurately for some tastes. Letters of protest began to reach the studios and the Hays Office from all the more respectable elements in communities across the country. Church groups, women's clubs and patriotic associations passed resolutions condemning the industry. Editorials appeared in the newspapers and sermons were preached from pulpits denouncing the growing immorality of the movies, urging the film producers to assume a greater social responsibility for the pictures they were turning out, prodding local censorship boards to increased vigilance and more rigorous standards. *Scarface* (1932), for example, at once one of the best and most brutal of the gangster films, was held up for months until the producers inserted several placatory scenes showing an aroused citizenry demanding action against what the film's subtitle described as "the shame of a nation." Even with these additions, *Scarface* was severely censored in many communities, banned outright in others.

As a result of such efforts the films became, if not more moral, at least more moralizing. Sermons on civic responsibility became the price one had to pay for pictures that dealt realistically with the more sensational aspects of the social scene. Under the sustained pressure of the protest groups, the wave of gangster films began to subside. During 1933 it gradually merged into another cycle, with the FBI men and other law enforcers as the new heroes. Actually, the G men were simply gangsters in disguise, acting with as little concern for "due process" as the gangsters they were hunting. But official morality was once more being served.

With the election of Franklin D. Roosevelt and the prompt introduction of NRA relief measures and reforms early in 1933, a new note of optimism appeared both in the country and in its films. The musicals, which only a short time before had been singing "Brother, Can You Spare a Dime?" and "Ten Cents a Dance," were now shouting out that "Happy Days Are Here Again" or "Stand Up and Cheer"—"good times are here!" Indeed, the musical comedies reflected this new optimism not only in their songs but in their themes as well. Typical of the era were the plots of *Footlight Parade* (1933) and *100 Men and a Girl* (1937), in which groups of starving musicians, singers and dancers were rounded up by Dick Powell or Deanna Durbin and prodded into putting on a show. Their success provided employment and happiness for all. In much the same way, King Vidor's *Our Daily Bread* (1934) showed a heterogeneous band of unemployed city people finding their salvation by working together on a farm co-operative. "Back to the soil" was reiterated as the solution to urban hard times in such films as *Stranger's Return* (1933), *State Fair* (1933) and *As the Earth Turns* (1934).

In keeping with the reformist trend of the NRA period, the topical films, the exposés of rackets, corruption and abuses of power took a more positive stand. Prohibition and gangsterism, juvenile delinquency, strikebreaking and prison reform were problems that an enlightened citizenry could do something about, once the facts were brought to their attention. It was in this spirit that the studios—and especially Warner Brothers—put into production such frankly controversial pictures as *Wild Boys of the Road* (1933), *Massacre* (1933), *Black Fury* (1935) and *The Black Legion* (1936), such vigorously antilynch films as *Winterset* (1936), *Fury* (1936) and *They Won't Forget* (1937).

While the predominantly affirmative and constructive outlook of these films was encouraged by the growing liberalism of the era, it is also true that a new sense of caution and constraint was forced upon the industry by the formation of the Legion of Decency during 1933, set up to implement a new Production Code. Drawn up by Catholic churchmen and lay members, the new Code was a thorough revision of the original structures established by the Hays Office during the "flaming" Twenties—but this time reinforced by the power of the Church to bring economic reprisals against any studio that violated its rulings. Sex and crime had become so prevalent on the screen that when at last the Legion of Decency made its official appearance, in April of 1934, many of the Protestant denominations were ready to support it in its announced campaign to clean up the movies. The Code, with but few minor revisions, has remained in force ever since.

With the rise of the Legion, many of the crude excesses of the tough, realistic school of film making were quickly eliminated; but at the same time much of the forthright honesty of the period also disappeared from the screen as well. Mae West was an early victim. Her good-humored vulgarity and frank sexuality in films like *She Done Him Wrong* (1933) made her irresistible to the reformers. The biggest box-office draw of 1933–1934, she became a prime target for the outraged forces of decency. To conform to the new Production Code, her scripts were so bowdlerized that by 1936 the Mae West character had lost its sex and her films their appeal. Her few subsequent screen appearances consisted of innocuous parodies of her former roles in pictures like *My Little Chickadee* (1940) with W. C. Fields. To avoid a similar fate, James Cagney, Clark Gable and Edward G. Robinson, the movies' favorite gangsters of the early Thirties, found it expedient to diversify their roles and lead more virtuous screen lives.

The industry itself quite consciously began laying greater emphasis on purely escapist themes—big Westerns, costume dramas, historical films and adaptations of the classics. While treatment of the social scene was suffused with what Richard Griffith has aptly termed "the fantasy of good will," the feeling that if everyone were kind and generous to his fellow man, the Depression could soon be overcome. This idea found its fullest and most popular expression in Frank Capra's *Mr. Deeds Goes to Town* (1936). Gary Cooper, a youthful millionaire, decides to give away his inherited fortune to the unemployed after discovering that his business associates are all parasites and cheats. The fact that no real-life millionaire has ever distributed his fortune with such openhearted innocence in no way diminished the attractiveness of the idea.

Mr. Deeds was one in a long cycle of films appearing during the mid-Thirties that came to be called "screwball" comedies, pictures that did anything and everything for a laugh. But while the action in these films was always wildly at odds with any conventional response to a similar situation, most of them had as their point of departure the terrible realities of that period—unemployment, hunger and fear. In *My Man Godfrey* (1936), for example, William Powell plays one of the "*nouveaux* poor," a man ruined by the crash and reduced to living in the city dumps. Some scatterbrained socialites find him on a scavenger hunt and make him their butler. Because of his own experience with poverty, Godfrey is able to enlighten his employers and transform them into useful, social-minded citizens. In *Easy Living* (1937), Jean Arthur, an unemployed secretary, suddenly finds herself in possession of a priceless mink coat flung out the window by a millionaire in a moment of pique; her scathing denunciation of his thoughtlessness while others are starving was the high point of the picture. And yet both of these were presented—and taken—as comedies. As Lewis Jacobs has written, "If 'screwball' comedies successfully turned the world on its ear, that was perhaps the way it already looked to a Depression generation which felt cheated of its birthright and apprehensively faced further loss in the steady approach of war."

As the Thirties wore on, these growing tensions produced a notable series of films that rode the mounting wave of liberalism without recourse to either the "fantasy of good will" or "screwball" subterfuge. Labor unrest, slum housing, unemployment and dislocation aggravated by the dust storms of the mid-Thirties—all of these were put on the screen with a directness that stressed the social and economic sources of such hardships. There were sympathy for the common man and new hope for a better tomorrow. In place of the contrived and improbable "happy endings" of the Depression musicals and "back to the soil" films, there was now a forthright expression of belief in the inherent strength of democracy to bring about national recovery and a solution to these problems. Characteristically, when John Steinbeck's bitter novel *The Grapes of Wrath* was filmed by John Ford in 1939, the picture faithfully transmitted the shocking and desperate plight of California's migratory workers, but material in the book was freely transposed so that the film might end on a strong declaration of faith in the ability of the American people to win through.

A belief in the democratic way of life was also implicit in an impressive and highly popular series of biographies that appeared throughout the late Thirties. Some of these films—such as John Ford's *Young Mr. Lincoln* (1939) or *Abe Lincoln in Illinois* (1940)—turned to American heroes whose lives and principles exemplified the democratic tradition. Others depicted great artists, scientists and political leaders in their battle with the bigots and reactionaries of their day. The careers of such international figures as Louis Pasteur, Dr. Ehrlich, Madame Curie, Emile Zola and Benito Juárez were presented as thinly veiled sermons on behalf of democracy and enlightenment. *The Life of Emile Zola* (1937), for example, reached its climax in Zola's classic *"J'accuse"* defense of Captain Dreyfus, a scathing denunciation of anti-Semitism and intolerance in all its forms. Underlying all these films was the awareness that our cultural and intellectual freedom was a precious heritage that the growing forces of fascism both at home and abroad were threatening to destroy.

DISASTER IN THE FARM LANDS

OF ALL the nation's resources, the land in the Thirties was in the most critical condition. The prairies had been overgrazed, the trees which once held moisture in the earth had been cut and not replaced, and in many sections of the country the land was exhausted from over-cultivation. Replenishment was over-due, but in some areas man had waited too long.

The first blow fell only a few months after the President took office; in South Dakota, on Armi-stice Day, 1933, a great dust storm boiled up over the land—the first of many that would sweep the Great Plains from Texas to Canada.

"By midmorning a gale was blow-ing, cold and black. By noon it was blacker than night. It was a wall of dirt one's eyes could not penetrate, but it could penetrate the eyes and ears and nose . . . and the lungs until one coughed up black.

"People were afraid, because they had never seen anything like this before . . .

"When the wind died and the sun shone forth again, it was on a dif-ferent world. There were no fields, only sand drifting into mounds and eddies that swirled in what was now but an autumn breeze. There was no longer a section-line road fifty feet from the front door. In the farm-yard, fences, machinery, and trees were gone, buried. The roofs of sheds stuck out through drifts deeper than a man is tall." *

FREDERICK LEWIS ALLEN

WHEN THE FARMS BLEW AWAY†

THE GREAT black blizzard of November 11, 1933—which darkened the sky in Chicago the following day and as far east as Albany, New York, the day after that—was only a prelude to disaster. During 1934 and 1935 thousands of square miles were to be laid waste and their inhabitants set adrift upon desperate migrations across the land. There was a long story of human error behind it.

During the latter part of the nineteenth century the Great Plains—a region of light rainfall, of sun and high winds, of waving grasses—had

* R. D. Lusk, "The Life and Death of 470 Acres," *The Saturday Evening Post,* Aug. 13, 1938.
† Excerpted from Frederick Lewis Allen's *Since Yesterday.*

been the great cattle country of the nation: a vast open area, unfenced at first, where the cowboys tended the cattle-kings' herds. Before the end of the century this range had been badly damaged by overgrazing; then the land was invaded by homesteaders, who tried to wring a living from the semiarid soil. World War I brought a huge demand for wheat, and tractors for large-scale machine farming became available, and the Plains began to come into their own as a crop-producing country. The sod covering which had protected them was plowed up on the grand scale. A new power era had come, it was said, to revolutionize American agriculture; factory methods were being triumphantly applied to the land.

To be sure, there wasn't much rain. The mean annual rainfall was only between 10 and 20 inches on the Plains (as compared with, for example, 20 to 40 in the Mississippi Valley region, and 40 to 50 in the North Atlantic). But there was a pretty favorable series of years during the 1920s and the farmers were not much disturbed.

Nineteen-thirty was a bad year in parts of this territory; 1931 was worse in the Dakotas: 1932 was better. Then came 1933: it was a swinger, hot and dry. During that first summer of the New Deal, farmers in South Dakota were finding that they couldn't raise even enough corn to feed the livestock. In western Kansas not a drop of rain fell for months. Already the topsoil was blowing; there were places in Kansas where it was said that farmers had to excavate their tractors before they could begin to plow. That fall came the Armistice Day black blizzard.

During 1934 and 1935, the thermometer in Kansas stayed week after week at 108 or above, and the black storms raged again and again. The drought continued acute during much of 1936. Oklahoma farms became great dunes of shifting sand. Housewives in the drought belt kept oiled cloths on the window sills and between the upper and lower sashes of the windows, and some of them tried to seal up every aperture in their houses with the gummed paper strips used in wrapping parcels, yet still the choking dust filtered in and lay in ripples on the kitchen floor.

A farmer, sitting at his window during a dust storm, remarked that he was counting the Kansas farms as they came by.

Westward fled the refugees from this new Sahara. In 1934 and 1935 Californians became aware of an increasing influx into their state of families traveling in ancient jalopies; but for years the streams of humanity continued to run. They came along U.S. Highway 30 through the Idaho hills, along Highway 66 across New Mexico and Arizona, along the Old Spanish Trail through El Paso, along all the other westward trails. They came in decrepit, square-shouldered 1925 Dodges and 1927 La Salles; in battered 1923 Model-T Fords that looked like relics of some antique culture; in trucks piled high with mattresses and cooking utensils and children, with suitcases, jugs and sacks strapped to the running boards.

They left behind them a half-depopulated countryside. A survey of the farmhouses in seven counties of southeastern Colorado made in 1936 showed 2,878 houses still occupied, 2,811 abandoned; and there were also, in that area, 1,522 abandoned homesites. As these wanderers moved along the highways they became a part of a vast and confused migratory movement. When they camped by the wayside they might find themselves next to a family of evicted white Alabama sharecroppers who had been on the move for four years, snatching seasonal farm-labor jobs wherever they could through the Southwest; or next to tenant families from the Arkansas Delta who had been "tractored off" their land—expelled in order that the owner might consolidate two or three farms and operate them with tractors and day labor; or next to lone wanderers who had once held industrial jobs and had now for years been on relief or on the road—jumping freights, hitchhiking, panhandling, shunting back and forth across the countryside in the faint hope of a durable job. And when these varied streams of migrants reached the Coast they found themselves in desperate competition for jobs with individuals or families who for years had been "fruit tramps," moving northward each year with the harvests from the Imperial Valley in southern California to the Sacramento Valley or even to the apple-picking in the Yakima Valley in Washington.

Here in the land of promise, agriculture had long been partly industrialized. Huge farms were in the control of absentee owners or banks or corporations, and were accustomed to depend upon the labor of migratory "fruit tramps," who had formerly been mostly Mexicans, Japanese, and other foreigners, but now were increasingly Americans. Those laborers who were lucky enough to get jobs picking cotton or peas or fruit would be sheltered temporarily in camps consisting typically of frame cabins in rows, with a water line between every two rows; they were very likely to find in their cabin no stove, no cots, no water pail. Even the best of the camps offered a way of life strikingly different from that of the ruggedly individualist farmer of the American tradition, who owned his farm or else was preparing, by working as a resident "hired man," or by renting a farm, for the chance of ultimate ownership. These pickers were homeless, voteless nomads, unwanted anywhere save at the harvest season.

When wave after wave of the new migrants reached California, the labor market became glutted, earnings were low, and jobs became so scarce that groups of poverty-stricken families would be found squatting in make-shift Hoovervilles or bunking miserably in their awkward old Fords by the roadside. Being Americans of native stock and accustomed to inde-pendence, they took the meager wages and the humiliation bitterly, sought to organize, talked of striking, sometimes struck. At every such threat, something like panic seized the growers. If this new proletariat were per-mitted to organize, and were to strike at picking time, they might ruin the whole season's output of a perishable crop. There followed antipicket-ing ordinances; the spectacle of armed deputies dislodging the migrants from their pitiful camps; violence by bands of vigilantes, to whom these ragged families were not fellow citizens who had suffered in a great Amer-ican disaster, but dirty, ignorant, superstitious outlanders, failures at life, easy dupes for "red" agitators. This engulfing tide of discontentment must be kept moving.

These unhappy wanderers of the West were only a small minority of the farmers of the United States.

The AAA [Agricultural Adjustment Administration] had begun the colossal task of making acreage-reduction agreements with millions of farmers in the hope of jacking up the prices of crops and thus restoring American agriculture to economic health. It made credit available to farm-ers and tried, through the Farm Mortgage Moratorium Act and other legislation, to free them of the immediate hazards of debt.

Farm prices rose. For example, the farmer who had received on the average only 33 cents a bushel for wheat in 1933 received 69 cents in 1934, 89 cents in 1935, 92 cents in 1936, $1.24 in 1937, and 88 cents in 1938. The cotton farmer who had received an average price of 5.6 cents a pound for his cotton in 1933 received between 10 and 13 cents during the next four years, and 7.9 cents in 1938. And certainly there was a gen-eral improvement in the condition of those farmers who owned their own farms—and lived outside the worst drought areas. There were gains in equipment and in comforts; more of these farms had electricity than in 1930, more had tractors and trucks, more had bathrooms, automobiles and radios. But this was not a complete picture of what had happened.

To begin with, quantities of farmers had lost their farms during the hideous early years of the Depression—lost them by reason of debt. These farms had mostly fallen into the hands of banks or insurance companies, or of small-town investors who had held the mortgages on them, or were being held by government bodies for nonpayment of taxes, or had been bought in at tax sales. As early as 1934, the National Resources Board stated that nearly 30 per cent of the total value of farm land in the West North Central States was owned by "creditor or government agencies which have been compelled to take over the property." At the small prairie city, the local representative of a big New York insurance company was a very busy man, supervising the management of tracts of property far and wide. In the callous old Wall Street phrase, the farms of the United States had been "passing into stronger hands"; and that meant that more and more of them, owned by people who did not live on them, were being operated by tenants.

For over half a century at least, farm tenancy had been on the increase in the United States. Back in 1880 only 25 per cent of American farms had been run by tenants. Slowly the percentage had increased; now, during the Depression, it reached 42. The growth of tenantry caused many misgivings. Tenants were not likely to put down roots, did not feel a full sense of responsibility for the land and equipment they used, were likely to let it deteriorate.

The passing of farms into "stronger hands" was accompanied by another change. More and more the farm owner, whether or not he operated his own farm, was coming to think of farming as a business. He was less likely to use his farm as a means of subsistence, more likely to use as much of it as possible for the growing of crops for sale.

In certain parts of the South and Southwest this trend toward mechanized farming took a form even more sinister; farm tenancy was becoming merely a way station on the road to farm industrialism. The tenants themselves were being eliminated. The AAA, strangely enough, was unwittingly assisting the process.

How easy for an owner of farm property, when the government offered him a check for reducing his acreage in production, to throw out some of his tenants or sharecroppers, buy a tractor with the check, and run his farm mechanically, with the aid of hired labor—not the sort of year-round hired labor which the old-time "hired man" had represented, but labor engaged only by the day when there happened to be work to be done.

Where did the displaced tenants go? Into the towns, some of them. In many rural areas, census figures showed an increased town population and simultaneously a depopulated countryside. Said the man at a gas station in a Texas town, "This relief is ruining the town. They come in from the country to get on relief." Some of them got jobs running tractors on other farms at $1.25 a day. Some went on to California—out of farming as a settled way of life into farming as big business dependent on a large, mobile supply of labor.

NEW WORLD A-COMIN'

PRESIDENT ROOSEVELT, in announcing his plan for the Tennessee Valley Authority, said it would have "the broadest duty of planning" for the good of everyone in the country. "This power development of war days leads logically to national planning for a complete river watershed involving many States and the future lives and welfare of millions. It touches and gives life to all forms of human concern."

And on the day the President signed the TVA bill, Senator Norris said, "It is emblematic of the dawning of that day when every rippling stream that flows down the mountainside and winds it way through the meadows to the sea shall be harnessed and made to work for the welfare and comfort of man."

Both men believed intensely in public power, and their eloquent words obviously were deeply felt; without their combined efforts one of the nation's greatest works would not have been accomplished. Perhaps it would not bring about a Utopia in the Tennessee Valley; neither would its success bring galloping socialism upon the country; but a most remarkable spirit of cooperation was evidenced once work had really begun in the Valley. In the words of Broadus Mitchell, "The TVA addressed itself to the greatest public-works project in history, with the engineer, the architect, the chemist and men of a score of other sciences commanded to lead the way. It was a union of heart and mind to restore what had been wasted. It was a social resurrection." *

DIXON WECTER

TVA†

FOR WHITE and black alike, the key to the South's economic welfare lay in using her natural resources with keener social intelligence. True, conservation was no novelty even in this prodigal, easygoing land. After the Civil War some South Carolinians had built up a modest but thriving industry in preparing phosphates for soil enrichment, and in 1918 Woodrow Wilson had caused the construction of a dam and two nitrate plants at Muscle Shoals on the Tennessee River in northern Alabama to make ex-

* Broadus Mitchell, *Depression Decade* (New York, Rinehart, 1947).
† Excerpted from Dixon Wecter's *The Age of the Great Depression*.

plosives and fertilizers for war and peace. Henry Ford and other industrialists long cast covetous eyes upon this development, and for years it
remained a bone of political contention. Meanwhile the Tennessee basin,
draining portions of seven Southern states, with a population of four and
a half million, continued like the rest of the South to denude its topsoil,
deny it replenishment and squander other resources like timber, minerals
and water power.

For this region, whose income and living standards were below the national average and even under the Southern median, a new destiny began
in May 1933. Thanks to a twelve-year battle waged by Senator George
W. Norris and other conservationists and to Roosevelt's conviction that
power resources belong to the people, the Tennessee Valley Authority was
created to promote flood control, navigation, electric-power production,
proper use of land and forest and "the economic and social well-being of
the people." The new agency was to deal with all natural resources as a
single big problem and make decisions without constant reference to
Washington. Interstate in character, it worked co-operatively with seven
state governments and scores of local ones. At last regional planning on a
large scale had been given the signal to go ahead.

Though the TVA could invoke the power of eminent domain in matters like flood control, the essence of its program affecting the people's
daily life was voluntary. Under a planning council six divisions—representing agriculture, forestry, industry, engineering and geology, land use,
social and economic aspects—maintained "demonstration units," which
became the chief means of individual persuasion. While still engaged in
building locks and dams and power plants, it began the retirement of
submarginal lands, soil conservation, afforestation, the introduction of
better farm machinery and the fostering of local manufactures, public
health and education.

The hill dweller of Tennessee, Alabama and North Carolina inclined
to stubbornness, conservatism, suspicion—the traits of ingrained sectional-
ism. In the lowlands a few oldsters at first avowed that, rather than move,
they would just sit in their rocking chairs till the water came up to drown
them. New-fangled methods of plowing and household gadgets also left
them dour. But as the program progressed—with vast works of concrete
and steel rising skyward and transmission wires spanning the valleys,
brown water turning deep blue, ragged hillsides changing into rich green—
inertia yielded to curiosity and then appreciation, with youth and the better
educated taking the lead. Sharecroppers, white and black, found jobs with
the TVA which gradually converted them into skilled craftsmen or me-

chanics; many were glad to exchange ramshackle cabins for the prefabricated workers' dwellings whose example began to raise housing standards in the Valley. Malaria control and the curbing of stream pollution enhanced regional health at the same time that the TVA health and safety department was supervising the medical needs of workers and setting a remarkable record of freedom from industrial accidents.

Instead of the capricious, destructive river and its tributaries of the old days, a chain of lakes presently stretched across the Valley, stocked with fish and offering nine thousand miles of shore line for recreation. A private organization called the Tennessee Valley Waterway Conference devised, with aid from TVA technical experts, a series of public-use terminals linking the railroads and truck highways with a navigable channel six hundred and fifty miles long.

Meanwhile the once backward region had become the second-largest producer of power in the United States, with municipalities and co-operatives in partnership with the TVA supplying electricity to consumers at three cents a kilowatt hour instead of ten. Responsibility for the distribution of this current fell largely to local boards made up of public-minded citizens. While home consumption of electricity for the nation increased 63 per cent between 1934 and 1942, that in the Tennessee Valley (beginning at 17 per cent below the national average) almost doubled. Freezing lockers, electric pumps, hay driers, motors to grind feed and cut wood— these were the sinews of new might, instruments for promoting agricultural efficiency and enhancing standards of living.

Although some branches of private industry, eager to sell more electric ranges and other appliances, rejoiced at these developments, the private purveyors of electric power abominated the new agency. Roosevelt's contention that TVA rates constituted "yardsticks so that the people of this country will know whether they are paying the proper price for electricity of all kinds" provided hot debate. Cost factors of the TVA could be figured variously—in terms, for example, of allocation between electric power, navigation and flood control, or of estimates for depreciation and amortization and the interest to be charged theoretically to the investment (since the TVA, financed largely by congressional appropriations, paid virtually no interest). Its bookkeeping was further complicated because it paid nothing for benefits provided by other federal services, such as materials and labor furnished by the WPA and Civilian Conservation Corps, workmen's compensation under the United States Employees' Compensation Commission, the franking privilege and low freight rates on land-grant railroads.

While its foes argued therefore that its rates did not cover true costs but flourished a yardstick as pliable as the "rubber dollar," its friends replied that TVA wholesale charges were actually high enough to cover all these disputed items, plus its payments to states and counties in lieu of property taxes of 12.5 per cent of gross revenues, roughly equivalent to taxes borne by private utilities. This issue, a matter of exhaustive congressional inquiry, was extremely complex. If, however, TVA rates failed to furnish an exact yardstick, they did serve to deflate excessive profits in the private-utility field, not only in the Tennessee Valley but through the nation. Thanks to this and other causes, the average residential rate for the whole country declined from 5.52 cents in 1933 to 3.67 in 1942.

For several years the TVA and local subsidiaries of Commonwealth and Southern, the chief utility corporation in this region, worked together in a precarious harness of enforced co-operation. But upon expiration in 1936 of the TVA's contracts to use private transmission lines, open war broke out, with the corporation's president Wendell Willkie leading the squadrons of private enterprise. A limited victory for the TVA, gained from a Supreme Court decision in 1936 holding that construction of the Wilson Dam was constitutional, was enormously re-enforced three years later when the tribunal ruled that private companies had no legal right to protection from TVA competition.

Through its power of appropriation Congress alone held a whip hand over this half-a-billion-dollar property. With a few notable exceptions, the majority of lawmakers acquiesced in the view of TVA Chairman David Lilienthal that "a river has no politics." Its personnel were chosen and promoted on the merit system under the TVA's exclusive responsibility, the sole instance of this method in the whole system of permanent federal agencies. Not only did the staff appear to be well insulated from political tampering but, in accord with the philosophy of regionalism, they represented a wide geographical selection, and were frequently loaned to junior projects, like the Northwest's Bonneville Dam or South Carolina's Santee-Cooper development.

The President and his National Resources Committee tended to stress the river valley as the unit of regional planning. On June 3, 1937, he recommended that Congress create six more projects, conceived at this stage, perhaps out of deference to congressional caution, less as "little TVA's" possessing executive authority than as planning boards.

In other respects as well, the conservation of the nation's natural resources under the second Roosevelt had gone forward even more swiftly than under the first.

FASHIONS—HIGH AND LOW

HOLLYWOOD STARS, from Shirley Temple to Greta Garbo, influenced the fashions of the day. In the past, new styles in clothes were often slow to take hold. Now, through newsreels and feature films, news of fashions quickly spread throughout the country. The manufacturer who thought small-town women did not know this year's styles from last was in trouble. "Previously," David Cohn says, "clothing merchants could trace the peregrinations of clothing styles as they slowly moved from Fifth Avenue down to Fourteenth Street, then to Main Street six to twelve months later. Now women wore the same style simultaneously, with variations brought about by cost and local divergencies of taste." *

This quick awareness encouraged acceptance of American designers, who previously had run a poor second to the French. Elizabeth Hawes opened the first all-American fashion show at Lord & Taylor's in New York City early in the decade, and helped the sale of her own originals, as well as other American designers, with her books about the fashion business.

Smart dressmakers began to give names to their dresses, as names are given to race horses, and the advertisers opened up full throttle. "The limits of the credulity of allegedly hardheaded women seeking youth and a fashionable figure have not been found. American women in

1935 in search of youthful bodies and slim, willowy figures continued to be of great comfort to the rubber planters of the world." *

The ideal girl of that year was Ginger Rogers, and this brought about the flat tummy, a slim young waist, and the realization of a corsetmaker's dream. Miss Rogers' slim lines and her glamorous costumes of the day influenced the production of corsets and allied garments to the tune of 67 million dollars. And the "slimming" of women forced closer-fitting and scantier undergarments.

There was a shift in the material used in women's undergarments from cotton to silk and rayon. In the Sears Roebuck catalogue, for instance, old-fashioned drawers were no longer advertised, and women were advised to wear Sears' "briefs —sleeker, smoother, skin-light, skin-tight!" The trend was helped by the success of the strip-teasers.

"One of the most successful [strippers] was Sally Rand, onetime leader in the Christian Endeavor Society from Kansas City, Missouri, whose bubble and fan dances at the World's Fair in Chicago, 1933, were so sensationally successful. Within a short time her earnings had jumped to $6,000 a week, which led her to observe that 'I never made any money until I took off my pants,' and to her confession that she was 'fanning her brother though college.' And children bounced their rubber balls to the rhyme,

* David L. Cohn, *The Good Old Days* (New York, Simon and Schuster, 1940).

"Sally Rand has lost her fan;
Give it back, you nasty man." *

Romance and youth were the stuff of women's fashions of the Thirties. The Sears catalogue confirmed it.

Moonlight Sonata—you, winsome and desirable in clouds of rayon net, your tiny waist sashed with whispering rayon taffeta.

Whispers in the Dark—you, pretty as a picture in a formal of celanese rayon ninon, agleam with rayon satin stripes. Proud puffed sleeves, softly shirred bodice, slashed in a V . . .*

And dresses were definitely designed for the young. Women, no matter what age, were willing to suffer any torture in the fitting salons, beauty parlors and even at the hands of the plastic surgeons: "Save the surface and you save all." *

Hairdos changed as well. By 1935 hardly a town in the United States was without at least one beauty parlor. With the development of the permanent wave, a regular visit to the hairdresser's was a matter of course.

"The American girl wanted her stockings sheerer and sheerer in transparency, and she was sold on the finest texture" * by endorsements by the Hollywood stars. At the beginning of the decade, American manufacturers were producing 300 million pairs of silk stockings annually, and the price per pair was approximately $1.50. By 1938 they were 91 cents. The price of raw silk had dropped, and technology had produced rayon. But there was a partial rollback of this "progress" in 1938 and 1939, when American women were asked to boycott silk, and to use cotton and lisle instead, as a protest against

Japan's invasion of China. Magazines and newspapers carried photographs of the American woman burning her silk stockings and flaunting her legs in lisle hosiery.

The girl of the Thirties began to show her curves again, to the satisfaction of men. Frederick Lewis Allen described her as "alert-looking rather than bored, with a pert, uptilted nose and an agreeably intelligent expression; she appeared alive to what was going on around her, ready to make an effort to give the company a good time." And "the prevailing style of hairdress (a shoulder-length page-boy or curled bob) was likewise simple, and lovely. In the years to come it may be that one of the most charming recollections of the period was that of hatless girls striding along like young blond goddesses, their hair tossing behind them. One recalls the complaint of a young man that almost every girl appeared good-looking—from behind!" †

Dresses and skirts had dipped to as low as ten inches off the floor in the early Thirties, but began to creep upward as the decade went on, until they were worn just below the knee. Most women now wore painted fingernails, without complaint from husband or escort, who had fought the good fight when the style was first introduced at the beginning of the decade.

Men's clothing, as usual, suffered no dramatic change, but stiff collars, garters, vests, spats and such were discarded in the interest of economy. Trousers were worn long and baggy, and the jacket with a belted back was successful for several seasons.

---

* David Cohn, *The Good Old Days.*
† Frederick Lewis Allen, *Since Yesterday.*

In the higher circles of fashion and design, there was apt to be experiment and capriciousness, exhibiting a kind of perverse humor, but adding up to damn' little, according to Cecil Beaton.

CECIL BEATON

FASHION AND DESIGN*

WOMEN'S FASHIONS in the name of practicability comprised street suits of indeterminate shape and length, "formal" pajamas, tea gowns with horse halters around the neck, and the creations so un-Parisian in taste of Schiaparelli. Yet Schiap was in her own way something of a genius. She injected a healthy note into the Thirties, inventing her own particular form of ugliness, and salubriously shocking a great many people. With colors that were aggressive and even upsetting, including a particular puce she referred to as her "shocking pink," Schiap began her revolution.

She used rough-looking materials, oaten linens, pebbly crashes, and heavy crepes—put nylon and other new materials to good purposes, and used synthetic fabrics for her dresses. Mrs. Diana Vreeland of *Harper's Bazaar* once sent a Schiap dress to the cleaner's. The next day she received a telephone call informing her with regret that the dress had been put into the cleaning fluid and there was nothing left of it.

Schiap was the first dressmaker to travel extensively, and wherever she went she brought back representative clothes of that country. On holiday in Switzerland she would make a mental note of the ski instructor's clothes —on her return, women would be given thick jerseys with padded square shoulders.

At one moment in the late Thirties, this capricious designer fell under the surrealist influence. In her shop a shocking-pink sofa became a pair of lips. She often put women in apparently unfeminine clothes, going so far as to introduce bus-conductor outfits. One suit, decorated with closed bureau drawers, was inspired by Dali. By 1938 fashion had gone into such a state of decadence that it seemed surely a last warning before the tower of Babel fell.

The Thirties, from the point of view of the arts and fashion, strikes one

* Condensed from Cecil Beaton's *The Glass of Fashion* (Garden City, N. Y., Doubleday, 1954).

as being perhaps the least interesting in recent decades: heavy wrought-iron doors, Knole sofas, backs bound with bandages of metal galloon and their adjustable ends held insecurely by tasseled knobs, placed cater-corner in even the smallest rooms; cigarettes were kept in disemboweled books; lamp shades were made of old music parchment; almost anything could be given a pseudoantique look by the simple expedient of applying a coat of yellow varnish.

There were the Chicago World's Fair and the New York World's Fair, both heralding the beginning of the acceptance of modern architecture with its straight lines, plain materials and obviation of detail. Interior decorating then went modern with a vengeance. But the mass-produced modern furniture was to be as impersonal as anything that had ever been turned out at Grand Rapids.

Fashion photographers came into their own. [My] own pictures became more and more rococo: like the souls in torment in Bosch's Hell, ladies of the upper crust were to be seen in published photographs fighting their way out of a hatbox or breaking through a huge sheet of white paper or torn screen, as though emerging from a nightmare, as seen through a plate-glass window which had been daubed with whitewash. White-on-white paper was often used as the background with a sheath of whitened branches.

Perfectly normal ladies were pictured in extremes of peril with one arm covering the face or thrust forward in exaggerated perspective straight toward the camera. Backgrounds were often exaggerated and often tasteless. Some of this meretricious work was inspired by a literary approach. Mannequins dressed to kill would be photographed with smoking guns, and smart witnesses would appear in the "witness box." At this time much unrestrained activity was afoot in the fields of decoration—night clubs were done up as bird cages, baroque excesses in plasterwork were allied to the plush luxuries of late Victorianism. Magentas and pinks together with bright yellows were favorite colors. Depression life in the Thirties had its highlights. Art, especially under the influence of such painters as Dali, Picasso and Berard, was impinging very closely on fashion.

Perhaps no other person [than Greta Garbo] has had such an influence on the appearance of a whole generation, though in fact the owner of this face possesses other qualities that cannot be improvised or imitated. The whole secret of her appeal seems to lie in an elusive and haunting sensitivity. We find ripples of feeling appearing at the surface, coming from some deep and unknown source. Though Garbo has been credited with having little clothes sense and obviously has paid no attention to the rules of current fashion, she had an innate flair with what is fitting for her and she possessed a great natural taste, being capable of appraising good clothes as well as appreciating them. At the time of her Hollywood advent, film makers attempted to make Garbo conform to their patterns, frizzing her hair and dressing her in impossible trappings. But by degrees, as she gained more authority, Garbo was able to assert her instinct and bring her real beauty to the fore, previously lost behind the unreal human façade Hollywood had devised for her as another of its temptresses.

[It was one of the paradoxes of fashion] that a woman who has not possessed an evening dress for twenty years should emerge as one of the leading influences on style of her day. And what Garbo achieved in clothes has been reflected also in make-up. Before Garbo, women's faces were pink and white. But her very simple and sparing use of cosmetics altered the face of the fashionable woman. For a number of years she used no lipstick or powder. It had been customary for stage people to use blue paint on their eyelids, but Garbo, by drawing a black line to accentuate the upper eyelashes, brought the line of the lid back into vogue.

In retrospect, the Thirties fashions were dull . . . and foolishness was widespread: Dali on a hot summer's afternoon read a lecture on surrealism in a diver's suit.

But brilliant personalities and artists were not lacking. Even in a low-pressure period they will turn water into wine, dross into gold, mutton chops into hats and meretricious material into art.

GOING TO COLLEGE

A COLLEGE DEGREE in the Thirties was not quite the help it is today in getting a job. No matter how much education a college graduate had, he might consider himself lucky, in the early years of the decade especially, just to land one of those marginal selling jobs (no guaranteed salary, commission only).

There was a hell of a lot of waiting—waiting to get an education, waiting to find a job, waiting to get married—all of which depended upon obtaining the money. Some people hung around the colleges, afraid to leave. Arthur Miller says he knew graduate students "who lived in an abandoned house, with no electricity or heat, and never took the boardings off the windows for fear of discovery, and one of them had been around so long he had gone through every course in the Lit school, but Roman band instruments." *

The colleges themselves did not have it easy. Their endowments had fallen off, as had the interest on their investments, and enrollments were down, and not until the middle of the decade would they rise. Yet, reactionary voices protested the government's program of assistance to students, through the National Youth Administration and the Federal Emergency Relief Administration.

ARTHUR MILLER AT MICHIGAN

Years later, Arthur Miller observed that he had attended the University of Michigan with the help of the NYA, but that within two months after leaving school, in 1938, he was on relief. Nevertheless, his college years obviously meant a lot to him. He says, "I thought I had accomplished something. I knew at least how much I did not know. I had found many friends and had the respect of the ones who mattered to me. It had been a small world, gentler than the real one, but tough enough." *

"I loved the idea of being separated from the nation, because the spirit of the nation, like its soil, was being blown by crazy winds. Friends of mine in New York, one of them a *cum laude* from Columbia, were aspiring to the city fireman's exam; but in Ann Arbor I saw that if it came to the worst a man could live on nothing for a long time. I earned $15 a month for feeding a building full of mice—the National Youth Administration footing the bill—and out of it I paid $1.75 a week for my room and squeezed the rest for my Granger tobacco (two packs for thirteen cents), my books, laundry and movies. For my meals I washed dishes in the co-op cafeteria. My eyeglasses were supplied by the Health Service, and my teeth were fixed for the cost of materials. The girls paid for themselves, including the one I married.

"I do not know whether the same thing happened at Harvard or Columbia or Yale, but when I was at Ann Arbor I felt I was at home. My

* "University of Michigan," *Holiday*, December 1953.

400

friends were the sons of die-makers, farmers, ranchers, bankers, lawyers, doctors, clothing workers and unemployed relief recipients. They came from every part of the country and brought all their prejudices and special wisdoms. It was always so wonderful to get up in the morning. I recall going to hear Kagawa, the Japanese philosopher, and how, suddenly, half the audience stood up and walked out because he had used the word Manchukuo, which is Japanese, for the Chinese province of Manchuria. As I watched the Chinese students excitely talking outside on the steps of Hill Auditorium, I felt something about the Japanese attack on China that I had not felt before.

"It was a time when the fraternities, like the football team, were losing their glamour. Life was too earnest. But I remember glancing with sadness at the photographs of Newman, Oosterbaan and the other gridiron heroes and secretly wishing that the gladiatorial age had not so completely disappeared. Instead, my generation thirsted for another kind of action, and we took great pleasure in the sit-down strikes that burst loose in Flint and Detroit, and we gasped when Roosevelt went over the line with the TVA, and we saw a new world coming every third morning, and some of the old residents thought we had gone stark raving mad.

"I tell you true, when I think of the Library I think of the sound of a stump speaker on the lawn outside because so many times I looked up from what I was reading to try to hear what issue they were debating now. The place was full of speeches, meetings and leaflets. It was jumping with Issues." *

YOUTH IN COLLEGE†

THE PRESENT-DAY *college generation is fatalistic.* Certain college presidents will deny this and they will be right in terms of sections of their own broods. But before any minute spectrum analysis is undertaken, the investigator is struck by the dominant and pervasive color of a generation that will not stick its neck out. It keeps its shirt on, its pants buttoned, its chin up, and its mouth shut. If we take the mean average to be the truth, it is a cautious, subdued, unadventurous generation, unwilling to storm heaven, afraid to make a fool of itself, unable to dramatize its predicament. It may be likened to a very intelligent turtle, skeptical of its biological

* "University of Michigan," *Holiday,* December 1953.
† Condensed from *Fortune,* June 1936. The magazine had conducted a poll of college youth in twenty-five American universities, and from the many interviews and questionnaires it attempted to ascertain the character of the composite college student.

inheritance, the shell, but determined not to be a bull, a bear, or a goat. The turtle has security and . . .

Security is the summum bonum *of the present college generation.* This may be convicting the average undergraduate of having good sense, yet security is usually thought of as the ideal of middle age. Yearners for security do not set foot on Everest or discover the Mountains of the Moon. They do not even defy the racketeers and start new wet-wash laundries. They want a haven in a . . .

Job that is guaranteed to be safe and permanent. The present-day average undergraduate is no chancy gambler. He doesn't expect to make much money. If the student decides on teaching or on a government job in the civil service, it is not only because he has ideals about molding the future generations or about helping his country. It is also because teaching and the civil service promise a relief from economic uncertainty. A professor's $5,000 per annum means—security. If the undergraduate selects a profession it is mainly because business seemingly does not offer opportunities for aggrandizement as it did in the golden Twenties. And if he does go into business he is perfectly willing to do what he is told without quibbling—and also without any attempt to force or insinuate his personality and values upon his superiors in the company that has employed him. He is, in brief, tractable corporation material. But are good corporation heads made out of tractable material? And if not, where are the future industrial and financial leaders coming from? Nice, decent, and willing boys may ultimately be a liability. Kingdoms often fall when they are in the hands of the epigoni.

We may have implied that it is an apathetic generation, but "passive" is an apter adjective. For, if one says to a young professor of economics, "You have a gutless gang of youngsters in your college," the professor will be perplexed. "Why, no," he will say, "the college boys of today are way ahead of those of ten years ago. They are much more interested in political and social questions. They know what is going on in the world. They read the papers intelligently. They take many more courses in economics and history and the social sciences." So another generalization may be set up. The undergraduate of today is . . .

Intellectually curious about the world. Does this contradict the passivity generalization? Seemingly, but when the inquiry is pressed one discovers that the impression of passivity and the impression of lively intellectual curiosity are two faces of the same coin. The answer one gets depends on what type of question is asked.

If one queries the average undergraduate about his chances for the future or if one talks with him about his ability to twist the world to his own desires, it is then that one will find him a fatalist—at least a stoic, at worst a whiner. Questions bearing on the personal equation bring out the facts that he doesn't think he will attain great heights in the world as it is constituted and that he doesn't think he can make that world over. He may deplore war, but he can't see himself thwarting the forces that make for war. Evidently he is a fit human paving stone for the juggernaut.

However, if one talks with the average undergraduate about the general *conditions* to be expected in the future, one will find oneself in the presence of a chatty, energetic, brightly curious young person. How can this be reconciled with the fatalism elicited by questions bearing on the personal equation? The answer is pat: a cautious, fatalistic person never moves into new country without first getting all the information he can about it. Our slave does not contemplate rebellion and a break for freedom; he merely wants to know the conditions of his servitude. Yet intellectual curiosity born of caution may, indeed, result in the crusades of tomorrow. At the moment the student sniffs the wind. He may be waiting to see how much life the business cycle—or series of business cycles—has in it. If jobs expand, the student will apparently go back to the *status quo ante* 1930. But it will be no complete spiritual reversion, for the student will have a background of political thinking that will forever prevent him from taking prosperity for granted. And if the prosperity fails to hold up . . .

The undergraduate will turn to new leaders. He is already doing so to some extent. The old-style campus big man no longer commands unqualified allegiance. The football star, the crew captain, the "muscular Christian" from the college Y.M.C.A., the smoothie from the big prep school who becomes track manager, the socially graceful prom leader—these still have honor and respect. But the intellectually curious person, who used to be considered queer or "wet" unless he had extraintellectual characteristics to recommend him, is climbing past the conventional big man. Englishmen, long accustomed to spotting future undersecretaries of the Foreign Office, future labor theoreticians, and even future Prime Ministers on visits to Cambridge or Oxford, have remarked on this mutation in American campus leadership and are inclined to set 1932 as the date at which the mutation became apparent.

This does not mean the colleges are becoming radicalized. Again it is important to emphasize, at least pro tem, the passive element. The new-style leader is more apt to demand courses in Communism, Fascism, and the works of Thomas Jefferson than he is to take a stand for or against a given type of social organization. The fact that students have been flocking to history, economics, and sociology courses does not mean that Leninism or Henry Georgeism is rampant under the elms. The new leaders limit intransigence to a demand for information. Tomorrow, if economic indexes turn downward, the demands may become more active in character. Meanwhile the student marks time and dallies with . . .

Culture and the Good Life. Unable to plot his future, the average undergraduate has turned to minor cultural and semicultural activities, in which there has been a great diffusion. Ping-pong, court tennis, squash rackets, rushing for the Berkshire snow train to get a weekend's practice in the telemark or slalom race, experiments with the Leica candid camera—the popularity of all such things is increasing by leaps and bounds. If it were not that they tend to displace a working direction, a major drive, in most instances, one might say that the Good Life had at least reached America. Yet the Good Life cannot be attained by making a cult of hobbies. The Good Life demands some animating . . .

Faith, with a dependent moral code. One might think that a lack of worldly faiths or an obscure terrestrial future could be counted upon to turn the undergraduate to thoughts of mystic matters. Yet—save for an occasional Buchmanite flurry—religion, as an institution, has taken a back seat. Too passive to be atheist, the undergraduate is vaguely deist. The girls' colleges show more religious hunger than the boys'.

Liquor and sex used to be part of the great triumvirate of campus topics that included religion. Today economics is to the fore as bull-session pabulum, with religion playing a minor role. Liquor as a conversational topic is passé. Less flamboyant drinking is the present-day rule; there is no prohibition law to defy, hence one can drink in peace. As for sex, it is, of course, still with us. But the campus takes it more casually than it did ten years ago. Sex is no longer news. And the fact that it is no longer news is news.

The family as such is no longer an object of derision, as it was in the early Twenties. Fathers and mothers are listened to once more, at least in the East and in the Middle West. (The Pacific Coast universities, which lag behind the colleges of the East, show less evidence of respect for parental dicta, but even on the coast the tide is beginning to turn.) Deference to the advice of father is part of the general yearning for security among the young. It is also part of a world hunger for certainty. And as the world wags, so wags the undergraduate.

THE CAMPUS WALKS AND TALKS

When the male undergraduate, 1936 model, gets up in the morning—at seven-thirty if he has early classes, at eight-thirty if not—he will, if he goes to a wealthy college, put on sloppy gray flannel bags and a tweed coat that is guaranteed to last for four years, or for the duration of the college course. The clothes, which represent an over-all investment of some $45, might be attributed by the cynical to a Depression fashion of imitating the proletariat. Economy in dress has cost Jack Feinstein and other college tailors many haggard nights. And when the undergraduate dashes quite barebeaded down the entry steps to breakfast, a recent rumor that some hat factories have shut down is readily credible.

Breakfast is a hurry-scurry matter of orange juice, eggs, toast, and coffee (the undergraduate has given up breakfasting on Coca-Cola), plus a quick glance at the college daily and an even quicker glance at some outside newspaper. This quick-flash gutting of the news is not limited to the sports page, for Hitler, Mussolini and Stalin have become quite as superficially exciting as the sports heroes.

After breakfast comes another dash, usually to classes. In some universities, however, compulsory chapel lingers on, at least for freshmen and sophomores. And in the colleges where the student is still fated to spend ten or fifteen minutes in putative worship, he does it with an air of extreme fatigue. The fatigue is so evident that when the enterprising editor of the *Daily Princetonian* recently assembled a Leica camera portfolio of typical worshipers—some half asleep, some tying shoes and neckties, some reading the New York *Herald Tribune,* some playing Salvo, some doing lessons, and some simply gawking at the rafters—it clinched the case against chapel with the Board of Trustees. By such persuasive methods has the undergraduate won his case against compulsory institutional religion in many of the universities.

The secular and contemporary orientation of the average undergraduate is apparent in the choice of courses to which he hurries after breakfast or chapel. He no longer preferably takes his scholastic eye opener with a professor who discourses on Platonism or "the best that has been thought and said" in the world's cultural history. Instead, he stampedes in preponderant droves to classes in the sciences, in sociology, in history, and in economics, and the teacher who does not illustrate a lecture with topical reference to the magazines and daily papers may be considered a dull fellow. If the student is pursuing culture, it is quite likely to be in a course on the contemporary novel that has been added to the curriculum at his own demand. Once the emphasis on history and the social sciences has been discounted, one is struck by the cultural diffusion represented by the choice of favorite subjects. Horticulture may appear on the elective schedule along with labor relations; ceramics and art interpretation may vie in popularity with a class in social-service work.

Since academic standards have been tightened up during the past decade, the average student who remains in college does some serious studying. Classroom horseplay still exists, and an antic student may try to snap a professor in action with a camera concealed by a couple of books, but there is less reading of *The Saturday Evening Post* in the back rows these days. Hence, the morning hours in college are largely devoted to constructive work. Around twelve o'clock comes a letdown that lasts well into the afternoon. The average undergraduate may turn up for lunch at his club or fraternity wearing an old sweater, if house rules made in a more formal day have been relaxed. He consumes large quantities of milk at lunch, and feels sleepy afterwards. When he gets up from the table it is to play pool, to read magazines, to listen to the radio—or to sit around and gas with his friends. If he is diligent about any particular line of work he may break the siesta tradition and bury himself in the library. But this is rare.

At three-thirty the tempo quickens. Today the typical undergraduate is a far healthier specimen than the one who tried to ruin himself before twenty-five in Charles Wertenbaker's 1928 college novel, *Boojum!*, and he may almost certainly be found on one of the playing fields by midafternoon. If he can't make a varsity squad he doesn't repine; he doesn't want to die of an athlete's heart any more than he wants to die of a drunkard's. But he likes to keep in mildly good shape and he goes in for a vast profusion of intramural games: touch football, softball, tennis, golf (it's more than your life is worth to walk across a college links), squash, handball, ping-pong (played vociferously), and scrub baseball. There are no special coaches for any of these sports, and no one cares greatly whether his side wins or loses. Lou Gehrig may make the "old college try" for an impossibly distant foul ball at the Yankee Stadium; but the old college try is absent from intramural athletics on the campus. The kids are out for mild fun, and they quit when they feel like it.

At six o'clock an infinitesimal number of undergraduates may serve cocktails (gin and lemon juice) in their rooms. But the typical student will go from his sports straight to dinner. After dinner there ensues a studious period for the majority, although on some nights the student will go to the movies. The Eastern undergraduate laughs derisively at the "collegiate" pictures produced by Hollywood directors who use the Pacific Coast campuses as location. (Anything that is "collegiate" is beneath the contempt of the Eastern collegians, in fact, and the campus sales of *College Humor* have dropped to almost nothing. Likewise the sale of banners, for which the student has no use. He prefers tasteful etchings in his room.)

When the movies are over, the prospective Phi Bete returns to work from his unwonted early evening relaxation. The college humorist goes off to adapt *The New Yorker* one-line joke (which has ousted the two-line joke except in jerkwater college weeklies) to the campus world, and the littérateur seeks solitude to blend the style of Hemingway with the influence of the *New Masses*. The less conscientious or ambitious student may play bridge (poker is only indulged in by a few "sports"), or he may go to the town taproom for a glass or two of beer and a bull session devoted to politics, sex, student personalities, and criticism of university policy. If he goes home to read, he will pick up Santayana's *The Last Puritan*, Vincent Sheean's *Personal History*, or some other national best seller. In F. Scott Fitzgerald's generation, student reading was often adventurously *sui generis*. It was the day of the campus popularity of the "quest book," which featured as its central character a Wellsian or a Compton Mackenzian young man in search of his soul. This type of book has ceased to be written. The modern blending of campus and national reading habits does not cover one item, an anonymous book called *The Psychology of Getting Grades*, which costs a dollar. This is unmentioned on the best-seller lists, but it is runner-up to Santayana on more than one campus. In it one can learn how to outguess the professor and even how to choose him before one has to outguess him.

Between ten-thirty and twelve-thirty the campus subsides into sleep. A few independent drunks, who care little for the Friday or Saturday night tradition, come roaring in at three, but the average undergraduate doesn't get tight until classes and study are over for the week. Weekends are not so frequent as they used to be, the obvious reason being that money has not been plentiful. But one doesn't have to go far away from college to drink. The stages of college inebriation are ranked as follows: high, tight, looping, stinking, plastered, out. Some would put tight after looping. But regardless of the grading of intermediate philological degrees of drunkenness, most of the drinking undergraduates think high is the desirable state of glow for a weekday night and even for the ordinary weekend. At spring house parties and at the football games the student can proceed to the tight and looping (or looping and tight) stages without causing any particular commotion.

When the college man meets the college girl, at the prom or the spring parties or in New York on a weekend, they dance very much as they danced some ten years ago. Those who would try to correlate styles in dancing with aspects of social change had better take warning from the fact that college dancing has passed arbitrarily back and forth between eras of high-speed jazz and the walking-talking-dancing slow movement of 1934. After the cheek-to-cheek business of the early Twenties came a variety of formations in which the girl's back was all but broken, with the lean-to formation winning the prize for most uncomfortable. Now, long after the demise of the jazz age, posteriors are back to a normal vertical, cheeks are back together, and the jazz tempo has been resumed. F. Scott Fitzgerald's Amory Blaine would still feel at home at a prom.

But it is doubtful that he would feel at home with the modern college girl if he came to know her away from the dance floor. Only girls referred to sarcastically as Midwestern sorority types dress up every day in a manner to suit Amory's Isabelles and Rosalinds. The typical Eastern college girl wears a tweed skirt and a sweater (probably knitted by herself) and low-heeled shoes. With no make-up and little lipstick, she presents a casual, even an untidy, appearance while on the campus. And the casualness is carried over into the girl's surface air of self-possession, which is unstudied.

The girl undergraduate gets up at eight, goes to classes conscientiously, and keeps her appointments with faculty people. At mealtime, and in between meals at the drugstores, where she eats a number of strange concoctions, she usually talks about what happens at school, and she may go on to discuss politics. Bull sessions on religion and sex are for more secluded moments. They are more frequent during freshman and sophomore years; upper-class girl students have too much work to do, have talked themselves out with their really good friends, and have discovered the advantages of getting enough sleep. Athletics do not bulk large in the girl student's life. She may do a little swimming, play a little tennis. A very few go in for golf. In the evening the girl student may go to the movies, but more often she retires to her room (she likes to live alone) or goes visiting. Late in the evening she makes tea (cocoa is no longer the midnight staple) and spreads some biscuits with jam. Although she is not allowed to smoke in her bedroom, the girl student consumes a large number of cigarettes during the day. In most ways she is behavioristically indistinguishable from many girls who don't go to college.

In the girls' colleges there is an inchoate hunger for religion or at least for philosophical certitude. But it is difficult to see much hope for institutional religion even among those who lust for certainty. God, to the undergraduate, is like the deity of the Unitarians—an "oblong blur."

So far as a moral code goes, the undergraduate, both male and female, seems to be fashioning one, without the aid of institutional religion. Ten years ago sexual promiscuity was either a fact or an idea that haunted the imagination. The backwash of war and the crumbling of the Victorian verities threw a generation into wild experiment or at least into lurid reading. Today the student takes sex more calmly, although on some male campuses, the sight of a pretty girl still provokes the usual scabrous ribaldry and cries of "fire, fire."

It is impossible to discover with any accuracy the actual sexual habits of a generation, but if the present-day undergraduate indulges in intercourse before marriage with any frequency he doesn't talk very much about it. Contraceptive knowledge is widespread, and the male undergraduate knows that contraceptive devices can be bought at filling stations. Hence, whether he uses his knowledge for practical purposes or whether he merely reassures himself for a distant future, a shadow has been lifted from his mind.

Fifteen years ago, when college girls sat up to the late hours of the night, they talked about careers and living their own lives. The trek to Greenwich Village was on. Today the prospect of marriage and children is popular again. Sixty per cent of the college girls and 50 per cent of the men would like to get married within a year or two after graduation, and 50 per cent of each sex would like to have children soon after marriage. On the subject of working wives, however, the divergence is sharp. For where only 15 per cent of the men think their future mates should hold paid jobs after marriage, 40 per cent of the girls look with favor upon continuing to work. Most girls are afraid of boredom; hence even if they have economic independence they want to be doing something. Forty per cent of the boys and 30 per cent of the girls consider two children per family the ideal number. Very few want no children at all; very few want more than four. Harvard, Princeton and Virginia, while not exactly for race suicide, have a low average desire of 2.8 children per male capita; Yale, "mother of men" and "mother of colleges," is considerably more philoprogenitive and desires an average of 3.2 offspring.

So far we have been considering the behavior and the sex mores of the animal. And in these respects there are some differences between this generation and its predecessor. But man is supposed to be a thinking animal, and the biggest difference between this generation and the one of the Twenties is in the subject that forms the content of its thought. That subject is the world crisis. Sometimes quite palpably, sometimes indefinably, it colors nearly everything the student does and says. Fear of the future and a vague sense of imminent frustration have taken the Fitzgeraldian cockiness out of the average undergraduate. If he drinks less and wenches less, it is because the stuff of the newspaper headlines is on his mind. A few have been enormously stimulated by the uncertainty of these years, but they are the exceptions. However, both the timid ones and the zestful ones have been mulling over the same social and economic problems. This mulling has not yet produced a definite youth movement, but the campus is a little—a very little—to the left of the country as a whole.

And because it is a little to the left, the Hearst newspapers have grown volubly excited about the "menace" of undergraduate radicalism. This excitement has resulted in considerable distortion of the truth. No ism has as yet altered the contours of the American university world. Undergraduate society is still shaped like a turnip. Liberals and democrats—or at least people who react favorably to the stimuli of liberal and democratic phrases —form the thick equatorial bulge of the turnip. These liberals and democrats are vaguely internationalist in their thinking; nationalism is out of fashion at the moment, for the student tends to identify it with imperialism and the suppression of alien populations.

At the taproot of the turnip is a numerically negligible group of Reds. The Fascist stem is even skinnier than the taproot. Announced conservatives make up a north temperate zone that is not quite as sizable as the south temperate zone of those vaguely interested in an ill-defined socialism. (When a Goucher girl says she is socialist it probably means that she has social good will, not that she is interested in the theories of Karl Marx.) Those who believe in the aristocratic principle balance the combined worshipers at Communist and Fascist shrines.

Curiosity about the conditions that will face the student after he has graduated has put new life into the arguments and attendance at many a campus political union. It was student curiosity that led to the widespread inflation of the sociology, history, and economics departments. But the increase in the number of instructors in the social sciences has not been sufficient to assuage the inquisitiveness of the thinking 5 or 10 per cent of the undergraduates. In many colleges—North Carolina, Minnesota,

Princeton, Yale and Dartmouth, to pick random examples—the cerebrating 5 to 10 per cent has, on its own initiative, invited guest speakers such as General Hugh S. Johnson, Harold Laski, Westbrook Pegler, Norman Thomas, Arthur Krock, Raymond Moley, George Soule, Jr., Fiorello La Guardia, Edmund Wilson, and Jouett Shouse. The inquisitive students are pretty much in the listening stage, and the question-and-answer periods that follow the speeches reveal more of a desire for information than any willingness to battle for or against specific ideas.

Although a nationwide college poll on Franklin D. Roosevelt would reveal more about sectional, class, and family backgrounds than about the political effect of university affiliation, the experimental ideas churned up by the New Deal propaganda have made a marked impress on the undergraduate mind. The New Deal has been dramatized so often as a youth movement that it has stimulated an interest in experimental government even among boys and girls who think Roosevelt is selling the country down the river. The young Republican who votes for Landon or whomsoever next fall will do so not for consciously reactionary motives, but with hopes that the Republican party will provide a liberalism in action that is less costly than the present Democratic brand. The thinking section of the undergraduate population definitely has its ear to the ground. And to some extent the impression of lassitude in the colleges springs paradoxically from the undergraduate eagerness to listen to propaganda for the new society. This propaganda, whether Communist, Fascist, or New Deal, continuously stresses the importance of state action, so quite naturally the listening student is apt to be left with the idea that he must sit around and wait for the Great White Father (or the Great Red Father) to give the nod.

Undoubtedly there is a good measure of lip service to liberalism among the undergraduates, but ten years ago there was not even lip service to any formulated political creed. When the Harvard *Lampoon* editors of 1935-36 apologized to the visiting Professor Laski for the attack made upon him by the 1919 editorial board in the days of the Boston police strike, they may have been indulging in an easy gesture. Yet the gesture is symbolic of the alteration that has come over the campus since the Twenties.

Of bona fide collectivist radicalism in the colleges there is at most only a chemical trace. There are, for example, some of the leaders of the American Student Union. This Union is the result of a merger of Socialist and Communist groups, but it has lost sectarian sharpness by its recent tactic of taking in liberals and progressives who are against war and Fascism but not necessarily for a socialistic organization of society.

Snobbery still prevails at Yale, Harvard and Princeton, though the girls' colleges no longer feel strongly about social prestige on the campus. At the wealthier men's liberal-arts colleges the campus is divided into the "white men" and the "black men." The black men are also known as "drips" and "meatballs." (Ten years ago the word was "wet smack"; twenty years ago, "the unwashed.")

Ten or twenty years ago campus snobbery often looked down upon the rough diamond who had brains. But the new orientation toward perplexing economic and political news has caused even the college snob to withdraw his objections to brains, which today need not be accompanied by social graces. Puzzled, unable to get satisfying answers from his teachers, the average student has ceased to regard the football star and the smoothie who qualifies for prom leader as the repositories of all virtue. The new orientation has produced a type of leader that contrasts vividly with the old-style campus headman. The Depression has brought the American college abreast of the English university at last, with the result that future administrators, politicos and thinkers can undoubtedly be spotted in sophomore year.

The shift in leadership is so clear and striking, so apparent in so many universities that it amounts to a structural change in the undergraduate world. The impact of the universal economic crisis on the campus obviously called forth the new leader. Hence referring to him as "English" is merely a way of explaining him by analogy, for he has, actually, sprung from the native soil. If a plateau of prosperity lies ahead for American business—and for the undergraduate who is seeking a job—the mutation will not have a mushroom growth in the near future. But it is undoubtedly here to stay: the fact that America has reached the end of pioneering and must henceforth grow intensively rather than extensively guarantees the new leader his niche and his influence.

A PRESIDENT WHO CARED

In 1933 the nation had witnessed an entirely new kind of leader as head of the government. John Gunther says that his best quality was his "extreme humanity." He defined humanity in terms of F.D.R.'s range from "amiability to compassion, from fertility in ideas to subtlety in personal relationships, from the happy expression of animal vitality to the deepest cognizance of suffering and primitive despair." *

He was a master politician, perhaps the best the country has ever had, and this was coupled with a great capacity to inspire idealism in people. Frances Perkins said that she and "everyone else came away from an interview with the President feeling better."

Furthermore, he was a President who was accessible to the people, not only to the members of his Administration but to the people at large. His oldest son, James, recalls F.D.R.'s policy:

"One of Father's first orders when he moved into the White House was symbolic of the New Deal's humanity. He circulated word to his staff, from the top secretaries to the telephone operators, that if persons in distress telephoned to appeal for help of any sort, they were not to be shut off but that someone was to talk with them. If a farmer in Iowa was about to have his mortgage foreclosed, if a homeowner in one of the big cities was about to lose his home, and they felt desperate enough about it to phone the White House, Father wanted help given them if a way possibly could be found; he was keenly cognizant of the suffering he had seen on his campaign trips.

"Many such calls were taken— sometimes by me, when I was in the White House, and occasionally by Mother. Often ways were found to cut red tape with some federal agency. After Father's death, Mother received letters from strangers, who told her how, in the dark Depression days, they telephoned their President and received aid." †

* John Gunther, *Roosevelt in Retrospect* (New York, Harper, 1950).
† James Roosevelt and Sidney Shalett, *Affectionately, FDR* (New York, Harcourt, Brace, 1960).

ARTHUR M. SCHLESINGER, JR.

F.D.R. AS PRESIDENT*

THE WHITE HOUSE routine had not altered much from 1933. The day still began for the President soon after eight o'clock with breakfast on a tray in his bedroom. Beside the narrow white iron bedstead was a plain white table, covered with telephone, pencils, memoranda, ash trays, cigarettes, nose drops and a glass of water. Ship prints and seascapes, old Roosevelt treasures, hung on the wall. Over the fireplace, on top of the marble mantelpiece with its grape carvings, was an assortment of family photographs, toy animals and whatever other mementos had caught the President's fancy. Like every room in any Roosevelt house, the presidential bedroom was hopelessly Victorian—old-fashioned and indiscriminate in its furnishings, cluttered in its *décor,* ugly and comfortable.

While breakfasting, the President looked rapidly through half a dozen leading newspapers, half of them bitterly critical of his administration (the New York *Herald Tribune,* the Washington *Times-Herald,* and the Chicago *Tribune*). He usually wore a sweater or cape, a dressing gown was too much trouble for a crippled man. The breakfast conferences of the Hundred Days were now pretty well abandoned, except in moments of emergency. Even Eleanor Roosevelt, pausing to see her husband on her way out, usually said no more than good morning; "he liked no conversation at this hour." The newspaper scanning was the first phase in Roosevelt's unceasing effort to get the feel of the government and the nation.

Between nine and nine-thirty his secretaries—Steve Early and Marvin McIntyre, with Louis Howe, until he became ill, and then usually Colonel Edwin M. Watson, better known as Pa, the President's military aide— came in to discuss the day's schedule. In the next half hour Roosevelt dressed and shaved. Often he combined this with business. Thus Harold Ickes:

When I got to his study, his valet ushered me into his bedroom, telling me that the President was shaving. He waved toward the bathroom and the President called out to me to come in. There he was, sitting before a mirror in front

* From Arthur M. Schlesinger, Jr.'s *The Coming of the New Deal* (Boston, Houghton Mifflin, 1959).

414

of the washstand, shaving. He invited me to sit on the toilet seat while we talked. When he was through shaving he was wheeled back to his room where he reclined on his bed while his valet proceeded to help him dress. . . . I was struck all over again with the unaffected simplicity and personal charm of the man. He was the President of the United States but he was also a plain human being, talking over with a friend matters of mutual interest while he shaved and dressed with the help of his valet. His disability didn't seem to concern him in the slightest degree or to disturb his urbanity.

Around ten-thirty he was ordinarily pushed in his wheelchair along the newly constructed ramps to the executive office in the west wing of the White House. Here, in the lovely oval room, he held his official appointments and spent most of his working day. The room had the usual Rooseveltian country-house informality. "You would think," said Emil Ludwig, "you were in the summer residence of the general manager of a steamship company, who has surrounded himself with mementos of the days when he was captain." On the wall hung Hudson River prints by Currier and Ives; ship models stood on the mantel: a litter of memoranda, government reports, books, toy pigs, donkeys and ship's rudders lay on his desk; on the floor, at the President's side, occasionally rising to be patted, were two fine Irish setters. The symbols of high office—the presidential flag, the Great Seal in the ceiling—were subdued and inconspicuous. Behind the President, light streamed softly in through great glass windows running down to the floor, and to the east, briefly glimpsed, were the quiet rose garden and the porticoes and the magnolia trees. In the commotion of Washington, this bright and open room had an astonishing serenity.

Most presidential appointments took place here in the two hours before lunch. The President aimed at seeing people at fifteen-minute intervals, but often fell behind, while visitors waited in the anteroom and McIntyre and Watson did their soft-spoken best to hurry things up. Lunch took place at his desk, with food served from a metal warming oven; it was often hash with a poached egg (when two eggs came, Roosevelt sometimes sent word to the housekeeper that this was a waste of food); lunch too was usually combined with business. In the afternoon there might be more appointments; then, about midafternoon, the President usually called in Grace Tully for an hour or two of dictation. About five o'clock during the first term, the office staff was briefly summoned for what he called "the children's hour," an interlude of relaxation and gossip. Soon after five-thirty, the office day ended; and the President took twenty minutes in the White House swimming pool, installed as a result of money raised in a campaign sponsored by the New York *Daily News*. Refreshed by exercise, the President prepared for dinner, ordinarily preceded by a martini or an old-fashioned. After dinner, he often went to his private study, a genial oval room on the second floor next to his bedroom, and dictated some more or read papers or held further conversations. Usually in bed before midnight, he quickly threw off the concerns of the day and in five minutes was deep in sleep. Unlike other Presidents, Roosevelt never allowed the Secret Service to lock the doors of his room at night.

Roosevelt's immediate staff was loyal and efficient. The longest in point of service, of course, was Louis Howe, who had worked for Roosevelt nearly a quarter of a century. Howe was only in his early sixties, but, frail and wizened, he was older than his years. His devotion to the President was more proprietary than ever, and his waspishness toward everyone else more insistent. But both Franklin and Eleanor Roosevelt cherished him. On certain matters, especially politics and patronage, Roosevelt continued greatly to value Howe's counsel; and on most matters he welcomed his opinions. "I am going to talk this over with Louis," he would say. "He has forty ideas a day and sometimes a few good ones." While the President often dodged Howe's advice, if he had to bypass his old friend he did so with incomparable tact.

As for Howe, he did not allow his protégé's eminence to constrain their relationship. Once McDuffie, the President's valet, brought him a message to which he replied snappishly, "Tell the President to go to hell." McDuffie, appalled, told his wife Lizzie, one of the White House maids, that he could not possibly deliver such a message to the President. Lizzie said she would fix it up; "Mr. President," she said, "Mr. Howe says that is a hell of a thing to do." The President laughed skeptically: "That isn't what Howe said, Lizzie. He told me to go to hell." Roosevelt's feeling toward Howe, as Richberg discerningly remarked, was that of a middle-aged son who still appreciated father's wisdom but was also impatient at father's efforts to keep him under parental guidance.

By the end of 1934, Howe's health, never good, grew steadily worse. He spent more and more of his time in his suite on the second floor of the White House. In February 1935 bronchial complications brought about a collapse. He was rushed to the Naval Hospital and put under an oxygen tent. Doctors despaired of him. "He seems to cling to life in the most astonishing manner," Eleanor Roosevelt wrote sadly to Molly Dewson, "but I am afraid it is the end." She underestimated his vitality. He rallied and, though he never left the hospital for long, he stayed alive another year. Much of this time he spent in bed, doubled up in an effort to reduce the pain; he let his beard grow into a straggling goatee which made his appearance more peculiar than ever. He continued to follow politics with sharp-eyed attention, sending out a flow of confusing directives to the National Committee and to Cabinet members. The Roosevelts visited him regularly. But he knew in his heart that he had not long to live. One day a friend told him that everyone counted on him for the 1936 campaign. "No," the old man said. "No, they'll have to run this campaign without me." He paused for a moment; then said, "Franklin's on his own now." In mid-April 1936, Louis Howe died.

Eleanor Roosevelt always felt that Howe's death left an irreparable gap in Franklin's life. Howe was almost alone, she believed, in being ready to follow through an argument with her husband, forcing him by peevish persistence to see unpleasant sides of an issue: "After Louis' death," she wrote, "Franklin frequently made his decisions without canvassing all sides of a question." Harold Ickes said the same thing: "Howe was the only one who dared to talk to him frankly and fearlessly. He not only could tell him what he believed to be the truth, but he could hang on like a pup to the root until he got results." Moreover, Howe unscrupulously organized campaigns to press his views; at his instigation, Eleanor Roosevelt, Farley, Ed Flynn and others would suddenly converge on the President and, as if by accident, make the same point. Eleanor Roosevelt felt in addition that her husband saw a better cross section of people and heard a greater variety of views when Howe was alive.

These things were probably true. Yet Howe's range was limited. "Louis knows nothing about economics," Roosevelt once said; in fact, he knew little of any aspect of public affairs, and was only vaguely aware what the New Deal was all about. Howe would have saved Roosevelt from mistakes in politics, but hardly from mistakes in policy. Still the subtraction of the most vehement nay-sayer from the entourage was certainly a misfortune.

Roosevelt had named Howe his Chief Secretary as a testimonial to his years of service. His other secretaries, Early and McIntyre, received the same salary as Howe and, as time went on, took over more and more of the day-to-day responsibility. Early, a tough, hard-driving, profane newspaperman just under fifty who had been for many years an ace for the Associated Press, had press relations as his main job. McIntyre, a gentle, agreeable man in his middle fifties, with a long and not especially distinguished background in newspaper work and public relations, was more or less in charge of political appointments (though, as in any Roosevelt operation, this seemed at times everybody's responsibility). Both Early and McIntyre were Southerners, Early from Virginia, McIntyre from Kentucky. Both had worked for Roosevelt in the 1920 vice-presidential campaign. Both were aggressively nonideological. Each preferred the political and business types with which they were familiar to the odd new breed of New Dealers; in McIntyre's case, an innocent fondness for the company of lobbyists was more than once a source of embarrassment to the White House. Both were loyal to Roosevelt rather than to his philosophy. But they kept out of policy questions and each strove to do as fair a job as possible.

Pa Watson, the military aide, who ran the general appointment schedule, was a more complex and subtle figure. An Alabaman in his early fifties who had been an aide to Wilson at Versailles, Watson was a man of winning personal charm. "I have never known anyone just like him," Ickes once said. ". . . He could be relied upon to keep us all in a mellow humor, and this without any effort on his part, but simply by being himself." People so adored the bubbling good nature that they sometimes missed the sophisticated awareness which lay beneath the quips and stories. Not a New Dealer, Watson had a greater understanding than Early and McIntyre of what the New Deal was about.

Of all the staff, Marguerite LeHand, the President's personal secretary, was undoubtedly closest to him and had most influence upon him. Missy was now in her late thirties, a tall, slender woman, prematurely gray, with a lovely face and attractive gray-blue eyes. She had worked for Roosevelt so long that she knew intimately his every expression and mood; his fondness for her was so great that he would listen to her as to few others on questions of appointments and even policy ("Mr. President, you really *must* do something about" so-and-so or such-and-such). She lived on the third floor of the White House and, when Eleanor Roosevelt was away, acted as White House hostess, inviting people who she thought might divert the President. Eleanor Roosevelt, while respecting Missy's abilities and understanding her value to her husband, felt that "occasionally her social contacts got mixed with her work and made it hard for her and others." People like Bill Bullitt and Tom Corcoran, she suggested, "exploited Missy's friendship" for their own purposes. But "though occasionally someone fooled her for a time, I always waited for enlightenment to come, with confidence born of long experience." Missy was pretty and gay and liked lively company; there can be no question that she brought an essential femininity as well as a sympathetic common sense into Roosevelt's life, and there is no evidence that she ever abused the affection and trust he reposed in her. An attack of rheumatic fever in 1926 had strained Missy's heart; and more and more of the office work, as, for example, taking dictation, fell to Grace Tully, another pretty and lively girl, who had worked for Roosevelt since the 1928 campaign. Both girls were Catholics, Miss LeHand of French, Miss Tully of Irish descent. They both cared deeply about the objectives of the New Deal. Both were exceptionally able and devoted women.

One other key White House figure was the executive clerk, Rudolph Forster, who had been there since the McKinley administration. His responsibility was the channeling of state papers, and he did this with an austere and frightening efficiency. For him the job was an end in itself; Presidents came and went, but papers went on forever. "You would be terrified," he once said to a Roosevelt assistant, "if you knew how little I care." (Yet even Forster, in the end, succumbed. In the 1944 campaign, as Roosevelt was leaving the White House on a political tour, Forster, with what Robert E. Sherwood described as "the air of one who was willfully breaking all of the Ten Commandments but prepared to take the consequences," shook the President's hand and wished him luck. Roosevelt, astonished and moved, said as the car drove away, "That's practically the first time in all these years that Rudolph has ever stepped out of character and spoken to me is if I were a human being instead of just another President.")

The next concentric circle beyond the White House staff in the President's constellation was the Cabinet. In the American system this had always been an ambiguous and unsatisfactory body. At the beginning of the republic, some conceived it as a sort of executive council. All grave and important matters, it was supposed, would be submitted to a Cabinet vote in which, as Jefferson put it, "the President counts himself but one." But Presidents, even Jefferson, recoiled from such a conception; and Jackson, in his general process of revolutionizing the Presidency, decisively redefined the relationship between the President and his Cabinet.

Jackson flatly declined, for example, to submit questions to vote. "I have accustomed myself to receive with respect the opinions of others," he said, "but always take the responsibility of deciding for myself." Lincoln, going even further, found Cabinet meetings so useless that he often avoided them and at one time seemed on the verge of doing away with them altogether. As for voting: "Ayes one, noes seven. The ayes have it" —or so the old story went. "There is really very little of a government here at this time so far as most of the Cabinet are concerned," complained Gideon Welles, Lincoln's Secretary of the Navy; "certainly but little consultation in this important period." Or again: "But little was before the Cabinet, which of late can hardly be called a council. Each Department conducts and manages its own affairs, informing the President to the extent it pleases." Theodore Roosevelt ignored his Cabinet on important issues. Woodrow Wilson did not even bother to discuss the sinking of the *Lusitania* or the declaration of war with it. "For some weeks," wrote his Secretary of the Interior, Franklin Lane, "we have spent our time at Cabinet meetings largely telling stories."

Roosevelt remained generally faithful to this tradition, though he made rather more effort than Lincoln or Wilson to recognize the Cabinet's existence. At first, he planned two Cabinet meetings a week on Tuesday and Friday afternoons. Effectively he had only one, however; the Tuesday meeting was first enlarged to include the heads of the emergency agencies and then dropped almost entirely. Sessions took place in an atmosphere of characteristic Roosevelt informality. The President ordinarily began with a recital of pleasantries, telling stories which tickled him or joshing Cabinet members about their latest appearances in the newspapers. Then he might throw out a problem for a generally rambling and inconclusive decision. Or, turning to the Secretary of State, he might say without ceremony, "Well, Cordell, what's on your mind today?" Then he would continue around the table in order of precedence.

The men—and one woman—sitting around the table were of varying qualities and abilities. They had conspicuously one thing in common—a high degree of personal rectitude. "For integrity and honesty of purpose," wrote Raymond Clapper after twenty years of covering Washington, "I'll put this Cabinet against any that has been in Washington since the war. It is one thing that does truly distinguish this group. There is not a shady one in the lot." Beyond that, the people around the table represented a variety of viewpoints and temperaments, held together only by a loyalty to, or at least a dependence on, the President. There was Garner (whom the President, to his later regret, invited to attend Cabinet meetings) with his complacent country sagacity; Hull, courteous and grave, always vigilant to defend his authority against real or fancied depredation; Henry Morgenthau, closest personally to the President, earnest, devoted, and demanding; the testy and aggressive Ickes; the preoccupied and thoughtful Wallace; Homer Cummings, bland, canny and unperturbed; Jesse Jones, wary and self-contained; the intelligent and articulate Miss Perkins (whose protracted discourses appeared to fascinate the President, but bored most of the others and at times enraged Ickes—"she talks in a perfect torrent, almost without pausing to take breath"); the amiable Farley, reacting only when politics came into the discussion—they were all forceful personalities, regarding each other with a show of conviviality which often only barely concealed depths of suspicion. For the most part, they chose problems of only middling—or else of highly general—significance to communicate to the group. This was partly because, in the inevitable jostling of bureaucracy, each felt that every man's hand was against him, and none wanted to expose vulnerabilities. It was also because the conviction grew that some members would "leak" tasty items—Garner to his cronies on the Hill, or Ickes to the columnist Drew Pearson. Questions that really troubled them they reserved for private discussion with the President afterward, a practice which Garner used to call "staying for prayer meeting." "Then you would stay behind," as Morgenthau described it, "and whisper in his ear and he would say yes or no."

The members of the Roosevelt Cabinet, as usual, suffered frustration and, as usual, thought their experience unique. In private, they echoed the familiar laments of Gideon Welles and Franklin Lane. "Only the barest routine matters were discussed," burst out Ickes in his diary after a meeting in 1935. "All of which leads me to set down what has been running in my mind for a long time, and that is just what use the Cabinet is under this administration. The cold fact is that on important matters we are seldom called upon for advice. We never discuss exhaustively any policy of government or question of political strategy. The President makes all of his own decisions. . . . As a matter of fact, I never think of bringing up even a serious departmental issue at Cabinet meetings." "It seemed to me," wrote William Phillips, sitting in occasionally for Hull, "that a great deal of time was wasted at Cabinet meetings and much of the talk was without any particular import." "The important things were never discussed at Cabinet," said Morgenthau. "The President treats them like children," Tugwell wrote in his diary, "and almost nothing of any importance was discussed."

The meetings evidently retained some obscure usefulness for the President. The reaction he got from this miscellany of administrators perhaps gave him some idea of the range of public opinion. It also helped him measure the capacity of his subordinates. Grace Tully reports, for example, that he preferred Henry Wallace's willingness to speak out on a wide variety of problems "to the reticence or indifference of some Cabinet members." But, like all strong presidents, Roosevelt regarded his Cabinet as a body of department heads, to be dealt with individually—or, sometimes, as a group of representative intelligent men, useful for a quick canvass of opinion—not as a council of constitutional advisers.

Beyond the Cabinet there stretched the Executive Branch of the government—an endless thicket of vested usage and vested interest, apportioned among a number of traditional jurisdictions, dominated by a number of traditional methods and objectives. This was, in the popular understanding, the government of the United States—the people and departments and agencies whose office it was to carry out the national laws and fulfill the national policies. The President had few more basic responsibilities than his supervision and operation of the machinery of government. Little fascinated Franklin Roosevelt more than the tasks of presidential administration. And in few things was he more generally reckoned a failure.

This verdict against Roosevelt derived ultimately from a philosophy of public administration—a philosophy held for many years after by Civil Service professionals, expounded in departments of political science, and commending itself plausibly to common sense. This school's faith was in logical organization of government, founded on rigid definitions of job and function and maintained by the sanctity of channels. Its weapons were the job description and the organization chart. Its unspoken assumption was that the problems of administration never change; and its consuming fear was improvisation, freewheeling or unpredictability—which is nearly to say creativity—in the administrative process. From this point of view, it need hardly be said, the Roosevelt government was a textbook case of poor administration. At one time or another, Roosevelt must surely have violated every rule in the sacred texts of the Bureau of the Budget.

And this conventional verdict found apparent support in much of the literature written by men who worked for Roosevelt. Though these reports differed on many other things, one thing on which they very often agreed was in their complaint about Roosevelt as an administrator. They agreed on one other thing too—the perspective from which they were written. Nearly all exhibited the problems of the Presidency from below—from the viewpoint of the subordinate rather than from that of the President. The picture created by this mass of individual stories, while vivid and overwhelming, was inevitably distorted and too often querulous. For no subordinate ever got what he wanted or thought he needed. In later years, George C. Marshall would talk of "localitis"—the conviction ardently held by every theater commander that the war was being won or lost in his own zone of responsibility, and that the withholding of whatever was necessary for local success was evidence of blindness, if not of imbecility, in the high command. "Localitis" in one form or another was the occupational disease of all subordinate officials; and, in a sense, it had to be, for each of them ought to demand everything he needed to do the best job he can. But "localitis" offered no solid ground for judgment of superiors, whose role it must inevitably be to frustrate the dreams of subordinates. The President occupied the apex of the pyramid of frustration. The essence of his job was to enforce priorities—and thereby to exasperate everybody. And, in Roosevelt's case, there is little left in the literature to emphasize the view from the summit, where any President had to make his decisions. As Grace Tully (whose book does something to redress the balance) commented on other memoirists, "None of them could know that for each minute they spent with the President he spent a hundred minutes by himself and a thousand more with scores of other people—to reject, improvise, weigh and match this against that until a decision was reached on a public policy."

The question remains whether the true test of an administrator may be, not his ability to design and respect organization charts, not his ability to keep within channels, but his ability to concert and release the energies of men for the attainment of public objectives. It might be argued that the essence of successful administration is: first, to acquire the ideas and information necessary for wise decisions; second, to maintain control over the actual making of the decisions; and, third, to mobilize men and women who can make the first two things possible—that is, who can provide effective ideas and information, and who can reliably put decisions into effect. It is conceivable that these things may be more important than preserving the chastity of administrative organization— that, indeed, an excessive insistence on the sacredness of channels and charts is likely to end in the stifling of imagination, the choking of vitality, and the deadening of creativity.

Franklin Roosevelt, at any rate, had some such philosophy of administration. The first task of an executive, as he evidently saw it, was to guarantee himself an effective flow of information and ideas. And Roosevelt's first insight—or, at least, his profound conviction—was that, for this purpose, the ordained channels, no matter how simply or how intricately designed, could never be enough. An executive relying on a single information system became inevitably the prisoner of that system. Roosevelt's persistent effort therefore was to check and balance information acquired through official channels by information acquired through a myriad of private, informal and unorthodox channels and espionage networks. At times, he seemed almost to pit his personal sources against his public sources. From the viewpoint of subordinates, this method was distracting when not positively demoralizing. But Roosevelt, with his voracity for facts and for ideas, required this approach to cross-check the official system and keep it alert as well as to assure himself the balanced and various product without which he could not comfortably reach decisions.

The official structure, of course, maintained a steady flow of intelligence. Roosevelt was, for a President, extraordinarily accessible. Almost a hundred persons could get through to him by telephone without stating their business to a secretary; and government officials with anything serious on their minds had little difficulty in getting appointments. In addition, he read an enormous number of official memoranda, State Department cables, and government reports, and always tried to glance at the *Congressional Record*. The flow was overwhelming, and he sought continually to make it manageable. "I learned a trick from Wilson," he remarked to Louis Brownlow. "He once told me: 'If you want your memoranda read, put it on one page.' So I, when I came here, issued a similar decree, if you want to call it that. But even at that I am now forced to handle, so the oldsters around tell me, approximately a hundred times as many papers as any of my predecessors." Certainly his subordinates paid little attention to the one-page rule.

What gave Roosevelt's administrative practice its distinctive quality was his systematic effort to augment the official intelligence. The clutter of newspapers on his bed each morning marked only the first stage in his battle for supplementary information. In this effort, reading was a useful but auxiliary weapon. Beyond government documents and newspapers, he read little. So far as current magazines were concerned, the President, according to Early, "sketches the field," whatever that meant. As for books, Roosevelt evidently read them only on holiday, and then not too seriously. When Frances Perkins sent him the Brookings study *America's Capacity to Produce*, he replied, "Many thanks. . . . I am taking it on the trip and will guarantee to browse through it but not of necessity to read every word!" On the whole, he preferred to acquire both information and ideas through conversation.

Many visitors, it is true, left Roosevelt with the impression that he had done all the talking. This was markedly less true, in his first term, however, than it would be later. Indeed, Henry Pringle, reporting the Washington view in 1934, wrote, "He is a little too willing to listen." And the complaint against Roosevelt's overtalking meant in some cases only that a visitor had run into a deliberate filibuster (thus William Randolph Hearst's baffled lament after a session with Roosevelt in 1933, "The President didn't give me a chance to make suggestions. He did all the talking"). "Words are a good enough barrage if you know how to use them," Roosevelt told one visitor. Like many talkers, moreover, Roosevelt absorbed attitudes and ideas by a mysterious osmosis on occasions when the visitor complained he hadn't got a word in edgewise.

Conversation gave him an indispensable means both of feeling out opinion and of clarifying his own ideas. He talked to everybody and about everything. His habits of conversation out of channels were sometimes disconcerting. He had little hesitation, if he heard of a bright man some-where down the line in a department, about summoning him to the White House. Ickes complained bitterly in his diary about "what he does so frequently, namely, calling in members of my staff for consultation on Department matters, without consulting me or advising with me." And often he bewildered visitors by asking their views on matters outside their jurisdiction. "He had a great habit," said Jesse Jones, "of talking to one caller about the subject matter of his immediately preceding interview." "I would go to see the President about something," wrote James P. War-burg, "and the fellow who was there before me talking about cotton would be told by the President, 'Well, why don't you stay.' Before we were through the guy who was there talking about cotton was telling him what to do about gold." All this, irritating as it was to tidy minds, enlarged the variety of reactions available to him in areas where no one was infallible and any intelligent person might make a contribution.

Moreover, at this time, at least, conversation around him was unusually free and candid. Always sensitive to public criticism, Roosevelt could take a large measure of private disagreement. Moley describes him as "patient, amenable to advice, moderate and smilingly indifferent to criticism." "In those days," wrote Richberg, "he enjoyed the frankness and lack of def-erence with which the original 'brain trusters' and I discussed problems." When people disagreed, they said so plainly and at length. "I had numer-ous quarrels with him," wrote Ed Flynn, who once (in 1940) hung up on him in the midst of a phone conversation. "However, as with sincere friends, the quarrels never impaired our friendship."

In seeking information, Roosevelt took care not to confuse the capital with the nation. "Pay no attention to what people are saying in Washing-ton," he once told Molly Dewson. "They are the last persons in the country to listen to." He loved going out to the country himself and got infinite stimulus from faces in crowds, from towns quietly glimpsed out of the windows of slow-moving trains, from chance conversations with ordinary people along the way. But polio and the Presidency limited his mobility. Instead, he had to urge others to get out of Washington. "Go and see what's happening," he told Tugwell. "See the end product of what we are doing. Talk to people; get the wind in your nose."

His first reliance was on his wife. From the first days after his disability, he trained her to do his looking for him. "That I became, as the years went by, a better and better reporter and a better and better observer," she later wrote, "was largely owing to the fact that Franklin's questions covered such a wide range. I found myself obliged to notice everything." While he sometimes doubted her judgment on policy and especially on timing, he had implicit faith in her observations. He would say at Cabinet, "My Missus says that they have typhoid fever in that district," or "My Missus says that people are working for wages way below the minimum set by NRA in the town she visited last week." "It was not unusual," said Grace Tully, "to hear him predicate an entire line of reasoning upon a statement that 'my Missus told me so and so.' " In addition, he liked detailed reports of the kind Lorena Hickok and Martha Gellhorn rendered on the situation of people on relief. And he listened with interest to any reasonably succinct account of human conditions anywhere.

Another great source of information was the mail. Five to eight thousand letters a day came normally to the White House; in times of anxiety, of course, many more. The mail was regularly analyzed in order to gauge fluctuations in public sentiment. From time to time, the President himself called for a random selection of letters in order to renew his sense of contact with raw opinion. As the White House mail clerk later wrote, "Mr. Roosevelt always showed a keen interest in the mail and kept close watch on its trend."

In all these ways, Roosevelt amassed an astonishing quantity of miscellaneous information and ideas about the government and the country. "No President," wrote Alben Barkley, "has ever surpassed him in personal knowledge of the details of every department"; and he could have added that probably no President surpassed him in specific knowledge of the geography, topography and people of the nation. Roosevelt took inordinate pride in this mastery of detail and often displayed it at length when those around him wished to get down to business. But, at the same time, the information—and the pride in it—signified the extraordinary receptivity which was one of his primary characteristics.

This receptivity produced the complex of information systems by which he protected himself from White House insulation. It oriented the administrative machinery away from routine and toward innovation. It made possible the intellectual excitement of the New Deal; it helped provoke a tempest of competing ideas within government because everyone felt that ideas stood and fell at the White House on their merit, not on whether they arrived through the proper channels. Good ideas might pop up from anywhere. "You sometimes find something pretty good in the lunatic fringe," Roosevelt once told his press conference: after all, America today was remade by "a whole lot of things which in my boyhood were considered lunatic fringe." Anyone with new theories had a sense that they were worth developing because, if good, they would find their way to the center. Sometimes this caused problems: Roosevelt was occasionally sold on harebrained ideas which more orderly procedures would have screened out and which taxed responsible officials before he could be unsold. But, on balance, benefits far outweighed disadvantages. H. G. Wells, who saw in Roosevelt's union of openness of mind and resolution of will the realization of his old dream of the Open Conspiracy, wrote with admiration in 1934, "He is, as it were, a ganglion for reception, expression, transmission, combination and realization, which I take it, is exactly what a modern government ought to be."

If information was the first responsibility of the executive, the second was decision. American Presidents fall into two types: those who like to make decisions, and those who don't. One type designs an administrative system which brings decisions to him; the other, a system which keeps decisions away from him. The second technique, under its more mellifluous designation of "delegation of authority," is regarded with favor in the conventional theory of public administration. Yet, pressed very far, "delegation of authority" obviously strikes at the roots of the Presidency. One can delegate routine, but one cannot delegate any part of the serious presidential responsibility. The whole theory of the Constitution makes the Chief Executive, in the words of Andrew Jackson, "accountable at the bar of public opinion for every act of his Administration," and thus presumably accountable in his own conscience for its every large decision.

Roosevelt, in any case, was pre-eminently of the first type. He evidently felt that both the dignity of his office and the coherence of his administration required that the key decisions be made by him, and not by others before him. He took great pride, for example, in a calculation of Rudolph Forster's that he made at least thirty-five decisions to each one made by Calvin Coolidge. Given this conception of the Presidency, he deliberately organized—or disorganized—his system of command to insure that important decisions were passed on to the top. His favorite technique was to keep grants of authority incomplete, jurisdictions uncertain, charters overlapping. The result of this competitive theory of administration was often confusion and exasperation on the operating level; but no other method could so reliably insure that in a large bureaucracy filled with ambitious men eager for power the decisions, and the power to make them, would remain with the President. This was in part on Roosevelt's side an instinct for self-preservation; in part, too, the temperamental expression of a restless, curious, and untidy personality. Co-existence with disorder was almost the pattern of his life. From the day of his marriage, he had lived in a household of unresolved jurisdictions, and it had never occurred to him to try to settle lines finally as between mother and wife. As Assistant Secretary of the Navy, he had indulged happily in the kind of administrative freewheeling which he was not much concerned to penalize in others now. As his doctor once said, Roosevelt "loved to know everything that was going on and delighted to have a finger in every pie."

Once the opportunity for decision came safely into his orbit, the actual process of deciding was involved and inscrutable. As Tugwell once put it, "Franklin allowed no one to discover the governing principle." He evidently felt that clear-cut administrative decisions would work only if they expressed equally clear-cut realities of administrative competence and vigor. If they did not, if the balance of administrative power would not sustain the decision, then decision would only compound confusion and discredit government. And the actualities of administrative power were to be discovered, not by writing—or by reading—executive orders, but by apprehending through intuition a vast constellation of political forces. His complex administrative sensibility, infinitely subtle and sensitive, was forever weighing questions of personal force, of political timing, of congressional concern, of partisan benefit, of public interest. Situations had to be permitted to develop, to crystallize, to clarify; the competing forces had to vindicate themselves in the actual pull and tug of conflict; public opinion had to face the question, consider it, pronounce upon it—only then, at the long, frazzled end, would the President's intuitions consolidate and precipitate a result.

Though he enjoyed giving the impression of snap decisions, Roosevelt actually made few. The more serious complaint against him was his weakness for postponement. This protraction of decision often appeared a technique of evasion. And sometimes it was. But sometimes dilemmas did not seem so urgent from above as they seemed below—a proposition evidently proved when they evaporated after the passage of time. And Roosevelt, in any case, justified, or rationalized, delay in terms of his own sense of timing. He knew from hard experience that a person could not regain health in a day or year; and he had no reason to suppose that a nation would mend any more quickly. "He could watch with enormous patience as a situation developed," wrote his wife, "and would wait for exactly the right moment to act." When people pressed proposals on him, he often answered (as he did to Frank Walker in 1936), "You are absolutely right. . . . It is simply a question of time." The tragedy of the Presidency in his view was the impotence of the President. Abraham Lincoln, Roosevelt said, "was a sad man because he couldn't get it all at once. And nobody can." He was responding informally to an important young questioner. "Maybe you would make a much better President than I have. Maybe you will, some day. If you ever sit here, you will learn that you cannot, just by shouting from the housetops, get what you want all the time."

Yet his caution was always within an assumption of constant advance. "We must keep the sheer momentum from slacking up too much," he told Colonel House in 1934, "and I have no intention of relinquishing the offensive." Woodrow Wilson had given him a cyclical conception of social change in America. Roosevelt told Robert H. Jackson that he had once suggested that Wilson withhold part of his reform program for his second term. Wilson replied in substance: We do not know that there will be a second term, and, if there is, it will be less progressive and constructive than the first. American history shows that a reform administration comes to office only once in every twenty years, and that its forward impulse does not outlast one term. Even if the same party and persons remain in power, they become complacent in a second term. "What we do not accomplish in the first term is not likely to be accomplished at all." (When Roosevelt told this story to his press conference in the first year of his second term, he lengthened the period of possible accomplishment from four to eight years.)

This technique of protraction was often wildly irritating to his subordinates, enlisted passionately on one side or another of an argument and perceiving with invincible clarity the logic of one or another course. It was equally irritating to his opponents, who enjoyed the advantages of over-simplification which come from observation without responsibility. But the President's dilatory tactics were, in a sense, the means by which he absorbed country-wide conflict of pressures, of fears, of hopes. His intelligence was not analytical. He did not systematically assess pros and cons in his own mind. What for others might be an interior dialogue had to be externalized for Roosevelt; and it was externalized most conveniently by hearing strong exponents of divergent viewpoints. Listening amiably to all sides, watching the opposing views undergo the test of practice, digesting the evidence, he gradually felt his way toward a conclusion. And even this would not often be clear-cut. "He hated to make sharp decisions between conflicting claims for power among his subordinates," noted Francis Biddle, "and decided them, almost always, in a spirit of arbitration: each side should have part of the morsel." Quite often, he ordered the contestants to work out their own compromise, as in NRA and on farm policy. In this connection he liked to cite Al Smith: "He said if you can get the parties into one room with a big table and make them take their coats off and put their feet up on the table, and give each one of them a good cigar, you can always make them agree."

With the conclusion, however reached, a new phase began. When Garner once tried to argue after Roosevelt had made up his mind, the President said, "You tend to your office and I'll tend to mine." ("I didn't take offense at that," said Garner, "because he was right.") "You could fight with Roosevelt and argue with him up to a certain point," said Morgenthau, "—but at no time during his waking hours was he anything else but a ruler." Wayne Coy, who was a Roosevelt assistant for some years, observed that one could say exactly what one thought to Roosevelt, so long as he was saying only "in my judgment" or "I think." When he said "The President thinks," the time for discussion was over. To another assistant, James Rowe, who insisted that he should do something a particular way, Roosevelt said, "I do not have to do it your way and I will tell you the reason why. The reason is that, although they may have made a mistake, the people of the United States elected me President, not you."

Often he announced his decisions with bravado. He liked to tell advisers, "I'm going to spring a bombshell," and then startle them with novel proposals—or rather with proposals novel to them, not perhaps to another set of advisers. "He delights in surprises—clever, cunning and quick," said Hugh Johnson. "He likes to shock friends as well as enemies with something they never expected." But he seems rarely to have supposed that any particular decision was in a final sense correct, or even terribly important. "I have no expectation of making a hit every time I come to bat. What I seek is the highest possible batting average." He remembered Theodore Roosevelt's saying to him, "If I can be right 75 per cent of the time I shall come up to the fullest measure of my hopes." "You'll have to learn that public life takes a lot of sweat," he told Tugwell, "but it doesn't need to worry you. You won't always be right, but you mustn't suffer from being wrong. That's what kills people like us." After all, Roosevelt said, suppose a truck driver were doing your job; 50 per cent of his decisions would be right on average. "You aren't a truck driver. You've had some preparation. Your percentage is bound to be higher." And he knew that the refusal to decide was itself a form of decision. "This is very bad," he said to Frances Perkins, "but one thing is sure. We have to do something. We have to do the best we know how to do at the moment." Then, after a pause: "If it doesn't turn out right, we can modify it as we go along."

This dislike of firm commitments, this belief in alternatives, further reduced the significance of any single decision. As Miss Perkins observed, "He rarely got himself sewed tight to a program from which there was no turning back." The very ambiguity of his scheme of organization—the overlapping jurisdictions and duplicated responsibilities—made flexibility easy. If things started to go bad, he could reshuffle people and functions with speed which would have been impossible in a government of clear-cut assignments and rigid chains of command. Under the competitive theory, he always retained room for administrative maneuver.

Only a man of limitless energy and resource could hold such a system together. Even Roosevelt at times was hard put to keep it from flying apart. But he did succeed, as no modern President has done, in concentrating the power of executive decision where the Constitution intended it should be. "I've never known any President," said W. M. Kiplinger, "who was as omnipresent as this Roosevelt." "Most people acting for Roosevelt were messenger boys," said Ed Flynn. "He really made his own decisions."

ELECTION YEAR—1936

AMERICANS soon had an opportunity to express their opinion of F.D.R. Nineteen thirty-six was an election year. To many people, so much had happened since March 1933, it was hard to remember the Presidency in the hands of anyone other than F.D.R. To most of us, there wasn't much doubt that Roosevelt would be re-elected. There was no one of any stature within the Democratic party to give him any real competition for the nomination. There were some disgruntled Democrats, such as Al Smith, who had turned against the New Deal and Roosevelt, but none of them presented a serious challenge.

The Republicans had a choice among former President Hoover, Senators Borah and Vandenberg, Colonel Frank Knox, publisher of the Chicago *Daily News,* and Governor Alf Landon of Kansas. Landon, not entering the primaries or really fighting for the nomination, won it quite easily; Knox was chosen as his running mate. Their slogans for the campaign were "Stop Roosevelt," and "The Holy Crusade for Liberty."

F.D.R. formally accepted the renomination by the Democrats in Philadelphia on June 27, and John Garner was chosen as his running mate again.

MARQUIS CHILDS

CAMPAIGN*

ONCE EVERY two or three decades comes an election that is for the party in power no more than a high-spirited picnic. Such was the campaign of 1936. If Mr. Roosevelt's political enemies had wanted to make it impossible for him to be defeated, they proceeded on exactly the right course. The background was the unbelievably inept Liberty League with its ermine-and-emeralds dinner at the Mayflower Hotel in Washington. Sage old Jack Garner said when it was all over that the Democratic party needn't have spent a cent, needn't have made a single speech. It was all done by an opposition that lacked any understanding of the temper of the American people.

From the beginning a buoyant sense of confidence ran through the

* From Marquis Childs's *I Write from Washington* (New York, Harper, 1942).

Democratic party. At Philadelphia in June the emirs and the pashas of the city machines gathered for what would be a roistering ratification meeting. They were all there—Hague of New Jersey, Kelly and Nash of Chicago, Pendergast of Missouri, Crump of Tennessee, and the lesser figures—to make as much noise as possible. They knew which side their political bread was buttered on. The vast expenditures of the New Deal had put into their hands power they had hitherto scarcely dreamed of.

A political convention, even when there is a real contest in sight, is a curious institution. This one was purely circus, a circus with only one act and that act a set piece out of the origins of American political history. Yet it took an orthodox five days padded with traditional gestures to build up to that ancient climax.

Spreading their tents, surrounded by their retinues, the emirs and the pashas were prepared to enjoy this comfortable occasion. In the Bellevue-Stratford, in the Ritz-Carlton, in the Benjamin Franklin, they set up headquarters where whisky and good will were dispensed with equal liberality. To fill in the dull hours they gossiped with each other, moving from one royal suite to another like reigning monarchs gathered for a coronation. They were formidable men. They controlled millions of votes and votes were power. You approached them with respect and caution.

In certain respects Tom Pendergast of Kansas City was the most formidable of them all. A thick, squat man with a head set solidly on a short bull neck, he moved with commanding dignity through crowded hotel lobbies. I had been assigned to do a roundup story on the bosses. "Let's get them all in," said O. K. Bovard, then managing editor of the *Post-Dispatch.* "Let's show what all this is based on." But I was to omit Pendergast who was to have special treatment from Spencer McCulloch of the St. Louis staff. There were several reasons why I was to leave out the Missouri boss, one of them being that Pendergast had sworn to knock me down on sight, and he was a man of his word.

That had come out of an encounter a year before. I had seen him off on the maiden crossing of the *Normandie,* it being one of his specialties to make the first eastward crossing on each new luxury liner. Hints of the scandal that was to dethrone him were already in the air and I followed him from his apartment in the Waldorf-Astoria Towers to the boat to ask some pointed questions. At the hotel he had been belligerent. "Yes, I told O'Malley to approve that insurance deal, and what're you going to do about it?" he growled.

At the boat it was different. For one thing I brought up to his suite Comte Bertrand de Jouvenel of *Paris-Soir* who was making the round trip on the great, gaudy new boat. Pendergast and the very blond Mrs. Pendergast were ensconced in the living room of their suite which was almost literally filled with flowers, orchids and lilies of the valley, expensive flowers. This was Pendergast, the Maharajah of Missouri, in all his glory.

Under Bertrand's suave, flattering manner, his charm turned on full force, they both expanded. De Jouvenel had come on board with a small trunk full of books on American politics. I had advised him to forget about them and concentrate during the four-day crossing on the massive little man who was in himself an encyclopedia of American political practice.

"I am told," said De Jouvenel, "that you are the ruler of Missouri, Mr. Pendergast. Can you tell me how it is that you do it?"

From an American, Pendergast might have taken the question as an effrontery, as *lèse majesté*. But this was a foreigner. You could see him turning it over in his mind.

"Well, I'll tell you how I do it," he said with a look of pride on his face. "It's a very simple thing when you come down to it. There's people that need things, lots of 'em, and I see to it that they get 'em. I go to my office on South Main Street in Kansas City at seven o'clock in the morning and I stay there when I'm in town till about six o'clock at night and during that time I see maybe two hundred, maybe three hundred people. One needs a half a ton of coal. Another woman's gotta get a job for her boy. I see to it that they get those things. That's all there is to it."

There was more in the same vein as the old man grew expansive. Set against the background of the orchids and the lilies of the valley, the amboina and macassar modern fittings of the B-deck suite, it made a wonderful story and I rushed off the boat just before sailing to write it. If he had seen it cold when he returned a few weeks later, Pendergast might have taken it in his stride. But one of his henchmen back in Missouri must have radioed to him the full text of the story. When I saw De Jouvenel in Paris some months later he told me that on the following morning while he was being shaved in the barbershop, Pendergast had descended on him, making wild and threatening gestures and brandishing a sheaf of radiograms. Poor Bertrand never quite understood the wrath of the ruler of Missouri. That was the reason I gave Boss Tom a wide berth at the Philadelphia convention.

There was as yet no sign of his dissolution. He was riding high and so were all the others. They had come into the promised land and they proposed to stay there; forever, if that were possible.

President Roosevelt arrived on a special train from Washington to be the star of that last and anticlimactic act. And so great was his histrionic ability, his sense of timing, his sense of crowd reaction, that he converted a foregone conclusion into something like a triumph. The crowd, a hundred thousand or more, stretched away into the darkness of Franklin Field, cheering wildly at each pause, as though the roar out of the warm, sticky night came from a single throat.

That was the beginning of a big succession of triumphs, of roaring crowds, of streets full of cheering people. The President himself could scarcely have had any illusions as to the outcome of the campaign. He is too shrewd a politician, too keen a judge of trends and tempers, to have failed to realize that it was a walkaway.

At Cleveland the Republicans had nominated Governor Alf Landon of Kansas, a pleasant, cheerful man who had been waiting in the proper expectant attitude for the lightning to strike. The truth was that the really ambitious men in the party, men like Vandenberg of Michigan, had ducked the nomination. They sensed that it spelt not merely defeat but disaster. The contest in Cleveland was almost as lame as the one at Philadelphia. There were men who wanted the honor but none with any weight. Landon, looking discomfited and out of place in the glare of the floodlights and the popping of the flash bulbs, was Hobson's choice.

President Roosevelt set out in early October on a major campaign tour that was to take him as far west as Sheridan, Wyoming. The atmosphere on the ten-car campaign train that rolled out of Union Station in Washington was a gala one. The President knew that he was going to like this expedition. His campaign technique had been perfected over the years until it was almost second nature with him. Moreover, he was to visit the fiefdoms of his chief lieutenants and he knew that everywhere a royal welcome was being prepared.

Perhaps no man in American political history had ever started on a campaign under a more fortunate augury. The city bosses were preparing to put on a kind of popularity contest, each one trying to outdo the other. Earlier in Jersey City, Mayor Hague had turned out the town and half the state in an imitation of a Roman triumph. From the moment that the procession of cars rolled out of the Holland Tunnel the thunder of bombs assaulted the ear, and the whole city under a cloudless blue sky seemed one mass of flag-waving humanity. Hague, an iron-jawed master of ceremonies, rode in the presidential car with the President to Hague's great public hospital and clinic in the center of the city that Hague regarded, with the simple possessive sense of a medieval baron, as his city.

The train rolled westward. Denver was big. St. Louis, on the return, was colossal. But it remained for Mayor Kelly in Chicago to put on an act that made everything else look like a halfhearted rehearsal. In the early evening the President rode for five miles in an open car through streets so crowded that only a narrow lane was left. In spite of the protests of the Secret Service, people had been allowed to swarm off the curbs and it was all that the motorcycle police could do to force a way through for the presidential cavalcade.

This was King Crowd. They were out to have a large time and they had it. Every kind of band—bagpipes, piano accordions, jazz, fife-and-drum, bugle corps—lined the narrow lane of humanity through which the presidential party passed. As the parade turned off Michigan Boulevard into West Madison Street the mass of people became denser and noisier. They shrieked from rooftops; they sang and danced; they leaned from tenement windows and loft windows to wave and shout. And all the time a rain of torn paper fluttered down, like gray snow in the half-lighted streets.

If King Crowd had its hero, it also had its hated and despised foe. Not the least remarkable thing about this extraordinary demonstration was the hostility shown toward the Chicago *Tribune,* and, in a lesser degree, toward William Randolph Hearst's Chicago *Herald-Examiner.* Because news photographers with their cameras clung to the outside of nearly every car, the crowd could spot the press. "Where's the *Tribune?*" "Down with the *Tribune!*" "To Hell with the *Tribune!*" These shouts were heard along the entire line of march but particularly in the slum areas on West Madison Street.

King Crowd in the streets was remarkable, but the real spectacle was at the stadium where the President was to deliver his address. The entire front of the great hulking building was illuminated with huge calcium flares that threw an eerie blue light for blocks around. As the presidential party arrived, earsplitting bombs burst overhead and the crowd, a hundred thousand strong, surged up in an almost irresistible tide. Sweating police struggled to keep a way clear so that the President's car could be driven into the stadium. When he appeared on the platform a blare of sound swept up and for a moment seemed to overwhelm him by its intensity. For once the composure of this master of crowds appeared shaken and it was not until he began to speak that he slipped into his customary confident manner.

In the course of this tremendous outpouring so well prepared by Mayor Kelly there was evident that iconology which was to manifest itself many times again. All along the line of march photographs and drawings of President Roosevelt were held up on sticks and poles, waved frantically as he passed. Back again on the campaign train the Secret Service men who had ridden on the running board of his car looked as though they had been through a football scrimmage, their clothes torn and bedraggled. They admitted it was the worst experience they had ever been through.

A campaign train is like nothing else under the sun. It is a transcontinental sound wagon, a glorified road company of the greatest show on earth, a traveling convention of politicians and minor prophets. Around the voice and the personality in the last car the whole machine revolves. Each climax is built up to his appearance. For the thirty or thirty-five reporters on the train, and especially for the press association men, it is a grueling, exhausting grind.

Yet it has its compensations. If there is a good crowd on board you can be sure of something diverting or something funny every minute of the day. The candidate himself is likely to supply a good many laughs. Roosevelt did this deliberately. He knew that back in the press car we were parodying the perfection of his technique. In the two dining cars were loud speakers, and for ordinary whistle stops most correspondents did not get off the train to go back to the rear platform but heard the speech via the loud speaker.

The little drama was almost always the same. When the microphones on the rear platform were switched on, after the train had ground to a stop, you could hear the murmur of the crowd, a vast buzzing noise, punctuated here and there by shrill cries and shouts. Then, as Roosevelt emerged from the door of the car onto the platform, on the arm of his son Jimmy or escorted, perhaps, by a local politician, the noise of the crowd would swell to a roar, here and there individual voices carrying over the roar, "We want Roosevelt," "We're for you, Mr. Roosevelt . . ." Customarily a local bigwig, the congressman from the district, or the governor, would gallop through a conventional introduction full of loud encomiums. Then the roar again, and Roosevelt waiting until it died down, his infallible sense of timing . . . "My friends, I'm happy to be here in ——. The last time I was here was ——. I see your —— looked excellent as I came along. . . ."

We back in the dining car knew this formula so well that someone would invariably supply a facetious name or a facetious date well in advance of the benign voice out of the loud speaker. Another device of the old master was to remind his audience that at some time in the past one or more of his relatives had been connected with local history, usually the settling of the place. It was difficult to believe that so many Roosevelts and Delanos could have been in so many different places.

The universe within a universe being drawn across the continent in slightly shabby Pullman cars was a center for ceaseless gossip and rumor. We had in the end car one of the most extraordinary figures of our time who was engaged in exhibiting himself to millions of people in the midst of that greatest of all American institutions, a presidential election. With him was his wife, herself no mean public figure. It was about these two that most of the gossip centered. We watched them lead their curious public lives and we speculated endlessly about their private lives. Every scrap of information, every rumor, every report, became a part of the legend of these two principals.

They were surrounded by lesser characters who took on importance and coloration from their proximity to the principals. Marvin McIntyre, wraith-like, his voice husky with fatigue, would play poker or bridge until five or six in the morning back in one of the press cars; then, cheerful as a cricket, would greet the local politicians who came on board at the first stop of the day. Judge Rosenman, the ubiquitous Sammy the Rose, was one of the speech writers on the train. Senator Wheeler of Montana, so soon to be an enemy, was part of the entourage for a time; he was afraid that Roosevelt was being too timid. Jimmy, the ebullient, the glad-faced, the smiling, the hand-shaking Jimmy, was on board and so was his wife, the gentle Betsy. This was an easy, comfortable family excursion.

The train wound back through the Middle West, through Michigan where in each industrial city thousands of men and women stood along the railroad tracks just to catch a glimpse of the President. But of course, said the wise old heads on the train, he would never carry Michigan. What was it they said about the visitation of politicians? People would come out to look certainly; they would come out to look at a dead whale on a flatcar. That was what the knowing correspondents said and we tended to agree with them. Look at the crowds that turned out to see Al Smith.

In Detroit, in Cadillac Square, was the same huge, yelling, roaring, almost uncontrollable crowd, or a Detroit version of it; the same struggling police lines, the same wild, frenzied cheering, the same smile from Roosevelt, the same easy, almost casual, wave of his hand. We were weary of crowds, we in the press cars. There had been no opportunity to service the Pullmans. Water flowed from the tap in trickles. The lights were a dim blur.

The contrast with Landon was painful. He had apparently never realized that campaigning in the era of the news reel and the radio calls for a technique as deliberate as that of a Hollywood star. You could be homely and homespun but if you didn't know how to put it across you looked merely inept and foolish. Landon was utterly unprepared for the fierce white light that beat on him after his nomination, just as he was unprepared to make the vital decisions that are called for each day in a national race.

Briefly, I was on the Landon train where the atmosphere was sober and uncertain. We went to Portland, Maine, for a fling at the Maine electorate just before Maine's presidential balloting (old saw: "As Maine goes, so goes the Nation"). I haven't the slightest recollection what Landon talked about. I only remember feeling pained at realizing how badly the Republicans managed these things. The rally was held in a baseball park outside of Portland and the speaker's stand had been constructed at what would be approximately center field. This left most of the audience, in the grandstand and the bleachers, removed by a considerable distance from the candidate. And about the time the speaker was to mount the rostrum a thick fog rolled in from the sea. Poor Landon might as well have been speaking from the bottom of the ocean for all the personal relationship he established with his listeners. As he began to speak, hedged in by a battery of microphones, two or three news photographers climbed a two by four not ten feet away and aimed at him. It wobbled uncertainly with their weight and Landon, glancing up from his manuscript, whispered several times audibly, "Get down from there, get down, I tell you!" He had the unhappy look of a man who has just taken his seat in the dental chair for what is certain to be a long and painful ordeal.

There were no amateurs in the Roosevelt camp. The President finished his strenuous tour in a warm glow of self-confidence, with the roars of the crowd still echoing from far out across America. It had been as successful as anyone had dared to hope and yet the strange thing was that, removed a little from the tumult and the shouting, it was difficult to realize why it had all happened. What made the enthusiasm of the tour seem all the more extraordinary was the fact that only by stretching the meaning of the phrase could Roosevelt's talks be called political speeches. They were more like the friendly sermons of a bishop come to make his quadrennial diocesan call. Bishop Roosevelt reported on the excellent state of health enjoyed throughout this vast diocese, particularly as compared with the miserable state that had prevailed before he took high office.

This was the central theme of almost every talk he made. The issues of the campaign and the policies to be followed in the future were touched upon only incidentally, if at all. The President promised crop insurance and crop control of some sort. He told the motor manufacturers that they must increase the annual wage paid to their workers through "planning." He said that work relief was important. But other than this he scarcely mentioned issues. And almost invariably he referred to his Republican opposition as one would speak of the forces of darkness, the embodiment of an almost abstract evil, and yet tolerantly as of an inevitable counterpoise to the good life for which he, the President, spoke. These forces of darkness had been beaten by the New Deal Saint George, and the President assumed in his talks that of course no one would be so deluded as to invite the dragon back again. Sometimes he asked the direct question of his audiences—do you want the powers of reaction in office again? Always a roaring chorus of noes came back.

For the last day or two Jim Farley joined the caravan. The meaning of the crowds and the cheers and the rain of torn-up telephone books had not escaped the big fellow. We sat with him in a drawing room on the last afternoon and talked it over. He was in a jovial mood. The big expanse of his bald head glistened and the tempo of his gum chewing was if anything faster than normal. Big Jim had worked hard for this. It was all over, he said. Nothing that the President could do or say in the two and a half weeks that remained could lose the election for him. The only question now was how large his majority would be, and although Farley had not yet got down to predicting states, he was certain that it would be large.

The Roosevelt campaign of that year was essentially Farley's kind of campaign. There were those within the Roosevelt inner circle who believed that issues should be discussed; the people should be educated on the big questions that the country faced. Henry Wallace was one of those who thought there should be more discussion of the state of the nation. But the practical politicians scoffed at such suggestions. A campaign, they said, was how you got elected. It had nothing to do with education. Hadn't the Republicans talked about the full dinner pail for forty years or more and got away with it four times out of five? This was Roosevelt prosperity, New Deal prosperity, and the Farleys in the party proposed to ride it through.

That was what Roosevelt did in the autumn of 1936. After the Middle West we went to New England. Same company, same show, same crowd. At Providence they swarmed like ants over the capitol plaza and the approaches to it. Boston Common just at dusk appeared to be packed solid with humanity. Motoring through Cambridge in the early darkness we heard a strange and alien sound. From the sons of Harvard on the curbstone came loud boos for that other son of Harvard in the front car. He was all those things the fathers of young Harvard men called him; a renegade, a traitor to his class.

We had been motoring since eight o'clock in the morning in a long furious procession that frequently got out of control of state police; fighting the crowds through mill towns all of the way. Yet the principal appeared as blithe and confident that evening before a huge crowd in Worcester as though it had been the first speech of the day instead of the twenty-first. We conceded that he could take it.

Curiosities were always turning up. In the course of that motor tour of New England a bland, supremely self-centered, young Englishman joined the party as a reporter, of sorts, to have a look at the quaint American system of electioneering. His name was Randolph Churchill and he was the son of a Tory politician named Winston Churchill. Young Randolph had inherited a generous share of his father's poise and self-assurance which American newspapermen found rather hard to take. On the train one night, the motoring over for the day, Heywood Broun put Churchill through a mild hazing, but so bland was this young aristocrat's exterior that it had no effect whatsoever. He was a little irritating and the next day the boys saw to it that as the hours wore on he was relegated to cars successively further back in the procession, until by midafternoon he might just as well not have been with the party at all.

This was one kind of campaigning. That same fall I was to see another kind. On orders from Bovard I sampled Norman Thomas's technique. If the Roosevelt campaign was almost straight showmanship of a very high order, the Thomas tour was a political Chautauqua. Norman and his courageous wife traveled without benefit of retinue, he in an upper berth, she in the lower. They traveled that way for weeks on end, Norman speaking from twelve to fourteen times a day, with a kind of endurance that only politicians must be endowed with. At each stop they would be met by earnest disciples who would take them in hand for the day's events. Often Thomas talked at schools and public forums, taking advantage of an audience wherever he could find one.

Almost invariably he gave them a rapid-fire harangue. The New Deal, built on the corrupt city machines, was no more suited to save the country than the reactionary G.O.P. They were both corrupt and dead, and only Socialism could save democracy, Thomas told his listeners, his voice growing hoarse, his talk sounding more like a scratchy phonograph record as he repeated it for the sixth or seventh time. His audiences were of course small. Six or seven hundred students or teachers, crowded into the auditorium of Antioch College at Yellow Springs, Ohio, was the high mark of a day of speechmaking in Ohio. Through the party organization and through the funds the party could command, through the prestige of his high office and the magnetic appeal of his personality, Roosevelt reached millions directly and on the air while the Socialist, Norman Thomas, spoke to thousands.

In the closing days the President carried his campaign to Pennsylvania. Pennsylvania was considered a doubtful state. In Pennsylvania lived the Republican party's great angel, Joseph Pew of the Sun Oil Company, who was out to elect Landon at whatever cost. But the Democrats too had an angel in Pennsylvania. On the platform with Roosevelt at Harrisburg sat John L. Lewis. I seem to recall that he had a slightly possessive air as though this had been a *fête de Versailles* that he had ordered and paid for, as indeed he had. I am frank to add, however, that this may have been merely an interpretation read into that grim and mysterious physiognomy in the light of the later knowledge that its owner had given a half-million dollars out of the United Mine Workers' Treasury to the Democratic war chest. For that matter John L. Lewis always looks possessive, and with good reason, for he has made the largest trade-union in the United States his personal property. On the platform on that blowy day, with his miner cohorts in the crowd before him, John L. may well have dreamed dreams of imperial grandeur. This was Franklin Roosevelt's inning. John L. Lewis's would come next.

One of the extraordinary things about a political campaign is the way in which the partisans are able to hypnotize themselves. Anyone with the slightest knowledge of what the American people were saying and thinking could have known that Landon hadn't a Chinaman's chance. Yet he himself was persuaded of his victory and so were many of the people around him. Weren't the newspapers for him?

The Republicans in the closing week made stupid mistakes that I believe Landon would not have made if the ultimate decisions had not long since passed out of his reach. For one thing there were the pay-roll notices threatening workers with the loss of their jobs if Roosevelt should win. Similarly the Social Security pay-roll deductions were made to seem part of an evil conspiracy to curtail the average man's income. Anyone with ordinary political judgment should have known that that kind of thing would produce an effect exactly opposite from the one intended.

It gave Roosevelt a chance to end his campaign in a blaze of emotion. Landon had had a huge rally earlier in Madison Square Garden. Of necessity Roosevelt's meeting had to be half again as big and twice as loud—and it was. They hate me, said Franklin Roosevelt of the rich and the mighty, and I welcome their hatred. The packed Garden exploded in a steamy torrent of sound. Only in this last speech did the President open up the New Deal stops—housing, work relief, social security—promising that these gains would be held and new goals set.

On the night of the great victory the clan Roosevelt was gathered at Hyde Park. Forty-six states in the Roosevelt column, that was something that the simplest mind could understand. Even before midnight the wise-money boys were looking for a place in the Roosevelt van, repenting their sins of omission and commission. William Randolph Hearst telephoned from California to tell the ebullient Jimmy how astonished and happy he was that the man he had sought to defeat through every kind of editorial trick and incessant salvos of type a foot high was actually the choice of the American people and by so overwhelming a majority.

In this moment of triumph all the oddly assorted elements within the Democratic party sang hosannahs. The President in his campaign had covered them all in; no one had been excluded. And nothing had been altered by the great tide of votes rolled up by the personality and the voice and the hope they implied.

THE PRESS AND THE CAMPAIGN

MOST OF the press in the big cities was for Landon. Publisher William Randolph Hearst said: "I'll stake my reputation as a political prophet on Landon's victory," and ran editorials suggesting that the Communists were, under instructions from Moscow, going to vote for Roosevelt. This line of attack gathered momentum during the campaign.

And the news magazine the *Literary Digest* said, "Our poll indicates that Landon will win 32 states, 54 per cent of the popular vote and 370 electoral votes."

The New York *Times* stayed with Roosevelt, and among the small-circulation papers there was a standoff between Roosevelt and Landon. Among the columnists, Walter Lippmann was for Landon, Westbrook Pegler for F.D.R. And while the polls of Gallup and Roper began to register a swing to the Democrats, predicting a sizable victory, that "disturber of the peace," H. L. Mencken, the Baltimore *Evening Sun* columnist, announced, with customary boldness, "They can beat him [F.D.R.] with a Chinaman."

H. L. MENCKEN

THE CHOICE TOMORROW*

NEVERTHELESS, and despite all Hell's angels, I shall vote for the Hon. Mr. Landon tomorrow. To a lifelong Democrat, of course, it will be something of a wrench. But it seems to me that the choice is one that genuine Democrats are almost bound to make. On the one side are all the basic principles of their party, handed down from its first days and tried over and over again in the fires of experience; on the other side is a gallimaufry of transparent quackeries, puerile in theory and dangerous in practice. To vote Democratic this year it is necessary, by an unhappy irony, to vote for a Republican. But to vote with the party is to vote for a gang of mountebanks who are no more Democrats than a turkey buzzard is an archangel.

This exchange of principles, with the party labels unchanged, is naturally confusing, but it is certainly not so confusing that it goes unpenetrated.

* From the Baltimore *Evening Sun,* Nov. 2, 1936, as reprinted in H. L. Mencken's *A Carnival of Buncombe* (Baltimore, Johns Hopkins Press, 1956).

Plenty of Republicans who believe sincerely in a strong federal government are going to vote tomorrow for the Hon. Mr. Roosevelt, and plenty of Democrats who believe sincerely in the autonomy of the states and a rigid limitation of the federal power are going to vote, as I shall, for the Hon. Mr. Landon. Whether the shift that confronts us will be permanent remains to be seen. But while it lasts it is manifestly very real, and those who let party loyalties blind them to its reality will be voting very foolishly.

The issue tends to be confused by a distrust of both presidential candidates, inevitable under the circumstances. There are those who believe that the Hon. Mr. Roosevelt, if he is re-elected, will abandon the socialistic folderol that he has been advocating since 1933 and go back to the traditional program of his party, and there are those who believe that the Hon. Mr. Landon, if elected, will quickly turn out to be only another Harding, Hoover or McKinley. Both notions, it seems to me, represent little more than a naïve sort of wishful thinking. Landon, I am convinced, will actually stay put, and so will Roosevelt. Roosevelt, to be sure, has flopped once, but he has now gone too far down his new road to turn back again.

The defense commonly made of him is that he confronted, in 1933, an unprecedented situation, and so had to resort to new and even revolutionary devices in dealing with it. There is no truth in either half of that theory. The situation that he confronted differed only quantitatively, and not at all qualitatively, from others that had been confronted in the past. And of all the devices he employed in dealing with it the only ones that really worked were those that had been tried before.

I am aware that there are many undoubtedly intelligent persons who believe otherwise. The fact, indeed, is not to be wondered at, for the intelligent, like the unintelligent, are responsive to propaganda, and all the propaganda since 1933 has been running one way. But it still remains historically true that all the major problems before the country when Hoover blew up were intrinsically simple and familiar ones, and it still remains true that those which were not tackled in tried and rational ways still remain unsolved.

All the rest was quackery pure and unadulterated. The situation of the country was exaggerated in precisely the same way that a quack doctor exaggerates the illness of his patient, and for exactly the same reason. And the showy and preposterous treatments that were whooped up had no more virtue in them, at bottom, than his pills and liniments. We then and there entered upon an era of quackery that yet afflicts and exhausts the country. We'll not get clear of it until all the quacks are thrown out.

Whether that will happen tomorrow I do not know. The probabilities, as anyone can see, are largely against it. But soon or late the business will have to be undertaken, and the longer it is delayed the more difficult it will become. For people in the mass soon grow used to anything, including even being swindled. There comes a time when the patter of the quack becomes as natural and as indubitable to their ears as the texts of Holy Writ, and when that time comes it is a dreadful job debamboozling them.

The *bona fides* of the Hon. Mr. Roosevelt was pretty generally assumed in the first days of his Presidentiad. He was, to be sure, excessively melodramatic, but observers remembered that he was a Roosevelt, and that a talent for drama was thus in his blood. Even his closing of the banks—in retrospect, a highly dubious measure—was accepted without serious protest, even by bankers. The NRA, when it was first announced, seemed a plausible if somewhat violent remedy for admitted evils, and most of his other devices of those days got the same tolerant reception.

But as his administration closed its first year, and he gradually extended and elaborated his program, it began to be evident that he was going far beyond the borders of the reasonable, and that the theory underlying some of his major operations, as it was expounded by his principal agents, was becoming increasingly fantastic and absurd. Bit by bit, the purpose of restoring the country to its normal manner and ease of life was submerged in the purpose of bringing in a brummage Utopia, fashioned in part out of the idiotic hallucinations of the cow states and in part out of the gaudy evangel of Moscow. And simultaneously, the welfare of the American people as a whole began to be forgotten in a special concern for special classes and categories of them, all of manifestly inferior status and all willing to vote right for goods in hand.

In brief, the New Deal became a political racket, and that is what it is today—that and nothing more. Its chief practical business is to search out groups that can be brought into the Hon. Jim Farley's machine by grants out of the public treasury, which is to say, out of the pockets of the rest of us. To serve that lofty end the national currency has been debased, the national credit has been imperiled and a crushing burden has been put on every man who wants to pay his own way in the world and asks only to be let alone. The excuse that a grave emergency justified such pillage is now abandoned. The emergency is past, but the pillage goes on.

At tomorrow's plebiscite this grandiose and excessively dangerous Tammanyizing of the country will come to judgment, with the chances, as I have said, in favor of its ratification. That it will be supported heartily by all its beneficiaries goes without saying. Every dole-bird in the country, of whatever sort, will certainly vote for it. It will get the suffrage of all the gimme pseudo-farmers in the Middle West, of all the half-witted share-croppers in the South, of all the professional uplifters and of all the job-holders on Farley's ever-swelling roll. It will be whooped up by every politician who lives and thrives by promising to turn loose A in B's corn-field. It will have the kindly aid of all other varieties of professional mes-siahs, ranging from the fantoddish prophets of millenniums to the down-right thieves.

Will there be enough of them to ratify it? Probably not. It will meet also some support by honest if deluded men and women. Thousands of them, I gather, are in the ranks of the labor organizations. They have been told that the New Deal saved them their jobs, which it didn't, and that it will prosper them hereafter, which it won't, and large numbers of them have believed. The actual fact is that they are not, and can never be, the beneficiaries of any such carnival of loot; they can only be its goats. In the long run the cost of the whole show will settle down upon them. In the long run every man and woman who works will have to pay for the upkeep of some Farley heeler who has been taught that working is foolish and unnecessary and even a shade immoral.

The Brain Trust brethren, of course, still promise that all the bills will be sent to the rich. Well, they were so sent in Russia, and paid in full. But when they had been paid, more money was still needed, and it is now being provided by the Russian workers. Living in filthy and miserable dens, and badly fed on poor and monotonous food, they labor under a brutal stretch-out system which yields them the equivalent of ten American dollars a month. That is what Utopia always comes to in the end.

THE NEW DEAL AND THE SUPREME
COURT

TOWARD the middle of 1935 it seemed that the New Deal had won its fight against the Depression and that the Roosevelt reforms were now a permanent part of the country's laws. Business was good, industrial production was up, more people were working, more money was available for investment, stock prices were climbing and corporation dividends were increasing. Political pressures had abated, and everywhere people seemed to be settling back into their traditional attitude toward federal government as something to be debated more or less amiably around election time and then to be left to the politicians, something that one *should* know about but never finds the time to keep tabs on. Happy days were here again!

There were, of course, thunderings on the Right and rumblings on the Left; but in the main these manifestations were confined to relatively small groups—the rarefied circles of financial and industrial command on the one side, and the dedicated partisans of small, doctrinaire political movements on the other. Both sides found effective individual support in the various sectors of American life, but neither achieved any active mass following among the great body of the American people.

But the Roosevelt Administration soon found its whole legislative program threatened, from an area that had been considered almost negligible in the political life of the nation —the federal courts, where a new kind of offensive was being launched against the New Deal. It was not, at first, the kind of action that made front-page headlines; it was, rather, a long series of undramatic little actions conducted according to rules that the ordinary citizens did not understand. But, in their possible consequences, these isolated actions were as important as a national election, for they were to determine whether the New Deal was constitutionally valid.

In 1935 and 1936 such actions in the federal district courts produced more than sixteen hundred injunctions restraining the executive branch of the government from enforcing the enactments of the legislative branch. Never before had the judiciary so freely overruled the Congress and the President; equally remarkable to informed observers was the number of sweeping denunciations of New Deal philosophy that accompanied the judges' decisions. Not surprisingly, therefore, the Administration saw substantial significance in the fact that of the more than 250 district court judges only about one fourth had been appointed by Democratic Presidents.

As the offensive grew, it developed a new technique by which New Deal representation in these cases was effectively eliminated. A corporation, for example, that might wish to have the government restrained from enforcing an onerous federal statute did not itself apply to the court for an injunction, but encouraged its stockholders to seek an injunction restraining the corporation from complying with the law's provisions, on the grounds—as before—that the provisions were unconstitutional.

Eventually, all of this litigation would be adjudged by the Supreme Court, and there the Administration soon found an almost equal readiness to nullify New Deal laws. In 1935 the Court vetoed the government's regulation of the petroleum industry and the National Industrial Recovery Act; in 1936 it invalidated the AAA crop control program and the Guffey Coal Act; and during this period it also ruled unconstitutional a number of state enactments relating to employment practices and social welfare.

To many observers the Court's decisions went far beyond the traditional limits observed by Supreme Court justices in the exercise of their right of judicial review. Critics of the Court pointed out inconsistencies, and even outright contradictions, in several decisions. New Deal partisans went further and charged that the Court had based their decisions on political bias rather than on strict interpretation of the Constitution. Roosevelt himself avoided the question of motivation, but complained that the judges were putting the country back into the "horse-and-buggy days."

Inevitably, some critics called into question the Court's authority to determine the constitutionality of Congressional or Presidential actions. And, indeed, the Constitution does not grant that power to the Supreme Court; but tradition and precedent have amply established it, and no one would seriously suggest that it

be taken away. Nevertheless, the proper limits to the exercise of that function had long been the subject of debate, much of it conducted by judges themselves who advocated most rigorous self-restraint.

Members of the Administration, however, were not encouraged by what they had seen of judicial self-restraint on the part of the conservative majority in the Court. They were well aware that the Constitution afforded Congress several methods of dealing with a frustrating Court. Through legislation the Court's right to rule on the constitutionality of federal legislation could be drastically curtailed; for the Constitution states that in all "the other Cases before mentioned"—that is, other than cases affecting ambassadors, other public ministers and consuls, and those in which a state is a party —"the supreme Court shall have appellate Jurisdiction, both as to Law and Fact, with such Exceptions, and under such Regulations as the Congress shall make."

Further, the Constitution does not say how many justices there may be in the Supreme Court; the Congress may determine that. And through the years the number of judges has several times been changed. In 1789, when the Court was established, the number was six; in 1807 it was raised to seven, in 1837 to nine, in 1863 to ten; in 1866 it was lowered to eight; and in 1869 it was raised to nine.

But a difficult problem remained: On what grounds could they persuade the Congress and the public to support any change in the Court? For some reason the charge that the judges had fallen behind the times did not seem adequate; something more concrete was desired. Advanced age might be an argument, for the judges ranged in age from sixty to seventy-nine in 1935—"nine old men," indeed. Unhappily for that argument, however, the oldest of them, Justice Brandeis, was one of the three judges who regularly sided with the liberal minority—himself and Justices Stone and Cardozo.

The argument that only two of the justices had been appointed by a Democratic President was even weaker, because one of the two was a member of the solid conservative bloc in the Court, while two Republican appointees—Justices Stone and Cardozo—were steadfast liberals.

For the purpose of an outright legislative move to curtail the power of the Court, the record of the Court's decisions might have furnished some support, for it shows, besides many inconsistencies and contradictions, many instances of decisions handed down on a vote of five to four—which opens the question whether the one judge who completed the majority was rightly given the power to determine the disposition of legislation that had been enacted by a large number of elected representatives of the people. But arguments like that are difficult at best; they require many steps in proving them, and Roosevelt knew that brevity is the key to success in public debate.

Roosevelt was not the first President to become embroiled in open dispute with the Supreme Court. Jefferson, Jackson, Lincoln, and Theodore Roosevelt, all had clashed with the Court. Franklin Roosevelt was well informed on the history of the problem that he faced. How he went about solving that problem is presented in the following selection, by James MacGregor Burns.

JAMES MACGREGOR BURNS

COURT PACKING: THE MISCALCULATED RISK*

WAS IT AN omen? The famous Roosevelt luck seemed to forsake the President on the January day in 1937 when he entered his second term. Bursts of cold rain soaked the gay inaugural decorations, furled the sodden flags around their staffs, and drenched dignitaries and spectators alike while they gathered below the Capitol rotunda. The rain drummed on the cellophane that covered Roosevelt's old family Bible, as he stood with upraised hand facing Chief Justice Hughes.

* From James MacGregor Burns's The Lion and the Fox (New York, Harcourt, Brace, 1956).

They eyed each other, the old judge, his wet whiskers quivering in the wind, the resolute President, jaw stuck out. Hughes read the oath with slow and rising emphasis as he came to the words "promise to support the Constitution of the United States." Roosevelt gave the words equal force as he repeated the oath. At this point, he said later, he wanted to cry out, "Yes, but it's the Constitution as *I* understand it, flexible enough to meet any new problem of democracy—not the kind of Constitution your Court has raised up as a barrier to progress and democracy."

The President turned to the rain-spattered pages of his inaugural address. "When four years ago we met to inaugurate a President, the Republic, single-minded in anxiety, stood in spirit here. We dedicated ourselves to the fulfillment of a vision—to speed the time when there would be for all the people that security and peace essential to the pursuit of happiness. We of the Republic pledged ourselves to drive from the temple of our ancient faith those who had profaned it; to end by action, tireless and unafraid, the stagnation and despair of that day. We did those first things first."

But the covenant "with ourselves" did not stop there. "Instinctively we recognized a deeper need—the need to find through government the instrument of our united purpose to solve for the individual the ever-rising problems of a complex civilization. Repeated attempts at their solution without the aid of government had left us baffled and bewildered. For, without that aid, we had been unable to create those moral controls over the services of science which are necessary to make science a useful servant instead of a ruthless master of mankind. To do this we knew that we must find practical controls over blind economic forces and blindly selfish men."

The rain poured down, dripped off Roosevelt's bare head, dulled the cutting edge of some of his sentences. As the intricacies of human relationships increased, he said, so power to govern them also must increase—power to stop evil, power to do good. "The essential democracy of our Nation and the safety of our people depend not upon the absence of power, but upon lodging it with those whom the people can change or continue at stated intervals through an honest and free system of elections." Did the Chief Justice, sitting a few feet away on the President's right, catch the faint warning in the sentence?

The President was turning now to the future. "Shall we pause now and turn our back upon the road that lies ahead?" He looked at the crowd. "Many voices are heard as we face a great decision. Comfort says, 'Tarry a while.' Opportunism says, 'This is a good spot.' Timidity asks, 'How

451

difficult is the road ahead?' " The nation had come far since the days of stagnation. But dulled conscience, irresponsibility, and ruthless self-interest already were reappearing. Here was the challenge to American democracy:

"In this nation I see tens of millions of its citizens—a substantial part of its whole population—who at this very moment are denied the greater part of what the very lowest standards of today call the necessities of life.

"I see millions of families trying to live on incomes so meager that the pall of family disaster hangs over them day by day.

"I see millions whose daily lives in city and on farm continue under conditions labeled indecent by a so-called polite society half a century ago.

"I see millions denied education, recreation, and the opportunity to better their lot and the lot of their children.

"I see millions lacking the means to buy the products of farm and factory and by their poverty denying work and productiveness to many other millions.

"I see one-third of a nation ill-housed, ill-clad, ill-nourished.

"It is not in despair that I paint you that picture. I paint it for you in hope—because the Nation, seeing and understanding the injustice in it, proposes to paint it out. . . .

"To maintain a democracy of effort requires a vast amount of patience in dealing with differing methods, a vast amount of humility. But out of the confusion of many voices rises an understanding of dominant public need. Then political leadership can voice common ideals, and aid in their realization.

"In taking again the oath of office as President of the United States, I assume the solemn obligation of leading the American people forward along the road over which they have chosen to advance. . . ."

BOMBSHELL

Just two weeks later Roosevelt and Hughes faced each other once again— this time in the gracious, brilliantly lighted East Room of the White House. It was the President's annual dinner for the judiciary. At the center of the scene were the President, jauntily waving his cigarette holder to point up his stories, and the great jurist. Both were in a jovial mood; the talk ran fast and free. Around them were banked others of the nation's great— cabinet members, judges, senators, bankers, even the Gene Tunneys.

The jollity barely concealed a certain tension in the air. Key New Deal measures were crowding the Supreme Court's docket. Rumors were running through Washington that Roosevelt, armed with his huge popular endorsement, was aiming some kind of attack on the Court. Besides the President, only a handful present knew the truth of the rumors. Watching Roosevelt and Hughes, Attorney General Cummings wished the secret were out. "I feel too much like a conspirator," he complained to Rosenman. Roosevelt, on the other hand, was probably savoring the irony of the moment. On the eve of a great battle the commander of one side was giving a banquet to his adversaries.

But the President was a bit nervous too. During the next two days he pored over his message to Congress, adding, erasing, shifting phrases and sentences. His main concern was to keep his plan secret; he had not told some of his closest aides. On February 4 he called an extraordinary meeting of Cabinet members and congressional leaders for the following day. Amazed White House stenographers were told to report at 6:30 the next morning to mimeograph documents for this meeting and for a press conference.

Next morning the Cabinet and congressmen waited wonderingly in the long, low-ceilinged Cabinet room. The President was quickly wheeled in. He called out cheery greetings, then turned directly to the business at hand. Announcing his intention to meet the challenge posed by the Court, he read excerpts from his message that would go to Congress in an hour.

Amid dead silence, he outlined his plan. For every Supreme Court justice who failed to quit the bench within six months after reaching seventy, the President would be empowered to appoint a new justice up to a total of six. The message to Congress talked much of judicial efficiency, congestion in the courts, the need for new blood, the problem of injunctions; and the President's bill involved new appointments at the district and circuit court level too. But the crux of the proposal leaped out from the long legal phrases—the power Roosevelt was asking to flank Hughes and his brethren with six New Deal justices.

The meeting was a study in mixed emotions. Ickes was elated that the President had moved at last. Cummings, twiddling his pince-nez with a slightly self-important air, was pleased to have long been a part of the unfolding drama. But the congressional delegation sat as if stunned. Garner and Rayburn said not a word. Robinson, deep concern written on his face, gave a feeble indication of approval. Henry Ashurst, chairman of the Senate Judiciary Committee, must have thought of his heated denial during the campaign that Roosevelt would try to pack the Court, but he loyally spoke out in support of the bill. Speaker Bankhead bore a poker face throughout.

There was virtually no discussion; the President solicited no opinions from his party's leadership. At the end he wheeled off to meet a waiting group of newspapermen. Over this session Roosevelt presided like an impresario. Again and again bursts of laughter punctuated his reading of his message to Congress, as he interpolated telling little points; the President threw his head back and joined in the laughter. Once again he demanded absolute secrecy until the message was released.

Driving back to Capitol Hill from the White House, Garner and his colleagues were still silent. Suddenly Hatton Sumners of Texas, chairman of the House Judiciary Committee, turned to the others. "Boys," he said, "here's where I cash in." The group took the news to Congress with them. By the time the message was read, the cloakrooms were filled with little knots of legislators asking one another, "What do you think of it?" In the first hours it seemed as though the proposal cut through each House, down the middle. Two sons of Texas signalized the extremes. In the House, New Deal Representative Maury Maverick grabbed a mimeographed copy of the bill, scribbled his name on it, and threw it into the bill hopper almost before the reading clerk was finished. In the Senate lobby Garner held his nose with one hand and vigorously shook his turned-down thumb.

A messenger hurried across the plaza to the Supreme Court building. Inside, the justices were hearing an argument. Only Brandeis had heard the news; just before the justices entered the Court, Corcoran, with Roosevelt's consent, had "crashed the sacred robing room" to tell him, and Brandeis had instantly expressed his disapproval. Now a page slipped through the draperies behind the dais and handed a paper to each justice. The attorney at bar, sensing the sudden tension on the bench, paused a moment. Hughes shifted restlessly in his chair, Van Devanter looked grim, Butler seemed to chuckle. But judicial mien quickly reappeared, and proceedings continued.

Blazing headlines carried the news to the people during the afternoon. Next morning, reading the newspapers in bed over his breakfast tray, the President was not surprised at the howls of anguish in the editorial columns. He had expected this; what he was banking on was the approval of the people. As it turned out, the proposal at the outset split the American people neatly in half. Could Roosevelt mobilize a popular majority behind his plan? Could he convert such a majority into congressional action?

The suddenness of Roosevelt's move, the obvious pleasure he found in presenting his handiwork, and the utter secrecy that surrounded its preparation all gave the impression of a proposal that had been hastily cooked up after the election. Actually Roosevelt had been considering judicial reform for over two years.

Even before the Court's all-out attack on the New Deal in 1935 Roosevelt was thinking of enlarging the Court to protect his legislation. That he would not brook judicial opposition on a crucial matter was apparent from the radio address to the nation he planned in the event that the Court found against him in the gold cases. Only the Court's slim vote in his favor turned him from defiance of the Court through presidential proclamation and an appeal to Congress. When the Court voided the NRA and other measures, the President's view that action must be taken steadily hardened.

But what to do? For a while Roosevelt had toyed with the idea of a constitutional amendment. Various types were possible: directly enlarging congressional authority in specific economic and social fields; granting Congress power to re-enact and thus "constitutionalize" a measure voided by the Court; requiring a six to three or even a seven to two vote in the Supreme Court to strike down an act of Congress; setting an age limit on judges or giving them terms instead of appointments for life. Eventually Roosevelt decided against the amendment method. At best it would take too long. More likely, an amendment, even if it won two-thirds majorities in House and Senate, would never hurdle the barriers carefully contrived by the framers of the Constitution—three-quarters of the state legislatures or of state conventions—especially since these assemblies tended to over-represent conservative, small-town interests and attitudes.

"Give me ten million dollars," the President said later, "and I can prevent any amendment to the Constitution from being ratified by the necessary number of states."

Could an act of Congress do the trick? A measure that directly challenged the High Court by trying to curb its power would probably be voided by the Court itself. There was another method, however, that seemed certainly constitutional because it was sanctioned by precedent. This was to enlarge the Court's membership, as previous presidents had done, by inducing Congress to authorize new appointments. At first, packing the Court seemed distasteful to the President, perhaps because the objective would be so transparent. But he kept returning to the idea. He was fascinated by a historical precedent—Asquith's and Lloyd George's threat through the King to pack the House of Lords with new Peers if that chamber refused to bow to the supremacy of the House of Commons.

Clearly the President feared a direct assault on the Court. Perhaps he sensed—as polls indicated—that in late 1935 most of the people opposed restriction on the Court's veto power. The Democratic platform of 1936 had come out only for some "clarifying amendment." During the campaign Hoover and others demanded that the President confirm or deny that he planned to pack the Court. Roosevelt not only ignored the specific question—as a seasoned campaigner would—but he skirted the whole problem of the Supreme Court. Doubtless his silence helped him roll up his great majority—but it also meant that he gained no explicit mandate to act on the Court.

At the first Cabinet meeting after the election Roosevelt raised the Court issue. He expected, he said with mock glumness, that McReynolds would still be on the bench at the age of one hundred and five. An appeal to the people might be necessary. The problem "must be faced," he wrote to Joseph Patterson of the New York *Daily News*. But how to face it? Before Roosevelt left on his cruise to South America, he set Cummings to work in Washington poring over a sheaf of plans for overcoming the nine old men—or at least five of them.

Mulling over various proposals one December morning, Cummings ran across a recommendation that Attorney General—now Justice—McReynolds had made in 1913 that when any federal judge, except Supreme Court justices, failed to retire at the age provided by law, the President should appoint another judge to preside over the Court and to hold precedence over the older one. Why not, thought Cummings, apply the idea to the Supreme Court?

"The answer to a maiden's prayer!" Roosevelt reportedly exclaimed when Cummings brought in his idea. And so it must have seemed. The plan was clearly constitutional. It was, compared with most of the other proposals, quite moderate in character, involving no change in the venerable system of checks and balances. Most important, the plan could be presented to the country as part of a broader program of reconstructing the whole federal judiciary in the name not of liberalism but of greater efficiency and expedition in the courts. And Roosevelt, with his penchant for personalizing the political opposition, must have delighted in the thought of hoisting McReynolds by his own petard.

All that remained was the matter of how to present the plan. Why did Roosevelt insist on almost conspiratorial secrecy? Why did he spring the plan suddenly on Robinson, who would have to manage the fight in the Senate; on Ashurst, who just before had hotly denied that Roosevelt had any plans for packing the Court, on his old progressive ally Norris, on Brandeis and Stone, on Rayburn and Garner, on Farley and Ickes, even on McIntyre and Early? Roosevelt explained to Farley that he feared premature disclosure by the press. This explanation is unconvincing.

Roosevelt was too astute a politician to think that secrecy was worth the price of excluding key leaders from the decision-making conferences. Moreover, Roosevelt himself had leaked the essence of the plan to a *Collier's* writer a few weeks before the announcement.

The explanation lies deeper—deep in Roosevelt's personality. He had won what he considered to be a personal election victory over the Old Guard. Now the Old Guard remained entrenched in the ramparts of the judiciary. The stage was set for a Rooseveltian onslaught against the citadel as exhilarating and triumphant as his rout of the Republicans. He set the stage with his old flair for timing and suspense. His final presentation combined in a curious fashion two Rooseveltian traits—his instinct for the dramatic and his instinct for the adroit and circuitous stratagem rather than the frontal assault.

Both instincts failed him. "Too clever—too damned clever," said one pro-New Deal newspaper. The President's liberal friends were disturbed. Some of them had hoped that Roosevelt would make a direct attack on the Court's conservative veto. Others used his disingenuousness as an excuse to desert the cause. Still others disagreed with his particular plan. Years before, Roosevelt had lamented that reform came slowly because liberals had such difficulty in agreeing on means. His words would fly back to mock him in 1937.

GUERRILLA WARFARE

Battle lines formed quickly but not in a way that was to Roosevelt's liking. He was not surprised that Republicans and conservative Democrats flared up in opposition. This was to be expected. But alarming reports reached the White House from the Senate. Two noted progressives, Burt Wheeler and Hiram Johnson, were opposed. So were Democrats Joseph O'Mahoney of Wyoming, Tom Connally of Texas, Bennett Clark of Missouri, Ed Burke of Nebraska, and a dozen others of the kind of men on whose loyalty the President had counted. And—worst blow of all—Norris. Although in the end he supported the bill, the old Nebraskan, within a few hours of Roosevelt's announcement, said quietly, "I am not in sympathy with the plan to enlarge the Supreme Court."

Something was happening to the Grand Coalition that had carried Roosevelt to his election triumph. Something was happening to the Republicans too. Knowing that their little band in Congress could not overcome the President in a straight party fight, they resolved to stay silent and let the Democrats fight one another. When Hoover, Landon, and other national leaders wanted to rush to the microphone and make the court plan a party issue, congressional Republicans McNary, Borah, and Vandenberg, acting quickly, headed them off. The Liberty League, moribund after November 1936, was silent. Roosevelt found himself aligned not against Republicans but against his own fellow partisans.

"What a grand fight it is going to be!" Roosevelt wrote Creel. "We need everything we have got to put in it!" To visitors he declared confidently that "the people are with me." Were they? Within a few days it was clear that the proposal had struck deep into the complex of American emotions. There was a crescendo of protest. The New York *Herald Tribune* gave seven of its eight front-page columns to the proposal. Patriotic groups moved quickly into action. New England town fathers called mass meetings. Bar associations met and denounced. Mail flooded congressional offices; some senators received over a thousand letters a day. What amazed congressmen was less the amount of opposition than the intensity of it. There was a pervasive element of fear—"fear of the unknown," columnist Raymond Clapper thought—and a deep reverence for the Supreme Court.

Many of the protestants cited their middle-class background, their little property holdings, their fear of labor and radical elements. Events helped sharpen these fears. During the early months of 1937 a rash of sit-down strikes broke out. The picture of grinning, insolent workers barricading factories against the owners was disturbing to people who wanted law and order, and a curious, emotional link was created in the conservative middle-class mind between the court plan and labor turbulence. For the first time, William Allen White wrote Norris, opposition to Roosevelt was coming "not from the plug hat section but from the grass roots."

The protest was not wholly spontaneous. Busily stoking the fires were Roosevelt's old friend Frank Gannett and other prominent conservatives. "Get busy fast!" Borah urged Gannett; the New York publisher put $49,-000 into the campaign and raised almost $150,000 more from several thousand contributors. Full-page advertisements blossomed in the newspapers; fervent oratory filled the air waves; speeches were franked by the tens of thousands through congressional offices and out to the country. And still the hand of Republican leaders was hardly visible.

One early effect of this surge of protest was to strip Roosevelt's proposal of its "efficiency" façade and to show it plainly as an attempt to liberalize the Court. Abruptly shifting his tactics, the President decided to wage his campaign squarely on this basic issue. And he resolved on a direct appeal to the country. "The source of criticism is concentrated," he wrote a friend late in February, "and I feel that as we get the story to the general public the whole matter will be given wide support."

Significantly, his first appeal was to his party. Addressing a resplendent Democratic victory dinner at the Mayflower Hotel on March 4, the President summoned his partisans to defend his proposal. Roosevelt seemed in the best of humor, but his voice was stern and commanding. He warned his party that it would celebrate victories in the future only if it kept faith with the majority that had elected it. "We gave warning last November that we had only just begun to fight. Did some people really believe we did not mean it? Well—I meant it, and you meant it."

A new crisis was at hand, the President asserted—a crisis different from but even graver than four years before. It was the ever-accelerating speed of social forces now gathering headway. The President dwelt at length on the fate of remedial measures at the hands of the courts. Then he brought his speech to a stunning climax:

"It will take courage to let our minds be bold and find the ways to meet the needs of the Nation. But for our Party, now as always, the counsel of courage is the counsel of wisdom.

"If we do not have the courage to lead the American people where they want to go, someone else will.

"Here is one-third of a Nation ill-nourished, ill-clad, ill-housed—NOW!

"Here are thousands upon thousands of farmers wondering whether next year's prices will meet their mortgage interest—NOW!

"Here are thousands upon thousands of men and women laboring for long hours in factories for inadequate pay—NOW!

"Here are thousands upon thousands of children who should be at school, working in mines and mills—NOW!

"Here are strikes more far-reaching than we have ever known, costing millions of dollars—NOW!

"Here are Spring floods threatening to roll again down our river valleys —NOW!

"Here is the Dust Bowl beginning to blow again—NOW!

"If we would keep faith with those who had faith in us, if we would make democracy succeed, I say we must act—NOW!"

The President's fireside chat a few days later was more pallid and more defensive. Again he dwelt on the conditions of four years before, the "quiet crisis" that faced the country, the failure of the Supreme Court to pull together with the other horses in the "three-horse team" of the national government. The Constitution must be saved from the Court, and the Court from itself. He directly met the charge of packing the Court by denying that he had any intention of appointing "spineless puppets." He explained at length why he had not chosen the amendment alternative. He pointed to his own record of devotion to civil and religious liberty.

"You who know me will accept my solemn assurance that in a world in which democracy is under attack, I seek to make American democracy succeed. You and I will do our part."

The President was not depending on oratory alone. From the outset a special White House staff, under Roosevelt's close direction, managed an aggressive campaign. They dispatched speakers to the country, channeled ideas and arguments to friendly legislators, and put pressure on senators hostile or silent on the measure. The form of this pressure was a subject of open wrangling among Democrats. At the very least, Corcoran and the other Administration agents put it up to senators in stiff terms to back up the President. Senators were tempted with new patronage arrangements and with federal projects for their states, and even with judicial appointments for themselves. Pressure was also brought to bear on a number of senators through Democratic organizations in their home states, including Chicago's Kelly-Nash machine and Pendergast's Kansas City organization. Some senators—certainly Robinson himself—could hardly forget that passage of the measure would mean that the President could allot six Supreme Court judgeships—the most highly prized appointive job in America.

Roosevelt's appeal to the people had some impact. Support for the plan reached its highest point in mid-March. But the actual deciding would be done on Capitol Hill, and here things were not going so well.

Roosevelt's aides were not operating on Capitol Hill with their usual efficiency. Part of the trouble was caused by James Roosevelt, whom his father had appointed as an assistant early in 1937. Eleanor Roosevelt, foreseeing the pressures amid which James would have to work, opposed the appointment, but her husband saw no reason why the fact that he was President should deprive him of his oldest son's help. Eleanor's doubts were vindicated. James made promises that seemed to have special authenticity but in fact did not; the efforts of the other aides on the Hill were undermined; and congressional friction and bitterness increased.

The senatorial opposition, on the other hand, was functioning with extraordinary skill and smoothness. The Republicans were still relatively quiet. On the Democratic side Carter Glass supplied the moral indignation and Wheeler and O'Mahoney the liberal veneer, while middle-of-the-road Democrats like Royal S. Copeland of New York, Frederick Van

Nuys of Indiana, and Connally furnished the anchor line of votes. Against them was aligned a solid core of New Dealers and a group of senators who went along with the bill largely out of personal loyalty to the President. A score of senators were—openly, at least—on the fence.

In mid-March the seat of battle shifted to the reverberant, multi-columned Senate caucus room, where the Judiciary Committee held hearings on the measure. Cummings led off for the Administration with a statement that reflected the President's original plea for a more efficient judiciary. He was followed by Assistant Attorney General Robert H. Jackson, who tried valiantly to bring the subject back to the issue of liberalizing the Court. Both were subjected to a barrage of unfriendly questions. So effective was the cross-examination that a dozen experts from the American Bar Association were rumored to be in Washington furnishing ammunition. Other Administration witnesses testified over the next ten days, including President Green of the A. F. of L., political scientists Edward S. Corwin and Charles Grove Haines, Editor Irving Brant of the St. Louis *Star-Times*. Then it was the opposition's turn.

Shrewdly handled, the congressional hearing can be a powerful weapon against the executive. Although not himself a member of the Judiciary Committee, Wheeler was ready, through his friends on the committee, to use it to turn the Administration's flank. A veteran of Montana's stormy politics, he was a man temperamentally at his best in opposition: tireless, vengeful, resourceful, and often choleric. Despite his protestations of love for the President, he had reason to feel disgruntled; an early and strenuous worker for Roosevelt's nomination, he had had little recognition, and he knew that he—who had been, after all, the Progressive party running mate of the great La Follette in 1924—had taken a more liberal position than the President on many relief and reform measures.

Wheeler opened the attack on the Court bill before the committee. Suddenly he produced the opposition's bombshell—a letter from Chief Justice Hughes showing categorically that the Supreme Court was abreast of its work and arguing that a larger Court would lower its efficiency. In the few minutes the letter took to read it made three things clear: that a coalition had been forged between the senatorial opposition and the politicians of the judiciary, who were quietly doing what they could against the plan; that this coalition was attacking Roosevelt on his weakest salient, his original charge of inefficiency; and that the political skill of Hughes himself had been thrown into the fight.

Outwardly Hughes had preserved his usual benignity in the face of the Court plan. "If they want me to preside over a convention," he said, "I

461

can do it." But the old politician's fighting instincts were aroused. He wished to speak out—but how could he in the face of the restraints that tradition imposed on the Court? Roosevelt's use of the inefficiency argument gave him the perfect opportunity to attack the plan in the guise of supplying data. The Chief Justice was ready even to appear personally before the committee, but Brandeis objected, so a letter had to do. Working feverishly over a weekend to meet Wheeler's timetable, the Chief Justice turned the letter over to the Senator with a smile. "The baby is born."

Hughes's political leadership and shrewdness matched Roosevelt's. He had not been able, he informed the committee, to consult with every member of the Court, but he was confident that his letter was in accord with their views. Actually, at least one justice, Stone, resented Hughes's failure to consult him and disagreed with part of the letter. Perhaps the Chief Justice knew or suspected that Stone disparaged Hughes's reputation as a liberal Justice, that Stone, through Irving Brant of the St. Louis *Star-Times*, was letting his views be known to the White House. In any event, Hughes's strategy was perfectly executed.

Dismayed by Hughes's counterthrust, the Administration had to sit by idly while the committee heard witness after witness. For days on end their arguments against the President's plan filled the press and radio. Roosevelt hoped that "things would move faster from now on," as he wrote a friend, but the opposition saw the advantages of delay. To make matters worse, the Administration had no one on the committee with Borah's or Wheeler's or Connally's brilliance in cross-examination. Here, too, the President was paying a price for his secrecy; Senator Hugo Black, a tenacious and resourceful parliamentarian, had left the Judiciary Committee at the beginning of the year.

During the critical weeks of late March and early April popular support for the plan slowly, steadily ebbed away. The backing that Roosevelt aroused in his two speeches lacked stability and depth; it simply disintegrated as the long fight wore on. Much of the trouble lay in the deep fissures running through workers and farmers, the two great group interests that Roosevelt had counted on because of their unhappy experiences with the Court. The A. F. of L. was now locked in trench warfare with the C. I. O., and labor rallies organized by the Administration fell apart in the face of this split, local Democratic party quarrels, and general apathy. The farm organizations were not acting as though there had ever been an AAA decision. Leaders of the powerful Farm Bureau Federation were silent; the Grange was against the plan; and—worst of all—the Farmers Union was divided. Evidently the farm leaders were responding less to a sense of calculated self-interest than to the currents of feeling sweeping middle-class America: respect for the "vestal virgins of the court"; fear of labor turbulence; concern for law and order and property rights.

In this extremity Roosevelt turned to the Democratic party. Farley industriously toured the party circuit, trying to build grass fires behind lagging Democratic congressmen and vaguely threatening punishment to deserters. All in vain—on this issue the party lacked vigor and militance. Moreover, prominent Democratic leaders outside the Senate were decamping on the court issue. In the cabinet itself Hull was quietly hostile. In Roosevelt's own state his old comrade in arms Governor Lehman came out against the bill, and even Boss Flynn of the Bronx, the most stolid of party war horses, was opposed.

At the beginning of April the President was still optimistic. Corcoran, Pittman, La Follette, and others had been reporting enthusiastically on the chances of victory. When Senator Black warned him of the opposition's determination and tactics of delay, Roosevelt replied: "We'll smoke 'em out. If delay helps them, we must press for an early vote."

BREACHES IN THE GRAND COALITION

Roosevelt was wrong. By April the chances for the Court plan were almost nil. The President simply could not command the needed votes in either Senate or House. Then on April 12 came a clinching blow. In a tense, packed courtroom Hughes read the Supreme Court's judgment sustaining the Wagner Act.

If Roosevelt had been as acutely sensitive to political crosscurrents during this period as he usually was, the Court's shift would not have surprised him. A few weeks after the election, while Roosevelt and Cummings were leafing through Court plans, Roberts had told the Chief Justice privately that he would vote to sustain a Washington minimum-wage law and overturn a contrary decision of a few months back. Hughes was so pleased he almost hugged him. Final decision was delayed, however, because Stone was ill for some time, and because Hughes saw the disadvantages of appearing to yield before the Court-packing plan. By the end of March the time seemed ripe for the decision on this case and on three others favorable to the Administration. Still, these were only straws in the wind, and they had little effect on Roosevelt's plans. The Wagner Act decision two weeks later, however, showed the decisive alignment of Hughes and Roberts with the three liberals.

Once again the Chief Justice had outfoxed the President. How much he changed his technical position to meet the tactical needs of the hour is a subject of some dispute among constitutional experts. Certainly Hughes's position on the companion cases to the main case of April 12 seemed a long jump from some of his earlier judgments; on the other hand, the Chief Justice, like most politician-judges, had been flexible enough in his positions to make the jump possible. His new position was more important politically than legalistically. He had consolidated a majority of the Court behind him; he had taken the heart out of the President's argument; he had upheld a measure dear to labor and thus reduced even further its concern over the Court—and he had done all this without undue sacrifice of the Court's dignity.

Outwardly Roosevelt's reaction to the Court's move was gleeful. "I have been chortling all morning," he told reporters. "I have been having a perfectly grand time." He compared the *Herald Tribune*'s enthusiastic hailing of the decision with its approval two years before of the Liberty League lawyers' opinion against the constitutionality of the Wagner Act.

"Well, I have been having more fun!" Roosevelt went on amid repeated guffaws from the reporters. "And I haven't read the Washington *Post*, and I haven't got the Chicago *Tribune* yet. Or the Boston *Herald*. Today is a very, very happy day. . . ." He quoted with relish a remark a friend had made to him: the No Man's Land had been eliminated but "we are now in 'Roberts' Land.' "

Inwardly the President was more puzzled than pleased. Should he press on with the Court fight? He must have sensed immediately that Hughes had given the plan's chances a punishing blow; he had hoped for a complete veto of New Deal legislation so that the issue would be sharpened for the people. He soon learned, moreover, that Robinson and others of his lieutenants were talking compromise. "This bill's raising hell in the Senate," Robinson reportedly told a White House representative. "Now it's going to be worse than ever, but if the President wants to compromise, I can get him a couple of extra justices tomorrow." On the other hand, Robinson himself posed a problem. It had long been understood that the doughty Arkansan would receive the first vacant justiceship and thus fulfill a life ambition. But the Senator's appointment would clearly be a recognition of service to Roosevelt rather than a recognition of legal distinction or ingrained liberalism; once on the Court, moreover, Robinson might swing right. To offset this appointment there must be others.

Roosevelt had further reasons to stand pat on his proposal. He was now in the fight to the hilt, and compromise would be interpreted as defeat for him and victory for Wheeler and the other rebels. He still hankered for six of his own appointees—liberal-minded judges with whom he could establish friendly personal relations such as he had enjoyed with the state judges when he was governor. Crucial New Deal measures were still to come before the Court, and the justices might swing right again if the pistol at their head was unloaded. Finally, the President still thought that he could win. Had he not saved many a measure during the first term, when prospects looked bleak, simply by sticking to his guns?

So the order was full speed ahead. "We must keep up—and strengthen—the fight," the President wrote Congressman David Lewis. As if to flaunt his confidence over the outcome he made plans to fish in the Gulf of Mexico at the end of April. Roosevelt's manner was still buoyant.

"I am delighted to have your rural rhapsody of April twelfth and to know that the French Government has spring fever," he wrote on April 21 to Ambassador William C. Bullitt in Paris. "Spring has come to Washington also and even the Senators, who were biting each other over the Supreme Court, are saying 'Alphonse' and 'Gaston' to each other. . . .

"I, too, am influenced by this beautiful spring day. I haven't a care in the world which is going some for a President who is said by the newspapers to be a remorseless dictator driving his government into hopeless bankruptcy."

The Supreme Court turnabout marked a decisive shift in the character of the Court fight. No longer was the issue one of Roosevelt New Deal versus Old Guard Court. Now the fight lay between the President and Congress. When the Court upheld the Social Security Act a few weeks later, it served to take the Court as an institution even further out of the struggle. But not its members. In May and June, Hughes made speeches that were hardly veiled assaults on the Court proposal.

Roosevelt returned from his fishing in mid-May. He was in a militant mood. After talking with precinct committeemen during the train trip back, he told the Cabinet, he was as certain as ever that the people were still behind the bill. Democrats in Congress who opposed it, he added, might expect defeat at the polls. Roosevelt warned Garner privately that he, the President, had brought a lot of congressmen in on his coattails, and that he might openly oppose Democrats who were against the bill. He had Robinson and other leaders in, laughed off their fears, explained away the defections they gloomily reported, and sent them back to the battle.

That battle was still going badly. Shipstead came out against the bill, as did several other senators on whom Roosevelt was relying. Party leaders were warning of a deepening split among the Democrats. Even White

House assistants were losing confidence and counseling compromise. Other New Deal measures were being pulled down with the Court bill. Then, on May 18, the opposition played another card. Wheeler and Borah, knowing of Van Devanter's wish to retire, got word to the justice that a resignation timed to coincide with an expected vote by the Judiciary Committee against the Court bill would help the plan's opponents. For Wheeler knew what that vote would be. A few minutes after Roosevelt read Van Devanter's notice of retirement on the morning of May 18 and had written in longhand a cool but polite note of acceptance, the Senate Judiciary Committee met in executive session. After brushing aside several compromise measures it voted 10-8 that the President's bill "do not pass." The committee line-up symbolized the split in the ranks of the Grand Coalition: six Democrats of diverse ideological hues deserted the President.

Face to face with this deepening split, Roosevelt executed one of the rapid tactical shifts that so often threw his opponents off guard. He turned to the possibility of compromise. But his freedom of maneuver here was unhappily narrowed by a conjunction of circumstances that stemmed partly from sheer bad luck and partly from the way in which he had handled matters. Van Devanter's retirement not only knocked one more prop from under the President's plea for new blood on the Court; it also precipitated in acute form the old problem of rewarding Robinson with a justiceship without alienating the "true" liberals and making a mockery of Roosevelt's arguments for the bill. Within a few hours of Van Devanter's retirement, almost as if by plan, both opposition senators and supporters of the bill were crowding around Robinson's front-row desk in the Senate chamber, pumping his hand, calling him "Mr. Justice." The Senate was in effect nominating Robinson to fill the vacancy.

In this extremity Roosevelt turned to the direct person-to-person persuasion for which he had such a flair. Against the advice of Corcoran and Jackson, who wanted him to let the bill go over to another session or even to accept defeat and take the issue to the country, the President decided on a shrewd but risky tactical move. Through Farley he let it be known to Robinson that the Senator could expect to take Van Devanter's place. Then the President called Robinson in and agreed to accept a compromise on the bill, but he added that if there was a bride there must be bridesmaids. He asked Robinson to take full leadership of the fight for a compromise bill. The President was now seeking to turn the senatorial support for Robinson's appointment to his own advantage. If the senators wanted to help their old colleague, they would have to provide some extra appointments as well. The danger in the plan was that everything depended on Robinson.

And the President did not fully trust the majority leader. He complained to Ickes that Robinson had lost his punch, that there was no leadership in Congress. Speaker Bankhead was not strong in the House, he said, and Rayburn was so anxious to succeed to the speakership that he feared to offend anyone. The President was especially upset about Garner. Exclaiming that "my ears are buzzing and ringing," the Vice-President had left on a long-planned vacation in Texas just as the fight in the Senate was coming to a head. But the President never expressed his feelings directly to Garner. Instead, after the Vice-President had been away several weeks Roosevelt urged his return in a letter that offered every bait that might lure the sulking Texan. Knowing of Garner's fears about government spending and labor violence, and his old populist distrust of bankers, the President predicted a balanced budget for the coming year and declared that the public was "pretty sick of the extremists which exist both in the C.I.O. and some of the A.F. of L. unions and also of the extremists like Girdler and some of his associates backed by the Guarantee [sic] Trust Co., etc." Roosevelt ended his appeal on a personal note.

"And finally, just to clinch the argument for your return, I want to tell you again how much I miss you because of you, yourself, and also because of the great help that you have given and continue to give to the working out *peacefully* of a mass of problems greater than the Nation has ever had before." But the Vice-President stayed in Texas.

Garner's own sit-down strike signalized the state of the Democratic party. It was not the Court plan alone that was splitting apart the Grand Coalition. The attack on the plan served as a rallying cry for the conservatives who feared the rising tide of labor turbulence, for the "old" liberals who disliked the President's indirections and his personal handling of party matters, for New Deal liberals who prized orderly processes and constitutional traditions. Seeking to placate these elements Roosevelt, when asked about the deadlock between labor and management, said calculatedly, "A plague on both your houses." Lewis's howl of indignation and the icy silence of the party Old Guard indicated that in striving to veer between the various factions Roosevelt was keeping the warm support of none.

At the end of June Roosevelt tried another tack—and one that again illustrated his preference for direct personal handling of affairs. A grand political picnic was arranged at Jefferson Island in Chesapeake Bay, to which Democratic congressmen were invited. The plan was to submerge intraparty bickering in three days of good fellowship. The President was at his best. Seated in an armchair under a big locust tree, he chatted congenially and drank beer with groups of shirt-sleeved legislators. He even allowed Martin Dies of Texas to induct him into the Demagogue's Club, involving a pledge to favor all spending bills and no tax bills, to do nothing to harm his chances for a third term, never to be consistent—and not to send controversial proposals to Congress.

In sharp contrast to this bucolic scene was the grim atmosphere of the Senate. There, day after day, Robinson was making the rounds of the Democrats, pleading with them to support his compromise plan. The new measure was mild enough, allowing the President to appoint only one coadjutor justice a year for any justice who had passed seventy-five and failed to retire. Even so, Robinson found it hard going, and often he had to resort to a personal plea to embarrassed senators for help in realizing his life ambition. When Robinson opened debate on the bill in the Senate he seemed to reporters, as he sawed the air with violent gestures and beat off his interrogators, like an aging bull tormented by the fast-moving picadors around him and stung by their *banderillas*. Day after day Robinson roared his arguments and threats at the opposition, meanwhile desperately counting and recounting the small majority he had lined up. But he had come to the end of his road. On the morning of July 14 he rose from his hotel bed, took one step, and fell dead, a copy of the *Congressional Record* in his hand.

The stroke that ruptured Robinson's heart ruptured as well the bonds of personal loyalty on which the majority leader had been depending for his compromise plan. There was a sudden rush away from the bill. Even as Robinson was buried in Little Rock the congressmen who had escorted the body out on the funeral train were busy sparring over the bill. On the train back to Washington, Garner, who had joined the delegation in Little Rock, went down the aisles systematically counting noses. On the morning of July 20 he reported to the President.

"How did you find the Court situation, Jack?" Roosevelt asked.

"Do you want it with the bark on or off, Cap'n?"

"The rough way," Roosevelt said with a laugh.

"All right. You are beat. You haven't got the votes."

NOT WITH A BANG BUT A WHIMPER

The end of the Court fight was anticlimactic. Roosevelt asked Garner to arrange the best compromise that he could. Whether the Vice-President tried to salvage something out of the bill or simply surrendered is shrouded in the obscure maneuvering of the last days. By now Congress was outside anyone's control; "everything on the Hill seems to be at sixes and sevens," Ickes complained. Appropriately enough, the Judiciary Committee served as executioner by offering a motion to recommit the Court bill. Only twenty senators voted against recommittal. A week later the Senate rushed through an emasculated bill, making minor reforms and improvements, which the President halfheartedly signed into law.

The last episodes of the Court fight were entangled with a struggle over the Democratic leadership in the Senate. Pat Harrison of Mississippi and Alben W. Barkley of Kentucky were vying for Robinson's mantle in one of those contests that become all the more bitter because they cleave the membership of an intimate club. The Court fight sharpened tempers of the opposing factions. Roosevelt was on good terms with both senators, but he had several reasons to prefer Barkley. The Kentuckian was a more reliable New Dealer and was personally more loyal to Roosevelt; he had, for example, given active support to the Court bill while Harrison was passive. And if Harrison won the position, he would probably have to vacate chairmanship of the Senate Finance Committee and this vital post would fall into the hands of a conservative Democrat.

Clearly Roosevelt had his preferences—but could he act upon them? Not if he was to follow the custom that forbids presidential interference in the Senate's internal affairs. Roosevelt's method of resolving this problem was characteristic. Openly he took a neutral position; to be sure, he addressed a letter to "My Dear Alben" urging a continued fight for the principles of the Court bill, but Barkley's position as acting majority leader permitted this public show of friendship.

Privately the President was not neutral at all. A check showed that Senate Democrats were split almost evenly between the two candidates. Every vote would count. An obvious weak link in Harrison's ranks was Senator William H. Dietrich, who owed his Senate seat largely to Boss Ed Kelly of Chicago. Roosevelt asked Farley to telephone Kelly to use his influence with Dietrich. Farley refused on the grounds that he had promised the principals that he would keep hands off. The President thereupon turned to Hopkins and Corcoran, who threw White House pressure on Dietrich and others. The Harrison forces mobilized pressure too. Senator Harry Truman, who had pledged his vote to Barkley, had to ask the Kentuckian to be released of his promise. Among the shifters was Dietrich— from Harrison to Barkley. Barkley's victory by one vote was an important victory for the President, but one that sharpened the ill temper of the Senate.

The Court fight over, Roosevelt sought to regain direction of his general legislative program. Congress, he told his Cabinet, must take responsibility for what was done and what was left undone. The President was especially concerned about the farm situation. If farm prices fell next year, he said, a good many Democrats would be defeated in the next election. While Roosevelt talked, Ickes scribbled on a piece of paper and passed it to Farley: "The President seems to be indulging in a curtain lecture for the benefit of the Vice-President."

Congress was still wallowing in confusion. Earlier in the session it had passed, under Roosevelt's proddings, several important bills. One of these was the Guffey-Vinson bituminous coal bill providing for governmental and private co-operation in marketing, price control, and trade practices. Others were a revised Neutrality Act and renewal of the Trade Agreements Act. Congress had also enacted the Farm Tenancy bill, authorizing federal loans to farm tenants, sharecroppers and laborers, to help them buy their own farms. This was work done, but it seemed strikingly small in the light of the President's broad challenge, in his inaugural, of "one third of a nation ill-housed, ill-clad, ill-nourished."

Could that challenge still be met? By the end of July five Administration measures awaited action in Congress: wages and hours, low-cost housing, executive reorganization, comprehensive farm program, and creation of seven regional agencies patterned somewhat after the TVA. When Congress adjourned late in August, only one of these measures had been made into law. This was the Wagner Housing bill. It was significant that this lone Administration victory was due far more to Wagner and an indefatigable group of public-housing enthusiasts and lobbyists than to the President. Roosevelt, to be sure, did help persuade a key chairman in the House to report the bill out of committee, but only after weeks of backing and filling in the White House.

Equally significant was the reason that the rest of Roosevelt's program failed. In part that failure stemmed from Roosevelt's original calculation that Court reform would have a better chance if other major bills were postponed in its behalf. Later he appeared to swing to the opposite view that at least one of the measures—wage-hour regulation—would be so popular that it would unify Democratic ranks split over Court reform. Both calculations proved wrong.

But there was a more important reason for Roosevelt's legislative difficulties—a reason that reflected the strategic weakness of his political position. The trouble was that the ample coalition that he had summoned to his personal support in November—and which had responded to that sum-mons—was already falling apart.

The blocking of the wage-hour bill showed how extensive were the fractures in the coalition. When Senator Black introduced his proposed Fair Labor Standards Act late in May, Roosevelt vigorously urged passage. "We have promised it," he said. "We cannot stand still." Quickly the bill ran into snags. Southerners from low-wage states, including Harrison, deserted the President on the issue. Sharp differences developed among labor groups, not only between A. F. of L. and C.I.O. leaders but also within the two organizations. As if all this was not enough, a fight broke out between low-tariff and high-tariff Democrats over a protectionist clause in the bill. Pressure against the bill was put on Farley and Roosevelt through Democratic leaders in the South. After a struggle the bill passed the Senate, and by calling in President Green of the A.F. of L. and acceding to his major demands Roosevelt was able to ease the bill through the House Labor Committee. Then the bill stalled in the face of a coalition of Republicans and Southern Democrats on the Rules Committee. In vain Democratic leaders summoned a caucus to put force behind the bill; not enough Democrats showed up to make it an official caucus.

By mid-August the President was ready to give up the fight for the rest of his program. He decided to call Congress back in special session during the fall. Let the congressmen get back to their districts, he said, and they would return with a strengthened feeling for the New Deal.

But one task remained for the President before adjournment—and a most pleasant task. Van Devanter's seat on the Court was still open.

A pleasant task—but not an easy one. Roosevelt wanted a durable New Dealer, a relatively young man, either a Southerner or Westerner, and a competent lawyer, who at the same time would clear the Senate without difficulty. This last was the rub, for in the sweltering Washington heat the senators seemed to be more bitter and unpredictable than ever. For this reason the President leaned toward a New Deal Senator. He finally chose Black over other senatorial possibilities mainly because the Alabaman had gone down the line for Roosevelt's policies; the President felt drawn to Black also because he faced a hard battle for re-election and perhaps because Black had an only child suffering from deafness. While Roosevelt did not rate Black's legal talents very high, he was more concerned about seasoned liberalism than expertness. Despite some grumbling in the Senate, the usual clubby feeling prevailed, and after a brief debate Black was readily confirmed.

"So Hugo Black becomes a member of the Supreme Court of the United States while the economic royalists fume and squirm and the President rolls his tongue around in his cheek," Ickes crowed in his diary. The President was not to roll his tongue long. A week or so later, after Black had left for a vacation in Europe, a Pittsburgh newspaper produced categorical proof that the new Justice had been a member of the Ku Klux Klan. The rumors that Black had neither confirmed nor denied during the confirmation debate were true. The press exploded with shrill attacks on both Black and the President.

"I did not know that Black belonged to the Ku Klux Klan," Roosevelt said to a friend. "This is very serious." The President was deeply disturbed. He told reporters that nothing could be said until Black returned from Europe. Privately he did what he could. He asked Ickes to go to Borah and see if he would help out. Wheeler and others had been demanding that the President investigate Black, and Roosevelt particularly wanted Borah's backing for the proposition that the President had no right to make such an investigation. Borah fully agreed. By the time Black returned from Europe Roosevelt had left on a Western tour, and all eyes were on the justice.

Harried by reporters, Black turned to the radio and laid his case before perhaps fifty million people. He denounced intolerance, and pointed to his congressional record in defense of civil liberties. Then, in his soft, strained Southern voice he admitted that he had been a member of the Klan, but asserted that he had long ago dissociated himself from it. After referring again to his civil liberties record, he ended with a sad "good night."

And thus ended Roosevelt's battle against the Court.

Roosevelt's enemies could not help gloating. Surely the President had suffered a dizzy fall in the short span of six months. At the beginning of the year he had towered over the political scene, with his colossal vote of approval in November and with his huge majorities in Congress. Then he seemed invincible. Yet now he had been beaten.

Why had this political colossus stumbled and fallen? Roosevelt's critics were quick with an explanation: Pride goeth before a fall. Intoxicated with success, Roosevelt had recklessly attacked a venerable American institution. Overly sure of himself, he had made mistake after careless mistake. His potency had gone to his head. Learned pundits quoted Lord Acton: "Power tends to corrupt, and absolute power corrupts absolutely."

Was it really so simple? A closer look at the Court fight showed that the real story was much more complex than this morality tale suggested.

Roosevelt did not go about the job of Court reform recklessly. Quite the contrary—he struck at the Court only after a long period of waiting, and under what he considered to be the best possible conditions. His plan was not hastily conceived; he had searched through a variety of proposals to find one that would have a good chance of clearing Congress and at the same time achieve his purpose. Nor was his plan a radical one. Compared with some of the constitutional and legislative proposals of the day, it was mild indeed.

That Roosevelt's cocksureness led to mistake after mistake and thus defeated the plan was another explanation of the time—and one that was assiduously promoted by those who, like Hopkins and Ickes, had little to do with conducting the fight for the Court bill. Such a view fails to explain, among other things, why the remarkably astute Roosevelt of 1936 became the bungler of 1937. The theory that Roosevelt did not direct the fight personally and the mistakes were made by subordinates is incorrect; he was in command throughout. Much was made of Roosevelt's stubbornness in clinging to the original plan; but this stubbornness was precisely the quality that had saved measures in previous terms—when it had been called firmness or resoluteness. Certainly Roosevelt made mistakes in the Court fight, but so did his opponents.

All such explanations ignored the probability that the original Court plan never had a chance of passing. This was the crucial point. For—if the plan was indeed doomed from the start—the Court's switch and Van Devanter's resignation and Robinson's death became mere stages in the death of the bill rather than causes of that death.

That the Court bill probably never had a chance of passing seems now quite clear. Roosevelt's original proposal evidently never commanded a majority in the Senate. In the House it would have run up against the unyielding Sumners, and then against a conservative Rules Committee capable of blocking the bill for weeks. From the start Democratic leaders in the House were worried about the bill's prospects in that chamber. Robinson's compromise plan might have gone through the Senate if he had lived. More likely, though, it would have failed in the face of a dogged Senate filibuster, or later in the House.

Any kind of Court reform would have had hard going. The popular reverence for the Constitution, the conception of the Supreme Court as its guardian, the ability of the judges—especially Hughes—to counterattack in their own way, the deep-seated legal tradition in a Congress composed of a large number of lawyers—all these were obstacles. Yet there was tremendous support in Congress and in the country for curbing the

Court's excess. Undoubtedly some kind of moderate Court reform could have gone through.

The fatal weakness of Roosevelt's plan lay partly in its content and partly in the way it was proposed. The plan itself seemed an evasive, disingenuous way of meeting a clear-cut problem. It talked about judicial efficiency rather than ideology; it was aimed at immediate personalities on the Court rather than long-run problems posed by the Court. The manner of presentation—the surprise, Roosevelt's failure to pose the issue more concretely in the election, his obvious relish in the job, his unwillingness to ask his Cabinet and his congressional leaders for advice—alienated some potential supporters. More important, this method of presentation prevented Roosevelt from building a broad coalition behind the bill and ironing out multifarious tactical details before springing the attack— behind-the-scenes activities in which Roosevelt was highly adept.

That this masterly politician should make such errors even before his bill was born is explained partly by Roosevelt's personality, partly by his view of the political circumstances at the end of 1936.

Clearly Roosevelt had come to love—perhaps he had always loved— the drama, the suspense, the theatrical touches, and his own commanding role in projects that astonished the country and riled the enemy. But it was more than this. Roosevelt had fought the campaign on a highly personal basis. And he had built a winning coalition around himself—not the Democratic party, not the Democratic platform, not the liberal ideology— but around himself. He had won a stunning victory in spite of the doubters, the rebels, and the perfectionists. The master strokes in the campaign were largely of his own devising.

Roosevelt's handling of the Court fight was the logical extension of his presidential campaign. But now he met a new set of factors, and some of the old tricks did not work. Now he was trying to push a controversial bill through Congress, not win popular votes for himself as a beloved leader. He could not maneuver as he once had; victory depended on conciliating key congressmen and clearing labyrinthine channels. The Grand Coalition seemed to have shriveled away. With the President's blessing, Stanley High tried to activate the Good Neighbor League—it failed to respond. The mighty legions of farm and labor, so powerful in November, seemed to melt away in the spring. Roosevelt turned to the Democratic party; it was a scattered and disorganized army. He appealed for support on the basis of a "quiet crisis," but people saw no crisis. It was not March 1933.

The Black appointment repeated the whole problem in minor theme.

Here again Roosevelt consulted only with two or three persons, and not with his congressional leaders. It was well known on Capitol Hill that the Alabaman had had Klan connections, and as Ickes said after the sensation broke, the leaders could have helped protect the President if Roosevelt had let them in on the decision beforehand. As it was, Roosevelt had to take personal responsibility for a personal appointment. Black went on to make a distinguished record as a justice, especially in the field of civil liberties—but this could not help Roosevelt at the time.

All in all, the Court fight was a stunning defeat for the President. Whether or not it was a fatal or irretrievable one, however, depended on the events to follow. Two years later, with his eye on a string of pro-New Deal Court decisions, the President exulted that he had lost the battle but won the war. As matters turned out in Congress and party, it could better be said that he lost the battle, won the campaign, but lost the war.

THE C.I.O. TAKES THE OFFENSIVE

By 1935, workers in many parts of the country were persuaded, as never before, of the importance of solidarity. Unionization had brought substantial gains to garment workers, coal miners, and newspapermen. Furthermore, they undertook to exert political influence as a group; John L. Lewis and his United Mine Workers contributed a half-million dollars through Labor's Non-Partisan League to help re-elect F.D.R. and sustain the New Deal.

But Detroit, the home of the automobile, the greatest center of industry in the country, was virtually untouched by the rising tide of unionism. The American Federation of Labor, organized around the craft unions, had no place for the unskilled and semiskilled workers from the mass-production industries. In November 1935, eight unions, led by John L. Lewis, formed the Committee for Industrial Organization within the A. F. of L., for the express purpose of organizing these unskilled workers. The following year they were expelled from the A. F. of L.

The first target of the new C.I.O. was to be the steel industry in Pittsburgh, known as "Big Steel." A half-million dollars was allotted by the union to organize the steel workers. Surprisingly, the "Big Steel" companies decided not to fight the C.I.O.'s request to negotiate a contract, and the steel workers won wage increases, the eight-hour day, the forty-hour week, vacations with pay, and seniority rights. However, the "Little Steel" companies in Ohio and Illinois were another matter; last-ditch battles were fought over a period of four years before the unions gained recognition and a contract.

Meanwhile, in Detroit the United Automobile Workers Union, now affiliated with the C.I.O., was agitating to establish their right to organize and bargain. They, too, were faced with a formidable antagonist.

The General Motors management had been making plans to meet the threat of unionization; from January 1934 through July 1936 they had spent almost a million dollars in the employment of private detectives and company spies.

HERBERT HARRIS

WORKING IN THE DETROIT AUTO PLANTS*

THE MASS production of automobiles for a long time has been the platitudinous symbol of American "progress," a word which is almost always associated with mobility alone.

Until the beginning of 1937, however, there was very little which resembled progress in the management-labor relations of our four-billion-dollar motor industry. The 433,000 men and 18,000 women employed in making passenger cars, trucks, hearses, tanks, station wagons, tractors, buses, taxicabs and ambulances faced, and in part still face, conditions more medieval than modern.

Despite the widely publicized five- and six-dollar-a-day minima, and hourly rates which, for a few, reached highs of $1.09, annual earnings of auto workers averaged less than $1,300 in the prosperity year of 1926 and less than $1,000 in the depression year of 1935. The feeling of insecurity generated by such incomes and by the irregular employment they reveal was described by an Italian punch-press operator named Rizzo:

I worka six years with this job, but all that time eight months is the longest I ever go steady in one year. For more than one year I only worka two or three days a week. Everybody say here, "Why don't you save when you worka?" But how can you save when you no worka steady? If I could get $5 a day all year, I could put this little pieca for the coal, this little pieca for the rent, this little pieca for the electric and maybe then I can putta this away for to save and know where I go. But now you work, you make something; you stop. You spend what you got save. You getta the debts. Then you get a job. You pay the debts. You save a little. You stop. And now I stop too long this time. Me, I don't drink. I stay home nights with the keeds.

Even so, the wages in motors are relatively good when compared with those paid elsewhere. On the other hand it takes all the makeshifts of a poverty more shabby than genteel to stretch them over the seasonal lay-offs to which the industry, by its own promotion of gadget consciousness and the annual model fetish, and its acute sensitivity to any rise or decline in national purchasing power, has become particularly prone.

However, it was not against the size of the pay envelope, per se, that General Motors workers staged a series of sit-downs at the end of 1936.

* From Herbert Harris' *American Labor* (New Haven, Yale University Press, 1938).

The cause for this spectacular strike, which lasted forty-four days, involving 40,000 workers directly and 110,000 indirectly, and paralyzed sixty plants of a giant corporation in fourteen different states, went deeper into the secret places of the psyche than the question of so much cash return for so much work done.

It expressed the pent-up resentments of men in revolt against being dehumanized, against being only a badge, a number, a robot in thrall to a vast and intricate succubus of machinery, draining them of energy, threatening to cast them on the scrap heap after a few short years. It reflected a long-simmering rebellion against humiliations inflicted by the impersonality of a great corporation which, no more callous than its rivals, sapped the health and vitality of its workers and then turned them over to the government to support as soon as approaching middle age began to diminish their usefulness.

Today [in 1938], for instance, motorcar manufacturers still lack, toward their workers, even that rudimentary sense of responsibility which prompts any dirt farmer to pasture a faithful horse; they remain indifferent to how fast the men wear out as long as there are others to replace them, and appear equally indifferent to the inadequacy of their buying power.

Inside vast oblong buildings of brick, glass, and stone, under the hot glare of arc lights, amid the whir and chug-chump of wheels, the automobile workers stand alongside great belt lines which move in front of them inexorably at the touch of a distant control button.

In the interior of a body plant, for example, at the far end of the belt, a new frame, a metal skeleton, bolt-sinewed, begins its journey. It reaches the first man who puts on a rim, goes to another who sets a fender, while underneath, men on their backs on little roller carts tighten axle bolts, each man doing the same thing, eyes fixed on the chassis, sweat rolling from his face, jaws clamped, lift, turn, screw, liftturnscrew, with the tempo often imperceptibly quickened, unable to leave the line to go to the toilet, to get a drink of water, hour on hour, with the straw boss warning step lively, you're slipping fella, with the fear of losing the job if you don't keep up, making you strain tired muscles till your own body is a single throbbing ache while the belt, detached as a river coursing between its banks, flows smoothly on.

In other departments, even in the assembly of standardized units for crankcases, radiators, cushions, such scenes constantly occur, especially at times of peak production, and are virtually the same whether the individual plant is owned by Ford, General Motors, or Chrysler, who between them control 93 per cent of the domestic business, or by independents like Nash,

Hudson, Packard, Studebaker, and Graham who divide the remaining 7 per cent of American auto sales.

When the shift is over the workers tumble half-dead with fatigue into buses, trolleys, or their own cars, mainly secondhand. Some acquire nervous twitchings popularly called "the shakes." They get home "too tired to do anything but eat and go to bed."* They are too all-in even to read the paper, or take in a movie with the wife, or shoot a game of pool with the boys, or play cards with friends.

"It takes your guts out, that line," and "The speed-up, that's the trouble," form the dual refrain of auto workers in Detroit, Flint, Hamtramck, Saginaw, Pontiac, and other Michigan communities.

In recent years the auto workers have been increasingly recruited from the hills of Tennessee and Kentucky and from the farms of Michigan and Ohio. Beginning in 1922 and tapering off in 1930, the migration of these men to Detroit and other towns accounted for forty-seven out of every one hundred automobile employees. During the same period an appreciable influx of Negroes from the South reached its apex in 1926 when nearly 10 per cent of all Ford employees were colored and assigned to the harder, heavier tasks such as "sanding" and "foundry work." Many of the workers, of course, are transients comprising the so-called "suitcase battalions" and "bundle brigades" who rush in at the first rumors of a busy season and largely vanish at the first signs of slackening schedules.

The young backwoods men and women who flocked to motordom's Mecca were lured by visions of what, by agricultural standards, was a Big Money paradise. Mainly of "good American stock," they tended to be as parochial as they were healthy and strong. They knew nothing of unionism, often regarded their jobs as temporary, as a means of "getting some money saved" and then buying a farm or opening a little business on their own. They were also unskilled, nor did they have to be otherwise. With the mounting mechanization of the industry, about 45 per cent of its jobs can be learned within two or three days; about 35 per cent within

---

* During the Flint sit-downs a group of women were interviewed at Cook's restaurant, commissary for the strikers. A dumpy, motherly woman of German descent, with straw-colored hair and pale-blue eyes, declared, "I'd like to shout from the housetops what the company's doing to our men. My husband, he's a torch solderer; they call 'em welders, but that's not what he is; he solders. You should see him come home at night, him and the rest of the men in the buses. So tired like they was dead, and irritable. My John's not like that. He's a good, kind man. But the children don't dare go near him, he's so nervous and his temper's bad. And then at night in bed, he shakes, his whole body, he shakes."

"Yes," chimed in her companion, a sharp-faced brunette, "they're not men any more if you know what I mean. They're not men. My husband he's only thirty, but to look at him you'd think he was fifty and all played out. And unless we have the union things will get worse."

a week; some 7 per cent within two weeks, and the remaining 13 per cent within a month to a year or longer.

The old-time craftsman's sense of creative satisfaction in the work of his hands is therefore a lost emotion for the majority of the industry's workers. They rarely see, or can recognize, the finished product to which they have contributed their own minute and regimented share. Often they handle only a part of a part of another part; for in this sphere the division of labor has attained a degree of specialization that is at once an engineering feat of a high order and an object lesson in how the technics of a civilization outstrip its ethics and its social values.

During the past two decades the industry's emphasis upon youth, with its greater speed and endurance, has kept displacing older employees at an ever-accelerating rate. In the Detroit region small-loan firms refuse to consider auto workers over forty as acceptable risks, despite the amazing number of hair-dyeing specialists who flourish in the vicinity; for to the auto worker the discovery of the first "silver threads" is perhaps even more tragic than the same discovery by the professional beauty.

But this disregard of seniority rights—rights which mean simply that the man longest on the job has a prior claim to it, especially at a time of rehiring after a slack season—is only one among many grievances plaguing the industry's labor since the end of the World War. Others include the "incentive" or bonus plan by which a group of workers, geared to the human metronome of the fastest among them, receive extra money for extra "lump" output. In this operation calculations for figuring the return of each worker are so abstruse that often they have no way of finding out how much they earn.

But more injurious to individual self-esteem on the job is the practice of espionage. In this the motor manufacturers were among the most conspicuous offenders until revelations of the LaFollette Senate subcommittee, investigating civil liberties, caused cancellation of many contracts with such private detective firms as the Pinkerton Agency to which General Motors, over a period of three years, paid $419,850, or Corporations Auxiliary which cost Chrysler $72,611 for 1935 alone.*

* There are 228 other detective agencies dispensing what is euphemistically named "industrial service." It is, of course, nice work if you can get it as the $50,000 and $60,000 a year salaries of executives in such concerns attest. Among certain legal theorists, the fact that American corporations have spent as much as $80,000,000 a year for this espionage activity would seem to call into question their right to remain incorporated under the laws of any state in the union. All the states—along with the Federal government—guarantee civil liberties, which have rarely been so flagrantly violated as in this setting of men to spy upon workers and "report" their efforts to form a union of their choice by exercising their constitutional rights of freedom of speech and of conscience.

Henry Ford, supreme individualist, who does his own financing and owns his own steel, cement, electric power and light, and assembly plants, his own coke ovens, and the like, also "rolls his own" in matters of espionage. He has hired Harry Bennett, an ex-sailor, ex-pugilist, to establish a spying and stool-pigeon system which works in the plant and also in large measure dominates the police and politics in Dearborn, Michigan. The favorite pursuit of Bennett and his boys is ganging up on union organizers, trying literally to beat them down, and otherwise forestall the coming of collective barganing to Ford's.

On May 26, 1937, for example, Walter Reuther and Richard Frankensteen, top officials of the United Automobile Workers, who had secured a city permit to distribute union leaflets to Ford workers as they changed shifts, took their places atop a street overpass debouching from one of the gates of the great River Rouge plant. Newsmen and photographers who had learned of their intention chatted with them for a moment and shot a few pictures. Suddenly, Frankensteen and Reuther and their companions observed that a crowd of some one hundred and fifty men had converged on an adjacent platform, and were lounging about. They had seemed to materialize as if in response to a signal. They definitely didn't appear to be workers, for, as Reuther later testified at a National Labor Relations Board hearing,

. . . they had no lunch baskets and wore no badges. . . . After the pictures were taken we were approached by some of these men on all sides. . . . One called out that we were on private property and to get the hell off of there. Frankensteen and I turned to get off the bridge in obedience to the command. I had hardly taken three steps when I was slugged on the back of the head. I tried to shield my face by crossing my arms. They pounded me over the head and body. . . . I was knocked to the ground and beaten. . . .

They picked me up and threw me bodily on the concrete floor of the platform. Then they kicked me again and again. They tried to tear my legs apart. Seven times they raised me off the concrete and threw me down on it. They pinned my arms and shot . . . jabs to my face. I was dragged to the stairway. I grabbed the railing and they wrenched me loose. I was thrown down the first flight of iron steps. Then they kicked me down the other two flights. . . .

Frankensteen was given a similar "workout" and one of his aides had his "innards smashed."

Whereas Ford's public-relations staff strove mightily to convey the impression that Frankensteen and Reuther had been repulsed by "loyal employees" incensed by union efforts to convert them, the testimony given by reporters and cameramen, along with Dr. Sanford of the Chicago Federation of Churches who happened to be on the scene, revealed that "thugs, hoodlums" and "brass-knuckle-men" of Bennett's "Ford Service" organization were responsible for this vicious attack.

Moreover, despite the fact that a Grand Jury has indicted the Ford Motor Company and members of Bennett's strong-arm squad for willful intent to do bodily harm, Bennett still retains his post as "personnel director" of the company and still boasts that if a Ford worker joins a union, he knows the particulars within twenty-four hours and has arranged for the man's discharge within forty-eight.

The general knowledge among auto workers that the man next to them on the line may be a secret agent, eager to amplify a kind word about unionism into a plot to "take over the factory" and impelled to make up lies out of whole cloth to justify his pay, freezes the warmth of normal human intercourse among men sharing a common enterprise.

Furthermore, under the division of executive authority that prevails in the industry, the foreman, who is management's surrogate, right on the job, exerts a tremendous power. He sometimes exacts tribute from the workers, allowing them to keep their jobs by kicking in so much a week, or "selling" the less strenuous assignments.

Early in 1933, goaded by wage cuts, layoffs, inhuman resort to the speed-up, workers began to walk out in a congeries of minor, intradepartment strikes that were yet portents of more to come. On September 22, the Mechanics Educational Society, an independent union which had enrolled nearly all of the industry's highly skilled tool and die makers, pulled out hundreds of its adherents in protest against incomes which had shrunk from an average of $2,717 in 1929 to $1,300 in 1933. In the Detroit region such "aristocrats" of labor, accompanied by many commoners, walked out at Buick, Chevrolet, A. and C. Spark Plug, Fisher Body, Cadillac, Dodge, Hudson, Plymouth, Packard, and extended their strike to Ford at Edgewater, New Jersey, and to Nash at Kenosha, Wisconsin.

Meantime the NRA codes for the motor industry were being formulated in the summer of 1933. The weather was hot, the atmosphere electric and the codes displayed both characteristics. They were transparently pro-employer—to such an extent, indeed, that it was the auto workers who first rechristened the NRA the "National Run Around."

Angered, the auto workers cast about for guidance toward unionism's goal. They had a confusion of choices. The I.W.W., the Socialist party, the Communist party, the American Industrial Association all entered the arena with at least paper organizations eager to enlist members. At last the

A. F. of L. itself yawned out of its somnolence, stretched, and stumbled into activity.

Its organizers, however, were largely men who had been graduated from the brown derby, "I'm tough, see, have a cigar, leave it all to me, boys" school of the old-time pot-bellied walking delegate. They were also hobbled at every step by the jurisdictional jealousies of the various crafts. Despite such handicaps, however, an estimated 210,000 auto workers more or less quietly joined the Federation's "federal unions."

But the new unionists were bewildered. They couldn't get their questions answered. They asked if they were going to become a nationwide industrial union, or whether they were to be kept waiting until the membership was subdivided into craft groups. Nobody seemed to know, least of all the field organizers. The A. F. of L. didn't know either. It was marking time, its most costly and colossal luxury from its earliest days.

Meanwhile, to forestall the growth of any genuine unionism and to comply with the letter, and not the intent, of the collective bargaining provisions in the NRA codes, the employers started to fashion "company" unions, often forcing men to join them on pain of forfeiting their jobs. Meanwhile, too, as the speed-up and longer hours for but slightly increased pay continued, the A. F. of L., prodded by rank-and-file insistence, set March 1934, as the date on which auto workers all over the country were to go on strike and with a single bold stroke end company unions and all the fraud and chicane they implied.

At President Roosevelt's request, however, this "threat to returning prosperity" was averted by Federation leaders and many long days of muddled mediation ensued. For a time, the inertia of the Automobile Labor Board, the craft squabbles within the A. F. of L., the organization conflicts outside of it, provoked an estimated 75,000 unionists into turning in or tearing up their union cards.

Elections held early in 1935 under the Board's auspices clearly reflected the prevailing temper of the nation's auto workers. Out of a total of 154,-780 ballots cast, 111,878 workers voted for "unaffiliated representation." In other words, the majority were so fed up with the clamors of competition for their allegiance that they didn't want any of the existing unions to act as their agents. Only 14,057 voted for the A. F. of L., 7,071 for other legitimate unions, and 21,774 for the company-run kind. Hundreds of thousands of workers refrained from thus registering their will, apparently in their discouragement believing even this gesture a waste of time.

Yet the deep desire to be unionized swirled like a strong current temporarily dammed up. The A. F. of L.'s federal locals had meanwhile begun banding together in what was, at first, a loose alliance under the name of the United Automobile Workers. It was directed by Francis J. Dillon, an A. F. of L. veteran business agent hand-picked by William Green against the majority votes of delegates to the U.A.W.'s convention at Detroit in August of 1935. The convention reluctantly agreed to permit Dillon to remain at the helm until an appeal citing his unfitness could be considered by the executive council of the A. F. of L. which was scheduled to convene at the Federation's own annual sessions in Atlantic City two months later.

But this appeal somehow was sidetracked in the tumult that surrounded the withdrawal of John L. Lewis and company from the A. F. of L. to form their Committee for Industrial Organization. In any event Green insisted on keeping Dillon in command of the United Automobile Workers, a tactical blunder of the first magnitude. For Dillon epitomized the old-fashioned approach to unionism adhered to by the more Victorian-minded craft leaders. On the other hand, the United Automobile Workers were more and more convinced that unionizing techniques devised for the nineteenth century were not applicable to the twentieth. In one of its earliest pamphlets, addressed to the worker, it declared, ". . . No man today is alone an automobile maker. You join with thousands of others in a collective productive effort. Does the manufacturer hire you, put you at a bench or forge, give you a heap of iron ore, a pile of cloth, a supply of raw rubber and a few sheets of glass, and then tell you to get to work and make automobiles individually? . . ."

Animated by this outlook, the auto workers in general were heartened by the creation of the C.I.O., founded as it was on the premise that either mass-production workers were to be organized, and speedily, or that "labor's voice" would soon be modulated down from at best a mild forte to a very soft and plaintive pianissimo, if it were to be heard at all.

Various other unions, such as the Coughlin-sponsored Automobile Industrial Workers Association and the Associated Automobile Workers of America, called the "Greer bunch" after the name of its principal, shared the affection of the U.A.W. for the industrial idea. All three groups began to talk about a fusion of forces, looking to the C.I.O. for guidance. They didn't get it, at first. The C.I.O. was already embroiled in fifty-seven different varieties of controversy and had to feel its way cautiously for some six or seven months. By the time Roosevelt was re-elected, however, it was sending scouts and advisers into Detroit to assist the U.A.W. in ousting

Dillon and hence to shatter A. F. of L. prestige and influence for many miles around.

In the spring of 1936 the U.A.W. supplanted him by electing Homer S. Martin as its president. He was thirty-four years old, a former minister emotionally identified with the underdog.

Late in December 1936, after a vigorous organizing campaign, the U.A.W. sent a letter to Mr. William S. Knudsen, then executive vice-president of General Motors, asking for a conference on the general subject of collective bargaining. The letter enumerated the auto workers' complaints and pointed out that local attempts to settle questions of wages, hours, and work conditions with branch officials had always arrived nowhere.

The company replied, through Mr. Knudsen, that it could not talk, and suggested that Martin and his followers seek adjustment of grievances with local plant managers. This was, in Martin's view, nonsense. The corporation's industrial relations policy was explicitly determined at the top and local administrators merely carried out the orders of their superiors.

"It's the merry run-around again," muttered U.A.W. members and in exasperation many of them spontaneously sat down in the Fisher Body Plant at Cleveland, Ohio, on December 28, 1936—ringing up the curtain upon the most spectacular and significant capital-labor drama of the post-crash period.

Next day the sit-down was extended to Fisher Body Plant No. 2 in Flint, Michigan, where the U.A.W. had submitted a sample contract to the plant manager with the request that he ponder its terms as the basis for future discussion. In reply he discharged five stanch unionists. Enraged by this "sock in the teeth," U.A.W. members and others also sat down. Next morning workers in Fisher Body Plant No. 1, also in Flint, heard the rumor that the company had begun to remove necessary tools and dies to weaker union places, to Pontiac, Michigan, and even to Atlanta, Georgia, to forestall production stoppages and to have the workers in these places break the Flint strike. In protest, U.A.W. men and their well-wishers sat down in Fisher Body Plant No. 1 with a gaiety that was later transformed into a grim tenacity of purpose, while the movement caromed to Anderson, Indiana, to Kansas City, Missouri, to Norwood, Ohio, and to Atlanta, Georgia, spreading from one General Motors plant to another throughout the country.

The high command of the C.I.O. which had recently annexed the United Automobile Workers was surprised and shaken by the suddenness of this sit-down epidemic and would have preferred smallpox or something simple instead. From the standpoint of John L. Lewis and his aides, the timing of this strike in motors couldn't have been more maladroit. At the moment the C.I.O. was hurling nearly all of its new might in money and men into the Steel Workers Organizing Committee's drive on steel, proceeding on the theory that if this "most impregnable fortress of the open-shop" could be made to yield to the C.I.O.'s assault, the whole industrial salient could be more readily conquered. To Lewis, as to his Marshal Ney, Scotch-born Philip Murray, success or failure in unionizing steel was to be Austerlitz or Waterloo. They hadn't reckoned on any new major engagements on a new front.

Yet they were duty bound to send succor to Homer Martin and the U.A.W., which as a union was still very young. Its leaders were honest and intelligent but they by and large lacked experience in all the multifarious activity, from publicity releases to maintenance of morale, that any big strike entails. With misgivings, Lewis dispatched John Brophy, Director of Organization for the C.I.O., to U.A.W. headquarters in the Hoffman Building in Detroit as the herald of more reinforcements and supplies to come, and later wired the Flint sit-downers that the C.I.O. and its affiliates "pledge you complete and unanimous support in the conduct of the strike. . . . You men are undoubtedly carrying on through one of the most heroic battles that has ever been undertaken by strikers in an industrial dispute. The attention of the entire American public is focused upon you. . . ."

With the stubborn and desperate courage of men carrying the banners of a new crusade, the Flint sit-downers refused to be dislodged for weeks that stirred headline writers to new heights, editorial writers, columnists, and radio commentators to new hysterias, provided bitter debates in the Senate and House, and divided most of the population into two emotionally overstrung camps, warring over the subject of the strikers' favorite song:

> *When they tie a can to a union man,*
> *Sit-down! Sit-down!*
> *When they give him the sack, they'll take him back,*
> *Sit-down! Sit-down!*
>
> *When the speed-up comes, just twiddle your thumbs,*
> *Sit-down! Sit-down!*
> *When the boss won't talk, don't take a walk,*
> *Sit-down! Sit-down!*

BRUCE BLIVEN

STRIKE AT THE FLINT PLANT*

To GET INSIDE a plant while a sit-down is in progress is a hard job. On the day I entered Fisher Body No. 1, the strikers had been holding the fort for two weeks. In that time not a soul had entered the building without their consent, and very few under any circumstances. When our car pulled up at the curb before the big, modern structure, set back in a green lawn like a Middle Western high school, a reception committee of five or six sturdy men was waiting. They promptly searched our party, and the car, for weapons. Only when they had been reassured as to our identity were we allowed to go up the walk to the plant itself. All the doors had been shut and heavily barricaded, two weeks earlier. To get in, you climbed on a pile of packing boxes, and swung yourself over the lower third of a heavy window of steel and opaque glass, hinged horizontally at the top. On a platform just inside was another reception committee, friendly enough on the surface but with grim undertones in their voices as they checked over our credentials. During the whole period of the sit-down, nobody left or entered the plant without a pass, and without being searched on his way out and in.

The room in which we found ourselves was a vast oblong, used for building automobile bodies. A double line of these extended the length of the plant, close together, looking with their uniform gray color and their smooth and bulging contours a little like so many kneeling elephants, trunk to tail. As you went forward along the line, each of these bodies was a trifle closer to completion than the one behind it; those at the very end even had the colors they will bear when chassis, engine and wheels have been added and they are off to the road.

Fifteen hundred men had lived for two weeks in a building never intended to be lived in at all, yet the place was remarkably neat and tidy, at least as clean as it is under normal conditions. Beds were made up on the floor of each car, the seats being removed if necessary, and the members of the night shift of guards were sound asleep in the haphazard quarters. They had no weapons of any kind except braided leather billies im-

* From "Sitting Down in Flint," *The New Republic*, Jan. 27, 1937.

provised inside the plant after the sit-down had started. The guards off duty slept in their clothes, with these billies thrust into a pocket or, sometimes, loosely grasped in the sleeper's hand.

The degree of organization among these men was something to think about. An elected strike committee was in general control. Every man had specified duties, to be performed at specified hours. Meals were prepared with food brought by friends on the outside and passed in through a window, these meals being served in the plant cafeteria at stipulated hours. A barbershop was in operation in one of the rest rooms. Liquor was absolutely forbidden. An emergency post office was set up and there was a heavy movement of mail in both directions—all of it censored by a special committee.

For recreation, the men played cards or listened to the radio, or to a daily concert by the members of the workmen's band, who were staying in. Hundreds of friends and relatives of the strikers visited them every day. With characteristic Yankee ingenuity, the strikers had rigged up a loud-speaker system throughout the plant, with a microphone at the "main entrance." When a visitor called to see any given striker, he was paged over the loud-speaker system. When meetings of all the strikers (except the guards on duty) were held, the union leaders or the members of the strike committee also used a microphone, to make sure of being heard by their listeners, sitting on the floor in the odd bits of space not occupied by machines. I could not see—and I looked for it carefully—the slightest damage done anywhere to any property of the General Motors Corporation. The nearly completed car bodies, for example, were as clean as they would be in the salesroom, their glass and metal shining.

HERBERT HARRIS

SIT-DOWN AT GENERAL MOTORS*

THE "SIT-DOWN" which between September 1, 1936, and June 1, 1937, involved 484,711 American workers not only in motors but in rubber, steel, textiles, shipbuilding, subways, oil refining, shoes, newspaper publishing, baking, aircraft, and countless other manufacturing service and retail-

* From Herbert Harris' *American Labor* (New Haven, Yale University Press, 1938).

ing spheres, is a strike of a very special kind. Whereas in the everyday variety employees leave mill or mine or store or factory to picket outside their place of business, in the sit-down they remain inside at or near their usual posts but do no work. They just sit or stretch out on the floor or benches or loll around on their feet. And if a sit-down lasts long enough—dozens of them in mass-production plants last only a few minutes or a few hours—it becomes a stay-in, properly speaking, though the term "sit-down" is already a colloquialism used to describe this technique, per se, whatever its duration.

Its advantages are obvious. Police and militia can more easily disperse a picket line in the open than an "occupied" plant where windows may be barricaded and gates barred. "You can't ride a horse through a brick wall," remarked a grizzled old unionist in Detroit during the General Motors stay-ins. "With the sit-down today the boys don't have to put up with that, anyway."

Sit-down psychology differs profoundly from that of any other strike tactic. In the first place, the men stay together all the time instead of meeting irregularly at a hall or union headquarters or in the street. They talk, become better acquainted, generate feelings of unity and co-operation, "one for all, and all for one." In the second place, the sit-down gives the individual worker a new and rare sense of power—especially in highly mechanized industries where relatively few men can literally "tie up the works." Gongs go bonging, phones shrill, straw bosses storm, managers get flurried and mad and machinery is idle—all because of what he and his companions have done.

Contrary to popular impression, the sit-down is not an instrument designed and patented by the C.I.O., although its widespread use in this country happened to coincide with the high spots of the C.I.O.'s organizing campaign during 1936 and 1937 especially.

Len DeCaux, editor of the *Union News Service,* the movement's official news bureau, declared:

As a matter of fact the first experience of the C.I.O. with sit-downs was in discouraging them. This was in the Akron rubber industry, after the Goodyear strike. C.I.O. representatives cautioned . . . the new unionists against sit-downs on the ground that they should use such channels for negotiating grievances as the agreement provided.

And in supporting this general approach, John L. Lewis at about the same time announced that "the C.I.O. stands for punctilious observance of contracts, but we are not losing any sleep about strikes where employers refuse to recognize well-defined principles of collective bargaining. A

C.I.O. contract is adequate protection against sit-downs, lie-downs, or any other kind of strike."

Despite William Green's statement that "both personally and officially I disavow the sit-down strike as a part of the economic or organization policy of the A. F. of L.," numerous Federation unions, notably electricians, hotel and restaurant, theatrical and building service employees engaged in sit-downs to protect their wage scales and for other reasons. It is, furthermore, a tactic resorted to mainly in industries that have been, or are, vigorously anti-union. During the period previously mentioned, that from September 1, 1936, to June 1, 1937, which witnessed the greatest extent of sit-downing, motors—which had been historically open shop—had about a quarter of a million sitters; rubber, which for a generation has been a "No Man's Land" for unionism, had about forty-five thousand; and textiles, still a battleground for pro- and anti-union forces, had about twenty-five thousand. On the other hand, in coal mining, where the United Mine Workers is well established, there were only 270 workers who sought to use the sit-down, and none at all in the extremely well-organized men's clothing and women's wear trades.

The American sit-down, in short, affirms not the right to the factory (which is not operated but kept in a state of quiescence) but the right to the job, a "vested interest" in it, and the attempt to protect this work territory against the invasion of others, strikebreakers, pending the settlement of differences between labor and management. The sit-down does not challenge ownership of productive equipment; but it does challenge the privilege of the "employer," whether corporation or individual, to retain within his (or its) own hands the enormous powers over employees that result from the fact that most families of wage earners live from hand to mouth, through no fault of their own, and often are but a few days removed from starvation.

From the mists and fogs of emotion-charged words marking the discussion of the sit-down one clear question emerges: Is purely legal title to a producing property the only right that should be recognized in the American democracy?

In Flint, Michigan, the power of General Motors was arrayed against the implications of this view in a community where, out of 165,000 inhabitants, 50,000 depended directly upon the company for livelihoods gained from Buick, Chevrolet, and Fisher Body plants. Anti-sit-down sentiment, after the first days of the strike, was crystallized by an organization called the Flint Alliance. It was composed of "loyal employees," most of whom somehow contrived to resemble bar-flies and poolroom toughs from nearby

Detroit, a sprinkling of General Motors executives and subadministrators and people from its technical and commercial divisions, some local businessmen, and almost all the vigilante-minded personalities in the vicinity. The Alliance's propaganda was fabricated by the high-pressure, high-priced Floyd E. Williamson who, himself an "outsider" imported from Manhattan, based a large part of his anti-union blasts upon the "un-American activities" of "outside" organizers. As the sit-down progressed, Alliance spokesmen grew daily more vociferous in their demands for violence, some of them promising that soon law-and-order committees of indignant citizenry would forciby evict the sit-downers who by the thousand had dug in for a long siege.

To oust the strikers, General Motors had secured from Judge Edward Black an injunction which commanded them to vacate company property and also forbade picketing. Although he owned nearly $200,000 worth of General Motors stock, Judge Black considered himself sufficiently impartial to issue his edict, a belief not entirely in accord with the more commendable traditions of the American bench. When Sheriff Wolcott delivered the Black doument to the sit-downers he was jeered and good-naturedly told to go home. Meantime, company officials, both local and national, and U.A.W. and C.I.O. leaders were busy fencing, mustering all their skill for parry and riposte, all of them with an eye on the public gallery.

On January 12, the company shut off the heat in Fisher Body Plant No. 2, and its own gray-uniformed police, reinforced by regulars from the local Flint force, were instructed to prevent the shipment of food into the building. It was hoped that this "diet of cold and hunger" would break the morale of the sit-downers.

Inside the plant, the men missed their lunch, shivered, and grew restive at the prospect of being also deprived of their dinner. Shortly before seven o'clock that evening, a United Automobile Workers sound truck rolled up before the great rectangle of Fisher No. 2, with Victor Reuther, a topnotch organizer for the union, at the microphone. At first he politely asked the police, both public and private, for permission to have food sent in to the sit-downers from the union's kitchen. The metallic lungs of the amplifier lifted his voice high above the sounds of the street until everyone within a half-mile radius could hear his plea. The officers, both the gray and the blue, were mute. Reuther tried another tack. He appealed to them as workers, urging the necessity for co-operation among all kinds and degrees of labor. There was no response, save the cheers of the sit-downers. He then became more aggressive, assuring the officers that strikers outside the plant would get food to the sitters. Some fifteen minutes later a group of pickets carrying pails of coffee and cartons of buns, like an oversized backfield, starting on an end run, bowled over the police guarding the door to the plant and brought food to their famished friends.

At 8:45 some sixty policemen set upon pickets stationed at plant entrances, clubbed them with night-sticks, and drove them inside the building. A sergeant smashed a glass pane in one of the doors and thrust the nozzle of a tear-gas gun through the jagged space, pumping shells into the vast interior. Other officers fired buckshot into pickets and men clustered near the door, wounding fourteen who were later removed to the hospital.

The sit-downers replied to this attack with literally everything they had: coffee-mugs, pop-bottles, and steel automobile hinges weighing two pounds each. At the beginning of the battle, a clarion voice from the sound truck cried: "We wanted peace. General Motors chose war. Give it to 'em!" In the road strikers formed a phalanx around the sound truck, repelled all efforts of police to dismantle it, and overturned three police cars and another belonging to the sheriff.

At midnight the policemen closed in their ranks and, with guns cracking, tried to rush the main entrance, only to be met by a devastating stream of water from a big fire hose which, along with the steel-hinge missiles, compelled them to retreat and finally to abandon their assault. This affair was promptly named "The Battle of the Running Bulls."

The bloodshed of that night, and the fears of more violence to come, resulted in the appearance of 1,500 of Michigan's National Guardsmen in Flint. Acting under instructions from the cool-headed, humanitarian Governor Murphy who was valiantly seeking to settle the strike by pacific means, they managed on the whole to preserve order almost impartially.*

Meantime—after the strikers by a ruse had captured the crucial Chevrolet motor assembly plant No. 4, and John L. Lewis had called on President Roosevelt to intercede for them against the "economic royalists represented by General Motors and the Du Ponts," who had opposed his re-election with the same fervor that the auto workers had supported it; and after Washington conferences between Secretary of Labor Frances Perkins and Alfred P. Sloan, president, and William S. Knudsen, vice-president of the company, had produced mutual recriminations—General Motors obtained from Circuit Judge Paul V. Gadola a significant and sweeping court order. It directed the sit-downers to evacuate company-

---

* One major, however, confessed his bitter disappointment that he was unable to test the value of his pet idea, shooting vomiting gas into the sit-downers via the plants' ventilating systems.

owned plants under penalty of imprisonment for contempt of court and a fine of $15,000,000, the estimated value of the invested properties. Again Sheriff Wolcott served to mocking and derisive groups of determined men the order that set 3 P.M. on February 3 as the deadline for leaving the struck plants.

In reply the sit-downers sent telegrams to Governor Murphy. The message from Fisher Body Plant No. 1 read in part:

> We the workers . . . have carried on a stay-in strike over a month in order to make General Motors Corporation obey the law and engage in collective bargaining. . . . Unarmed as we are, the introduction of the militia, sheriffs, or police with murderous weapons will mean a blood-bath of unarmed workers. . . . We have decided to stay. . . . We have no illusions about the sacrifices which this decision will entail. We fully expect that if a violent effort to oust us is made many of us will be killed, and we take this means of making it known to our wives, our children, to the people of the state of Michigan and the country that if this result follows from the attempt to eject us, you are the one who must be held responsible for our deaths.

The night before the "zero hour" day of February 3, the sit-downers, pallid under blazing arc lights, listened grimly to their radios, or played cards or parcheesi or checkers or dominoes, or tried to lose themselves in newspapers or magazines, or talked in subdued tones. Many were convinced that the morrow meant massacre. For defense against expected machine guns, inadequate clubs dangled from their belts. An air of almost Oriental passivity, as of men who wait in resignation for the beat of destiny's drum, hung over them. Their faces were stern and thoughtful, and few slept.

In the morning roads leading into Flint were filled with cars and trucks carrying union sympathizers from Akron, Lansing, Detroit and Toledo who by the thousand swarmed over the town and had to take over the direction of traffic themselves, for no policemen were in sight. The visitors moved toward the various sit-down plants, and only the women's emergency brigades, with their red and green berets, brought color to a somber procession that for weapons held pokers, broom handles and pieces of pipe.

While Flint's clocks ticked on toward the showdown hour of three in the afternoon, Governor Murphy in Detroit finally succeeded in arranging a conference between William S. Knudsen for the company and John L. Lewis for the United Automobile Workers. To Sheriff Wolcott, who had the duty of enforcing the Gadola eviction order, Governor Murphy wired that everything should be held in abeyance during the Knudsen-Lewis conversations; and the Sheriff, more than pleased to oblige, suddenly discovered that he lacked proper legal sanction, anyway, along with a sufficient force to carry out the Gadola edict, although the Flint Alliance and the company's legal staff in Flint assured him that they could together remedy both deficiencies.

When this turn of events was made known, sit-downers, pickets, and unionists from other cities made high holiday. Their violins, saxophones, banjos, cornets struck up hillbilly airs and square-dance tunes, and men and women swung partners joyously over the frozen lawns surrounding the various plants.

Next day the company complied with President Roosevelt's request that in the public interest its representatives should again meet with spokesmen of the strikers. A wearing week of conferences ensued between William S. Knudsen, G. Donaldson Brown and John Thomas Smith for General Motors, and John L. Lewis, Lee Pressman (general counsel for the C.I.O.), Homer Martin and Wyndham Mortimer for the strikers. Time after time only the moral strength and suasions of Governor Murphy, who presided over the negotiations, prevented their collapse, and cigarette and cigar ashes spilled over trays amid the temper-fraying clashes of strong wills and stronger wants.

Eight days later, the Governor, his face haggard with strain and lack of sleep, had the great personal triumph of seeing at long last a meeting of minds out of which came the agreement terminating one of the most important capital-labor disputes in recent times.

The contract signed by General Motors and the United Automobile Workers was a great step forward for unionism in motors and contained seven basic provisions: (1) recognition was to be granted to the U.A.W. for its members only, and not as sole collective bargaining agent; (2) straight seniority rules were to prevail after six months of service; (3) shop committees were to be set up to smooth out grievances on the job; (4) a survey of speed-up evils was to be made; (5) the forty-hour week was to continue in force; (6) time and a half for overtime was to prevail; (7) no discrimination was to be exercised against unionists, who could wear their union buttons and talk about their organization during lunch hours.

The union requests for a uniform minimum wage, affecting plants in all parts of the country, and for the thirty-hour week were both denied.

Primarily as the result of its sit-downers' forty-four-day defiance of General Motors, the United Automobile Workers (late in 1938) had some 370,000 dues-paying members out of an industry-wide maximum potential of 450,000. It is thus the third largest among the C.I.O. unions. It has collective bargaining agreements with all of the independents and with two of the Big Three, General Motors and Chrysler. Currently it is trying to unionize Ford* against an opposition as stubborn as a peasant's prejudice and as strong as a billion dollars.

The U.A.W. is doubly young—both in its short time of existence as a union and in its membership, since the industry still places a premium upon speed and endurance in its workers, attributes most generally found in men and women under forty, even under thirty-five. The union's maverick sit-downs, condemned by motor magnates and (some of them) by Martin himself, have derived from a new sense of liberation from oppression; from flawed methods of adjusting "line" and departmental grievances; from foreman-worker antagonisms that had been piling up for years and were often aggravated by both the self-assertion of the new unionists and the desire of the straw boss to show them that he was still top-dog. Many of the pettier officials, indeed, still believe it their purpose in life to bring obloquy upon the union whenever possible; and neither side has as yet been "educated up" to the patience and will to good will necessary for a harmonious management-union relationship.

* The union's campaign culminated in a contract signed in June 1941.—ED.

BOOKSELLING AND BEST SELLERS

IN THE Depression years millions of readers rediscovered the public library. Three to four million more people borrowed books in 1933 than in 1929, and the total circulation of library books increased nearly forty per cent. These same years saw the development of the private circulating library, where a book could be rented for three cents a day. To many readers the ownership of a new book had become an impracticable luxury.

In consequence, the sale of books to the general public amounted to 22 million dollars in 1933, about half of that in 1929. Cheap hard-cover reprints of best sellers found a ready market (successful paperback editions would not appear until 1939); book clubs offering selected new books at reduced prices began to flourish as more and more book buyers subscribed to the beneficent authority of the "library judges."

The desire to "escape" was clearly reflected in the general book buyer's choice. In the opinion of Frederick Lewis Allen, "*The Good Earth* by Pearl Buck, which led the fiction best-seller list in 1931 and 1932, probably had an additional appeal because it took readers away to China. The appearance of *The Fountain* by Charles Morgan, on the same list for 1932, may have been partly due to the fact that it told of a man who escaped from the outward world of ugly circumstance into a world of inward reflection." * The same might be said about the success of James

Hilton's *Lost Horizons*, which made the best-seller list in 1935. The historical novel too offered escape. *Anthony Adverse* by Hervey Allen led the best-seller lists of 1933 and 1934, while *Gone With the Wind* by Margaret Mitchell was number one in 1936 and 1937. *Northwest Passage* (1937) by Kenneth Roberts and *Drums Along the Mohawk* (1936) by Walter D. Edmonds were also long-lasting favorites.

During the same time, superb biographies were published—Carl Van Doren's *Benjamin Franklin*, Marquis James's *Andrew Jackson*, Carl Sandburg's *Lincoln*, Douglas Southall Freeman's *R. E. Lee*, to name but a few.

Guidebooks to. personal success were popular: *Live Alone and Like It* by Marjorie Hillis, *Wake Up and Live* by Dorothea Brande, and *How to Win Friends and Influence People* by Dale Carnegie were huge successes.

Books by journalists reporting on conditions in Europe indicated a growing general interest in foreign lands. Among the best of these works were Vincent Sheean's *Personal History* (1935), Negley Farson's *Way of a Transgressor* (1936), John Gunther's *Inside Europe* (1936) and Pierre van Paassen's *Days of Our Years* (1939).

These titles are a sampling of the best sellers of the decade. What did the author have to look forward to in terms of income if he were lucky enough to get a best seller?

* Frederick Lewis Allen, *Since Yesterday.*

EDWARD WEEKS

HARD TIMES AND THE AUTHOR*

IN NORMAL times the financial status of our author admits of three levels.
At the top are a small group of what I might call literary magnates—
E. Phillips Oppenheim, Zane Grey, Mary Roberts Rinehart, Willa Cather,
Sinclair Lewis, Louis Bromfield, Kathleen Norris—each one of whom in
full production might earn in the neighborhood of $70,000 a year. A
fellow publisher has made a composite picture of the income of a popular
novelist whose new book has just sold 50,000 copies and who is eager to
pursue every offer. Before you read these figures, let me caution you that
mighty few moguls are capable of this earning power and still fewer of
them can maintain it for long.

Royalty at 15% of $2.50	$18,750
Motion picture rights	25,000
Sale of serial rights on next novel	15,000
Misc. short stories, all written but up to now rejected .	3,000
Contract for 6 short stories	6,000
Lectures (net)	2,500
Misc. rights (English, foreign, second serial)	2,500
Motion picture contract for editorial work for 10 weeks	
at $500 a week	5,000
	$77,750

I doubt if in any year as much as one per cent of the writing profession
is capable of reaching this maximum figure. In 1934 there were exactly
fifteen authors whose books sold 50,000 copies or more in the United
States.

On the plane next below will be found a group of well-known novelists
and short-story writers, authors of the best technical books and the standard juveniles, and a few exceptional biographers who with utmost industry
are able to average an earned income of between $10,000 and $15,000 a
year. They comprise perhaps 12 per cent of the writing profession.

By simple subtraction, 87 per cent of our army of writers are to be
found on the third and lowest plane. To put it generously, the annual

* Condensed from the *Atlantic Monthly*, May 1935.

proceeds of their writing range somewhere between $800 and $5,000. The Authors Guild puts their average earning in *good times* at $2,500 a year. Since many of them are people of maturity with families to support, it goes without saying that the members of this third estate must depend either upon private incomes or part-time jobs if their bills are to be met. For them literature is a poor staff and a not altogether reliable crutch.

The pinch of hard times was of course felt on each of these levels. The shrinkage of advertising and circulation compelled magazine editors to economize. That is to say, they reduced the size of their publications, they printed material they had paid for but never used; they bought, in short, about half as much new material as they had needed in the happy days. Magazine writers who had been living in assumed security suddenly realized that their markets were disappearing and—worse—that even when a sale was made they were likely to receive a price smaller by 50 per cent than what they had been accustomed to.

Meanwhile the book writers were facing their own particular grief. Readers were losing the habit of buying the many books they wanted; they had suddenly become price-conscious. They bought only the irresistible books; the others were borrowed from the public libraries or rented from the circulating libraries in the bookstores. The royalties of even the best established writers came down on the toboggan; the royalties of authors whose books customarily sold over 10,000 copies suddenly dropped 50 per cent below the 1929 return. The royalties of unestablished writers, by which I mean first novelists, young poets, beginning biographers, dwindled to the vanishing point. "Fewer and better books" was an ideal rule to enforce if booksellers and publishers were to survive. But, reduced to financial terms, it meant that mature authors had to tighten their belts and beginning authors had to surmount a higher wall than heretofore.

MAJOR NOVELISTS

How DID the Depression affect the serious writers of the period?

Many had left the United States in the Twenties because they could not do their best work in the boom atmosphere. Malcolm Cowley, writing in the *New Republic* in 1939, put it another way: The Thirties had brought a "sense of relief" to the writers, who "had been unhappy in the boom days, which were dominated by their enemies, the businessmen." Cowley went on to say:

"The Depression brought hundreds of writers home from Europe. Though their reason for returning was in many cases merely that their money had run out, they showed the usual tendency of writers to find historical motives. . . . They rediscovered America, in one book after another, and it was a different America from the country they had deserted early in the 1920s. To carry the process one step farther, European writers began to follow them westward, as political refugees or tourists, so that New York became a capital of world literature. Its importance began to be recognized abroad." *

Among the returning writers were three major novelists who, while primarily identified with the Twenties, would influence the new generation; they were F. Scott Fitzgerald, Ernest Hemingway and John Dos Passos.

FITZGERALD

Fitzgerald's influence was on the wane; the publication of his novel *Tender Is the Night* in 1936 received little attention, and many reviewers found it disappointing. Not until his death, and the posthumous publication of the unfinished *The Last Tycoon* in 1941, would his star begin to rise again. Fitzgerald's predilection for self-destruction was incompatible with the mood of the Thirties. Writers were inclined to be impatient with his asocial writings, and unsympathetic with his absorption with himself as an artist. Nevertheless, he was producing important work in this period, and must be considered part of it.

HEMINGWAY

When Hemingway went off to Europe in the early Twenties, he was seeking an environment of the greatest possible isolation, a condition he considered essential for the creative artist. This did not mean isolation in the physical sense, for he enjoyed relationships with other expatriates; rather he saw himself and the protagonists of his work as individuals who must stand apart from the society to which they belonged. Only by doing this could an individual be free to discover the true meaning of the self.

Maxwell Geismar believes Hemingway marks the end of the cult of the individual, which was an integral part of the lost-generation syndrome. The Depression forced writers, Hemingway included, out of isolation and made them aware, as Geismar says, of "the transience of our materialistic

* Malcolm Cowley, "A Farewell to the Thirties," *The New Republic*, Nov. 8, 1939.

power which they had felt so inimical to creative values."

Hemingway's novel *To Have and Have Not*, published in 1937, was set in a Florida resort town during the Depression and bore signs of his new concern with social problems. While it was not ranked with his best work, it was reviewed as part of the "social protest" fiction of the time. The turnabout in Hemingway was detected when, as Harry Morgan, the protagonist, lies dying at the end of the story, he says, "No matter how . . . a man ain't got no bloody . . . chance." And Hemingway adds, "It had taken him a long time to get it out and . . . all of his life to learn it."

Hemingway published only one novel in the Thirties, but he continued to write and publish superb short fiction, along with two nonfiction works—*The Green Hills of Africa* (1935) and *Death in the Afternoon* (1932).

It was Hemingway's style, however, rather than his social protest, which had a powerful influence upon other writers, from newspaper reporter to aspiring novelist. When they worked to simulate it, they usually ran aground, unable to equal the simplicity of expression that Hemingway had achieved only after years of struggle to make the words fit the experience. And while some writers, particularly the hard-boiled (which included John O'Hara and James M. Cain) managed to match its glittering surface, their work frequently bogged down in violence for its own sake.

DOS PASSOS

It is in the work of John Dos Passos that a connection can be found linking the writers of the Twenties and the writers of the Depression. Dos Passos shifted the focus away from the lonely individual to society itself; the dominant theme was not the failure of the individual but the failure of society to provide a healthy environment for the successful development of all human beings. In his trilogy, *U.S.A.*, Dos Passos was the first to combine in one huge orchestration all the manifestations of our modern industrial society.

By the use of certain technical devices, like the "Newsreels," the "Camera Eye," and "Biographies," he widened the scope of the novel. And yet, as Maxwell Geismar says, "though the exposition in *U.S.A.* was brilliant and its picture of American life was full and varied, the novelist's conclusion was simple, and not encouraging. Filled as the three volumes were with achievements of urban power, in the land of power, the 'Newsreels' became ever more sensational and chaotic, while the 'Biographies' of our national heroes formed only the record of their disinheritance [and] the 'Novels' recounted only the disintegration of these average lives, from the obscure merchant seaman Joe Williams to the publicity wizard J. Ward Moorehouse; and the reflections of the author in 'The Camera Eye' became in turn increasingly desolate. Thus the immense national energy which had built up such a remarkable society within so short a period had apparently become centrifugal: the elaborate system was shaking itself apart. In fact, just as each novel of the trilogy was better than its predecessor, each was more despairing." *

* From *Literary History of the United States* (New York, Macmillan, 1953).

Dos Passos wrote about the emptiness of the American success myth and the appeal of radicalism, but he overlooked the majority of Americans who are attracted to neither, who live between the two poles and give society its stable center. It is Geismar's observation that the characters in *U.S.A.* "are not in their entirety accurate historical creations but very often the symbols of a bleak and despairing view of life." For if they were accurate representations "there would be little value in the catharsis of social revolution . . . for such a revolution implies the freeing of human traits which the present social order is crushing. But in these American protagonists, what is there to free? Where are the little moments of human warmth, generosity, decency? If this is an accurate portrait of the race, then we may also say that the Capitalism which Dos Passos is attacking, if it is the cause of these social types, seems also to be their proper orbit." *

Nevertheless, *U.S.A.* was a landmark among the social novels that were written in the Thirties and its influence is still seen today in the work of many young writers.

FAULKNER

In the work of William Faulkner, concern about the individual's isolation is successfully blended with criticism of the industrial society. Of course, the society is one that is peculiar to the deep South. Within his imaginary county, Yoknapatawpha, he creates all life.

The Yoknapatawpha saga was begun with the novels *Sartoris* and *The Sound and the Fury*, both published in 1929; then followed *As I*

Lay Dying* (1930), *Sanctuary* (1931), *Light in August* (1932), *Absalom, Absalom!* (1936), and a collection of stories in *The Unvanquished* (1939). This alone represents an impressive production, but there were also two more volumes of stories, *These Thirteen* (1931) and *Dr. Martino* (1934), and two other novels, *Pylon* (1935) and *The Wild Palms* (1939), all unrelated to the saga.

According to Geismar, " 'Jefferson,' Mississippi, is the capital of this world which reaches backward in time to the origins of Southern culture and forward to the horrid prophecies of its extinction, and which ranges down in social strata from dying landed aristocracy, the Sartoris and Compson families, to the new commercial oligarchy of the Snopeses, down to the poor-white Bundrens of *As I Lay Dying*, to the pervert Popeye of *Sanctuary* and to the Negro Joe Christmas of *Light in August*, turned brute again by the society which had raised him from the animal.

"[It is in] these ancestral halls in which echo only the sobs of the possessed and demented . . . [that] Faulkner built his work on an even grander scale than Dos Passos. He related even his minor personages with one another, elaborated their genealogy from generation to generation, gave them a countryside: a deep land of Baptists, of brothels, of attic secrets, of swamps and shadows." †

If his writing was tortuous, and his characters sometimes grotesque, his work had qualities that are seldom found in the work of other writers. In Faulkner's world the reader will find a pervasive element

* Maxwell Geismar, *Writers in Crisis* (Boston, Houghton Mifflin, 1947).
† From *Literary History of the United States.*

of deep family affection and a range of sensitively shaded emotional relations between the very young and the old, both Negro and white. There is also a rare, wonderful backwoods humor, evident not only in the novels but also in the short stories.

Most readers reacted strongly to Faulkner's work (as they still do today), in admiration or complete rejection. The great cry against him was his lack of discipline and his constant experimentation. But he is the kind of author who writes only when moved by the inner voice, and probably he should then be judged, as Malcolm Cowley has said, as "an epic or bardic poet in prose, a creator of myths . . . [which] he weaves together into a legend of the South."

WOLFE

Thomas Wolfe was very early recognized as one of the important spokesmen of the younger generation. His four huge novels, more than a million words in length, may be considered a single work, a story of his life, thinly disguised as fiction. *Look Homeward, Angel* (1929), a family chronicle of the Gants, reviews the author's early years in North Carolina through the eyes of Eugene Gant. *Of Time and the River* (1935) tells of Eugene's years at Harvard, his return home at the time of his father's death, and his visit to Europe in the early years of Hitlerism. The posthumously published *The Web and the Rock* (1939) and *You Can't Go Home Again* (1940) continued the story (with the protagonist's name now changed to George Webber) almost to the point where, in real life, it was ended by the author's death in 1938.

"This huge novel," Geismar says, "multiformed and sometimes inchoate as it was, with its alterations, always in progress, formed a central document of the period. Just as Dos Passos reinvigorated the naturalistic novel by means of the symbolist techniques, so Wolfe regenerated the whole tradition of native realism through the electric charge of curiosity, of lyricism, of anger and protest, and perhaps even of pure excitement which he put into it." *

Many readers are irritated by Wolfe's overwriting, and his overdramatization of experience; others describe his writing as rich, sensuous rhetoric. F. Scott Fitzgerald was not of the latter group; he suggested that Wolfe could benefit from a consideration of Flaubert's concise style. Wolfe's answer was a defense of the "putter-inner" as against the "taker-outers." "I want to be a better artist," he said. "I want to be a more selective artist . . . but Flaubert me no Flauberts, Bovary me no Bovarys. . . ." And he went on to defend his intense appetite for all experience. In the opinion of Frederick J. Hoffman, "He wished to make from quantity a qualitative assertion concerning the meaning of life in its American cultural setting."

But if his novels lacked artistic structure, to many readers the lyrical prose passages were filled with color and tone—in a day when other writers were pruning their works to the lean, hard sinews so popular with the hard-boiled school. And Wolfe's partisans were moved by his laments over the transience of joy and the brevity of the individual life in the infinite river of time.

Who, since Whitman, has cele-

* From *Literary History of the United States.*

brated the glamorous pageantry of America, who has so unblushingly cried out over the "everlasting, living dream"? "I think the true discovery of America is before us," Wolfe wrote. "I think the true fulfillment of our spirit, of our people, of our mighty and immortal land, is yet to come. I think the true discovery of our own democracy is still before us. And I think that all these things are certain as the morning, as inevitable as noon."

His faith in America did not derive merely from some mystical promise of our land. At the time of his death, he had begun to achieve, as Geismar says, "the merging of the artist with his material: humanity." Wolfe indicated that identification when he wrote, "Mankind was fashioned for eternity, but it is with present evils that he is now concerned. And the essence of all faith . . . for such a man as I, the essence of all religion for people of my belief, is that man's life can be, and will be, better."

FARRELL

To discover *Studs Lonigan* now is probably not the overwhelming experience it was for some of us in the Thirties. Here was another massive novel—this time a documentary of the spiritually impoverished in an Irish-Catholic section of Chicago—which shocked the reader with its unglossed picture of the drab and vicious underlife of our cities. *Studs Lonigan* is one of the most striking examples of Depression literature; it is a raw, bitter exposition of the failure of the important institutions—home, church, school and playground—in the education of young men. The street and the poolroom had become the potent educative factors,

and our awareness of tragedy was strong as we watched Studs fall victim to his environment.

Farrell is often compared with Dreiser, and it is not hard to draw a parallel between his Studs and Dreiser's Clyde in *An American Tragedy*. Alfred Kazin believes that the difference between the two writers is that Dreiser, despite his awkward style, manifested a deep sense of poetry, while Farrell, less sentient, demonstrated a "literalness of mind which showed all through the Depression literature in the surrender of imagination and in the attraction to pure force."

Farrell continued to write about his section of Chicago for most of the Thirties, bringing out such novels as *A World I Never Made* (1936) and *No Star Is Lost* (1938), which began a new series about Danny O'Neill, clearly patterned on the author himself. Eventually readers complained that his style was clumsy and that he was tone-deaf in his choice of words and rhythms. Perhaps if he had gone outside his South Side Chicago environment in search of fresh settings the critics might have dwelt less insistently on his style. At any rate, Farrell served an important purpose then, one that can still be appreciated today, by calling attention to the spirit-stifling misery and demoralizing meanness that pervades so much of lower-middle-class city life.

STEINBECK

John Steinbeck, author of the most popular novel about the Thirties, *The Grapes of Wrath* (1939), was born in California, went to college at Stanford, but did not stay long enough to get his degree; he worked as a carpenter, painter, newspaperman, ranch hand, and wrote his first novel, *Cup of Gold* (1929), about the pirate Henry Morgan.

For his second novel, *Pastures of Heaven* (1932), he chose his own California valley country as the setting for a loosely connected group of stories. Later, in *Tortilla Flat* (1935), he wrote with ironic humor of the *paisanos* who reject hard work and competition (capitalism) and live off the land or the sea—or off anyone they can.

In Dubious Battle (1936), a "proletarian" novel, told the story of a strike conducted by migrant fruit pickers. In the following year he brought out an entirely different kind of novel, *Of Mice and Men* (1937), about the strange companionship of the powerful but feeble-minded giant Lennie and his friend and protector George. The success of this book, Steinbeck's first best seller, was due, at least in part, to its being about men who desired no more than enough to eat and a place to sleep.

In 1939, *The Grapes of Wrath* was immediately acclaimed "a great novel." It sold more than 300,000 copies in its first year and continued a best seller into the following year. It told the story of an Oklahoma family, the Joads, who lost their tenant farm in the Dust Bowl and migrated to California in search of employment as itinerant farm workers. "Readers who had thought of migrant workers as so many negligible thousands on the road or at work in masses," Carl Van Doren said, "now suddenly realized that they were not that at all. The Joads might have been any ordinary farm family uprooted and turned out to

drift over the continent. This novel did more than any other Depression novel to revise the picture of America as Americans imagined it." *

The novel may have been a kind of social tract, as some reviewers said it was, but to many thousands of readers it was a moving experience, and Steinbeck's powerful indignation at the sight of human suffering found a warm response in their hearts.

THE NEXT IN LINE

There were many other novelists of the decade whose work was important and still is read today. Some of them have had a surprising influence on later writers. Witness, for example, the novels of Nathaniel West with their satirical observations of life in the Thirties, and Horace McCoy's short novel *They Shoot Horses, Don't They?* (1935) with its setting a marathon-dance contest—in France the existentialists call it "great."

In the opinion of some critics, the work of John O'Hara and Erskine Caldwell in the Thirties is still their best. O'Hara's *Appointment in Samarra* (1934) and *Butterfield 8* (1935) put him in the front rank of the "hard-boiled" school. Caldwell's *Tobacco Road* (1932) and *God's Little Acre* (1933), and his many short stories, showed a deep concern about the injustices experienced by the Southern sharecroppers, but he chose to deal with them ironically, combining a grim humor with outrageous situations.

Many other novels of the Thirties, and some collections of short stories, have come back into print, and have had wide circulation in paperback

---

* Carl Van Doren, *The American Novel* (New York, Macmillan, 1940).

editions. It is worth recalling some of them:

William Saroyan's early collections of short stories—*The Man on the Flying Trapeze* (1934), *Inhale, Exhale* (1936), *Love, Here Is My Hat* (1938), and *The Trouble with Tigers* (1938).

James M. Cain's slick, tough, immensely readable novels—*The Postman Always Rings Twice* (1934) and *Serenade* (1937).

Marjorie Kinnan Rawlings' novels of Florida backwoods people—*South Moon Under* (1933) and *The Yearling* (1938).

Richard Wright's *Uncle Tom's Children* (1936)—his best work, *Native Son*, which placed him among the great writers of his time, did not appear until 1940.

Jerome Weidman's novels of rapacious enterprise in the New York City clothing industry—*I Can Get It for You Wholesale* (1937) and its sequel *What's in It For Me* (1938).

John Marquand's *The Late George Apley* (1937) and *Wickford Point* (1939), both of which started a new career for him as a serious novelist after years of success as a writer for the popular magazines.

Katherine Anne Porter's two collections of stories—*Flowering Judas* (1931) and *Pale Horse, Pale Rider* (1939).

The Thirties also saw the emergence of James Gould Cozzens, Jesse Stuart and Conrad Richter, as important novelists. And, of course, those novelists with reputations already firmly established continued to publish throughout the decade—Elizabeth Madox Roberts, Thornton Wilder, Sinclair Lewis, Ellen Glasgow, Stephen Vincent Benét, and Robert Nathan, to mention a few.

THE WRITERS' PROJECT

AN ENORMOUS body of writing was produced between 1935 and 1939 under the auspices of the WPA's Federal Writers' Project. Over six thousand writers of all kinds produced 378 books and pamphlets. Major efforts were the guidebooks to states, cities and waterways.

"The WPA's Historical Records Survey, instituted in 1936," Dixon Wecter reported, "sent forth relief workers to take inventories of local public records stored in city hall cellars, courthouse garrets and library lofts, to index old newspaper files, to make abstracts of court cases wherein nuggets of local history were embedded, to examine business archives and church records and even to scrutinize moldering tombstones for vital statistics. The allied survey of federal archives combed the land for national administrative and historical documents. Luckily, the recent perfecting of microfilm rendered possible the photographic preservation of millions of pages crumbling into decay." *

Out of all this emerged an America hitherto unknown.

ROBERT CANTWELL

THE GUIDES†

IT IS doubtful if there has ever been assembled anywhere such a portrait, so laboriously and carefully documented, of such a fanciful, impulsive, childlike, absent-minded, capricious and ingenious people, or of a land in which so many prominent citizens built big houses (usually called someone's folly) that promptly fell into ruins when the owners backed inventions that didn't work.

There was unquestionably something secretive and mysterious about them, but it was counteracted by an odd, clownish, lunatic sense of humor —they composed irreverent jingles for their tombstones, made up jocular names for their villages and farms, and were continually deciding boundary

* Dixon Wecter, *The Age of the Great Depression.*
† Excerpted from Robert Cantwell's "America and the Writers' Project" in *The New Republic*, Apr. 28, 1939.

lines, the locations of county seats and the ownership of plantations by flipping a coin.

They were great builders of spite fences, spite churches, spite towns—their captains of industry even built spite railroads. The four hundred citizens of Ilo, Idaho, moved their whole town a mile and a half to set it up across the railroad tracks from another town and for thirty years refused to incorporate with it.

Scattered through these volumes are brief biographies of prominent, notorious, or merely eccentric individuals who once swung weight in their own communities and whose marks—whether they be the Shot Tower of old Dubuque, or the addresses of prominent prostitutes scratched on the transoms of New Orleans—still remain.

The Guides have no rigorous standards to determine inclusion; people are mentioned whether they succeeded or failed, whether their inventions worked or not, whether they won or lost their duels, made money inside or outside the law: the only test seems to be that some living evidence of their presence, if only a legend or the name of a street, still persists in their own towns.

How has it happened that nobody ever thought before to trace the careers of the vast majority who guessed wrong—the leading bankers who put their money in canals in 1840 and in Maine shipyards in 1856, who plunged on slaves in 1859, and bet that Florence, in Baboon Gulch, Idaho, would be the leading city of the state? What a fine group of far-sighted financiers have really turned up in the Guides! They bought lots in Indianola, Texas, and refused to let the railroad enter Cantwell's Bridge, Delaware; they invested in river steamers, stagecoach companies, pony expresses, whale fishing, or cannon-ball foundries, or like Captain Hauser of South Dakota shot foul gases into the air to bring on rain.

It is a grand, melancholy, formless democratic anthology of frustration and idiosyncrasy, a majestic roll call of national failure, a terrible and yet engaging corrective to the success stories that dominate our literature.

History in relation to place also has the effect of transforming the roles of the leading actors. You can read a dozen biographies of Grant and get less insight into his early career than is supplied by a history of Galena—no biography communicates the sense of the boom environment in which he functioned, or pits him so clearly against the hard-drinking, violent, amoral get-rich-quick world that formed his character. When you read Grant's biography in relation to his own development, you wonder why he lent himself to the schemes of speculators; when you consider it in relation to the history of Galena, you wonder how he could have been expected to do otherwise.

If [the Federal Writers' Project] continues,* if the state guides can be completed and organized nationally, if the state encyclopedias can be brought out in consistent forms, and if the material in the files can be segregated and indexed for historians—there can be no question of the Project's value. It will revolutionize the writing of American history and enormously influence the direction and character of our imaginative literature.

* It didn't; it ended June 30, 1939.—ED.

THEATER—THE FABULOUS INVALID

THE commercial theater, as represented on Broadway, was beset by economic trouble, as usual. Caught between rising unemployment and high prices at the box office, the independent producers could do very little about either; they contended that high prices were dictated by rigid charges for theater rental and by union-fixed salary levels for the actors and stagehands. Consequently, many erstwhile theatergoers, those who could not afford the standard prices of $2.20 and $1.10, no longer went to the plays.

As a result of competition from ever-increasing numbers of motion-picture houses, more and more theaters throughout the country had been forced to close their doors; vaudeville was a thing of the past, and its musicians and stagehands had swollen the ranks of the unemployed. Some of these people found work in Hollywood, but there the average employment for the 22,000 actors registered with casting agencies was only seventy days a year.

Help was forthcoming once the Works Progress Administration was established in 1935; one of its provisos was to qualify relief efforts by helping the "employables" to find work within their own skills or trades; to create jobs for theatrical workers, a system of regional theaters was organized under the Federal Theater, and funds appropriated to produce plays at small admission prices.

It was argued by many in the commercial theater that there were no people with talent on the relief rolls to act in government-produced plays. Time would prove them wrong.

The Federal Theater survived many attacks within Congress; on June 30, 1939, however, an amendment was added, as a sop to the critics of work relief, to the new WPA appropriations bill cutting off funds for the Theater Project.

Sometime later Miss Hallie Flanagan, former director of the project, received a telephone call from a Congressman. She expected that he wanted to offer his sympathy; instead he wanted to talk about the theater project in his state. She said, "But, Congressman, there is no Federal Theater. You voted it out of existence."

A stunned silence. Then, *"What?"*

"It was abolished on June 30 by Act of Congress."

Again, silence. Then a shocked and heavy voice said, "Was *that* the Federal Theater?"

HAROLD CLURMAN

THEATER GROUPS

THE GROUP THEATER *

RECENTLY, in his sumptuous apartment in Paris, Irwin Shaw, whose lyric, antiwar play *Bury the Dead* was first produced by one of the smaller theater groups in 1936, very nearly sighed as he remarked to his guests, "How exciting the theater was in the Thirties. We all thought of what we wanted to express and what had to be said rather than about success." That was very nearly the truth of the matter.

The Group Theater—which I founded together with Cheryl Crawford and Lee Strasberg—began its career on Broadway, where it remained for ten years. The Group was the "elder statesman" among the new organizations that gave the Thirties its particular theatrical character. But the Group did not represent Broadway any more than the Neighborhood Playhouse, the Provincetown Players, the early Theater Guild, the Civic Repertory Theater—organizations typical of the Twenties, whose houses were all south of Times Square—were off-Broadway enterprises in the sense that we think of such enterprises today. Even the younger, smaller, less enduring groups of the Thirties—the Theater Union, Theater Collective, Theater of Action—though they all functioned more or less in the vicinity of lower Manhattan, were not what we today consider off-Broadway operations. For though most of those brave bands were terribly poor—always on the verge of extinction—they were enormously ambitious. Ambition gave even the least valid of their productions a certain ardor and flare that communicated genuine excitement.

The ambition I speak of in the theater of the Thirties—whether physically on or off Broadway—was a moral, social, artistic ambition. When Stella and Luther Adler, J. Edward Bromberg, Morris Carnovsky, Margaret Barker, Franchot Tone, Mary Morris, Alexander Kirkland and others joined the Group Theater's acting company, they were already well known. They chose the Group, and in the main were loyal to it through thick and thin, because the Group's policy in plays, in acting technique, in organizational setup, in social seriousness, appealed to them as artists and

* From "Groups, Projects, Collectives," *Theatre Arts*, September 1960.

citizens. The Group—and most of the other organizations I have named— wanted to make the theater vitally expressive of the American scene, of the life of the times. They also hoped—this was especially the Group's aim—to develop actors as conscious artists, and eventually to produce new playwrights.

ODETS *

Although *Awake and Sing!* was a modest one-set play, Odets was unable to raise the money to produce it. Neither was I, when I addressed myself to backers interested in the "better things" in the theater. The play, which showed people grappling with the petty details that mess up their lives, seemed in script form to make an unpleasant, harsh impression. The pettiness and mess were more apparent than the play's tenderness and pathos.

I decided to appeal to Franchot Tone† in Hollywood. I called him by phone, and told him we needed five thousand dollars to produce Odets' play. He asked me to send a script on to him for reading. I promised to do so, but I insisted that he send the money without waiting for the script. Franchot laughed and agreed.

Though it is true that everything at this time was done *con amore*, a few trifling circumstances cast shadows to highlight the generally creative atmosphere of our work. During the first week of rehearsal J. Edward Bromberg asked if we could release him for an engagement in Hollywood, since his part in our play was only a secondary one. When I rejected the very thought of this, he said no more about it.

I was living with Odets on Horatio Street, and after rehearsal he kept me up nights to discuss the progress of the play. (We promised each other that if the play prospered, we would move to more respectable quarters.) I hardly slept at all. Because of overconcentration and the rapid pace of production—the play was rehearsed less than four weeks—I was in a state of almost complete exhaustion as opening night approached.

There were only nine members of the Group company in *Awake and Sing!* Most of the others were busy with rehearsals of *Waiting for Lefty* under the direction of Sanford Meisner and Clifford Odets. It was to be given at a benefit for the *New Theatre Magazine*, unofficial organ of the new insurgent movement in the theater.

Sunday night, January 5, 1935, at the old Civic Repertory Theater on Fourteenth Street, an event took place to be noted in the annals of the American theater. The evening had opened with a mildly amusing one-act

* From Harold Clurman's *The Fervent Years* (New York, Knopf, 1945).
† Franchot Tone had joined the Group Theater in its first year, 1931.

play by Paul Green. The audience, though attracted by the guest appearance of a good part of the Group company, had no idea of what was to follow.

The first scene of *Lefty* had not played two minutes when a shock of delighted recognition struck the audience like a tidal wave. Deep laughter, hot assent, a kind of joyous fervor seemed to sweep the audience toward the stage. The actors no longer performed; they were being carried along as if by an exultancy of communication such as I had never witnessed in the theater before. Audience and actors had become one. Line after line brought applause, whistles, bravos, and heartfelt shouts of kinship.

The taxi strike of February 1934 had been a minor incident in the labor crisis of this period. There were very few taxi drivers in that first audience, I am sure; very few indeed who had ever been directly connected with such an event as the union meeting that provided the play its pivotal situation. When the audience at the end of the play responded to the militant question from the stage: "Well, what's the answer?" with a spontaneous roar of "Strike! Strike!" it was something more than a tribute to the play's effectiveness, more even than a testimony of the audience's hunger for constructive social action. It was the birth cry of the Thirties. Our youth had found its voice. It was a call to join the good fight for a greater measure of life in a world free of economic fear, falsehood, and craven servitude to stupidity and greed. "Strike!" was *Lefty's* lyric message, not alone for a few extra pennies of wages or for shorter hours of work, strike for greater dignity, strike for a bolder humanity, strike for the full stature of man.

The audience, I say, was delirious. It stormed the stage, which I persuaded the stunned author to mount. People went from the theater dazed and happy: a new awareness and confidence had entered their lives.

A series of *Lefty* performances was given every Sunday thereafter at the Civic Repertory Theater—all of them benefits. Finally on February 10 the press was invited to see *Lefty*, given together with the Group's experimental sketches.

The reviewers liked *Lefty* very much. At this time, after the Theater Union had done three productions, and the Jewish workers' group known as Artef had won a degree of esoteric fame, one or two commentators noted that "the progress of the revolutionary drama in New York City during the last two seasons is the most recent development in the theater."

Awake and Sing!, which had been in rehearsal about ten days when *Lefty* was first presented, opened on February 19, 1935. It was accorded a very favorable but not sensational newspaper reception. In the New York *Times* Brooks Atkinson, after calling Odets the Group's "most congenial

512

playwright," went on to say: "Although he is very much awake, he does not sing with the ease and clarity of a man who has mastered his score. Although his dialogue has uncommon strength, his drama in the first two acts is wanting in the ordinary fluidity of a play. . . . To this student of the arts *Awake and Sing!* is inexplicably deficient in plain theater emotion."

Awake and Sing! was written out of the distress of the 1932 Depression (not to mention Odets' whole youth). It was completed in 1933 and belatedly produced in 1935. Yet only when it was revived in 1939 did the same reviewer say: "When Clifford Odets's *Awake and Sing!* burst in the face of an unsuspecting public four years ago, some of the misanthropes complained that it was praised too highly. Misanthropes are always wrong. For it is plain after a glimpse of the revival last evening that *Awake and Sing!* cannot be praised too highly. . . . When it was first produced, it seemed febrile as a whole and dogmatic in conclusion. It does not seem so now; it seems thoroughly normal, reasonable, true."

Now when no one ever mentions the possibility or desirability of a repertory theater,* it might be pointed out that there can hardly be any true theater culture without it, since most judgments in the theater are as spotty and short-sighted as those Mr. Atkinson confessed. Indeed, the judgment of any work of art on the basis of a single hasty contact would be as frivolous as most theater opinion. And, since I have paused to make the point, I might add that only by constant repetition through the seasons did the plays of Chekhov become box-office in Russia.

A bit of loose talk about Chekhov's influence on Odets cropped up in some reviews. Odets knew very little of Chekhov's work at this time, but quite a lot about Lawson's *Success Story*, in which he had served as Luther Adler's understudy. It was Lawson's play that brought Odets an awareness of a new kind of theater dialogue. It was a compound of lofty moral feeling, anger and the feverish argot of the big city. It bespoke a warm heart, an outraged spirit and a rough tongue.

But the talk of Chekhov's influence on Odets' work was a minor note in the reception of his plays. Far more common was the bugaboo of Marxism or Communism. They constituted the specter that haunted the Thirties. Rumor on these subjects was so prevalent that it reached even the daily theatrical columns. One reviewer, for example, spoke of "the simplicity of his (Odets') communist panaceas." He preferred *Awake and Sing!* to *Lefty* because in the latter "one finds Mr. Odets working now as a party member."

The Left press at the time of Odets' first success granted his importance,

* Mr. Clurman was writing in 1945.—ED.

but was careful to make serious reservations about *Lefty*, spoke gingerly of *Awake and Sing!* (in the *New Masses*), and called it "a comedown for the Group Theater, an unimportant play whichever way you look at it," in the *Daily Worker*.

Odets became the central figure of the so-called Left movement in the theater. But the relation of his work to Marxism or Communism was of a special sort not to be understood in terms of glib political commentary. The Marxist drift of the Thirties no more "caused" *Lefty* or *Awake and Sing!* in January and February of 1935 than *Lefty* and *Awake and Sing!* caused the organization of the CIO in November of that year. All these phenomena, including also the NRA and the later acts of the New Deal (the National Labor Relations Act, and so on), were an outgrowth of and a response to a common dislocation that convulsed our whole society. They were all undoubtedly related, but they are by no means comprehensible if they are lumped together mechanically as if they were identical.

Odets' work from the beginning contained "a protest that is also prophecy." There was in it a fervor that derived from the hope and expectation of change and the desire for it. But there was rarely any expression of political consciousness in it, no deep commitment to a coherent philosophy of life, no pleading for a panacea. "A tendril of revolt" runs through all of Odets' work, but that is not the same thing as a consistent revolutionary conviction. Odets' work is not even proletarian in the sense that Gorky's work is. Rather is it profoundly of the lower middle class with all its vacillation, dual allegiance, fears, groping, self-distrust, dejection, spurts of energy, hosannas, vows of conversion, and prayers for release. The "enlightenment" of the Thirties, its effort to come to a clearer understanding of and control over the anarchy of our society, brought Odets a new mental perspective, but it is his emotional experience, not his thought, that gives his plays their special expressiveness and significance. His thought, the product chiefly of his four years with the Group and the new channels they led to, furnished Odets with the more conscious bits of his vocabulary, with an occasional epithet or slogan that were never fully integrated in his work. The feel of middle-class (and perhaps universal) disquiet in Odets' plays is sharp and specific; the ideas are general and hortatory. The Left movement provided Odets with a platform and a loud-speaker; the music that came through was that of a vast population of restive souls, unaware of its own mind, seeking help. To this Odets added the determination of youth. The quality of his plays is young, lyrical, yearning—as of someone on the threshold of life.

It was nonsense for the New York *Sun's* reviewer, in order to challenge the validity of *Lefty*, to check with a taxi driver on his average earnings. *Lefty* was not basically about the hackman's low wages, but about every impediment to that full life for which youth hungers. Hence the play's wide appeal.

Perhaps Odets privately harbored the belief that socialism offers the only solution for our social-economic problems. Perhaps his desire to share a comradely closeness to his fellow men might attract him to those who hoped to bring about a socialist society, but he must also have suspected that temperamentally he might prove a trial to any well-knit party. Instead of being an adherent of a fixed program, a disciplined devotee of a set strategy or system, Odets possessed a talent that always had an ambiguous character. If because of all this the regular press was misled into chatter about his "Marxism" while the Left press was frankly perplexed and troubled by him, it may also be guessed that Odets too was pretty much in the dark on this score.

On the one hand, Odets felt himself very close to the people—the great majority of Americans—even in his bent for the "good old theater"; on the other hand, his heart was always with the rebels. But who precisely were the rebels, and what did they demand of him? Those he knew were a small minority, and they marked out a line for him that he could not altogether accept. After the first flurry of Odets' success had passed, everyone discovered a "change" in him. The conventional reviewers were glad; the Left was disconcerted. But, in the sense they had in mind, both were wrong—Odets had not changed.

Perhaps the truth is that the vast majority, to which Odets felt he belonged as much as to any rebellious few, had not yet created for itself a cultural clarity or form, not to speak of other kinds of clarity or form— had not, for example, yet made for itself a theater in which he could function freely. Perhaps the "few" who often criticized him more harshly than anyone else did not know how much they had in common with those they professed to scorn.

Whatever later wisdom might declare, Odets in the spring of 1935 was the man of the hour. Theatrically speaking, the climax of the Odets vogue came with the production of *Lefty* as a regular show on Broadway.

Since *Lefty* was only an hour long, we had to have a companion piece to go with it. Odets himself supplied this by dramatizing a short story purporting to be a letter from Nazi Germany he had read in the *New Masses*. The play, written to order, was finished in less than a week. Cheryl Crawford directed it, and the setting was designed by an unofficial Group apprentice, Paul Morison, who had performed similar services for us at Green Mansions.

This twin bill opened at the Longacre Theater on March 26, 1935, at a price range from fifty cents to a dollar and a half—something of an innovation on Broadway.

In order not to disturb the casting of *Awake and Sing!*, all the actors not engaged in that play took over the production of *Lefty* and *Till the Day I Die*, which, incidentally, was one of the first serious anti-Nazi plays to reach the New York stage.

Odets himself played Dr. Benjamin in *Lefty* (originally played by Luther Adler), and on opening night his appearance was greeted by an ovation. This was the last acting assignment of his career. Lee Strasberg under an assumed name played a small part in the anti-Nazi play. In the new *Lefty* cast Elia Kazan, replacing Bromberg, was thunderously effective. Everyone was sure we had picked him off a taxi to play the part— our "discovery" from Constantinople, Williams College and Yale!

The new play was respectfully received though the New York *Times* reviewer thought: "If you want to register an emotional protest against Nazi policy, Mr. Odets requires that you join the Communist brethren"— a rather peculiar interpretation of a play that at most called for a united front against Nazism. But the plea for such a front in those days was chiefly associated with Communists.

The play actually was a rather old-fashioned piece of theater in a style that derived from the swell of Odets' sentiment, an unavowed inclination toward romantic drama, and a feeling for social currents. It was a little artificial, yet not without some qualities of youthful sweetness and idealism.

Awake and Sing! never made much money. Odets believed the failure of *Awake and Sing!* to become a box-office smash was due to the Group's lack of business ability. He was wrong; the play attracted an important but small part of the theatergoing public: those who bought the cheaper tickets. *Lefty* and *Till the Day I Die* were seen by a devoted and intelligent public still too small (and poor), alas, to furnish box-office comfort.

Yet, except for their bewildered backers, the plays were an enormous success. They were the talk of the town, the thing-to-see for all who wished to remain abreast of the times. If we hadn't known this through reviews, interviews, public clamor, and an excited correspondence, I at least should have guessed it by the constant buzzing of the phone in the University Place apartment I shared with Odets.

The lion hunters were on the trail. Actresses, publicists, bankers, novelists, editors, wanted to meet the boy wonder. There was a difference in his situation as compared to that of a young writer like Thomas Wolfe, who was similarly sought after on the publication of *Look Homeward, Angel.* The difference was that while Odets was regarded by many as the dramatic find of the day, he was in addition that new phenomenon, a radical, a revolutionary, a Red.

An interest in an important new playwright was altogether normal for people like Tallulah Bankhead, Ruth Gordon, Beatrice Lillie, Helen Hayes, Charles MacArthur, Clare Boothe (Luce). But when Bernard Baruch began to examine him, when Edna Ferber asked that he be invited to a party that she might simply "take a look" at him, when Walter Winchell sought him out to have him explain the meaning of Communism (only to decide that he preferred to get the information from the "top man," Stalin himself), we were confronted with a sign of the times as significant as it was comic.

Odets was in a whirl, pleasant at first no doubt, a little terrifying later. He bought himself more records and virtually doped himself with music. Little girls he had known in the days of our jaunts to Stewart's Cafeteria on Sheridan Square now approached him timidly (or suspiciously) and asked if they could still speak to him. This infuriated and bruised him. He began to feel rather shut off, isolated.

At the time *Awake and Sing!* was written, a Hollywood scout offered him $500 a week on the gold coast. Odets asked me if it wasn't "unrealistic" to refuse it. I replied that it wasn't, if for no other reason than that he would be offered more later. When, despite all the acclaim, his earnings were relatively modest, though greater than they had ever been before, his agent called to tell him that M-G-M was willing to go as high as $3,000 weekly, perhaps even higher. Like a conspirator he whispered that he might be willing to consider it.

I overheard this conversation and was troubled by it. When I was at sea on my way abroad in April, I wrote him a letter confessing my reaction. It was his duty to himself, to his colleagues, and to his audience to go on writing plays. The three first plays, and the recently completed *Paradise Lost*, were a mere beginning. Odets answered that he was happy I had written him as I did. Indeed such criticism as my letter implied was always welcomed by him: it made him feel responsible. In 1937, after the success of *Golden Boy*, when I wrote him a letter in which I was very severe with him for not making better use of his time than he was wont to do at such periods, he said to me: "I received your letter. I loved it."

517

Perhaps not all artists are so, but many flourish only when they feel a concern for their work that is eager, jealous, essential.

People from all over the country swarmed into our offices. They wanted to join us, they said, because they were in sympathy with our aims. It was often a rude shock to them when I pointed out that we were a theater, not a cult, and that talent was still the first requirement for work with us.

The actors were now riding the crest of the wave. I do not mean this in any material sense, since most of the Group had as vague an understanding of their own economic situation as I did. They never worried over money except when they were broke, in which case a few dollars in their pockets would make them feel affluent again. They were thriving with a sense of fulfillment, the feeling that they were part of the main current, which to an extent they had helped create.

Our activity was incessant. A few of our people made experimental films with Ralph Steiner. Others helped direct plays for new groups. Kazan, for example, did this for the Theater of Action, which produced *The Young Go First*, a play about the CCC camps. We arranged a symposium of lectures at the New School for Social Research. Lee Strasberg gave a course on stage direction at the Theater Collective School. At Mecca Temple Morris Carnovsky did a monologue by Odets called *I Can't Sleep*, one of the pages of Odets' work most significant for its indication of the source of his inspiration—the troubled conscience of the middle class in the Depression period. At the same time a playlet by Art Smith called *The Tide Rises* based on the San Francisco marine strike used the talents of the younger people in the Group and showed the Odets influence already at work.

New theater societies were being formed all over the country to give the three Odets plays. Group Theaters shot up like mushrooms: in Chicago, Hollywood, New Orleans, San Francisco. A Negro People's Theater was set up in Harlem to give *Lefty* under the direction of our own Bill Challee. All in all, *Lefty* was being done in some sixty towns which had never before witnessed a theatrical performance. Thirty-two cities were seeing the twin bill of *Lefty* and *Till the Day I Die* at the same time.

Even suppressions, bans, arrests on grounds of "unlawful assembly" or "profanity," served to increase the play's prestige. These occurred in Philadelphia, Boston, New Haven, Newark, Dorchester, Chelsea and Roxbury. On the West Coast Will Geer, managing a small enterprise that had announced *Till the Day I Die*, received a menacing note: "You know what we do to the enemies of the New Germany." He produced the play, and was severely beaten up by Bundist hoodlums. In New York Odets put an extra heavy lock on the door of our apartment.

From a political or sensational standpoint, all this came to a boil when Odets went down to Cuba as head of a committee to study labor and social conditions, with emphasis on the status of students under the reactionary Mendieta regime. The visit—under the auspices of the League of American Writers—was supposed to last two weeks. It lasted a few hours; on the arrival of the *S.S. Oriente* the entire committee, composed of timid little white-collar workers and teachers, were arrested as "agitators."

The story made the headlines. Telegrams of protest were sent, meetings held, petitions signed. When I heard that some of the Group actors had called a protest meeting for the acting profession and saw one of them haranguing the small audience, beer-hall fashion, I became almost as annoyed as I had been amused.

Odets had been chosen to head the committee because in six months he had become a name. To be used in this way flattered him and appealed to his Hugoesque imagination. He wrote a few amusing reports on the matter for the New York *Post*, made highly inflammatory statements, and sounded off generally like a gay hothead in the Parisian Forties of last century. He soon became bored with his own busyness, temperamentally foreign to his introverted nature.

Odets' plays aroused interest not only in theatrical and minor political circles but in the literary world generally. The book reviewers devoted columns to him: he was being read in the same spirit as were the novels of Dos Passos, James Farrell, Erskine Caldwell, John Steinbeck, Robert Cantwell and Thomas Wolfe. The Group as a whole drew strength from this graduation from Broadway onto the larger American scene. It also drew some false conclusions from it.

This became evident in its reaction to new plays—for example, *Winterset*. Maxwell Anderson was contemplating letting the Group, for which he had an abiding affection, produce the play if it would cast Burgess Meredith in the leading role. Despite interesting production possibilities and a fine basic theme, it left me rather cold. I could not make myself comfortable in its atmosphere of an "Elizabethan" East Side! But, considering the state of American drama, it was not a play to be dismissed lightly.

We decided, therefore, to read the play to our company. With the exception of two or three people the actors were more averse to the play than I. Though its theme was Justice and its idea sprang from a prolonged pondering on the historic Sacco-Vanzetti case, they felt no immediacy, no true life in the play, only a filtering of these matters through a sentimental literary imagination.

Lee Strasberg did not so much disagree with this reaction as he feared its consequences on the course of our development as a practical theater. Because he felt himself under a cloud at this time, he failed to fight for his opinion. Two years later, when I admitted to the company that we had made a mistake in not doing the play, for all our reservations, since the function of a producing organization cannot be equated with that of the critic in his chair, the company maintained the integrity of its character and expressed shock at my change of view.

Yet it must not be assumed from this that the actors had become altogether complacent because of their newly won acclaim. On the contrary, there was a strong urge to make further progress.

GROUPS *

I have not yet mentioned—except in passing—the extraordinary phenomenon of the Federal Theater, which began its career on October 1, 1935, only to end it because of political pressure on July 1, 1939. Under the direction of the doughty Hallie Flanagan, the Federal Theater Project was the first (so far, the only) nationwide government-sponsored theater in the United States. This project, born not out of a love or appreciation of the theater, but as part of the Works Progress Administration, which was established to give employment to needy people in socially useful jobs, made a contribution to our theater the significance of which has to this day not been fully recognized. For the Federal Theater, often harshly criticized by professional show folk and politicians who suspected it of being too useful to the Roosevelt administration, proved what might be accomplished in a creative sense by a government-promoted theater organization in the hands of devoted craftsmen.

"Aren't very many of the Federal Theater productions amateurish?" I was once asked at a lecture I gave at the time. My answer then—as it would be today—was: "Yes—and so are many Broadway productions." Though most of the Federal Theater personnel came from relief rolls, and nine out of ten dollars were spent for wages, the Federal Theater employed ten thousand people, operated theaters in forty states, published a nationally distributed theater magazine, conducted a research bureau serving not only its own theaters but twenty thousand schools, churches and community theaters throughout America, and played to audiences totaling millions.

* From "Groups, Projects, Collectives," *Theatre Arts*, September 1960.

The project invented the "Living Newspaper," a cinematic and journalistic type of production dealing with such subjects as agriculture, flood control and housing. *One Third of a Nation* (designed by Howard Bay) was in every respect a thrilling show, which attracted large audiences on Broadway at something like a dollar top.

It was in the Federal Theater that Orson Welles first displayed his lavish talent (with the Negro *Macbeth, Doctor Faustus* and *Horse Eats Hat*). Later, with the indispensable aid of John Houseman, he formed the Mercury Theater—the last of the outstanding ventures of the Thirties. The Mercury's first production, *Julius Caesar* (in which Martin Gabel, Joseph Cotten, Hiram Sherman and George Coulouris appeared, along with Welles himself), was an example of how gratifying the social enthusiasm of the Thirties could be when applied to Shakespeare.

The Federal Theater produced T. S. Eliot's *Murder in the Cathedral, The Swing Mikado,* a dramatization of Sinclair Lewis' *It Can't Happen Here,* the first American performance of Bernard Shaw's *On the Rocks* and Paul Green's *The Lost Colony.*

Perhaps the most succinct testimony to the swell of fervor the project aroused in the country was published in *Federal Theater Magazine,* written by a member of the audience: "We're a hundred thousand kids who never saw a play before. We're students in colleges, housewives in the Bronx, lumberjacks in Oregon, sharecroppers in Georgia. . . . We're the Caravan Theater in the parks, Shakespeare on a hillside, Gilbert and Sullivan on a lagoon, the circus under canvas, Toller on a truck. . . . We're the Living Newspaper; we're the Negro theater, the Yiddish theater and theaters throughout America playing not only in English but in French, German, Italian and Spanish; we're the file, we're the record, we're theater history."

The theater of the Thirties was often referred to as a "left theater," a "Roosevelt theater," a theater of "creeping socialism," or worse. The record shows that this was mostly eyewash. The theater then reflected what was going on in the world around it. What was going on affected everybody and resulted in many changes that are not only permanent but universally approved. The theater movement of the Thirties, often verbose, hotheaded, loudmouthed, bumptious and possibly "pretentious," did not produce Communism in our midst; it produced a creative ferment that is still the best part of whatever we have in our present strangulated and impractical theater.

WARD MOREHOUSE

THE PLAYS OF THE THIRTIES*

PLAY production in the 1930s shrank, dropping from an average of around 250 plays a season to about half of that total. Hollywood continued its merciless raids upon the Broadway scene, signing dramatists, actors, directors. Theater building in Manhattan came to an abrupt halt shortly before the decade arrived; there were empty playhouses from ocean to ocean as the great era of touring plays and stock productions began a steady decline; theaters in New York and elsewhere were demolished to make way for parking lots and garages, and many became movie houses. Vaudeville was near starvation (the Palace in New York changed its two-a-day policy in 1932, when it added films, and for much of the Thirties, films were the sole attraction there). Producers went broke, as did the actors (broker than usual), but there were no mass suicides.

The American dramatist revealed a consuming interest in a wide variety of subjects, and he did not hesitate to grapple with vital, contemporary issues. There was a trend toward the social-minded theater, and a widespread appreciation of nostalgia, which was revealed in such pieces as *One Sunday Afternoon, Ah, Wilderness!* and *The Star-Wagon*. The critics, taking themselves and their profession very seriously, started the New York Drama Critics' Circle. The organization actually came into being as a result of the disgust over the inane choice of Zoë Akins' *The Old Maid* for the Pulitzer prize of the season of 1934–35 in preference to Lillian Hellman's *The Children's Hour*.

Perhaps the leader of the new playwrights was the same Lillian Hellman, who first flashed into the town's consciousness with *The Children's Hour*, a sound and adult drama, and who was represented again later by *The Little Foxes*, a masterpiece of construction, which also was the first of her studies of predatory Southern families. Sidney Kingsley arrived on the scene with two resounding successes, the realistic *Men in White* and *Dead End*. Clifford Odets revealed a capacity for vivid characterization and flaming dialogue in *Awake and Sing!* and *Golden Boy*.

Among the established dramatists, Maxwell Anderson emerged as a one-man theater with the historical pieces *Elizabeth the Queen* and *Mary of*

* From "These Full Lean Years," *Theatre Arts*, September 1960.

Scotland; the political, and sharply satirical *Both Your Houses*, a Pulitzer prize winner; and the imaginative and poetic *Winterset* and *High Tor*, which won the first two best-play awards of the new Critics' Circle in successive seasons. Wit and urbanity went into S. N. Behrman's polished writing in *Biography* and *No Time for Comedy*. Eugene O'Neill contributed two vastly important—and highly interesting—works, *Mourning Becomes Electra* and *Ah, Wilderness!* There was unforgettable poignance in Thornton Wilder's *Our Town,* which deals with love and marriage, life and death in a small community in the long, long ago, and which has been recurrent in the theater, professional and amateur, ever since its première in 1938. The redoubtable Robert E. Sherwood had a productive time of it; his output ranged from the high comedy of *Reunion in Vienna* to the mingling of philosophy and melodrama of *The Petrified Forest* (written after a stay in Reno), to *Idiot's Delight,* with its prophecy of the approaching war, and to the exalted drama of *Abe Lincoln in Illinois.* Paul Osborn turned out a touching and whimsical theater piece, *On Borrowed Time*; Howard Lindsay and Russel Crouse achieved the long-run wonder of all time with *Life with Father,* dealing with the reminiscences of Clarence Day (the decade produced another marathon work in *Tobacco Road*); James Thurber and Elliott Nugent wrote a vastly entertaining comedy of college life, *The Male Animal,* and in 1939 the stocky, thick-browed and explosive William Saroyan, one of the newcomers, contributed that sensitive and observant—and funny—work, *The Time of Your Life.* The locale was a saloon; the characters were people who just drifted in. He won the award of the Critics' Circle and that of the Pulitzer committee, but resolutely returned the Pulitzer check for $1,000.

The decade was a romp for the playwriting team of George S. Kaufman and Moss Hart. They gave Broadway the hilarious *You Can't Take It with You, Once in a Lifetime, Merrily We Roll Along, I'd Rather Be Right, The Fabulous Invalid, The American Way* and *The Man Who Came to Dinner.* Josephine Hull, playing the unmethodical Mrs. Sycamore in *You Can't Take It with You,* who became a playwright because a typewriter was delivered at her home by mistake, was wonderful in that comedy, doing just about as much for it as the authors did.

The first Pulitzer prize winner of the Thirties, Marc Connelly's *The Green Pastures,* drew its material from Roark Bradford's *Ol' Man Adam and His Chillun.* It was performed for five years, in New York and on tour, yet Connelly had great trouble getting it produced at all; the script specified an all-Negro cast (his characters included De Lawd and the Angel Gabriel, Noah and the King of Babylon and Ol' King Pharaoh, the Stout

Angel and the Thin Angel and the Custard Maker and the children of the Heavenly Fish Fry).

The careers of some famous producers ended in the Thirties. David Belasco's fifty-year reign in New York came to a close with his death in 1931, during the run of his last offering, *Tonight or Never*, with Melvyn Douglas and Helen Gahagan. Florenz Ziegfeld died in 1932, though several editions of the *Follies* were presented later in the decade. And George M. Cohan, tired, confused and steadily losing interest, continued to act, but his producing and writing activity dwindled; he knew that he was on his way out. But Lee Shubert seemed ready to go on forever. He was still taking his daily sun-lamp treatments at the Astor barbershop, still reporting at his circular cubicle in the Shubert Theater building, and still staying up until 2 A.M. It was during the early Thirties that he said to me:

"The Shuberts have thirty-five theaters in New York and we have to keep getting plays into these theaters. We can't stop; we've got to go on always. We have seventeen hundred actors now working for us, and next season we'll have more. A man who produces hits must also have failures. I expect 10 per cent of my productions to be successful, 20 per cent to be moderately successful, and the rest unsuccessful. That's the average from season to season. The taste of the theatergoing public is now changing everywhere. There's a demand for class; the sensational type of play doesn't go any more."

Some others among the older managements were still in business. Sam H. Harris was very active, and so were John Golden, Arthur Hopkins, William A. Brady and Arch Selwyn. The Theater Guild was by now a well-established producer—and a leading one—along with Gilbert Miller, Herman Shumlin, George Abbott, Jed Harris, Richard Aldrich, Dwight Deere Wiman, Alfred de Liagre, Jr., and Brock Pemberton. The New York Theater now belonged to them, just as it had been the domain of Belasco and the others who were departing. I remember calling at the offices of George C. Tyler a few years before his death. He popped up from behind a battered roll-top desk, something that he must have had since he was starring William Hodge in *The Man from Home*. He was an aging, emaciated, self-pitying figure. "You've come to see me?" he said incredulously. "Why in the world would anybody want to come to see me?" He moved from his desk to a window overlooking Forty-second Street, once a great theatrical thoroughfare. "Just come here and see this awful street. It was so wonderful. Now it's cheap and tawdry and only half alive. What's happened to the theater I knew and loved? What's happened to all the world?"

What was happening was that the theater was shrinking, physically. Gone, too, were the stock companies from such strongholds as New Haven and Worcester, Newark and Washington, Pittsburgh and Atlanta. But the decade witnessed the rise of summer theaters as we know them today— package shows, touring stars (many of them cast off by Hollywood), apprentices, and schools for actors and technicians. In the second half of the Thirties there were thirty-odd legitimate playhouses in New York—a little more than half the total in the Twenties. But their marquees carried the names of some of the finest actors this country has known. The Thirties produced many newcomers who went on to fame. But there were also many well-established favorites among the roster of players, which included Alfred Lunt, Lynn Fontanne, Katharine Cornell, Helen Hayes, Ina Claire, Tallulah Bankhead, Gertrude Lawrence, Judith Anderson, Walter Huston, Noel Coward, Paul Muni, Ruth Gordon, Luther Adler, Eva Le Gallienne, Alice Brady, Leslie Howard, Josephine Hull, Monty Woolley, Raymond Massey, Jane Cowl, Lillian and Dorothy Gish, Howard Lindsay, Dorothy Stickney and George M. Cohan. And that's merely a cross section.

GUY BOLTON

THE MUSICALS*

IN RESPECT to musical comedy, there is a school of thought that maintains life began at '43, the year *Oklahoma!* was born. Without intending any reflection on that fine show, I would like to ask: In what way is it superior to the *Porgy and Bess* of 1935? Has it a better score? Is its artistry greater? Are its musical numbers more firmly integrated with the story? Are its characters more vivid, better drawn?

An outstanding difference between the musicals of yesterday and today is one of size. Small musicals like *Peggy-Ann*, *Music in the Air* and *Leave It to Jane* are gone, which seems to me a pity. Charm, which we, who wrote in the Twenties and Thirties, considered a prime essential, was easier to capture in the smaller dimension.

In the Thirties, air conditioning was not standard equipment in the musical theater, by any means, and runs were shorter. But there was talent.

* From "Musicals Too Were Memorable," *Theatre Arts,* September 1960.

Rodgers and Hart turned out some memorable shows: *On Your Toes*, *Babes in Arms*, *I'd Rather Be Right* (with George Kaufman and Moss Hart), *I Married an Angel* (their own long-run champion of the decade, with 338 performances) and *The Boys from Syracuse*. Good as their contribution was—and all of those musicals came within a three-year span: 1936–38—I think the palm should go to George Gershwin. In the Thirties he wrote the scores of *Girl Crazy* (1930), *Of Thee I Sing* (1931), the first musical to win the Pulitzer prize, and *Porgy and Bess*. Gershwin's remarkable range is illustrated by those three achievements. Among so-called light scores, I doubt that *Girl Crazy* has yet been beaten; in the field of near opera, *Porgy and Bess* is outstanding; the satire in *Of Thee I Sing* extends from lyrics to music, the recitatives being an amusing burlesque of grand opera (in such numbers as "I'm About to Be a Mother" and "Wintergreen for President," the music is as much a source of laughter as the words). Jerome Kern wrote two outstanding numbers, "All the Things You Are" (from *Very Warm for May*, 1939) and "Smoke Gets in Your Eyes" (*Roberta*, 1933), but the scores as such were no match for *Show Boat*, or his earlier musicals. Gershwin's *Girl Crazy*, presented at the Alvin Theater exactly one year after the historic Wall Street crash, introduced Ethel Merman to the New York stage; it also brought forward another newcomer, Ginger Rogers. With the exception of *Porgy and Bess*, this was Gershwin's top score. In general there was a greater emphasis on comedy in the musicals of the Thirties than there is in those of today. One sad and significant fact was the loss of houses for legitimate productions, a trend that worked a particular hardship on the musical stage.

The only notable change that has occurred since the Thirties involves the use of ballet and trained ballet dancers. The musicals of the Thirties may have been of lighter substance than those of today, but they followed the Gilbert and Sullivan tradition by aiming at satire more than do the current shows. Larry Hart, Rodgers' partner, was particularly gifted in this field, and the travesty of the New Deal, *I'd Rather Be Right*, provided him with an excellent subject for spoofing.

The one really memorable musical of 1934 was Cole Porter's *Anything Goes*. It ran for 420 Broadway performances. Cole's next show, *Leave It to Me* (1938), was a pasquinade dealing with the Soviet Union, a subject he tackled again, seventeen years later, in *Silk Stockings*. *Leave It to Me* is chiefly memorable as the show that introduced Mary Martin and "My Heart Belongs to Daddy." And the chorus included two young men named Van Johnson and Gene Kelly. Kelly's presence in a chorus illustrates a point in regard to the dancing ensemble of the Thirties. The dominant choreographer was Bob Alton; it was he who staged the numbers of *Leave It to Me* and *Anything Goes*, both of which were rightly famed for their work in that department. Alton had devised the idea of making up a chorus line of solo dancers who had not yet achieved solo rank. In that way he was able to bring individual artists forward to compete in succession, much in the manner of a challenge dance. Naturally such highly trained specialists could not be expected to be vocalists as well, so another troupe of specialists, trained singers, were engaged, the two groups taking the place of the largely untrained dancers-singers of the Twenties. Part harmony and special choral effects came into use, as a result, and such a division of the chorus was maintained through the years, though the present-day chorus members must have talent in more directions than ever before. Another requisite of pre-Alton days suffered to some degree when the new order arose in the Thirties; not all the trained vocalists were beauties. I remember Channing Pollock's somewhat acid comment: "The moment I looked at the chorus, I knew they could sing."

DANIEL BLUM

NEW FACES*

FEW PERSONS noticed a thin, freckled girl who played the maid in *A Month in the Country* at the Guild Theater (now the Anta) in the spring of 1930. The girl had graduated from Bryn Mawr, appeared with a Baltimore stock company, and had a few roles on Broadway, including the job of understudying Hope Williams in *Holiday*, before she was seen in the Turgenev play. But in the fall of that year, when the same girl supported Jane Cowl in *Art and Mrs. Bottle*, the critics tossed a few posies at Katharine Hepburn. Two years later she received greater acclaim in *The Warrior's Husband*; from that point she went on to stardom in Hollywood and has returned to the stage periodically.

Little mention is made of the appearance of Bob Hope in *Smiles* (1930) or *Ballyhoo of 1932*. But in 1933 he came into his own in *Roberta*. Playing supporting roles with Bob were George Murphy and Fred MacMurray. *Say When!* and an edition of the *Ziegfeld Follies* followed, and by 1936 Hope was starring in *Red, Hot and Blue*.

* From "New Faces Became Old Favorites," *Theatre Arts*, September 1960.

Another star of that show was Ethel Merman. Six years earlier she had left a stenographer's desk in Astoria to become an overnight sensation in *Girl Crazy*, singing "I Got Rhythm" and "Sam and Delilah." She popularized "Life Is Just a Bowl of Cherries" in *George White's Scandals* (1931), and "Eadie Was a Lady," "Rise 'n' Shine" and "You're An Old Smoothie" in *Take A Chance* (1932). Then came *Anything Goes*, two years later, and Merman more than had it made.

The program of *Forsaking All Others* (1933) lists "A Gentleman— Henry Fonda." The role was a walk-on. Prior to that he had gained experience with the Omaha Community Playhouse, spent several summer seasons with the University Players at West Falmouth, Cape Cod, and appeared in small parts in two New York productions, including *The Game of Love and Death*. In 1934 he was in the first *New Faces*. Success came in the same year with *The Farmer Takes a Wife*, in which he appeared with June Walker. A year later he was in Hollywood, making the film version, and he returned to Broadway once more during the decade— in *Blow Ye Winds*, a flop, in 1937. During his four years at Princeton, James Stewart was active in college theater (his tenor voice and his accordion playing won him great popularity in the Triangle Club). A summer season at West Falmouth girded him for storming producers' offices. When *Carry Nation* opened at the Biltmore Theater in New York on October 29, 1932, young Stewart was playing Constable Gano. It was his Broadway debut; the production ran seventeen performances. It was also the metropolitan bow for Joshua L. Logan, Mildred Natwick and Myron McCormick. Stewart's next role was the chauffeur in *Goodbye Again*. He appeared in *Spring in Autumn*, *All Good Americans*, *Yellow Jack*, *Divided by Three*, *Page Miss Glory* and *A Journey at Night*, and in 1935 he departed for the film capital.

Logan, McCormick, Miss Natwick and Margaret Sullavan, together with Stewart and Fonda, had all served their apprenticeships with the University Players at West Falmouth. Miss Sullavan made her first New York appearance in 1931 in *A Modern Virgin*. Four more flops followed, but the critics were much aware of this lovely girl with the throaty voice. In 1933 she replaced Marguerite Churchill in *Dinner at Eight*, and then went to Hollywood, returning to Broadway in 1936 as the star of *Stage Door*.

Josh Logan was not the only struggling actor of the Thirties who went on to success as a director. The Group Theater produced a number of others. Elia Kazan, Robert Lewis and Sanford Meisner were actors in such Group offerings as *Men in White*, *Waiting for Lefty*, *Till the Day I Die*, *Weep for the Virgins*, *Paradise Lost*, *The Case of Clyde Griffiths* and

Golden Boy. John Garfield was another who came to the fore with the Group in the mid-Thirties. During the same period, another noted playwright-director, Garson Kanin, was a young actor in such George Abbott successes as *Three Men on a Horse* and *Boy Meets Girl.* Director Sidney Lumet was an eleven-year-old actor in *Dead End,* one of the dramatic hits of the decade. He was also in the Max Reinhardt production of *The Eternal Road* (1937), together with Kurt Kasznar and Lotte Lenya.

The Federal Theater Project of the WPA (1935–39) helped the careers of such then unknowns as Orson Welles, Joseph Cotten, Arlene Francis and Hiram Sherman. The last three appeared in the WPA production of *Horse Eats Hat* that Welles directed. The same actors were prominent in the brief but exciting career of the Mercury Theater, established in 1937 by Welles and John Houseman.

The first edition of the revue *New Faces,* which opened March 15, 1934, was a stepping stone for other young performers: Imogene Coca, Nancy Hamilton, Charles Walters, who has become a well-known film director, and Alan Handley, the television producer. And it helped to establish producer-talent-hunter Leonard Sillman and a show that has had three other successful editions through the years.

In 1934 the *Page Miss Glory* program had this entry: "Reporter from *The Telegram*—Betty Field." The part was a walk-on, and her New York debut. But soon George Abbott employed her in *Three Men on a Horse, Boy Meets Girl, Room Service* and *What a Life,* long-run hits, one and all.

José Ferrer was the Second Policeman in *A Slight Case of Murder* (1935). It was his first assignment on Broadway. By the end of the following year, he was given a paddle to wield in *Brother Rat,* another memorable Abbott farce comedy of the era. Eddie Albert was also in the cast.

In Montgomery Clift's first professional appearance on the New York stage, he was one of Thomas Mitchell's precocious brats in *Fly Away Home* (1935). The success he won served to break down the parental objections to his going into the theater. *Jubilee, Yr. Obedient Husband, The Mother* and *Dame Nature* provided him with other juvenile roles for the next five years.

On November 9, 1938, the critics and the usual rude first-night audience gathered at the Imperial Theater to witness the opening of a musical, little knowing that they were about to witness theatrical history, but before the final curtain, the hit of the evening was a newcomer from Texas named Mary Martin, even though the cast included such veterans as Sophie Tucker, Victor Moore and William Gaxton. The Texas girl stopped the show—Cole Porter's *Leave It to Me*—with "My Heart Belongs to Daddy."

GUNS AND IDEALISTS

AMERICANS who sympathized with labor and the political Left were usually strongly anti-Fascist, and the Spanish Civil War aroused many of them to action. They pressed for help to the Loyalist government; they wrote letters, argued, and stirred up controversies to make others conscious of the significance of this struggle against the Fascists: here was an opportunity to stand fast against fascism, perhaps to halt the fateful tide toward war. Eventually, three thousand Americans went to Spain and took up arms against the Fascists. They wrote a page in our history quite unlike any other.

On July 17, 1936, several garrisons of the Spanish army in Spanish Morocco rose against the civil government. The coup might have been defeated if Mussolini had not immediately supplied the insurgents, led by Generalissimo Franco, with the necessary materiel for making war—planes, ammunition, and even troops. While the civil government and their faithful, to be known as the Loyalists, rallied a good deal of support, many of the Spanish institutions and organizations fought for themselves at first, and the resultant state of anarchy enabled Franco to move steadily through the country, sweeping up all opposition. In early November, he reached the outskirts of Madrid and here, with their backs to the wall, the Loyalists mustered a stubborn opposition.

Volunteers from many countries had arrived to fight against fascism and Franco. While they were small in number—never amounting to more than fifteen thousand men—they provided an inspiring and effective defense against Franco at the gates of Madrid. They were known as the International Brigades.

The Internationals were never a major force in the Loyalist armies—the Spaniards did most of the fighting on both sides. But they were often used as shock troops, which meant that their casualties were as high as 70 per cent.

Perhaps this was the first time since the Crusades that men all over the world felt a need to stand and fight for an ideal. Many volunteers were Communists, but even a Communist was under no compulsion to give his life for Spain. Idealism was a factor.

The largest nationality in the Brigades was the French, partly because of their proximity to Spain and partly because of an overwhelming sympathy many French had for the Loyalist cause. Americans began arriving in December, but did not go into action until February. By then there were enough for a battalion of 450, and they chose the name Abraham Lincoln Battalion. Later a second group called itself the George Washington Battalion.

The Americans were ill prepared for combat; the United States at that time did not have universal military training—one of the few countries at that time which did not. Supposedly they were to get three months' training at least, but they were placed in action too soon to receive it. Herbert L. Matthews, distinguished foreign correspondent of the New York *Times,* has described some of the action in which American volunteers were involved:

"In the middle of February when the rebel advance [Franco's men] seemed almost irresistible, the Lincoln Battalion, along with other fresh Internationals, were withdrawn from their training center and rushed into the line. On February 16, Americans took their places in the Fifteenth Brigade along with what was left of the English battalion that had fought since early November. . . .

"I used to go down to Morata, because the hub of the world struggle against fascism had temporarily been moved from the capital to that little town, for all the Internationals were there engaged in barring the way to Madrid once again. Both sides were locked in an immovable grip. The fiercest fighting occurred around Pingarron Hill, to the northwest of Morata. It was a dominant position which the rebels had occupied and fortified strongly and despite fierce exchanges they remained in possession of it. Pingarron Hill evidently weighed heavy on the stomach of the Loyalist general, and he determined to assault it.

"Bob Merriman, California teacher of economics, was ordered to take the Lincoln Battalion across an open terrain and over a preliminary rise 'at all costs.' The attack started shortly after dawn on February 27. The aerial bombardment was ineffectual, the artillery weak, and the tanks either refused or were not ready to go. But Merriman had his orders. At zero hour, as the men moved forward, he was wounded and an English officer with World War I experience took the first wave of Americans over himself, and gained the preliminary position with hardly the loss of a man. A Spanish battalion was on the right, and an English battalion to the right of the Spanish. The English drove forward well, but the Spanish held back. That meant catastrophe, for as the Americans came forward they met not only the fire from the positions ahead but a murderous crossfire from their right.

"The result was almost literally a massacre. Of the succeeding waves of Americans hardly any reached that first position. One hundred and twenty-seven men were killed and approximately 175 wounded. One American, Robert J. Raven, was wounded from two grenades, one of which mangled his feet while the other burst almost in his face. A nurse told him later that he was permanently blinded. He was silent for a moment. Then he said, 'I came to Spain prepared to give my life; I won't squeal because I've lost my eyes.' " *

The battalion was reduced to approximately 135 men but it stayed in the lines, where the men who lived soon learned how to take cover and perform the other rudimentary acts to save themselves in combat.

Later Matthews visited the area when there was a period of idleness and found the Americans playing ping-pong, baseball and so on to pass the time. They had dug in strongly now, and he was impressed with their trenches. He complimented a New York Irishman who said, "Sure, we aren't going to pay rent after this

* Herbert L. Matthews, *Two Wars and More to Come* (New York, Carrick & Evans, 1938).

war. We'll just build dugouts in Battery Park."
One of the American soldiers was

Alvah Bessie. He describes combat in Spain, beginning with the movement up to the lines in March 1937.

ALVAH C. BESSIE

FIGHTING IN SPAIN*

TWO NIGHTS before, there had been a fiesta around a huge bonfire, and singing and a cheap French champagne that tasted more like sour hard cider, and there were *avellanos* to eat and shells to toss in the fire, and there were speeches. Young girls had come up from Barcelona to visit us, representatives of the Unified Socialist Youth, and though at that time we knew little enough Spanish, one of them, a small, plain girl, was able to fire us with immense enthusiasm. There was also a young man, every inch a man, who had been impressed into Franco's army in the north and had managed to escape to us with a Fiat machine gun and three other armed men.

"We must be moving," the older men said, "When they throw a fiesta for you, it never fails."

At five in the morning of the thirtieth we were up and lined up and marched down toward the road, where there were cases and cases of unused Russian rifles, packed in grease. These were issued to the men, and as we had no rags with which to clean them we tore wide strips off our underwear, wiped barrel, stock and bolt, ran strips through the bore. My rifle, whose metal work bore the stamp of the Russian Imperial Eagle, was numbered 59034. Under the partly obliterated Imperial emblem was a new stamp, the hammer and sickle of the Soviet Union.

There was no time to clean the arms adequately; we cleaned and wiped them as we marched. We halted for a moment to receive little paper packs of cartridges, 165 rounds a man, which the men stuffed in their pockets or packed into their blanket rolls. We halted again to take on a load of hand grenades, a modification of the World War Mills bomb, made of segmented cast iron and provided with a lever and a pin. None of us had ever tossed a live grenade. We went onto the main road and marched in artillery formation on either side of the road, the scouts going ahead at

* Condensed from Alvah C. Bessie's *Men in Battle* (New York, Scribner, 1939).

the point and on the flanks, the main body moving slowly along. Every fifteen minutes there were "avion" warnings, and we scattered off the road into the ditches and the fields, lying on our faces till the whistle blew.

LATER

We had one section of Spanish boys attached to each company, and lying there in the line I caught a glimpse of one of them crawling through the underbrush, his mountainous pack-sack swaying like the howdah on an elephant's back. He came from behind me, and to the right and was crawling toward Tabb's machine-gun squad, saying, "I want to see the machine gun working." I heard Tabb shout to him to get down, that he was in the line of fire, but the boy kept coming at him, smiling, saying, "I want to see the machine gun," and then he rolled onto his side, his hands seeking his groin, shouting. "Mama mia! Ai! Mama mia!" Tabb's gun let a burst fly at the rough crest opposite, and I looked across and could see where the bullets hit the stone, but there were no men in sight.

I was sent on patrol alone, and when I got back the Spanish boy was still lying in front of our lines, groaning. Dick told me to get a stretcher-bearer and I went back down the hill, sweating and grunting to myself, but momentarily relieved by being out of the line of fire. Below, there was a first-aid man, but no stretcher-bearer was available and the *practicante* was reluctant to come back up the hill. "Bring him down," he said, and I said, "We can't you'll have to go up," and all the way back up the hill he kept saying, "Keep down, be careful, look out, the fire's pretty hot up here, where is he?" It got on my nerves and I felt good thinking of him alone out there, dressing the wound, while I could drop back behind the hill and sit down and light a cigarette.

When I got back, Dick said, "Look over there; there's a mountain. There are a lot of troops behind that hill, but we don't know who they are, ours or theirs. Go over and find out and try to get back by dark."

The body felt light; the head detached from the body; the feet a long way below and carrying the detached body along by their own independent effort.

There was a sniper who followed me along through the edge of the woods and across the open space, and I kept thinking, This is too close for comfort, you bastard; and then I entered the woods and promptly lost my way. (I wonder what it's like in Brooklyn now, I thought; and how much do they get on relief, and do the kids get enough orange juice and corn flakes and does she get enough to eat or does she scrimp on her own chow to line the kids' bellies?)

I looked back, but the hill on which the Battalion had taken up positions was hidden, and I stood there, thinking. When I left I was going due west into the sun, and the mountain was somewhat north of west, and now the sun is on my left when it should be on my right—and what is it like in Brooklyn? I sat down and rolled a cigarette. Letting my mind play with the compass directions, and then Luke Hinman came along. He was a Battalion scout and had given me a few simple lessons in scouting a few days before, and so I asked him about the directions watching his hard, kind face with the broken nose, the firm lips, the blue eyes. He didn't talk much.

Moving through the woods quietly with your rifle at the ready was good. Then I came across a guy we can call Hal, another Battalion scout, who was sitting in the woods, or rather lying on his back with his eyes closed. "What're you up to?" I asked; and he said, smiling, "I'm on patrol." So I moved on and found the hill and came cautiously behind it. There was another company of Lincolns there, the third. I started back through the woods and located Hal again, who was still lying on his back. "How's the patrol going?" I said, and he said, "Couldn't be better." Goldbrick was the word that came into my mind, and I laughed to myself as I went along, thinking would they shoot him for that if I said anything which I won't but would they?

On the hill behind ours I met Hank Wentworth. "Dick's worried about you," Hank said, "Where you been all this time?" "Well to tell you the truth," I said, "when I started out I saw the kitchen truck at Headquarters and I got something to eat." "What'd they have?" he said. "Nothing came up to the line yet." "Oh, salad, steak and rice and French fried potatoes and wine and cookies and nuts and coffee—" "No crap," Hank said.

Just before dark, Dick received a message from Battalion which read, "Advise that enemy is expected to attack on your right flank; place a light machine gun on your right with instructions not to fire till they are 50 meters from you." And because I'd been over the terrain he sent me out with Sid, who was Tabb's gunner, and kept Tabb, Johnson and Taubman on the hill.

Sid had received a glancing blow on the head earlier that afternoon, and he had a handkerchief around his forehead that kept slipping over his eyes as we doubled down the back side of our hill and along through the wood that bordered the olive field. He was short and slim. But a sniper had seen us moving and he followed us through the wood as we went ducking around and under the low spruces, getting caught in the brambles, and scratching our hands and faces. I was praying for the sun to set but it was still high over the western hill.

When we reached the point where we would have to cross the open space, we looked at one another. There was Sid, small and scared, and the black, wet face of the the Negro, Johnson (my God, I thought, he must be fifty years old) and Moish Taubman, who used to say he was the laziest man in the Battalion, but had guts of cast iron. We crouched near the opening, waiting for each other to suggest some way of getting across. The bullets were hissing high or cracking low, and Moish said, "That son of a bitch is going to hurt somebody if he ain't careful"; and Sid said to me, "You're stronger than I am, suppose you take the gun, and go across first."

I took the light machine gun in my arms like an infant and faced the hundred meters of ploughed earth ahead. I took a deep breath and crouching low, started to run. I was crouched too low, felt myself falling, stumbling, lifted my head and shoulders so I could take longer strides, and zigzagged stumbling over the heavy clods of earth, thinking, fifty meters is awful close; if we wait till they get that close . . . Dick had said, "Bring the gun back, and come back yourselves."

The fascist machine gun spoke and the dirt kicked up around me; I ran, seeing the little wooded clump ahead, wondering if the others were right behind. When I reached the wood I fell flat on the gun and dug my face into the hard ground. The machine-gun bullets were snarling overhead and I lay there waiting, counting in my head, one two three four five, holding my breath for them to stop. Twigs and leaves kept dropping, and looking behind I could see where the slugs were kicking up the dirt, whining off the stones like a plucked piano string. No one had followed, so I lay face downward on the gun. Then they came panting almost grunting with the effort, and threw themselves down all around. After a while the fascist gun stopped firing.

We sat in the heavy darkness, tending the gun that faced up the valley, waiting. For a time we whispered about the possibility of the Battalion moving off without us, but there was no reason for this; we had taken two hills that day and there was nothing to worry about. We scouted about individually in the dark. We couldn't smoke; we couldn't talk. We listened till our ears hurt and no one came.

"I'll lead the way back," Sid said, and started confidently off. "Wrong way," I said, but Sid didn't answer. "You're going the wrong way," I said, and Sid stopped, waited for me to come up close, then said, "I'm in command of this squad." "O.K.," I said, "but you're going the wrong way anyhow."

We picked our way up the side of a hill, slipping on the exposed stones, dead tired and aching with the long day's tension. Johnson was carrying the gun, moaning quietly to himself. When we reached a halt on the side of the hill, he said, "Comrade, this comrade says you're going the wrong way. He brought us here; maybe he ought to know the way back. Maybe you better let him take us back, comrade. I'm done in," he said and sat down with the gun cradled in his lap.

APRIL 1937—IN THE HILLS ABOVE TORTOSA

Below us there were hundreds of men from the British, the Canadian Battalions; a food truck had come up, and they were being fed. A new roadster drove around the hill and stopped near us, and two men got out we recognized. One was tall, thin, dressed in brown corduroy, wearing horn-shelled glasses. He had a long ascetic face, firm lips, a gloomy look about him. The other was taller, heavy, red-faced, one of the largest men you will see; he wore steel-rimmed glasses and a bushy mustache. Herbert Matthews of the New York *Times*, and Ernest Hemingway. We introduced ourselves and they asked questions. They had cigarettes; they gave us Lucky Strikes and Chesterfields.

Hemingway did not seem to be discouraged, but Matthews was. Hemingway said, Sure they would get to the sea, but that was nothing to worry about. It had been foreseen; it would be taken care of; methods had already been worked out for communication between Catalonia and the rest of Spain; by ship, by plane, everything would be all right. Roosevelt, he said, had made an unofficial offer—or so he had been told—to ship 200 planes to France, if France would ship them to Spain. That was one of the best things we had ever heard of Roosevelt, but where were they? The war will enter a new phase now, Hemingway said; the Government's resistance will redouble, the people of Spain and Catalonia were fighting mad; the political organizations and trade unions were rounding up new replacements; the people wanted to counterattack; in mid-March Barcelona had been bombed 18 times within 48 hours, and 1,300 had been killed, 2,000 wounded. The Pope expressed his horror and his Christian indignation. All over the world popular sentiment, for the Loyalists from the start, and despite floods of Catholic and fascist propaganda, was growing stronger with every defeat the Government had suffered. There were huge demonstrations in London, Paris, Prague, Moscow and New York; the decent people everywhere were putting pressure on their governments to come to the assistance of Spain, but what can the decent people do?

We began to be aware of exactly how bad the situation was. The Brigade had gone in with about 2,000 men, and come out with 1,300; the Lincoln Battalion went in with about 500, and now we had about 120. Most of those who had come up from Tarrazona with me for their first action were gone.

AUGUST 1937

There was still some light in the sky as we moved out of the rest camp under the olive trees along the narrow trail leading over the low hills toward Gandesa. Then we turned off the main road onto a goat path that led into the hills. For two and a half hours we bent to a forty-degree angle, twisting and turning, slipping and stumbling up the almost impassable way. There was one thought in our minds: It's going to be hell getting food, water and munitions up this hill; it's going to be tough for the wounded.

With the dawn we could really see what we had to work with; a bare mountainside thrust into the empty sky, facing a concealed enemy slightly below. All day, we waited in the heat; there was no water. Then water came up—water disinfected with iodine and mixed with Spanish cognac. A squadron of fascist planes came over and unloaded upon the men on our left.

LATER

It was bitter cold, and we lay on the bare rocks, waiting, waiting for what, we did not know. They were singing over on their hills, a weird Moorish song that curdled your blood and made your spine run cold.

We listened to them singing, and we watched the sudden moon come from behind the wet clouds and then disappear again. The wind came up and blew the clouds away and we lay strewn all over the hilltop like the dead, waiting.

Dawn came up through the heavy fog. Fog meant no airplanes, so we could relax. But by ten in the morning we could hear them, and Curtis, flat in the next hole, said, "Here they come." "Don't worry," I said. "There's no ceiling; they can't see through the fog"; and so we remained silent and listened to them droning and droning overhead. And then, suddenly, there was the familiar whistling and a load fell directly into the *barranco* behind the hill, across the way from us, and the earth rose under us and threw us off and we fell back again, our hands clasped over our heads, hearing the falling rocks and dirt, waiting to be hit, our ears ringing.

Later that day, the ceiling was unlimited, but there were no further planes; the afternoon grew deathly quiet and the heat grew intense, but nothing happened. No rifle fire, and no shelling. That was the end of our third day in that hole.

THE NEXT DAY

We were crouched in the shallow *refugios* alongside the cliff; I was lying on my back and Dick was catching a little sleep at my feet, with Archie behind him with Sans. It had just passed noon when they opened up, and from the start they had our range. We could count about seven batteries at work, all of them concentrated on our sector, that was no more than 500 yards wide. They came, you heard them from the start to the end, the three low harmless thumps of the faraway guns, then a brief silence, then a low hissing, growing crescendo into a riffling whistle (a scream if they were coming close), and then a deafening crash that reverberated between the two slopes that enclosed the *barranco* behind the hill.

"That was close," Curtis said. "They've got us spotted."

He was in the next hole with the telephonist, Felix. I turned onto my back, saw Aaron's automatic pistol tucked between the two rocks where I had put it.

I heard them coming again, and closed my eyes, put my arms over my face and waited. You felt nothing at such moments except a tightening of the belly, and you drew up your legs instinctively and then it was all over. There were occasional duds; occasionally a shell whistling close overhead would suddenly lose its twirling motion and, turning end over end, go scuffling through the air making a noise like a small boy blowing air between his lips. You wanted to laugh when you heard those.

From where I was lying, if I lifted my head, I could see the built-up parapets of the other men in the *plana mayor*, the stretcher-bearers, the barber, the quartermaster Lara. When the shells were coming they were nowhere to be seen; after they had landed and the shrapnel had stopped screeching and smacking at the stone, they all sat up, sticking their heads over the parapet as though they were puppets in a Punch and Judy show.

"What about it?" Archie yelled; and Dick shouted, "What about what?"

"We ought to be up in the line," the commissar said; then they both ducked, and the thing went off and deafened us and the stones fell in on us from where the shrapnel and concussion had chipped away the cliff.

There was a terrific tearing smash and everything was black and a voice was screaming, screaming. I went out for a moment and came to and put my hand on top of my head and looked at my hand, but there was no blood on it. It was difficult to see, the air was clogged with rock dust and smoke and the ringing was continuous and the voice kept screaming on a high note. Far away, I heard Dick say, "Who got it? You, Bess?" And I said, "I don't think so," and sat up.

The screaming came from behind me so I got up and looked, and there was Curtis, lying on his belly, his buttocks torn away, holding them with his hands, his face turned to me, dead white and powdered with rock dust, and his mouth open, his eyes looking at me, his mouth open screaming. I could not take my eyes away from his.

Felix lay behind Curtis, his legs bloody and his face still, and I climbed over the few stones that remained standing between us, and Felix said, "Take him first, he's worse." Curtis kept screaming although his mouth did not move, looking at me with his eyes wide and staring and I was saying, Take it easy take it easy take it easy, and suddenly it was good to be moving, good to be doing something instead of just lying there waiting for something to happen. I yelled for the *practicante,* but he was up in the lines; I yelled for a bandage and was handed a small one-inch roll that was worthless. I called the stretcher-bearers who came and we lifted Curtis out under the arms and knees, and they went away with him through the fire that was falling before us, behind us.

Felix's legs were badly torn and his foot was broken to bits, the bone stuck through the torn leather of his shoes. I gave him a cigarette and tried with my wet red hands to light it for him, succeeding after a time.

They were pounding the shallow lines on the hill crest; with artillery and antitank shells they were hammering away from left to right, and back again, and it hurt to watch; it hurt in much the same way that a sore knee hurts when you clumsily bang it again and again.

All day, hour after hour, they kept it up. They covered our parapets and every inch of the back side of the hill. They wanted by the sheer weight of their steel to blow us off that hill. The body was utterly exhausted and indifferent to conscious fear but straining to the snapping point. There was sweat, and there was internal pain.

It all seems very far away and meaningless, although you know the meaning or you would not be there; there is no immediate reality in this. You can think of Times Square with all its cars and all its people, and the focus narrows down and you can see their faces, ordinary commonplace faces like the faces you have known all your life, like the faces of the Spanish men and women and children you have seen in the cities and the small towns and the country, who are waiting back of the lines now, maybe reading a newspaper: our forces in the sector of X . . . repulsed, with heavy casualties. And what does it mean, tell me, and do you know? Faces, do they care about us over here? And do they even think of us with love? The women and the children and the men—do they know we are so far away from them and dying for them? Do they know this is their struggle too? There is no connection between the fact of war and people; not when you are in it. It seems to be something taking place upon another, insulated plane of existence that does not, while you live it, touch the people whom it really touches. You think of love.

For it is love alone that can, for even a moment of our time, give you the illusion that you are not alone, penetrate your loneliness and separate it from you for that moment. And you are afraid that you will die without that love; you are not just afraid to die. And this is the meaning of it all (the people's war); these men behind these fragile rocks, these men whose tender flesh is torn to pieces by the hot and ragged steel; they could not accept their death with such good grace if they did not love so deeply and so well—were not determined that love must come alive into the world. What other reason could there be for dying? What other reason for this blood upon your hands?

A CERTAIN KIND OF IDEALIST

A COOL reception awaited the Spanish Civil War veterans upon their return to America. They had gone to Spain despite official disapproval by the United States government, and some of its branches would give them a hard time for years to come. The State Department, for instance, refused to issue passports to Americans who had served with the Loyalists. A few years later, when the United States was arming for war, such Americans were considered poor risks at the induction centers; if you had fought in Spain, you were, *ipso facto*, a Communist.

Years later, at the time of the McCarthy hearings, Morris Ernst and David Loth wrote *Report on the American Communist*, in which they examined the "homogeneous" character of the Communist party member. It was their opinion that there was a strong strain of idealism in many of those interviewed, and that, in their way, they were "selfless, dedicated" people. The following story, told by a veteran of the Spanish Civil War, indicates that this very idealism was apt to be cynically exploited by the Communist party.

MORRIS ERNST AND DAVID LOTH

REPORT ON AN AMERICAN COMMUNIST*

"I JOINED the Communist party in the early Thirties. I was twenty-four at the time and worked for the federal government. Probably the thing that pushed me into the party was that I felt terribly guilty at being employed when there were so many unemployed.

"My difficulties with the party began when I went to Spain to fight with the Lincoln Brigade. The trouble probably started with the fact that I have a gift for languages. I learned to speak Spanish and to read it fluently in a fairly short time. As a result, I was able to read the Spanish papers and to talk to Spaniards.

"I began correcting my previous conception of the Spanish situation,

* From Ernst and Loth's *Report on the American Communist* (New York, Holt, 1952).

which I had gotten completely from the American Communist party. I learned, for example, that the Popular Front was a hoax. Nobody believed in it except schmoes who had never learned to read Spanish. I found that while the other groups in the Popular Front were adhering to its terms, the Communists were going right ahead and doing the very things they had agreed not to do which made the Popular Front possible. For example, none of the member organizations were supposed to recruit, proselytize, or use high-pressure tactics to win new members. The Communists were the only group which consistently violated this agreement. They viewed the Popular Front solely as an instrumentality, and used it accordingly. They gave lip service to the Popular Front idea and did just enough grandstand stuff to enable them to point with pride to their militant devotion to the Popular Front. The difference between what the party professed to do and what it really did made it pretty confusing for me for a while until the whole thing began to emerge in my own mind for what it was—probably one of the worst examples of organized large-scale hypocrisy in history.

"During this period when I was trying to sort things out in my own mind, I started getting in trouble at party meetings of the Brigade. I sounded off on a number of issues and rapidly became unpopular. Luckily I had a couple of old friends who had risen to important posts in the party who came to my defense when my deviationist attitude was reported, with reassurances that I was just a slightly crazy guy, not a disrupter or a spy. Dozens of boys in the Lincoln Brigade were executed for deviationist tendencies, sometimes on the pretext that they were deserters.

"When I got back to the United States in 1938, I was intellectually certain of where I stood with regard to the party. I didn't sever my connection, however, immediately in the sense of formally resigning. I just stopped going to meetings. The Friends of the Lincoln Brigade at that time had a tremendous amount of money at their disposal which was supposed to be used to help veterans. I made two speeches for them for which I was paid, but after that they obviously didn't trust me not to shoot my mouth off and didn't give me any more speaking engagements.

"After a few months I was notified to appear before the Control Commission. This was the disciplinary body which investigated grievances against members, carried on personnel investigations, and selected people for special duty or Comintern work. Notices to appear before the Commission were never sent out by mail, but by word of mouth. When the message reached you, you either kept the appointment or left town or just holed up and worried yourself to death, depending on what kind of a guy you were. I kept the appointment. I had no intention of making a big dramatic thing out of it and going into details of why I could no longer accept the party line. I just played indifferent. The man who interviewed me was very solicitous at first.

" 'What's the matter, comrade? Aren't you feeling well?'

"He said I was probably suffering from shell shock and offered to arrange for me to have a long vacation at Camp Kinderland, the party country resort. He held out the lure of possible re-employment by the party; I didn't have a job at the time. When none of this broke down the indifferent attitude I had assumed, he warned me that if I didn't pull myself together and start behaving properly, I would be expelled. Nobody had to explain to me what this involved. For people like me it meant complete ostracism and being cut off from all of the people who had been my friends. Even though I was sure where I stood in principle, I must admit this prospect gave me many hours of doubt as to what I should do. At some points I was almost convinced that the fault was with me, that it was my weakness not any defect in the party that was precipitating the break.

"The ostracism was as bad as my worst anticipations. Men I had lived with passed me on the street without speaking to me. Even a man whose life I had saved in Spain refused to talk to me. He had been wounded in battle, and I carried him to safety on my back for 15 kilometers from early morning to sunset, holding my pants up with one hand because I had used my belt as a tourniquet for his arm. The first time I met him on the street after my interview with the Commission, he passed me by. The second time, he couldn't stand it and asked me to have a cup of coffee with him. He justified himself by saying:

" 'I stick to the party.'

"Once that was off his chest, he never talked to me again. Things were so bad that I became suspicious of the few people who would still talk to me. I thought they had probably been assigned to keep tabs on me.

"Up to this point I had continued attending meetings of the Veterans of the Lincoln Brigade. While I still had no wish for an open clash with the party, I had not been able to sit quietly and watch the men who had fought fascism in Spain follow the pro-Fascist party line of neutrality toward the war in Europe. This was, of course, well before the invasion of Russia caused an overnight switch in the line.

"I suddenly found myself brought up on charges for expulsion from the Veterans of the Lincoln Brigade. To my astonishment I found my importance blown up to fantastic proportions. Earl Browder was the chief speaker against me. He called me the successor to Trotsky and described me as a cunning manipulator who had cultivated a bland exterior to cover up his devious and widespread machinations. The charges were seconded by John Gates, who delivered a speech reporting practically every word I had ever said during the years in Spain. He even had a detailed account of a meeting at which I had queried La Pasionaria's evaluation of a certain battle. [She was the fiery woman leader of Spanish Communists.] It was one of those damned petty semantic squabbles that people sometimes get into. But to hear Gates tell it, I was a disrupter whose object had been to lose the war in Spain. When I tried to speak in self-defense, I was physically escorted to the door."

A TURN FOR THE WORSE

BY THE beginning of 1937, Americans felt they had left the Depression far behind them. The President, in his budget message in January, announced that the matter of continuing recovery in the economy could be safely turned over to the businessmen. The relief rolls were to be cut, and some of the Public Works projects would be reduced.

Even the budget might be balanced soon; the President made it clear, however, that the balancing of the budget would not be had at the expense of any needed relief measures.

Before the sound-money men in the country could clap hands, however, the economy suddenly took a nose dive in the fall of that year. Stock prices fell, until by March 1938, A. T. & T., which had been selling around $170 a share, was down to $110. What happened to the national recovery?

FREDERICK LEWIS ALLEN

RECESSION*

DURING the latter part of 1936 and the early part of 1937 there were sharp increases in the prices of goods. Business concerns had been accumulating big inventories. When the time came to sell these goods at retail to the public, the purchasing power to absorb them just wasn't there.

New investments had lagged; and what was more, the government spending campaign had been virtually halted; Secretary of the Treasury Henry Morgenthau had persuaded President Roosevelt to make a real attempt to balance the budget.

Result: the goods which were piled up on the shelves moved slowly. Businessmen became alarmed and cut production. Two million men were thrown out of work in the space of a few months—and became all the less able to buy what was for sale. Thus out of that apparently clear sky—no great speculative boom in stocks or real estate, no tightness in credit, no overexpansion of capacity for making capital goods (in fact, not nearly enough expansion)—came the Recession.

* From Frederick Lewis Allen's *Since Yesterday* (New York, Harper, 1940).

It brought its ironies. Precisely a year after the beginning of the great sit-down strikes in General Motors, the president of the corporation announced that about 30,000 production men were to be laid off immediately, and the remaining men would be reduced to a three-day week. What price CIO gains now?

Another irony was provided by the collapse of values on the New York Stock Exchange. On Tuesday, March 8, 1938, just as trading for the day was beginning, President Gay of the Exchange mounted the rostrum, and, as the gong rang to halt the brokers, read the amazing announcement that Richard Whitney and Company were suspended for "conduct inconsistent with just and equitable principles of trade." Whitney had been the leader of the Old Guard of the Exchange. With his downfall the last opposition to a reorganization of the Exchange crumbled—in accordance with the wishes of Chairman William O. Douglas of the Securities and Exchange Commission.

There was irony, too, in the earnest effort of Administration leaders to remain calm and hopeful-looking as they issued statements predicting an early upturn, while the economic landslide was roaring downhill. Hadn't there been another Administration, not so many years before, which they had ridiculed for doing much the same thing?

As the Recession deepened, there rose angry voices from the business community and the conservative press. The whole thing was the Administration's fault. This was a "Roosevelt Depression."

As 1937 turned into 1938 Roosevelt was still trying to balance the budget and to refrain from proposing measures which would frighten businessmen unduly, but slowly the Administration leaders were becoming convinced that no policy of retrenchment and appeasement would bear fruit.

All the while the New Dealers were urging a resumption of deficit spending, and on April 2—as things were getting worse and worse—the President threw in the sponge. At lunch on the train from Warm Springs to Washington he told Harry Hopkins and Aubrey Williams that he was ready to abandon the budget-balancing effort and go in for heavy spending again. On April 14 he went on the radio to explain that he was asking Congress to appropriate three billion dollars for relief, public works, housing, flood control, and other recovery efforts.

That spring the legislation went through Congress, and simultaneously business began to show faint signs of improvement. In the latter half of June the stock market sprang to life. Recovery began again.

But the Administration as a whole had been struck a very heavy blow by the Recession. Meeting a new economic crisis, it had disclosed itself as neither able to generate "confidence" in businessmen nor to concoct any new and effective measures of recovery. The best it could do was to take down from the shelf a bottle of medicine to which it had been addicted for years—pump-priming.

THE WRATHFUL ELEMENTS

It was a rare year that at least one of the country's major rivers didn't reach flood crest and spill over on the land, creating havoc in the homes, and taking the lives of people who lived along its banks. Congress frequently passed flood control bills, but they were usually only stopgap measures.

Finally, on June 22, 1936, Congress passed legislation which established an over-all national flood-control policy, and authorized construction of some two hundred control-works on the rivers. Before major progress was accomplished, however, the Ohio River went on a rampage in January 1937, which produced perhaps the worst flood damage in American history.

At Cincinnati the water rose almost eight feet higher than it had ever risen there before; at Louisville, almost seven feet higher. Nine hundred people lost their lives; five hundred thousand families were driven from their homes; and a month after the crisis almost three hundred thousand were still homeless.

"But these figures," Frederick Lewis Allen wrote, "give no impression whatever of what men and women experienced in each town during the latter days of January as the swirling waters rose till the Ohio seemed a great rushing muddy lake full of floating wreckage, and the cold rain drizzled inexorably down, and every stream added its swollen contribution to the torrent. Railroad tracks and roads washed away. Towns darkened as the electric-light plants were submerged. Business halted, food supplies stopped, fires raging out of control, disease threatening. The city of Portsmouth, Ohio, opening six great sewer valves and letting seven feet of water rush into its business district, lest its famous concrete flood wall be destroyed. Cincinnati giving City Manager Dykstra dictatorial powers. The radio being used to direct rescue work and issue warnings and instructions to the population as other means of communication failed: a calm voice at the microphone telling rescuers to row to such-and-such an address and take a family off the roof, to row somewhere else and help an old woman out of a second-story window. Breadlines. The Red Cross, the Coast Guard, the WPA aiding in the work of rescue and reorganization. Martial law. Churches above the water line being used as refuges. Mud everywhere, as the waters receded—mud and stench.

"Most dramatic of all, perhaps, the triumphant fight to save Cairo, Illinois: men piling more and more sandbags atop the levee, standing guard day and night, rushing to strengthen the wall of defense wherever it weakened, as the waters rose and rose—and did not quite break over." *

The only river in the East and Midwest areas of the nation that did not produce comparable damage was

* From Frederick Lewis Allen's *Since Yesterday*.

548

the Tennessee, now harnessed by the TVA.

The flood damage was barely cleared away, and the recession well on the way to being licked, when, in the fall of 1938, a hurricane suddenly struck the East Coast of the nation with savage force, killing 700 people, and destroying over two billion trees.

There was almost no warning—the present network of storm warnings did not exist then. People were caught in their beach houses and on vulnerable lowlands. Great South Bay was completely sucked dry by the vacuum created by the onrush of the first winds, and then when the tidal waves burst over Fire Island, hundreds of houses were smashed to kindling.

One woman hiding under her bed all night long looked out the window at daylight to observe she was now residing in the next town. And one family marooned on Fire Island clung to the stunted, gnarled beach trees the night through, watching the wind and waters wash away their house.

JOHN Q. STEWART

NEW ENGLAND HURRICANE*

NEWSPAPERS, especially outside New England, gave the stupendous hurricane of Wednesday, September 21, very inadequate treatment. For two or three days immediately following the disaster bits of it were front-page items, but the whole account was not available until the neurotic interests of editors had jumped to fresher happenings. Only in scattered fragments was the storm's story published at the time. The limitations imposed on reporting by excessive mania for speed never have been illustrated more emphatically.

The first hurried headlines the next morning, "Storm Hits Atlantic Coast," are about all that inattentive newspaper readers from New York City west are likely to remember of a catastrophe as dramatic and horrible as any ever accomplished by wind and sea and rain. Spectral fleets of aerial bombers over Czechoslovakia were made more real to the American public than the actual low-flying blasts of the typhoon.

"For twenty-five cents I'll listen to your story of the hurricane." A bored sandwich man is rumored to have paraded Boston Common with this sign. Yet no narrator would be able to supply him with an altogether complete and trustworthy description. History moved on September 21 too

* From *Harper's* Magazine, January 1939.

fast to follow across New England, and the telegraph lines in tatters went down behind her. The wind's destruction commenced about 2:30 P.M., along the south shore of Long Island, and ceased above the Canadian border after midnight. The disaster was threefold. Over sea beaches storm waves of the hurricane, few in number but towering as high as forty feet, swept everything away. Terrific winds carried destruction inland. Torrential rains swelled streams already flooding from earlier downpours.

Seven states, and the Province of Quebec, counted close to seven hundred fatalities. A seaboard as wealthy as any in the world, and its hinterland, heavily provided with telephones, radios, coast guards, and state police, felt the shock. There had been no warning worth the mentioning; telephones and coast guards were scarcely called to service. A sophisticated population died by hundreds with little or no knowledge of what raw shape of death this was which struck from the sky and the tide.

In the long and laudable annals of the government's weather forecasters that day's record makes what must be the sorriest page. Hindsight is easy. The routine responsibilities of the United States Weather Bureau are so important that criticism of the failure of this splendid body of men to rise to an unprecedented emergency is not altogether justified. Yet suppose that the broadcasting of adequate advance notice of storms had been the New York Stock Exchange's duty instead of the duty of a branch of the Federal Department of Agriculture! The outcry from Washington over the insufficiency of the warning which was given would have been immediate, bitter, and voluminous. Scores of previous lifesaving predictions of hurricanes along the sparsely populated Southern coasts would have been dismissed as insignificant.

Those storms which are the most terrible are brewed by salt air and sunshine, by the damp sea air and the warmth of the sun and the earth's turning. Hurricanes, the extreme violences to which the earth's atmosphere is subject, are formed in a narrow belt near the equator, the doldrums. There the air is the most stagnant on the planet. To the making of their vortical energies go thousands of billions of horsepower hours—tigerhours —of sunlight.

In different oceans these disturbances bear different local names, hurricanes, typhoons, willy-willies, cyclones. "Tropical cyclone" is the technical name. In the early morning of September 21, Long Island and New England, unaware of the danger, lay fully exposed in the probable path of a West Indian hurricane advancing off Cape Hatteras.

Northward that morning at forty-five miles an hour in the Atlantic the windless central hub of the whirling wind was approaching. It swept over the aroused sea and, successively, along the Carolinas, Virginia, Delaware, New Jersey barometers would dip and rise again as it passed. The Weather Bureau's routine observations at 8:30 A.M., E.D.S.T., alone ought to have been glaring warning. Already then the storm's circular isobars—or lines of equal barometric pressure—were sketched as lengthened into ovals with their long axes pointing north. During the preceding twelve hours, this weather map for Wednesday morning showed, the tropical cyclone as a whole had been moving at an average speed of thirty-five miles an hour. Continuation of the rapid advance was indicated, northward into a fatal barometric trough across New England between two high-pressure areas. The wind at Hatteras at 8:30 A.M. Wednesday was blowing from the northwest fifty miles an hour; and Cape Hatteras was scores of miles west of the hurricane's center on its less violent side. What if meteorological statistics of many years did indicate that September tropical cyclones in the north Atlantic, if they curve from Florida as this one did, nearly always curve again eastward and out to empty sea? This one's course eastward evidently would be blocked by that potent Nova Scotia high. Not for the hardy accustomed captains of the north Atlantic steamer lanes would be the task of dealing with this particular whirlwind.

The triangle of ocean from Long Island to Bermuda to Georgia bore few ships that day, or at any rate no radio officers who troubled to communicate, after early morning, wind speeds and barometer readings. Here was the Weather Bureau's undefended sector. A violent hurricane was known to be at large in it, but officialdom's undisturbed routines were not adjusted to disclose just where it headed. In the tropics these storms move more slowly than twenty miles an hour, but accelerated advances are not unusual in northern waters. Telephone lines south along the coast remained undamaged and available, but were apparently unused for the emergency assembling of weather data. Meteorology is not a very exact science; but to estimate from wind and barometer the approach of a hurricane center is an elementary exercise, and has long been an essential part of the training of navigators at sea.

In the northern hemisphere the winds blow round the center in the direction opposite to that which the hands of a huge clock lying on the ground would take. "Face the wind, then the center is to your right." The winds are strongest near the center and the barometric pressure is lowest there. Rising heated air accounts for that low, and the gyroscopic force of the earth's rotation starts the whirl. In the southern hemisphere it is always clockwise. The whole vortex, once formed, may travel for thousands of miles with unchanged structure. Air friction continually takes toll of its energy stored from the sun's evaporation of the sea, and forces the low-level winds to move inward to fill the central vacuum. Yet for a week or two the condensing water vapor of the rain releases power enough to maintain the reduced pressures at the center, and while that nuclear vacuum is maintained the rotating earth continues to urge the incoming winds around it. In this wise, long before James Watt, nature had harnessed steam.

Not until almost midafternoon September 21 did the rapid fall of barometers in New York City itself suggest to Weather Bureau officials cloistered in office buildings that the dreadful invader from the south had refused to follow precedent by recurving northeast to open sea. At 3 P.M. the warning went out from New York City that a hurricane center would pass over Long Island and Connecticut "late this afternoon or tonight, attended by shifting gales." Even this tardy notice was not adequately spread, and already the inner spirals of the wind were screaming against Long Island.

Days before, while the fledgling hurricane still was swooping northwestward from its nest in the doldrums, experienced Florida had battened down. But there were no preparations made Wednesday afternoon from Cape May to Maine. Dwellers in summer cottages and fishing settlements remained uninformed of peril until the unchained wind and sea informed them. Meteorology long has taught what the effects are when a hurricane crosses a coastline. For far too many people that afternoon the knowledge came too vividly and too late.

II

The breadth of the inner circle of devastating blasts was a hundred miles and more. From a stratosphere balloon poised precariously above the turmoil the murky winds would have been seen directed counterclockwise over the ground, around huge concentric curves within this circle. As the center moved north at fifty miles an hour across middle Long Island, the blow to the westward of the center was approximately from the north. To eastward it was from the south, and in that quadrant the hissing gales were ridden by steep "storm waves" from the Atlantic. Ahead the winds were roughly east, and they were west behind. The eastern half of this great anticlock was its "dangerous semicircle," where the northern advance of the hub added its speed to the far more rapid whirlings of the wheel. The western semicircle, which crossed New Jersey, eastern Pennsylvania, and eastern New York, was less destructive by much; for there the hub's northern speed subtracted from the southern rotation of the wheel. Even in a hurricane one hundred miles an hour is an important differential. Severe damage therefore principally was to the eastward of the hub's course. Next morning's weather chart would map the track of the center through New Haven, and just west of Hartford, over lower Vermont, and on toward Montreal. The worst damage did not extend much west of these points.

At 3:30 P.M., the Boston Weather Bureau issued a mild radio warning. It gave no indication that terror and death were beginning to blast the Long Island and Rhode Island and Cape Cod coasts. New Hampshire received no urgent word. There ought to have been steady repetition until radio masts went down, "Tell your neighbor—close your shutters—park your car away from trees—don't let the wind get in your house—tell your neighbor!"

In Randolph, in northern New Hampshire, we are nearly three hundred miles north-northeast of Long Island. High in the White Mountains, we can watch ebbs and flows of the clouds with a personal interest for which it appears bureaucratic routines are inadequate substitute. Already at 10:30 A.M. that Wednesday a marked change was evident in the character of the unpleasant weather which had prevailed since the previous Sunday. Several of us identified the new disturbance as probably a hurricane approaching from the south. We did not take it upon ourselves to communicate with Portland or Boston. We expected the developing storm to be an interesting but not a dangerous experience.

The temperature, for a September blow in northern New England, was ominously high, 64° at our altitude of 1,800 feet. The wind, from a little south of east, had a weight and a gustiness characteristic even of the outer circles of a tropical cyclone. Once known, such squalls are recognized again. We had had days of remarkable clarity: Sunday, Monday, and Tuesday, beneath low clouds the mountains had been curiously distinct whenever the unwelcome rains would cease. Hurricanes as a rule weaken rapidly over land. The vapory ground, sodden from a rainy summer, was ready to nourish this one as dreadfully as though New England had been the very Caribbean.

The development of the storm Wednesday morning and early afternoon at Randolph followed precisely standard textbook descriptions of the approach of a hurricane. The whipping raindrops were characteristically fine, like mist. The temperature held constant. The barometer fell slowly at first, but after 4 P.M. at 0.1 inch an hour. The wind then really began to build, and the rain slanted in blizzards. It seemed inconceivable that an intense

553

disturbance should be coming, for there had been days' newspaper notice of the arrival of the almost worn-out hurricane of August 1933—but here it came.

"The center will pass attended by shifting gales." Northern New England was ignorant of this bland announcement. As night groped through the storm's twilight, catastrophic frenzy replaced our mountain air. Still the direction of the wind held to the south of east. At about 8:15 P.M. the barometer sharply stopped falling at 29.0 (corrected to sea level). Rapidly then the wind hauled round and soon the gale was tearing at the southern instead of the eastern shutters of our cottage. An amateur in meteorology knew by wind shift and barometer that the fearful anticlock whirl of the alien storm was rushing toward Canada with its hub passing to our south and west.

Out of the night's steady bellowing that one soon became unconscious of, every few minutes would rise a whine which demanded all attention as it drove directly at our thin south wooden walls and raved at every window crack. It seemed that the next gust or the next would breach our frail defenses. After 11:30 P.M. patches of stars appeared through thinning clouds; the wind rapidly lessened and, still strong and persistent, turned southwest. The barometer began rising as fast as it had fallen before, and it went to 29.5 by 7 A.M. Thursday as the never-so-welcome sun rose at its equinox in an almost cloudless sky. This had been no ordinary "equinoctial storm," but with New England casualness the inhabitants of the countryside set about removing its wreckage. The wind during the night had blown itself out at last in southern Quebec. Not for a day or two did we learn how comparatively fortunate our neighborhood had been.

The rapid northern advance of the storm had shortened its duration. Instead of the dozen hours of maximum tempest which Miami would have known, New England had but four or five. Only dwellers by salt water experienced the sea's unbelievable wildness, which across tropical islands is the gravest danger of these atmospheric vortices. The whole duration of the blow was perhaps twenty hours. The rain in Randolph was torrential between 4 and 6 P.M.; after that scarcely two more inches fell. The cyclone pressed at the heels of earlier heavy rains, and even without its deluge dangerous floods would have swept the lower river valleys.

III

Many of the most spectacular incidents of that afternoon and night in the northern hurricane's track will never be collected, for their central participants are dead. The danger of death brushed close to millions of others, how close we never shall know. New York City felt only the edge of the storm.

Along the New Jersey coast in mid-afternoon the barometer fell 0.4 inch in an hour as the center passed at sea. The wind there blew from the north during the early afternoon and then shifted toward west. Coast Guard stations appeared as uninformed as laymen. Over the sandspit which separates Barnegat Bay from the ocean, several gigantic waves reared in close succession about 5:30 P.M. They followed surf and high water which normally would have been accounted very violent. They were examples of the terrible "storm waves" which accompany hurricanes, and had been heaped up doubtless by the tempest's eastern semicircle, seventy-five miles or so offshore, when the blow was toward the coast. Reduced atmospheric pressure at the center may have helped form these waves. They hammered in at forty miles an hour against the opposing west winds of the western semicircle. They annihilated boardwalks and slapped debris against the sand dunes.

The south shore of Long Island and the exposed Connecticut and Rhode Island shores east of Montauk Point faced the full force of far stronger seas. Along these coasts beach after beach was scoured. At West Hampton, of thirty-room mansions no single vestige remained. Seventeen refugees huddled chest-deep in sea water on the second floor of one when the walls at last gave way. Survivors lost not only their houses; many lost houses and lots; for the beach was deeply channeled. In Suffolk County the reduction in assessed valuation of real estate is estimated at $50,000,000. Elaborate lawns a mile from the sea at Quogue were under breakers two feet high; a cottage washed across with ten people on its roof. Soon after 4 P.M. the eye, or center, was seen crossing Long Island there; for fifteen minutes the sky was blue, breezes were light, and people thought the storm had passed. While the center was approaching a barometer needle dipped toward 28 "like the second-hand of a watch."

Inland, at Wesleyan College in Middletown, Connecticut, the old stone tower of the chapel blew down after the audience had departed from the opening exercises of the term. A dozen of New England's beautiful campuses, and many more old village greens, were scarred with trees shattered or uprooted. Most buildings inland were undamaged, but where gusts were most turbulent windows were blown in, shingles were loosened, roofs were stripped off, barns rolled over. Slides blocked roads in the hills, and bursting dams ripped roads in the valleys. Gushing streams broke highway and railway bridges and poured down village streets. Mountain forests beloved of trampers and skiers underwent in four hours more damage than would have accumulated from the gales and freshets of a score of winters and springs. And in New London, Worcester, and Peterborough (New Hampshire), fires abetted the wind.

Long Island Sound was beaten to one unbroken sheet of foam. Both shores were invaded by wind-driven tides. A family who lived in Darien, Connecticut, caught by the gale on their schooner in the Sound, weathered it but found that the water had ruined their house on the shore. Along the mainland coasts from Stonington to Buzzards Bay, where Long Island no longer served as breakwater, the storm waves were murderous. Narragansett Bay suddenly flooded downtown Providence. People who watched the surf were snatched into the sea, even from behind the steering wheels of their cars. One fortunate family at Misquamicut, fleeing by automobile toward high ground at fifty miles an hour, barely outran the pursuing sea. From a hilltop house at Watch Hill a woman looked from her window and saw a giant wave approaching "like a fog bank coming fast." It came ahead of the wind; this was soon after 4 P.M., and three hours of horror followed. That house stood, but disintegrated leaves and grass covered it with gray-green paste.

When the water had receded, owners on lower ground at Watch Hill were unable to identify the sites where their houses had been. Among a crowd who innocently had dared the sea's edge there to gaze at the huge breakers, one young woman had the following experience. She saw that massive wave rushing in and knew that she would die; there was nothing to do. The impact threw her into the crossarms of a telephone pole, breaking her arm and injuring her leg. As the pole went down the whipping wire entangled her fast, and from afternoon until next morning she floated to a rescue across Little Narragansett Bay.

If this storm had struck before Labor Day, at the height of the seaside season, the list of the dead along these coasts might have exceeded the six thousand lost in the Galveston hurricane of 1900.

Widespread tragedy is never devoid of lighter accompaniment. A gentleman of Stockbridge, in the Berkshires, an ardent amateur of bad weather, was visiting in Florida; he wired his unsympathetic wife that he would lengthen his stay to see the hurricane. He missed it; his wife and children in Stockbridge had to leave their house by boat.

From the seacoast to the border, from western Maine to eastern New York, there was wicked damage to trees. As examples: of a grove of 40 noble white pines around a cottage on Lake Winnepesaukee, 39 are down, several across the cottage. Of 3,000 sugar maples in one planting in central Vermont, 100 were counted standing. In hilly country the damage was spotty, but nearly everywhere a fraction, negligible or tragic, of the trees are lying snapped off or uprooted. Natural forests of trees of all ages and sizes seem to have suffered less than plantings of identical trees.

Telephone, telegraph, and power lines were out of action for days. Even water mains were broken. Passengers along the New Haven's Shore Line two weeks after the disaster had to take to buses where the rails still failed. Some villages were without restoration of full mail service for eight days, whatever the proud inscription above the portals of New York City's central post office may proclaim. The Blue Hill Meteorological Observatory, near Boston, successfully measured winds flying 186 miles an hour.

IV

To the Northeast hurricanes no longer are an exotic and romantic phenomenon. From August to November is the season for West Indian hurricanes, and many have penetrated north before. Extensive lists given by Ivan Ray Tannehill, the marine meteorologist of the Weather Bureau, include the following since 1900 which reached New England: September 9, 1934; August 24, 1933; October 3, 1929; October 1, 1920; September 16, 1912; September 15, 1904; June 30, 1902. In most of these, however, winds in New England did not reach seventy-five miles an hour, which is the threshold of devastation—the number 12, or "hurricane," of the seaman's scale.

The combination of chances which made the storm of 1938 unusually severe undoubtedly will recur; although, it is to be hoped, not soon. There was comparable violence on September 3, 1821, along a path a few score miles west of 1938's. A little farther west, in September 1896, another remarkable hurricane spread havoc and death from Florida and Georgia north through amazed central Pennsylvania. Yet even in the most afflicted regions of the South, the probabilities have been stated as 20 to 1 against a destructive blow in any given year.

What were the factors which made the New England hurricane of 1938 so destructive? As regards loss of human life it stands apparently fourth among similar storms in the United States. As regards property damage— several hundred million dollars—it was far and away the worst in all history. No trustworthy explanation of its severity across New England can be given, but the following four factors were involved.

First, there was the unfortunate barometric high which for several days had been laggard east of Maine when it should have been rolling its hooped isobars across the Atlantic. (The expert meteorologist names these highs "extratropical anticyclones." Previous instances are on record of their apparent interference with the paths of tropical cyclones. The ordinary barometric low on our weather maps is an "extratropical cyclone"; usually it is a comparatively trifling disturbance.)

Second, this hurricane all along its path was a major one. It was of great intensity while still in southern waters, where the cruise liner *Carinthia* went through it on the Monday.

Third, the worst of the storm at many points along the northern coasts unluckily coincided with the local hour of high tide. With the moon only twenty-eight hours short of new, high tides that afternoon would normally have been greater than average. The exact configuration of a shoreline, as well as the state of the tide, always is important in determining how destructive the miscalled "tidal waves" become in hurricanes. Funnel-shaped harbors which lie open toward an oncoming blow offer a hazard especially serious. No mathematician can predict storm waves in detail, can integrate the sea's excitation by the swirls and vacuums of an advancing whirlwind.

Finally, hurricanes require humid air for their sustenance, and it may have been the already soaking ground across New England which conserved this one's force to points so far inland.

Forecasting can save the lives of people and can effectively reduce the damage to property. But nothing in our power can save the trees in a hurricane—except hasty guy-wires rigged for tame trees here and there. There are residences in New England which three months ago were showplaces for their trees and are now surrounded by stumps. Orchard trees are lying uprooted, pushed over from every point of the compass. Irreplaceable great trees with trunks four feet thick are down: birch, elm, oak, maple, spruce and pine. New England mourns for her trees; but with this solace: not all the resources of science could have saved them.

OLD-TIME RADIO

THE RADIO, with its tremendously varied "free" entertainment, seemed a wonderful investment in the Depression years. About 12 million sets were in operation in 1929. Between 1930 and 1932, 4 million sets were sold, and by the end of the decade 28 million homes were equipped. What other plaything took, daily, four and a half hours of a family's time—assuming the human ear was paying attention? (By the end of the Thirties most of us had discovered that little switch placed so conveniently in the inner ear, enabling us to escape the drone and rumble of the "hard sell," the newscaster, or just plain bad music.)

It is small comfort to the American public to recall that at the beginning of the Thirties the sales value of radio broadcasting was still considered a matter for argument. Sponsors were hesitant to utilize the hard sell. By 1932, with cutbacks in the sales of consumer goods, all pretense was dropped, and, led by George Washington Hill (bent on selling his cigars and Lucky Strike cigarettes, come hell or high water) the advertisers swallowed the medium whole. Product identification, when Ovaltine meant Little Orphan Annie and vice versa, was just around the corner.

Let's admit that the monster— many people called it that—was insidious in its daily impact; still, there were marvels here and there, particularly if you were young and impressionable. Nowadays it is fashionable to be nostalgic and sentimental about the old radio serials, and even about the old wooden console set—that rococo horror that dominated the living rooms of the 1930s.

In the beginning, it wasn't just the young who listened; the whole nation used to tune in every evening to hear Amos and Andy, and people would be heard saying the next day, "I'se regusted." Before the soaps and serials took over completely, there were some pretty amusing episodes in the lives of such as Lum and Abner, Vic and Sade, Myrt and Marge, and the Goldbergs. But who would have suspected, when G. Washington coffee introduced its genteel crime series based on the Sherlock Holmes cases, that we were in for a daily diet of mysterious murders.

But give radio its due. The fine thing about it, to quote Brock Brower, was that "the listener produced half the show right in his own head, taking his lead from a range of voices, a musical bridge, and a few sound effects." *

* "A Lament for Old-Time Radio," *Esquire*, April 1960.

559

FRANCIS CHASE, JR.

SOUND AND FURY*

THE WORD came from Washington. On Sunday, March 12, 1933—eight days after his inauguration—the President would speak. Reassuringly, he called it a "fireside chat." Americans turned on their radios and listened—sixty million hopeful, anxious Americans sat by their loud-speakers and listened. The White House announcer said, "Now, the President of the United States. . . ."

In simple language, the President explained the practices of banking, scored those few unscrupulous bankers who had gambled away other people's money, and explained his purposes in calling the national bank holiday. He ended with a plea for the confidence of the people.

For all practical purposes, that was the first broadcast from the White House. There had been other broadcasts originating there; even Calvin Coolidge had stood before the microphone and spoken to the people. But the people hadn't listened. The combination of a drab speaker and dull issues drove listeners to the livelier competition provided by "Amos 'n' Andy." Hoover didn't lack issues, but his total disregard of the human equation in talking before the microphone, the almost slide-rule precision and monotony of his talks, proved no listener magnet. In fact, during the period between 1929 and 1932, Hoover made ninety-five radio appearances—only nine less than Roosevelt made from 1932 to 1936. Few, if any, will recall the subject of one such talk.

Despite the President's gift for making complicated problems of government and economics understandable to the masses of listeners-in; despite the magnetism of his finely pitched radio voice, there were many who neither believed in his policies nor listened to his persuasive chats. The unfortunate thing then was that such opponents of the President's policies not only refused to listen to the President but they had no way of making their own views and policies known. Of course, they could buy time on the air; many stations would even give them time.

One night in the spring of 1934, after George V. Denny, Jr.—then assistant director of the League for Political Education—and a friend had been listening to a fireside chat, the friend told Denny of a neighbor who

* Excerpted from Francis Chase, Jr.'s *Sound and Fury* (New York, Harper, 1942).

refused to listen to anything Roosevelt had to say. Denny, upon consideration of that neighbor's attitude, together with the Fascist blasts against democratic processes and the growing belief among many Americans that democracy was a thing of the past, decided to convert this one man's intolerance into a bright sword unsheathed on behalf of a living democracy—the Town Meeting of the Air.

To Denny, would-be actor, the reasons for democracy's failure to function—as expressed in such acts of intolerance as refusal to hear the other side—stemmed first from a failure on the part of the nation's leaders, as a group, to dramatize their messages. In the second place, the spirit of fair play inherent in the American make-up was not being appealed to. The first program went on the air on May 30, 1935, over NBC, with Denny acting as moderator. The first subject was, "Which Way America—Fascism, Communism, Socialism or Democracy?"

The broadcast originated in the auditorium of New York's Town Hall, where some fifteen hundred could gather. Before the program, the audience was warmed to the discussion by an hour of free-for-all debate on the issue by the audience. A neat arrangement of portable microphones permitted people in all parts of the auditorium to take part in the discussion. The same system permitted them to question the speakers during the question period following the debate. The first broadcast—which went on the air without publicity—drew a response of three thousand letters. Town Meeting of the Air answered some of the arguments that radio was not free and that its stand on controversial discussion was a milk-and-water half measure. Town Meeting was built solely on controversy. It boasted an audience far in excess of the collective editorial pages of the American press at the time.

Ironically, one of the warmest discussions ever to find its way over Town Meeting—or any other—microphone was on the subject, "Do We Have a Free Press?" Frank E. Gannett, publisher of reactionary newspapers, defended the press; Harold L. Ickes continued his role as a press critic.

The American press is as free as it wishes to be (Ickes argued). So far as government control is concerned, the American press is free. . . . In fact, the American government annually pays an enormous subsidy to the press in the form of less-than-cost postage rates. . . .

Yet, while the American press is free as far as the government is concerned, it is nevertheless far from free. . . . Mr. Ickes then listed three accusations which, he maintained, the people level against the press:

First, the press has financial affiliations or is subject to financial pres-

561

sure which limits its freedom. Second, it is subject to the influence of advertisers, causing omission, distortion or improper slanting of news and affecting its editorial opinions. Third, it is unfair to certain groups of citizens, especially workmen, whose interests conflict with those of the newspaper or its financial backers or advertisers.

Mr. Ickes then became specific. Town Meeting folk loved facts, and Ickes set out to show how Mr. Gannett's papers, in particular, were under such influence as he listed. He cited the Federal Trade Commission's investigation showing certain Gannett papers were largely financed by the International Paper and Power Company. He charged that such financing muzzled any free discussion by those papers of the power situation. He also pointed out the part Gannett's papers had played in opposing passage of the Pure Food and Drug Act, in 1933, when many of the large advertisers were against its enactment. For the third accusation, Mr. Ickes produced an article from a Gannett paper reporting a Town Meeting program a year before in which Gannett had engaged in debate with Edward O'Neal, of Illinois, a farm leader. The newspaper had a column and a half of Gannett's remarks but not a single reference to O'Neal.

Mr. Gannett's replies were largely in generalities, although he did assert that the financial arrangements for his newspapers were made with the International Paper Company, not International Paper and Power Company—a fact which Ickes, in rebuttal, denied. He dwelt upon the services of the press, accused Ickes of denouncing the press because the press had "defeated" the Roosevelt "court-packing" bill.

It was an Ickes night. No one ever captivated a Town Meeting audience with generalities, and the Secretary of the Interior came loaded with buckshot. Gannett seemed to have forgotten even his gun.

When the question period for the Gannett-Ickes debate opened, a man arose.

Why, Mr. Moderator, was your policy changed tonight to permit a personal attack on a speaker?

Mr. Denny: The policy wasn't changed. I want to make this perfectly clear: there is a difference between an attack made anonymously from the floor on an individual, and a speaker who is well known saying his say from the platform. The man attacked is right here on the platform and can answer back.

Woman: (To Mr. Gannett) Do you think that distortion of the facts is the privilege of a free press, as manifested during the campaign for the Presidency in 1936?

Mr. Gannett: I don't think any real newspaperman distorts the facts deliberately. There may be a misunderstanding of the facts. I don't know what you refer to by the distortion of the facts in 1936. Freedom of the press is freedom to print. You can print your paper and I can print one. Thank God, we have that privilege in America.

Man: (To Ickes) Did you come here tonight to discuss a free press or to reap vengeance on a newspaperman who happens to disagree with you?

Before Ickes could answer, Mr. Denny spoke: "Now you see, that is the difference between an anonymous attack from a man you don't know and an attack by Mr. Ickes on Mr. Gannett—who is here to answer whatever Mr. Ickes has to say. That is a personal question. Don't take advantage of the fair play you are granted here by asking questions like that."

Woman: (After an exchange between Ickes and Gannett) Couldn't we have peace in the family? Mr. Ickes and Mr. Gannett, both, couldn't we have peace in the family?

Mr. Ickes: If the lady wants peace, I wonder why she came here.

Mr. Gannett: Yes, we could have peace in the family if we all approved of Mr. Ickes' New Deal papers.

This is democracy in action. Town Meeting's microphones broadcast the words of the nation's leaders in many fields—Earl Browder, Communist candidate for President; Senator Taft, Senator Wheeler, John T. Flynn, Wendell Willkie, Mrs. Roosevelt, Dorothy Thompson, Max Lerner, Norman Thomas, to list a few.

Across the country, listening groups—gathering in CCC camps, in Y.M.C.A.s, in schools, colleges, private homes—used the Town Meeting program as a jumping off place for their own discussions.

At the beginning of the decade, radio, drawing more and more upon the type of act formerly found only in vaudeville, had made the entertainment circuits an economically unsound proposition. Advent of the Depression and the disappearance of spare change from American pockets, far from reviving variety, was like the final spade pat on vaudeville's grave. Variety houses across the land closed their doors, darkened the bright lights of their marquees while workmen moved in and almost overnight transformed them into movie palaces.

But vaudeville was to prove a lively corpse. Collapse of the variety circuits proved only that people, hard-pressed for the necessities of life, could no longer afford the luxury of touring troupes. Laughter was still desired and radio could provide it cheaply.

It was not a peculiar development in the history of radio, then, that its greatest strides forward were made during the very depths of depression when other, older industries were closing their doors and turning their employees over to relief agencies. In fact, the development of radio in a period when other business failures were creating widespread unemployment is one of the logical and wholly normal aspects of the industry. Radio, by 1930, had taken two important steps toward meeting the public demands upon it for morale-building divertisement.

In the first place, manufacturers of receiving sets had made radio accessible to all. By the turn of the decade, factories were turning out the most efficient receivers at prices 40 per cent under the 1925 level. Even for those still unable to afford ownership of a radio set, listening was not out of the question. Loud-speakers blared out the baseball games from almost every corner cigar store; they were to be found in hotel lobbies, and, after the establishment of the National Emergency Relief Administration, radios became standard equipment in relief shelters and transient camps.

But making radio accessible to all was but the first step in radio's march. With the possible audience enhanced by millions, producers in the radio field were faced with the problem of broadcasting a type of program that would attract listeners. The matter of programming was further intensified by the growth of competition, for by now, radio was thoroughly commercial with three out of five shows sponsored by outside concerns. Shrewdly, radio executives realized that laughter was the prime need of the moment, and vaudeville, like Lazarus, rose from its grave and laughed a long, contagious laugh. Names which had come to mean much in the world of variety—Edgar Bergen, Fred Allen, Jack Benny, Burns and Allen—began to mean much more in radio. Where before, Jack Benny—by strenuous trouping—might have played to two hundred thousand people in the course of a season, he now found himself playing to as many as ten million on a single Sunday evening. Major Bowes particularly captivated the public fancy during those early Depression years with one of the oldest of vaudeville stunts, built upon the Cinderella motif—the amateur show.

The pioneer spirit so largely responsible for vaudeville's transition from the stage to the microphone was, oddly enough, neither a Keith nor a Sarnoff, but a youth with no deep-set roots in either vaudeville or radio. Rudy Vallee not only pioneered the radio variety show, but brought to radio such careful production, such fine showmanship and originality in both idea and presentation, that he might well be considered radio's first important producer. Beside his production efforts, his crooning accomplishments paled into an infinitesimal insignificance.

Among the stars he led for the first time to a microphone were Beatrice Lillie, Ezra Stone, Edgar Bergen, Carmen Miranda, Eddie Cantor, Milton Berle, Phil Baker, Olsen and Johnson. Ideas first presented on his broadcasts have led to independent radio shows when other producers developed them to the logical conclusion for which Rudy had no time. Notable among these are the universally popular "Aldrich Family" and "We the People." It is unfortunate that the greatest talent finder yet produced by radio has never been able to hold onto talent. Mr. Vallee was a hard man to work for, perhaps because of his own burning ambition to be a great dramatic star. On the very Thursday in 1929 when the stock market began to have palpitations of the heart, Rudy started his weekly, hour-long broadcast for Standard Brands under the title, "The Fleischmann Hour." On his second program he interviewed the Grand Duchess Marie, of Russia, following up on subsequent broadcasts with interviews with Max Baer, La Guardia, Heywood Broun and other notables outside the entertainment world. Soon, other programs were following suit and presenting such dignitaries, so Rudy turned to unknowns who had enjoyed some great experience or performed some feat of valor. In a few weeks, people were saying, "I was on the Vallee program," much as they would wear a Carnegie Medal. Years later, "We the People" was built into a popular network show along exactly the same lines.

Soon, too, listeners learned to watch the Vallee broadcasts for fresh talent. His talent scouts were busy searching out-of-the-way places for fresh voices and acts; they listened to local stations in all parts of the country, held countless auditions and hardly a top-notch variety network broadcast is heard today which hasn't at least one Vallee find in its cast. But his contributions were not to variety alone. He brought such stars of the theater as Helen Hayes, Ethel Barrymore, Eva Le Gallienne and Walter Huston to the microphone, not in scenes from Broadway plays (as was the radio custom) but in short dramas written especially for broadcast.

Radio Public Entertainer Number One of the U.S.A. and its Number One Salesman was Jack Benny.

After the war, Jack had taken up vaudeville seriously, playing the fiddle less and less and talking more and more. It was a long, slow process of accumulating gags, eliminating those which didn't click, polishing up those that did. For six years, in whistle-stop towns, he used the same opening gag. He'd walk out on the stage and ask the orchestra leader how the show was.

"Fine up to now," the primed leader would reply.

"I'll fix that," was Jack's comeback.

By 1930, vaudeville was on the way out but Benny—to whom vaudeville was everything—stayed on until there just wasn't any more vaudeville. In February 1932, Ed Sullivan had Jack on his radio program as guest. The public response was fair, and he began to study radio technique and to alter his routine to fit it. In May 1932, Canada Dry sponsored him in a program which was not too successful. Chevrolet and General Tires each gave him a turn on the air, but not until 1934, when General Foods, makers of Jell-O, hired him, was Benny ready, and the upsweep in Jell-O sales was one of the miracles of radio.

Benny knows that the public will always laugh at the cocky smart aleck who gets it in the neck, so he's the smart aleck. You are glad to see him get his due, and yet, you feel sort of sorry for him. He might, but for the goodness of God, be you or me. It was life transformed into ether waves every Sunday night.

His jokes were planted so expertly that even a child could grasp them; his timing perfect; his supporting cast good, well-paid and happy.

But if Jack Benny's broadcasts were the results of careful blueprinting, those of his public enemy and private friend, Fred Allen, were anything but planned. Allen was a wry-faced fellow with the most apt and buoyant wit on the air. Jack Benny or Bob Hope might keep a corps of writers busy. Fred Allen wasn't too certain of what he would say until it popped out, and his show was resultantly spontaneous. His program was built around a "Town Hall" sequence, in which a hick-town show was presented. Fred—tobacco-chewing dealer in bowls of wisdom sprinkled liberally with Tabasco and garnished with gall—was the epitome of the small-town wit. He was a sharper, more pungent and biting edition of Will Rogers. One Wednesday night, after an Allen broadcast, Owen D. Young elbowed his way through the throng at NBC to get near the comic.

"I've been listening to your program for years," Young beamed, "and I've been lucky enough to be in your audience the last three broadcasts."

"Well, Mr. Young," said Allen, chewing away at his tobacco like a baseball player, "I can understand why a person might want to see one of my programs once, just for curiosity's sake. But anyone who could sit through it three times should see a phrenologist!"

But the man who made the most money out of radio variety was the gruff, acidulous Major Bowes. At a time when entertainment marts of New York were flooded with talent out of jobs; when one of the most overcrowded divisions of WPA was its theatrical project, Major Bowes was attracting hundreds of stage-struck youngsters to the metropolitan area with the promise of fame and fortune. "Around she goes," the Major used to chant over the air, "and where she stops, nobody knows." He was talking of the wheel of fortune, and certainly it was not the Major's fault if he was unable to deliver on the gilded promises it held out. Travelers along the highways in 1934 and 1935 became accustomed to the signs hitchhikers wore on their backs: "En route to New York to appear on Major Bowes' program."

Amateur shows have always had a wide public appeal, and Major Bowes became the fairy godfather to many a one-night Cinderella. Only, unlike Cinderella, there was no prince in most cases. As a matter of fact, a huge percentage of the Bowes amateurs weren't even amateurs, but professionals out of work. They were paid ten dollars if they were good enough to get on a broadcast (a figure far under the AFRA minimum for radio talent and far under the amount expended by shows like "We the People" on its guests) and a few of them managed to get into a Bowes vaudeville unit for a few weeks of touring at salaries in the neighborhood of fifty dollars per week. But Bowes's amateurs sold coffee for Chase and Sanborn and, later, automobiles for Chrysler. They made Major Bowes one of the richest men in radio with an average yearly income from broadcasts and his vaudeville troupes of a million dollars.

A program like Major Bowes's Amateur Hour wasn't the result of programming trends like the variety shows of Bob Hope, Jack Benny or Fred Allen. His Sunday morning program from the stage of the Capitol Theater, in New York City, had long been a favorite—and well-handled—program, and there has never been any question about Bowes' showmanship. The amateur show he started locally on WHN in 1934 evoked such tremendous response that NBC put it on the network. Murray Hill 8-9933 (the number where votes on the amateurs were received by a battery of telephone operators) became the most famous telephone number in the world. The Major Bowes Amateur Hour was something that just happened. Attempts to duplicate inevitably failed. Charlie McCarthy was another such novelty act and rash imitators of radio's Pinocchio have learned, to their sorrow, that Charlie isn't quintuplets. The same held true for the character of "Baby Snooks," created by Fanny Brice.

From a standpoint of real public interest and benefit, there were programs such as the NBC Symphony Orchestra, heard each Saturday night in presentations of the world's great music, an aggregation of America's finest musicians. These broadcasts had a tremendous role in making great classical music the peculiar property of any man owning a radio set. It was broadcast "in the public interest," undertaken weekly without commercial sponsorship by a group of radio stations which, in this way, repaid the people of America for the use of their ether waves.

Arturo Toscanini, its first conductor, was a musical perfectionist, a maestro with a fearful temper, an unfailing memory and the power to lash his musicians into frenzies of fine playing. For the services of this seventy-three-year-old musical genius, NBC dipped into its own pocket to the tune of $4,000 per broadcast plus the income tax payments due on that salary. Because Toscanini, more than most conductors, conducted with his hands and face—never with his body—guests (like the Will Hayses, the Gene Tunneys, the Fredric Marches, United States senators and congressmen and diplomats) used to come early to get seats close to the front where they might see his sometimes pleased, sometimes furious expression. Perspiration poured from his forehead during these broadcasts, dripped from the end of his nose until, at intermission, he would have to change clothes completely. Two broadcasters had the official NBC okay to run over their allotted time without being cut off the air—President Roosevelt and Toscanini.

CBS's comparable attraction was its weekly presentation of the New York Philharmonic Orchestra. The Metropolitan auditions were also broadcast, and over the networks and on local stations, more good music was made available to average Americans than an Italian or Viennese millionaire could hear in years.

But perhaps the best example of what radio was accomplishing in its efforts to make great music the everyday companion of the American listener was afforded by the Metropolitan Opera broadcasts.

At the end of the decade that hallowed sanctuary of culture, diamond necklaces and double chins was fighting for existence. A million dollars was needed to keep the monstrous house from becoming the dark habitat of memories instead of the world's finest voices. In desperation, its directors turned to American radio listeners who, for several years, had been receiving opera broadcasts each Saturday afternoon.

The difficulty in which the opera company found itself was due to its peculiar organization. The opera house itself was owned by a group known as the Metropolitan Opera and Real Estate Company. Operas, on the other hand, were produced by the Metropolitan Opera Association, a nonprofit corporation. Stockholders of the former company were the holders of swanky parterre boxes around the Golden Horseshoe which they accepted in lieu of cash rental payments on the opera house.

Most of these early stockholders were dead. Their stock had passed into the hands of estates, and these legal entities cared little for Bizet or Mozart. The Metropolitan Opera and Real Estate Company began to contemplate liquidation of its holdings and sale of the opera house. That, literally, would have set the opera out on the sidewalk.

The problem was put squarely up to the people, to the radio listeners in Sioux Falls and Oak Grove, in Omaha and Ogden. Could democracy support opera and did it want opera?

More than 150,000 contributions—many of them family contributions —were received. They amounted to almost a half million dollars. They were the small gifts of everyday listeners who had never sat in the Family Circle and peered down upon the great stage of the Met. What had really occurred—and radio was responsible—was a sort of revolution. Radio had given the opera, once the property of the elite, to the people; now the people were giving life to the opera, deserted by the elite.

Radio's big staple, the daytime serial, or soap opera, never had such troubles, for sponsors of programs aimed at selling merchandise to housewives discovered that adding listeners' teardrops to the dishwater was a big business. Daytime serials became the biggest thing in radio, whether you considered them from a standpoint of broadcast time, expenditure of the advertising dollar, listening interest, or effectiveness in selling what the sponsor had to offer.

The average network station by the end of the decade devoted five hours—in fifteen-minute segments—to daytime serials designed to entice women to buy household items. They examined most phases of American life in which dramatic possibilities inhere. One serial dealt with an orphanage, another with a woman member of Congress, another with a widowed mother seeking a place in the business world, et cetera. The only definite requirement was that it be deeply touching, that each sequel end with a suspenseful situation, that it sell products. The serial writers learned that tragic, heart-stirring events were more gripping than the joyful ones, and a day's listening to the soap operas gave one a distorted view that all is far from well with America and that happiness was an unknown blessing. Some of the most successful and longest-running were "Young Doctor Malone," "Women in White," "Guiding Light," and so on.

At about the same time the daytime serials were beginning to take hold, a different type of late afternoon and early evening serial was finding its way to the airways. These were the kid shows; and in those early years, they were almost entirely of the blood-and-thunder variety. Invariably, these broadcasts were sponsored by advertisers who had something to sell for the household. The psychology was: Sell the kids and let the kids sell their parents. The device employed most effectively was the give-away.

Cereals, dairy products, flashlights all used this type of program effectively. We all remember serials such as "Little Orphan Annie," "Gang-busters," "Jack Armstrong—All American Boy," "The Lone Ranger," and dozens of others. At the end of the show, the announcer would tell his audience that, with each box top or wrapper of a certain product sent in, the sender would receive a badge making him a full-fledged member of the So-and-so Club (linked to the program) or a mask or pocketknife, exact replicas of those used by the character in the serial. Here, again, the advertiser had uncovered an effective means of merchandising, and while kid shows, even at their commercial height, reached only a frac-tional part of the popularity enjoyed by daytime serials (in 1938, less than five million dollars was spent on such programs), still they were an im-portant part of radio.

Important radio drama came into being only late in the Thirties with the arrival of Orson Welles, Arch Oboler, and Norman Corwin. Radio produced other dramas of course. Dropping the time consumed by day-time serials, approximately 20 per cent of broadcasting time during the earlier years was given over to broadcast drama, but it was of a cut-and-dried pattern. "First Nighter," a weekly show on which boy-meets-girl and boy-gets-girl fifty-two times a year, was also a part of the broadcasting pattern. It was on "First Nighter" that Don Ameche, radio's first matinee idol, achieved recognition. There were many such shows on the air, and for light listening, they served a good purpose. One of the earliest and most successful dramatic shows of this type to hit the air was Louella Parsons' "Hollywood Hotel." The best remembered, perhaps, was Cecil B. De Mille's "Lux Radio Theater."

Arch Oboler's contributions to radio drama were twofold. He was the first writer to successfully employ the stream-of-consciousness type of writ-ing in radio dialogue, and he brought to the air a type of imagery, almost fantasy, with which he clothed even the most realistic themes. Many, since the advent of Oboler, felt that fantasy is perhaps the field to which radio drama may best adapt itself. Oboler, himself, is not one of these. Oboler's writings had a terrifically wide range, perhaps because all radio writers were only a hop, skip and jump ahead of the microphone, which con-sumed words unmercifully. It was Oboler who wrote the famous lines which caused Mae West's banishment from the air.

"It wasn't the lines," Oboler insisted, "which were bawdy, but her man-ner of giving them." Then he quoted the lines.

"I want something to happen, a little excitement—a little adventure. A girl's got to have a little fun once in a while. . . . There's no future under a fig tree.

"A couple of months of peace and security and a woman's bored all the way down to the bottom of her marriage certificate. . . . If trouble means something that makes you catch your breath—if trouble means something that makes your blood race through your veins like seltzer water —mmm, Adam, my man, give me trouble!"

Most radio writers and actors worked under a cloak of anonymity, and only occasionally would an Orson Welles or an Arch Oboler or a Norman Corwin come along to rise above that cloak and make a name important.

But the most important dramatic broadcast from an experimental standpoint was a radio show not dominated by any one individual but the Columbia Workshop, where any writer, actor, producer or director with the creative spark might find voice. The Workshop was started as a now-and-then proposition in 1936 and, two years later, had become such an important training station for talent and testing ground for new techniques that it became a regular sustaining feature of the network. The prime importance of this group is that its efforts were directed toward developing radio drama fashioned to the medium rather than the mere adaptation of plays and motion pictures.

Sound, for the Workshop producers and writers, was a special and unique medium of expression, and sound effects on their programs are a composition in their own right. Sound is used to promote thought and emotion and, used this way, may develop into an art quite apart from the field of music.

To the microphones of the Workshop came plays from the pens of William Saroyan and Archibald MacLeish, whose *The Fall of the City* was recognized by critics as one of the best things on radio. Other plays heard on the series include Lord Dunsany's *The Use of Man*; Irving Reis's (Reis was one of the founders and guiding lights of the group) *Meridian 7-1212*; *A Drink of Water*, by Wilbur Daniel Steele; a number of Ambrose Bierce's eerie short stories adapted to the microphone; and Dorothy Parker's *Apartment to Let*.

If the Workshop had made no contribution to dramatic art in broadcasting, its contributions in the field of sound effects would more than justify its existence. *The Fall of the City* was staged in a Los Angeles armory to effect the hollow, reverberating sound which conveys the feel of great space. In *Alice in Wonderland*, during the scene in which Alice fell down the rabbit hole, the hollow sound her voice would have in such a predicament was effected by placing a box over the actress' head. When a man was stabbed on *The Ghost of Benjamin Sweet,* the sound of the dagger striking home was obtained by striking a knife into a watermelon. For a hospital scene, a microphone was actually placed against a man's heart and amplified many times.

But the Workshop's contributions to broadcasting went beyond that. It was in the Workshop that young Orson Welles learned much of his technique for broadcasting, working with Reis and Robson and others who grew up with broadcasting. Here, too, Max Wylie, Douglas Coulter and Davidson Taylor—all important names in radio production—found an opportunity to test ideas which became broadcasting tenets. And while Columbia Workshop was a co-operative affair in which all voices were heard and heeded, it, too, developed dominating individualities at various stages of its growth. Perhaps Norman Corwin was its most important voice.

Corwin was essentially a poet, and his plays were written with a lyrical beauty few other radio writers achieved.

At CBS, Corwin originated, wrote and produced *Words Without Music,* but he didn't come into his own until his rhymed fantasy, *The Plot to Overthrow Christmas,* was aired on Christmas Day, 1938. Audience mail poured into the studio and Corwin was given a free hand to develop his dramatic offerings. Perhaps the best Corwin piece was *They Fly Through the Air with the Greatest of Ease,* which was inspired by Vittorio Mussolini's relish at seeing men and horses in Ethiopia blown up by bombs he dropped. A part of the opening narration follows:

> All right, so it is morning.
>
> It is morning on a level field, still wet with dew;
>
> A field once used for haying, flown over one time by birds going north or birds going south to build homes;
>
> A meadow mowed upon by men, buzzed in by bees, and lingered on by lovers in the moonlight.
>
> Here, where last year stood the windrows of the hay,
>
> Is now such an aviary of birds as God had never dreamed of when He made the skies.
>
> Look close and you will see one now.
>
> They are wheeling it out of the hangar,
>
> Carefully . . .

Easily the most sensational figure in radio drama was Orson Welles.

Here was the man who dressed Julius Caesar in a blue business suit, rewrote Shakespeare (for the WPA theater), and gave Broadway a modern treatise on Fascism which made money. Who, when the WPA authorities decided a half hour before curtain time that he could not put on a labor opera with a leftist tinge: *The Cradle Will Rock*—simply loaded the cast, and costumes, scenery and properties (which belonged to Uncle Sam), along with a piano, into a truck and found a new theater that same evening, and the audience following him like the Pied Piper to the new theater in high glee.

A short time later his Mercury group of players was given a regular Sunday night feature on CBS. It was here that he developed the first-person narrative device for bringing radio drama intimately into the home and, whenever he could, Welles himself served as narrator. Hadn't he got his training as the hideous and insidious laugh in "The Shadow," an earlier radio mystery show, and as a part-time performer on the "March of Time" show? All this served to provide a proper overture to his famous dramatization of H. G. Wells's novel *The War of the Worlds*, which threw the Eastern seaboard of the United States into a complete tizzy. To understand partially why the country reacted so frantically, it is necessary to examine the state of jitters the American public had undergone in the Munich crisis.

September 1938 found a world harassed by the most serious problem since Sarajevo. Radio listeners of the day still remember the twenty days leading to Munich. Those intimately associated with radio—and particularly those in the news departments of the great networks—will never forget them. For during that period, radio—as a news medium—came of age.

Technically, the industry had long been ready to perform the job which the Czech crisis precipitated. In the spring of 1938, the Columbia Broadcasting System, in order to give listeners a better and more intimate picture of the Austrian *Anschluss*, had set up what it called its "European Roundup." Representatives of CBS, as well as newspapermen, stationed in important European capitals, were thus permitted to talk directly with the American listening audience and give on-the-spot interpretations of world-shaking events as they were happening by short-wave radio.

In 1936, radio newsmen, with portable transmitters, had stood among the crowds keeping vigil outside Buckingham Palace to learn of the condition of King George V. When death came for the beloved monarch who had guided his people safely through World War I, NBC was first on the air with the tragic news.

Later, when Edward VIII chose "the woman I love" above the seat of the mighty, his abdication was an epochal event not only in its historical significance and deeply touching nuances, but also because it was the first time that any king, anywhere, had used radio to explain his action.

That year, radio had felt its way, too, amidst shellfire and rattle of machine guns in on-the-spot descriptions of battles being fought between Fascist and Loyalist forces in Spain's Civil War.

In such events as these, newsrooms of the large networks were being molded and tempered and formed. Men like Abe Schechter, NBC's special-events chief, and Paul White, of CBS, had built up their organizations until they covered the world as completely as the city staffs of large daily newspapers covered their own cities. These skilled observers, winnowed through a long trial-and-error process, sat close to their teletype machines on the morning of September 12, 1938, for confidential reports from networks correspondents abroad indicated that *der Tag* was close at hand.

On the surface, and to the average American listener, the stream of American life flowed smoothly enough. Only the Tuesday night before, America had thrilled to a new type of program—"Information Please." The ideal of the program was to stump a board of experts consisting of John Kieran, sports writer; F. P. Adams, conductor of the famous "Conning Tower" column; Oscar Levant, wisecracking musical genius. Learned Clifton Fadiman, literary critic of *The New Yorker* magazine, presided as master of ceremonies. The board—or their guest experts—strove to answer all questions submitted by listeners or pay a cash penalty. Among the program's first guests were Paul de Kruif, scientist-writer; Stuart Chase, economist and author; Marc Connelly, playwright; and John Gunther, journalist and international observer. More than sixty thousand listeners sent in questions for the "Information Please" experts to answer that first week.

But under the surface, dire events were already in the making. On the afternoon of September 12, at two-fifteen, announcers on the various networks interrupted the regularly scheduled programs to announce that the world-awaited talk on Germany's foreign policy to be delivered to the Nazi Congress at Nuremberg by Adolf Hitler was now to be broadcast.

Then, before a fervent assemblage of his followers, Adolf Hitler began, in his guttural, half-hysterical style, an address which was to launch the world upon twenty nerve-racking days, days in which the stream of events flowed from one climax on to another with such rapidity that even the winged words of radio had difficulty in keeping pace. For several months, Hitler's demands upon the Czechs for special rights and privileges for the

Sudeten German minority had been growing. Now, at Nuremberg, in terms which were unmistakable, the Chancellor was to tell the world his latest demands and leave no question of the fact that the full weight of the growing German military machine stood squarely behind each spoken word.

During these twenty days, in more than a thousand broadcasts from important world centers by more than two hundred newsmen, radio followed wherever the finger of history pointed. American listeners heard Adolf Hitler, Neville Chamberlain, Édouard Daladier, Benito Mussolini, Eduard Beneš. Across the troubled lands of Europe journeyed men with microphones—by train, plane, automobile, horse cart. Americans, for the first time, realized how close were London and Prague, Paris and Berlin. They could hear a man breathe in Rome and a paper rustle in Munich. They heard, during these twenty days, broadcasts from Geneva, Nuremberg, Trieste, Stratford-on-Avon, Warsaw, Budapest, Clydebank and Castel Gondolfo. From minute to minute, as the world waited for the armies of Europe to move, American listeners heard—and understood—the development of the growing crisis.

Until Munich, there had been only an apathetic interest in world affairs on the part of the American listening public and commercial sponsors for European broadcasts were unheard of.

After Munich, the networks had little trouble selling news programs to sponsors, but at the moment it is fairly well established that the networks and their associated stations undertook the tremendous task of placing the troubled world in a showcase for its listeners without any idea that, someday, their investment would pay big dividends.

It was four o'clock in the afternoon when Hitler finished speaking. At 4:05 P.M., a news commenator in CBS's New York studios took the air. His name was H. V. Kaltenborn, and while radio listeners up until now were familiar with his voice, perhaps with his name, this tall, dignified master linguist and ad-lib artist was seizing in his two big hands a priceless moment. During the next twenty days, he refused to leave the studio, catnapping on hard lounges there, having his meals brought in to him, munching on cold sandwiches, sipping black coffee while he studied teletype messages, cables and talked by long-distance telephone across the ocean to CBS newsmen in Europe and Asia. When the twenty days were finished and the peace of Munich had descended upon a still half-trusting world, Kaltenborn's name was a household word throughout America.

Now, grasping the contents of Hitler's spoken words, with only five minutes in which to translate them from German and digest them, Kaltenborn went on the air.

"Adolf Hitler has spoken [he told an America which had not yet had time to study and understand the meaning of the address], and the world has listened, because it feared that the speech might mean war. And it may mean war, but not immediate war. Certainly if there is one thing clear in what Hitler has said . . . it is that there is no immediate intention of forcing a crisis. There was nothing in his speech tantamount to an immediate ultimatum. There was in it—and through it—a very definite declaration that Germany would no longer tolerate the oppression, as he called it, of the Sudeten Germans in Czechoslovakia. . . . "

Other networks offered similar analyses following the Nuremberg address, but no other analyst of that period possessed the quick clarity, the easy, fluent manner of Kaltenborn in making complicated declarations— declarations perhaps purposely couched in vague and uncertain terms for the war of nerves Hitler was fighting—simple and understandable to the mass of listeners.

On the evening of September 12, radio's newsmen, speaking from foreign capitals, reported to the American public on reactions of the various peoples concerned. CBS's Ed Murrow, speaking from London, said:

"There is little indication that Herr Hitler's speech this evening has decreased tension here. However, once again the British have demonstrated their ability to fly into a great calm at a time of crisis. . . . Feeling is widespread that the British Government will urge Czechoslovakia to do everything short of dismembering the country to prevent war."

In Berlin, commentators unanimously pointed out that the Germans in the street awaited the speech of their Chancellor with as many fears as did the rest of the world. From Prague, Iowa-born William L Shirer, who had witnessed the Austrian *Anschluss,* told his listeners that President Beneš had listened to the address in the palace, the cabinet members in their private homes and that demonstrations by the Sudeten Germans had been mild, with no arrests, nobody hurt. John T. Whittaker, crack member of the Chicago *Daily News* foreign staff, gave the reaction of the French from Paris:

"When Frenchmen heard what Hitler said about Czechoslovakia's alleged brutality to the Sudeten German minority and about the alleged conspiracy of the democracies against Germany, they smiled. What interests Frenchmen is that, though it was a menacing and provocative speech, it was not precise. . . . "

But on September 13, events moved rapidly as if to counter these opinions. The Czech Government declared martial law in five Sudeten German towns. Fourteen minutes after the communiqué had been handed to American newsmen, American radio listeners knew of it. In London, Prime Minister Chamberlain called his Cabinet to Number Ten Downing Street for a conference. The Sudeten German party delivered an ultimatum to the Czech Government at 7:30 P.M. and twenty-six minutes after the document was delivered, Americans knew of it. The ultimatum demanded that martial law be lifted within six hours.

Late on the afternoon of September 14, with war seemingly minutes away and actual fighting going on in Czechoslovakia, the world was informed in a radio news flash that Prime Minister Chamberlain would fly to Germany next day for a personal interview with Adolf Hitler in a final effort to ward off a European war. Again radio was reporting—and first—a première performance. For the first time in history, the head of a great government would plead personally with another government's leader in a war crisis!

Just before entering the plane, Mr. Chamberlain gave a farewell message to the British people which, as was becoming habit now, was heard also on American radio.

"I am going to see the German Chancellor," he said, "because the situation seems to me one in which discussions between him and me may have a useful consequence and the Fuehrer's reply to my suggestion encourages me to hope that my visit to him will not be without results."

For the first time, Europe was close to America—minutes away. And America was relearning its geography at the loud-speaker (and through "crisis" maps provided by the networks upon request), studying again the history which, a few years back, seemed unimportant and remote. For the echoes of medieval history were still reverberating in the ether waves, and the yellowed pages of dusty tomes on high library shelves came vividly alive in all these broadcasts. The roots of what was happening now had been planted long years ago.

And then, as the affairs of the world reached a most crucial point, something happened to radio. Short-wave transmission, never as perfect or as certain as the ordinary frequencies, can be utterly inaudible when atmospheric conditions are not favorable. Between September 15 and September 30, frequent electric storms over the Atlantic caused such interference that broadcasts did not come through and radio's news departments were forced to rely upon the same overcrowded cables and telephone lines as the newspapers for their news dispatches. This meant that radio, if the storms continued, would be only a short time ahead of the newspapers—the time it took newspapers to set type and print, to be exact.

In this situation, Jack Hartley, of the NBC news staff, ingeniously arranged a circuit for that network which completely confused its opposition for several days and resulted in NBC's scoring several notable beats. He had broadcasts sent to Capetown, South Africa; relayed from there to Buenos Aires, across the South Atlantic; and from Buenos Aires to New York, all by short-wave transmission. Broadcasts traveled three times as far as usual, but arrived only a few seconds later than if they had been sent directly from London or Berlin or Prague to New York.

Reports from Berchtesgaden, where Chamberlain and Hitler were meeting, were meager, trimmed by the fine hand of the German censor. Speculation and rumor—reported as such to listeners—took the place of fact. Then, dramatically, came the cold announcement that Chamberlain would return to London after only a few hours with Hitler. Experts guessed that Hitler's demands were more than Chamberlain could grant.

A reporter for the British Broadcasting Company, who was heard by rebroadcast over American networks at noon, September 16, described the return of Chamberlain to the airport at Heston.

Glancing around the field out in front of the airdrome building he said, "I see Lord Halifax standing there and the German Chargé d'Affaires, Dr. Cross, and a crowd of people talking animatedly down below me . . . and at last the aircraft comes into sight. Now she is right to the southerly side and she is swinging round and she'll come across another full circle of the airdrome and land to the west. It's a tremendously dramatic moment!"

Prime Minister Chamberlain, worn and tired and bearing the umbrella which had already become his peculiar mark, stepped down from the plane and spoke into a microphone.

"I have come back again, rather quicker than I expected," he said, in a weary voice. "Yesterday afternoon I had a long talk with Herr Hitler. It was a frank talk but a friendly one, and I feel satisfied now that each of us understands what is in the mind of the other. You won't, of course, expect me to discuss now what may be the results of that talk. . . . I am going to have another talk with Herr Hitler, only this time he has told me that it is his intention to come halfway to meet me. He wishes to spare an old man another such long journey."

History was being made within earshot of the loud-speaker, and loud-speakers had become standard equipment in almost every American home.

To bring through the air and across thousands of miles of ocean the sound of Europe tearing up her maps was not an easy task despite the facile way in which it seemed to be handled by those who listened in. In Prague, the lobby of the Ambassador Hotel, where diplomats and newsmen gathered, was an indescribable madhouse of rumor, tension and confusion. Radio reporters, with their engineers and technical aides close at hand and ready to go on the air at the drop of a hat—or an ultimatum—milled around, tried to get telephone calls through to the frontier, to Berlin, to the government offices in Prague, itself. One lone Czech switchboard girl bravely strove to keep track of a hundred placed calls.

The six-hour ultimatum given the Czech Government had almost run its course. At about ten o'clock, one of the American correspondents managed to get a call through to his office in Berlin. Nothing was known there of the ultimatum. The German Government was issuing no news at all. A few minutes later, word came through from the first of the correspondents who had rushed up to the Sudeten territory. He said that revolt had broken out there and that police and troops, with machine guns and hand grenades, were striving to keep order.

On one score, all newsmen in Czechoslovakia were agreed: the Czechs were determined to fight to preserve their democracy and, if it became necessary, they would sell their freedom dearly. But the decision taken in Czhoslovakia to fight seemed already to have been voided in London where Chamberlain and Daladier were meeting. Even as the Henlein ultimatum reached its expiration hour, a joint communiqué of the British and French Governments was flashed to the world from London.

"Britain and France have reached complete agreement with regard to a policy aimed at promoting a peaceful solution of the Czechoslovakian question."

The communiqué added that the two governments hoped that thereafter "it will be possible to consider a more general settlement of European peace."

For six days, American radio listeners had watched the crisis grow, were aware of all the fine nuances and shadings behind the verbal barrages laid down in this war of nerves. Informed as perhaps no other people have ever been in such a time of crisis, they realized that the communiqué meant that the allies were prepared to sacrifice Czechoslovakia to save themselves, if Hitler did not demand too much.

Three more tense days of waiting followed. Negotiations upon which the decision—peace or war—hung, took place behind closed doors at the Hotel Dreesen, in Godesberg, where Chamberlain and Hitler held their second meeting. And again their meeting was brought into the sharp focus of the world's eye by radio.

During these days, CBS added a new wrinkle to radio news coverage when it put the two-way conversation (used as an anniversary stunt by NBC three years before) to practical use. Kaltenborn would talk from New York with correspondents in the various world capitals, ask questions, receive answers—and both ends of the conversation were heard instantaneously by American listeners. Radio fans heard from the lips of those on the ground the thoughts and reactions of people who, a short year later, were to be shedding their blood in a bitter war.

Radio men speak of this period as "The Munich Crisis." But in reality, it was a series of crises with one following another in rapid procession. Expiration of the ultimatum and the joint Franco-British communiqué brought one crisis to an end and laid the groundwork for the next which, even now, brewed and boiled behind locked doors at Godesberg.

Then, on the evening of September 23, listeners heard these quiet but dangerous words in an announcement from Godesberg:

"Mr. Chamberlain went to pay a farewell call on Adolf Hitler at ten o'clock tonight, which is five-thirty by New York time. So far, there is no word as to what transpired at this visit. A report throughout Europe is that negotiations between Chamberlain and Hitler are definitely ended."

The following day, Mr. Chamberlain returned to London. War seemed inevitable, hours away, and from Washington, President Roosevelt sent a direct message to Adolf Hitler and President Beneš, of Czechoslovakia, appealing for peaceful negotiation.

On September 27, Kaltenborn informed listeners that Hitler had ordered full mobilization for the following day and that he stood ready to strike on October 1 unless Czechoslovakia acceded to his demands. In London, by the light of flares and automobile headlights, trenches were being dug in the parks. There was a tight, tired look about the eyes of Londoners, and gas masks were being issued by air-raid-precaution men.

Next morning, Mr. Chamberlain reported for the first time to Parliament on his negotiations with Hitler. A running account of his statement, as the words fell from his lips, was being transmitted to the American people by an observer from a vantage point in the House of Commons. And listeners may have noticed in the public speeches of diplomats during this period a quality which had never been contained in even the most important utterances of the past's great statesmen. With Chamberlain—as with Hitler, Mussolini and Beneš—was the certain knowledge that the words he spoke were being heard in all corners of the earth; and that men in high and low places, the peoples of the earth, were passing judgment upon him. His speech was a justification of his efforts, an attempt to show that he had sacrificed dignity in flying to Munich and again to Godesberg, but that no sacrifice was too great if peace could be preserved. It was a skillfully worded plea for the sympathy and support of a world he knew was hanging upon his every word.

Just as he reached the point in his address where he declared that, in spite of all he had been able to do, war seemed inevitable, Sir John Simon handed him a penciled note. Members of Parliament, newsmen, a world that was all but present in the vivid word pictures being painted for it, sensed the importance of the missive and waited breathlessly as he unfolded it and read.

It was an invitation from Hitler to attend a conference the following day in Munich at which representatives of England, Germany, France and Italy would try, by peaceful negotiation, to avert war. Czechoslovakia, the nation most concerned in the negotiations, was significantly omitted from the list of conferring nations.

A scene unprecedented in British Parliamentary history followed. Never before was there such a tumult in the House of Commons. Amid cheers, shouts, crying and waving of papers, Chamberlain, tears streaming down his cheeks, sat down.

The same thorough coverage which had marked earlier developments in the crisis continued at Munich with the teamwork of on-the-spot reporters feeding news to commentators drilled in condensing, clarifying and interpreting it for the mass mind.

Then, suddenly, word came that the conference was about to close and that a protocol had been signed by the four parties. Newsmen and radio men rushed to the hotels where the various delegations were staying to receive their press releases, American reporters going to the British delegation's headquarters. Prior to the breaking up of the conference, however, Jordan, NBC's European news chief, had spoken to Sir William Strang, of the British group, and arranged to receive whatever releases that group made. When word that the conference had broken up and that the Italian delegation was already rushing from the building to catch its train reached the newsmen, they rushed for their waiting cars.

But on the way out, Jordan saw Sir William on the pavement, noticed that Sir Horace Wilson, with Strang, carried prepared releases. He asked for his copy and Strang, taking one from Wilson, handed it to him. Back up the stairs at breakneck speed raced Jordan, but in the improvised broadcasting room, a new difficulty confronted him. The German radio official in charge did not believe that he had an official text of the agreement at first and, later, when he was convinced, didn't like the idea of Jordan broadcasting it to America before the German text had been released to German listeners.

Tearfully, Jordan pleaded; then he became angry and a fist fight almost ensued. But Jordan's eloquence finally won out and, eight minutes after the release had been handed him, it was being heard by American listeners. The NBC broadcast was forty-six minutes ahead of all competition, and listeners tuned to NBC stations knew of the end of the free democracy which was Czechoslovakia before many of the correspondents who were present in Munich!

Statesmen throughout the world hastened to pay tribute to the power of radio. They said that radio, by keeping the world so fully informed, had forced the choice of negotiation upon leaders, who, twenty years before, might well have chosen war.

The palms which were being hung upon radio, as a medium of public information, after Munich were merited, and the developments of the months following Munich and leading to the outbreak of World War II amply bear out this statement. Americans were the best-informed people in the world during those fateful twenty days. Americans knew every move that was made as it was made, enjoyed brilliant interpretations of these moves by students of government and economics and international affairs. But American radio is a competitive and free institution.

What happened abroad?

In England, during the crisis, a prominent magazine recommended that readers who wanted to know the truth about Czechoslovakia should tune to the short-wave broadcasts from American stations! When Winston Churchill wanted to talk about the crisis, the British Broadcasting Company refused to carry his speech, which was heard only in America. When Anthony Eden discussed the subject from London, an American network made his words heard all across America—but not one Englishman, unless tuned to an American station, could hear his voice.

How well the French radio acquainted its listeners with vital facts is best illustrated by an American exchange student at the Sorbonne who, leaving France at the height of the crisis and two days after almost complete mobilization had been ordered, had her first knowledge of the mobilization and the fact that France was on the verge of war after she boarded an American liner.

In Germany, listening to foreign broadcasts had long been a misdemeanor. Hitler's one-tube sets were designed to pick up local signals only, and German listeners heard Nazi party exhortations, tales of Germans being killed and maltreated in Sudetenland and emotional outbursts by Nazi bigwigs.

The twenty nerve-racking days just ended had evidenced the growth to mature stature of radio newscasting. The necessity of the moment had molded into a finely organized and supersensitive sounding board various processes which had been building over eighteen experimental years.

Two weeks after the peace of Munich, radio gave a laboratory demonstration of how heavy that peace hung over the heads of Americans who had followed it from beginning to end; and of how effective the new technique of news broadcasting had become. Orson Welles, youthful writer-producer-director of the Mercury Theater, presented his group in H. G. Wells's *The War of the Worlds,* on Sunday evening, October 30. And to make it vivid, he simulated a news broadcast.

JOHN HOUSEMAN

THE MEN FROM MARS*

RADIO WAR TERRORIZES U.S.—New York *Daily News,* October 31, 1938

Everybody was excited I felt as if I was going crazy and kept on saying what can we do what difference does it make whether we die sooner or later? We were holding each other. Everything seemed unimportant in the face of death. I was afraid to die, just kept on listening.—*A listener*

Nothing about the broadcast was in the least credible.—Dorothy Thompson

THE SHOW came off. There is no doubt about that. It set out to dramatize, in terms of popular apprehension, an attempted invasion of our world by hostile forces from the planet Mars. It succeeded. Of the several million American citizens who, on the evening of October 30, 1938, milled about the streets, clung sobbing to one another or drove wildly in all directions to avoid asphyxiation and flaming death, approximately one-half were in

* From *Harper's* Magazine, December 1948.

terror of Martians—not of Germans, Japanese or unknown enemies—but, specifically, of Martians. Later, when the excitement was over and the shadow of the gallows had lifted, some of us were inclined to take credit for more deliberate and premeditated villainy than we deserved. The truth is that at the time, nobody was more surprised than we were. In fact, one of the most remarkable things about the broadcast was the quite haphazard nature of its birth.

In October 1938, the Mercury Theater, of which Orson Welles and I were the founding partners, had been in existence for less than a year. Our first Broadway season had been shatteringly successful—*Julius Caesar, The Cradle Will Rock, Shoemaker's Holiday,* and *Heartbreak House* in the order of their appearance. In April, Orson, in a straggly white beard, made the cover of *Time* Magazine. In June, the Columbia Broadcasting System offered him a radio show—The Mercury Theater on the Air, a series of classic dramatizations in the first person singular with Orson as master of ceremonies, star, narrator, writer, director and producer. He accepted. So, now, in addition to an empty theater, a movie in progress, two plays in rehearsal, and all seven of the chronicle plays of William Shakespeare in preparation, we had a radio show.

We opened on July 11. Among our first thirteen shows were *Treasure Island, 39 Steps, Abraham Lincoln, Three Short Stories* (by Saki, Sherwood Anderson, and Carl Ewald), *Jane Eyre, Julius Caesar* (with running commentary by Kaltenborn out of Plutarch), and *The Man Who Was Thursday.* Our second series, in the fall, began with Booth Tarkington's *Seventeen, Around the World in Eighty Days,* and *Oliver Twist.* Our fifth show was to be *Life with Father.* Our fourth was *The War of the Worlds.*

No one, as I remember, was very enthusiastic about it. But it seemed good programming, between the terrors of Dickens' London slums, and the charm of Clarence Day's New York in the Nineties, to throw in something of a contrasting and pseudoscientific nature. We thought of Shiel's *Purple Cloud,* Conan Doyle's *Lost World,* and several others before we settled on H. G. Wells's twenty-year-old novel, which neither of us, as it turned out later, remembered at all clearly. It is just possible that neither of us had ever read it.

II

Those were our golden days of unsponsored radio. We had no advertising agency to harass us, no client to cut our withers. Partly because we were perpetually overworked and partly because that was the way we did things at the Mercury, we never seemed to get more than a single jump ahead of ourselves. Shows were created week after week under conditions of soul-and health-destroying pressure. On the whole they were good shows. And we *did* develop a system—of sorts.

It worked as follows: I was editor of the series. With Welles, I chose the shows and then laid them out. The writing, most of it, was done by Howard Koch—earnest, spindly, six-foot-two—a Westchester lawyer turned playwright. To write the first draft of an hour's radio script took him about five days, working about fifteen hours a day. Our associate producer was Paul Stewart, a Broadway actor turned director. His function was to put the broadcast through its first paces and preliminary rehearsals. Every Thursday, musicless and with rudimentary sound effects, a wax record of the show was cut. From this record, played back later that night, Orson would give us his reactions and revisions. In the next thirty-six hours the script would be reshaped and rewritten, sometimes drastically. Saturday afternoon there was another rehearsal, with sound—with or without Welles. It was not until the last day that Orson really took over.

Sundays, at eight, we went on the air. Beginning in the early afternoon—when Bernard Herrmann arrived with his orchestra of twenty-seven high-grade symphony players—two simultaneous dramas were regularly unfolded in the stale, tense air of Studio Number One: the minor drama of the current show and the major drama of Orson's Gargantuan struggle to get it on. Sweating, howling, disheveled, and single-handed he wrestled with Chaos and Time—always conveying an effect of being alone, traduced by his collaborators, surrounded by treachery, ignorance, sloth, indifference, incompetence and—more often than not—downright sabotage! Every Sunday it was touch and go. As the hands of the clock moved relentlessly toward air time the crisis grew more extreme, the peril more desperate. Often violence broke out. Scripts flew through the air, doors were slammed, batons smashed. Scheduled for six—but usually nearer seven—there was a dress rehearsal, a thing of wild improvisations and irrevocable disaster. (One show was found to be twenty-one minutes overlength, another fourteen and one half minutes short.)

After that, with only a few minutes to go, there was a final frenzy of correction and reparation, of utter confusion and absolute horror, aggravated by the gobbling of sandwiches and the bolting of oversized milk shakes. By now it was less than a minute to air time. . . .

At that instant, quite regularly week after week—with not one second to spare . . . the titanic buffoonery stopped. Suddenly out of chaos, the show emerged—delicately poised, meticulously executed, precise as clockwork, and smooth as satin. And above us all, like a rainbow over storm clouds, stood Orson on his podium, sonorous and heroic, a leader of men surrounded by his band of loyal followers; a giant in action, serene and radiant with the joy of a hard battle bravely fought—a great victory snatched from the jaws of disaster.

In later years, when the Men from Mars had passed into history, there was some bickering among members of the Mercury as to who, exactly, had contributed precisely what, to that particular evening's entertainment. The truth is that a number of us made a number of essential and incalculable contributions to the broadcast. (Who can accurately assess, for instance, the part played by Johnny Dietz's perfect engineering, in keeping unbroken the shifting illusion of imperfect reality? How much did the original old H. G. Wells, who noisily repudiated us, have to do with it? Or the second assistant sound man? Or individual actors? Or Dr. Goebbels? Or Charlie McCarthy?) Orson Welles had virtually nothing to do with the writing of the script and less than usual to do with its preliminary rehearsals. Yet first and last it was his creation. If there had been a lynching that night, it is Welles the outraged populace would have strung up—and rightly so. Orson was the Mercury. *The War of the Worlds,* like everything we did, was his show.

Actually, it was a narrow squeak. Those Men from Mars barely escaped being stillborn. Tuesday afternoon—five days before the show—Howard Koch telephoned. He was in deep distress. After three days of slaving on H. G. Wells's scientific fantasy he was ready to give up. Under no circumstances, he declared, could it be made interesting or in any way credible to modern American ears. Koch was not given to habitual alarmism. To confirm his fears, Annie, our secretary, came to the phone. She was an acid and emphatic girl from Smith College with fine blond hair, who smelled of fading spring flowers. "You can't do it!" she whined. "Those old Martians are just a lot of nonsense. It's all too silly! We're going to make fools of ourselves! Absolute fools!"

For some reason which I do not clearly remember our only possible alternative for that week was a dreary one—*Lorna Doone.* I tried to reach Welles. He was at the theater and wouldn't come to the phone.

The reason he wouldn't come to the phone was that he was in his thirty-sixth successive hour of dress-rehearsing *Danton's Death,* a beautiful, fragmentary play by Georg Buechner out of which Max Reinhardt, in an augmented form, had made a successful mass-spectacle in the Twenties. Not to be outdone, Orson had glued seventeen hundred masks on to the back wall of the Mercury Theater, and ripped out the entire stage. Day after day actors fell headlong into the rat-ridden basement, leaped on and off erratically moving elevators, and chanted the "Carmagnole" in chorus under the supervision of Marc Blitzstein.

Unable to reach Welles, I called Koch back. I was severe. I taxed him with defeatism. I gave him false comfort. I promised to come up and help. When I finally got there—around two the next morning—things were better. He was beginning to have fun laying waste the State of New Jersey. Annie had stopped grinding her teeth. We worked all night and through the next day. Wednesday at sunset the script was finished.

Thursday, as usual, Paul Stewart rehearsed the show, then made a record. We listened to it rather gloomily, long after midnight in Orson's room at the St. Regis, sitting on the floor because all the chairs were covered with coils of unrolled and unedited film. We agreed it was a dull show. We all felt its only chance of coming off lay in emphasizing its newscast style—its simultaneous, eyewitness quality.

All night we sat up, spicing the script with circumstantial allusions and authentic detail. Friday afternoon it went over to CBS to be passed by the network censor. Certain name alterations were requested. Under protest and with a deep sense of grievance we changed the Hotel Biltmore to a nonexistent Park Plaza, Trans-America to Intercontinent, the Columbia Broadcasting Building to Broadcasting Building. Then the script went over to mimeograph and we went to bed. We had done our best and, after all, a show is just a show. . . .

Saturday afternoon Paul Stewart rehearsed with sound effects but without Welles. He worked for a long time on the crowd scenes, the roar of cannon echoing in the Watchung Hills and the sound of New York Harbor as the ships with the last remaining survivors put out to sea.

Around six we left the studio. Orson, phoning from the theater a few minutes later to find out how things were going, was told by one of the CBS sound men, who had stayed behind to pack up his equipment, that it was not one of our better shows. Confidentially, the man opined, it just didn't come off. Twenty-seven hours later, quite a few of his employers would have found themselves a good deal happier if he had turned out to be right.

III

On Sunday, October 30, at 8:00 P.M., E.S.T., in a studio littered with coffee cartons and sandwich paper, Orson swallowed a second container of pineapple juice, put on his earphones, raised his long white fingers and threw the cue for the Mercury theme—the Tchaikovsky Piano Concerto in B Flat Minor #1. After the music dipped, there were routine introductions—then the announcement that a dramatization of H. G. Wells's famous novel, *The War of the Worlds,* was about to be performed. Around 8:01 Orson began to speak, as follows:

WELLES

We know now that in the early years of the twentieth century this world was being watched closely by intelligences greater than man's and yet as mortal as his own. We know now that as human beings busied themselves about their various concerns they were scrutinized and studied, perhaps almost as narrowly as a man with a microscope might scrutinize the transient creatures that swarm and multiply in a drop of water. With infinite complacence people went to and fro over the earth about their little affairs, serene in the assurance of their dominion over this small spinning fragment of solar driftwood which by chance or design man has inherited out of the dark mystery of Time and Space. Yet across an immense ethereal gulf minds that are to our minds as ours are to the beasts in the jungle, intellects vast, cool, and unsympathetic regarded this earth with envious eyes and slowly and surely drew their plans against us. In the thirty-ninth year of the twentieth century came the great disillusionment.

It was near the end of October. Business was better. The war scare was over. More men were back at work. Sales were picking up. On this particular evening, October 30, the Crossley service estimated that thirty-two million people were listening in on their radios. . . .

Neatly, without perceptible transition, he was followed on the air by an anonymous announcer caught in a routine bulletin:

ANNOUNCER

. . . for the next twenty-four hours not much change in temperature. A slight atmospheric disturbance of undetermined origin is reported over Nova Scotia, causing a low pressure area to move down rather rapidly over the northeastern states, bringing a forecast of rain, accompanied by winds of light gale force. Maximum temperature 66; minimum 48. This weather report comes to you from the Government Weather Bureau. . . . We now take you to the Meridian Room in the Hotel Park Plaza in downtown New York, where you will be entertained by the music of Ramon Raquello and his orchestra.

At which cue, Bernard Herrmann led the massed men of the CBS house orchestra in a thunderous rendition of "La Cumparsita." The entire hoax might well have exploded there and then—but for the fact that hardly anyone was listening. They were being entertained by Charlie McCarthy—then at the height of his success.

The Crossley census, taken about a week before the broadcast, had given us 3.6 per cent of the listening audience to Edgar Bergen's 34.7 per cent. What the Crossley Institute (that hireling of the advertising agencies) deliberately ignored, was the healthy American habit of dial-twisting. On that particular evening, Edgar Bergen in the person of Charlie McCarthy temporarily left the air about 8:12 P.M., E.S.T., yielding place to a new and not very popular singer. At that point, and during the following minutes, a large number of listeners started twisting their dials in search of other entertainment. Many of them turned to us—and when they did, they stayed put! For by this time the mysterious meteorite had fallen at Grovers Mill in New Jersey, the Martians had begun to show their foul leathery heads above the ground, and the New Jersey State Police were racing to the spot. Within a few minutes people all over the United States were praying, crying, fleeing frantically to escape death from the Martians. Some remembered to rescue loved ones, others telephoned farewells or warnings, hurried to inform neighbors, sought information from newspapers or radio stations, summoned ambulances and police cars.

The reaction was strongest at points nearest the tragedy—in Newark, New Jersey, in a single block, more than twenty families rushed out of their houses with wet handkerchiefs and towels over their faces. Some began moving household furniture. Police switchboards were flooded with calls inquiring, "Shall I close my windows?" "Have the police any extra gas masks?" Police found one family waiting in the yard with wet cloths on faces contorted with hysteria. As one woman reported later:

I was terribly frightened. I wanted to pack and take my child in my arms, gather up my friends and get in the car and just go north as far as we could. But what I did was just sit by one window, praying, listening, and scared stiff, and my husband by the other sniffling and looking out to see if people were running. . . .

In New York hundreds of people on Riverside Drive left their homes ready for flight. Bus terminals were crowded. A woman calling up the Dixie Bus Terminal for information said impatiently, "Hurry, please, the world is coming to an end and I have a lot to do."

In the parlor churches of Harlem evening service became "end of the world" prayer meetings. Many turned to God in that moment:

I held a crucifix in my hand and prayed while looking out of my open window for falling meteors. . . . When the monsters were wading across the Hudson River and coming into New York, I wanted to run up on my roof to see what they looked like, but I couldn't leave my radio while it was telling me of their whereabouts.

Aunt Grace began to pray with Uncle Henry. Lily got sick to her stomach. I don't know what I did exactly but I know I prayed harder and more earnestly than ever before. Just as soon as we were convinced that this thing was real, how petty all things on this earth seemed; how soon we put our trust in God!

The panic moved upstate. One man called up the Mt. Vernon Police

Headquarters to find out "where the forty policemen were killed." Another took time out to philosophize:

I thought the whole human race was going to be wiped out—that seemed more important than the fact that we were going to die. It seemed awful that everything that had been worked on for years was going to be lost forever.

In Rhode Island weeping and hysterical women swamped the switchboard of the Providence *Journal* for details of the massacre, and officials of the electric light company received a score of calls urging them to turn off all lights so that the city would be safe from the enemy. The Boston *Globe* received a call from one woman "who could see the fire." A man in Pittsburgh hurried home in the midst of the broadcast and found his wife in the bathroom, a bottle of poison in her hand, screaming, "I'd rather die this way than that." In Minneapolis a woman ran into church screaming, "New York destroyed this is the end of the world. You might as well go home to die I just heard it on the radio."

The Kansas City Bureau of the Associated Press received inquiries about the "meteors" from Los Angeles; Salt Lake City; Beaumont, Texas; and St. Joseph, Missouri. In San Francisco the general impression of listeners seemed to be that an overwhelming force had invaded the United States from the air—was in process of destroying New York and threatening to move westward. "My God," roared an inquirer into a telephone, "where can I volunteer my services, we've got to stop this awful thing!"

As far south as Birmingham, Alabama, people gathered in churches and prayed. On the campus of a Southeastern college—

The girls in the sorority houses and dormitories huddled around their radios trembling and weeping in each other's arms. They separated themselves from their friends only to take their turn at the telephones to make long distance calls to their parents, saying goodbye for what they thought might be the last time. . . .

There are hundreds of such bits of testimony, gathered from coast to coast.

IV

At least one book* and quite a pile of sociological literature has appeared on the subject of "The invasion from Mars." Many theories have been put forward to explain the "tidal wave" of panic that swept the nation. I know of two factors that largely contributed to the broadcast's extraordinarily violent effect. First, its historical timing. It came within thirty-five days of the Munich crisis. For weeks, the American people had been hanging on

* *The Invasion from Mars* by Hadley Cantril, Princeton University Press, from which many of the above quotations were taken.

their radios, getting most of their news no longer from the press, but over the air. A new technique of "on-the-spot" reporting had been developed and eagerly accepted by an anxious and news-hungry world. The Mercury Theater on the Air by faithfully copying every detail of the new technique —including its imperfections—found an already enervated audience ready to accept its wildest fantasies. The second factor was the show's sheer technical brilliance. To this day it is impossible to sit in a room and hear the scratched, worn, off-the-air recording of the broadcast without feeling in the back of your neck some slight draft left over from that great wind of terror that swept the nation. Even with the element of credibility totally removed it remains a surprisingly frightening show.

Radio drama was taken seriously in the Thirties—before the Quiz and the Giveaway became the lords of the air. In the work of such directors as Reis, Corwin, Fickett, Welles, Robson, Spier and Oboler there was an eager, excited drive to get the most out of this new, all too rapidly freezing medium. But what happened that Sunday, up on the twentieth floor of the CBS building, was something quite special. Beginning around two, when the show started to take shape under Orson's hands, a strange fever seemed to invade the studio—part childish mischief, part professional zeal.

First to feel it were the actors. I remember Frank Readick (who played the part of Carl Phillips, the network's special reporter) going down to the record library and digging up the Morrison recording of the explosion of the Hindenburg at Lakehurst. This is a classic reportage—one of those wonderful, unpredictable accidents of eyewitness description. The broadcaster is casually describing a routine landing of the giant gasbag. Suddenly he sees something. A flash of flame! An instant later the whole thing explodes. It takes him time—a full second—to react at all. Then seconds more of sputtering ejaculations before he can make the adjustment between brain and tongue. He starts to describe the terrible things he sees—the writhing human figures twisting and squirming as they fall from the white burning wreckage. He stops, fumbles, vomits, then quickly continues. Readick played the record to himself, over and over. Then, re-creating the emotion in his own terms, he described the Martian meteorite as he saw it lying inert and harmless in a field at Grovers Mills, lit up by the headlights of a hundred cars—the coppery cylinder suddenly opening, revealing the leathery tentacles and the terrible pale-eyed faces of the Martians within. As they begin to emerge he freezes, unable to translate his vision into words; he fumbles, retches—and then after a second continues.

A few moments later Carl Phillips lay dead, tumbling over the microphone in his fall—one of the first victims of the Martian Ray. There followed a moment of absolute silence—an eternity of waiting. Then, without warning, the network's emergency fill-in was heard—somewhere in a quiet studio, a piano, close on mike, playing "Clair de Lune," soft and sweet as honey, for many seconds, while the fate of the universe hung in the balance. Finally it was interrupted by the manly reassuring voice of Brigadier General Montgomery Smith, Commander of the New Jersey State Militia, speaking from Trenton, and placing "the counties of Mercer and Middlesex as far west as Princeton and east to Jamesburg" under Martial Law! Tension—release—then renewed tension. For soon after that came an eyewitness account of the fatal battle of the Watchung Hills; and then, once again, that lone piano was heard—now a symbol of terror, shattering the dead air with its ominous tinkle. As it played, on and on, its effect became increasingly sinister—a thin band of suspense stretched almost beyond endurance.

That piano was the neatest trick of the show—a fine specimen of the theatrical "retard," boldly conceived and exploited to the full. It was one of the many devices with which Welles succeeded in compelling not merely the attention, but also the belief of his invisible audience. *The War of the Worlds* was a magic act, one of the world's greatest, and Orson was just the man to bring it off.

For Welles is at heart a magician whose particular talent lies not so much in his creative imagination (which is considerable) as in his proven ability to stretch the familiar elements of theatrical effect far beyond their normal point of tension. For this reason his productions require more elaborate preparation and more perfect execution than most. At that—like all complicated magic tricks—they remain, till the last moment, in a state of precarious balance. When they come off, they give—by virtue of the unusually high intensity—an impression of great brilliance and power; when they fail—when something in their balance goes wrong or the original structure proves to have been unsound—they provoke, among their audience, a particularly violent reaction of unease and revulsion. Welles's flops are louder than other men's. The Mars broadcast was one of his unqualified successes.

Among the columnists and public figures who discussed the affair during the next few days (some praising us for the public service we had rendered, some condemning us as sinister scoundrels) the most general reaction was one of amazement at the "incredible stupidity" and "gullibility" of the American public, who had accepted as real, in this single broadcast, incidents which in actual fact would have taken days or even weeks to occur. "Nothing about the broadcast," wrote Dorothy Thompson with her usual aplomb, "was in the least credible." She was wrong. The first few minutes of our broadcast were, in point of fact, strictly realistic in time and perfectly credible, though somewhat boring, in content. Herein lay the great tensile strength of the show; it was the structural device that made the whole illusion possible. And it could have been carried off in no other medium than radio.

Our actual broadcasting time, from the first mention of the meteorites to the fall of New York City, was less than forty minutes. During that time men traveled long distances, large bodies of troops were mobilized, Cabinet meetings were held, savage battles fought on land and in the air. And millions of people accepted it—emotionally if not logically.

There is nothing so very strange about that. Most of us do the same thing, to some degree, most days of our lives—every time we look at a movie or listen to a broadcast. Not even the realistic theater observes the literal unities; motion pictures and, particularly, radio (where neither place or time exists save in the imagination of the listener) have no difficulty in getting their audiences to accept the telescoped reality of dramatic time. Our special hazard lay in the fact that we purported to be, not a play, but reality. In order to take advantage of the accepted convention, we had to slide swiftly and imperceptibly out of the "real" time of a news report into the "dramatic" time of fictional broadcast. Once that was achieved—without losing the audience's attention or arousing their skepticism, if they could be sufficiently absorbed and bewitched not to notice the transition—then, we felt, there was no extreme of fantasy through which they would not follow us. We were keenly aware of our problem; we found what we believed was the key to its solution. And if, that night, the American public proved "gullible," it was because enormous pains and a great deal of thought had been spent to make it so.

In the script, *The War of the Worlds* started extremely slowly—dull meteorological and astronomical bulletins alternating with musical interludes. These were followed by a colorless scientific interview and still another stretch of dance music. These first few minutes of routine broadcasting "within the existing standards of judgment of the listener" were intended to lull (or maybe bore) the audience into a false security and to furnish a solid base of realistic time from which to accelerate later. Orson, in making over the show, extended this slow movement far beyond our original conception. "La Cumparsita," rendered by "Ramon Raquello, from the Meridian Room of the Hotel Park Plaza in downtown New York," had been thought of as running only a few seconds; "Bobby Millette playing first 'Stardust' from the Hotel Martinet in Brooklyn," even less. At rehearsal

Orson stretched both these numbers to what seemed to us, in the control room, an almost unbearable length. We objected. The interview in the Princeton Observatory—the clockwork ticking monotonously overhead, the woolly-minded professor mumbling vague replies to the reporters' uninformed questions—this, too, he dragged out to a point of tedium. Over our protests, lines were restored that had been cut at earlier rehearsals. We cried there would not be a listener left. Welles stretched them out even longer.

He was right. His sense of tempo, that night, was infallible. When the flashed news of the cylinder's landing finally came—almost fifteen minutes after the beginning of a fairly dull show—he was able suddenly to spiral his action to a speed as wild and reckless as its base was solid. The appearance of the Martians; their first treacherous act; the death of Carl Phillips; the arrival of the militia; the battle of the Watchung Hills; the destruction of New Jersey—all these were telescoped into a space of twelve minutes without ever stretching the listener's emotional credulity. The broadcast, by then, had its own reality, the reality of emotionally felt time and space.

V

At the height of the crisis, around 8:31, the Secretary of the Interior came on the air with an exhortation to the American people. His words, as you read them now, ten years later, have a Voltairean ring. (They were admirably spoken—in a voice just faintly reminiscent of the President's—by a young man named Kenneth Delmar, who has since grown rich and famous as Senator Claghorn.)

THE SECRETARY

Citizens of the nation: I shall not try to conceal the gravity of the situation that confronts the country, nor the concern of your Government in protecting the lives and property of its people. However, I wish to impress upon you— private citizens and public officials, all of you—the urgent need of calm and resourceful action. Fortunately, this formidable enemy is still confined to a comparatively small area, and we may place our faith in the military forces to keep them there. In the meantime placing our trust in God, we must continue the performance of our duties, each and every one of us, so that we may confront this destructive adversary with a nation united, courageous, and consecrated to the preservation of human supremacy on this earth. I thank you.

Toward the end of his speech (*circa* 8:32, E.S.T.) Davidson Taylor, supervisor of the broadcast for the Columbia Broadcasting System, received a phone call in the control room, creased his lips and hurriedly left the studio. By the time he returned, a few moments later—pale as death— clouds of heavy smoke were rising from Newark, New Jersey, and the

Martians, tall as skyscrapers, were astride the Pulaski Highway preparatory to wading the Hudson River. To us in the studio the show seemed to be progressing splendidly—how splendidly Davidson Taylor had just learned outside. For several minutes now, a kind of madness had seemed to be sweeping the continent—somehow connected with our show. The CBS switchboards had been swamped into uselessness but from outside sources vague rumors were coming in of deaths and suicides and panic injuries.

Taylor had requests to interrupt the show immediately with an explanatory station-announcement. By now the Martians were across the Hudson and gas was blanketing the city. The end was near. We were less than a minute from the Station Break. The organ was allowed to swirl out under the slackening fingers of its failing organist and Ray Collins, superb as the "last announcer," choked heroically to death on the roof of Broadcasting Building. The boats were all whistling for a while as the last of the refugees perished in New York Harbor. Finally, as they died away, an amateur short-wave operator was heard, from heaven knows where, weakly reaching out for human companionship across the empty world:

> 2X2L Calling CQ
> 2X2L Calling CQ
> 2X2L Calling CQ
> Isn't there anyone on the air?
> Isn't there anyone?

Five seconds of absolute silence. Then, shattering the reality of World's End—the Announcer's voice was heard, suave and bright:

ANNOUNCER
You are listening to the CBS presentation of Orson Welles and the Mercury Theater on the Air in an original dramatization of *The War of the Worlds*, by H. G. Wells. The performance will continue after a brief intermission.

The second part of the show was extremely well written and most sensitively played—but nobody heard it. It recounted the adventures of a lone survivor, with interesting observations on the nature of human society; it described the eventual death of the Martian Invaders, slain—"after all man's defenses had failed by the humblest thing that God in his wisdom had put upon this earth"—by bacteriological action; it told of the rebuilding of a brave new world. After a stirring musical finale, Welles, in his own person, delivered a charming informal little speech about Halloween, which it happened to be.

I remember, during the playing of the final theme, the phone starting to ring in the control room and a shrill voice through the receiver announcing itself as belonging to the mayor of some Midwestern city, one of the big ones. He is screaming for Welles. Choking with fury, he reports mobs in the streets of his city, women and children huddled in the churches, violence and looting. If, as he now learns, the whole thing is nothing but a crummy joke—then he, personally, is coming up to New York to punch the author of it on the nose! Orson hangs up quickly. For we are off the air now and the studio door bursts open. The following hours are a nightmare. The building is suddenly full of people and dark blue uniforms. We are hurried out of the studio, downstairs, into a back office. Here we sit incommunicado while network employees are busily collecting, destroying, or locking up all scripts and records of the broadcast. Then the press is let loose upon us, ravening for horror. How many deaths have *we* heard of? (Implying they know of thousands.) What do *we* know of the fatal stampede in a Jersey hall? (Implying it is one of many.) What traffic deaths? (The ditches must be choked with corpses.) The suicides? (Haven't you heard about the one on Riverside Drive?) It is all quite vague in my memory and quite terrible.

Hours later, instead of arresting us, they let us out a back way. We scurry down to the theater like hunted animals to their hole. It is surprising to see life going on as usual in the midnight streets, cars stopping for traffic, people walking. At the Mercury the company is still stoically rehearsing—falling downstairs and singing the "Carmagnole." Welles goes up on stage, where photographers, lying in wait, catch him with his eyes raised up to heaven, his arms outstretched in an attitude of crucifixion. Thus he appeared in a tabloid that morning over the caption, "I Didn't Know What I Was DOING!" The New York *Times* quoted him as saying, "I don't think we will choose anything like this again."

We were on the front page for two days. Having had to bow to radio as a news source during the Munich crisis, the press was now only too eager to expose the perilous irresponsibilities of the new medium. Orson was their whipping boy. They quizzed and badgered him. Condemnatory editorials were delivered by our press-clipping bureau in bushel baskets. There was talk, for a while, of criminal action.

Then gradually, after about two weeks, the excitement subsided. By then it had been discovered that the casualties were not as numerous or as serious as had at first been supposed. One young woman had fallen and broken her arm running downstairs. Later the Federal Communications Commission held some hearings and passed some regulations. The Columbia Broadcasting System made a public apology. With that the offical aspects of the incident were closed.

As to the Mercury—our new play, *Danton's Death,* finally opened after five postponements. Not even our fantastic publicity was able to offset its generally unfavorable notices. On the other hand, that same week the Mercury Theater on the Air was signed up by Campbell Soups at a most lavish figure.

Of the suits that were brought against us—amounting to over three quarters of a million dollars for damages, injuries, miscarriages and distresses of various kinds—none was substantiated or legally proved. We did settle one claim, however, against the advice of our lawyers. It was the particularly affecting case of a man in Massachusetts, who wrote:

"I thought the best thing to do was to go away. So I took three dollars twenty-five cents out of my savings and bought a ticket. After I had gone sixty miles I knew it was a play. Now I don't have money left for the shoes I was saving up for. Will you please have someone send me a pair of black shoes size 9B!"

We did.

NO RISKS, NO COMMITMENTS

THE POSITION of the United States in world power politics in the 1930s was not one of leadership, as it is today; there was plenty of opportunity to influence the squabbling countries in Europe, but F.D.R.'s attitude was apt to be "watch and worry." Personally, F.D.R. was intensely interested but, as James MacGregor Burns says, he was "unwilling to throw his weight into the balance, [he] was still confined to a policy of pinpricks and righteous protest. No risks, no commitments, was the motto of the White House." *

In Burns's judgment, F.D.R. had opportunities to reorient the people's fear of war and "direct it toward internationalist policies" rather than allow the drift to continue toward isolationism.

But as one remembers the state of the country at the time, with its neutrality debates and pacifist sentiment, it is doubtful that public opinion could have been changed substan-

tially. In 1937 over a half-million college students reputedly signed a pledge not to support the United States in the event of war. And in a poll taken in the same year, nineteen out of twenty people answered "No" to the question, Should the U.S. enter another war?

Also, one is apt to forget the national distaste, prevalent at that time, for military spending. According to *Fortune,* the United States Army on June 30, 1935, consisted of "165,000 men, 67 generals, enough rifles for one regiment, and a handful of effective tanks." † Next year the Army's plans for expansion via new equipment were limited to purchasing another 1,870 rifles.

It all seems like a bad dream now; but to the men who would have to fight the delaying actions in the Pacific in 1941 and 1942, the American people must have seemed the prize idiots of all time.

How did we get that way?

DEXTER PERKINS

THE RELUCTANT WORLD POWER‡

THERE HAVE BEEN periods in the history of the United States when foreign policy occupied a subordinate place, but the age of Roosevelt was not one of them. Withdrawal or participation—that was the choice confronting the

* J. M. Burns's *The Lion and the Fox.*
† "Who's in the Army Now?" *Fortune,* October 1935.
‡ Condensed from Dexter Perkins' *The New Age of Franklin Roosevelt* (Chicago, University of Chicago Press, 1957).

American people. They began by wishing to evade all responsibility for the world outside their borders. They ended by accepting responsibility as a major world power. The America of 1933 turned in on itself. The story of this change is central and fundamental to an understanding of the times.

We begin with what has been called American isolationism, but behind the conduct of nations, as behind the conduct of individuals, lies an emotional state, which, as a rule, transcends the logical processes by which it is justified. To put the matter another way, the mood of a nation is often as important as its opinions; public sentiment is often as important as public judgment.

There were many reasons why the United States should be isolationist in 1933. The Great Depression itself was the best of all reasons. Confronting the most serious problems of internal adjustment that they had ever faced, the American people were reluctant to project their gaze beyond the seas. It was easier to ignore overseas events because, of all the great nations, America had the most naïve view of the role of force in international affairs. The nation had risen to greatness without engaging in large-scale war, and "power politics" in the European sense had played very little part in the process. Without experience in this field, Americans viewed the competitions of Europe as a sinister game which they neither desired nor felt compelled to play. Moreover, the experience of intervention in World War I had not been a particularly enheartening one. The generation most influential politically in the Thirties had seen the idealistic program of Woodrow Wilson roughly handled at Paris; it had seen selfishness supplant altruism; and it had seen, just as President Roosevelt entered office, the nations of the Old World repudiate their indebtedness to the United States. Had Americans crossed the seas in 1917 and 1918, given money and blood for the relief of Europe from German oppression, only to come to this result? The complaint could be, and was, pushed further. Since scapegoats are always useful in this world, it was easy to believe, as President Hoover believed, that America would have emerged much sooner from the Depression if it had not been for the European economic crisis of 1931, if the wrangling nations of the Old World had not deepened their own economic difficulties by political rivalries, if they had not intensified their own misery by folly and the game of power. And, on top of all this, there subsisted, as there still subsists today, the notion that there is something unique about the political and economic order of the United States and that only contamination could come from closer association with the wicked world outside American borders.

In his inaugural address President Roosevelt had defined his foreign policy as the policy of the "good neighbor." The phrase was meant to have a universal and not a restricted geographical application, but it was so pat a description of his course of action in the Western Hemisphere that it soon became closely identified with that area. Here, as in other matters, Roosevelt sensed the public mood and translated it into action.

In his policy toward Latin America Roosevelt was much assisted by his two principal aides in the field of foreign affairs. Cordell Hull, the Secretary of State from 1933 to 1944, was precisely the kind of man to become enthusiastic over the good-neighbor policy. There have been few secretaries of state so prone to think in abstract principles, so attached to broad formulas of action, so persistent in expressing American policy in terms of aspirations and ideals. Possibly this was so because his grasp of facts and his experience were limited when he came to office. Moreover, Hull had been a devoted follower of Woodrow Wilson. Despite Wilson's lapses from idealism in his dealings with the republics to the south, the spirit of his diplomacy had often reflected that regard for the rights of other states which was to become an essential element in the diplomacy of the new Administration. Hull found in his memories of the past a strong support for the policies which he was to put into action.

But another figure strongly influenced the development of United States relations with Latin America. Sumner Wells, the Under-Secretary of State, had been, long before 1933, a sturdy opponent of the interventions in the Caribbean. At a time when interest in Latin-American affairs was at a somewhat low ebb among professional diplomats, he had made a specialty of these matters and had been chief of the Latin-American Affairs Division of the Department of State in 1921-22. He had gone to the same private school as the President, and to the same university as well. More sophisticated than Hull, closer to Roosevelt personally, ambitious and vigorous, he was a person to be reckoned with even at the outset, when he was only an assistant secretary. And though he and Hull were frequently to be at swords' points in the ten years of their association, though the President's habit of bypassing the Secretary of State was to introduce a painful element into the relations of Hull and Welles, each supplemented the other in our dealings with the republics to the south. Welles knew much more than Hull; but Hull, as a veteran politician and a former congressman and senator, was better qualified to translate the policy of the Administration into terms that could be understood and appreciated on Capitol Hill.

What was the essence of the good-neighbor policy? The root principle was the principle of noninterference in the affairs of independent states. It would, however, have been one thing to enunciate this principle in general terms; it was an entirely different matter to incorporate it in a formal diplomatic document. The Latin-American states had clamored for such a commitment at the Pan-American conference at Havana in 1928; and it had needed all the lawyerlike ability and diplomatic skill of Charles Evans Hughes to stave off action. But at the conference of Montevideo in 1933 and again at Buenos Aires in 1936, Secretary Hull gave them what they asked for. His manners and methods in dealing with the sometimes sticky pride of Latin-American diplomats were widely applauded; even the vainest of foreign ministers, Saavedra Lamas of Argentina, succumbed to his homely charm; and at home the Secretary had the satisfaction of seeing the agreements that he signed ratified unanimously by the Senate. Moreover, the United States gave early proof of its sincerity. In spite of great temptation, on account of the large American interests involved, it made no move toward intervention when a somewhat radical regime arose in Cuba; and, in 1934, when that regime was succeeded by a more conservative one, the United States agreed to the abrogation of the Platt amendment by which, as far back as 1901, it had reserved the right to intervene in the affairs of the island. In 1934 came the evacuation of Haiti and the departure of the last of the marines from the soil of any independent state. In 1936 an agreement with Panama ended American tutelage of that republic.

A second principle of the good-neighbor policy was inter-American co-operation. At Buenos Aires the nations of the New World (Argentina reluctantly consenting) agreed to consult together in the event of an international war "which might menace the peace of the American hemisphere." Two years later machinery was provided to carry this pledge into effect, and on this second occasion, at Lima, a resounding declaration of American principles was adopted.

A third aspect of the good-neighbor policy was the lowering of trade barriers. This was a favorite idea of Secretary Hull. Unsuccessful in imposing it on the President in 1933, Hull continued to press for action, and the result was the Reciprocal Trade Agreement Act of 1934 which authorized a 50 per cent reduction of tariff duties by presidential action in understandings with other states. To such a country as Cuba, heavily dependent on the American market, this was a decided boon.

Finally, the good-neighbor policy was characterized by a remarkable tolerance toward the economic policies of the Latin-American republics. The Administration stood aloof from the controversies raised by the defaults of many of these republics on their debts, and it pursued a most restrained policy when they handled American interests roughly. When, for example, the Bolivian government expropriated the holdings of the Standard Oil Company in Bolivia, the State Department raised no great protest. And when, in a measure much more far-reaching in effect, the Mexican government followed the same course, no particular outcry came from Washington, though a very limited settlement of American claims was made in 1940. When America entered the war in 1941, it was to reap its rewards in the remarkable solidarity of the American states.

The successes of American policy toward Latin America were hardly matched either in Asia or in Europe. In our outstanding controversy with Japan the President could hardly retreat from the position assumed by his predecessor, namely, that the United States would not recognize the new situation created by the Japanese occupation of Manchuria. But neither could he take positive action of any kind. The country was in no mood for a policy of adventure, and Roosevelt reflected the mood.

The temper of American opinion with regard to the Far East in these years was shown by the strong desire manifested in Congress to get out of the Philippines. It was in consonance with American promises and American ideals that the islands should some day receive their independence, but the movement in this direction in the Thirties was motivated by no such lofty conceptions. A combination of interests, especially the beet-sugar interests, which suffered from Filipino competition, and of isolationists who hoped for an abdication of responsibility in the Far East was responsible for the bill that passed Congress in 1934. In the course of the debate the argument was frequently used that the islands represented a dangerous commitment on which the American taxpayer would never be willing to make good. The independence measure provided for the withdrawal of the United States from its military bases at the end of ten years and left for future discussion the question of naval bases. In the meantime Congress neglected the defenses of Guam, the island outpost in the Pacific.

The Administration by no means entirely consented to the course of events in the Orient. Hull, according to his custom, addressed numerous moral homilies to the Japanese government, which, however eloquent, changed not a tittle the actual posture of affairs. The President sought ever larger and larger appropriations for the Navy, and by 1936–37 and 1937–38 these had become the greatest in history. In the fall of 1937, moreover, he sought to arouse American opinion. Speaking in the Middle West, in the midst of the region most isolationist in sentiment, he declared that "peace-loving nations" must "make a concerted effort in opposition to those violations of treaties and those ignorings of humane instincts which are today creating a state of international anarchy and instability from which there is no escape through mere isolation or neutrality." War, he went on to argue, must be quarantined like an epidemic disease. But it is no exaggeration to say that the speech fell flat, and the President himself seemed to skate away from any concrete application of his formula when press correspondents sought to elicit further information as to his intentions.

If it was not easy to rouse the American public where flagrant aggression had already taken place and where the interests of the United States were clearly menaced, it is not surprising that the Roosevelt Administration made no great effort to shape its European policy along lines of co-operative effort. Both in the field of armaments and in the field of economic policy, the President and his advisers were powerless to check the ominous course of events.

In the matter of armaments the situation was this. For some time Germany, disarmed by the treaty of Versailles, had been clamoring for the lifting of the restrictions on its armed forces. A conference had been convened in 1932 and was again in session in the spring of 1933. The French, justly suspicious of the great power across the Rhine, and especially of the new Reich of Adolf Hitler, wished some kind of guaranty against aggression in exchange for a grant of permission to the Germans to expand their military establishment. But such a guaranty was impossible for the United States to give. The utmost that the President could do was to declare, through his special representative Norman Davis, that in case the League of Nations applied sanctions against Germany, the United States would not interfere with such sanctions. Such a statement was pitifully inadequate to meet the situation. When, shortly after the Roosevelt offer, Germany abandoned the conference and a few months later withdrew from the League, it was clear that a new period of arms competition was at hand. The most farsighted observers already saw the dangers in the path ahead.

In March 1934, the magazine *Fortune* published a sensational article on the armaments business. Most of what it had to say concerned the tie-up between European arms manufacturers and politicians, often an unpleasant story. But the activity of the American steel companies at the Geneva naval conference of 1927 was also recalled. Hard on the appearance of this article the Senate voted to investigate the arms traffic. By a curious mental operation on the part of Senator Pittman, who was the chairman of the Foreign Affairs Committee, Senator Nye of North Dakota, a Republican of distinctly isolationist slant, was chosen to direct the inquiry. The chief investigator and informal counsel for the committee was Stephen Raushenbush, and under his spur the investigation went far beyond its original purpose. The policies of the Woodrow Wilson Administration were sharply criticized, and the thesis that American entry into the war was the work of wicked Wall Street bankers, aided and abetted by sinister arms barons, gained headway accordingly with American public opinion. The thesis, it is worthwhile to remark, was unsound. But in public affairs it is not the accuracy but the force of a belief that counts, and there can be little doubt that the tide was running strongly toward revisionism in 1934 and 1935.

In such circumstances Congress reacted in vigorous fashion to the drift of public opinion. Cordell Hull, with his Wilsonian background, was by no means enthusiastic about what began to be called "neutrality legislation," but President Roosevelt, opportunist politician that he often was, made no attempt to stem the developing movement. The first discussions turned on an embargo against the munitions traffic in time of war. Such an embargo, framed in absolute terms, was sure to benefit the most heavily armed and therefore, in all probability, the aggressor nation, and it would run squarely athwart any coercive action by the League of Nations against a law-breaking state. In the House these considerations had weight, and the imposition of the embargo was left to the discretion of the President, but the Senate took the bit in its teeth, and, in its final form, the arms legislation left no choice to the executive but to apply the prohibition on arms export to all nations at war without distinction. The President, aware of the strength of congressional feeling, signed the law with a commentary on its provisions and the expression of a hope that "more permanent legislation might provide for greater flexibility." He was later very much to regret his action.

The temper of Congress in the session of 1935 was demonstrated in another fashion. For a period of more than a decade the question of American adhesion to the protocol setting up the World Court had been much discussed. Nothing could have been more innocent than this proposal; for the court was a court of voluntary jurisdiction, and action on the protocol did not bind the United States to submit any specific question whatsoever to the international tribunal. Yet, from its first appearance in 1923, the court issue seemed to rouse substantial opposition. The court judges were elected by League machinery, and to the foes of the League, including such powerful senators as Borah, this alone was enough to condemn the whole idea. In 1926 the Senate had ratified the protocol but with reservations that proved distasteful to the many nations who had accepted the court. Painful negotiation followed on the reservations, and, when accord was reached, long delay followed on that accord. It was not until the spring of 1935 that the new agreement came before the Senate for ratification. And then occurred a most astounding phenomenon. A flood of protests swept into Washington, spearheaded by the nationalistic publisher William

Randolph Hearst and by Father Coughlin. Some 200,000 telegrams came to senators in a few days—40,000 in a single day—all of them expressing bitter opposition to the court. In the face of such a demonstration the Senate capitulated. The protocol failed of ratification by a vote of 52 to 36. Very rarely has a vote been accompanied by so much unreason.

Throughout the debate on the court the President had maintained an indifferent attitude. He had no mind to breast the tide of sentiment; the vote on the subject only confirmed the Administration in its extremely cautious attitude with regard to the whole problem of neutrality. This circumspection was soon to be demonstrated in a matter of far greater significance.

The League of Nations had been powerless to check the aggression of Japan. In 1935 and 1936 it was to be put to a new test. The Italian dictator Benito Mussolini had for some time coveted Ethiopia. Five days after the Italian troops crossed the frontier, the League Council found by a unanimous vote that Italy had violated the Covenant and committed an act of aggression. On November 18 the members of the League, acting with extraordinary accord, declared an arms embargo, an embargo on credits, a ban on Italian imports, and a partial ban on exports. But there was a serious weakness in its operations. The most vital of all exports to Italy was oil. And this the Italians were allowed to continue to buy from the outside world. Moreover, in the face of threat of war, the League leaders began to take fright. The League never did muster its courage to carry through a decisive program, and in due course the movement for sanctions collapsed. The Emperor of Ethiopia, the unfortunate Haile Selassie, was compelled to bow before the power of the new Rome.

What was the attitude of the Roosevelt Administration during the course of these events? It is fair to say that it was less co-operative, so far as the League was concerned, than the attitude of Secretary Stimson in 1931. "With the isolationist sentiment so strong," says Secretary Hull in his memoirs, "it was impossible to join any League body considering sanctions. I preferred that any action we took should be entirely independent and not even seem to be suggested by the League." This attitude was maintained throughout the whole Ethiopian imbroglio, and it was approved by the President himself.

In the United States the breakdown of sanctions confirmed the isolationists in their point of view. Congress in 1936 enacted further neutrality legislation which, in addition to its embargo provisions, forbade the extending of loans to belligerents. When civil war broke out in Spain in the summer of 1936, the same formula was applied. The prevailing philosophy that the way to avoid war was to refuse to assist either of the belligerents was futile and even dangerous. In the case of an international war, as we have said, it would mean strengthening the aggressor against his victim, and in a civil war it tended to encourage revolt against an established government by denying arms to constituted authority. But the majorities in favor of this course were overwhelming, and the President hesitated to put his prestige to the test by vetoing such legislation.

The tide of sentiment represented by the Neutrality Acts did not cease to flow in 1936, but in 1937 and 1938 there were some signs, though only slight, of a reaction. When the national legislature set about framing a permanent statute in the first of these years, conflicting points of view were evident. Apart from the fact that the restriction on trade militated against a victim of aggression, there was the fact that commerce in time of war might be of great benefit to the United States and that to cut it off entirely might work serious damage to the national economy. A certain ambivalence was evident in the action of Congress. In pursuance of its objective of preventing (on the basis of American experience in the last war) involvement in the next one, the new legislation made it mandatory for the President to warn Americans off belligerent merchant ships. But with regard to trade, it was finally decided that the middle course was to permit belligerents to buy in the American market, provided that they paid in cash and carried away their purchases in their own vessels. The list of commodities to which this provision was to apply was to be fixed by the President himself.

There was to be a final expression of the isolationist philosophy in 1938. The most extraordinary of all proposals of this extraordinary epoch is what came to be known as the Ludlow amendment to the Constitution. This amendment, introduced by an Indiana congressman, provided that the United States could enter a war only after a national referendum. The American people, faced perhaps by some instant danger, were supposed to debate the issue in every part of the land, expose their divisions to the possible enemy, and fracture their national unity in time of peril by sharp and perhaps bitter discussion. Moreover, if such a measure were not dangerous, it would prove to be futile. For as the history of the United States demonstrates, the actual declaration of war usually follows protracted negotiation which, under our constitutional forms, is in the hands of the President. Wars do not come about suddenly. A long train of events makes up the issues on which the final decision depends. A wise President will be guided by public opinion in determining these issues, but the nation will doubtless in the future, as in the past, wish to sustain the Chief Executive.

Nevertheless, the idea contained in the Ludlow amendment had much support. A public opinion poll showed that 75 per cent of those questioned were in favor of the principle in 1935, 68 per cent in 1938. When the issue was brought to the floor of the House in the latter year, it was clear that a great parliamentary battle impended. The President spoke out against the proposal; so, too, did the Secretary of State. When the vote was taken, the count stood 209 in the affirmative and 188 in the negative (a two-thirds vote being required). Three out of every four Republicans had been recorded as in favor of this remarkable measure, and three out of every eight Democrats had taken the same position.

The Ludlow amendment represents the isolationist sentiment in its most extreme form. It was based on distrust of the executive, on a conception of foreign policy which would have accentuated internal division and made effective action impossible, on that kind of fear of war which encourages others to war. It was the high-water mark of the movement of American withdrawal. But before many months had gone by, the scene shifted drastically, and a new era arrived. Events in Europe set the stage for great changes in the orientation of American diplomacy.

THE DECLINE OF TIN PAN ALLEY

DORON K. ANTRIM, writing about Tin Pan Alley in *Scribner's* Magazine in 1936, charged that "the major music publishers are now subsidiaries of the motion-picture companies; and 80 per cent of the popular songs turned out today are written for pictures. The leading song writers are in Hollywood under contract, or are free-lancing there.

"Since the advent of radio the sale of sheet music has steadily declined. Prior to 1925, the life of a hit song was sixteen months, with a total sale of slightly over a million copies. Since 1931, a song is considered good if it keeps on top for three months with a total sale of around 230,000. The publishers have other sources of revenue—such as the royalties paid for performing rights (via ASCAP)—but more and more songs must come from the mill in view of the short life of each song.

"The new output runs mostly to smartness and sophistication. Mabel, who used to play the sweet simplic-

ities of the bicycle era on the upright piano, would experience difficulties negotiating the modern, tricky harmonies and rhythms; songs are not written for Mabel any more. They are fashioned for the singing stars in films, such as Bing Crosby and Grace Moore, according to their styles, likes and dislikes." *

Record sales had followed much the same dismal declining sales curve as sheet music, but when the record player was attached to an electrical motor early in the decade, sales began to increase again. Records were played in the juke boxes and over radio. Then we had the "Lucky Strike Hit Parade." When a song made the list of the ten most popular in the nation, it was played over and over again, week after week, *ad nauseam,* until mercifully it fell out of favor with the public.

In contrast to songwriting today, the Thirties was surely a rich period. Lots of songs written then are still being heard today.

SONGS OF THE THIRTIES†

1930

THE Gershwin brothers wrote music for two Broadway musicals, *Strike Up the Band* and *Girl Crazy,* from

which "The Man I Love," "I Got Rhythm," "Embraceable You," and "Bidin' My Time" were hits. In the first *Little Show,* two outstanding

* "Tin Pan Alley," *Scribner's,* February 1936.
† Song titles from Sigmund Spaeth's *A History of Popular Music in America* (New York, Random House, 1948).

show tunes were "Body and Soul" and "Something to Remember You By." Other hits from Broadway were "Cheerful Little Earful" and "Would You Like to Take a Walk" from *Sweet and Low*, and, from less memorable offerings, Rodgers and Hart gave us "Ten Cents a Dance," and Cole Porter, "Love for Sale."

From the movies came "Three Little Words" and "It Happened in Monterey."

From Tin Pan Alley, "Time On My Hands," "You're Driving Me Crazy," "The Waltz You Saved for Me" (Wayne King's theme song) and "Bye Bye Blues." Two flamboyant numbers were "The Peanut Vendor" and "Around the Corner."

1931

The Broadway musical *Of Thee I Sing* provided "Wintergreen for President," and *The Band Wagon* gave us "Dancing in the Dark"; Rodgers and Hart were again represented with "I've Got Five Dollars" from *America's Sweetheart*. Earl Carroll's *Vanities* gave us "Goodnight, Sweetheart," and George White's *Scandals* had "Life Is Just a Bowl of Cherries," "That's Why Darkies Are Born," and "My Song." Billy Rose was co-composer of a great hit in "I Found a Million Dollar Baby."

Successful pop tunes were "Mama Don't Want No Peas and Rice and Cocoanut Oil," "All of Me," "I Love a Parade," "Sweet and Lovely," and "River, Stay Way From My Door." Also "As Time Goes By," the song that would be rediscovered by Dooley Wilson in the motion picture *Casablanca* in 1943. And the song Eddie Cantor helped make famous: "Now's the Time to Fall in Love (Potatoes Are Cheaper)"; plus "Who's Your Little Whoozis" and "'Swonderful."

1932

The decade's best-remembered song (and perhaps least played these days) was "Brother, Can You Spare a Dime?"

Ethel Merman in *Take a Chance* introduced "Eadie Was a Lady" and "You're an Old Smoothie." Cole Porter wrote "Night and Day" for *Gay Divorcee*.

The film *Forty-second Street* supplied "Shuffle Off to Buffalo" and "You're Getting to be a Habit With Me"; and Rodgers and Hart wrote "Mimi" for *Love Me Tonight*.

Two memorable pop tunes were "Shanty in Old Shanty Town" and "I Cover the Waterfront."

1933

The popular stage musical, *Roberta*, gave us "Smoke Gets in Your Eyes" and "Yesterday," by Jerome Kern.

The movies had the catchy tune "Carioca" in *Flying Down to Rio*, "We're in the Money" and "Did You Ever See a Dream Walking?" in *Gold Diggers of 1933*, and "Temptation," from *Going Hollywood*.

Big hits from Tin Pan Alley were "The Last Round-up," by Billy Hill, and later in the year "The Old Spinning Wheel," both of which had gone begging for publishers for years; plus Hoagy Carmichael's "Lazybones," Rodgers and Hart's "Lover," and Harold Arlen's "Stormy Weather."

1934

From Broadway, Cole Porter's "I Get a Kick Out of You" and "You're the Top" out of *Anything Goes*. Also, from other shows, "Wagon Wheels" and "Swing Low, Sweet Chariot."

Hollywood provided "Little Man, You've Had a Busy Day," "Love in

Bloom," "June in January," "The Continental," "Stay as Sweet as You Are" and "Two Cigarettes in the Dark"; also "Cocktails for Two" and "All I Do Is Dream of You."

Memorable pop tunes were Duke Ellington's "Solitude"; and "Moonglow," "The Object of My Affection," and "Easy Come, Easy Go."

1935

This year was graced with Gershwin's great musical *Porgy and Bess* and its wonderful songs—"Summertime," "I Got Plenty of Nuttin'," "It Ain't Necessarily So" and "Bess, You Is My Woman."

And Cole Porter in *Jubilee* gave us "Begin the Beguine" and "Just One of Those Things."

In Hollywood, Irving Berlin's first movie score for *Top Hat* provided "Cheek to Cheek," "Isn't This a Lovely Day," and "Top Hat, White Tie, and Tails"; the film *Every Night at Eight* had "I'm in the Mood for Love"; and "Paris in the Spring" came from the film with the same name.

Pop tunes were "Red Sails in the Sunset," "When I Grow Too Old to Dream," "Deep Purple," "You Are My Lucky Star" and Ellington's "In a Sentimental Mood." The wackiest song of the year, and maybe any other, was "The Music Goes Round and Round."

1936

Cole Porter wrote "I've Got You under My Skin" and "It's De-Lovely" for Fred Astaire's film *Born to Dance* and Ethel Merman's Broadway musical *Red, Hot and Blue*, respectively. Rodgers and Hart had "There's a Small Hotel" in the Broadway production *On Your Toes*, and Jerome Kern, writing for the motion pictures, contributed "A Fine Romance" and "The Way You Look Tonight" to the film *Swing Time*. Bing Crosby sang "Pennies from Heaven" in the film of the same name, and Johnny Mercer satirized Western songs with "I'm an Old Cowhand." And Berlin wrote "I'm Putting All My Eggs in One Basket," "Let Yourself Go" and "Let's Face the Music and Dance" for the film *Follow the Fleet*.

Pop tunes were "Is It True What They Say about Dixie?" "It's a Sin to Tell a Lie," "Christopher Columbus," "Say Si Si," "Shoe Shine Boy," "I've Got a Feelin' You're Foolin' " and "Goody! Goody!"

1937

Rodgers and Hart wrote "The Lady Is a Tramp," "Where or When?" and "Johnny One-Note" for *Babes in Arms*, a Broadway musical.

Cole Porter supplied "In the Still of the Night" and "Rosalie" for the film *Rosalie*; Hollywood also gave us "That Old Feeling," "September in the Rain" and "Once in a While"; Bing Crosby introduced "Sweet Leilani" in the film *Waikiki Wedding*. And Irving Berlin's most memorable for the year was "I've Got My Love to Keep Me Warm."

Two crazy pop tunes were "Dipsy Doodle," by Larry Clinton, the bandleader, and "The Merry-Go-Round Broke Down"; Maxine Sullivan made "Loch Lomond" popular all over again. And Johnny Mercer's "Bob White (Whatcha Gonna Swing Tonight?)" was recorded by Bing Crosby and Connie Boswell, a rhythmic catchy tune. Last but not least were two songs, "Once in a While" and "Nice Work if You Can Get It," the last by the Gershwin brothers.

1938

The "Hit Parade" on radio could bring even an old song back to popularity, and this year saw the following revivals: "Little Sir Echo," "A Tisket, A Tasket" "Penny Serenade" and "Ti Pi Tin."

Rodgers and Hart had three shows playing simultaneously on Broadway: *I'd Rather Be Right*; *I Married an Angel*, with a title song of the same name; and *The Boys from Syracuse*, out of which came "This Can't Be Love" and "Sing for Your Supper."

In Hollywood, out of *The Big Broadcast of 1938*, we had "Thanks for the Memory." Walt Disney's *Snow White* had "Whistle While You Work," "Heigh Ho" and "Some Day My Prince Will Come"—all popular hits. Johnny Mercer wrote a couple of catchy tunes—"Jeepers Creepers (Where'd You Get Those Peepers?)" and "You Must Have Been a Beautiful Baby."

The far-out tune for the year was Slam Stewart's "Flat Foot Floogey with the Floy Floy."

1939

From Broadway shows, we heard "I Didn't Know What Time It Was" by Rodgers and Hart from *Too Many Girls*, and Jerome Kern's "All the Things You Are" from *Very Warm for May*.

The pop songs of the year included "The Beer Barrel Polka," Johnny Mercer's "And the Angels Sing," Hoagy Carmichael's "I Get Along Without You Very Well," Saxie Dowell's "Three Little Fishes," and "I'll Never Smile Again," "The Hut Sut Song," "Sunrise Serenade," "South of the Border," "Scatterbrain," "Stairway to the Stars," "Wishing" and "If I Didn't Care."

THE MARVELS OF ADVERTISING

In 1936 J. P. Morgan told the press that if "you destroy the leisure class, you destroy civilization. By the leisure class, I mean the families who employ one servant—twenty-five to thirty million families." Hardly were the words out of his mouth, when the housewives pounced on him to prove that he must have got his ideas of American domesticity from Hollywood. In the 1930 census there were fewer than thirty million families in the country, and fewer than two million servants to attend them.

While Mr. Morgan obviously had been misinformed, there was no doubt that millions of mechanical servants and labor-saving devices were available for the home: canning, baking, dressmaking, ironing, cleaning, lighting, heating, laundry, refrigeration—hardly any phase of home life was unaffected. Surely the salesman must be given his credit, and his ally the advertiser. If the advertising world ever should run out of products to plug, we can all be sure that in their genius they will invent others. As David Cohn says, "By 1930 all the common ills of the body, such as body odor, bad breath, dandruff, and so on, had in fact been spoken for by a group of powerful concerns; for other aspiring manufacturers there remained only the opportunity of inventing new ones. Up to this point the public had accepted the advertising of hitherto unmentionable products designed to remedy unmentionable ills, and—

wouldn't you know it?—by 1939, imaginative copy writers were inventing scores of new ills, and advertising the products to cure them." *

Listed below are some of the plagues which America saw itself confronted with in the pages of newspapers and magazines:

> Underarm Offense
> Pendulosis
> Undie Odor
> Paralyzed Pores
> Colon Collapse
> Ashtray Breath
> Office Hips
> Athlete's Foot

Early in the decade two monitors for the public good, Arthur Kallet and F. J. Schlink, armed with evidence from organizations devoted to research among consumers, published a book, *100,000,000 Guinea Pigs*, which took out after the advertisers, the food and drug industries, and even government agencies. They named names and set off charges against nationally advertised products such as mouth washes, antiseptic solutions, and tooth pastes, proclaiming them too feeble to justify the extravagant claims in their advertising; bran cereals touted for "roughage" were, they stated, too rough for sensitive intestines; and the amounts of sulfur dioxide used in preserving dried fruits were, according to their findings, dangerously above the maximum limit set by

* David L. Cohn, *The Good Old Days* (New York, Simon and Schuster, 1940).

the Food and Drug Administration. This kind of exposé, along with other efforts, put pressure on the businessmen of the day to tone down (temporarily, at least) some of their reckless claims.

DIXON WECTER

THE CONSUMER AND SCIENCE*

A STRIKING paradox lay in the contrast between the acute health-consciousness of the American people—mirrored in advertising, syndicated medical-advice columns, radio talks on hygiene, the huge drug-counter traffic and myriad symptoms of faddism—and the government's traditional timidity or parsimony in approaching public health.

The deepening of the Depression worsened conditions. In 1932–1933, for example, investigations showed that the highest sickness rate occurred among wage-earning families which had suffered abrupt losses in income and living standards, while in general it stood about forty per cent higher among the jobless than among the full-time employed. Childhood and youth naturally remained the principal victims, and in these years undoubtedly were sown many of the causes that led to the rejection in 1940–1941 by Army medical examiners of almost half the first two million registrants examined under selective service.

In February 1938, Senator Robert F. Wagner introduced a national health bill, proposing grants-in-aid to states to foster either tax-supported systems of general medical care or combinations of public medicine with universal health insurance. Meeting inflexible opposition from the American Medical Association, it failed of passage, even though a Gallup poll found a majority of doctors favorable to schemes of voluntary health insurance and Surgeon General Thomas Parran in July publicly observed that "at the present time people in general are beginning to take it for granted that an equal opportunity for health is a basic American right."

Short of compulsion, the putting of medical and hospital costs on an insurance basis was indeed the innovation which the Thirties brought to several million families, chiefly with modest incomes. Just as medical centers and private-group clinics were a prime development of the previous

* Excerpted from Dixon Wecter's *The Age of the Great Depression* (New York, Macmillan, 1948).

period, so that of the new decade was the group-health association and the hospitalization plan. By 1938 the plan had spread to about sixty cities, enrolling some three million subscribers.

The Twenties had brought extraordinary blatancy and meretriciousness to advertising, and one of the Depression's early effects upon many manufacturers was to promote the substitution of smaller containers, looser packing, subnormal weight, misbranding and inferior materials. With the consumer impelled as never before to spend his dollar advantageously, a profusion of books like Arthur Kallet and Frederick J. Schlink's *100,000,-000 Guinea Pigs* appeared to warn him of pitfalls. American Medical Association committees spearheaded reform in the drug market, while its committee on foods, created in 1929, awarded grudgingly its seal of approval, rejecting two out of every three products submitted and insisting upon revised labels and deflated advertising claims for most of the remainder.

The New Deal also took a hand in the matter. Besides short-lived efforts under the NRA, it set up the AAA's Consumers' Counsel, which in partnership with the Bureau of Agricultural Economics, Bureau of Home Economics and Bureau of Labor Statistics, inaugurated a biweekly bulletin called the *Consumer's Guide*. In addition, the Federal Trade Commission from 1934 onward obliged many advertisers to correct errors and temper the exuberance of their claims, and the Wheeler-Lea Act in 1938 considerably strengthened such controls. Meanwhile demands increased for a sweeping modernization of the Pure Food and Drug Act of 1906, notably after the death of over seventy users of an "Elixir Sulfanilamide" purveyed by a drug company. Despite apathy by the press and open hostility from many commercial concerns, but under urgent pressure from women's organizations, the Food, Drug and Cosmetic Act of June 24, 1938, scrapped obsolete legislation and widened the domain of federal authority, requiring adequate testing of new drugs before their introduction to the market, sharply defining adulteration and misbranding, and prohibiting deceptions effected by containers and labels.

If the consumer had the cash or credit, he could buy more commodities —for health, efficiency, convenience and luxury—than any earlier American had been able to command. Multiplying the marvels of synthetic chemistry, industrial research poured forth a stream of new attractive wares at low cost. Between 1920 and 1940 the number of industrial-research laboratories grew from three hundred to more than two thousand, the scientists and technical experts they employed from six thousand to sixty, with General Electric, Du Pont, Radio Corporation of America, and Westinghouse setting the pace. The miracles of applied chemistry shielded several big concerns from the worst consequences of the Depression, notably the Du Ponts, who embarked upon a sales campaign for the nonporous envelope called cellophane. The results were so successful that the public began to buy its prunes and caramels and cigarettes thus encased. The same concern pioneered a synthetic rubber under the name "duprene," utilizing a process devised by Dr. J. A. Nieuwland, announced in 1931. Its importance became evident ten years later when Japan sought to retaliate upon American oil and metal embargoes by choking off the flow of natural rubber across the Pacific.

In the novel field of chemurgy, which early caught the eye of Henry Ford as well as the Du Ponts, farm products ranging from soybeans to skim milk were converted into plastics, and in 1939 Congress subsidized regional laboratories for further research. From such materials as camphor, carbon, alcohol, urea, asbestos and formaldehyde still other synthetics were achieved. Nylon, a polyamide fiber made from coal, air and water, was introduced to an appreciative feminine public in 1939–1940, while coarser fibers of the same product went into toothbrushes. Plywood, fibers made from cellulose, and new steels containing molybdenum, vanadium, nickel, chromium and tungsten proved of immediate industrial and future military importance. Pyralin, fabrikoid, plexiglas, plastecele, lucite and vinylite were other innovations. Within a short space it dawned upon the average person that wonderful new substances now composed the fountain pen with which he wrote, the radio cabinet at his bedside, the sponge in his bathroom, the wheel by which he steered his car, his wife's dresses, and the motion-picture film which they saw projected on the screen. And, thanks to imaginative designers like Norman Bel Geddes, many such products tended to greater functionalism, beauty and clarity of color.

In the mid-Thirties the process of cracking heavy oils, after extraction of gas and gasoline, added millions of barrels of fuel for consumers' use as well as raw materials for industrial alcohol, lacquers, plastics and synthetic rubber. As still another aspect of laboratory conservation, polymerization, a technique causing combustible gases to combine into gasoline molecules, promised eventually to add nine billion gallons of gasoline to the nation's annual output.

Machines serving to replace man's senses, including the ability to gauge form and size and weight and to test pressure and temperature, were joined in 1930 by the first commercially practicable photoelectric cell. This Aladdin's lamp of modern science could see better and farther than the human eye, without error, fatigue or color blindness. It proved itself an incomparable servant for sorting articles, matching hues, counting passing objects, regulating light, automatically leveling elevators at floor stops, opening doors and guarding gates and prison walls.

In practical acoustics the radio telephone attained its majority, its use on planes and ships presaging the "walkie-talkie" of approaching war days. In 1937 the coaxial cable entered commercial use: a single wire by means of the crystal wave filter and the vacuum tube could now carry two hundred and forty simultaneous conversations.

New processes also affected eating habits. The commercial adoption in 1930 of solid carbon dioxide ("dry ice") made possible vastly longer shipments of fresh edibles by land and sea, for its gradual release of carbon-dioxide gas killed or checked bacterial growth. The extremely rapid freezing of foods, preserving them with their natural flavors, had been devised in 1925 by Clarence Birdseye, and the method, bought by General Foods, was introduced to the retail trade in 1930. Four years later ten million pounds of such frozen foods as peas, corn, berries, oysters and other perishables were being sold. By the end of the decade the costs of refrigeration had been reduced by over three fourths, and though prices still remained higher than for fresh foodstuffs, the volume had grown to two hundred million pounds.

Even more sweeping developments in the American dietary came from physiological and medical research concerning vitamins. These investigations had begun before the First World War, but the modest total of forty-seven papers published on that topic in 1911 had grown to fifteen hundred annually by 1930. Knowledge advanced swiftly in regard to vitamin complexes, relations of vitamins to each other and to hormones, and their general effect upon metabolism, health, susceptibility to disease and longevity. The nature of vitamin A remained largely a mystery until the important work done in 1929 by Yale's M. D. Tyson and Arthur H. Smith; in the next year its plant source was identified with the pigment carotin. Vitamins A and B_1 were synthesized in 1936 and, largely through the researches of the Texan Tom D. Spies, nicotinic acid within the B_2 complex was discovered to be the cure for the Southern poor whites' scourge, pellagra. In 1937 Edward A. Doisy of St. Louis isolated vitamin K from alfalfa, and shortly afterward showed its potency in checking hemorrhage. On the other hand, these years brought into use the drug heparin, having precisely the opposite effect, and in the latter Thirties this anticoagulant began to be employed with marked success in preventing thrombosis and in treating bacterial heart disease.

The publicity about vitamins helped to modify certain culinary practices. Housewives learned not to keep fresh foods too long before consumption as well as not to boil vegetables excessively and then throw out the water; increasing use of the pressure cooker was thought to preserve vitamins; and more vegetables were served raw than ever before.

Physiology and medicine also recorded other important advances. Greatest was the discovery of sulfa drugs, particularly sulfanilamide, sulfapyridine and sulfathiazole. Pioneered in Germany, they were perfected and applied to new uses in the United States.

The widespread use by hospitals of desiccated blood plasma, perfected about 1940, held immense significance for the future. Rapid gains occurred in the thoracic field. In 1930, for example, the artificial lung was invented, enabling those with paralyzed chest muscles to survive, and new surgical techniques rendered it possible to remove an entire lung to check cancerous growth.

Along the borders of physiology and psychiatry occurred certain fruitful developments, such as the adoption in 1937 of the insulin-shock treatment for schizophrenia.

Such innovations as air-conditioning equipment, plastics, prefabricated houses, the photoelectric cell, synthetic rubber, television, gasoline from coal, et cetera, made it plain that, during the time when millions vainly sought work and hosts of factories rusted in idleness, technology had marched sturdily forward. In 1937 twenty per cent more goods and services could be produced than in 1929, with no additions to the labor force, and one engineer reckoned that something less than a twenty-four-hour work week could be made to serve all American productive needs. A Gallup poll in June 1939, asking those on relief, "What do you blame for the present unemployment in this country?" reported that the largest percentage said, "machines taking the place of men"—a reason both dispassionate and intelligent.

Some of these marvels of technology were displayed by the three great fairs of these years. Chicago's "Century of Progress" drew about ten million admissions in its first season in 1933. Unlike her glorification of Old World Culture in the exposition of forty years earlier, this occasion featured native achievements in invention and engineering, and its Hall of Science drew the largest number of visitors. The summer of 1939, febrile last season before the catastrophe of the Second World War, saw parallel exhibitions on opposite shores of the continent, with railways taking advantage of the circumstance by offering excursion rates to "See Two World's Fairs." San Francisco's Golden Gate Exposition, true to its architectural motif drawn from pre-Columbian and Spanish America, tended somewhat to play down modernism and technology save for the most ambitious floodlighting in color ever attempted and a lavish aeronautical display.

Bigger and more catholic was New York's "World of Tomorrow," its emblem of trylon and perisphere (a spire rising from the globe) symbolizing "the theme of social reconstruction." Its twenty-nine million admissions in 1939, including the King and Queen of England on an unprecedented good-will tour, saw the début of fluorescent lighting on a large scale, radio broadcasting of facsimile newspapers and a ten-million-volt lightning bolt discharged at intervals "to show how man has chained the forces of nature." The "Town of Tomorrow," bristling with innovations in housing, and the "Electrified Farm," revealing the wonders of hydroponics (the soilless cultivation of plants), attracted millions. Foreign nations occupied twenty-two variegated pavilions flanking the Court of Peace, with Nazi Germany conspicuously missing. Czechoslovakia, her independence lately destroyed, attempted nevertheless to carry on; Italy featured a gigantic waterfall and Japan a Shinto shrine enclosing a replica of the Liberty Bell made of eleven thousand cultured pearls and four hundred diamonds; while over the Soviet building the colossal figure of a worker towered into the sky holding aloft the Red Star. It was indeed the World of Tomorrow in parables and ironies. But, whatever political allegories might have been fancied beneath the show, the triumph of technology stood clearly forth, with some forecast of its still unwritten and perhaps incalculable effect upon the fate of modern man.

"MAYBE YOU CAN EXPLAIN IT TO ME"

GREAT STRIDES had been made in science and medicine, and in other vital areas of the physical world. But men did not seem to know enough about how to live with each other compatibly. There was still poverty —the President announced toward the end of the decade that one third of the nation was still ill-housed, ill-clad, and ill-nourished. For instance, there were still a million-odd migrant farm workers; listen to one of them speaking to a *Fortune* writer in 1939:

"Mister, you been to college, you learned things there—maybe you can tell me what's to become of us. You see, back in Oklahoma we had a farm. There's me and the three kids and the old lady and my mother. We got along, yea, and then things started to happen. First came the Depression and we couldn't get nothin' for our crops. Make maybe two hundred dollars a year. Course the farm started to go downhill—to dry up—and fust thing I knowed the whole blamed farm had dried up and blown away. Course, it weren't quite as quick as all that. There were a couple of years when we tried mighty hard. Didn't eat much those years.

"Well, come '35 it weren't no use trying any longer so we just packed up and pulled out. Came out here cause we hear you could make fair money harvesting crops. And ya know we did make fair money the fust year. Ya see the kids are twelve, fourteen, and fifteen years old so all of us can work except my maw—when there's work to be got. Well, we picked peas in the Imperial and Santa Maria, potatoes at Stockton, and grapes at Napa. We made high as seventeen, eighteen dollars a day. Course it costs a lot to move around and there was a time when we couldn't get no work, but we done purty good. Then last year we made the same places but it weren't no good. They didn't pay so good last year. Cut from thirty-five to twenty-five cents an hour and piece work was lower. We got by, though. But, God, Mister, what's going to happen to us this year? Here it is March and I only worked about two weeks so far. I tried every place and everybody but it weren't no good. People has kept comin' in here so now there's six for every job—and darn few jobs. See that sign? Says forty-five cents for picking a hundred pounds o' cotton. Know how long it takes to pick a hundred pounds o' cotton down here? Well, it takes just about a whole day. You know you can't feed a family o' six on forty-five cents a day. It ain't my fault, is it? Jees, I worked hard since I was a kid. I allus done what I thought was right, and I think I know right from wrong. I allus tried to teach my kids right from wrong. But I'm beginnin' to wonder. I don't know what to do. There's nothin' back in Oklahoma for us to go to and now there's nothin' here. Somehow somethin' don't seem right—I want to work and I can't—I want to bring up my kids decent. You been to college, Mister, maybe you can explain it to me." *

And there was the festering cancer of race prejudice. Anti-semitism was already somewhat diminished when the trauma of Nazism roused people against its evils. Fissures were also beginning to appear in the old, hardened attitudes of white toward Negro Americans. And behind every little victory were individuals who would rally to the cause of free men regardless of color or creed.

WALTER WHITE

MARIAN ANDERSON AND THE D.A.R.†

ON AN early spring afternoon in Washington in March 1939 a vivacious, auburn-haired Washington newspaper correspondent, Mary Johnston, excitedly called me out of the Senate gallery, where I was listening to another filibuster. She had just come from an interview with the president of the Daughters of the American Revolution, Mrs. Henry M. Robert, Jr., who had bluntly told Miss Johnston that neither Marian Anderson nor any other Negro artist would be permitted to appear in Constitution Hall. Indignant at this lily-white policy, Miss Johnston wanted me to give her a statement which she could use in a story.

I had watched Miss Anderson's struggle against poverty and prejudice with more than ordinary interest. Following the success of Roland Hayes, she gave a recital in New York's Town Hall in 1925 which might better have been postponed a year or so. That evening Marian sang badly, though those who have listened to her in later years will find difficulty in believing that anyone with so great a voice could ever sing other than perfectly. Perhaps her performance that evening was due to stage fright. Some believe that the fault was due to the voice teacher with whom she was studying. He was a devotee of the *bel canto* school, and had attempted to raise Marian's voice a full octave. The New York critics that next day were harsh, even bitter. Most of them recognized the existence of a great voice, but some of them pontifically declared that it had been ruined.

Marian was so heartbroken that she vowed never to sing again. Some

---

* "I Wonder Where We Can Go Now," *Fortune,* April 1939.
† From Walter White's *A Man Called White* (New York, Viking, 1948).

months later the N.A.A.C.P. was holding its annual conference in Philadelphia. Roland Hayes was to be presented with the Spingarn Medal and the presentation was to be made by the provost of the University of Pennsylvania, the scholarly and eloquent Josiah H. Penniman. Harry T. Burleigh, the famous composer and baritone of New York's St. George's and Temple Emanu-El, was scheduled to accept the medal for Roland *in absentia*, as Roland was then on a concert tour in Europe. We invited Marian to sing, but received a flat refusal. It took long persuasion to induce her to change her mind. But on Spingarn Medal night in crowded Witherspoon Hall she sang superbly and was forced to give encore after encore and then to take curtain call after curtain call. When at last the applause had subsided and the ordeal ended, Marian burst into tears and exclaimed, "Thank God! I've got my faith again!"

Now I welcomed Mary Johnston's suggestion, but pointed out that no one would be surprised to learn that I was indignant at the action of the D.A.R., and suggested that we get statements instead from some of Miss Anderson's famous fellow artists.

Mary agreed. Utilizing one of the high window sills of the Senate gallery as a desk, we drafted a telegram and compiled a list of distinguished musicians whom we would telegraph for comments. With gratifying speed the replies poured in from Lawrence Tibbett, Leopold Stokowski, Walter Damrosch, Kirsten Flagstad, Geraldine Farrar, and others, all praising Miss Anderson as a great artist and expressing indignation and almost disbelief that the D.A.R. had taken the action we had reported.

On my return to New York, I found Sam Hurok, Miss Anderson's manager, as indignant as I have ever known him to be. He proposed that attention be focused on the bigotry of the Daughters of the American Revolution by asking Miss Anderson to sing an open-air, free concert in Washington.

The idea was exciting. The most logical place was the Lincoln Memorial. Mr. Hurok agreed, and asked Gerald Goode to go to Washington with me to see if arrangements could be made. Virginia-born Oscar Chapman, Assistant Secretary of the Interior, with characteristic intelligence was enormously enthusiastic. He made an immediate appointment with Harold Ickes, Secretary of the Interior and throughout his life an unequivocal battler for justice to the Negro. Mr. Ickes was equally excited over the prospect of such a demonstration of democracy. President Roosevelt was leaving that afternoon for Warm Springs. But Mr. Ickes would not let him leave until the President had permitted him to come to the White House to tell the story. Hearing it, the President gave his approval and told Mr. Ickes to provide whatever facilities were necessary to make the concert the greatest event of its kind ever held.

The engagement for which the Daughters of the American Revolution had refused the use of Constitution Hall had been arranged by Howard University. Since the university was dependent for support upon congressional appropriations, Mr. Hurok did not want to involve it in a protest which might have widespread repercussions. He therefore made a proposal which was more difficult to turn down than any other I have received in all the years of my connection with the Association. He suggested that the Lincoln Memorial concert be under the auspices of the N.A.A.C.P. It would have meant publicity for the Association which could not have been bought for many tens of thousands of dollars.

But there was a broader issue involved than publicity. Because the N.A.A.C.P. is known as a fighting propaganda agency, its sponsorship of the concert might have created the impression that propaganda for the Negro was the objective instead of the emphasizing of a principle. I, therefore, proposed that the concert be given under the most distinguished and nonpartisan auspices possible—namely, a sponsoring committee on which would be asked to serve such persons as members of the Cabinet and the Supreme Court, senators, congressmen, editors, artists, and others who believed that art should know no color line.

It was natural that we should think instantly of Mrs. Eleanor Roosevelt as chairman of such a sponsoring committee. She had invited me to her apartment in New York a few days before to ask my advice on her resigning from the D.A.R. in protest against the treatment accorded Miss Anderson. She had resigned, and this focused world-wide attention on the episode. However, I did not feel that Mrs. Roosevelt should put herself on the spot, particularly since reactionaries in the South were already pillorying her for her attitude on the Negro.

I therefore went to Mrs. Caroline O'Day, Congresswoman-at-large from New York State, whose Southern birth in Savannah, Georgia, and whose standing and integrity were such as to make her the next logical choice as chairman of the sponsoring committee. Mrs. O'Day enthusiastically accepted the chairmanship and turned over all the facilities of her office to us for use in sending telegraphic invitations to those selected to be asked to serve on the sponsoring committee.

A few politically minded individuals—chiefly in Congress—were cagey. Some had their secretaries wire that the invitations would be "brought to the attention" of their employers. A few sought refuge in excuses like "my position makes it unwise for me to participate in controversial issues of this character." But the overwhelming majority of those invited accepted membership with promptness and enthusiasm. Justices of the Supreme Court, top-flight artists of world reputation, writers, diplomats, Cabinet officers, congressmen and senators, men and women of lesser renown, agreed to serve and thereby express their admiration for Miss Anderson and their indignation at the cavalier treatment the D.A.R. had given her. Seldom in history had a more distinguished group of Americans rallied to affirmation of democracy.

Among the sponsors were Mrs. Franklin D. Roosevelt and many other nationally and internationally known figures.

I drove down to Washington on Easter Eve. The weather was crisp and cold but heavy with the promise of approaching spring. However, as I approached Washington sleet began to fall. With it fell my hopes. I went to bed low in spirits because of the snow piling up on the streets outside. Weeks of thought and all our hard work seemed about to be thwarted by nature. I was almost afraid to look out of the window when I awoke early the next morning. I shouted with happiness to see the sun.

The concert was scheduled to begin at five o'clock. We drove to the Lincoln Memorial, approaching it from the rear. We had to park the car blocks away because every available place near by had already been pre-empted. What a sight greeted us when we came around to the front of the Memorial! Every one of the several hundred chairs which had been placed on the lower platform was occupied. Seldom in the history even of Washington had a more distinguished group of sponsors been gathered. But much more important to us was the audience itself. Seventy-five thousand white and colored Americans not only from Washington but from cities, towns and villages within a radius of hundreds of miles had gathered at the Memorial of the Great Emancipator to hear a singer of whom Toscanini had said: "A voice like yours comes but once in a century."

No member of that audience will ever forget the sight of Miss Anderson emerging from a small anteroom beside Gaudens' statue of Lincoln. She was apparently calm, but those of us who knew her were aware of the great perturbation beneath her serene exterior. On her right was gentle Georgia-born Caroline O'Day. On her left was Virginia-born Oscar Chapman. A tremendous wave of applause rose from the vast throng, which was silenced only when Miss Anderson gently raised her hand to ask that the concert be permitted to begin. Amplifiers poured out the thunderous chords of the opening bars of "America." Clasping her hands before her Miss Anderson poured out in her superb voice "sweet land of liberty" almost as though it was a prayer.

As the last notes of "Nobody Knows the Trouble I've Seen" faded away the spell was broken by the rush of the audience toward Miss Anderson, which almost threatened tragedy. Oscar Chapman plowed through the crowd and directed me to the microphone to plead with them not to create a panic. As I did so, but with indifferent success, a single figure caught my eye in the mass of people below which seemed one of the most important and touching symbols of the occasion. It was a slender black girl dressed in somewhat too garishly hued Easter finery. Hers was not the face of one who had been the beneficiary of much education or opportunity. Her hands were particularly noticeable as she thrust them forward and upward, trying desperately, though she was some distance away from Miss Anderson, to touch the singer. They were hands which despite their youth had known only the dreary work of manual labor. Tears streamed down the girl's dark face. Her hat was askew, but in her eyes flamed hope bordering on ecstasy. Life which had been none too easy for her now held out greater hope because one who was also colored and who, like herself, had known poverty, privation and prejudice, had, by her genius, gone a long way toward conquering bigotry. If Marian Anderson could do it, the girl's eyes seemed to say, then I can, too.

THE NATION'S HEARTBEAT WAS NEVER
MORE LOUD AND CLEAR

WITH so much still to be done, there was to be no opportunity for the government and the people to work together to finish the job: war was to come some months later.

Those who have written about the Thirties end their narratives usually with the solemn announcement of imminent war. But war is neither an end nor a beginning; after the war, even bigger chores faced America. The international scene absorbed our attention before we could turn to our own problems.

The work was still there to be done, as we see clearly in this year, 1961—in conservation, better regulatory practices for business and labor, fairer taxation, integration— a list as long as one's arm.

Perhaps what had happened to America in the Thirties made it easier for us to understand the crises, the catastrophes and plain human suffering in other parts of the world; and, I hope, now in our own country.

I like to believe, as does Frank Brookhouser, "that in the Thirties, despite their troubles and their tragedies, the men, women and children in America loved more strongly, felt more deeply, generated more warmth, and held more compassion for their fellow men than ever in our history, before or since.

"The people had more character.

"It was, granted, a grim and heartbreaking period in many ways. But the people triumphed over the loss and the disappointment and the suffering and the heartache. And never was the nation's heartbeat more loud and clear." *

* Frank Brookhouser, *These Were Our Years* (Garden City, N. Y., Doubleday, 1959).

ABOUT THE EDITOR

DON CONGDON *spent his early years in Pennsylvania in a coal-mining valley near Butler, and later went to high school in a chair-factory town near Erie. He came to New York in 1935, where he found work as messenger in a literary agency. Later he was an Associate Fiction Editor at* Collier's *Magazine and an Editor at Simon and Schuster. For the past fourteen years he has been an associate in the Harold Matson Company, an agency handling the work of some of America's most distinguished authors.*

Mr. Congdon has edited several other anthologies, among them The Wild Sweet Wine, Stories for the Dead of Night, *and two volumes on World War II,* Combat: European Theatre *and* Combat: Pacific Theatre.